Unfinished
Business: Pressure Points
in the
Lives of Women

Also by Maggie Scarf:
BODY, MIND, BEHAVIOR

MAGGIE SCARF

Unfinished Business: Pressure Points in the Lives of Women

DOUBLEDAY & COMPANY, INC.
GARDEN CITY, NEW YORK
1980

Grateful acknowledgment is made to authors and publishers for permission to reprint the following copyrighted material:

Excerpts from "Sex-Role Stereotypes and Clinical Judgments of Mental Health" by Inge K. Broverman, Donald M. Broverman, Frank E. Clarkson, Paul S. Rosenkrantz and Susan R. Vogel which appeared in *Journal of Consulting & Clinical Psychology*, Vol. 34, pp. 1–7, 1970. Copyright © 1970 by the American Psychological Association. Reprinted by permission.

Excerpts from *Attachment and Loss*, Volume II, by John Bowlby, © 1973 by The Tavistock Clinic of Human Relations. Published in the U.S. by Basic Books, Inc.

Excerpt from *The Adolescent and His World* by Irene M. Josselyn, by permission of the publisher. Copyright 1952 by Family Service Association of America, New York.

Excerpt from "Of Love and Loss" in *Mothering* by Rudolph Schaffer (pp. 80–81). Copyright © 1977 by Rudolph Schaffer. Reprinted by permission of Harvard University Press.

Excerpts from *Loneliness: The Experience of Social and Emotional Isolation* by Robert Weiss. Copyright © 1973 by Massachusetts Institute of Technology. Reprinted by permission of The MIT Press, Cambridge, Massachusetts.

Excerpts from *Secrets in the Family*, copyright © 1977 by Lily Pincus and Christopher Dare. Reprinted by permission of Pantheon Books a Division of Random House, Inc.

ISBN: 0-385-12248-9
Library of Congress Catalog Card Number 78–22352

In memory of Norma

CONTENTS

Acknowledgments   xi

Foreword   xv

Prologue   1

IN THE TEENS

Chapter One/Departing Time: Anne   11

Chapter Two/Getting Back Home: Debra   39

Chapter Three/Of Love and Loss   68

IN THE TWENTIES

Chapter Four/The Winner: Marie   101

Chapter Five/On Promiscuity and Depression: Sandy   137

Chapter Six/Body and Mind   171

IN THE THIRTIES

Chapter Seven/Turning Thirty: Kath   189

Chapter Eight/Mood and Medicine: Judith (1)   229

Chapter Nine/Elation and Despair: Judith (2)   246

Chapter Ten/Postpartum Problems: Laurie (1)   274

Chapter Eleven/Great Mother/Bad Wife: Laurie (2)   292

IN THE FORTIES

Chapter Twelve/The Facts of a Life: Diana (1)   329

Chapter Thirteen/Femininity as Symptom   354

Chapter Fourteen/Does Anybody Want Diana to Live? Diana (2)   366

IN THE FIFTIES

Chapter Fifteen/The Time of Menopause: Doris (1)   395

Chapter Sixteen/Happily Ever After: Doris (2)   421

Chapter Seventeen/A Marital Crisis: Doris (3)   449

IN THE SIXTIES

Chapter Eighteen/Alone: Margaret Garvey   485
Letters   515
Surviving   527

Appendix I/Signs That You May Be Suffering from
    Depression   543
Appendix II/Do Numbers Lie?   551
Appendix III/Critical Periods   558
Selected Bibliography   560
Index   569

ACKNOWLEDGMENTS

I can't, like a new bride, throw the bouquet of my gratitude blithely off in any single direction. Too many people have been extraordinarily generous and helpful to me, and over too long a period of time. I'll have to bestow my thanks, blossom by blossom, upon the differing individuals and the differing institutions that have so assisted me along the way—and only hope to reach *most*, if not all, of the many who do merit a special kind of tribute.

Firstly, to my long-time friend and mentor, Dr. Gary Tucker, Chairman of the Department of Psychiatry at Dartmouth Medical School, I want to express an appreciation that I know he will consider maudlin and embarrassing. If I were to try to tell him how important his support was at the outset of what I considered a daunting and difficult project, he would undoubtedly turn my remarks away with the words: "Ridiculous, I've done nothing; what you've done you've done by yourself!" I want to forestall this conversation by thanking him in print.

Then, to my other guide and friend, Dr. Thomas Detre, Chairman of the Department of Psychiatry at the University of Pittsburgh Medical School, I want to express this same degree of appreciation—one which is so overriding that it leaves even a writer powerless, for it's beyond all customary words and expressions. Tom Detre's uncanny patience and untiring support have enriched my understanding and confidence throughout—throughout this project, in particular, and throughout my entire career as a psychiatric writer and journalist.

My initial research on this book was given a giant boost forward by a Nieman Fellowship in Journalism at Harvard University, granted me in the year 1975–76. During that time, I became connected with the "Walk-in" or Acute Psychiatric Service at the Massachusetts General Hospital (affiliated with Harvard Medical School) and was able to attend regular patient conferences, supervised by a superb and wise clinician, Dr. Gary Jacobson. That same year I sat, too, with the staff of the Somatic Therapies Unit, also at Massachusetts General, and under the direction of Dr. Michel Mandel. I learned a good deal there about the screening of depressed patients, and indications for the various types of anti-depressant therapy that are now available.

At the same time, through great good fortune (with a strong assist from a mutual friend, Dr. Herbert Benson, author of *The Relaxation Response*) I got to know Drs. Carol and Theodore Nadelson, both Harvard faculty members and both psychiatrists on the staff of the Harvard-affiliated Beth Israel Hospital. I began, during the spring term of my Nieman year, to attend various patient conferences, "intake" interviews, supervisions, and other events at Beth Israel, under their very understanding and welcome wing. I was also, during that year in Boston, spending many hours in discussions with Dr. Gerald Klerman, who was then Director of the Erich Lindemann Mental Health Center. Dr. Klerman, one of this nation's leading experts on the depressive disorders, is now Administrator of ADAMHA (Alcohol, Drug Abuse and Mental Health Administration). These conversations were sometimes almost dizzying in their range and scope, for Dr. Klerman, in a word, knew simply *everything*—everything about the clinical care of depressed patients, and everything about all of the copious research on depression that was going on in the United States as well as everywhere else in the world! His great gift to me was his intensely pressured time.

My activities, during that Nieman year, were not limited to Harvard-affiliated hospitals, or to the Erich Lindemann Mental Health Center (where I was also doing patient interviewing). For I was making extended visits throughout this entire period to the University of Pittsburgh Medical School and to the Dartmouth-Hitchcock Mental Health Center in Hanover, New Hampshire. At that latter facility I'd come to know another important mentor, Dr. Peter Whybrow, a researcher into the depressive disorders whose own thinking affected *my* thinking profoundly. I thank him for those many fascinating conversations, and for the hours of tutoring that he so willingly and graciously donated. I want to say, in parentheses, that if I seem to have been everywhere at once during that year, and talking to a great many disparate people at the same time, this is *true*. I was.

I found it, however, relatively easy to be engaged in all of these activities, for the best of reasons: I was gathering information, but I wasn't writing. The writing of this book became the hardest, most wrenching, most life-consuming part of the entire task. The writing was, in truth, more than a task—it became a journey, and one from which I eventually alighted, a very different person. I *felt* different, and looked at myself and my own life in far different ways. One couldn't, as I'd realized along my route, have hoped to reflect upon these painful interviews—or write about them—without touching upon one's own raw places, without inadvertently making connections with the most defended, vulnerable, hurtful, hidden parts of one's own inner self. I found myself listening, as an interviewer and writer; but reverberating, as a human being. Oddly enough, it was the writing that I found more treacherous than the talking, for it was then that I had to tease out the meaning that these events in *other women's lives* had for me . . . for me, as a human individual and for me, as a woman.

Some of the work, the writing work, on this book was done in the year 1976–77, during which I was in New Haven, and was attending clinical conferences at the Dana Psychiatric Clinic (part of the Yale University School of Medicine). But far more of the writing was accomplished during the following year, which was spent as a Fellow at the Center for Advanced Study in the Behavioral Sciences, at Stanford, California—a year during which I was supported by a grant from the National Science Foundation. At the Center for Advanced Study, I secured the aid and comfort of a wonderful secretary, Joan Warmbrunn: I also found excellent library services, an ever-ready and waiting Xerox machine, and excellent office space: much of my own blueprint for Heaven, should anyone ever ask me to design it!

I'd been certain, after surveying the excellent "working conditions" at the Center, that I could complete my book during that year. But when I left, the following September, there was still a great deal—both in terms of the research and in terms of the writing—that remained to be finished. This absorbed the greater part of the following year. And a fresh spate of traveling, interviewing, and writing was, to my great relief and gratitude, supported by a welcome grant from the Alicia Patterson Foundation.

During these past ten months of intensive work on this book, I've leaned, in every way, on the skills of my research assistant, secretarial helper, and pal, Felicia Naumann. My editor, Kate Medina, who predates this work in terms of friendship, was a skilled and intelligent friend throughout. When it came to the editing process itself, however, she emerged as one of the most creative and insightful practitioners of her craft that it has ever been my own good fortune to encounter. To Candida Donadio, my agent, and to Henry Bloomstein, I want to say a special thanks for a very special, mind-revolutionizing conversation about this book. You two remember, don't you, the conversation that I mean?

Dr. Myrna Weissman, Director of the Yale Depression Unit, who is one of America's foremost experts on the subject of women and depression, will be met with everywhere in these pages. Her impact upon *my* thinking can be inferred from the fact that, a few weeks before completing this manuscript, she and I were sitting on her dining-room floor and recording an interview about her most recent research!

Finally I want to thank the women whom you will meet here, women who were so entirely willing to share. Who are they? They are patients and therapists, friends and colleagues, people who found me, people whom *I* found; people who *are to be found* everywhere. They spoke with such candidness and bravery of their inmost secrets, and of their pain. On them—the individuals whose interviews appear in this book and the ones whose confessions rest with me and are part of my knowledge alone—I bestow these final flowers of my tribute, and of my profound appreciation.

Maggie Scarf
Jonathan Edwards College, Yale
July 1979

NOTE: There is one person whose name has had, alas, to be left out of this list of thanks. That is the name of my research assistant, during my Nieman year at Harvard: She became *part* of the book, and appears in the chapter entitled "The Winner" under the name of Marie Sirotta. Revealing her name in these acknowledgments might have been disturbing to her privacy. The other women whose interviews have been used in these pages have agreed to let their stories be told, with minor changes as far as identifying details (names, geographical locations in some cases, profession or husband's profession, etc.) are concerned. The case histories described here are, therefore, factual, aside from the omission or change of such unnecessarily specific and revealing information.

M.S.

Maggie Scarf's reputation as a science writer is richly deserved. She has the unique ability to gain complete mastery of a subject, and to present complex issues in a lucid and deceptively simple prose. Her book, *Unfinished Business*, sheds light on the problems that are endemic to the successive decades of women's lives—why, and when, a woman is likely to break down, and what crucial factors are apt to be involved.

Depression remains psychiatry's number one health problem—despite the proven efficacy of psychologic and biologic treatments. Case studies have repeatedly shown that many people who need help for depression do not seek it, and their families are often reluctant to take a stand and insist upon the necessity for outside help and guidance. Incidents of suicide, particularly among adolescents and young adults, are still on the rise. Crisis centers established in the United States and Canada to encourage self-referrals have done little to change this tragic situation.

All of us, at one time or another, have experienced a sense of despair —when we lost someone we cared for, when our hopes and expectations were not fulfilled. Our reluctance to view depression as a disorder (rather than as simply a condition of being human) is understandable, for this reason. But when one reads Maggie Scarf's book, it becomes clear that what might first appear as an ordinary reaction to grief or disappointment can, almost imperceptibly, evolve into a far more serious problem.

Unlike the feeling of sorrow, which leaves one joyless but does not alter our view of ourselves, when we become depressed we find ourselves looking into a strange mirror: all our real and believed misdeeds are brought into painfully sharp focus, and the memories of whatever unfinished business we left behind us on our way to adulthood are revived; even what we thought was good about ourselves is obliterated. The emerging sense of worthlessness, in turn, makes the depressed person mistrustful; he or she regards family members and friends (people who continue to see them as they really were and are) as insincere and false.

To make matters worse, the memory of this painful experience, like the pain of childbirth, is short-lived—as soon as we come out of our oppressive despair (and everyone who does not commit suicide ultimately *does*) we forget and want to turn away from confronting—even remembering—how helpless and lonely we felt.

As these moving accounts come to life, the women's stories convey the powerful message that while some of us are unusually vulnerable to depression, none of us is immune; and even the few of us who escape depression will sooner or later encounter a family member or a friend who has stopped believing (at least for a time) that there is a future. In *Unfinished Business* we learn to appreciate that women who, for whatever reasons, haven't managed to "grow up" completely and to become independent human beings, are ill prepared to cope with changes in their own lives and with their changing roles in society. Being a woman becomes, then, more a matter of increasing complications rather than widening opportunities: challenges that can never be met and successfully mastered.

Maggie Scarf's contribution, however, extends far beyond this series of absorbing descriptions of some painful and complex struggles. For hers is not only a deeply involving but a scientifically accurate book; and I believe its influence will be enduring. We—professionals and lay people alike—see ourselves, and our own lives, in these pages. *Unfinished Business* is outstanding, and it is important.

THOMAS DETRE, M.D.

*Unfinished
Business: Pressure Points
in the
Lives of Women*

Statistics, and a Game of Tennis

When I began to gather material for this book, it was to be about the problem of women and depression. The book that I have written is, however, simply a book *about women*.

This happened, I suppose, because the sorts of issues and concerns that kept cropping up in the intensive interviewing that I was doing—with women of differing ages, who were anywhere from mildly to very seriously depressed—were not discernibly different from the sorts of issues, concerns, and difficulties that preoccupy *women in general*.

The problems, as they were articulated time after time, had to do with power and dependency, love and hate; with the need to be cared for and the need to care for and to nurture others. They had to do with marriage and disappointment in marriage; with childbirth and menopause; with trust and betrayal; with moods, the menstrual cycle, widowhood, and loneliness; and with the difficulties associated with the handling of angry and aggressive feelings. They had to do, most crucially, with the search for security within the context of a set of vitally significant relationships.

Again and again, in the course of these interviews, the conversations seemed to return to a couple of underlying, interrelated leitmotifs, or life themes. One concerned the woman's struggle to liberate her self (or certain aspects of her self) from its thralldom to magical figures from the past—to liberate the adult person from the shackles of her childhood. The other recurring theme involved the demanding and sometimes daunting effort to develop an independent and autonomous sense of self: by which I mean, speaking broadly, that inner confidence that one will be able to survive on one's own emotional resources, should it become necessary to do so. (It will be seen in the pages that follow how agonizingly critical an issue this can be.)

These matters are not, obviously, the concerns and preoccupations of depressed women *only*. They are the issues, considerations and concerns of *most* women—and the powerful discussions that I was engaged in, throughout this time, were certainly evoking resonances and recognitions in *me*. During the same period, which stretched out to become several years, I was also consulting with biologists and psychologists, psychiatrists and psychiatric researchers, anthropologists, gynecologists, and others. I was reading in the rich psychiatric literature on the subject of depression; and reading about female psychological and biological development as well.

Eventually I could really *see*—comprehend—what I was seeing, hearing, reading. I began to recognize that there are certain psychological tasks to be negotiated, throughout the course of female adulthood; and that a woman's failure to deal with one of these periodic challenges, when it arises, can impede her seriously when it comes to meeting the subsequent set of life demands. I began to discern the kinds of problematic businesses that must be transacted and transcended, during the course of a woman's lifetime—and what it was that brought satisfaction, and what sorts of things could bring about a sense of meaninglessness, of self-disgust and despair. These matters became the subject of my book.

Concerning Loss

My research on this manuscript was begun, undoubtedly, at the moment when I first encountered those bizarre statistics on women and depression. I came across them by chance—I was actually doing some background work for an article on manic-depressive disturbance—and my initial reaction was one of wry disbelief. The figures seemed strange—strange almost to the point of absurdity. If they *were* accurate, though, the evidence was clear and overwhelming: women, from adolescence onward—and throughout every subsequent phase of the life cycle—are far more vulnerable to depression than are men.

Was it true? Or was there some hidden kink or bias in these peculiar statistics?

The same results or findings—more depressed females than males—turned up, I then found, in *every* study, carried out anywhere and everywhere. More women were in treatment for depression. It was so, in every institution—inpatient and outpatient—across the country. It was true in state and county facilities. It was the case in community mental health centers. It was simply true, across the board. And, when the figures were adjusted for age, or phase of life, or social class and economic circumstances (in other words, any which way) the outcome was still the same.

It cut across all other variables and was a constant factor. For every male diagnosed as suffering from depression, the head count was anywhere from *two to six times as many females*. The figures did show variation, depending on who had run the study, and in which particular geographical location, and what the criteria for "being depressed" actually had been. But the numbers of men who were depressed, and the numbers of women who were depressed, were *simply never equal*.

What did this consistent disparity—these sexually lopsided statistics —say, or mean? Were they considered true findings?

I called the late Professor Marcia Guttentag, who was then (in the spring of 1974) directing the Harvard Project on Women and Mental Health. She said that the figures represented the reality, and that depression was not only widespread among the American female population; it was present to a degree that she would call "epidemic."

The figures that she and her colleagues were analyzing, moreover, indicated that the rates of depression among women hadn't peaked or stabilized; they were rising. "Not only is there that excess of *treated* depressions," she observed, "but there are also vast numbers of women who are depressed for various reasons—and who have many of the clear-cut symptoms of depression—but who are walking around, not realizing they 'have' anything, and therefore not seeking, or *getting*, any treatment."

I hung up the telephone feeling dissatisfied, for she'd had no ready explanations to offer, nothing to say in answer to the question of "Why?" Why, after all, should one sex, the female one, be more prone to develop a depressive disorder than was the male? It really made no sense. It seemed, in a way, as odd as the idea of one sex getting flu, or measles, or appendicitis—or some other illness—far more frequently than the other. The only thing by way of a clue that Marcia Guttentag had had to offer (and it was mentioned almost as an aside toward the close of our conversation) came from an intriguing content-analysis that she and her co-workers were then carrying out.

They were sifting through materials in popular magazines being published for primarily male and primarily female markets, and looking for underlying themes. The idea was to search out—and to spell out—consistent differences in stories and articles directed toward men and toward women. And the differences they'd found, said Professor Guttentag, had been absolutely striking.

In the fiction and essays directed toward the male market, the material tended to concern adventure, the overcoming of obstacles; the preoccupations were with mastery and with triumph. While women characters did appear in much of what was being written for men, women were there as objects of fantasy.

The magazines being written *for women* had a very different orientation. The clear preoccupation, in these materials, was with the problem of Loss. While many women's articles and women's stories did have to do with relating to others emotionally and with pleasing others—"especially," said Guttentag ironically, "with pleasing *men*"—the theme of Losses, and how to handle losses, was omnipresent. It was simply everywhere, running through most of the fiction and the non-fiction being published for the women's market. Her analysis of these female-oriented materials revealed what Marcia Guttentag described as "huge concern" about disruption, or the threat of disruption of crucial emotional bonds.

The stories and articles mirrored concerns about other kinds of losses as well—loss of attractiveness, loss of effectiveness. But the melody running through all of the very disparate sorts of writing for women, and played upon in seemingly endless variation, was the deadly *seriousness* of such losses, the difficulties encountered in trying to overcome them. . . .

Similar themes were found *nowhere* in the material being written for men.

Did *she*, I asked, link that worry or sensitivity about losses to the enhanced vulnerability to depression among women? Guttentag acknowledged that she herself didn't know *what* to think. She was put off and perplexed by those statistics on women and depression; but she was convinced that the findings were accurate (see Appendix II: "Do Numbers Lie?" for a run-down of the many efforts to explain away those problematic figures). She was, she added, still in the middle of that magazine-content-analysis.

I was invited to come and talk with her in Cambridge, Massachusetts, and to meet with some of the other mental-health statisticians working on her project. She sounded uncertain. I myself might have let the whole matter drop there—as an unexplainable curiosity—if my friend Barbara hadn't stood me up, several days later, for a game of tennis.

Barbara and I are, among other things, both Yale faculty wives. We're both also tennis duffers, in the most extreme sense of that word. We used to play a weekly game that was punctuated with elaborate apologies; it was the funniest, most terrible game imaginable. We were so bad, in fact, that we'd had to find a tennis court (it was close by a newly-built housing project) that no one ever went to and which was, perhaps because it was still undiscovered, very rarely used. There we used to play out our preposterous and yet infinitely satisfying tennis game unseen.

The ball went everywhere. We ran all over our court, and the next court—and we claimed that our game was actually deteriorating as a result of the acquisition of so many newly acquired bad habits!

We were ridiculous, but we laughed a lot, and indisputably got a good deal of exercise. Thus, I wasn't prepared for it, and was hurt, when Barbara started arriving late, and with the flimsiest of excuses. One week she said she'd almost forgotten entirely—an apology that I found annihilating. I was angry even before arriving for our next week's appointment—and that time she didn't show up at all. I sat there fuming on that empty court for almost an hour.

But no Barbara . . . no explanation. . . . I thought about calling her that evening, but was still too furious and humiliated to venture putting these feelings into speech. What was wrong and what had I done? Had I said something? I suffered and sputtered; but knew it was the end. *Clearly* the end; the end of a valued friendship. Why? I kept searching through my mental files for some clue, some explanation. . . . Why did it *never* occur to me, I wonder in retrospect, that the explanation might have nothing at all to do with Barbara and myself, or with our relationship?

I don't know. But while I sat sulking on that tennis court, she lay in the hospital. She had tried to kill herself, two days earlier, with an overdose of sleeping pills. I never heard about it until over a week afterward, when someone whispered that news into my ear, at a faculty party.

My memory of that moment is that I happened to be standing near a staircase, and I sat down on a lower step, suddenly, as though all the air had been punched out of me. All that I remember saying is: "Oh." But I'd kept shaking my head disbelievingly, as if refusing the information; it was impossible. How could I place this inadmissible information side by side in my head with the pretty, witty, and amiable woman that I knew, and had known for a period of years?

"I've been very depressed for a very long time," Barbara was to tell me later. How had she managed to keep those feelings so well out of sight? How could the surface—and the reality—of her life have been so phenomenally different?

I couldn't understand it. I'd known, of course, many people—especially women—who'd suffered depressions of varying intensities, from the dull toothache to the flaring pain variety. But it was the shock and the suddenness, the frightening unexpectedness of Barbara's suicidal effort that shivered through me in another way, that rattled me down to the very roots of my being. It was as though an explosive light had illuminated the interior truths, the situation that was her inner existence. "I just got to feeling so desperate that I couldn't see my way to going on living," she said. A short while later, the "incident" was covered over. She stopped speaking about it, to me or to anybody . . . but she left it with me, her mystery.

Somehow, it was Barbara—and my pained comprehension of just a few of the things that were happening in her life—that set me to wondering again. . . . I went back to those remote graphs and tables on women and depression; and they now seemed to be something nearer, more pressing, more terrible. I'd looked at them through other eyes, a couple of weeks earlier.

Now I was wondering with a new intensity: *why?* Why should women, in the aggregate, be so much more vulnerable to depression than were men? I could, as a professional journalist, obsessive researcher, and careful writer, explore the matter as rigorously and honestly as possible. I could interview many different kinds of experts —clinicians, brain physiologists, hormone specialists, sociologists, and so forth—and I could interview depressed women of all ages and in all kinds of circumstances. But what I *couldn't* do, throughout the years of talking to people, reading, and writing that eventuated in this book, was to keep my own cool distance; I couldn't help really caring. Both the women I was speaking to and the subject that I was studying *mattered* to me, not for abstract reasons, but in a deep and personal way that I myself still don't fully understand.

My thoughts were to return, during my many long interviews for this book, to that odd first conversation with Marcia Guttentag—to what she'd said, I mean, about the thematic content of the articles and stories in magazines published primarily for women. The suggestion implicit in her remarks had been that women were, in some way, inherently more sensitized to losses, particularly losses in relationships —and I listened for this, as an underlying motif, as I struggled to understand what a particular woman's problem *was;* what her depression and despair were *about*.

It was in the course of this search for "themes" that I noticed something absolutely striking: the replies I was getting varied—in relatively systematic ways—with the various stages of the life cycle. That is, although there were certain overarching depressive themes and issues— issues which will be explored everywhere in this book, and which could crop up at *any point* in a woman's life—the issues and difficulties of the different life decades tended to fall into distinct psychological baskets. Women in the same phase of life were, by and large, depressed about similar sorts of things.

In adolescence, for example, the concerns usually had to do with such matters as the wrench of separation from one's parents, and with changing body-image—the frightening journey of transformation from child to sexual woman.

In the years of the twenties, focal preoccupations tended to be those having to do with the search for intimacy and commitment: the career costs that might be incurred, should one put the "loving" tasks ahead of the work ones—or, indeed, should one do things the opposite way around!

Issues of the thirties were, frequently, the mistakes that had already been made and the payment that had been exacted: an "I've been cheated" sense that the fantasies and dreams of girlhood had not been and might never *be* satisfied.

At mid-life, major preoccupations were with the loss of certain identity-conferring roles or ways of being—roles which, in many an instance, had been perceived as a person's sole source of interpersonal power or meaning. It might be that the fading of a woman's attractiveness was being experienced as an overwhelming assault. For she'd depended upon being sexually appealing in order to get herself needed attention: attention that wasn't merely needed for a sense of pleasure but was needed for emotional survival. Or it might be that a woman's depressive symptoms had emerged around the departure of a child, perhaps the youngest child—and the subsequent loss of the nurturant mothering role which she'd conceived of as her identity, her reason for being.

Depressions of the various decades do reflect underlying issues and concerns *of that decade of life:* what a depression is about has everything to do with an individual's place in her own existence, where she *is* in terms of life stage.

Seen over the perspective of a lifetime, a depressive disorder is a failure in adaptation; an inability to cope, at some juncture, with the ongoing inner and outer shifts and changes which each of us must confront throughout our human existence. As the wheel of the decades turns, so do a person's needs, desires, and tasks. Each of us does, in effect, strike a series of "deals" or compromises between the wants and longings of the inner self, and an outer environment that offers certain possibilities and sets certain limitations. But both the inner human being and the stability of outside circumstances are always in a process of change (which may be subtle to the point of imperceptibility, but which is nevertheless, there). As one way of existing inevitably alters and gives way to another, new adjustments and new adaptations are demanded. Depression makes such an ongoing adaptation difficult, if not to say impossible. To be depressed is, very simply, to be stopped short in one's life.

But when one *is* so stopped, the depression itself speaks a good deal about the stage of living in which one has become stranded. For a depressive disorder is, in a way, like one of those distorting or trick mirrors that can be found in funhouses: the depression blows up and enlarges—displays in fantastically oversized proportions—those psychological issues, tasks and dilemmas that are endemic to the differing ages or segments of the life-arc. What a mood disturbance is *about* is the stuff and substance of a particular phase of living—but written in a much larger, and for that reason far more legible, script.

It is for this reason that *Unfinished Business* and the women who appear in these pages—Anne, Debra, and Marie; Sandy, Kath, Judith, and Laurie; Diana, Doris, and Margaret Garvey—oughtn't to be viewed as a series of case studies of people who became depressed at some point of pressure, some stressful juncture of female living. For while these *are* their histories, and the subject matter has to do with what stressed and depressed *them*, this book is really a long reflection on girlhood, love, seductive parents, commitment. On promiscuity, divorce, childbearing, mood drugs. On impotence, reproductive hormones, and the loss of attractiveness . . . among other things. What it is, perhaps more than anything else, is a meditation about the realities of most women's lives, *as they are lived*, across chronological age and across time.

In the Teens

CHAPTER ONE

Departing Time: Anne

A Psychiatric Consultation

"Would you be able to tell me how you, Anne, see all of this?" Dr. Carol Nadelson's voice was gentle, almost not audible.

Anne Munson, a somewhat plump girl of almost seventeen, stared at the psychiatrist, her blue-gray eyes preternaturally widened. She pushed her harlequin-framed eyeglasses slightly down on the bridge of her pug nose, shrugged slightly: "I—don't know." Her voice was puzzled and childlike: "This just isn't my day, I guess." The patient was wearing a blue velveteen bathrobe that zipped up the front and seemed overly heavy for this strangely warm, almost hot, early April morning.

"This isn't your day." Dr. Nadelson had repeated the sentence, slowly and thoughtfully. She seemed to hesitate, but then asked: "Can you tell me a little more about *that?*"

Anne sighed. One of the medical students attending this psychiatric consultation coughed nervously into his hand; but the girl didn't turn her face toward the sound. Her eyes remained steadily fixed upon Dr. Nadelson, almost as if she were the only other living individual in the room. The rest of us—the nurses; the medical students; the social worker handling Anne Munson's case; myself—had been reduced to a mute human backdrop. We sat there, inactive as display dummies, waiting out what became an extended silence, in a welter of our own uncertainties and anxieties.

We weren't merely made uncomfortable by her silence; we were squirmingly *feeling* it. At last, though, she shifted in her seat and said almost offhandedly: "Well, I just woke up, y'know, this morning . . . and I knew it was going to be one of those *baaaad* days. I didn't. . . ." The sentence was left unfinished.

"Didn't what?"

Anne patted down the front of her brown-blond hair, cut in bangs over her forehead. "Oh," she answered dispiritedly, "I really didn't feel much like doing anything."

The miasma of her mood, like a spreading cloud, was beginning to create its own climate in the room. For a few moments, nothing further was said. Anne had begun fiddling with the blue satin belt of her velveteen robe. She untied and reknotted it, then placed the streamers carefully, in straight lines, down across her lap and over her knees. She smoothed them out, then smoothed down the blue material around them, setting herself to rights like someone waiting in an anteroom for an important interview. Noises—joyous voices—from the corridor floated in to take the place of our awful quiet.

Someone out there, a woman, made a comment that ended in laughter. Then another, a booming and deep male voice; and there was more laughter. No words were necessary; it was the happiness you can hear from around corners, without necessarily knowing what it's about. Here, however, no guesses were needed: we were meeting in the staff room of the obstetrics and gynecology ward at the Harvard-affiliated Beth Israel Hospital in Boston. Those excited voices out there were the voices of one or more new mothers. And who was the man, I wondered idly—a husband? A physician? They were all laughing again.

I looked, in sympathy, at seventeen-year-old Anne Munson, who'd been on this ward for almost a week and who'd been here to undergo a saline abortion. I wondered what she was feeling about the sounds of delight that were coming in to us from the hallway. Her face was a blank.

The saline procedure, of all abortion procedures, is the one that is used as infrequently as possible. There are simpler and less painful methods that can be used in the first weeks after conception—but Anne, confused and unsure about when and where to go for an abortion—hadn't consulted a doctor until she was too far along in her pregnancy to avail herself of one of them. Still, *that* part of the problem was over; she'd had the abortion, recovered easily from it, and she was fine. Physically speaking, it was all over: there'd been no complicating factors and she was in no bodily distress. Ordinarily, she'd have been discharged several days ago.

But the problem—and the reason for this psychiatric consultation—

was that she was refusing to leave the hospital. She had, she'd kept telling the nurses and the social worker, no place to go. She couldn't go back home to her family in Wisconsin; and she felt "too worthless" and "too out of things" to return to the boarding school, just outside Boston, that she'd been attending. She herself wasn't quite sure why, but she wanted—*needed*—to stay here.

Nobody seemed quite sure what it was that she had in mind—a state of permanent patienthood?

Assessing Danger

As everyone knew, there might be nothing at all to worry about. This young, physically healthy woman might be experiencing an upsurge of depression and anxiety which was merely temporary—a reaction to the abortion she'd recently undergone. These feelings might dissipate, quite naturally, in the course of the next couple of weeks; she could be absolutely fine. There was, on the other hand, always the possibility that the signs and symptoms of more serious pathology might be in the process of emerging. The social worker, Mrs. Hart, had spoken to the chief resident on the obstetrics and gynecology ward; and he, in turn, had asked for this psychiatric consultation. Dr. Nadelson had come in, then, to evaluate (if such an evaluation were possible) what it was that was happening to Anne Munson, and whether or not it was dangerous.

Anne's clear need to regress a bit, to remain here snug and protected in the enfolding care of the institution *might* be no cause for concern; but it could be an expression of her own dimly apprehended and yet deeply alarming impulses. She might want to stay here to protect herself *from herself* . . . from her own self-destructive and suicidal impulses. The hospital staff had to be sure.

For, if moods of feeling lost and abandoned, upset, sorrowful, frightened, all alone and depressed are common among adolescents—and they *are*—then so are difficulties in dealing with the control of sudden impulses. Upsurges of overwhelmingly powerful feelings—feelings that one wants to die, to disappear; that one "wants out" and can't go on—may propel the adolescent directly into action. Anne Munson could not reasonably be jollied out of here and back into her own world by means of a series of supportive pep talks. Not without a serious reading on where her "head was at," an assessment of her potential danger to herself.

"I Was Changing; I Knew I Was Changing."

It was Mrs. Hart, the social worker handling the Munson case, who intervened to end the silence. "This is the way it's been with Anne," she explained, glancing at the girl solicitously, as if asking permission to speak for her, to speak on her behalf. "She'll wake up some mornings feeling O.K. and then she'll have a lot of bounce and energy. When it's that way, then things are fine; she'll do things and enjoy keeping herself busy. . . ." Anne, without looking up from the streamers on her lap, was nodding her head in assent. Mrs. Hart, a woman with a soft aureole of gray hair framing an unlined, young face, continued: "But then, on other days—like today—she'll wake up feeling so low, so hopeless, so *guilty*. . . ."

"Yes," responded Dr. Nadelson, her expression calm. She was nodding her own head, as if to say "I agree" or perhaps, "I know all about that." She turned back to gaze at Anne; but Anne didn't lift her eyes, didn't return the glance. "Can you tell me," asked the psychiatrist quietly, "what are the *thoughts* that go through your mind when you're feeling those ways . . . I mean, kind of low and 'down'?"

Anne looked up swiftly, almost like a child caught at something mischievous; but her only reply was another of those "this is beyond me" shrugs. There was no feeling to be read upon a face whose expression was stolid and impassive. After what seemed an interminable time of waiting for her to answer—to say something—to say *anything* —I shifted uncomfortably in my seat.

So, I heard, did several other people. Witnessing the doctor's efforts to reach and involve this young woman was on the edge of being painful. Carol Nadelson might have been struggling toward Anne Munson through a waist-high layer of glue. The atmosphere in the room was growing increasingly charged; it was getting unbearably disconcerting. And then, just when the advent of a reply seemed totally improbable, the patient startled us all by speaking.

"When I'm feeling like this"—her voice was low and filled with shame—"and I'm back at school—I guess I don't like it too much. And I guess when I'm like that . . . I let other people do stuff for me, the stuff *I'm* supposed to be doing. 'Cause I'm feeling too bad, and like I just can't make it; I can't do anything. And I feel . . . so ugly. Like, you know," she added miserably, "I'm not feeling very *good* right now."

"Are you feeling perhaps," asked the doctor softly, "that *you're* a no-good person?"

Anne's eyes dropped again; she folded her hands in her lap and kept her eyes lowered. She was the image of (or was it the unwitting burlesque?) of the cooperative good little schoolgirl. I wondered why it was that she thought she was ugly? Realistically speaking, she was not —not even remotely—and yet she'd charged and convicted herself of this basest of female crimes! What did those feelings of ugliness refer to?

Were they old feelings or were they new? It might be that this self-concept of herself as someone "ugly" was a reaction to the abortion itself. She could be responding to the fact that something had happened to her body—been taken, literally, from *inside* her—with a sense that she had, somehow, been mutilated. "Right now," she was saying to Dr. Nadelson, as if in the hope of ending this conversation on the spot, "I'd just like to go back to bed and creep under the covers . . . and just . . . stay there all day."

The psychiatrist leaned forward, looked interested: "That's a feeling that just sort of comes over you from time to time?" A lock of dark hair had fallen forward over Carol Nadelson's eyes; she tried to blow it upward with a breath of air, then reached back, tucked the wave back into place. The strand of hair started slipping forward again.

"It—well, it comes and goes," said Anne evasively.

"Can you tell me—do you have any idea yourself—about *when* it's going to come?"

Anne shook her head in the negative, and added a "No." But she was beginning to seem more alert.

"Not really . . . because yesterday I felt pretty O.K.," she added thoughtfully. "In fact I felt really good. And then today I woke up and, oh, I just didn't want to open my eyes. I felt so *out* of it."

"And when you say 'out of it' what you're saying is that you felt very low, very 'down,' when you wakened this morning?"

"Right. Um, yeh." The young patient's voice was warming; a note of interest had crept into her responses. She seemed, in some subtle fashion, more present—more as if she were *here*, in her body, in this room. And a moment later she went so far as to acknowledge the handful of observers attending the conference: she permitted herself a pause, during which she scanned our faces with a long, sweeping look.

Dr. Nadelson had opened her mouth to speak; but at that moment her words, whatever they might have been, were drowned out by a sudden onslaught of noise from the street below. A tumult of beeping

horns and shouts—a man's voice screaming something angry and unintelligible—had washed up and broken over us through the large open
windows that fronted on busy Brookline Avenue. We all smiled and
someone laughed aloud. Then, as quickly as the wave of noise had
peaked and crashed, it seemed to resolve itself and to ripple away.
"What was that you were saying?" Anne asked the physician. "I
couldn't hear."

"I was asking what is was that you felt like *doing* when you got up
in the morning and were feeling those ways? I mean, so low and so
sad?" Nadelson was inclining her own body a fraction closer toward
Anne's.

The girl shrugged, let out a long breath or a sigh. "Oh . . . nothing
I guess. Like this morning when Mrs. Hart came into my room and
wanted to talk with me—"

She'd stopped, turned to look at the social worker, as if for
confirmation of this report: "And I was, just, well, *lying there*, wasn't
I?" Anne turned back to Dr. Nadelson, added dismally: "When I'm
low like that I just don't feel like doing anything. I don't, you know,
want to make any effort . . . 'cause it doesn't seem worth it. I'm *out*
of it," she summarized.

"And when you're in this kind of mood—and you're at home—or at
school—not in the hospital, at any rate—what is it that you do? You
just go back to bed and stay there all day?"

"Yes. *No*, I mean." Anne blinked several times in rapid succession;
she reached up to touch the edge of her white plastic harlequin-shaped
eyeglasses. "I can't, not at home, not when anyone's *around*. But I just
sorta walk, go from room to room. I don't really do much of anything
. . . I'm not *interested* in anything. . . ." The look on her face was
stricken.

"And when—if you should search backward in your memory—was
it that all of this started to happen? Do you think, if you could cast
your thoughts back in this way, and actually think about it hard, that
this is something you actually would *know?*"

"When it started to happen?" The young woman, parroting the
question, seemed taken aback by it.

"Yes. Can you remember—or even make any guesses about it?"

A dubious half-smile crossed Anne's face, as if she were being asked
to answer a question that was basically silly. She shrugged one of
those dismissive shrugs, said: "Oh, I don't know . . . four, maybe five
years ago."

"And what things—can you remember?—were happening in your
life around that time?"

"Happening? *Then?*" The partly mocking expression remained upon her face. "I was, I guess, in junior high school. And I guess I was pretty unhappy. My mother told me recently that when I was thirteen I blamed all my unhappiness on *her*—but I don't remember, I can't remember doing that. I don't think I really *did*. And what else? Oh. I remember trying to run away, but that was after my father spanked me. I can't think, now, what *that* was all about . . . but I do remember him spanking me—and he was hitting me *hard*—and I was starting to scream or cry or something. And he said: 'If you don't quiet down, I'll give you something to cry about!' and I kept thinking 'You stupid asshole, you *are* giving me something to cry about; you're *hitting* me!' But of course you can't say something like that to my father! You can't say that to *him* because he'll just hit you harder!"

"Was it in your mind, at that time," asked Dr. Nadelson gently, "that your father was out, somehow, to get you? Or did you think that he still loved you even though he could get very mad?"

"I guess I thought—" Anne paused, hitched her shoulders up and down in a brief, wry movement. "Well, that he was out to get me."

She was silent for a few moments. But she seemed, when she spoke again, to be thinking aloud—off on a treasure hunt to see what could be retrieved from the past. "What else was happening around that time? . . . . My schoolwork, I remember, was going down. I'd started slacking off a lot . . . I was feeling pretty lousy about myself. . . ."

She'd stopped speaking once again, but we all strained toward her. She had captured, and was holding, our attention. "Lousy? About what?" prompted the psychiatrist, trying to blow the lock of hair back up off her own forehead again.

"Scared, I guess. I was scared—a lot. Feeling kind of helpless about things. . . . Everybody else, the kids I knew, seemed so 'with it' . . . and I really wasn't. I can remember feeling *gross*. Like my body was gross and I was gross and I was a fat slob. Yeh, 'gross' and 'slob' are good words because that's how I really felt the whole time. And there was just this *frightened* feeling, you know—because I was changing. Obviously, I was changing. I was, um, getting breasts, y'know, and I'd already gotten my period—but I guess that at home they didn't *realize* I was changing. I mean, either they didn't know it or—I—I don't know what it is that I'm *trying* to say!"

"Maybe," put in the physician, "that you had the feeling that those changes weren't being welcomed? Or maybe even noticed?"

"Yes. *Yes.*" Anne sat forward in her chair, her eyes brightening with recognition. "It was as if, to them, I was still a little girl. But I *wasn't* . . . and I knew that, inside. It was awful; I hated everything in myself; I hated *myself* . . . I was so unhappy!"

"What else, specifically, was it that you so hated about yourself?"

"My nose; I hated my pug nose. And my not being 'with it.' I wasn't cool at all."

The Real Separation

In advance of the interview, there had been the usual brief outlining of Anne Munson's case and the particulars of her present situation. This public and formal synopsis had been presented to Dr. Nadelson, by the chief resident on the obstetrics and gynecology ward, just a few moments before the patient was invited to enter the room. In these few moments, the rest of those in attendance—the medical observers and myself—were invited to suggest any questions that happened to strike us or puzzle us. We were also, because this was to some large degree a teaching situation, asked to suggest the types of questions that we thought should be raised.

I myself had had a question; but hadn't voiced it. It had seemed to be such a minor question, and not pressing enough to demand the group's attention. Now, however, as the interview began picking up speed, it returned to perplex me again. Why, I kept wondering, had Anne Munson chosen a boarding school that was so very distant from her family and her home? Her parents and an older, married sister lived in Madison, Wisconsin; and here was Anne, in a boarding school just outside Boston. She was very far from home.

The reason, moreover, for that question's coming back to my mind, was that "independence" had soon manifested itself as perhaps the most highly charged of all issues. And there are two strategies that adolescents frequently resort to when they can't quite manage to achieve that real, that *inner* independence—the confidence that they can care for themselves and survive on their own resources—which is psychological in nature.

One strategy is that of remaining too close to the parents; and resting, so to speak, in the shade of their care. The person who goes this way may be able to separate from parents at some time later on—or may be able to do it never. The other strategy is that of putting *distance* between oneself and one's family: going *very far away* from the parents in order to create the façade of an achieved independence. But in this instance, as in the former instance, the psychological task of separation hasn't been completed.

The adolescent has gone far away, but she or he hasn't succeeded in making the real separation. Anne Munson was, indeed, far from home;

but her thoughts, as the interview was making very clear, were not; not at all. She'd moved from the subject of her parents to a discussion of her older, married sister, Sara. Sara, envied passionately and disliked passionately, had been the family's Good Girl as long as Anne could remember. "I admired her—oh, beyond all belief. Because she was my big sister and she could do things and had big friends and she was—*way* ahead of me. And I guess I've always felt the need to catch up with her and to be like her. I felt—oh—as if I had to please my folks, always, and make sure that I was just as good as my sister."

But she'd never, as Anne put it, been able to "make it" with her parents, been able to please them. Coming to boarding school in Boston had been a flight from the scene of that lost battle. She'd thought, really, that she'd be able to leave many of her problems—mostly, her bad feelings about herself—behind her, in Madison. But it hadn't quite worked out that way: the rotten feelings; her sense of alienation and isolation; that pervasive self-dislike had simply followed her here.

In some deep sense, she hadn't gotten away.

The Normal Misery of Adolescence

Were the episodes of despair that Anne Munson said she experienced —times of feeling miserable, low, gross, as if she wanted to crawl under the bedcovers and just huddle there all day—evidence of anything that could be termed "pathology"? Or was what we were seeing merely part of the normal misery of adolescence?

She was, after all, in a phase of human living that is *characterized* by wide mood-swings—by sudden, inexplicable bursts of high energy that alternate, unaccountably, with moods of unhappiness, sluggish apathy and hopeless, helpless boredom. Many adolescents feel, as Anne seemed to feel, that they're somehow different from other people, weird and alien. Many adolescents, because so much in their lives feels so out of control, suspect that they may be going a bit crazy. And very probably they are. For many experts view this period of the life cycle as one in which it's "normal" to be somewhat disorganized and maybe even a bit out of one's mind.

For surely, at this juncture of the life span, one is being called upon to cope with a vast array, an avalanche, of inner and outer changes. The rapid growth spurt of early puberty—on the order of three to four inches a year—calls, just in itself, for a good deal of adjustment and accommodation. One's body is out of one's control, becoming different. And of course girls usually show this growth spurt around eleven or twelve—*before* the boys do. They experience themselves, very often, as giants; big hulks of clumsiness. They feel like tall freaks, individuals who take up too much space. They feel gross.

But this "normal growth spurt of adolescence" is only one among the many biological surprises in store. *Everything* is changing; not only physical height, but all of the body's interior organs suddenly swiftly increase in size. Most strange and unnerving are the changes in hormonal status, for these bring about—in the female adolescent—the development of breasts, the appearance of pubic hair, the menarche—that whole set of disturbing changes that Anne believed her parents had either disapproved of, or not noticed.

This sudden flood of chemicals, newly circulating within the body, brings about shifts in thoughts and feelings as well. Such feelings are sexual, to a large degree; and they're aggressive, to some degree. Above all, though, they're foreign and "not nice" feelings; not the feelings that a girl, striving to please her mother, imagines that her mother would want her to be having. And so if Anne Munson had found such changes in her body and in her self rather unacceptable—and if she'd felt guilty, low, and down on herself—she surely wasn't the first developing teen-ager to have done so!

Those depressive episodes might be nothing more than growing pains.

Actresses and Actors in the World

Many adolescents do feel, as Anne described having done, like actresses or actors in the world; playing, for the benefit of parents, the role of the child they so recently were . . . while sensing that the person they really are is now someone different, unacceptable. At the same time there's frequently a feeling that this true inner self—who is alien and bad—may be too powerful to be contained. "She" may escape from within, become manifest to the parents and to the outer world at large. This sense of oneself as not a completely real person (but merely *playing* the role of being oneself) is very common among people in their young teens—and so is the conviction that no other being has ever felt these same ways before! It's all so fearful, so incomprehensible, so new and so profoundly lonely.

For, and this is crucial, the biological changes of puberty are being loosened upon a *child's* being. And, as adolescent specialist Dr. Richard Munich once commented to me, it is in a sense lucky that they *are*, because all of these physiological and social changes are impacting upon an immature ego. "If an adult mind had to cope with a vast flood of changes such as these," observed Munich, "in such a brief span of time, I think most individuals couldn't manage it." An adult, lacking the flexibility of the adolescent's unformed ego, might become psychotic if confronted with so many demands for change, all happening at once.

In the relatively short period of time that encompasses the adolescent years a dizzying restructuring and transformation—both physical and mental—is taking place. The stressfulness of this process is almost incalculable, close to impossible to describe. And yet this *hard* aspect of adolescence is something that so many people find it hard to recall, to remember, to believe is really there. There's just so much envious glorification of this phase of life! Of the freedom, of the physical beauty, of the potential and the future possibilities that are the inheritance of the emerging adolescent! It's very rarely that we think about those things that are being lost during this epoch or about the nature of the adolescent's pain.

Yet that pain is truly the underlying theme of these years. And the pain is, largely, the pain of separation.

Adolescents are, from the tenth or eleventh year of life—and until age sixteen or seventeen—engaged in the exquisitely hurtful task of separating out what is "myself" from what is "my parents." They are parting from the first powerful love attachments of human living. This involves loss and pain.

I have in fact never, during the course of my interviewing, encountered a depressed adolescent girl whose major concerns *did not* center about issues having to do with separating from the family of her origin. The difficulties that she was experiencing (whatever it was that had brought her to seek help or treatment) might seem, at first, remote from "unfinished parenting." But they never did turn out to be so—and this came to seem to me almost as predictable as if it had been an edict, laid down and enforced by law.

I will have much to say throughout this book on the topic of separation. For now, though, let me observe that most of us *do* tend to drag fragments of the love tie that once bound us so powerfully to our parents and siblings well forward into our adult lives. In most instances, the issues aren't pathological (although we do, as part of the business of every phase of life, work and rework them). But there are certainly a not insignificant number of women who suffer depressive breakdowns—and well past their adolescent years—over problems relating to an unachieved separation from Home Base. (Doris Nordlund, who will be met in Chapter Fifteen, and Margaret Garvey, who appears in Chapter Eighteen, are examples that readily spring to mind.)

Somewhere, lost in these women's histories, was a problem left unsolved, a growing-task never completed, a psychological bill left unpaid; important business that had been avoided or evaded, but never really transacted, never completed. In Anne Munson's case, the whole process of trying to escape experiencing the pain of the separation process—of trying to circumvent rather than work through the problem—was taking place under our noses.

For Anne, having denied her powerful dependency feelings, and having put much geographical mileage between herself and a psychological task that she'd found too difficult to confront, was acting out her stoutly denied need to be parented: that need was being expressed, in metaphor, in the form of her *behavior*. She didn't want—for reasons she herself couldn't articulate—to leave the hospital.

But in truth, she was being cared for there like a baby. Her need and wish to remain, days after recovering from the abortion, was in itself a pretty frank message. She was saying "*I* want and *I* need to be the baby for a while; I need to be loved and tended." It was as though she herself wanted to be the fetus that she'd just lost. Her situation here in the hospital had, in any case, some fairly obvious characteristics.

The most obvious ones were that her wants and her needs were being attended to—on a nice and predictable schedule. She'd been able to gain the concerned attention of the gentle and giving Mrs. Hart, her social worker; she had the sympathy and attention of the nurses and doctors as well. Everyone's job was that of caring for her; she was a patient. And if her world, like a child's world, was a simplified and circumscribed one, why, so was it safe and well-contained within fairly set limits. What Anne was clinging to, and finding it so difficult to separate from, was in effect a parody of the parenting process.

The mere fact that she felt, as she put it, "unready" to leave, was a statement. The statement, interpreted, was: "I'm finding it hard, oh so hard, to grow up." Anne almost said it, straight out, toward the close of that first interview. She had found, she remarked, in a somewhat puzzled voice, that going away from home had resulted in her feeling more, rather than less dependent.

"I thought, y'know, that it would be *easy* to get to be—oh, self-sufficient. I mean it looked easy, but really, it isn't. There's a whole lot more to it than I thought. And I sometimes do feel, honestly, that I'm just not going to make it. I *want* to . . . but I get so far, and I can't seem to get any further."

Notions of the Future

Shortly before getting pregnant, Anne Munson had—because she did, herself, have some not-quite-articulate notion about what things were happening and failing to happen in her life—had the idea of going back home to Madison, and finishing her last semester of high school *there*. "I have an extra half year to do," she explained to Dr. Nadelson, "because of the shifting of schools. And I guess I had the idea that maybe I should take that time to live with my parents and to . . . sorta grow up with them."

"So that then you'd be able to leave without this same sense, or feeling, of pressure?"

"Yes," replied the girl, staring. "Yes, I think—I guess—that's it." Her parents, however, had not been receptive to that suggestion. "They wanted me to stay in school here, and to finish up where I was. And I guess that made *me* feel they must be a whole lot happier with me away. It made me feel kind of selfish, too, because when I decided about coming East I really pushed *hard*. I didn't want to be around *them*, regardless of how they felt! . . . even though they, I don't think, really wanted me to leave at that time. . . ."

"So now," she resumed after a moment, "when I've been deciding I might want to come back and try again, they don't really want *me*. And I want to come back anyhow . . . which is, I guess, pretty *selfish*." Her cheeks had grown flushed. A silence followed this statement.

It was broken by the high, insistent note of a pocket bleeper. The intern sitting on the chair next to mine took the gadget out of his pocket, switched it off, and left the room to call in for his message. "If you, Anne, had your choice," Dr. Nadelson resumed, her voice equable, "about where you might like to find yourself in—oh, say, about three or four years from now—then where do you think that might be?"

When Anne didn't answer for a moment, the physician added: "What kind of a *person* do you think you'd like to be at that time? And what do you think you'd like to be doing? Do you have some ideas about that?"

Anne's facial expression was mainly blank, if slightly puzzled. She shook her head, fended off the question with one of those shrugs. "I guess who I was, in a few years from now, would depend a whole lot on whatever it was I *did happen* to be doing. And I can't, y'know, think of any one thing that'd be. Not any one thing in *particular. . . ."*

"There's nothing at all, then, that you might like to see yourself doing a few years from now? You've no ideas or thoughts about where you might like to be? What you might want to *be like* then?" Carol Nadelson's voice was mild—mildly interested, mildly surprised.

I was aware, however, that innocuous though these questions sounded, Anne's answers to them would be critical to making whatever judgments needed making about her present emotional state. For one must fear for the adolescent who isn't fantasying herself forward into an imagined future—who has no dream, no goal (however vaguely formed) to tempt her forward into adulthood. Such an individual may be, at some deep level, preoccupied with thoughts and notions of "ending the future." Anne might not only be feeling stuck and unable to move on—unable, even, to leave the hospital—but unable to envision "who she would be" because she wasn't really sure about going on being.

She had turned her gaze away from the psychiatrist and was looking out the window, staring at the scene behind me. I turned, too, saw a startlingly bright sky and a few hard-edged clouds, as brilliantly defined as if they'd been drawn by a cartoonist. "I don't know, I guess I haven't really thought about it that much," I heard Anne say dubiously; and I turned back again. "Maybe," she shrugged, "be a mother's helper . . . do something like that."

A lost, a waiflike expression had settled on her features. She seemed, on the instant, to have grown younger and even physically smaller—as though having retreated magically into an earlier stage of childhood. She murmured something to the effect that she really *enjoyed* taking care of babies and of children. She might really like it, she allowed, if she did find herself working somewhere, as a mother's helper, several years hence. It was, as a matter of fact, something she'd thought about doing after she graduated: "At least, y'know, for a while." Beyond that, she hadn't really thought; hadn't really made any plans. Being a mother's helper was, on balance, probably the best thing she could think of herself as doing.

Mother and Baby

Never once, during the entire session, had Anne Munson mentioned her lover. That aborted fetus must have had, nevertheless, a presumptive father! Her failure to refer to that male partner bordered, as someone remarked during the case discussion that followed this inter-view, almost on the preposterous! So much had Anne's concerns seemed to center upon her parents and envied older sister that her lover—whoever he might be—had been reduced to an irrelevancy. Her thoughts, her internal preoccupations at this time, seemed to hover around one kind of vision or image. And that image was "mother and baby."

Anne had, in the course of her initial remarks about her parents, said that she considered herself completely independent of them ("aside," as she'd added, "from the obvious *financial* dependence"). Later on, as we know, in acknowledging that she'd wanted to go home and finish her last year of high school, this statement had been partially recanted.

The picture that could be put together, though—piece by laborious piece—was that of an adolescent who'd believed that by putting geo-graphical space between herself and her parents, she would achieve in-dependence (of *them*) and autonomy. Of an adolescent who, more-over, saw her conflict as a struggle between being *who she really was* as opposed to being the person who'd be pleasing to her mother and fa-ther. But running away from such a dilemma doesn't really resolve it. Anne hadn't magically achieved that true subjective awareness of her-self as a being who is self-sufficient.

This is an inside feeling of independence: what she'd achieved was no more than an outer semblance. She could parade before the world as someone who was on her own, mature, grown-up, an adult person; someone responsible for making the host of daily decisions that con-cerned her. But the inside experiencing of her life was very different, for she was still "hooked" to those people far away, back at home, back in Madison. She hadn't yet achieved the inner separation; she hadn't divided herself from them psychologically, become an au-tonomous person. She was still very much their needy and dependent child. She might well have been, in that recent pregnancy, trying to play out—in the language of fantasy and behavioral metaphor—her own perplexity about being babied and being the mother.

It is, by the way, a truism of clinical practice that depression in ado-lescent women often does manifest itself in the form of "accidental" pregnancies. What is involved, often, is a most paradoxical form of problem-solving. That is, the juvenile girl who feels herself unloved, unwanted, uncared-for, fantasies lavishing upon *her own baby* the ten-derness and nurturance for which she herself so longs and aches. The nearest analogy to such a way of thinking and behaving would be that of buying a gift for someone else, which you desire for yourself, and then enjoying that person's pleasure in having it, by means of the process of empathy. It was this fantasy—of giving to her infant the mothering that *she* wanted—which had, I believe, led Anne to maintain her unwanted pregnancy until the eleventh hour (when the painful saline procedure became necessary).

Now, in the charged aftermath of the abortion, most of her bravado about her independence had failed her. Flimsy as cardboard at best, it had been swept away by the first strong winds of real experience. She was feeling so vulnerable and alone: Beth Israel was a refuge, a sanctum, a stand-in for the safe place of childhood. She'd sat before us, an almost-adult, a sexually mature young woman, responsible for herself to a substantial degree. But what had struck everyone, and struck us all so forcibly, was that her thoughts, wishes, hopes, angers, frustrations had all been about the people back home.

She remained entangled in the first love attachments of her life; and she seemed stuck in them—not moving through or beyond them—from a psychological, developmental point of view. She was stuck, or if she did have an emotional vector, it was backward—back into the family, and into a past she'd tried to step out of and walk away from, as if it were a dead snakeskin.

She hadn't made it; but then, the necessary inner work had been fled from, never completed. This accounted, to some large degree, for her feelings of helplessness and insufficiency at this moment. Like a young child she felt unsafe, not quite competent, not quite able to take charge of her own feeding and care.

Internal Voices

Most of us tend to think of adolescence in terms of an apprentice adulthood. That is to say, as a period of intensive trying out for later roles, later ways and styles of being. Part of the charm of adolescence *is* its very air of playfulness; its lack of dogged commitment, of permanency. Career goals, powerfully important relationships, cosmic creative aspirations, sweeping social ideals: all can be taken up with deadly earnestness, invested with overwhelming significance—and cast aside in boredom within the space of months, or even weeks. Commitments are, in some way that's difficult to articulate, not made with the same degree of investment as they will be later on, in adulthood. Reality itself isn't, at this phase of life, a hard-and-fast thing; it feels, somehow, reversible. The adult world, like a board-game one is just learning, can be rebegun if the first efforts don't work out.

A sense of not-being-completely-serious (although some of the things she or he is doing *may* have serious and real-life consequences) pervades the teen-ager's thoughts, feelings, actions. And this fundamental playfulness is, when one thinks about it, on the whole, adaptive. For it facilitates exploration of the environment, and the various strategies and ways of being *in* that environment. One plays—which is a form of practice—at becoming a certain kind of a person with certain sorts of interests. One plays at developing important love relationships outside the family. And while it's clear that in the pseudo-courtship that we call puppy-love, certain emotional components of later attachments—call them "depth of commitment" and "profundity of feeling"—are lacking—these early relationships are valuable trial runs for the later, deeper, more truly intimate attachments that will be forged in adulthood.

Its very air of imitation of adulthood; its very ephemeral quality is, in fact, what makes puppy-love so endearing and so humorous. To the adolescent, life is a game—a game that's going to turn serious. Or it is, on the other hand, a desperately serious business—which remains, at some level, a game. To phrase this still another way, the teen-ager, like an actor playing the role of a diner in a restaurant, goes through the motions of selecting from the menu of life's options—but this *feels*, in some deep sense, non-binding, like an "act." For the person hasn't really given up on many of the choices that *haven't* been selected—not only in terms of other possible important emotional relationships, but of possible career options, styles of being and living, and so forth. There is still something tentative about the entire scenario: if one doesn't like what appears on one's plate, there's an inner readiness to send it back and reorder.

And it can be done more easily than will be possible later on, for one isn't yet, irrevocably, "anyone." The adolescent retains, to some degree, that magical quality of childhood—of playing-at-being rather than really being a particular individual. The possibilities, especially early in the teen years, remain wide, for an ease in making what may be really huge shifts and changes is there. What accounts for this flexibility, this capability for change, is the lack of a fairly stable inner program.

For there isn't yet that relatively fixed and settled self-recognition of who one actually *is*, what one prefers, what one would like (or would not like to do) in the reasonably foreseeable future—and what might have to be given up in order to pursue one's goals. This inner settlement—a provisional one, to be sure—is only achieved in the closing years of the adolescent period. Before what can best be described as an inner integration takes place, the person's character is unfixed; the analogy is with soft wax, moldable clay.

The adolescent transformation involves a changing about, a shifting

of forms . . . the shaping and reshaping of successive selves. Only toward the conclusion of this personality-revolutionizing process can we
recognize the more or less permanent structure to which we give the
name Identity. What this encompasses is, according to the great
theorist of adolescence Dr. Peter Blos, that set of statements about the
self that can be subsumed and recognized by the person as: "Yes, this
is who I am. This is me."

Although such an inner settlement is, as I said, to some degree
provisional—to be elaborated upon in subsequent phases of life—this
sense of no longer playing-at but of *being oneself* is the great achievement of human adolescence.

It marks, in fact, the far pole of the adolescent journey.

What we fail to bear in mind, though, is that *at the other side of the
journey lies childhood.*

This critically important matter is frequently overlooked, or forgotten, or dismissed. For we become so bemused and enchanted, so angered, distressed and alienated by the antics of the adult-in-training,
that we tend to focus on the entire period as one in which the major
issues are all forward-oriented. Many of them *are*, of course. Adolescence *is* about "becoming grown up." But there's another, equally
fateful and yet far less obvious, set of issues and concerns to be dealt
with during this particular life period. And these center about the loss
of the Garden, of the "safe place"; they have to do with childhood's
ending.

The adolescent's struggle entails far more than the process of adapting psychologically to a transforming body in a strangely changing
world: it involves the painful effort to free ourselves emotionally from
those first nurturers who have caressed us and disciplined us, cared for
us and frustrated us since the beginnings of our memories. It is a time
of exile from the known country, the old country, with whose king
and queen, all-powerful in their giving, all-powerful in their denying,
we are—at least, at puberty's onset—still so inextricably intertwined.

At the dawn of adolescence, we are in thrall to these royal per-
sonages, our parents. This is a truth of human living, no matter how
wretchedly parented we may, in truth, have been. So are we still engaged, and deeply, with those other family courtiers, our siblings. And
thus, while the adolescent process does very clearly involve great
efforts directed toward becoming adult and becoming mature, there
are other matters—less recognized and less acknowledged—that are
happening in the below-stairs of consciousness. These have to do with
psychological separation, with the differentiating out of what is "me"
from what is "them."

No one could, I believe, exaggerate the pain or the complexity of this task. For separation involves loss, and loss involves suffering. The suffering may be invisible and inarticulate; but it is, nevertheless, happening. Adolescence is, as is widely recognized by mental health workers, a time of mourning and fear. The mourning is for the loss of childhood and the loss of one's childhood self. The fears are fears about independence and about one's ability to fare well and competently in that unknown world outside.

Let me focus on the mourning—the normal mourning—aspect of adolescence, for a moment. Mourning is, in and of itself, a wound-healing process of a psychological nature. That is to say, grieving involves a time of mental hurting and agony which has its wonderful human resolution: true mourning ends with what is called internalization, a "taking in" of the person who has been lost to us. It is thus true that, in the fantastically complicated process that goes on during adolescent separation, we are *parting psychologically* from our parents—with pain and with suffering—but in doing so, *making them a part of ourselves*.

We are not, then, really all alone in the world . . . they are guiding presences, living on within us.

If all has gone well, or even reasonably well, we aren't empty inside; we are filled with those parental presences. Just as their voices once came from outside, directing us and telling us what to do—how to behave in such and such a situation—we now experience them from inside. This is what makes it possible for us to leave, to make our own way in the world. For should an unknown set of circumstances arise there will be an authority-within to refer to. The answers one needs, if one has found it possible to identify with and be like one's parents, are to be found somewhere inside the self.

It is this phenomenon—internalization—that makes the task of psychological separation so crucial an aspect of the adolescent passage. Our parents, once there on the outside when we needed them, are now there on the inside when we need them. If one has been adequately parented, one can—as part of the resolution of the separation and mourning—take in one's parents' ways of thinking about things and dealing with life. One is emotionally provisioned, then, and ready to live an adult life of one's own. One can leave.

If, on the other hand, things have gone badly between parents (or *a* parent) and child, there can be a shrinking away, an avoidance of what looks like a too-scary, or potentially overwhelming task. There can be, as had happened in Anne Munson's instance, a flight *from* rather than a resolution of the issues.

Anne had, when confronted with the problem of her changing self —and the problem of trying to be the child that she perceived her

parents wanted her to be—tried to replace psychological with geographical separation. A paragraph from a diary that she was keeping
at the time of her departure will, I think, serve as a good example of
what I'm trying to say.

Anne gave me this diary, it should be said at once, several months
after the scene I've been describing. She had been, during this intervening period, receiving outpatient therapy, and she was doing very
well—back in boarding school, and feeling a great deal better. She and
I had been talking on a regular basis, for she'd opted to be interviewed
for the study I was doing. It was close to the conclusion of our series
of talks—she was about to leave for Madison for the summer—that
Anne asked me, somewhat shyly, if it "would be helpful, possibly, to
other girls" if she gave me the daily journal she'd been keeping ever
since she left home.

I said I would like to see it and be grateful to have it—and I was
struck, when I began reading it, by the very first entry. This had been
made, symbolically enough, on her first night away from home. It was
written at bedtime, at the new boarding school, on what was supposedly the eve of Anne's victory. She'd struggled for and fought for
and demanded this opportunity: to go away to this boarding high
school (a rather permissive one) and to be on her own and "do her
own thing." She had struck out for autonomy and independence.

But here, when she wrote in her diary, was what Anne Munson had
to say:

I feel odd now. Everyone's gone now and I feel strange. Homesickness hasn't crept up yet, so I don't feel like crying. I'd like to
talk to someone. I can't find my yellow fur doggie and yet, I was so
sure I'd brought it with me. I know I packed it, but I can't find it
anywhere. I've looked all over. I'm so tired and I want to sleep, but
really *need* my security-dog . . . HALF-HOUR LATER. I just
searched again, it simply isn't here! And how I miss it. I wish
Ruthie (Anne's room-mate) would come back so I could go to bed.
I'm very lonesome. The sheets are too short for this damned bed
too! Nothing could help my sinking feeling now, nothing could,
unless a friend came. I could use Tom now, anybody, anybody to
touch. I'm kind of freaking out. So exhausted. Tomorrow's Sunday,
I feel like crying now. I hope I can. Or else feel better. I can't write
to anyone now. I wish I could call someone. I wouldn't know who,
though . . . what *happened* to my old stuffed doggie?

That stuffed toy was, so clearly, Anne's link to childhood, to home,
to protection, to mother. And she never did discover what happened
to it: comments upon its strange disappearance, and her own dashed

sense of loss, resound throughout the diary. Her old toy doggie was gone, adrift in the world: "Probably," as she once wrote desolately, "tossed out in someone's garbage can."

A Mother's Helper

Anne had gone off to school to become, in one fell swoop, autonomous, independent, mature, grown up. Her need to view herself as *being* these things had led to the suppression of mighty longings—longings to be cared for and comforted. These were the wishes that had been, ultimately, expressed in the exotic code language of her "incomprehensible" desire to stay in the hospital. For where *else* can a person who considers herself mature go about getting herself babied?

It was fascinating, moreover, that the best future Anne was able to envision for herself was that of "mother's helper." Such an ambition did, in itself, say quite a lot. It surely conveyed her own sense of wanting to mother, and yet *not being ready* to nurture another human being. What, when one thinks about it, does a mother's helper actually *do?* She looks on and assists (without ultimately having responsibility) while a real mother cares for her baby.

Many girls want to do this apprentice mothering—and go through an impassioned phase of doing it—around the ages of ten, eleven, and twelve. For Anne, so waiflike, so much a child adrift in the world herself, it seemed to be a wonderful compromise formation. It was, this ambition of hers, a way of not being a mother herself and yet going about learning the things she'd need to know in order to one day become one. It was, perhaps most important of all, also a way of being some other mother's adopted daughter.

She'd left home, but was an unfinished person. She hadn't the inner tools, the psychological equipment, that would facilitate her independent survival. And she had the inner awareness that this was so. Anne had a goal for herself, to which she often referred; the goal was "becoming really mature."

Once I asked her what the word "mature" actually meant to her? "I mean," I explained, "what would you look like if you went to your bathroom mirror one morning, and saw yourself as a totally mature and adult person?"

Anne looked surprised but replied swiftly: "I would see my mother and my father." Then, as if taken aback by her own words, she'd objected at once: "Not that *they* are mature. But for me, maturity would mean . . . showing them that I *am* mature!"

"And would that involve," I pursued the matter slowly, "being *like* them? Would you have to be someone like your parents in order to be 'mature'?"

"Well, they keep giving me that feeling *a lot*. If I do something headstrong, for instance, my mother and father will *scorn* me." The statement erupted in an outburst of anxious, angry feeling; she sounded like a young and dependent child, fearing parental disapproval above all.

"Can I ask you something, Anne? Do you want to be like your mother? I mean, do you want to be someone similar to the person that she is?"

"I *want* to be," she shrugged, "in the sense that I won't then feel guilty about letting them down. But I don't want to be *like* my parents, either! I have other ideas—other goals—other things that make me happy."

"What makes you happy that they wouldn't understand?"

She frowned. "Oh, I love folk dancing and I don't think they ever really *understood* it. To them it's like there's just a bunch of strange people in odd-length skirts and queer materials. And they've all got hairy legs and they're dancing around and clapping . . . you know. I always get the feeling that they just don't, and never did, have any interest in who I really was or the things I was doing."

"And yet you say," I reminded her, "that to be 'mature' would be to look in the mirror and see someone very like your parents."

Anne smiled: "Yeah."

"But maybe maturity will be something very different, for you."

She didn't answer. "And I wonder if that's going to be painful for you, if it *is?* Because it's not going to be the same as for your mother and father?"

"Yeah," she said again, though without the smile. "I guess all I really want is for them to tell me that I'm okay."

"And you won't be okay unless they tell you that?"

"Yeah. That's the way I feel. Like—they are important to me, and I don't know why I *let* them be so important to me. But it's as if they've got something of mine—something that belongs to me. I mean, I *give* it to them, all of the power!"

Sex and Nurturance

Feelings of dependency have their origins, obviously, in the emotional attachment that binds the utterly helpless young and developing child to the all-powerful caretaking parent. It is this primary attachment that the adolescent, during the years of separating and detaching, is having to let go of . . . with such sorrow, pain and fear.

There is always a truly frightening aspect of feeling very needy. If one's well-being hangs in the balance of someone else's good opinion, then that other person has power and control over the regulation of one's self-esteem. The person on whom one depends has power over one's inner world. In the best of circumstances, in the best of relationships, some failures and some betrayals are inevitable. But in that situation in which one individual depends *utterly* upon the other, there is inevitably going to be a great deal of helplessness and rage. This feeling that one is powerless, that one is in the hands of the Other, is the psychological helplessness of the human infant.

The small baby can literally be destroyed by someone else's failing to care. This is a literal biological fact. And from it flow those many experiences, beginning in our largely obscured infancies and extending throughout our lives—experiences, I mean, of fearing for one's very survival. The young baby's fear of the loss of the caretaking and protecting Other becomes transformed, early in childhood, into the fear of the loss of the other person's *love*. And that primitive infant anxiety —that one will be annihilated by the absence of the nurturing parent —becomes transmuted, with growth and the passage of time, into its purely psychological equivalent.

This is the fear that one won't be able to survive the loss or rupture of the love-bond itself. Without that loving attachment, one will be alone, abandoned, without protection, left "hungry," and at the mercy of an unfeeling environment. The basic human horror is the feeling that one can't sustain oneself, on one's own; and that one is alone, isolated, in an uncaring universe. The terrible bargains that are made, in the effort to avoid confronting "aloneness," are in fact at the source of much female depression. This is a topic to which I will return—and return again and again.

During the letting-go years of adolescence, when one is renouncing —with very real pain—those fundamental first attachments to parents, psychic energies once invested *in them* are being inexorably withdrawn. There's an effort, which can be experienced as something truly driven and desperate, to find other "replacement" relationships, relationships that will be meaningful and satisfying. Relationships that will, moreover, diminish one's own terrible sense of neediness, of dependence *upon them* and *their* good opinion and good will for the maintaining of one's own sense of value and self-esteem. But the dependency is often still very much there—sometimes overpoweringly so. And paradoxically, the less sense of inner security a person has, the more she or he seems driven back to seek and reseek parental protection. The emotionally rich get richer, for they are less needful and thus better equipped for coping and caring for themselves! Those who fare badly outside the home base hurry back in defeat, feeling increasingly more dependent.

Anne Munson's "escape" to a boarding school far away, where she'd be forced to be grown up and therefore less tempted to succumb to her parents' power, had been at some level, an escape from her own frightening feelings of neediness—fears of being regressed and infantile. She'd been afraid of succumbing to a wish that *she* had, the wish to remain their baby.

But, having left, she still felt needy, like an abandoned infant or a very young child. And, when one thinks of it, why *is* it that a small child can't leave home? The answer to that question is ridiculously obvious: there *is* nothing else. A girl of six or seven may throw a temper tantrum and may *want* to run away, but she can't—for she can't make it in a complex environment which is well beyond her mental and physical coping capacities. That six-year-old can't leave, because she wouldn't be able to survive.

The same situation can exist with regard to a young woman of almost seventeen, like Anne Munson. A person who senses that she's not yet got the necessary inner tools—who feels she'll have difficulty making it in the outer world—can feel just as scared and alone as the small child. For she still needs, as does the young child, someone to tell her what to do and how to behave. Anne's request had been, finally, that the hospital be her parent—at least, for a while.

The point here is that, generally speaking, if a child has made a good indentification with the parent, then she'll have picked up enough of what to do, how to get along in life, so that, even though there may be some unsureness and some hesitancies, she'll be ready to go off to prep school, college, work, or marriage; that person will have enough inside her to enable her to find her own way.

How does a person acquire this inside substance? It flows from having grown up in a situation which could, in general, be counted upon: one in which it was safe to make mistakes so that—if the child did make them—the parent didn't punish her overly severely. A situation, moreover, in which expectations weren't unreasonably high: successes were usually rewarded and failures weren't too harshly dealt with; the developing individual was able to take risks and gamble and find out what things worked for her and what didn't—that is, of course, a *good* situation (though perhaps not as common a one as could be hoped!). It is a situation in which the child, in the process of separation, can identify with and "take in" the parents—and therefore take in a way of thinking about things and of dealing with life.

Anne, however, had little of substance—of such internal pictures, of such internal resources—within her. Hers was a pseudo-adulthood, without the inner realities of independence; without those qualities that would enable her to create a satisfying existence of her own. She had, for example, a sexual life (an adult enterprise) but it was without any of the joys that come from intimacy, love, involvement of the self, self-esteem-building feedback.

Anne was, at present, involved in a long affair with a boy whom she'd described as "just someone I know; a friend, whom I happen to be sleeping with." I asked her, at one point in our conversations, whether she'd ever had a relationship with a man she'd slept with that could be described as "intimate"? She'd shot me a puzzled glance, so I'd explained: "I mean 'intimate' in the sense that it was loving and trusting and all that kind of thing. Have you ever, would you say, been involved in *that* kind of a sexual relationship?"

She parried my question with one of her own: "Haven't you read that diary that I gave you yet?" (She'd given me her journal just a few days before this particular interview.)

"No," I admitted, "I haven't had a chance."

"Well—it's in there. I remember writing about that, in a number of places. I mean that it was really too bad that I didn't *like* the people I slept with—or maybe not 'like' but even 'love' them . . . because Tom —he was a kid I met on the bus—he was the first one I ever went to bed with. And I wrote it there, in my diary, that I didn't really *like* him." She hesitated, then shook her head swiftly, in the negative: "No, in that case I'd really say I liked him okay; but he just wasn't my favorite person. But I don't even *like* Scott, the boy that I'm sleeping with now. . . ."

She laughed: "I'm starting to think that he's a whole lot too much like my *father*" . . . she laughed again. "I've heard a lot of psychological theories about that, and I really am starting to *wonder!*"

In what ways, I'd asked, did Scott remind her of her father?

Anne answered promptly, and with asperity: "He likes to have the power! He's old-fashioned in a lot of ways. Like, just a couple of weeks ago, he was taking my nightgown off and I got myself stuck in it and couldn't get it off. And I said something like: 'Oh gee, looks as if I'm caught in something; I can't move.' And he said: 'Oh good, you're helpless'—in this really mean, *macho* sounding kind of voice! And I just looked at him, and I said 'Scott!' " The expression on her face was one of outrage.

She'd been worried, she added, about his "behaving as if he were superior to me" from the very outset of their relationship. She'd realized that there might be this sort of problem, from the first moments of their conversation; she'd warned herself, consciously, against getting into an involvement.

Had she ever, I asked her, spoken about the ways he behaved toward her to Scott directly? "Oh no." She shook her head, or nodded it, saying mildly (as if the whole matter was actually not that important): "We sleep together, you know, and we're friends. . . . We might go into the city together once in a while. But that really is all there is to it." The anger on her face had disappeared.

"Then you don't feel, Anne, that there's any question whatsoever of him loving you or you loving him . . . ?" I met her eyes.

"No, we don't love each other, but it's all right. I feel this relationship is actually okay, because I don't want anything long-lasting. I don't love *him*. He thought I was sleeping with other people, too, and I guess he was pretty surprised when I told him I wasn't. I mean, a couple of months back . . . he felt my stomach and he said: 'Oh, are you expecting?' And I said I was. And he asked: 'Who is it, that blond kid, the one with the motorcycle?' And I said: 'Scott, I haven't slept with anybody but *you* this term.' And he said: 'Uh.' "

It sounded bleak, even for a short-lasting relationship.

What was in it, I wondered, for *her?* Where was Anne's own sense of entitlement, of feeling that she *merited* Scott's concern, his caring about her? Why was she willing to continue, to live on the scant crumbs of her lover's emotional charity? A few days after we'd had this conversation I did begin reading the diary. At once I found myself ensnared by the first passages—the ones about the loss of her beloved stuffed dog.

They said a good deal, those desperate paragraphs. I thought at once of the writings of the late Dr. Donald W. Winnicott, a British psychoanalyst. Winnicott noted the significance and profound meaningfulness that certain favorite objects—a stuffed toy, a piece of blanket binding, etc.—can have in the mental life of the young child. Such soft or satiny objects become special to the infant because they symbolize "Mother." They are, in effect, what D. W. Winnicott described as *transitional* objects.

By this he meant that the special toy or blanket is real—it is a *thing* —and can be stroked, touched, caressed, kept by the baby's side at all times. It is also, however, a fantasy, because the real meaning it has to the child is "Mother." This makes it possible for Mother to go away— to leave the baby's room at bedtime—while the soft toy or the blanket edge, symbolizing her presence, gives the young child a way of keeping her close by. She "is" the beloved object.

The baby's transitional or special object thus fills the space between what is real and what is pretend. It can play the role of comforter, because as long as the child has the special toy or blanket, he or she can partake of Mother's presence. The wildly adored object substitutes, in a word, for her actual nearness, and permits her to move off from time to time—to not be with her dependent child constantly. Anne's attachment to a favorite comfort-object, left over from infant days, was of course no rarity.

For many of us do bring such old attachment-objects along with us into our adult lives. They are humorous, in a sense, and they are harmless, too. But what did strike me, on reading the diary, was the sorrowing bereftness of her statements. Anne sounded like a very little, very desperate, very homesick child. "I'm *so* lonesome," she wrote, that first evening, in her new bedroom in her new boarding school. "Nothing could help my sinking feeling now, nothing could, unless a friend came. I could use Tom now, anybody, anybody to touch. I'm kind of freaking out. . . ."

This was, to be sure, written on the first evening of her first day away; her mother and her married sister had left just a few hours earlier. Her stuffed doggie was nowhere to be found, so Anne yearned for a boy she'd me on a bus—whom she "liked" but didn't "love"—to cuddle and to hold and caress her.

Sexual Barter

In a scientific paper intriguingly titled "Body Contact and Sexual Enticement," psychiatrist Marc Hollender describes a phenomenon that can best be called sexual barter. Some women, suggests Dr. Hollender, consciously or unconsciously, trade being held and stroked for sexual intercourse. Among a sample of female subjects interviewed by Hollender and his co-workers, a number said that they frequently would agree to having sex when they were well aware that what they wanted was *to be held*. They wanted fondling, touching and holding —to be enclosed in someone's arms. Body contact, plain and simple, was what they were after: "But," wrote Hollender et al., "the wish to be held and cuddled in a maternal manner . . . (was) . . . felt to be too childish, and so to avoid embarrassment or shame, women convert (ed) it into a longing to be held by a man as part of an adult activity, sexual intercourse."

And in another, rather similar, study—this one involving a sample of twenty women, all of whom had had three or more illegitimate pregnancies—Hollender and colleagues found that almost half the subjects interviewed were *consciously aware* that they routinely traded sex for bodily touching and stroking. The women really, they acknowledged, desired the tender contact that initiated and marked the close of the coital sequence. They were far less interested in the sexual act *per se*.

They desired parenting—tender stroking—far more than they did the love of a peer. Anne Munson was trading sex for this strange semblance of nurturing. For her sexuality was reflective of her incapacity *to be*, to exist on her own. Her thoughts had moved in so straight a line from that felt need for her stuffed doggie to a felt need for Tom —or "anybody"—to touch and caress her! Her sexual behavior, by which I mean the relationship that had developed with Scott, bespoke both her terrible neediness and her lack of self-esteem. Her depressive symptoms were both cause and effect of such utter neediness—as, in truth, the common symptom of "loss of self-esteem" is both a cause and effect of depression. (In Chapter Five, we'll meet a woman whose depression was intertwined with her promiscuity, and whose issues were very very similar to Anne's.)

Unwanted pregnancy is, as I mentioned earlier, a fairly common behavioral expression of an underlying depressive disorder among female adolescents. Sex and pregnancy represent despairing efforts to fill up an inner emptiness and loneliness—with something that is living, vital, and kicking. "Mistakes" such as the one Anne Munson had made are, in some strange way, a means of counteracting the awful isolation that exists within—of getting company inside one's skin.

CHAPTER TWO

Getting Back Home: Debra

The Early Laboratory of Love

Anne Munson had spoken laughingly of those "psychological theories" that suggested a link between the kind of lover she'd chosen (someone who wanted her to be inferior and helpless; who considered himself "superior" to her) and the kind of man she perceived her own father to be. The idea that she might be attempting to resolve, in the context of her relationship with Scott—who "wasn't that important to her anyhow"—questions rooted in her relationship with her *father*, had struck her as highly comical.

And so it is, in a way: but the joke is a very human joke, a joke played upon all of us. The sometimes farcical, sometimes tragic, sometimes tender, sometimes awful truth is that the family is the early laboratory of love. It is there that we perform our first clumsy experiments; there we learn the outline, the shape, the process, the generalized patterns that adult loving will one day "feel like" it should take. Is it, therefore, so surprising, so astonishing that at puberty—when a novel hormonal status is not only exerting its effects upon thought, idea, and feeling, but is kneading the body into a new, unfamiliar, exotically more adult shape—that erotic longings might become mixed in with the girl's old, dependent, childhood attachment . . . her love for her father?

The advent of adolescence heralds, most reliably, an upsurge of frightening and delicious and supremely dangerous feelings. There is an underground, and usually completely unconscious fantasy romance that springs up between the daughter, and the heterosexual love object —the male parent. At this particular stage in the girl's development, which is to say at around twelve or thirteen, the domestic atmosphere is *inevitably* going to become charged. She is changing, and her parents know it; her parents are in the process of reacting and responding to her changing self; she feels, experiences their response. And, while the daughter is unlikely to be (as a consequence of that chemically based rise in sexual ideas and feelings) entertaining "forbidden" notions consciously, the air becomes laden with repudiated ideas, thoughts that are unthinkable. I'm not suggesting, by any means, that the daughter is aware of being attracted to the father, of wanting him for herself. Just that the atmosphere has become dangerous, and has been made so by mutual, dimly sensed alarums.

A twelve- or thirteen-year-old daughter in a household spells, in the best of circumstances, a hard time for everyone. She is in turmoil and arousing turmoil. Often, at a conscious level, those intense feelings for the father will be transformed into the long and painful crush, the yearning for the inaccessible someone. That mental stand-in for the father may be—frequently is—a movie or rock star; what's most crucial is that he be (like Father) totally out of her reach. Even so, the adolescent's competitiveness, anger, and frustration will, as a matter of course, be expressed in the context of her relationship with her successful rival. Who is, obviously, her mother.

The dilemma is a developmental one: funny, if the mature participants (the parents) happen to find it so. But the father may be, on his own part, unconsciously stirred by his daughter's ripening womanhood. Not infrequently the father himself is frightened by unacceptable feelings and he draws back from his child somewhat: she, then, finds *him* unaccountably rejecting and remote. And as psychiatrist Albert J. Solnit, the director of the Child Study Center at Yale, pointed out to me, this pullback on the father's part occurs while his daughter is experiencing a heightened longing for closeness. "One of the things that, unfortunately, you find fathers most insensitive to," observed Solnit, "is the fact that if they're at all critical or disapproving, or if they reprimand their daughter, this can be perceived as the most terrible of humiliations. And that isn't because the reproof is so enormous; it's because that incredible sensitivity to him is there."

The situation is further complicated by the fact that the child-cum-woman is in the process of losing her exaggerated confidence—the child's confidence—in her parents' magical all-knowingness, all-powerfulness. Mom and Dad's human limitations are, in fact, becoming increasingly apparent to the sensitive eye and ear and growingly sophisticated thought processes of the adolescent. Her parents are *not*, as they once were in her eyes, perfect. They aren't in charge of the world and able to solve all of the problems that could possibly arise.

And so, while the daughter is experiencing an upsurge of emotional neediness and attraction to the father, the scales of her childish overevaluation of him are also falling from her eyes. She is torn, said Dr. Solnit, between the vision of her father as a marvelous being, a great guy, and the alternative view of him as a fraud or a fool.

Whatever turn matters now take will have much to do with the mother's own feelings about the girl's suddenly emergent sexuality . . . with the daughter's new aggressiveness as well. The child who could be controlled by her mother is fast disappearing; a critical and sometimes hostile stranger seems to be taking her place. Whether or not the mother responds to her daughter's rage and competitiveness with unconscious—or very conscious—anger of her own will depend on a variety of factors. A crucial one will be the quality of the relationship that she, as wife, has with her husband. Can she be tolerant of her daughter, and share his attentions with her for a while?

In those circumstances where things are *not* going optimally between the couple—and the mother herself is, perhaps, feeling needy and starved for her husband's attention, his concern—the two females may quickly find themselves in a totally adversary position. For Mother may, at this moment in her own and her daughter's life, fall prey to fears and fantasies about this blossoming competitor—and the loss of youth and attractiveness attendant upon her own aging process. It's easy to see how readily the Primeval Threesome may become fragmented and polarized.

All of these things will be going on, moreover, at a time when that part of the adolescent which is still "child" still needs her mother's love and emotional protection. The daughter will necessarily be modeling her own sense of herself as a female person on that most crucial of adult models: her mother. The girl will, as well, be appraising her own feminine characteristics (particularly, how attractive and lovable she is) in relation to the kinds of feedback she's getting from The Man; that is, her father. Needless to say, with this type of emotional tinderwood lying about, the potential for flareups, and in fact for real disaster, is high.

In situations which become pathological, two members of the "family triangle" can line up against the third. Very frequently, according to Dr. Solnit, it is the mother and father who line up against their child. "Both of them see her," he said, "as threatening and competitive. It's not only because of the way the daughter is *behaving* towards the mother that they've gotten this feeling. Often, a good part of the struggle is their own. They find themselves banding together against her because it's so *hard*, for both of them, to think of their little girl as a sexually interesting, live and busy person."

This can become so problematic, so intolerable, that the parents simply aren't able to cope with it. They act as if they *must* eject that child from the household; they must rid themselves of her presence, if only for a while.

This was what had happened, it appeared, in the case of young Debra Thierry, whom I interviewed at the University of Pittsburgh's Western Psychiatric Institute and Clinic. Debra, whom we'll be discussing throughout much of this chapter, was nineteen at the time of our conversations: she was still dealing, though, with the aftereffects of a crucial summer in her life—the summer when she'd just turned thirteen.

Debra had been shipped off to a horseback-riding camp that summer, much against her own desires and will, and with an abrupt insistence that had startled and confused her. Overprotected prior to that exile, the timid young girl had begged to be allowed to come home. Her parents, however, refused to consider the possibility: since Debra had begun camp, she must finish it.

What followed was catastrophic for them all.

What a tale Debra's actually was! It was as though her parents' powerful need—to have her out of the house that thirteenth summer —had opened a family dike. What ensued had been overwhelming; and, more than six years later, the damaging aftereffects had surely not been all cleared away. Debra was, although approaching the close of the adolescent phase in terms of years, still wrestling with that child's sense of herself as a still very needful being who was not yet capable of surviving on her own.

She had not yet, at age nineteen, achieved the relative equilibrium— the sense of having become the Person That I Am—that rings down the maturational curtain on the adolescent years. She had not, as Anne Munson had not, graduated from her childhood; her apprenticeship for adult living wasn't over, in the sense that there was no inner confidence that she could (if necessary) make it alone. She was still unfinished and unready.

Psychoanalyst Sandor Lorand has said what I'm trying to say in an article called "Adolescent Depression." Writes Dr. Lorand: "The painful psychic achievement of the adolescent—his detachment from parental authority—is so painful precisely because he experiences it not as a liberation but as an abandonment by those . . . whom he relies on for guidance and support. Hence the reluctance (to separate) sets in, accompanied by feelings of aloneness, emptiness and helplessness, and a resentment towards the idea of abandoning the past. . . ."

For Debra Thierry, as for Anne Munson, detaching from the parents was more than difficult and painful; it was terrifying. Neither of them had progressed beyond the phase of being the dependent child: separation wasn't, for them, experienced as liberation—a freeing up of the self into a future that would be of one's own making—it was experienced as a sense of being adrift in a vast and meaningless void. It *felt*, because the inner knowledge (which is psychological in nature) that she *could* survive on her own hadn't yet emerged, like an unbelievably unfaceable process. Separation, because the business of childhood really wasn't completed, was less like freedom than desertion.

Excess Matter in the Universe

Debra was an adopted child, "acquired," as she phrased it, at the age of three weeks. Thus, although her adoptive mother could tell her that she'd been "chosen," she was prey to feelings that her mother really regretted that choice. "I am not the daughter my mother wanted," she would repeat, from time to time, as if she considered herself to have been some sort of defective purchase. Not only had she been a "bad buy" for the woman who'd taken over responsibility for her; her natural mother hadn't wanted her enough to keep her.

Debra had an inmost image of herself—that of the unwanted baby. She had, in fact, in one of our conversations, described herself as something superfluous in the world; she thought of herself, she said, as something like "litter."

"Litter?" I had repeated that word uncertainly.

"Yes," she said, and went on to explain: "Like drifting newspaper, you know. Something that's just floating around, underfoot, being kicked aside. Unnecessary. Because it isn't—isn't—"

She stopped, unable to supply the word. "Isn't 'wanted,' do you mean?" I asked. She nodded, but looked doubtful. "Yesss . . . that's about as close as I can come to saying it, I guess."

I stared at her. If I'd been asked to describe this person, the woman who talked of herself in this fashion—and if I'd had no other basis for my description than the ways she *described herself*—I'd have said the poor creature who felt this way inside her skin must be pasty-faced, withdrawn, mousy, small, retiring, and perhaps somewhat hunched or crouched in posture. She sounded as if she must be physically unattractive, an unfortunate—one of life's sad losers. But what was amazing was that she was, on the contrary, an unusually lovely person. Debra had wide, very startling blue eyes, ringed with a fringe of dark makeup. She had long, perfectly straight dark hair, from which stray strands of copper red shot off momentary flicks of differing lights.

She was small in stature, effortlessly slender. Her features were thin, not classically regular—a sharp, aquiline nose, a widely curving mouth —but she was one of those people who, by means of some transformational magic, become more perfect the longer one looks at them. At least I remember thinking, as she spoke of herself as "litter," that she was indeed a remarkably beautiful woman.

And I had to struggle to match this, my own perception, with hers. For whatever was good, attractive about her, an asset, seemed to exist outside her own awareness. That devastatingly low estimate of her worthfulness, which seemed to pervade much or all of her mental life, had left her with the feeling that she was—like a sheet of stray newspaper being blown across a sidewalk—a kind of excess matter in the universe.

In from the Sky

I met her during the context of an "emergency." At least her parents, who'd phoned in to the University of Pittsburgh's Western Psychiatric Institute for an immediate appointment, had feared this might be one. Debra had, within the past several days, had several out-of-control tearful episodes. She'd been talking, (later she said it had been more metaphoric than serious) about wanting to simply give up and die. Her mother and father had, understandably, taken the whole thing extremely seriously. She'd been so depressed in the preceding forty-eight hours: possibly, this could escalate into a suicidal crisis. Their daughter reacted to "partings" with almost unbearable anxiety and distress . . . and her boy friend had just departed. On the face of it, not much had happened: Paul had simply gone back to college (it was the end of the summer) in the Far West.

But Debra had reacted, nevertheless, with something like inconsolable mourning and grief. She seemed frighteningly miserable. Her parents were . . . frightened. They'd called Western Psych, begging for space in her doctor's busy schedule. She needed time with him, *now*, no matter how limited it might be. *Someone* had to make contact with her, talk to her, help her to regain her equilibrium!

Whatever might be happening (and who could say for sure what it was?) they needed help in handling it. Her mother had, as one of the office receptionists later told me, been calling in frantically ever since early that morning. For Debra had, in the past, attempted to kill herself. Such talk, such remarks as "not seeing why it was worth it going on living" were, when she was feeling this desolated and abandoned, nothing that could possibly be dismissed. And so, although she'd been doing very well this past summer and up until this recent departure, one couldn't be sure how seriously to take this emotional reversal. She might be readying herself for some dramatic, self-hating, self-hurting gesture right *now*. . . .

The Western Psychiatric Institute and Clinic, on O'Hara Street in Pittsburgh, is affiliated with the School of Medicine at the University of Pittsburgh. The morning that Debra Thierry came in, I was interviewing the Institute's director, Dr. Thomas Detre. I remember the feeling I had, when I met her—that she'd just dropped in from the sky. For it was only toward the close of my recorded talk with Dr. Detre that he suggested I might want to remain and sit in on an upcoming therapeutic session. That is, if the patient herself agreed to my doing so (and he believed that she would).

My reaction initially was one of frank reluctance. I was following, on that particular day, a bulging schedule of patients and clinicians; it was late morning, now, and I was feeling somewhat interviewed-out. This would, moreover, take up the following hour—my only time to catch my breath and to grab whatever might pass in the guise of lunch.

Debra would, Tom Detre was saying, probably be most interested in speaking with someone who was engaged in studying depression among women. But I still felt resistant, for the intensive talking, begun early that morning, had left me feeling so pressured, so harassed and over-wound up that the thought of adding even one more item made me feel almost dizzy. I didn't, on the other hand, want to be rude. And so, almost for no other reason than to be polite to my host on this research visit, I agreed to remain here for the patient interview. That is, if Debra Thierry was interested in having me do so.

As it developed, she was. But, before going out to the waiting room to ask her about this, Detre gave me a few brief facts. She was nineteen years old. She was adopted. She thought of herself as an unwanted baby. "I think you'll find," said the physician, "that Debra's almost a walking illustration of the depressive themes of adolescence that you and I have just been talking about." He smiled, as if acknowledging his awareness of my ambivalence about staying. "But you'll see *that* for yourself. . . ."

He opened the office door, but then appeared to think of something; he closed it quietly. "You should know, by the way, that she's going to be, today, in what I believe will be a short-lived regression. She's been making good strides this past summer . . . and this is a temporary setback. But Debra will, I'm afraid, be extraordinarily sensitive about partings and separations throughout her entire life. . . . Well, wait here; you'll see."

Outer Facts and Inner Realities: A Lost Child

She was full of fear. Not that the sorts of things she was saying weren't the usual kinds of depressive talking—expressions of unhappiness, of an inner worthlessness, of helplessness, of "what's the point of anything?"—as well as that general sense that she might not be able to make it, to go on getting her particular show on the road, to keep getting up each morning, to deal with the trivia, setbacks, problems of daily existence. Her thoughts certainly went round and round in those well-recognized ways; a part of her surely wanted to fold up and quit.

But, bubbling up through all else that she said, like the mysterious source of energy that keeps a whirlpool in motion, was the constant pumping forth of fear. One could pick it up, almost, in one's own gut; I felt myself, like a human violin string, reverberating to Debra's panic. And if I could have given a name to that feeling—located it and tried to articulate what I thought it was about and where it was coming from—I'd have said it was the fear that she'd be abandoned. She'd be deserted, desolated; utterly, unspeakably alone. And that would be, for her, unbearable. It would be something she could not survive.

Realistically speaking, though, astonishingly little had happened. In terms of real events that had actually occurred, her boy friend Paul had gone back to college a couple of days earlier. There had been, apparently, no rupture in their relationship. As far as current planning went, they'd be seeing each other again at Christmas. This was the outer truth.

The inner truth was that she simply had no belief that he'd return to her, having once gone away. She *felt* this to be so, experienced it as logical and demonstrable fact—for she had no confidence whatsoever in the caring of others. She had, indeed, in the way that young children do, interpreted "going away" as "rejection." And she seemed, again childishly, incapable of forming a self-comforting image; she couldn't quite visualize his return, their reunion at Christmas. It was as if Paul were disappearing into a void that stretched across the totality of her mental horizon: he was gone now, beyond her immediate view.

This meant the end; it had come, the inevitable and expected catastrophe. Of course it had come! She was, as she always had been, an unloved and unlovable nobody. Alone . . . nobody caring. Paul's departure had, as so much else had, served to prove that beyond any doubting.

"When he was here, there was a *reason* for me to hang on," explained Debra, opening her arms, palms upward, as if to entreat understanding. "I mean, I couldn't get really badly depressed—or let him know, even, that I sometimes could do that. So, though I might not *want* to get out of bed in the morning I'd never have let him come out to the house, and find me staying there . . . find out the ways I really felt." She shook her head swiftly, decisively: "But I knew that as soon as he went away, I wasn't going to have that reason for getting up anymore." Tears were starting to form in her eyes. "And then, when he did go—I felt—I started to feel . . . that I wouldn't ever *see* him again. . . ." She blinked, touched at each eye with one of her fingers. She looked as scared, as vulnerable as a lost child.

She sounded sure—absolutely certain—that the relationship with Paul was finished. He was gone; whatever web of daily activities had connected them was hopelessly ruptured. And Debra knew "in her bones" that the unrolling of time was going to bring into clear view the proof of her emotional logic. Paul would not be back with her at the holidays: he'd find someone else—someone better for him—during the course of the coming semester. She had her reasons for believing this: "Before he met me," Debra leaned toward the physician intently, "he was kind of fat; he was really very *unattractive*. And now, you know, that's all different—he's different. He really hadn't gone out with many girls before; and I—I'm just no bargain. All he'll have to do *now* is go out with some other girls, ones he meets at school, and he'll realize that. He could be a *whole lot* better off without me. . . ." I could hear the grief twanging in the notes of her voice; hers was the most critical, the most self-directed of cruelties.

The worst, in her inner experiential world, had already happened. If, in actuality, their separation was temporary, she couldn't at this moment recognize it as such. In her fantasies, her imaginations of her future, the loss of Paul was final. And it was from *this* blow, which seemed to be as real to her as if it had actually occurred, that Debra was presently suffering.

Here, to explain some of the vivid and painful images in her head, were some of the mental scenes with which she was preoccupied: she saw herself, a few weeks hence, going back to school. Feeling terrible. Feeling lonely and not quite sure she could cope. She saw herself, at some later point in the year, receiving that letter from Paul saying that he was so sorry; there was now someone else. This brief imaginary skit was followed, inevitably, with a vision of her deciding to kill herself. And never was there any suggestion of the equal, or perhaps more probable alternative: that her boy friend might simply go on

loving and caring for her, and might return at Christmas with everything between them completely unchanged.

"Of course," Detre was suggesting, with a little shrug, "one can't
predict the future, or what's actually going to have happened to a person a few months hence. But if one were to try to do so—and to base
the predictions on what's happened in the past—I'd say that Paul's
seemed, throughout this past spring and summer, to care a lot . . . to
be very committed to you."

"But that's because he doesn't know he could get others!" she objected passionately. "He still hasn't gone out with enough girls to *realize!*" She hitched up her fragile, bony shoulders briefly, dropped
them, was silent.

"Well, I can understand how vulnerable you are feeling," put in the
psychiatrist, after a moment. "It must be hard—when you aren't,
yourself, feeling too much like a worthwhile person—to conceive of
being wanted and needed by somebody else."

Debra shifted in her chair. It was a hot day in late August; she was
wearing a dark sundress with a pattern of small yellow flowers. "He's
never really gone out—he had only *one other* girl friend and even that
wasn't—" She shrugged, fingered the narrow gold chain around her
neck.

On what basis, what facts, Dr. Detre was asking her, had she based
her belief that everything was over? How had Paul actually said his
good-byes? Had he left her suddenly, with a curt abruptness? What
had been the general tone of the farewell? As these questions cascaded
over her head, Debra shook it rapidly, as if she were a dog shaking off
excess water: "No, no, that's not the point! What I'm saying is that he
still hasn't realized it yet! That now he's going to find that he's *attractive* to a whole lot of girls. . . ."

"O.K." The therapist smiled. "But still, you haven't answered my
questions. How did he say good-bye? Was there anything said, or
done, that indicated that he felt caring and affectionate? Or, perhaps,
that he didn't?" She was staring at him, the dark centers of her blue
eyes huge. "Oh, he showed affection all right!" she answered dismis-
sively. "But that's not what I'm trying to say!"

"Well, wait a moment; what did he do to indicate his affection?"

"He gave me something." She flushed, slightly, began to smile em-
barrassedly.

"What did he give you?"

"A ring."

"Oh, a ring. May I see it?" The clinician's voice was amused. And as

Debra held the piece of jewelry forward to be seen, we all burst out laughing. It was a handsome aquamarine in a silver oval setting. "Does *that* demonstrate to you that Paul's not planning to see you again?" When she didn't reply, he continued drolly: "*When* did he give it to you? A year ago or so? And has he soured on you since that time?"

"No. You don't *understand*," protested Debra, still laughing, as we all were. She could recognize, in the "joke," the patent absurdity of the disconnection between outer facts and inner realities. She glanced at the ring finger of her right hand with pleasure and pride.

"I'm sure I don't," retorted the doctor amiably. "I sure do twist things around a lot, don't I?"

She could enjoy a laugh on herself; the anguish she felt really could recede. But then, like a wave drawing outward momentarily, the pain crested again, crashed over, swept forward in the instants that followed. The sense of grief, of having lost something irretrievable, overwhelmed her: "I do understand what you're saying and I know what you're telling me. You're saying, 'this thing that you fear; it's not going to happen, and it's really not true' . . . and I know that's the way you're seeing it. But underneath, you know, I'm still seeing it *my* way. Because you don't have to listen to the thoughts in my head . . . and *feel* the ways that what I'm thinking is making me *feel!* . . ."

Detre was nodding his head, not objecting; it was as if he were agreeing, or conceding, that Yes, he had not been looking at her world through her eyes throughout this amusing little sequence. And Debra went on: "I mean, I do believe you—you make me see—that there isn't any good reason for me to be getting upset. But deep down, inside me, there's a person who's very . . . *scared.* And that person *believes,* no matter how much I may laugh when you point out that it sounds cockeyed, that she might really never see Paul, ever again . . . ?" Her statement, like a plea, a request for reassurance, had ended on a questioning note.

The doctor shrugged, took out a cigarette, quietly lit it from a standing silver and onyx lighter sitting on the low table before him. "And you can't," he inquired evenly, "entertain seriously the far more likely sounding possibility? That Paul will be back in Pittsburgh, at the holidays, just as he said he would? And that nothing between the two of you will have changed in the slightest? Or if it has, it will have changed for the better—because in the meanwhile, he'll have missed you as much as you've been missing him? Eh?"

Debra's eyes were fixed upon him, and she looked startled. It was as if someone had been trying to explain to her the most novel, the most unimaginable and unthought-of set of propositions. Detre, a thin stream of smoke emerging from his nostrils, sat silently, the sides of his mouth turned up slightly, so that he looked like a statue, an oracle. But he coughed then, slightly, on the smoke.

They Just Wanted Me Out of the House

Debra and I left that interview, went down in the elevator together. She was feeling visibly better; but she dismissed the notion that she'd really been "seriously suicidal" in the first place. The things she'd been saying at home, such as "not seeing the point of anything" had only been what she called her depressive ravings; she didn't actually, she told me with a careless shrug, *mean* it; she'd never gotten to the point, in all of this, of feeling that she'd really hurt herself. "It's my folks, my mother," she explained, her voice sounding somewhat scornful, "who, every time I get the least bit upset or hassled tries to blow the whole thing up into an MGM spectacular." She looked annoyed. "Sometimes I think she really *wants* me to go on being depressed— 'poor sick little Debra'—so that she'll have, you know, something to do with her own life. Because when I'm well, she really gets kind of antsy. They both do. They don't, I believe, know what else to *do* with their time!"

We went out into O'Hara Street, stood there talking, sweating in the white-hot August sun. The stone staircase in front of the Western Psychiatric Institute was crowded, busy with the comings and goings of the after-lunchtime throng. As we stood chatting, being jostled by an occasional passerby, we might have seemed to be two casual friends cheerfully fixing the date of our next meeting. We were, in fact, setting a time aside to get together: we had more to say, wanted to have a few conversations by ourselves.

It was getting late, a little past one o'clock; I was already overdue for an appointment in the nearby Department of Psychology. Lunch was, by then, a forgotten hope. And yet, though we'd settled on a time and place that we could meet—a couple of days later—I lingered, feeling held by what seemed like an almost Ancient Mariner kind of spell.

There was something that Debra appeared to have to say to me, and now, at this moment, before we parted. There was something she wanted to tell me. But all that she *did* say, and it sounded fairly bland, was that she'd had a "lot of upset" in her life since the summer that she'd turned thirteen. "They—my parents—shipped me off to horseback-riding camp that year. I didn't want to go there at *all*. If I went anywhere, which I didn't want to do anyhow, I wanted to go to a different camp, along with another girl that I knew. But they sent me *there*, to that place. And maybe it'd have been O.K. if it hadn't rained all summer. As it was, there wasn't much to do except to sit around and think about how lonely I was, how scared of the other kids, too. . . . Finally, it got so desperate that I ran away from that camp. But my parents said I had to go back; if I didn't, I wouldn't be finishing up something that I'd started out to do. *I* didn't care about that . . . it wouldn't have mattered to me that much. But I think," she added, her voice charged with hurt and anger, "that they *really* just wanted me out of the house."

We separated then, and I hurried on—literally ran—to try to overtake my schedule. But as I was scurrying along O'Hara Street, my thoughts still hovered around Debra's last statement. What was the significance of what she'd said? Why had it seemed so important to her to tell me, at that moment, about a horseback-riding camp she'd been sent to some five—no, six, for she was nineteen—summers ago? I wondered.

When we met again, the following Thursday, Debra was looking subtly healthier. Her mood, she said, had been "shifting about" in the interim; but she'd never gotten back into a really low state. I asked her about that horseback-riding camp, first thing.

"I pleaded hard with my parents," she responded promptly, as ready as a pupil who's been preparing the important answers in advance. "I didn't *want* to go away that summer." The summer before, when she was twelve, a mere two weeks away—at a Girl Scout Camp—had been a terrifying, almost overwhelming, experience. She was, said Debra, an extraordinarily overprotected child—and she was almost pathologically shy.

"I was scared to the point of being *petrified* before I ever went," she related. "And so when I got to that horseback-riding camp, I don't know if it was because of my personality or because I was *that* scared, but no one talked to me. And I didn't talk to the people there. I was just so scared of camps."

Driven, after a couple of weeks of intense loneliness and homesickness, to attempting to run away, she'd been sent back again by her parents. She must, they'd counseled her, "finish up what had been started." And so she'd remained docilely where she was: By August, however, she'd begun the sleeping. She got to sleeping, and sleeping, and sleeping. It reached the point, said Debra, where the counselors "just weren't able to wake me up."

The camp administrators, growing concerned, sent her home for a week of rest and recovery. To the growing girl, this event was probably crucial: it marked her discovery that she could manipulate the environment through "illnesses." But this time, Debra, grown wiser about the ways in which one could get wishes met, no longer said that she didn't want to return to camp. She pretended that she wanted very much to go back; and she did so, by the second week of that month.

"But why," I asked, "did you say you wanted to go back if you didn't want to?"

"I felt like if I said I didn't want to go, they'd send me anyhow. So I *did* go. But then I stopped eating, and got so sick that they had to put me in the hospital. Also, I started hyperventilating—breathing in this funny, very fast, shallow way; the way you breathe when you've been running—and no one could figure out what it was all about. So I was moved to another hospital, back here in Pittsburgh; they pinned the whole thing on my thyroid. And after that, I was given some pills and I was sent home. . . ."

She blushed slightly. "I was *home!* And after that, I was fine. But the reason I'd gotten home was because I'd been so sick. That, oh *that* stuck in my head!" Her face held an expression of bitter triumph. Like Gretel, in the fairy tale, she'd outfoxed her rejecting parents. They had tried to lose her, to send her away; and off into the woods of the world outside. But she, clever girl, had found the particular trail of breadcrumbs that would get her, without fail, back to where she belonged. It was "being ill." And after that time, explained Debra, "I just *knew* it. Being sick gave me the opportunity to get out of things . . . and, y'know, to stay home and be taken care of. I *took* that opportunity."

She hesitated, looking embarrassed. So much so, indeed, that I asked in puzzlement: "Like—what, for example?" Debra, staring at me, said: "A bizarre opportunity." She stopped again. I waited.

When she said nothing, I leaned forward in my chair, bent my head to one side questioningly. She began to fiddle with the thin chain at her neck, smiled a bit ruefully, then said: "It was this. The following November, a few months after all that stuff at camp had happened, I cut my leg shaving. And I'd heard that if you wrap something tight around it, it stops the bleeding. So I did that; I put a real tight bandage around it. But I put it on *so* tightly that when I woke up the next morning, my whole leg was swollen. . . . Well, you know, I did that myself. But I realized at once that I could use it to pretend something was wrong, and to get out of going to school. I was afraid of the other kids, anyhow, and I didn't much want to go. So, here it was: the whole thing had fallen into my lap. I didn't have to go to school, after all; I was *sick*."

It was with this minor event—having put on that bandage too tightly—that, as I soon was to realize, a complex, costly and crazy family saga originated. For Debra's mother, naturally, took her to the doctor. And the family doctor, unable to figure out what might be causing that mysterious swelling, recommended a specialist. The specialist, in turn, sent mother and daughter to *another* specialist: no one could, however, discover what lay at the source of that disturbing swelling in the thirteen-year-old Debra's leg. Test after test, of course, turned up no medical explanation. Until eventually, the physicians the family was consulting came to the conclusion that the girl must be suffering from something fairly serious. "I guess," shrugged Debra now, "that you can take just so many tests on people and then you're going to find something wrong *somewhere.*" And this was what, apparently, had happened.

She'd been diagnosed as suffering from the fatal disease lupus arthritis.

Debra was, in short, "dying." And, as their fatally ill child, she was managing to *extract* from her parents all of the nurturing, tenderness and care which had been so suddenly withdrawn from her the summer before—the summer that she'd turned thirteen. Her fourteenth birthday now passed, but of course that "lupus arthritis" wasn't following its usual and expected course. The disease itself wasn't, in fact, going anywhere . . . and yet that swelling in the young patient's leg persisted. "It was," recounted Debra, "like being caught up in a whirlwind: I just couldn't *get out.*" She'd set a strange scene into motion, and now was, herself, unable to escape it. Her parents were, on their part, unable to bend their necks to the axe of that diagnosis. They couldn't accept it, couldn't believe it: they'd flown her, in the following months, to several medical facilities in other parts of the country. But now, as a result of these efforts, a new diagnosis was being suggested. Debra had, the doctors now thought, a brain eruption, an aneurism. There was, alas, little hope for her in the long run. "I knew *exactly* what was going on," she recounted. "But I was torn between —I couldn't—I was far too deeply into it to *ever* tell them the truth."

"What symptoms," I asked her, "did you have at this point?"

She flushed: "Well, my leg was swollen. I was still putting the bandage on it."

I started, looked at her in astonishment: "Every night? Even in the hospital?" I think I started to laugh then, and so did she. "I know it sounds funny," she protested nevertheless, "but it was *awful.* Awful not knowing when it was that I was going to be found out . . . and feeling too trapped, caught in the whole mess, to get out of it myself! How *could* I do it? How could I say to my parents—who'd just paid off a huge hospital bill—that *I'd* been doing it; fooling them; fooling all those big doctors the entire time? It was like—I had some superhuman powers—"

"Evil powers?" I interrupted.

"Yes. Yes. Meanwhile, too, I *was* getting out of school. I was out, for months at a time, for pretty much the entire next year. And I—I was getting friends out of *pity.* . . . But I was amazed, myself, about —you know—having gotten away with all of it. And I didn't know what I could do *next!*" Like many another successful inventor, she'd been taken aback, truly, by the beauty and power of her own discovery. It *was*, of course, that—a creative invention, a cleverly original strategy designed to secure her parents' concern, attention and care. It was a way, when one thinks about what purpose it actually was serving, to get back home and to stay at home, and to make sure she'd get herself *taken care of*.

But events were now getting, very seriously, out of Debra's control. For X-rays of her brain, done at a "fancy medical clinic," had led to the scheduling of brain surgery. *Was* there, in fact, something wrong inside her brain? Had the physicians she was seeing, although on what she knew were false premises, *still* discovered (accidentally) a tumor or growth that actually was there? She herself was confused: "I had no control over what they found inside my head. But the thing was, they were getting ready to operate: and I sure wasn't going to go through with that!"

Was she sick, in reality, or wasn't she? Was she going to live or to die? Debra wasn't, any longer, certain herself. The brain aneurism *could* be there independently of the leg bandaging—by the most eerie of coincidences, the latter could have revealed the presence of the former. It wasn't unlikely, really, that she would die: it would be better, too, if she *did* die.

There was no longer any way, or none that she could think of, out of this complete mess, this morass of lies.

Debra, in the hospital, wrote a letter of confession to her parents; she sent it out. Then she went into the hospital bathroom and gulped down a carefully hoarded overdose of sleeping pills. She was, at this point, just a couple of months short of turning fifteen.

Finishing Up What One Has Started

She's been quickly discovered, found out, "saved." But then, Debra's attempt on her life had only been semi-serious. The timing on that letter to her parents was such that she'd never have had a chance to perish in advance of their receiving and responding to it. And then, a hospital bathroom isn't really the most private place for trying to commit suicide. Hers had been clearly the kind of suicidal gesture which is termed the "cry for help." It reflects an urgent need to turn some set of circumstances around far more than it does a person's real wish to end her or his life.

Still, the show was over; her defensive campaign had collapsed. The method she'd been using, and using so successfully, to gain the love and concern of others, simply would not work any longer. She was exposed for what she was. And, shortly afterward, hospitalized briefly on a psychiatric unit (due to that suicidal effort), she felt the bottom dropping out of everything. "I suddenly realized that I had *nothing.* I had done all those things. I knew my parents would lay it on me, about them, about what I'd done, once I came home. I was nowhere; I had no one. I really hit the basement, then; I mean I *was* suicidal. That was the time, oh, the time when I really *did* want to die! I'd have done anything—jumped out the window if I could—I simply hated myself. I just couldn't bear it . . . I stopped eating. They had to feed me intravenously. More than anything, anything, I really wanted to die."

Debra sat up very straight in her chair, suddenly, as if someone had just spoken to her about her posture. She drew in a long, very deep breath, like a diver preparing to go under. "But then," she continued, "I got out of that violent, that really self-attacking kind of phase. I just got terribly depressed . . . gave up . . . couldn't do anything."

Her career as medical patient had ended; now, a new career as psychiatric patient was getting underway. Debra, profoundly depressed, was transferred to a longer-stay psychiatric facility: one that specialized in various forms of drug therapy used in the treatment of depression. "No one ever *asked* me if I wanted to go there; I was just sent," she said now, looking angry. "I felt like some hunk of leather or something that anybody could just beat around. And they kept trying out different drugs on me . . . which made me feel *more* like a piece of leather. I think I went in and out of every drug known for about the following two years."

Nothing helped.

She was sixteen now, hating herself, hating everyone around her: "Above all, I hated my parents." They'd been, in the meanwhile, impoverished by their daughter's medical and psychiatric saga. And, toward the close of her stay on that drug-therapy unit, Debra became violently self-destructive again; she'd made several wrist-slashing attempts, turning all of that fury into attacks on her self. "My parents, at a hundred and fifty dollars per day, couldn't go on keeping me where I was," she said soberly, "and yet I *wasn't* in any kind of shape where they thought they could handle me, and care for me at home." She ran a long slender hand through the back of her hair, lifting it up momentarily: the brown, dark strands fell silently into place.

"They were forced, then, to put me into a community hospital—which was, I think, what saved my life. Because there they decided that I was *addicted* to all the drugs I'd been getting as 'treatment.' And so, although I wasn't a typical kind of a drug addict, they did put me into a drug rehab center." The life of the rehabilitation unit was one which was highly structured: this form of live-in treatment is one in which schedules and routines are closely adhered to and very important.

This type of setting provided the kinds of outer support, of limit-setting, that the young woman so sorely needed. "It helped me," reflected Debra, "it really did. I got off all those medicines. And I learned that the only way to get out of the depression was to really *psych* myself in the mornings. To get up and start doing *things*. . . ."

Part of the closing phase of the treatment process involved, however, getting the patient to admit, openly, to her or his drug dependency . . . to being an addict. This she adamantly refused to do. She hadn't, she insisted, taken those drugs voluntarily. They had been *prescribed* to her by a physician. Because of this intellectual disagreement, she had to leave the rehabilitation unit without having properly "graduated." "My parents were dead set against my doing that too," she smiled wryly. "Because, it was the same as my leaving summer camp that summer; I wouldn't be finishing up something that I'd started!"

She paused, then added bitterly: "I knew, by then, that they could shove that down their throats. I was leaving, and on my own terms, and I didn't care."

Healing the Self

If one were to assess a life course, in terms of its vector, its general direction, then Debra Thierry's, at age sixteen-plus, sounded nothing short of frightening. So much had happened, and was continuing to happen, that it was confusing to try to figure out who had done what to whom . . . and why. Certainly, as we spoke, I could feel my sympathies (and my "blame") shifting backward and forward, between the parties. Clearly, her parents had cared more for their daughter's carrying through a meaningless rite—"finishing what she'd started"—than they had been able to respond to her real distress and despair. And Debra, still somewhat shy, still uncertain, appeared to have emerged from a family atmosphere in which no sense of her own independence seemed ever to have been fostered . . . or perhaps, even permitted. Cast out suddenly, as she had been in that terrible summer, she'd responded to the trauma in a fashion as ingenious as it had been bizarre. Her strategy had, in the short run, succeeded in defending her against the dangers (strange people, strange situations) she so desperately feared. And if, in the long run, this method of coping *had* to be unworkable, why, she herself was still largely a child when she'd devised or invented it. And the time sense of children doesn't, as we know, stretch far beyond the immediate.

Debra had been thirteen when the long struggle to "get home" had started; when she left the drug-dependence unit, she was moving toward the close of the teens. It was at this point that, seemingly harassed and driven by currents beyond her own ability to deal with or to handle, she'd suddenly taken over in a new way; she came, quite unexpectedly, into a far greater, and unexpected, degree of control. Dating from her stay at the drug-dependence unit, she began moving through another stretch of sea. She'd come past something. Her thoughts, ideas, feelings, emotions were less prone to scuttle her, to send her whirling about dizzily in riptides of self-hatred and self-disgust. She was becoming capable, though with occasional reverses (and for reasons that defied explanation) of taking greater care of herself. She was just growing better—which is to say, growing up.

Of course it's true, as psychiatrist E. James Anthony has noted, that it is during adolescence that the potential for "healing the self" in this way does first arise. In early childhood, we haven't the capacity for repairing (or salving) our own psychological hurts and wounds. We aren't able to truly look within, to introspect and communicate with our inner selves. In the preschool years, we master anxieties and distresses by dealing with them in play—that is, we play them out, in games. Older children, which is to say children in the latency years (six to twelve) deal with problems and difficulties by *not* dealing with them; in other words, they try to avoid thinking about matters that may be painful or frightening, and to keep busy with preoccupations of a variety of sorts (the "collecting, classifying and counting" of things is, according to Dr. Anthony, the kind of activity that absorbs the latency-age child).

But at puberty we come into contact with—and confrontation of— the inner self. A person has, by this period of life, become capable of analyzing, thinking abstractly, making deductions and hypotheses— and begins constructing theories about whatever things are happening to her, or to him. These are truly new sorts of capacities. In the adolescent years, moreover, childhood's defenses (which include the magical sense that the parents are all-powerful and can take care of anything) are crumbling, while the fortifying guns of our adult defenses are not yet firmly in place. As adolescent specialist Anthony phrases it: "Sandwiched between the defenses of latency and adult life, never again will the adolescent experience the same sense of closeness with his inner being, aside from periods of crisis and catastrophe. . . . adolescence is the peak period for self-psychotherapy."

The potential for restoration and self-healing are, during this phase of life, as present and powerful as the potential for self-hate and for destructiveness. And so it was that, in the wake of Debra's sojourn at the rehabilitation center, the healthiness that was *also* within her began to manifest itself, to surface. What can best be termed a developmental miracle had, somehow, begun taking place. She started (to borrow a term used by psychiatrist Anthony) to "hatch away" from the symbiotic, too-close union—that excessively dependent, ambivalently overangry-and-hating and overloving-and-needy relationship that she had with her mother.

Debra, when we spoke, credited the drug-dependence unit with the new strides that she had, at age sixteen, found herself capable of making. But who knows, in truth, what had made that forward leap possible? It could have been no more than the passage of a period of time. . . . But she *had* moved into the dizzying business of self-transformation; she was growing, with whatever pain and whatever occasional backslidings, into someone who could survive on her own. Why, at that moment?

The best answer to this question is, simply, "because." As Dr. Anthony, an extraordinarily sensitive writer on the subject of adolescence, has put it: "Many of us have survived the great developmental transition without being aware of how we did it. Adolescence becomes one of our dead selves, and we apparently neither miss it nor mourn it. . . ." We aren't always able to explain how it happened, or why, in terms of the tasks and the timing. But during this transition in our lives, we learn something about "self-empathy" or taking-care-of-the-inner-self.

Getting Away

That year, said Debra, she made some far-reaching decisions. Most important among them was, she believed, her decision to go back to high school and to graduate. She was behind, of course, but with effort could finish a year behind her former class. "I was really gung ho on everything, that year," she recounted. "And I did it all, set up a high school that I could go to—*not* my old school; I felt I couldn't go back there—and I kept thinking, all throughout, that at the other end there would *be* a Happy Ending! I thought, more than anything, that at last I'd be getting away, really *away*, from everything that had been happening to me, everything that *I'd* done, too. And that's all, I think, that was on my mind the whole time. Getting away! I felt I wasn't living, simply *existing;* and that I'd start to live when I left home. That was going to be *it*, to be so wonderful—and the only thing I was working and living for was graduating! I was going to go to college five hundred miles away, to *get* away. I'd even had plastic surgery done on my wrists, where I'd hurt myself, so that no one would ask me about the scars."

Now, however, her mother seemed to be going through some kind of sea change too. She didn't like, or at least seemed worried—sometimes to the point of being provoked—by her daughter's sudden moves toward autonomy and independence. She felt that Debra wasn't well enough, really, to care for herself: she needed lots of help, nurturance, assistance. The tasks that a normal girl of her age might reasonably be expected to perform, were, or so Debra's mother's behavior implied, ones that could stress *this* girl far beyond her capacities! "My mother liked doing things for me," she observed now, with a sigh. "She liked it to the point that, actually, I didn't have to do a single thing for myself. She'd clean my room for me, type my papers; she'd even *eat* for me, I think, if it could have come down to that. And I, in the beginning, had enough of my own strength built up so that this didn't bother me. I mean, I could fight it. But then, I started slipping. It got me down. I didn't want to do anything, to bother taking care of myself, if *she* was going to do it for me. I felt I could just lie back, let everything sort of happen. . . ."

As she spoke her voice grew softer, diminished, almost that of an uncertain child. "What other sorts of things did your mother do for you?" I asked, trying to bring her back by sounding brisk.

"Oh, wash. She did my wash. And getting up in the morning. . . ."

I laughed. "She did your getting up for you?"

Debra smiled, but the smile disappeared rapidly. She shook her head: "No, getting *me* up. In college, when I finally did get there, I quickly learned that if you don't get out of bed yourself, nobody *is* going to get you out!" She looked somber. "You know, I'd been looking forward to this, so much; being on my own, I mean. I'd spent the whole year before thinking of nothing else, only graduating, getting away from home! I'd gone *far away*, too, so that I couldn't go running back if I felt shaky. This was it: I had to do everything for myself, and all I'd been dreaming about was how wonderful that was going to *be.* . . ."

She gave me a wry look. "But then, when I really made it, really *was* away, I started feeling—overwhelmed. I was—so scared. And I did screwy things at first. I'd do things like stay in bed and sleep for five days. . . ." She paused. "My whole perception of my mother changed, during that time, too."

Faced, during this first experience of *really* being away from home (for Debra had, during the entirety of her adolescent odyssey, been either with her parents or squarely under the gaze of some hospital or other institutional eye) the new freshman now saw her mother as "not a nag, so much, but as someone who cared, who really *was* concerned. It's amazing how," she added reflectively, "because I was feeling so absolutely petrified, I came to see my mother in such a different way." The "self-caring-for" activities, such as laundry, getting up in the morning, etc., were ones that her mother had been taking charge of for her. No one else here was going to do them. She had, somehow, to navigate these tasks on her own.

In the course of those first days at school, she'd shifted in and out of moods of neediness and of competence; of feeling that she couldn't make it, and of feeling that she'd outgrown, at last, that desperate reliance on her mother's caretaking. "I'd talk to her on the telephone, and I'd be very self-assured and feel just fine. But then, somehow, it would come over me . . . I'd become so *frightened*." It was during this time, that is, the early weeks of her freshman year, that the young student, at the suggestion of an adviser, began seeing a school psychologist.

It was a healthy move. It was an admission, true, that she wasn't "independent" in the sense that she couldn't depend on and take care of herself without aid. But it was, on the other hand, not developmental defeat: she hadn't run back to mother. And the therapy she'd had then was, said Debra, something that she'd found really helpful—even though it didn't succeed in utterly vanquishing that regressive pull, that powerful impulse to retreat to a simpler time of her life. For some "child part" of her still craved a nurturer, a guardian. That part of her yearned for a concerned and problem-solving magical-parent who would calm excessive fears, take care of whatever dangerous or threatening situations might arise. . . .

So fantasies of reunion with her parents, especially her mother, continued to alternate with fears of submitting to these seductive, ultimately jeopardizing desires. To drop out of school, to flee homeward, might mean being a child forever; it would be experienced as a kind of surrender. If the pull homeward was, for this dependent and needy girl, an exceptionally forceful and magnetic one, it was by no means exceptional—at her age—to be feeling some degree of "pull." For every adolescent does experience, at some stage in the separating process, strong wishes to return home, to be the protected child again (and most especially is this felt in the wake of blows and defeats out in the world).

Most parents, too, experience similar kinds of wishes; that is, the wish, whether in or out of awareness, that the child return and *be* a child once again. (As the above-quoted Dr. Anthony has observed, the parable of the prodigal son is "as pertinent to the parent as to the child.") There are, in the inner world of both parents and offspring, often profound reservoirs of yearning for and unconscious fantasies about the restoration of union. There are powerful impulses, on both sides, to return to the way it was in early childhood's Eden.

But to really *do* it, to flee backward now, would have been Debra's acknowledgment of psychic defeat. The Gates of the Garden, once opening to welcome her on her return, might close again; she'd be imprisoned, possibly always, tied to babyhood and dependence. Going back, much as part of her wanted to in those early days, would have proven—to herself and to her parents—that she was unfinished, unable to survive on her own.

The sessions with the psychologist, during those first weeks of college served as a sort of emotional inner tube. They kept her afloat, if nothing else, head bobbing above the possibly engulfing waters. And eventually, with the passing of time and the growth of some degree of self-trust, the therapist succeeded in establishing contact with the "non-child" parts of Debra's personality. He was able to tap into the more autonomous, healthier, less dependent aspects of her being. "I started doing a lot more things on my own after a while," she told me, "and I was feeling really *good* about that. In fact I was feeling swell all the way up until about Thanksgiving; I thought I'd *made* it; I actually did. But then, at the holiday, my parents came out all of a sudden. They came, you know, just for a visit. My mother took one look at me, and she said, as if I'd really done something *wrong*: 'You've grown up too fast.' And, oh God, when she said that, it hurt me. I mean, that really hit the spot."

The growing-up that had been accomplished during the painful first weeks of the semester wasn't (for some reason) the right or acceptable kind of growing up that a young woman should do! And the sense of "having done it wrong" stuck in her thoughts like a thorn or a nail in soft flesh; it remained with her long after the holiday's end. It became, again like a thorn, increasingly painful. "But I got by, I managed until Christmas," she said, "when I went home. Then, I just gave up, felt awful, hadn't the energy for anything. I felt as if some plug in my system had just gotten lost somehow, and all the energy had leaked or drained right out of me. My mother was doing *everything* for me, just like before I left."

Ten Million Expectations

Did Mrs. Thierry, I wondered, even recall having made that depressogenic remark—"You've grown up too fast"—to her daughter? I wondered, too, exactly what she'd meant when she'd said it? It seemed to have had monstrous significance for Debra, and I asked *her*, at some point, what she thought her mother's intent and her own feelings had been at the moment that she'd said it?

The question seemed to startle her. She stared at me, then said slowly: "When she said that, actually, we'd already been together for a while. We'd been alone, just the two of us, 'cause my Dad went to take a walk and look, you know, around the campus. I was feeling good, really excited actually, about school. I'd gotten myself into pretty good shape, and I'd *done* it myself; she hadn't done a thing. So I had this happy feeling, and I suppose I must have been showing off a bit, sort of saying: 'Look, now, see how well I've done!' . . . But then, when she said that to me, in that cold kind of way I thought: 'Wow, maybe I never *did* do so well as I thought.' Maybe I'm not the right kind of *person* . . . for some reason, the floor just fell out from under me."

"Why, do you think, were you so devastated by that remark of hers?" I asked Debra now.

She seemed puzzled. "I—can't answer for sure. Maybe it's that I rely on her approval to such an extent. The only thing I can come up with in my own thinking is the idea that maybe she didn't like me the way I was. I still wasn't the daughter she wanted me to be."

We fell silent. She was thinking her own thoughts and I was thinking mine. The most impenetrable of mysteries was, it seemed to me, Debra's parents' motives in suddenly exiling her, and remaining fixed in their decision to enforce it, the year of her thirteenth summer. For her mother had been, before that time, an excessively careful kind of a mother, who tended to "do for" rather than permit her daughter to "do." Had Debra's normal biological maturing been seen as threatening, untenable, an attack or misbehavior of some kind? Had her parents been experiencing, that summer, serious problems of some kind that their daughter (even now) knew nothing whatsoever about? Or was the truth some combination of these, and perhaps other unknown elements? I hadn't the answers nor, when Debra tried thinking about them, had *she* any. But if her own behavior, after that terrible summer, had demonstrated that she was having pain in separating from her mother, so did her mother's behavior do so at this moment.

For that cruel, dismissive comment—"You've grown up too fast"— said pretty clearly that she was angered and offended by her child's show of independence. Her mother was finding it difficult to separate from *Debra*. Doing things on her own, and making developmental strides forward was seen, for this reason, as evidence of badness or wrongness (defined as "growing up too fast") on the daughter's part. Debra had of course, in her bragging, been openly soliciting her mother's encouragement and approval. But what she'd gotten had been the opposite: it had been the confirmation of her worst fears about herself.

These had to do with not being able to make it, to leave, to separate, to survive on her own. The growing she'd done, which she'd thought to be good growing, had in fact been done wrongly!

Now, starting to speak again, most haltingly, as if dredging every word heavily upward from a quarry of hidden stone thoughts deep within her mind, Debra said: "My mother and I—I think—we have the same problem. She wants a daughter that I'm not and—I want a mother that *she's* not. . . ." Her gaze, flickering over the beige wall of the borrowed office we were sitting in, was turned upon me suddenly; her eyes met mine directly. "You know, I was adopted, very young," she stated.

"Yes. How young?"

"I was three weeks old. And my mother already had ten million expectations put on me the day that she adopted me. She adopted me for a reason: she wanted to fill a need that *she* had. I don't fill that need the way she wants me to. And I've reached the point, you know, where I no longer care."

"What needs do you think your mother wants you to fill?" I asked. We'd both leaned forward in our chairs; we were staring hard at one another. Debra started twisting, nervously, the going-away ring that her boy friend Paul had given her. "She wants a daughter who really *needs her*," she answered. "And you know, I do need her. But I won't ever, not ever, let her know that."

"And you," I responded quickly, "what is it that you want in a mother?"

"I want a mother who will show me how to do things on my own, and not do them *for* me. But my mother won't ever do that. I could never ask her to show me how to do something, because she *wouldn't* show me—she'd *do* it for me instead. And the thing is, I used to be angry with her because she was that way. But what good is it, being angry? What good is it ever going to do me?"

Her voice was rising, in anger, in uncertainty. At the same time, she opened her arms outward in that "Hear me! Listen!" entreating kind of a gesture. As she did so, my glance fell on her wrists; and I realized, with a start, that the plastic surgery had not been 100 per cent successful. There were very thin, pale pink lines there; stigmata of the suffering that had gone before. I felt, on seeing them, a combination of revulsion and sadness. "You know, when my mother said that thing, about my growing up too fast, I thought first of all that she'd said it because she didn't want me growing up *at all* . . . she wanted to be in control of me forever." Debra, sweeping onward, spoke as if she hadn't noticed my involuntary start (though I believe she had).

"Then I guess I started thinking," she said, "and mulling it all over in my head afterward. And I thought that—I don't know, maybe there *was* something wrong with the things I was doing. Or maybe," she added searchingly, turning the statement into a question, "I was doing the right things but doing them in the wrong ways?" She looked at me searchingly: "Maybe there are, uh, certain *ways* of doing things?"

I wasn't sure, for a moment, whether or not she was serious. But then I realized that she was—absolutely. She was, in fact, asking me whether there was a "right" way and a "wrong" way that a person ought to go about the business of growing up.

The Daughter My Mother Wanted

Perhaps the reader, glancing back through the "facts" of Debra Thierry's life, sees them as something alien—signposts in a foreign language; unreadable; stretching through a territory too different from normality ever to be truly comprehensible. It might be easy to shrug this Debra off as a strange being, unlike ordinary people—"crazy" or "sick." But this is what, if you'd sat with her, as I did; and gotten a good sense of the person she was, as I did, you would realize at once was untrue.

For she wasn't unintelligible, mad, "seriously disturbed," out-of-touch. She had been through what can only be named Hell, and she bore the marks (not only on her wrists) of where she had sojourned.

It was clear that she'd always been highly sensitive and vulnerable about "losses of relationship"; and that she wouldn't ever be very good at the inevitable business of separations and partings. Still, she was more "like you and me," by a long shot, than she was not.

I know that there's a certain temptation (we all feel it) to explain such strangely self-destructive behavior in terms of "ill brains" and similar biological mysteries. And certainly "biology" may play into situations such as this in terms of a person's general vulnerability in times of high stress. But still, I don't believe it's necessary to invoke "disease of the mind" explanations in order to make distance between ourselves and Debra.

We can understand, without such "labeling-and-filing-away" devices, a very great deal about the underlying *sources* of her powerfully self-directed rage, and of her great fear, her awful sense that she'd be deserted and "left to die" in the psychological sense of that expression. The entire past six years of her life (almost a third of her lifetime, when one thought about it!) had been devoted to the surmounting of a particularly traumatic happening.

She'd been shoved from the nest, in that thirteenth summer, while still feeling scared and unready. The fury aroused by that event hadn't, then, been consciously experienced as anger she felt *toward* her parents (that would come later, when the sick-show was over and she'd become frankly depressed). For at that time she still depended upon and needed them too much to dare to perceive or to "know" about the depth of the hostile feelings churning within. These feelings would be expressed, over the years, in terms of the sham illnesses; these fooled her mother and father, wrung their loving, caring and concern from them almost as if against their will. The hatred would surface, finally, in her frank depression—expressed now as hatred of the self.

For a part of the girl wanted desperately to be the "daughter my mother wanted." She'd even, remember, played the part of *that* girl by pretending that she really did want to return to camp after the week of rest and recovery she'd extorted by oversleeping and appearing run-down and ill. A part of Debra strove, in other words, for some magical reincorporation into the family. She'd been exiled precipitously, and for unimaginable reasons—perhaps she was "bad," unwanted at home—and afterward, for a time at least, tried hard to be good enough to be "pardoned" . . . to achieve reunion. If she were aware, consciously, of her feelings of inner fury there never *could* be a real coming-home again! One can see why those hostile impulses, which couldn't be allowed into awareness, were being systematically diverted and stifled, to emerge eventually in a somewhat disguised and distorted fashion.

In her thirteenth year, this immature creature hadn't been "at liberty" to be angry at her parents; she was still too needy and unfinished. She had, moreover, a sense of herself as being somewhat defective and incapable and "not the right sort of person" (in translation: "Not the daughter my mother wanted"). And even now, at a time in her life when she really had made a certain amount of growth headway—in terms of detaching herself from her parents (at least the old, superpotent, omniscient parents of her childhood) and working on becoming an individual in her own right—Debra could still be quite backward and clumsy in her capacity to perceive and to process her responses of rightful anger.

For when I observed to her that I thought her mother's statement (about having "grown up too fast") was pretty devastating, she looked at me with sudden eagerness. She didn't say anything, though, so I added, shrugging: "Is there something wrong, really, in a daughter's growing up and not being dependent all the time? I guess you don't sound too fast, as far as timing's concerned, to *me*." I shrugged again.

"Yes, it's funny," she replied, "because at first, when she said that, I felt as if it were *her* problem and her way of looking at it; maybe her own insecurities that were making it hard for her to let go. That was the *first* thing that came into my mind. But then, after that, I got to thinking . . . and I got the idea that there must be *something* the matter with the way I did things. Maybe I really wasn't doing them right. I don't know. The only answer I could come up with, finally, was that she didn't like the way I *was*. I wasn't the kind of child she'd wanted. And so I guess I decided, finally, that there must be something . . . something dreadfully wrong with *me*."

Even then, over six years later, she was having problems in perceiving and expressing her hurt and angry feelings directly. It never had occurred to Debra to say to her mother that that had sounded like a most unkind statement, and to ask her exactly what she meant! And Debra's image of herself was still, to a large extent, the child's image; that is to say, the one mirrored in her mother's eyes.

I'm not suggesting, that Debra's history is "ordinary"—or that every thirteen-year-old girl, sent away, sulking, to horseback-riding camp, will eventually end up on a psychiatric ward, depressed and frankly suicidal! Her tale is, undoubtedly, to some degree the story of an extreme. But it does illustrate—as extreme examples can do with such starkness and clarity—the nature of what are universal and underlying themes. These revolve around dependency, immaturity, problems in recognizing and dealing with one's own hostile feelings (we all have hostile, angry feelings from time to time; but *some* people are taught, early in their lives, not to dare to recognize or acknowledge such wicked and impermissible feelings, thoughts, ideas). They have to do with the experience of the self, at the age of thirteen, in a strangely foreign body filled with strange new sexual and aggressive feelings—feelings that ought, perhaps, to be punished. They have to do with the profound loneliness of the separation process as well: that yearning backward toward childhood and those receding figures on its shores who could (if they would) make one feel not lonely and unprotected and scared anymore.

They have to do, finally, with the meeting of parental expectations. In Debra's instance, that thirteenth summer, she somehow perceived herself as having been presented with a choice. She could be independent and somewhat rebellious and cantankerous—as thirteen-year-old girls often tend to be—and in that case, she could get out of the house. Or she could be utterly needful, a sick and dependent little girl, who cannot survive without her mother's cherishing and protecting care. Her choice, her way of "being the daughter her mother wanted her to be," was, of course, the latter.

She'd played out, with the uncanny theatrical abilities of the adolescent, the role of the mortally ill, beloved, and nurtured child. Her mother's role, the complementary one, was that of the caretaker who is needed in the most absolute and desperate of senses (and who will *always* be needed). In this duet of pretenses, both parts were crucially interdependent, and both players were cuing one another; but both of the players were fooled, taken in by the scene that they themselves had created.

Debra was, at the age of nineteen, just beginning to understand the import of some of the dialogue and to discern the underlying nature of the plot. She was beginning to question the importance of her depressive illness *to her mother*—and in fact, the meaning that her remaining depressed, incompetent, and needful might have in the greater context of her parents' relationship with each other. These were, it seemed to me, good questions; the questions she most needed to ask.

CHAPTER THREE

Of Love and Loss

The Forming and Mourning of Love-Bonds

In terms of that smaller "cycle within the life cycle"—i.e., the great biological arc of the female's reproductive years—Anne Munson and Debra Thierry were clearly at one end of a spectrum. At the opposite end were those depressed women whose grown or almost-grown children were leaving or preparing to leave: these women were into what has been called the "launching phase" of the family life cycle (because it is the phase during which the offspring are being launched off into their own independent adulthood). Many of these women were in their middle or late forties.

Curiously enough, however, both the "prereproductive" and "postreproductive" females were frequently struggling with issues that—if one looked closely at the deep structure of the depressive themes—were actually strikingly similar. Or, to rephrase what I'm saying in musical terms, the individual variations and elaborations—the notes sounded by a sixteen-year-old woman as distinct from those sounded by a forty-seven-year-old—might seem to be awfully *different*, when one first heard them, but the underlying themes and motifs were often the same. These motifs had to do with the loss or letting go of crucial emotional relationships and with the letting go of the idea of oneself as the person *in and defined by those relationships*.

In the instances of Anne and Debra, those love-bonds were the most primitive ones of human living. They were the ties of the "first love" relationship in which each one of us engages: that richly charged first love of human life which is the child's ferocious and powerful attachment to the caretaking parents. It was this primary love-connection that these young women somehow hadn't been able to truly relinquish. Anne had, though she'd "left home," achieved only the façade, the outer semblance of independence and autonomy. She hadn't, in an inner psychological sense, really ever made it away from home base. Debra's bitterly inarticulate battle—never understood, it seemed, by any of the terrified and furious participants—had been to get back home and extract the nurturing that she needed, the nurturing that would someday make it possible for her to leave.

A reluctance to separate had set in, to requote Sandor Lorand, accompanied by feelings of an inner lonesomeness, emptiness, and helplessness, and "a resentment towards the idea of abandoning the past. . . ." This same description could, however, have been used to describe many of the depressed *older* women that I was interviewing: for, in many instances, the pained source of their despair was an inner aloneness, a vacuum, an empty center at the very heart of the being.

"Emptiness," Erik Erikson has written, "is the female form of perdition." This is not, I believe, a universal truth about women in their postreproductive years, but it is a fair assessment of what *certain* midlife depressions are about. That is, about a sense of inner void—an inner world emptied of value and meaning. It may be that the depressed, postmothering woman has been trying to "fill up" that cavernous inner vacuum with a newly charged, freshly-revitalized relationship with her spouse.

Diana Pharr Dahlgren, who'll be met with later on, had adopted this strategy for dealing with what was, in effect, a massive existential crisis. But the strategy hadn't worked (as Diana's alcoholism and suicidal attempts proclaimed), not at all. If anything, those desperate efforts to connect with her husband in a new way had only amplified her sense of loss. Bereft of her identity as Mother (with all that role's attendant tasks and status) she felt bereft of meaning; she felt "like a nothing." She felt like a superfluous blob on the face of the earth, with a name and an address, but no inner substance or reality. Diana, in her forties, seemed stuck in the concept of herself as Mother—in the same way that Anne and Debra seemed frozen into the role of Child.

Of course we all are, during the process of growing, developing, living our lives, engaged in the periodic forming and mourning of our love-bonds. A parent learns to love a child, and then must know how to let go of her or him: the child's emotional task is the complementary one. A great part of the "normal suffering" of adolescence has to do with this: the fledgling adult is being forced, in distress and sorrow, to part with passionate relationships, a hitherto familiar identity as child, and to move into the strange and immensely frightening wider world. A new self, involved in new loving relationships, must be found—somehow, somewhere.

But what, so beats the underlying bass drum of fear, if this *doesn't happen?* Suppose instead (terrifying idea) that one finds oneself alone and abandoned—stranded between the lost world of childhood and isolated in an indifferent universe of adults? The notion itself is so frightening—and the regressive pull into the protected, nurtured world of infancy so powerful—that many young people, at the very edge of their adult lives, turn and beat a sudden retreat. Bette Glassman, a twenty-year-old woman who was hospitalized for depression at the Dartmouth-Hitchcock Mental Health Center in Hanover, New Hampshire, spoke of an almost "physical need to keep returning to my mother and my father. I feel as if I'm being pulled back to them," she said, "and especially to my mother. It's as if I were at the end of a long invisible string, somehow—as if I were at the end of a yo-yo."

She, like Anne and Debra, was "caught" or "trapped" in momentous emotional relationships that were in the process of winding down, changing. So were many of the older women I was speaking with, as well; but they could not grieve and let go. There was, in both younger and older groups, a pervasive sense that there would be no way *to be* in the world, that was different from what had been before. An old way of being was disintegrating, and a new one had to be constructed; but it was as though, beyond being Child or Mother, there was no way of existing that could be envisioned or encompassed.

The loss of certain kinds of emotional relatedness was experienced as amputation—as the loss of valuable chunks or parts of the self. It was as if being "me" had everything to do with "being me for them" in terms of a very few, very intensely charged loving relationships. And without "them" in the picture, each woman's sense of "me" was painfully diminished . . . inevitably, for it was toward "them" that her entire existence had been oriented, and upon which her own sense of self—her identity—was based.

Her self, then, without those relationships, was being experienced as without meaning. Her self no longer mattered; it faded into a melancholically indistinct landscape. The winding down or ending of these powerfully important relationships was being perceived as the loss of everything good and valuable in her life—of self-esteem, of self-worth and of much that had given purpose and significance to living. She'd become marooned, where she was, while her supplies of hope and optimism drained remorselessly away.

About Human Attachment

Let me return to that remark of Bette Glassman's, quoted a bit earlier, in which she described her experience of being "pulled back, as if by an invisible string" into the web of her earliest relations—into that most primitive of human bonds, the child's tie to the caretakers. This is, and I'll repeat it once more, truly the first love of any individual's existence—what we call the "first love" or "first awakening" of adolescence isn't so much an awakening as it is a *reawakening*—of intense passion, first experienced beyond the reach of conscious memory and buried now, for the most part, in the distant, distorted, dreamlike world of infancy.

It was of course Freud who first drew attention to the potency and force of this early infantile love attachment—and to its grave significance for later psychological and sexual development. In a way this "first love" is an apprenticeship and a model for later love relations, the love-bonds formed in adulthood. And "the Way It Was" in this crucial first experience of emotional bonding can provide so deeply ingrained a pattern-for-loving that the person, almost mesmerically, constructs and reconstructs the "family romance" over and over, throughout a lifetime. Among the women that I've interviewed I've seen many who—almost trancelike in their behavior—have replaced a "remote and unreachable parent" with a "remote and unreachable spouse." Parent and Spouse may seem, on the surface, to be totally different kinds of people. But for the woman *in* that love relationship the emotional climate is the same.

That we should repeat this first experience of loving in many forms and guises later on in life isn't, however, something really very surprising . . . not when one thinks about it. Our basic training for the important business of loving does occur in this particular context—in this earliest love-bond, this earliest emotional connection of human living. We learn about "loving" from our first caretakers, and what wonderful students we are! For, in many instances, it seems to take half, or more, or all of a person's lifetime to discover (if that person ever *does* make the discovery) that "loving" can be anything *otherwise* from what he or she learned it to be, long ago, far in the past, way back then.

Now a fascinating question, and one that has puzzled many a wise head, is how and why we humans *do* learn—so readily and so early in life—to love? That we do become enamored of our caretakers, and do so as soon as we can "recognize Mother" and are psychologically organized enough to invest this recognition with feeling (which happens, generally speaking, at about the sixth month of life) is not a matter which is in any dispute. But what is it, exactly, that makes this powerful love-bond spring into being? On what *basis* does this momentous emotional connection—I mean, the child's tie to the parent—first form and emerge?

This sounds, I know, like a fairly simple question . . . so simple as to be hardly worth asking. The question of why Bette Glassman was "stuck" in her childhood attachment to her parents—even though the season of these relationships' intensity ought to have passed—seems far more interesting, a far more complex issue to ponder. But the question I'm raising now is not anything to do with why Bette wasn't able to let go of those early love-bonds. It is this: why had she, and why do we all, learn to care so desperately about our caretakers, to love our caretakers in the first place?

The answer must seem self-evident. It's the kind of question, I know, that makes one want to shrug and say: "Because." We humans form strong emotional attachments, early in our lives, to those who nurture us. And we do it because . . . that is what human beings *do*.

But is it so simple? On what basis, actually, does this emotional relationship form—what brings the baby-caretaker bond into being? Most psychoanalytic writers, while holding varying views on the underlying nature of the infant's tie to the mother, are in general agreement on two very fundamental points. The first is that this early love-bond is the very foundation stone of the personality. And the second is that "love," from the baby's point of view, forms, takes shape and emerges in all of its intensity in the context of the feeding experience.

In other words, the human infant becomes emotionally attached to the caretaker (usually, the Mother) because she brings gratification and relief of internally experienced tensions—particularly the overwhelming tension of hunger. And, as the baby comes to recognize her and to associate her with "satiation" and "nurturance," a strong emotional connection emerges, linking the "cared-for" and "caring" persons deeply and profoundly. The idea is, in short, that we first experience "love" in the context of being fed. The earliest, most critical, most "life-tone-setting" love-attachment that we form is formed because we feel love for the person who feeds us (by and large, Mother). This view of what baby love is all about—and why we learn to love in the first place—has been called the "cupboard theory of loving."

But relatively recently, by which I mean in the late 1960s, a new view of "why babies learn to love" definitely entered the intellectual arena. This is called "attachment theory" and the person whose name is most prominently associated with it is Dr. John Bowlby. Bowlby, an English psychoanalyst, has constructed a theory of love-bonding which leans heavily on ethology—the study of animal behavior in the wild. And it is his intriguing suggestion that the human baby, like infants in closely related species (including apes and monkeys) forms an emotionally toned attachment to the mother because *we are, as a species, preprogrammed to do so*.

This is an evolutionary argument. The idea here is that we don't learn to love our caretaker, early in life, because she feeds us. We learn to love, and to volubly display our feelings, because such a behavior pattern has been, from a species'-survival point of view, *adaptive*. The infant who manages to enslave and enchant the mother—to bind her to him or her lovingly—will actually manage to keep that mother close by. And thus, the reasoning goes, throughout aeons of human prehistory during which our ancestors roamed the primitive environment, those babies whose behavior kept the protective parents close at hand were the ones whose survival chances were "upped." The infant who was pre-adapted for setting up a rich emotional communication with the caretaker was the one who had a better chance for living long enough to reproduce. In this way, forming an "attachment" or love-bond in the early months of existence was a behavior pattern that was bred into our species.

Babies do show a strong tendency—perhaps a psychological *need* is closer to the truth—to form an intense emotional connection with a caretaking figure. This need to create a bond or tie with mother first manifests itself at about six or seven months of age. The love-bond that comes into being somewhere around this period becomes ever stronger and more absorbing and exciting: it reaches its peak of intensity, for the child, during the second year of life. What is called "attachment behavior" (that is, behavior directed toward keeping the parent close by) becomes slightly less exaggerated after about the age of three; but it is still very much a part of the scene until the fourth or fifth year. Thus, from infancy onward and to about the fifth year, much that the child *does* is—when one observes it coolly—directed toward a single and overriding goal. And this is keeping the caretaking and guardian mother as closely at hand as is possible. The baby experiences her presence as "satisfying" and "security-enhancing," suggests Bowlby, because—during the long prehistory of our species—her presence ensured protection *against predators*.

Much of human behavior has the effect of ensuring protection. This is a notion, as attachment theorist Bowlby told me, that we "tend to lose sight of in our safe Western civilizations. But it would be hard to understand the behavior of an animal except by reference to the environment in which it evolved. Now suppose a child is frightened; what will he do? He'll run to his mother. Why does he choose to do that particular thing? Because in the primitive environment, that behavior was adaptive; it promoted survival. We can see similar things in our physiology; when it's hot out, for example, we sweat. We don't sit down and think about why we're doing it, we just do it. But sweating is a physiological adaptation which has the effect of keeping body temperature constant."

So is staying close to the beloved (and protection-giving) parent. Dr. Bowlby, whom I interviewed at great length during a visit to England, phrased it this way: "The fact is that in the natural habitat, the need for protection is paramount. You can wait till tomorrow for food, if necessary. You can wait six months for sex. But if a predator threatens, the top priority is protection—or you won't *be* there to-morrow."

The idea is that learning-to-love may arise far more out of an an-cient need for protection than it comes about as a consequence of being fed. And because "mother's love" has had, throughout evolu-tionary millennia, an underlying and real survival value, the *human baby experiences mother's presence as necessary for psychological sur-vival*. It is true, certainly, that babies who are regularly fed and well-housed, but *are unable to form a bond with a caretaking person*, show astonishing and alarming mental and physical deficits. For example in a study of foundling-home infants, carried out in the mid-1940s by Dr. René Spitz, it was shown that babies being cared for in a hygienically isolated environment—with one nurse assigned to every eight infants —showed profound physical and psychological retardation by the end of the first year of life.

These babies, who'd been separated from their prison-inmate mothers at age four months (i.e., before they were capable of forming a "love-bond") were unable to sit or stand, cried frequently, never smiled, and had no beginnings of speech. They were apathetic and unresponsive, caught infections easily, and had a high mortality rate. It was as if these human creatures, never yet having *known* love, were still capable of suffering and dying from its lack!

The conundrum, when one thinks about it, is this: that the love-bonding of infant and mother may well have evolved from a species' survival need having to do with keeping "the couple"—mother, child —in loving proximity to one another. But in the instance cited by Spitz, that is, one in which no "attachment figure" was available, the babies were literally dying from the absence of that protective and absorbing emotional tie.

Protest, Despair, Detachment

It is now well recognized (largely through the work of Bowlby and a colleague, James Robertson, at London's Tavistock Clinic) that young children who are separated from their parents go through experiences of terrible suffering that are very analogous to the pain of adult grief and mourning. A brief stay in a hospital or in a residential nursery can —for the child from age six months to age four or five—usher in a period of profound psychological agony. A film made of one little girl, Laura, during a brief separation from her parents (for a small operation) demonstrates this truth well. The movie, filmed by James Robertson, is a psychiatric classic; and it is absolutely harrowing. For small Laura's behavior is indistinguishable from that of an adult who's been plunged, suddenly and horribly, into a state of inconsolable bereavement.

What has now become clear, both as a result of Robertson's moving and awful "documentary" and as a result of other observations of children in "separation experiences," is that the youngster's adaptation to the absence of the beloved parent occurs in three very distinct phases (which resemble, to some degree, the successive phases of adult mourning).

The first is Protest, a frantic attempt to find and rejoin the mother.

The second is Despair, a state of increasing hopelessness, similar to the deep grief of the bereaved adult.

The third is Detachment, during which the child takes more interest in the surroundings—in the nurses and doctors, say, if he or she happens to be in the hospital—but seems to lose interest in the mother. Should she (the mother) visit at this point, her baby is liable to turn from her listlessly and apathetically. This move away from the affectional bond into "not caring" is termed the "affectionless state." If the separation doesn't go on for too extended a period of time, it reverses itself. And, at home once again, the young child will go through a phase of intense and desperate clinging.

Preprogrammed for Loving

The biological tendency for the baby to form a powerful emotional bond with the caretaker is, to restate the matter briefly, keyed to a set of genetic instructions whose "evolutionary payoff" involves keeping-mother-close-by during the long helpless period of human infancy. So-called "attachment behavior" is, argues Bowlby, "instinctual" inasmuch as human beings are pre-adapted to establish this love-bond early in life. It is almost as if the infant organism were set to promote such an occurrence. For example, babies' smiles, which are potent "social releasers"—that is, responses that bring about social interactions;

in this case, affectionate love-play—are elicited by human faces more than they are by anything else. An infant, smiling up at Mother, usually has an effect upon her which is absolutely enchanting and enslaving. And yet, does the very young and happily smiling baby actually "recognize" her?

Probably not. There have been numerous studies of what evokes smiling in young infants and it appears that it is nothing other than the visual configuration—two eyes, a mouth—of the human face (rather than recognition of a *particular* human face). One study, carried out in the late 1940s, demonstrated that when infants were presented with different masks they smiled at the ones which had two eyes, in the right places, and a mouthlike slit. They would *not* smile at a human face (or a mask) in profile. They would not smile at their mother's face in profile.

It was almost as if babies were programmed to respond to certain stimuli in the environment . . . those resembling a human face. And this "smiling response," perceived by the mother with such delight and joy, acted to open and maintain emotional communication *with* her!

Babies smile most at what most resembles the human face. They also tend, as psychological experiments have shown, to respond more to those sound frequencies that are most like the human voice. Not only that, but there is also some evidence that they respond better to the higher frequencies of speech—in the female voice range. This is truly curious because we adults seem, almost instinctively, to *know* that. Most of us talk to young infants in abnormally high "kitchy koo" tones of voice and then, without giving the matter much thought, return to our usual voice pitch when talking to older children or to adults.

Human infants would appear to be born with a sensory apparatus that is *selective*. They enter the world ready to be attracted by stimuli resembling the human face (what they seem most fascinated by are the eyes) and tend to respond with attention and interest to sound frequencies in the range of the human female. It is not unlikely that the newborn baby is, as psychologist Rudolph Schaffer has recently suggested, "socially preadapted" in such a way that he or she will "respond particularly to human characteristics" thus ensuring that the parents will assume a special significance from the moment of birth onward.

As the infant grows, and does come to "know" the caretakers—particularly, the mother—he or she soon develops the typical range of familiar "attachment behaviors." That is, from about six months onward, the baby's set of instinctual responses (crying, sucking, smiling, etc.) appear to focus and become integrated. They center firmly upon the mothering person. The baby will then protest and cry when she goes away—and greet her joyously on her return (thereby "punishing" departures and "rewarding" returns). He will cling to her when frightened, will try to follow after her when he becomes able, and whenever it is at all possible. This "human baby behavior" resembles, as Bowlby told me during our series of conversations, the behavior of our monkey and ape cousins.

Studies of infant primates in the wild show that they, too, stay in close proximity to their mothers and rush to her side at the least sign of alarm. The intense need to keep the mother nearby is, he observed, based on a biologically rooted behavior pattern. "It's my belief," commented Bowlby, "that 'keeping mother close by' is in itself a psychologically satisfying thing for the infant; it's an end result, ensuring safety, especially from predators." And, if one carefully observes the baby's behavior—from about six months onward—it *does* look as if it had a set goal. That is, of course, to keep the mother within close range—where her child can see her and hear her . . . and her protection and care is, thus, readily available. The notion, a hard-line evolutionary one, is that "human love" is a behavioral mechanism: the lovebond *binds* the parent to her offspring throughout the extended "helpless" period of infancy. The baby's smiles and the baby's cries are communications that bring about powerful responses on the part of the mother: they challenge her into social interactions with her infant, encourage the growth of that "emotional connection" that will keep her near to her utterly dependent child. "It isn't exactly chance, you know," said Dr. Bowlby wryly, "that what makes a baby smile most is the sight of a human face."

Mothers in Love

Mothers are, on their own part, ready to fall in love with their newborns. Such is nature's lovely synchrony. If babies appear to be impelled toward forming a strong bond with their attachment figures, why it's obvious that most mothers seem equally drawn to do so. This general happening, this shared behavior pattern of mother and offspring, promotes not only survival of that baby, but of the social group and of the species. It works out: unless things go awry in the environment, and a particular mother and her infant are separated or simply fail, in some way, to set up a good emotional communication.

This can happen, surely, in particular instances. But nature's way is the way of generalities, of likelihoods; of what has proven most useful, for a particular species, in the sets of environmental circumstances that have been "expectable." And there is, in both human parents and human offspring's behavior, that shared impetus, that mutual surge toward loving. As psychologist Rudolph Schaffer pointed out in his recent book (*Mothering*):

> Love means a preoccupation with its object; a wish to be in the other's presence, a great enjoyment of his company . . . a dislike of being separated for long, and a continuing orientation even in his absence. In mother love we therefore have the reciprocal of the child's attachment, which is also rooted in a need for physical proximity. But the mother's actions are not merely a reaction to the child's need; they represent rather a genuine expression of her own requirements—witness the mother creeping up to her sleeping baby to steal a look. . . . We have given much attention in recent years to the child's side of the relationship, particularly by observing his behavior during enforced breaks in that relationship; yet this information has only rarely been complemented by including data from the mother's point of view about her need for "togetherness. . . ." Anyone who has ever been in love knows of the increased awareness it brings of the other's person, of the absorption in him that makes it so much easier to sense his moods, feeling, needs and wishes. To be attuned to the child is part of mother love. . . .

The human female's predisposition—not only a "psychological" but a hormonally and neurally mediated tendency—to form an intense love-bond with her baby is a behavior pattern that we share with our simian relatives, the social apes and monkeys. And, as anyone who has seen the "experimental separation" (for purposes of research) of a monkey mother-infant pair can attest, nothing is so human-looking as the agitated mother in her distress—unless it is the appearance and behavior of the separated monkey baby. This is truly a faithful image of human grief and despair.

There have been a number of descriptions of infant monkeys undergoing separation experiences: I'll quote from just one, a report on the behavior of four macaques (pigtail) whose respective mothers were removed from the social colony when the babies were between three and four months old:

> During the first phase pacing, searching head movements, frequent trips to the door and windows, sporadic and short bursts of erratic play, and brief movements toward other members of the group

seemed constant. Cooing, the rather plaintive distress call of the young macaque, was frequent. There was an increased amount of self-directed behavior, such as sucking of digits (i.e., finger and thumb sucking), and mouthing and handling of other parts of the body including the genitals. The reaction persisted throughout the first day, during which time the infant did not sleep.

After 24 to 36 hours the pattern in three infants changed strikingly. Each infant sat hunched over, almost rolled into a ball, with his head often down between his legs. Movement was rare except when the infant was actually displaced. . . . The infant appeared disinterested in and disengaged from the environment. Occasionally he would look up and coo. After persisting unchanged for 5 to 6 days the depression gradually began to lift. The recovery started with a resumption of a more upright posture and a resurgence of interest in the inanimate environment. Slow tentative exploration appeared with increasing frequency. Gradually, the motherless infant also began to interact with his social environment primarily with peers, and then he began to play once again. The depression continued, but in an abated form. Periods of depression alternated with periods of inanimate-object exploration and play. Movement increased in amount and tempo. Toward the end of the month the infant appeared alert and active a great deal of the time, yet he still did not behave like a typical infant of that age.*

When the monkey mothers were then reintroduced, report animal behaviorists I. C. Kaufman and L. A. Rosenblum, another dramatic change occurred. There was a "tremendous reassertion" of the mother-infant relationship, with desperate clinging on the part of the monkey baby. The resemblance to the Protest/Despair/Detachment sequence of the separated human child—as well as that intense hanging on and clutching after reunion—was absolutely striking.

This thing we humans call "love" would seem to have its roots in our animal past. At least insofar as this first emotional attachment of living is concerned—that is, the infant's tie to the parent—humans and other primates not only share the tendency to *form* the love-bond but to become distressed, upset, perhaps even ill in instances of the bond's disruption. Jane Goodall, the first animal watcher to observe chimpanzees (our closest primate relatives) in the wild, thought she'd seen a juvenile chimp actually *die* of grief after the death of its mother. During a conversation that we had in the early 1970s, Goodall described the young male Flint's death to me:

* Kaufman, I. C., Rosenblum, L. A. "Depression in Infant Monkeys Separated from their Mothers," cited in Bowlby, John, *Attachment and Loss*, Volume II, Basic Books: New York, 1973 (pp. 64–65).

Flo (Flint's mother) lay down on a rock, toward the side of a stream and simply expired. She was quite old. Flint stayed near her corpse; he groomed one of her arms and tried to pull her up by the hand. The night of her death he slept close to the body, and, by the following morning, he showed signs of extreme depression.

After that, no matter where he might wander off to, he kept returning to his mother's body. It was the maggots which, at last, drove him away; he'd tried to shake the maggots off her and they would swarm onto him. Finally, he stopped coming back. But he did remain in an area comprising about fifty square yards; and he wouldn't move any further away from the place where Flo had died. And in ten days he had lost about a third of his body weight. He also developed a strange, glazed look.

At last Flint died too; he died very close to the spot where his mother had died. In fact, the day before he had returned to sit on the very rock where Flo had lain down. . . .

Distress such as this sounds very—*human*. And it may be, as some evolutionary theorists believe, that primate behavior patterns—such as the tendency of the mother to form an intense emotional attachment to the offspring—have evolved in much the same fashion as body-and-brain structures have evolved. It is possible that "love-bonding" among primates came into being as a means of coping with what is a very extended period of infant immaturity. All primates enter existence utterly dependent upon their mothers' nurturance and care; and certainly, the human infant is the most helpless newborn creature in nature. The intense tie that springs up between mother and offspring makes both of them *feel* that the other is necessary for well-being and security. This motivates the mother (whether she be monkey, ape, or human) to protect and provide for her baby; and the baby to want to stay close by and to seek the mother's protection. In short an experienced "psychological need" (to remain in close proximity; to reunite if separated) brings about behaviors, on the part of both individuals, that will keep the offspring within close range until he, she, or it has learned those lessons about the environment that will be crucial to independent survival.

Thus it is that loving—this state of feeling that seems more human than almost anything else that is human—may be in essence an adaptive primate response to the long dependency and helplessness of the infant and growing juvenile. "Love" may be, in its origins, an evolutionary solution to the problem of the baby's need for security, protection, and care. In human terms, of course, there are many varieties of love that have nothing—obviously!—to do with the mother-infant pair bond nor with the exigencies of infant survival. But what I am saying is that "emotional attachments" probably arose in the context of solving what were life-and-death primate dilemmas. And it is in this respect, this deep link to feelings of security (or, conversely, to fears, anxieties, and terrors) that we *experience* our profound emotional attachments. Our loving relationships aid us, from infancy onward, in orienting to the world . . . and sometimes these relationships—or *one* such relationship—seems to constitute *everything* in a particular person's world.

That love-bond is, then, perceived as something necessary for going on, for survival. And its loss, or its threatened loss, is equated to the loss of everything—including any reason for further existence.

The Depressive Theorem

To be depressed is to be in a state of emotional paralysis, to dare nothing, to try nothing, to freeze. The painfulness of it, that noxious state of vulnerability and inferiority, is real—as real as any form of physical pain. Like physical pain, it will often command a person's complete attention. How often I've spoken with women who seemed "preoccupied," even befuddled, whose energies were being totally absorbed by the effort to retain some equilibrium despite the awful hurting going on within! That hurting, when intense, would dominate consciousness with its urgency, its demand. When less severe, the hurting might be forgotten in the distractions that life happened to offer . . . but it had to be returned to, always, at the diversion's end.

Some women, when I talked with them, were finding it impossible to see beyond the suffering of the moment. Others, less seriously depressed, found it possible to "get out of it for a while," but only in the knowledge that they'd be returning home to where the pain was . . . to the wounded Self.

The depressed person *is* wounded, though the injury can't be seen or located. That person is "changed," diminished; he or she has usually experienced a morbid drop in confidence. Guilt, anxiety, irritability, hostility: these are common ingredients, in variable proportions, that may be found in the depressive stew. It is, experientially, a fairly horrible mixture. And the person suffering from depression, coping with this feast of dysphoric feelings (about the Self; about others, frequently, too) is—as one might imagine—far less flexible, far less able to cope in the *outer* world . . . to negotiate.

The depressed person, like the individual who's been injured physically, does have to operate with less-than-normal energies and capacities. And, because there is that true diminishment in adaptability—a genuinely *lessened* ability to deal with events, interactions, all sorts of "real life" circumstances—the person's dealings with the environment tend to become erratic, off-the-mark, and often genuinely self-defeating. "Feeling bad," then, has plenty of consequences: it brings about situations in which bad things happen. How frequently, in the course of interviewing many women, I recognized that a person's state of mind had gotten her locked into a situation in which she was either doomed to go on pedaling-in-place in her life (expending great effort and getting *nowhere* in terms of personal satisfaction) or losing very valuable ground.

What seemed to happen often was that an individual's mental set—that self-critical, self-devaluating mood—brought about unwelcome sequelae—which then served to deepen the depression, to confirm the many rotten things she already knew about herself. Among the many women that I came to know, women I spoke with for either brief or extended periods of time, I found a sizable proportion who'd gotten into such a vicious negative-feedback cycle, who were constantly setting themselves up in ways that would prove once again what they already knew so well: that they were valueless individuals, worthy of little or no consideration. This was something I came to call the "depressive theorem." Anyone can prove it, to her own satisfaction and with the greatest of rigor, if only she patterns her life in such a way that this will happen—that her worst premises and suppositions about herself can be "objectively" supported and validated!

Yet the person's own experience will be, very often, that something is happening *to* her. She will fail to make a connection between the kinds of feedback she's getting from the men she is seeing, and anything that *she herself* is doing or feeling.

Helen

Helen Girard, a divorcée in her mid-twenties, once observed, in the course of a conversation: "There's something about me, somehow, that seems to *invite* emotional catastrophe." It hadn't occurred to her, at that point in our interviews, that she herself might be issuing the invitations. She, who felt herself to be a "deeply flawed and wanting" individual had—during a postdivorce depression—been managing to get herself *treated* like someone who is flawed, wanting, and without value. But before coming for treatment of her depressed state, she hadn't recognized that she was setting herself up for failure-feedback in every relationship she had with a man.

All that she'd recognized was that there was, in the wake of each short-lived effort to create some emotional involvement, a further lowering of her self-esteem . . . and that she felt helpless to halt that downward spiral. She had, however, enough insight into her situation to say: "The lousier you feel about yourself, it seems—and the more you need other people—the more unattractive and obnoxious you actually *become*." Nothing, in truth, fails like the downward cycle of failure (just as nothing succeeds like success).

But if one is feeling sad, bad, useless, like a nothing, one subtly projects this interior vision into the world of hard facts and objective circumstances—creating, oneself, a setup for depressive feedback. Helen was not quite aware that she was doing this in the interactions she had with the men she was meeting, or already knew. But again and again, as her depressed mood deepened, she'd managed to get herself involved with "people who would use me and then discard me. . . ." It was almost as if she were, like a careful lawyer for the prosecution, meticulously arranging all of the evidence that would, once and for all, demonstrate how worthless and discardable a person she actually *was*.

As far as the business of loving was concerned, Helen Girard almost seemed to be in it *for the grief!*

As her despair and self-hatred had flowered—a kind of jungle growth that had sprung up in the wake of her final decree—she'd run through a series of short and hurtful relationships that almost seemed designed to demonstrate the worst things she already knew or suspected about herself. She'd gotten herself treated like a piece of turd; and therefore, clearly, she *was* one.

Turning Into a Witch

When she came in, for help, to a Harvard-affiliated crisis clinic, Helen Girard was feeling slowed down, lethargic, unable to concentrate on her work. She had a good job, one in which she was learning to be a printer; but she'd been coming in for criticisms recently, mostly on the grounds of being "distracted" and "not all there; my mind's else-where." She'd been suffering from bouts of crying, which frightened her: "Sometimes I feel as if I'm never going to stop, that I'll never get

hold or get to the end of the tears. . . ." It was the crying jags, primarily, that had brought her to the Acute Psychiatric Service at Massachusetts General Hospital in Boston. But there was also her shameful behavior with her three-year-old son, Rob.

She was being horrible to Robbie, and *knew* that none of what was
happening was his fault! "I feel, sometimes, like I'm turning into a
witch," she confessed. "Or if not that . . . going crazy." It was, then,
her relationship with her son, and those sobbing episodes, that motivated her to seek treatment. But Helen had a number of other physical
and psychological symptoms. She'd not tied them to anything so specific as "depression."

She was feeling low, a bit lost, disappointed; she was jumpy and
vulnerable to small slights. She felt unhappy, in need of help and support and as if, in some vague manner, she'd done a lot of things in her
life that were wrong. These were her "feeling" symptoms.

The physical ones included digestive problems, insomnia, constipation.

Helen was, too, experiencing bouts of anxious terror. Later, when
they'd diminished quite a lot in intensity, she described these feelings
as something like "being on the edge of nothing . . . like you're falling off the side of time or space."

Bouts of panic such as these aren't uncommon in states of depression. Sometimes, in fact, they confuse the diagnosis. The therapist
can't decide whether the person's become depressed secondary to an
anxiety neurosis, or anxious secondary to a depressive attack! But
while anxiety is frequently present *in* depression, it oughtn't to be
confused *with* depression. There's a very important distinction to be
made between these two major affects or emotional states.

Anxiety can be likened to an early-warning device. Anxious feelings
are part of an important biological alarm system which—in humans
and in other animals—alerts an organism to the presence of threat or
danger. Anxiety signals the existence of a problem: some matter which
must be dealt with, and which will require attention, activity on one's
own part, mastery—before whatever it is that has aroused alarm,
alertness, watchful worry, manages to get out of hand, and nothing
further can be done. Perhaps this can be explained most easily by
means of a simple example. If I happened to be walking alone in a
park and I started to take note of unexplained noises (twigs crunching
in the bushes, say, just out of my sight) I'd surely experience intensely
anxious feelings. My anxious reaction would, in turn, involve a host of
instantaneous psychological and physical responses, promoting a state
of heightened wariness, acuity, energy, readiness to flee, or to meet and
attempt to deal with the threat.

At once, whatever might have claimed my attention before—the blueness of the sky, the birdlife, the wildflowers I'd been examining—I'd begin concentrating on whatever had made me feel anxious. In my state of heightened attention, I'd review what I knew about dangers in the park, the nearest access to other people, the ways in which I might check out whether or not someone suspicious were moving along close by me . . . and strategies for dealing with the situation if I felt myself seriously endangered. The spurt of anxiety would, in brief, allow me a spate of planning time, on a mental and physical High Alert, before actually confronting my dilemma. *Without* this kind of anxiety-reaction (which we humans do, as we all know, experience in terms of threats to one's psychological as well as one's physical safety and integrity) it's doubtful that any organism could adapt to the real pitfalls and dangers of the environment.

Anxiety is an important survival mechanism. It is, despite its bad reputation, a necessary part of any animal's (human or otherwise) reactive repertoire. And while feeling too much of this noxious stimulation is obviously maladaptive—because it puts one's physical and mental resources under constant strain and pressure—feeling *too little* anxiety would present a far greater potential for disaster. Seen from this point of view, our anxious feelings have their positive aspects. And some experts, emphasizing its adaptive function, have termed anxiety a "biological call to battle."

Depression is, contrariwise, a state of "after the battle is over." It has been likened to defeat at the end of a war, to desolation, to a state of having given in and given up. And here is the important distinction to be made between anxiety and depression: when one is feeling highly anxious, the inner urges are toward taking action, doing something, solving some problem; trying to identify and to deal with whatever it is that one *experiences* as threatening. But the person who is depressed is dominated by other feelings—by feelings of hopelessness, helplessness, worthlessness and the impulse to take no action because nothing can help and the problems are insoluble in any case. In the so-called "middle states," which are very common, the anxiously depressed person is held in thrall by the two powerfully warring motivations.

That is, there is the impulse to take action and the desire to do nothing—to *not rock the boat* in a situation which is perceived as potentially overwhelming. Among most of the depressed women I was interviewing and relating to, that latter set of impulses—to stillness and inaction—were the ones that tended to become dominant. But this quiescence, from the point of view of outward behavior, was being experienced with a terrible inward violence.

The depressed woman was someone who had lost. She had lost something. The tone was of something profoundly significant having been taken away, of some crucial life territory's having been surrendered. And what emerged, with what came to seem to me an amazing regularity, was that the loss in question was the loss of an important, self-defining, powerful, and binding emotional relationship.

Despite the complex, varying, dizzyingly diverse matters and difficulties that any person could potentially become depressed about, it appears to be *one kind* of a loss, more than any other, that can trigger depressive episodes in women. And this is the loss of a love-bond.

What Matters Most

It's puzzling, but almost axiomatically the case: depressions, when they happen in women, happen in one kind of context more than any other. This context is the loss of emotional relatedness: something changing, perhaps because of an expectable life transition; something going awry; something ending. *Attachments* are the critical variable: they seem to be, among both non-working and working and highly professional women, what really *do matter most*. It is in terms of highly invested and extraordinarily important loving attachments that most women's secret self-assessments and interior appraisals of self-worth seem to be made.

For men, the depressive themes tend to be different—and I'll say more about this in a moment. But I just want to note that some writers have speculated that a much greater investment in one's emotional attachments might simply go along with culturally transmitted sex role expectations correlated with "being feminine." Women are *supposed* to be warmer, more expressive, more eager to relate on a personal level and so forth. The suggestion is that they might, due to intensive early femininity training show a greater propensity to put more of themselves into—and therefore at risk—in a few powerful and powerfully important relationships.

To fail in those relationships, or to have them end, then, becomes equated with failing in everything; to slip here can mean a headlong slide downward into desperation and misery. It is around *losses of love* that the clouds of despair tend to converge, hover, and darken. Important figures leaving or dying; the inability to establish another meaningful bond with a peer-partner; being forced, by a natural transition in life, to relinquish an important love-tie; a marriage that is ruptured, threatening to rupture, or simply growing progressively distant; the splintering of a love affair or recognition that it is souring and will come to nothing . . . these are among the commonest causes of female depression. It is around *attachment issues*, more than any other sorts of issues, that depressive episodes in women tend to emerge.

And conversely, as a recent study of London women demonstrated, the existence of a confiding, intimate, sexual relationship—a confidante with whom one is sexually involved—provides protection against depressive symptoms. For among the sample of Englishwomen studied, many of whom were being confronted with fairly severe real-life stresses, those who had a "friend" in their husbands or lovers, developed significantly fewer symptoms of depression. (A friend, alone, wasn't enough; the confidante had to be someone with whom one was tied in an intimate and *sexually* intimate relationship.)

Men don't, with such predictable regularity, become depressed over the rupture or threatened rupture of emotional bonds. Again, this could have much to do with expectations about what being masculine involves—independence, action, aggressiveness, and a high motivation toward competing, winning, achieving. For men, the depressive motifs frequently have to do with work issues, status and success difficulties, with "making it" out there in the world at large. The career-impasse situation, a deadly and virulent depressogenic issue for many men, doesn't touch the same tender nerve of concern in women.

I am not, of course, suggesting that men never become seriously depressed over the loss of a love-bond, nor am I saying that women can't do so over a career setback—a failure at school or at work. I'm only noting that career issues, while they may be matters of significance and importance to a woman, don't set the stage for severe depression in the relatively clear way that the loss of a powerful affectional bond can do.

And the experience of *being depressed* is probably qualitatively different, in some important respects, for men and for women. One recent survey of college students, carried out at Yale University, noted that females, when depressed, suffered "significantly higher levels of . . . experiences of loneliness, helplessness, dependency and the need for external sources of security." But for the males, in contrast, depression had to do much more with "self-criticism and the failure to live up to expectations."

Women become depressed about the loss of the Other.

Men become depressed about failing to "make it," to gain control of and mastery over the environment.

A Real Woman

Males and females may, in short, be marching to very different kinds of inner music. It is possible that, as Harvard psychologist Jerome Kagan has suggested, the two sexes are "sensitive to different aspects of experience and gratified by different profiles of events." Everyone does, clearly, keep his or her interior score card, a running self-assessment which continuously monitors the question: "How am I doing?" It appears to be the case, however, that for males and for females, the grading systems are very different.

Getting back to that notion of the feminine sex-role ideal—I mean our culturally shared notions about the traits of the Perfect Woman—it's quite evident that She is someone who is warm, expressive, and who gives out to others. Many or even most women do feel (and behave) as if being assertive and aggressive on their own behalf isn't a very nice thing to be or to do. Being aggressive and competitive *on behalf of those one loves* is all right, however; it's even "good." As four woman psychiatrists pointed out in a recent paper ("Some Formulations on Aggression in Feminine Development") "Women channel their impulses toward direct action into the making of, and preserving of relationships. In itself, this is an adaptive and constructive mechanism. However, the problem arises when the relationships substitute for activity and actions, and thus serve a secondary goal. They (that is, the woman's love relations) become the means by which she can feel some sense of power and effectiveness, and thus are the source of her self-esteem. . . ."

Which is fine, point out the four physician-authors (Dr. Jean Baker Miller, Dr. Carol Nadelson, Dr. Malkah Notman, Dr. Joan Zilbach) as long as those relationships are providing enough good feedback in terms of satisfied feelings about the self.

Should a valued and important love-bond grow sour, however, or fail utterly, the woman who's poured her "self" into it finds that "self" dissipating—as if her aggression, vitality, and energy had been, like a supply of water, spilled out heedlessly onto sand. "The loss of important relationships," note psychiatrists Miller, Nadelson, Notman, and Zilbach, "and consequently the lowering of self-esteem, are important factors in the development of depression, which is more frequent in women."

In the aftermath of the loss of love, there is not only this diminished or depleted sense of "self": the woman must contend, as well, with those newly released aggressive and competitive impulses which have been channeled into the lost affectional relationship. Women, on the other side of an important love-bond, not only feel impaired but bad, full of an inner poison. They experience, in a novel way, the unleashed ambition, competitiveness, energy, aggression, that's been poured out into support of the Other.

"What I had to learn," Helen Girard told me, "wasn't only that I had a Self that could survive it when Tony and I broke up; but that I had a Self *at all!* I wasn't honestly sure that, when we two were separate, there would be anything there that *was me*." She shook her head ruefully, smiled. She was, at the time of this particular talk, well out of the depressive episode that had brought her for treatment a few months earlier.

That episode hadn't been the first of her depressions. Helen had gotten depressed in the months just after her son Robbie was born. "Tony said that no wife of his was going to work if she had a baby at home," said Helen, running a distracted hand through her short, wavy hair. "So I said 'All right.' . . . I stayed home for a year, and it was sheer hell. He—Anthony—was drinking a lot, and there wasn't any communication between us at all."

"How do you mean that—'no communication'?" I asked.

"Well he, you know, was going through about half a gallon of booze a week. And drinking at work, too, as I later realized. I was pretty much left to myself, with the baby; I didn't venture out that often. We were living way out in the suburbs and he took the car; I depended on Tony for everything. I don't think, now, that he could handle the responsibility . . . and so he got to drinking more."

She hesitated. "Now, though, that I'm at a distance, so to speak, from everything that was happening between us, I don't believe that we *ever* communicated. At all. I always had the impression there was something bothering him constantly, and he never would let *on*." Her voice, as she said these things, held a wobbly, injured, questioning note.

Helen had, after that year, packed her bags and taken her baby; she and Rob had gone to Ohio, to her parents, for a "visit." The visit stretched on from weeks to months: she found it easier to stay where she was, for she needed help in caring for Robbie. "I guess I'd resented Rob from the moment he was born," she admitted. "Because whatever problems Tony and I were having *before* then, things went downhill from there awfully fast afterwards. I felt trapped. *Exasperation.* I wanted to get out of the house. Anthony would come home from work in the evening—he was working for a contractor—and he'd be tired and I'd be just so desperate to get out. I couldn't just go out myself: I didn't think *he* was capable of taking care of the baby. I mean, he never really did do anything with Robbie. He was always *my* responsibility—*my* kid, not Tony's."

For the duration of her stay in Ohio she and her husband were, said Helen, in fairly constant touch with one another. "He seemed very congenial over the phone and even happy to hear from me. *I* always did the calling; he never called. And the day that I was ready to come back to Boston—which was about the middle of May or so—he came all the way to Ohio just to drive us back."

Helen laughed: "I was *ecstatic*. I mean, he'd come all the way there just to bring us back and I thought: 'Wow! He really cares!' But then, when we got back home, we got into a discussion . . . we discussed everything we'd never been able to talk about before."

Nothing, she said flatly, was solved.

All that she'd learned was that the marriage, painful for her, wasn't working for her husband either. Anthony felt as deeply alienated as *she* did. There seemed to be something going on, something happening; and yet it was out of her reach somehow, ungraspable, not to be comprehended. But, by the following September, their relationship had become so insupportable that she'd decided to take Robbie and to move out. "I said to myself 'That's it; it's not *going* to resolve itself and I'm a fool for staying here!' And I left. That was when I finally discovered what I ought to have realized much earlier. Which was that Tony had been having an affair with a woman at work for a year and a half."

Helen scowled, adding: "We'd been separated for about four or five months when I found out about that. And you know the next time I saw him I walked up to him very calmly, put my hands on his throat and said: 'You son-of-a-bitch.' And I was choking him. . . .'"

I smiled, because Helen Girard is a slight, not strong-looking woman, as slender as a comma. Tony was, as she'd described him, tall, slightly on the heavy side, muscular. "What did he do?" I asked.

"Ahhhh. He just said 'I'm sorry.'"

She shook her head rapidly, as if chasing away annoying and pesky memories. "In a way," she said, "it was kind of a relief. I'd gotten to a point where I could honestly say: '*I hate your guts!*' . . . But then to find that everyone who knew us had known, the whole time, all about it! I felt humiliated. I just couldn't *believe* it: wow, all our friends knew and nobody told me! I felt just like a fool. And then, after that, I went through a succession of different phases. Ones in which I hated him; ones in which I was calling him up every night. It went on and on."

She had been dipping, since the separation, in and out of depression.

After the divorce was final, she fell into a mood she couldn't seem to struggle free of: that was when her crying jags, a new development in her life, had begun. "I felt," Helen recounted starkly, "as if I'd been deserted by everyone. Total desertion—as if here I was, on this desert island. I knew, I really did, that all I had to do was pick up my phone and call someone . . . but I didn't, I *couldn't*. I was exhausted, wanted only to sleep. I'd come in from work, feed Robbie, feed myself, turn out the lights and go to sleep. Except for, sometimes, I'd start crying —for no special reason, or because I'd seen something sad in the newspaper." Helen shrugged: "Once I started to cry when reading about a kid with leukemia who was having her last Christmas in the hospital. And it's O.K., I mean, to shed a tear for someone else, someone you don't know. But my problem was, I couldn't *stop*."

There were no men in her life at that time either. "I'd always had dates," she explained, "and there'd always been someone to *go out with*, at the very least, from the time that Tony and I split. The men . . . came and went. When one left, another showed up. But then, that one always left too . . . I was miserable. And all of a sudden there just didn't seem to be *anyone*. My relationship with Robbie was a disaster. I was taking everything out on him."

The two years during which she was separated, not yet divorced, had found Helen moving into and out of relationships rapidly. She'd been "scaring men off," she now believed, by the intensity of her needs. In the days after the dissolution of her marriage had become final and legalized, she'd felt no longer needy but desperate. She couldn't seem to conceal or control her desire for a protector, someone to care for her and her son. (Of course, though I may be accused of anthropomorphizing for mentioning it, mothers of infants—among practically all species of social primates—are accorded extra special status, protection, and care. A nursing chimp mother will *never* be attacked by another female, although such quarrels occur quite routinely otherwise. In instances where the entire group is threatened by attack—by a predator—the dominant males range themselves on the outer edges of the band while the mothers and young babies are in the most protected, well-guarded inner places. In nature, the mother and infant pair appear to be seen as both very special and attractive, and extremely vulnerable.)

In any case, that profound neediness and vulnerability seemed to come across to the men she was meeting against Helen's own will: it was, she said, like a psychological information-leak. And the men had, on their parts, responded with fears about being co-opted into having to take care of her. "I didn't know what I was doing," she said. "I was looking too hard, I think, for someone else to tell me where I was at. I couldn't find the person that was 'me'; at least not in terms of a single personality. I'd passed from being my parents' child to being Anthony's wife. This was the way I thought about myself, I suppose, and the way I thought others were thinking of *me*."

She cocked her head to one side thoughtfully: "So when I *wasn't* his wife, I think I just assumed some other guy would come along and say 'Marry me' and then I'd become *that man's wife*. It's taken me a long time, and a lot of hard times, to find that I—all by myself—could have any identity. That I could want things, do things, achieve things all on my own and *for me*. It was just the most difficult of all the lessons I've had to learn—and one I still am learning—I mean, *not to be* this desperate woman with a child who wants a husband. To be able to live life without having someone else there to live it *through*. To experience things directly and not through that kind of a filter—a *man*." She giggled lightly, as if to mitigate the force of what she was saying.

"But you know," added Helen, "the idea of being ambitious for my own self, and trying to get forward on my own behalf—it still doesn't feel completely right. Something about it is really unnatural to me: I can get to feeling panicky and—" She lifted her shoulders briefly. Her hazel eyes, which had been moving restlessly around the room, which hadn't met mine during this burst of speech, now settled upon the cuticles of her fingernails. Her last sentence left unfinished, in suspension, Helen began absently pushing back the loose skin around the half-moons at the bottoms of her nails. She'd begun a spate of that nervous self-grooming that humans and other animals engage in; they're a self-calming, self-stroking sort of device. (Cats, for example, lick their fur when stressed.) We all do this routinely for self-reassurance: men stroke their beards; men and women run their hands over, or twist locks of their hair. Many people will scratch small itches, stroke their cheeks, pat their own knees, and so forth. It's an action-message, from the self to the self, and the message is: "Calm down; it's O.K."

After a few moments of silence between us, occupied by Helen's thus "putting herself in order," her gaze swung up to focus upon mine. She stared at me fully and frankly: "I seem to have to learn and to relearn that 'getting things'—succeeding in my own right—won't make me unattractive, or a 'bad' or unfeminine person. Because there's still something deeply threatening to me about doing things on my own *for myself*. At the present time, I'm being pushed ahead in my work—and I'm learning the printing business rapidly and well—but I think I'd feel far less conflicted about the whole thing if I were having this success as *Tony's wife*. For him, not for me." She stopped momentarily, as if she'd grown perplexed or confused.

"Maybe it's just the notion of not being like my mother was," she then resumed. She was trying the same set of feelings from a different angle. "Maybe it's not living *my* life in the way that she lived hers. Being different or . . . odd. But something in me *has* that belief: I mean, that you can't go out there in the world and do the things you want to do and remain, well, a real *woman*."

Helen's voice trailed off and she looked at me uncertainly: "Does what I'm saying make any sense to you whatsoever?"

A Hurricane's Coming!

Among her most pressing issues, when Helen Girard came in for treatment, had been her embittered relationship with her small son Rob. Her own capacity to mother her son had been profoundly disturbed by the marital disruptions that she believed had been caused by Robbie's birth: she behaved toward her child in ways that had made her feel that "I must be either abnormal or crazy."

"All of my frustrations used to come out on him," Helen was able to admit now. "I used to scream at him for no reason at all. At first, you know—I mean, just after the split with Tony—I became crazily dependent on Robbie. I tried desperately to get involved in his life, even though I'd already begun working. I took time, when I came in at night, to spend with him. I mean, what with Anthony's not really caring, I turned to Robbie, I guess. I was keeping a diary at that time, and I remember writing in it: 'What can a little child *know* about what's happening?' And yet here I was, depending upon him emotionally."

As she'd begun dating more and more frequently, however, the small boy had gotten put aside. "I never really found any guy that I dated who took an interest in Rob," said the baby's mother, "and so I think I started to reject him myself. I was feeling that . . . he was holding me back. From finding someone to love me. And so here was this little kid," she shook her head rapidly as if to shake away *that* inadmissible thought, "whom I really loved dearly; and yet I'd begun hating him, yelling at him, telling him that he was just ruining my life."

Helen had, when she'd begun her therapy, been seriously thinking about giving Robbie up completely. The brief relationships that she was having, with a procession of men, weren't truly bringing her satisfaction. The bed-hopping life, with its consistent emotional boomeranging, kept leaving her with an aftertaste of new failures and

even tattier, sorrier losses. Still she believed that Rob (and, in some obscure way, her ex-husband, Anthony) were what stood between her
and her happiness. It was, she now thought, an "almost revengeful act
that I had in mind. I suppose I had the idea that by sticking Robbie on
his father I'd be able to prevent Tony from doing what he was doing
—running free, screwing around all the time." She smiled wanly. "I
think I wanted him to know how hard caring for a child actually *is*."

To the men she'd gone out with, since the time of her separation,
Helen had presented a docilely feminine image of compliance and
sweetness. It was only Rob who'd been seeing the other side of the
mirror—her rage, fury, fear, and guilt. If she experienced anger toward any of the people she became involved with, that person never
knew it. "I simply threw myself away," was all she could say about
what had been happening. "I let myself be used, and I did it because
all I wanted was to be held. Just that, to be cuddled, to be held . . . I
needed the warmth."

Underneath, though, bubbled the poisonous feelings—fury at Tony,
at her own "remote and unreachable" father, at the untrusted and un-
trustworthy series of rejecting and unloving men who seemed to be
merely crossing through her life. If Helen could express her anger to
no one but her small son, though, it was Rob who *could* show anger
toward her male visitors! Robbie had taken to attacking any man who
came into the house, rushing at the guest, socking and kicking him.
He'd even attempted to knock one person, a friend Helen had met at
work, from the chair he sat in at their dinner table!

Thus, when that period of emotional drought had occurred—when
there'd been nobody around to care or to reflect the mildest interest
or sense that she mattered—Helen had her scapegoat at hand . . .
she'd blamed, been enraged at, her son.

"Now," she said, "when I come in from work, and I'm tired, I have
more resilience and can show a little more patience. But even so, it can
get tough. Because when I *do* sit down to play, he still can throw tan-
trums. Like last night: we worked for hours, building a great big hospital building out of his blocks. It had—oh, lots of different wards and
an operating room. A courtyard where the patients could rest while
they were getting better. And I wanted to put in his little toy people
—to be the patients, and to finish the whole thing off."

She pulled a curl from behind her ear, began to twist it in her finger
absentmindedly. "It really was *beautiful* . . . but Robbie suddenly
started yelling that a big hurricane was coming, and he started kicking
and knocked the whole thing down!" She'd put the lock of hair back
behind her ear with a harsh gesture, and was frowning angrily: "He
literally *tore* that whole damned thing apart!" Helen stared at me, not

quite seeing me, eyes dilating in the memory of her rage: "Sometimes I think," she said tensely, "that he wants to destroy *everything* that I'm trying to build."

"What's Robbie so afraid of, do you think?" I asked her.

"Sometimes I feel like—like I'm going to choke him," was the answer she gave me. "I know how that must sound . . . but when he's like that, the way he was last night, I really feel afraid that I might *do* it."

I shook my head, gave her a puzzled look. "But what's he so afraid of?"

This time Helen seemed to hear, and to consider the question. I could almost watch the anger deflating, almost hear it hiss out of her body, like air leaving a tire. "That I'll destroy him, I suppose," she answered carefully. And added, a moment later: "By leaving him." She shrugged. "But I *won't.*"

She'd confronted, early in her treatment, the choice: she'd either be a real mother to Robbie or give her son's care over to her husband. And, when it was laid out on the table by her therapist in that way, Helen had realized that there never *had* been any choice. "When it came right down to packing his little toys and clothes and shipping him to his father, it was out of the question. And so the obvious thing for me to do was to start working on repairing my relationship with Rob."

The truth was that she'd made a good deal of progress in this direction, though with an occasional bad setback, such as the one that had happened in the block-building the night before. Robbie had surely become, in the short span of his troubled existence, an extraordinarily distressed and needy child. And his mother still had, in terms of emotional capital, little to give out . . . especially when so little was coming in to her. At times she felt unable to handle things, drained, and in danger of being overwhelmed.

But these moods were now sporadic: she wasn't, as she had been, engulfed in a sense of her incompetence, her worthlessness, her despair. She was back into a social network, was seeing friends—both men and women. Helen was, as she put it, "definitely well on my way out of the pits." And if she had an occasional slideback, she resumed her climb upward pretty rapidly.

In terms of gains, however, the most dramatic had been the disappearance of Robbie's frightening nightmares. He'd been having them, without cease, since the time of his parents' separation. According to Helen he had, with regularity, woken several times a week, screaming for her in a kind of primitive terror. "I'd run into his room and find him so hysterical that I couldn't wake him up," she said, "and he'd be screaming: 'Mommy! Mommy!' I couldn't wake him up enough so that he'd realize I was *there* . . . couldn't get him to the point of recognizing that Mommy was there *with him!*" She drew in a breath sharply, gave me a wondering, if fearful look. "I think, maybe, he was dreaming that I was gone."

In the time since she'd been receiving therapy, his mother had made the decision that she was not—ever—really going to give him up. And Robbie's fear-dreams, those dreams of being left behind, softly in the night, had ended.

Loving Is Too Dangerous

It had been in the wake of the final divorce decree—that public announcement of the severing of her attachment to Tony—that Helen Girard's spirits had sunk so precipitously and so low. The force of this event's impact upon her, and her own desolation at the rupture of the bond, were nowhere made so manifest as in her relationship with her baby. She'd been behaving toward Robbie—the creature whom she would naturally have loved—as if she hated him. But then Helen, herself abandoned and deprived, had been attempting, without success, to deal with her own grief and anger, her sense of inferiority and failure. And she seemed, almost, to be responding to the ripping away of her own emotional moorings, by teaching Robbie that love was too treacherous. She'd been telling him that *he* couldn't depend on her—just as she'd not been able to depend on his father. Intimacy, mutuality, the desire for emotional union—were risky. Love-bonds meant mutual dependency. She'd depended, once, upon Tony . . . and that had been a dangerous mistake.

Rejection had left her feeling: "If someone needs to love *me* I'll reject *him.*" And so perverting and pervasive had these feelings been that she'd come to hate and feel contempt for her own Self: she'd felt depressed, after the divorce had come through, in a way that she'd never been depressed before.

Like a climber who's suddenly lost all foothold, she'd felt her control and sense of balance vanishing. The experiential sense of that depression had been, as Helen had put it, "like falling off the side of time or space. . . ." Such a reaction to the loss of a love-bond is, as I've said, by no means infrequent among women. And it may be, as I and certainly many others have suggested, that women are *inherently more sensitized* to the loss—or threatened loss—of important emotional relationships. What I'm saying is that it is perfectly plausible that there's a biological bias in this direction.

Again, I'm thinking in terms of evolutionary considerations. We have seen how the human infant's inborn tendency—to form a powerful attachment to Mother—could have been, during the prehistory of our species in the wild, a behavior pattern that *promoted survival*. That is, because intense feelings for one another have the effect of keeping individuals near to each other, the bond kept the protective parent close to her baby. By securing the mother's affection and attention, the infant was actually achieving physical security and survival. To be alone was, on the other hand, to be exposed to real danger . . . to become a likelier victim, to become prey. (Is this, I wonder, why loneliness *feels* so threatening? [Isn't there, perhaps, some atavistic input that underlies the "crazy thinking" of the very lonely person, who may experience his or her loneliness as so menacing to existence itself, as so fundamentally dangerous?] It may be that we feel loneliness to be so potentially annihilating because, to the lone human—and above all, the lone human infant or child—being alone *was* death.)

There is at present a good deal of evidence from fossil and archaeological records which supports the notion that our human modes of behavior did evolve in much the same ways that our bodies and bodily organs—such as the brain, heart, liver—did. Or, to phrase it another way: behavior patterns that worked; that is, were adaptive, in the harsh realities of the primitive environment, led to survival of the young and the passing on of those same behavioral tendencies. Females, for instance, who were inclined in the direction of forming powerful emotional attachments (not only with the helpless offspring but with the protection-giving male partner) were those whose own babies had an enhanced chance of surviving to reproduce. And females who *didn't* display this type of behavioral bias were *less* likely to pass on their own motivational traits (because their offspring were less likely to live long enough to reproduce).

In brief, a tendency to form and maintain powerful emotional attachments might have been bred into the human female genotype.

Merely surviving, in the unrelenting environment in which our species evolved, appears to have demanded a strict differentiation of sexually assigned tasks and roles. Early human groups, gathered in so-called hunter-gatherer bands, came together for mutual food-getting and for safety. The women took responsibility for the bearing and caretaking of children: they also tended fires and gathered plant foods and fuel. The men were responsible for protection—against predators and against other human bands—as well as for hunting meat, for fishing, and for those tasks requiring more than female strength. Psychologist Frank Beach has speculated that, as human evolution proceeded, the genetic differences between males and females widened and grew more pronounced. Such a trend, Dr. Beach has written, may have "improved the capacities of the two sexes to perform their separate roles, and thus increased the effectiveness of the social group as a survival mechanism."

Thus, sexual differences—in terms of emotional tendencies, of profiles of events that are experienced as satisfying and rewarding—could have become part and parcel of "being male" or "being female," because these led to survival. They were biologically adaptive in terms of each individual carrying out his or her own tasks as efficiently as possible, and they were therefore adaptive for the human group as a whole.

Of course, behavior patterns suited to the strict demands of the natural habitat must differ from those suited for apartment life in New York or for life on a farm in Wisconsin! But it must be remembered that the primitive environment was the one in which we humans became human. Civilization is a relatively recent development. As far as can be ascertained, it accounts—in terms of time—for no more than *one per cent* of the history of our species! And there is *no* evidence whatsoever that humans have undergone biological changes during this infinitesimal bit of evolutionary time.

Perhaps this ancient hunter-gatherer division of sexual labors accounts for that greater masculine sensitivity about "making it," about gaining control in the wider world, mastering the environment. Does it relate, I wonder, to the fact that men seem to get far more seriously depressed about "goal failure" issues than they do about problems in emotional relationships? And does it correspond, I wonder, to the female's apparently greater affiliative needs, her sensitivity to fluctuations in her love attachments, and her greater input of Self into her important relationships?

And does this, in turn, explain that dominant theme running through much of the magazine material being printed for women—that concern about and fascination with the topic of Losses (particularly emotional losses, and how to overcome them) which was noted in puzzlement by Marcia Guttentag and her Harvard colleagues? It may be that women are differentially intrigued by the topics of Separation and Loss because they know these to be the areas of their greatest vulnerability, the sphere of highest risk. Women *do* tend to develop depressive symptoms in the "rupture of a powerful attachment" context far more than they do in any other.

In the Twenties

CHAPTER FOUR

The Winner: Marie

Dark Closet and Shut Trunks of the Mind

The struggle to become oneself is, for every human individual, so staggeringly complex a task. For, in the years preceding puberty, life and growth and development have been *fostered* by our emotional immersion in that love bath, that bond, that powerfully experienced relationship of child and parents. And then, with the suddenness of a biological thunderclap, the onset of physiological and psychic changes announces the ending of life as we have known it. We're given notice that all that we've been, and all that we *are*, must alter profoundly. We are going to—we must—grow up.

The solid earth; one's sense of oneself: all is in flux, all sliding. Complicated inner (hormonal *and* psychological) and outer (changing body-size and form, and the environment's responses *to* those changes) warnings and indicators let us know that unstoppable processes are under way. Now there is pressure to relinquish much that has given protection, security, nourishment, stability . . . meaning. And the child's ancient desire to be loved, cared for, approved of, and such, begins to shift. There are the old yearnings, surely, to be cherished and protected. But there are new yearnings and ineffable, intangible, sweet, unnameable wishes. There is the desire to be "in love."

With the advent of adolescence, the romantic threesome—I mean that eternal triangle that is the child, the same-sex parent and the opposite-sex parent—seems to heat up, to illuminate, to grow red-hot; the "triangle" becomes, for the nonce, an emotional grill. Now, as the ideas and impulses related to "being in love" swim into the foreground of consciousness, the "forbidden love" (which is the attraction to the opposite-sex parent) must be given up once and for all, decisively renounced. This attraction and renunciation isn't anything, I hasten to say, that will happen at a conscious level; such ideas are unthinkable—literally. But powerful fantasies relating to *replacing* the same-sex parent will be, nevertheless, simmering below the surface stream of awareness, conscious thoughts, ideas, impulses. They are so shameful, so unacceptable, that they rarely if ever manage to thrust themselves upward into the psychic daylight. Untenable notions such as these must be kept away, out of knowledge, in the dark closets and shut trunks of our minds.

They are subsectioned off from consciousness . . . but they are there. If we consider this matter in terms of the daughter, she is, at some fantasy level, imagining or dreaming of blissful union with the father (and fearing, too, the retaliation of Mother, who is at once hated rival and still one's needed protector and one's caretaker). The mother herself, responding to her child's anger, may be feeling angry, rivalrous too. She may react with rage at having been thus betrayed. The father is, on his own part, liable to be feeling guilty, intrigued. He may be experiencing, subliminally, a certain attraction toward his sexually maturing child—stirrings of interest which will very likely cause him to draw back in fear and alarm; this may result in his abruptly becoming more remote from his daughter, electing to stay out of the brouhaha erupting between mother and child. Or, as mentioned earlier (in the discussion of Debra Thierry), the father and mother, mutually alarmed, may band together in affronted and threatened concert against their suddenly developing, suddenly more womanly and uncontrollable offspring.

What happens next will be of fateful import to the emerging adult —who is, much as everyone, transfixed by her breast and body changes, might have forgotten it—still in large degree an immature and dependent being. And the variations on how this basic life task is handled—the task being the psychic separation of child from first caretakers—can range from the strange to the awful to the humorous to the tragic to the dizzying. In Debra Thierry's case, which partook of the strange and the near-tragic, the parents—moved by God-knows-what inner alarums and fears—had needed to get her out of the house for a while. They'd needed, at that moment in time, to cool down the family heat, to lower the emotional thermostat. Whatever might have been going on among the three of them (and Debra, still puzzled about what had happened, could fix on no particular episodes that had precipitated her ejection) her mother and father had *acted*, and done so in unison. She'd experienced that as their acting *against* her; their solving their own problem (whatever it was) by throwing her out, getting her totally away from the scene.

But the same problem, i.e., that of the painful psychological hatching of child from the parental nest-egg, can be handled in radically differing kinds of styles. For Marie Sirotta, who was twenty-eight when we did our interviews, and who was my research assistant during a Nieman year at Harvard, the experience of puberty had been utterly the opposite. There was no drawing up of sides between child and parents: Marie's father *preferred* her company to that of her mother's. He simply enjoyed his daughter, as a person, far more than he did his wife. He made no bones about that; everyone in the family knew it; and this, as will be seen, presented the adolescent girl with difficulties that she was—almost two full decades later—just becoming able to confront and to tackle. But she was, by then, in her late twenties and behind her there was lots of pain and spilled time.

Victorious Rival

In his *Three Essays on the Theory of Sexuality*, Freud describes the process of *detaching from parental authority* as the most critical, as well as the most agonizing, psychic work of adolescence. The achievement of an independent self; that is, a self that's no longer dependent upon and emotionally merged (as it is in childhood) with that of the parents, is clearly the great end and achievement of this period of living. In the view of some experts studying adolescent depression it is this important and central battle—the struggle to make it away, to separate and to become autonomous—that is of the greatest significance in determining whether or not a person ultimately falls within the range of what is considered normal . . . or, on the other hand, whether she or he will become maladjusted in one, or more, important areas of living.

Now others may view this as an overstatement of the importance of the separation process. Some researchers would surely take exception to it. For my part, I don't. For I've now seen and spoken to far too many women who seem to be, somehow, trapped in the wrenching task of trying to liberate "who they are" from whatever part or role they took, (or were assigned) in the Family Drama. Marie Sirotta's role, psychologically a very dangerous one, was that of victorious rival.

For Marie had realized a rather frightening triumph over her mother (who was, during this phase of the daughter's life, the evil queen). Marie's own sense of being the person whom Daddy *truly* preferred was delicious and heady, undeniably; but there were, at the same time, accompanying feelings—of guilt (though she'd done nothing wrong) and of an almost overwhelming sadness. And feelings of being profoundly alone.

She was, on the one hand, the star of the family situation. And yet . . . still . . . there were fears that she might really *be* the nasty, hateful bitch her mother seemed to think she was. Marie might be someone who *deserved* and ought to be punished.

Detaching

The process of detaching from our first love-bonds is, as I've said and believe, a major work of adolescence . . . which may stretch into the years of early adulthood, too. Much as I have seen this to be so, in my encounters with depressed adolescents—and with women who, while grown up and matured in terms of years and accomplishments, are still mired and enmeshed in separation issues—the ubiquity and intensity of this particular struggle never fails to astonish me. I have seen, in fact, women in their sixties struggling to separate Self from parents (or *a* parent) in these latter years of their lives! Margaret Garvey (to be discussed in Chapter Eighteen) was such a person. It is the strangest coming due of a psychic bill that has never been paid—and the carrying charges are expensive! For, until the inner separation has been accomplished, there's a sense of not yet having become "me, myself": one is nobody, because one isn't *anybody* yet. To become the-person-that-one-is would require giving up the child's dependent relationship with the parents. But the adolescent—or the adult woman who's trapped, as was Marie Sirotta, in protracted adolescence—resists this, consciously or unconsciously.

She must make a new self who'll live in a new world of her own devising: but the suffering is centered around the problem of her not being able to move into the future because she *has not yet found it possible to give up the past.*

What is strange is how, very frequently, those women who have this type of problem the most seem to know about it the least! I have listened, so often, to people who, while describing their life mood as one of stagnancy and unhappiness, seem to have made no connection between *those* feelings and what are very salient issues relating to unresolved dilemmas, unfinished business, concerning a parent or parents. Feelings of isolation pervade, like a poisonous haze that stands trapped in the inward air; the person feels trapped and *is* trapped, in those still powerful, still powerfully operative, old emotional relationships. My sense of what is happening is that such a woman is caught in a phase, a season of living: a season that ought to be over but has, weirdly, failed to end.

In Marie's case, the season was early adolescence; and the rich emotional life of the romantic threesome had reached its full growth, its culmination. But it had continued to proliferate, to elaborate, to grow thick and choked, confused and jungly. Ultimately, it stank with psychological danger. And here, in this dense, rank, shut-off area of the Self were her preoccupations and yearnings; her hidden angers, her unconscionable hopes. Here, as well, was the source of her pain and the answer to her riddle. But Marie, frightened, had hardly dare approach or explore it; she couldn't look within for she might discover things that were too terrible to know. Nothing, she told me later, could have made her return to resurvey the painful scenes of her early adolescence—nothing but the pain of her depression. But at some point she'd understood that simply going on with her life would require her knowing what the time of early puberty—and the "eight disastrous years" of her marriage—had really been all about.

She knew, at some level, that her relationship with her father and the disaster of Carl Sirotta, were inevitably and inextricably linked.

"How Often Do You Get to Raise a Daughter Twice?" or, Second Adolescence

"Eight Disastrous Years"—this was the title, given by Marie, to the time of her life between age eighteen and age twenty-six. It encompassed the period of her first meeting Carl, their marriage, and it ended with her decision to leave him. But I was struck, in my talks with Marie, by the large and circular course her life had taken if one started even further back—five years earlier, in puberty—and ended at the present, when she was twenty-eight.

"You seemed," I once said to her, curious, "to have been fanning out in all directions at about twelve, thirteen, and fourteen years. You were experimenting with getting to know people from different sorts of backgrounds, and of different faiths, and so forth." She'd seemed to be moving away, in junior high and in her high school years, from a tightly knit, fairly limited and disadvantaged Sicilian milieu—one that she found terribly constricting, especially for a woman. From our interviews, I'd gotten the sense that she'd been taking on, in the high school period, a wholly different sense of her future and her self. "And yet," I said, "you went off into a marriage that was, as you yourself believed at the time you did it, destined to keep you in much the same place and position you'd been trying so hard to escape from! And from that place, too, there was another retreat . . . it looks, you know, as if you've described this full circle, and come around, again, to where you were at its beginning. Living at home . . . a 'daughter.' . . ."

I stopped and looked at her curiously, for Marie was smiling. "What?" I asked.

"The whole joke is that my father was, you know, *delighted* when he learned that my marriage was breaking up. He was simply ecstatic —there's no other word for it! And you know what he said? He said, 'How often is it that you get to raise a daughter twice?' "

But then Marie was silent; she seemed thoughtful, gave a shrug. "I think that maybe this was something necessary—I just had to go back home again and do it all differently: relive my childhood again . . . except as an adult, this time around, someone having *input* into the things that are happening. And the thing that is coming out of this second adolescence, the really important thing, is that my mother and I have now become really good friends. We don't find this need to *compete* with one another anymore: I've realized, too, that my father was never a bed of roses. I love him, but he can sure be a son-of-a bitch."

The smile had faded. "It's the first time I've been able to see things from my mother's point of view, and yet not turn completely against my father. And it's just—I can see them, now, much more clearly than I did back there, when I was younger. I'm back in the nest, true, and I *am* their child. But it's completely different. It's an adult relationship, a three-way adult relationship."

"Do you think," I asked her, "that it was, somehow, necessary for you to go back there and *have* that experience in order to be able to leave in a good way?"

"Yes," said Marie, "I really do. Because throughout my adolescence, things between my mother and myself had gotten so bad. The relationship had deteriorated, actually, to the point where we wouldn't speak for months at a time. And I think that it was that—more than anything—which drove me into my marriage. It was only," she added soberly, "after I myself was married that I began to realize . . . having married someone so much like my father . . . that she had been put down an awful lot. Also that . . ." She'd reached into her leather purse, pulled out a pack of cigarettes, lit one.

I waited. "That what?" I asked at last.

"Well, that *I* had put her down a lot." She exhaled, coughed.

"For what things? I mean, what were you putting her down for?"

Marie blushed slightly. "For being a bit dumb. But I found out how easy it is to *look* dumb oneself, when one is in the same position. And I did, too. I was, once I'd married, in exactly the same situation as hers: expected to be subservient; expected to sit home and wait with dinner in the oven—three, four, five hours; it didn't make any difference. My husband was only half Sicilian—his mother was German, a Lutheran—but it was the same thing for the woman. You're not supposed to complain, not supposed to have an opinion of your own. And it was only when I had these expectations laid upon me that I realized how unhappy they'd made *her*—that she really didn't like being and living these ways. Moving back home; it's done wonders for the relationship between the two of us. I know what she's feeling and we get along more now—as adults." I handed Marie an ashtray, silently, and she tapped the end of her cigarette off with a flick. "I'm also considering moving back out," she said.

I looked at her in surprise. "What led to that?"

"Oh," she answered composedly, "I think I've finally gotten the relationship that I want with them; I think we understand one another. Now, I can manage . . . can accomplish, oh, more of the things that I want to accomplish. I think we've gotten much clearer about one another. I can move back out again."

The way in which she said these words made me think: "Oh yes, perhaps she's ready to go." The issue itself didn't sound as if it were a hot-wire issue: she was just, in the deepest sense, becoming able to and preparing to depart. But there had been times, as I already knew, when dying would have looked a good deal easier. The idea of existing on her own, throughout that time of her life that she'd named "the eight disastrous years" would have appeared plainly impossible.

It was during this period—from her courtship to marriage and to the ultimate decision to leave Carl—that Marie had been anywhere from mildly to pretty desperately depressed. She'd been seriously suicidal as well; she'd gathered, and on one occasion been close to using, that especially female anodyne for life's hurts and ills. She'd been preparing to kill herself (despite strong Catholic objections to the act) with sleeping pills.

But if her marriage was the occasion for depression, it was also, as Marie herself had long since realized, linked to a "whole lot of stuff that had been going in the house way before I ever *laid eyes* on Carl." Her bad feelings about herself ("I used to think of them as my 'foggy moods'") had become a part of her inner world somewhere around the age of twelve or thirteen. Her ability to provoke quarrels between her parents—because her father so clearly favored her, and took her side—was proving both delicious and terrifying.

It made her feel Evil. It made her feel as if she had a wicked, a sweeping sort of power. Oh, she could get them fighting! And knew all of the tricks for making that happen. After managing to get a family battle going, she related, in the musing voice of remembered wonder, "it felt kind of good for a while. I mean I'd be really *happy*, and I'd have this gut feeling: 'Wow, I really did it!' I'd feel pretty satisfied when I'd get the two of them arguing . . . or when I could get my dad to be bad to my mother. . . ."

Her expressive brown eyes had brightened as she'd said these things: she'd jammed out her cigarette, leaned forward, looking expectant and excited. But then, as she sat back, her voice became lower and her words came out more slowly: "After I'd done it, though, I would feel really guilty. I'd think a lot about what a rotten person I was, and how I'd caused all that trouble. I guess I did spend a lot of time *wanting* to get all those arguments going . . . but I spent as much time feeling just rotten. Thinking about what a mean and miserable individual I myself really was. . . ."

To win, in this kind of situation, is to lose quite a lot. There is, as one comes to realize, something intensely dangerous—and thrilling—in the situation of the Daughter Triumphant. The thrilling part has to do, of course, with having captured the affections of *that particular man*. As Marie herself had stated it, "Wow!" To steal one's mother's husband; one must be powerful, indeed, to achieve such a feat! But the psychologically fearful and dangerous aspect of the same situation is that the pubescent daughter is also busily modeling her own femininity—her own core sense of herself as a female—upon her critically important role model, her mother; that is, upon a model who is, at the very same time, being rejected, devalued, and cast aside.

The daughter is thus in a no-win dilemma. For if the psychological work of this period of living includes making an identification with the mother (that is, becoming "like mother," first of all, and then moving on from there to more fully develop as "one's own female self") then the identification is scary; Mother looks too degraded. The girl will shy away from being-like-her, avoid "taking Mother in" as a psychological presence—one whose guidance will serve her later on in life, when she is on her own.

The result, psychically speaking, of *not* internalizing Mother, will be that dreadful sense of inner emptiness; the feeling of having nothing inside, of being profoundly needy and alone. The choice, then, for the daughter, is awful. She can identify with her mother as a powerless, castoff, often depressed individual. Or, she can fail to do so and be more like Daddy; be closer to Daddy; be his girl; win him over. But this involves guile, suffering, and the experience of inward disaster.

The daughter-winner is, in the adolescent family triangle, inevitably careening toward a long subsequent period of working it out. For this particular family constellation—father and daughter involved in a fantasy; mother left out in the cold—appears to be a natural setup for much romance, eventual misery, and internal pain.

A Spoiled, Impossible Baby

Marie Angelina DaCosta (whom I knew later as Marie Sirotta) was, according to the family legend, a baby who'd been born "naturally difficult." The first child of her parents, Marie had been (or was told that she'd been) a terrible trauma. "They told me that I never slept. I never ate, either; I was colicky right from the start. I've *always* been described, among the relatives, as someone different from anyone else in the family. They were all even-tempered and I was, supposedly, a hellion. My mother, for the first four years of my life, dragged me around from one doctor to another; they were all trying to figure out what was wrong with me."

Her parents hadn't, apparently, known what to *do* with her; she was awake some sixteen out of twenty-four hours a day. "Then," said Marie, "when my sister Antonia was born, I really got much worse. I wanted *so much* attention—and it got so intense—that my mother was sure something was seriously wrong with me. She even thought about taking me to a psychiatrist—which is, for a Sicilian family, really an unheard-of thing." Marie laughed. "But our family pediatrician, who's really old school, and a friend of the family, disagreed. He said I didn't need a psychiatrist; I needed a good Smash."

I looked at her. "And did they deliver that Smash?"

She smiled wryly. "He said the problem was sibling rivalry. Jealousy over losing my place. I'd been spoiled because I was a waited-for child—my parents had tried for four years to have me—and through being a first grandchild. And then, because I'd been so difficult a baby, they'd given in to me . . . but that had all had to change when Antonia came along. My mother couldn't, any longer, *give* me that sixteen out of twenty-four hours a day; she didn't have that kind of time to deal with me. So the Smash was that the doctor told them that the best way to keep me down and asleep in the nighttime was to tie me to my crib. And this, crazy as it sounds, is something they evidently did."

The story told later to Marie was that she'd screamed, for one night, throughout the entire night. And for the next night, she'd screamed through half the night. The screaming time had decreased progressively, until she'd learned that, when put in the crib, it was time for her to go to bed and to sleep. After that, it seemed, she'd always slept through the night. "They never had trouble after that," she said, adding: "I don't remember any of this at all."

It was, I replied, a rather awful sort of a story.

She ran a quick hand through her short, bobbed hair, took out another cigarette. "I was difficult from Day One, it seems. My mother says that when they handed me to her at the hospital, the head nurse said she was never so glad to see a baby leaving—that I'd screamed constantly for the four days that I'd been in the newborn nursery. And you know, like my mother used to say to me," Marie laughed, " 'You never shut up; you just never shut up!' " The family was living downstairs from cousins of the new parents; the families had been life-long friends. "My mother's cousins used to come upstairs, at night, to pace the floor with me; they'd do it, you know, to give my mom a break. My father was out of town a lot of the time; he *worked* out of town until I was about eight. So these relatives of my mother's, who had babies of their own, took turns with me . . . treated me as if I were theirs."

What did she make of this whole story now? I raised that question with Marie, adding: "Do you think you were in some pain, or what's your own hypothesis about what might have been going on?"

She answered promptly, as if she'd thought about having an answer ready, that she had just been a temperamental baby. "So temperamental," I asked, "that you *screamed* all day . . . ?"

She hesitated, then looked at me hard. "I don't think I was in any kind of physical pain."

This was what I, too, had been wondering about. Marie said slowly: "I don't know how much emphasis to put upon it, but after taking a Growth and Development course and learning that . . . well, that a mother who's upset can affect her unborn baby . . . I went home and asked my mom if she'd been *glad* that I was pregnant. . . ."

"That 'I' was pregnant?" I intervened.

"Oh!" She laughed, looked embarrassed. "No, I mean that *she* was pregnant with me! She answered that she had really wanted me, but that it had been an extraordinarily hard pregnancy. She wasn't getting along with my dad at the time; and she had, before then, wanted so *badly* to get pregnant! But then, to find the wish coming true at the *worst time* in their marriage . . . well, it really upset her. And what my dad did then was—and this is funny because it's what my own husband did to *me*, years later, although I wasn't pregnant when it began happening—he started spending more and more time away from home." Marie jabbed out her second cigarette, although she'd barely smoked two puffs of it. It continued burning, stinking acridly in the tray; I reached over, ground it out absently myself.

"Which, of course, upset my mother all the more," she continued. "And in a way she blames me as the instigating factor for him staying out more and more, on the town, with the boys. She felt that it was *my* fault, y'know. . . ." Marie's eyes met mine, and almost as if I'd asked the next question aloud, she shook her head in the negative decisively: "I don't think—there's never been any talk—about his having run around. But then, I don't think she'd admit that to me anyway."

Marie Sirotta, a second-year master's degree candidate at Boston University (subject: psychology) during the year she worked for me, had been much affected by that Growth and Development course. She'd begun to wonder if that baby jumpiness and baby irritability of which her relatives had so loudly complained might have been traceable back to things that had been going on in *her mother's life* during that difficult pregnancy. "I suppose," she said carefully, "that I began to blame my own 'nerviness' on her 'nerviness,' and decided that this was just a thing that might have crossed the placental barrier. I know now that she was having a miserable time, both with my father, and with the pregnancy. She did have bleeding, at two different times; and she did have to go and stay in bed."

"So that the time when you came into the world was truly a very hard time for her?"

"Yes," replied Marie quietly, "yes; it really was."

"And is it your belief that *she* might have been depressed . . . ?"

"Yes. Oh, yes."

There had been what felt like a barricade, an unscalable obstacle, between mother and daughter; this had been there from the outset. It was as if, from time immemorial, there had been a natural choosing up of sides. "I was my father's favorite; we were always very, very close," said Marie. Her younger sister Antonia had not belonged, so to speak, to either parent decisively (and had gotten into the habit of saying, when in her teens, that "nobody loves a middle child"). Mike, the youngest of the siblings, had been co-opted to the mother's side "My dad sees my brother as competition in just the way that my mother saw *me* as competition . . . and the time that my mother spent with my brother, he resented."

She hesitated, then, as if forming a thought, or perhaps wondering whether to speak it. "You know," Marie broke the uncertain pause, but seemed to consider each word separately as she added it to the sentence, "My father does not care for my brother; he hasn't, ever. He's never mistreated him, and I suppose he does love him . . . but he doesn't *like* him. And he really always put Michael down, no matter what it was that he'd done, or what he'd said. It was always wrong, you know. It could have been better. And so," she said sadly, "by the time my brother was fifteen years old, he'd just faded out—that was it. If he'd had his way he really would have dropped out of the whole human race; I really do think so. But he just stopped trying, and bounced around . . . it's only now, in his late twenties, that I think he's beginning to worry about things like a future, and about maybe *making* something out of his life."

As for Antonia, married now, and working as an executive secretary, Marie believed that the joking about "nobody loves a middle child" had been full of real and hurtful meaning to her sister. But the family sides had been drawn very clearly and sharply; she, Marie, was exclusively on the father's team. There had been, from as far backward as she could possibly stretch memory, a special sort of closeness between them. "We can read one another's moods instantaneously," she explained, adding that she'd been more aware of this than ever since her return home.

There'd always been a kind of wordless communication between them; an understanding of what the other was feeling. "From the time one of us opens the door and comes in we are simply *aware* of where the other person's at." She smiled, ran her hand over her short hair absently: "He can give me advice, for example; and he's one of the few people who can do it without my getting extremely defensive. And that works in the other direction as well. My mother will often work through me to get what she wants, because she knows he'll be much more reasonable with me than he will with her. Like, if she wants him to go to the doctor's, *I'm* the one who has to do the cajoling. It would just automatically irritate him if she were to attempt to do it."

A bemused, amused, flattered expression had settled on her features. "We just are—always have been—very, very close. I remember that when he would come home (he was on the road most of the time, as a journeyman welder) I'd be with him, oh, just constantly. He'd take me around, even take me into the back room of bars—something which *infuriated* my mother! She thought that was no place for a little girl to *be!* . . . And we'd come back, and there'd be a big argument and he'd say: 'I want her with me! Here I am, home for a short while, and I *want* her to be with me.'"

There was a note of joy in her voice: "Once, apparently—I don't remember this—but it seems he spent their last thirty dollars buying me a jacket. A little Eisenhower jacket: on one of those Saturday jaunts, you know. And there was a *huge* quarrel after that happened. . . ." Her father, said Marie, would take her out for lunches and to bars, where he'd have a few beers. She recalled being given peanuts, on one occasion, and then being asked to sing. He loved to show her off to his cronies.

"It sounds, doesn't it," I asked her, "as if you were being invited to fill your mother's place—as companion—weren't you?"

"I was his companion, yes." She tossed her head, went to her purse for her pack of cigarettes. "*Her* job was to stay home, and keep house, and that was supposed to be the thing that made her happy. I know now that it never did. . . ."

In Enemy Territory

Throughout much of her childhood, during the long weeks when her father was away, Marie had lived under the care, protection, and power of the Enemy. She'd realized, long before the family brew came to a full boil in her adolescence, that her mother saw her as competitor, as someone wicked and dangerous. "We would go for days, my mother and I, without her saying much more to me than 'Eat your bologna sandwich' or 'It's time to go to bed.' Or she might ask me: 'Have you done your homework?' . . . things like that. But we never hugged, never kissed—we never even *talked*, for that matter." Marie's face, transformed from the pleasure of a few moments past, now assumed the downturning features of sorrow. It was almost as if she'd just been demonstrating to me the caricatured expressions on the faces of the Greek masks: so quickly had she moved from the joy and aliveness of comedy to the pain and stillness of tragedy. She took a drag of her cigarette, said quietly: "She loved me, I suppose, but to this very day if I were to reach over and embrace my mother, she'd get flustered. She'd blush. She just does not show any outward physical emotions."

"Then how was she able, when you were a child, I mean, to make you *aware* of her love?" I asked.

Marie thought about that briefly. "Through the fact that—well, I suppose because we are such good friends now. But as a child, I didn't

believe . . . I don't think I ever felt that she *did* love me. She loved
my kid sister. She loved Antonia."

"What did she do that made you think she loved Antonia and that
she didn't love you?" I shook my own head, puzzled. And as I did so,
I almost *watched* a group of memories opening up in my companion's
mind; it was as if a mental file had been pushed open; she held up a
hand as if to amend a former statement. "I guess, come to think of it,
that she *did* hug Tonia quite a lot. But then Antonia was a really
lovely child; so cuddly; and she *liked* to be rocked and held. I was,"
she laughed a somewhat shrill, self-deprecating laugh, "all elbows and
knees; big *feet*, too . . . I was always awkward."

I gave her a dubious smile. "Maybe so, at twelve or thirteen. You
probably were. But you know, it's hard to imagine a small baby—say,
of age one or two or three—that's all elbows and knees. Isn't it?"
Shrugging, I looked into her eyes questioningly, adding that that idea
didn't make, truly, a whole lot of sense to me.

"She never *did* want to hold me, though," reiterated Marie, "I think
she always saw me as competition. Antonia wasn't, somehow, because
my father had *already* taken sides. And I was his." Her eyes, cloudy
and darkish brown, had fixated intensely on mine. But I had the feeling that she wasn't, in truth, speaking to me so much as she was speaking to herself.

Now You Are a Woman

Such, then, was the outline of Marie DaCosta's family circumstances,
as she began experiencing the great energic spurt that comes with puberty's onset. Here was that dizzying slew of biological changes: in
height, weight, and body musculature (the female, a couple of years
earlier, has begun showing an average of three to four inches increase
in height and a gain of roughly eleven pounds per year; this all implies
revolutionary change in the plain matter of *size!*). And of course, the
development of breasts and of pubic hair (never discussed, or even
mentioned in a conversation between Marie and her mother). And the
important event, both in its symbolic and its reality aspects signifying
the attainment of womanhood and femininity—the onset of menstruation. To this event, Marie reported, her mother had reacted with one
cold comment: 'Now you are a woman'; and there had been no further word. Such patent physical changes entailed, as clearly they had
to, changes in emotion, perception, and thought. A girl's altering
body-image must bring about a re-evaluation of herself in the light of

so many strange new capacities and powers. In terms, too, of a changing internal biochemical state—for a shifting body and brain physiology is promoting, in its turn, the experience of strange and confusing new sensations.

In the *best* of situations, which Marie's was so far from being, there are now complex psychic tasks to be undertaken. As Dr. Irene Josselyn has written (in *The Adolescent and His World*) the mother is, at this juncture of her child's life, both the daughter's competitor and her role model. The father is "the ideal, but forbidden sexual object. While she (i.e., the daughter) feels drawn toward the father, she must deny this attraction. Yet she cannot judge other men with confidence except by standards calibrated according to her concept of the father. She does not dare to be like her mother; she must deny her mother's virtues in order to assure herself of her own superiority to her mother. Yet her clearest definition of femininity is that with which her mother has acquainted her, and which she has accepted as a model for herself. She vacillates between contempt for her mother and father, idealization of her mother and father, contempt for her father and idealization of her mother, idealization of her father and contempt for her mother. . . ." This ambiguity and conflict-ridden agenda *must* cause distress even in the most benign and tolerant and unequivocal of environments.

In Marie's instance, however, psychological and physical development were occurring within the context of—and in a setting where—certain rules and a game plan had already been ordained. She wasn't, for these reasons, able to engage in a great deal of the vacillation of which Dr. Josselyn speaks. Her father, whom she correctly perceived as the person-with-power in the household, obviously preferred her company to her mother's. She could share in this, *his* power, by means of her own feminine influence and sway; she could coyly twist this personage around her own little finger.

She was, in this particular plot, given the part of daughter-seductress and child-woman. And surely, at a fantasy level, she'd triumphed (in terms of being an attractive female) rather decisively over her mother.

The price was, as it had to be, a good deal of anxiety and guilt. There was, too, that other psychological cost to be paid in such circumstances: the difficulty involved in identifying with the mother (an identification which is part of the normal maturational process) in attempting to come into one's own and fulfill one's own role as a mature woman. For in Marie's instance, there had been a defeat of the mother. And so the most important "model for womanhood" that she had before her was looking sorry and dilapidated indeed!

Would becoming a woman entail, one day, replicating the existence that was her mother's? If Marie's own life were ordained to follow a similar course, what was there, really, to beckon her forward into the future? At a subliminal level, the young girl had to be dealing with such issues. For she was emerging from one phase of her life and moving on to another, and, as Dr. Helene Deutsch has rightly observed, the important experiences of our lives are "not isolated but linked together in a long chain." The mother's own person, and her way of being, were her daughter's most salient model; they comprised, in short, the developing adult's most important "pattern for future living."

And yet, as Dr. Irene Josselyn, in her discussion of this "role-modeling" aspect of mothering, writes (in *The Adolescent and His World*): "Too often a woman finds that biological fertility results in sterility in other aspects of her life. It is as if an excellent cake were covered with a bitter or tasteless frosting. As a consequence, many women fail to find a desirable and adequate means of self-fulfillment. . . . They imply to their daughters that to succumb to the temptation of being a wife and mother is to expose oneself to slavery under an indifferent, if not a cruel, master. . . ."

Other women are, notes Josselyn, "martyrs to their biological and social roles"; they view their own femininity and its cultural demands as a cross to be borne. "Their destructiveness towards themselves and others makes them," says the psychologist, "like all martyrs, difficult to endure. If the mother has not found rich and multiple gratifications in her own femininity, identification with the mother inevitably creates a conflictual struggle for the girl."

The choice, in other words, can seem to be one between the devil and the deep blue sea. "Normal psychological development" implies an identification with the mother, whose figure, whose way-of-being ought to invite the daughter to become a woman, "become a person like me." But being-like-mother, if she's devalued and defeated (perhaps depressed too), looms as a fearful and unpalatable option or decision. And to complicate matters even further there was, in Marie's case, a conscious or unconscious certainty that much of her mother's unhappiness and lowered family status had to do with her father's own obvious preference for *herself*.

If there was (and there had to be) much unconscious anxiety and guilt about her success in the jealous competition for her father's attention, Marie was discomfited on other grounds as well. Culturally speaking, in the tight-knit and gossipy Sicilian community from which she sprang, a girl who was interested in bettering herself intellectually was viewed as an oddity. And she was, by far, the brightest child in the family. She was far more capable, in terms of shining in the class-room and bringing home good grades, than was her younger brother, Michael . . . another cause for her mother's antipathy and resentment.

When Marie, in grade nine, opted to take a college prep rather than a commercial course, the family's neighbors, and the girl's grand-parents, and other relatives frowned upon and objected to the deci-sion. Her own parents were attacked for permitting her to do such a thing. According to Marie the talk was: "What do you *mean*, a girl, and you're letting her do such a thing? She's not going to be a secre-tary or a hairdresser?"

This had been taken, related Marie, as yet another proof of her pe-culiarity.

Beating Mother Out

Her mother had, though, come to her defense in this matter; both her parents had defended her choice. The difficulty was, however, that from that point onward there was not even an outward semblance of amiability; she and her mother didn't get along *at all*.

"I don't think," said Marie, "that we talked civilly from the time I was thirteen until . . . maybe we did when I was eighteen. It was just backbiting before then; screaming and yelling all the time. I wanted to do things, to go places; she wouldn't let me do them. I wanted to date: 'No, you can't date'; *she* didn't go out on dates until she was eight-een.

"I couldn't, because of that, go out until I was sixteen. And it was everything—'What do you mean, you want to wear lipstick? No, you're *not* wearing lipstick, not until you're sixteen!' That's how it went, we fought about everything—and really, it was *bad*."

School, too, was another area in which she was conquering in terms of "beating mother out." For Marie was opting for a future that would be very different from the style of her mother's life; she would do something, quite possibly, in terms of a career. And this was, from her mother's point of view, perhaps being perceived as a rejection of what had been her own way of living. In any event, though, Marie was clearly able to do well and even excel in certain areas of life that had never been presented as *options* to her mother.

Marie was doing everything differently, for a nice Sicilian girl. She was bringing home tangible evidence of successes at learning that would one day be translatable to successes in the world outside the home. Such strivings had been unthinkable, forbidden to the mother, in *her* own youth. In some way, and to some degree, the direction the daughter's life was taking involved a negation of much of the older woman's past, her ways of functioning and doing, and being. Both child and parent knew it.

For the bottom line was this: Marie wasn't becoming a "feminine person" in the prearranged and prescribed fashion that her mother would easily have understood. She was being different (guilty, bad, etc.). This was another factor feeding into the two females' mutual fear, dislike, and discomfort.

Marie was, at the threshold of puberty, struggling with still another disadvantage which ought not to go unmentioned. She had never, during the preadolescent years (roughly, between ages eight and eleven) developed one of those close relationships with a same-sex peer that the great psychiatrist Harry Stack Sullivan considered a *prerequisite* for later intimacies. Sullivan saw what he called "chumship" as a necessary emotional way-stage on the developmental path leading to heterosexual bond-forming (falling in love) of the later adolescent and adult years.

But there hadn't been, for Marie, any such loving pal. She'd been a seclusive child throughout, and although she performed well as a student, she described herself as uncertain and frightened—"actually terrified"—when it came to the business of making friends. Why would any other girl *want* to make friends with her? She'd thought of herself, during the years when her father was away on the road much of the time and she was left home with her mother and siblings, to be someone who was simply not lovable. She was odd, peculiar; not really a girl that the other girls would have any desire to get to know.

It is in these years—and I'm speaking now of the time just prior to puberty—that an individual can, according to Harry Stack Sullivan, first truly suffer the "really intimidating experience of loneliness—the need for intimate exchange with a fellow being, whom we may describe as a chum, a friend. . . ." It is in the first loving friendship, suggests Sullivan, that a kind of mutual validation occurs. Here is a chance, as well, to look at oneself through the caring friend's eyes. Such intense two-way relationships give both parties a chance to affirm one another's personal worth. Not only do they affirm one's value, they reinforce it: that is: "My friend, whom *I* idealize, finds me acceptable and attractive; therefore I must be O.K., and maybe even someone better than I'd thought."

So powerful a psychic balm are these first experiences of empathy and loving, remarks Sullivan, that (says he): "I would hope that preadolescent relationships were intense enough for each of the two chums literally to get to know practically everything about the other one that could possibly be exposed in an intimate relationship, because that remedies a good deal of the often illusory, usually morbid, feeling of being different, which is such a striking part of rationalizations of insecurity" (i.e., explanations given to the self about why it is that one feels so anxious and unhappy) "in later life."

Marie DaCosta had had no such close friend; there'd been no person to tell her that she was, by and large, all right. Speaking, years later, of that period of her life, she said: "I cried myself to sleep more times than I can remember. I felt . . . deserted. I felt—oh, as if I were missing something that was very important to me. And this, whatever it might've been, was something my mother just couldn't provide."

Losing and Finding

The main themes of adolescence, according to the brilliant psychoanalytic theorist Dr. Peter Blos, are those of "object relinquishment" and "object finding." That is, "*love* object relinquishment" and "*love* object finding"; letting go of the intense love relations of early childhood and searching out new emotional bonds. This work is the work of adaptation: of creating one's own place, emotionally speaking, in the world outside the family.

Earlier, however, in the preadolescent "emotional way-station" posited by Harry Stack Sullivan—the intensely powerful first experience of intimacy that he called chumship—there's been what almost seems like a practice run at loving. The whole notion of chumship suggests, in fact, that the emerging human individual takes the Bucket of Love (so to speak) which must ultimately be wrested away from the relationship with the parents, and tests it out, experiments with its uses, in this tryout experience with an intimate and idealized friend. Chumship could, if it *is* an important intermediary place between childhood and adult love, be seen as a developmental stage *beyond* child-parent bonding and *preceding* intimate heterosexual commitment. In the passionate friendships of later childhood and early adolescence we prepare ourselves for "object relinquishment" and gear ourselves for the great search involved in new-love-object finding.

The painful acceptance of the end of childhood gives way, during the adolescent years, to a need for a different kind of human closeness. Now there is what may be recognized as the searching process, the quest for a certain someone . . . someone to love and to care for, who will, in turn, love and care for oneself. New bonds, if they're benign and if they're working, are what facilitate the awful task of letting go. Still, letting go of the "child" part of the self will inevitably present some degree of difficulty, distress, and suffering. "The realization of the finality of the end of childhood, of the binding nature of commitments," writes Blos, and "of the definite limitation to individual existence itself—this realization creates a sense of urgency, fear and panic. Consequently, many an adolescent tries to remain indefinitely in a transitional stage of development; this condition is called prolonged adolescence. . . ."

This was where Marie Sirotta was, at the time that we began our interviews. It was something she herself was aware of, for, when proposing herself as a subject in my study, she said quite breezily: "I'm, you know, in what you'd call 'delayed adolescence.'" She was living at home, and thinking about moving; but somehow hadn't gotten around to formulating any definite plans to do so. For the meanwhile she was a daughter—a twenty-eight-year-old daughter—whose parents still loomed very importantly in her thought processes and in her life.

Exploring

One wouldn't have predicted, from the picture she'd presented at ages thirteen and fourteen, that Marie would be where she was at the time that her late twenties rolled around. For she seemed, judging from her descriptions of what life had been like for her then, to have been the model of the well-adapted, busily exploring, busily moving-outward adolescent.

The underground themes which were, eventually, to manifest themselves in the "eight disastrous years" (i.e., the guilt and anxiety associated with that fantasy-triumph over her mother; and the dependency and *need* for her mother's love, masked even from Marie herself, by pretenses that she "didn't care anyhow") had not yet given signs or notice of their existence. But if her guilt about the conquest over Mother was unconscious, so was the daughter's later expiation to be so. For Marie did atone, much later on, in her twenties. She did it, essentially, by working herself into an identical position.

She "paid" by becoming a sister-in-suffering; by getting into and then empathizing with her mother's situation. This was, then, her means of winning her mother's affection—the caring and empathy which, back in the early teens, Marie had denied even wanting or being concerned about.

A Real Family

Early in puberty, when she was about twelve, a thing that she'd hoped and prayed for ever since she could remember actually *did* happen. Her father stopped his constant traveling and found steady work nearby. Now, at last, they could all be a real family. When this change took place, recalled Marie, "I felt as if the dream of my entire life were coming true." But it didn't, apparently, solve many of the real problems that already existed.

"Our family just never 'worked' as a family," she explained, "and I'm still very sensitive to that. The truth is that we all—all of us kids, I mean—were played off against one another right from the start. I was in Dad's camp; Michael was in Mom's. And Antonia . . . she was just Tonia, acting as if she didn't want to belong in *anybody's* camp and to hell with us all. But nobody really talked to anyone. I don't think any of us knew how to get *through* to the others! Not that there were any knock-down battles: there weren't. My folks didn't believe in doing that, at least not in front of the kids. But there were long, long spells in which they wouldn't talk . . . and I can remember wishing they'd go ahead and *fight!* All of us knew they weren't getting along, and we'd sit down to dinner, and no one would speak to anyone else. That kind of thing. You know, it frightened us. . . . We were afraid to open our mouths."

The young adolescent's hope that the family might draw together now—her father having at last come off the road—soon had to be given up, completely abandoned. But then, in her early teens, the family was something she was putting more and more into the background. The pace of her activities was quickening; and the vector was definitely outward and away from the "whole sorry mess at home." Marie was busily exploring an environment that was strange, fascinating, and full of curiosities. As she entered high school, she began meeting new kinds of people, learning about "all sorts of things I hadn't realized existed," hearing a lot of intellectual discussions about things that she'd not known of before: "I heard things being talked about, for the first time in my life, in an other-than-Sicilian-and-Catholic framework. This was, for me, a totally novel point of view."

Her mother didn't like it. And she herself was, admitted Marie, feeling pretty cocky at that time. "O.K., so my mother was tearing her hair out, but who cared? I was excited, meeting all these new people— Jewish kids, black kids, all kinds of kids I'd never met before! And that was—oh, *wonderful* for me!" Marie was beginning to date, too, though only in groups at first: at the magic age of sixteen she was finally permitted to have a boy friend.

"Of course," she smiled, "he was Jewish. To this day I don't know whether I got involved with him because I liked him or because I knew that was the way to get *them*. You know, not only was he not Catholic; by God, he was Jewish! . . . We went together for a year and a half. And for the first year, it worked out really well; we were inseparable. But it wasn't just the two of us; there was a whole group. And that, also, was new for me. I mean, a whole group of us would decide: 'Let's go to the basketball game' or: 'Let's go out and get hamburgers.' I hadn't had that kind of freedom before. Steve drove; he had his own car."

It was a first love, a first taste of freedom, a first experience of belonging—of really *being* valued, cherished, protected. And for that first year, during which she and Steve were "inseparable," things really did go well. But this long stretch of happiness was succeeded by a six-month period during which the relationship started breaking apart. By then, according to Marie, she'd become "kind of dependent" on her boy friend. "*Kind* of!" She laughed as soon as she'd said the word: "I was *absolutely* dependent upon him!" A former girl friend of Steve's had appeared on the scene—someone he'd dated and broken up with before meeting Marie. Now, during what became six long months of emotional teeter-tottering, she found herself "vying with this girl, competing for him constantly." A whole world; the center of which was herself-and-Steve and the periphery of which was "the crowd," hung in jeopardy. As he continued to vacillate between herself and his old love, Marie began experiencing the panic of possible aloneness and abandonment.

Those old and denied feelings of dependency—the feelings of the child who, unable to depend upon and trust the mother, had secluded and "taken care of herself"—were surging up, with renewed force and passion, in this first serious boy-girl relationship of her life.

The extent and urgency of her needs, she now believes, truly frightened him; like many a person who senses that too much is at stake to be borne, she had begun to behave badly. "I was feeling shitty, really shitty, about myself; and I couldn't go to my family with any of it, because none of this was really part of them. The set of friends that I was going around with were—they were brighter. They had more money, more going for them in terms of just being smart; they had nicer clothes. And I really felt that I was, myself, as far as the group was concerned, marginal; I thought I'd only been accepted because of Steve. But going around with this crowd had been, from the word

'Go,' a betrayal of my family . . . and now here *he* was, betraying me! I think I believed, deep down, that I was being punished, because here was what I'd done . . . and this is what happened *to* me. . . ."

"But in what ways," I asked, "would you say that your overdependency made you behave badly in that relationship?"

She hesitated, thought for a moment. "A friend of Steve's told me, much later, that I was really far more responsible for the breakup than he was. My attitude had changed toward the end of the first year, but I just didn't realize it at the time. I'd gotten very aloof and very cool —also, sarcastic. Then, when his old girl friend entered the picture, it was all about *showing* him that I didn't care! And so I'd go on and on, putting him down about everything. . . ." His ex-girl friend was, on the other hand, known for her sweet nature and for her adoration of Steve. Marie thought, on reflecting about that situation, that the contrast between the two of them had finally been too much.

Her vulnerability had led to this elaborately defensive show of "not caring" (as she'd once "not cared" in the relationship with her remote and embittered mother). But her brittle, angry behavior toward Steve, at this time, was also fueled by churning anxieties about the sexual explorations in which the two of them had been engaging. "I was really very concerned about the sexual aspects of the relationship. I knew that—according to my religion and my upbringing—the things we were doing were dead wrong. And I think it was that, more than anything else, that made me want to turn the whole thing off."

What they were "doing" had been no more than a lot of heavy petting. But Marie, still ignorant about sex, believed it was possible for her to become pregnant that way. In a way, by behaving badly, she'd been trying to end it by forcing *him* to end it. "Do you think," I wondered, "that you were doing that? So that in a sense, he'd have that responsibility and *you'd* still be being punished for all those awful, rotten sexual things you'd been doing?" I laughed, and she did too.

"Yes," she answered. "And it's really astonishing the way, years later, the tables turned. Because that's exactly how my husband got out of our marriage—by being so impossible that he forced *me* to make the moves!"

Betrayals

The relationship with Steven Glass was forbidden and doomed for other, deeper reasons. He was truly the antithesis of her father; and

Marie had had, always, a special closeness with her father. She'd felt, from the outset of her romance with Steve that there'd been treachery on her part; it was, in a sense, a way of saying, "No, I want other qualities in a man."

Her father was, as she described him, a small person, "blustery and kind of wiry." He could express feelings in hugging, tickling, kissing; but he was unable to articulate his feelings verbally. "Steve was the first person I'd ever been able to talk to, really to *talk*, as far as opening up feelings was concerned. He was sensitive, and just—a very nice human being. He was the first male I'd ever known who had been that way. . . ." Marie shook her head as if to say "forget it"; but she looked wistful.

"And you, do you ever regret," I followed after the unspoken thought, "that things *didn't* go on . . . that they didn't work out with Steve?"

"Yes, I do," replied Marie. "I do, to this day."

The two had parted with finality during the first half of her senior high school year. It was, for her, a period of crying episodes, severe stomach pains, feelings of not wanting to get out of bed in the mornings. She had developed an ovarian cyst and had had to spend several weeks in the hospital. She was lagging behind in her schoolwork, unable to cope with the loss of Steve and finding no solace—nothing to fall back on—in the family. Her attempt to escape them had come, clearly, to naught. She was being disciplined, she felt vaguely, for ever having had the audacity to *try*.

Most hurtful of all hurts, that senior year in high school was, of course, the breakup with Steve. He was back with his old girl friend: Marie, feeling desperately betrayed, had cried about it for weeks, felt that people were talking about her behind her back. Surely no one in the crowd would like her or have anything more to do with her *now!* "I think," she said, "that if ever in my life I was paranoid, it was during this particular time. I found out very slowly, after I became able to look around and to listen to people again, that that wasn't actually true. People liked me; I hadn't only been included in the group because of Steve."

During the next six months, however, she'd begun playing very manipulative, aggressive games with other boys that she knew. She would, for example, make two dates for the same night and then call both people up, saying she had a headache: "I was calling all the shots now, I guess. I really was *very* angry."

The following September she was to start college. She had wanted to go away to school but there simply wasn't the money to send her. And to Marie, that was "defeating my own purpose. Because what I actually wanted was to get away. Not to commute back and forth to school, and to hold a part-time job . . . that was too much like going to high school. But that was, it turned out, the only way it was going to *be* possible—so it had to be O.K."

That was the summer, though, that she'd met Carl Sirotta.

And that meeting had, in effect, changed pretty much everything in her life.

Letting Go of the Power

I haven't described Marie Sirotta's physical appearance, and perhaps the mention of her Sicilian ancestry has conjured up a mental picture: dark eyes; dark hair; the olive-tinted hues of a Mediterranean complexion. She was, however, one of the exceptions to the stereotypic expectation that one encounters. Her eyes were, it is true, dark and brown; but her skin was on the fair side and her hair an improbable auburn (a souvenir, undoubtedly, of the long-ago Norman invasion of the isle of Sicily, and the long period of Norman domination).

That hair of Marie's, that handsome red-brown hair—she kept it clipped short, almost as short as a man would wear it. And as soon as a softening wave began to make its appearance, it was surrendered immediately to the shears. The serviceable clothes she wore did, by and large, communicate a similar "no-nonsense" message. Everything about her seemed to say quite frankly, "I am the person that I am, and I'm not going to dress up for the boys, nor am I going to play cutie-pie. So don't try anything funny, or to put me into any special categories. I am an independent woman—and I don't want anyone, male or female, to dare to forget it."

Gone was any trace of that dependent, leaning, needing, probably somewhat cajoling eighteen-year-old girl who was first introduced to Carl Sirotta that summer. And, of all qualities that Marie disliked in my *other* "subjects"—whose interviews she was, at that time, transcribing and typing—it was the quality of dependence. I had noticed this shortly after she began working as my research assistant. She, who was usually so richly empathetic, so concerned with the lives and beings of the women whose talks she was laboriously transcribing, became almost angry when someone talked into my tape recorder *that* way!

I'd become amused finally, and pointed this out to her, saying: "You know, Marie, when you react badly to one of the women I've interviewed it's *always* about the same thing . . . have you noticed?"

And she'd blushed, admitted that, yes, she did know. It was always in reaction to a someone letting go of the power. A woman who was handing everything that she was, or that she hoped to be, over to *someone else*—and that someone being a man.

"No Name"

She had disliked him on sight, this person she was to marry. A girl friend of hers was entranced by him at the time, and they'd happened to catch sight of him after a movie one evening. "Betsy called him over to the car, and he came right over. I can remember his walking towards us, and me muttering to her: 'Where's your taste?' She said, under her own breath, 'Mmm, he's adorable.' And I said: 'He looks fourteen years old; he's got a cut on his face, and he's got the stupidest blue eyes.' She said she thought he was gorgeous; I said I thought she was crazy. He came over to the car and said: 'Hi, Bets; who's your friend?' And I said 'No Name.' And he said, 'Hi No Name, I'm Carl.' But I totally ignored him; I thought he was dumb and ugly."

But what had caused, I asked her, such a strong reaction in what seemed to be a casual encounter? "I don't know," Marie answered slowly. "I just had this immediate antipathy—a real distaste that was something almost chemical." She stared at me, shaking her head slowly as if in eternal puzzlement. Her expression itself seemed to ask the question, "How could I have ended by marrying the man? How did the thing ever come about?"

I nodded my own head wonderingly in response.

The relationship with Carl was something that, in retrospect, seemed to have happened by means of small, almost imperceptible advances. For about a month after that first chance meeting the two of them had simply kept running into one another. Marie had seen him, in fact, a day or so later, at a neighborhood young people's party; he'd tried to get her to go out for a ride with him and she'd rebuffed him with hardly a thought. "Then—I don't know how it got started—but he was picking me up at work. I had, I suppose, told him where I was working that summer, and what time I got out. So I guess that, through that violent dislike, I still must have been interested. Because I'd let him know where I would be . . . and when."

They had begun to date, in a desultory fashion at first; and then, as the months passed, with a growing exclusivity. The realization that she would marry Carl, reflected Marie, came to appear to be something that was—and always had been—her fate. Not a chosen fate exactly;

but a fate, inasmuch as it was going to *happen* willy-nilly. They'd become lovers after a year of going out together although she was, she said, "decidedly *not* sexually attracted to him."

"Then—why?"

A helpless and vulnerable expression crossed her features: "Well, I'm still not sure. We'd been dating, then, for about a year and everybody else was either getting married or sleeping with people. And I was worried—about being a virgin. Thinking, you know, that there had to be something wrong with me. . . ." She laughed wryly.

"So you went to bed with him because you just felt it was about time?" I smiled. "And how was that?"

She shook her head very hard, as if to reject the memory: "Yes I did it because it was 'time.' And it was simply *awful*. It hurt."

In the Palm of His Hand

She had gone to college in the fall, done very well for the first year, and then dropped out. She and Carl were eventually going to marry. Her family insisted that there wasn't much point in her spending the next three years studying. It seemed far more sensible to go to work and make some money. And Marie agreed, thinking that she'd get married and could then be independent of her family and have everything she wanted. "Marriage, not school, became the goal ahead of me; I was going to live happily ever after." Carl was already working steadily as a carpenter and contractor; he was in no rush at all to marry. "But I did want to get married," said Marie. "I decided I'd had it with this sleeping together; and I was going to force his hand. I told him, you either marry me—because I want to be married before I get pregnant—or I'm calling the whole thing off!"

She'd been leaning forward intently but now sat back: "Well, he laughed. And he said: 'You're not calling it off; I've got you right in the palm of my hand. You're not going anywhere! . . .'" Carl knew that, because they were lovers, this strictly brought up young woman was convinced she had to marry him. He also knew, remarked Marie, that she had become extremely dependent upon him.

"I was never a very independent person; and I'd gotten to count upon him for everything," she admitted. "I couldn't get to the *corner drugstore* unless he was driving me there! And so things continued that way for a while—me wanting to get married; he postponing it—until I met someone else, a young executive at the bank where I was working. This guy had asked me out, and I'd refused, saying that I was almost engaged." She laughed, reached in her purse for a cigarette. "He said, though, that 'practically' or 'almost' didn't count. And I really *was* very attracted to him."

She'd begun seeing this new admirer; and before long, had broken off her relationship with Carl. Eventually, a series of delightful dates became a deeply satisfying sexual love affair. There was never any question of permanence; that had been agreed upon at the outset. But when, after three months, her lover was transferred to an office in Manhattan, she learned that the affair was going to end abruptly. That was all. When she protested, she was reminded that they'd said, in advance, that this was to involve no commitments. "It's true," said Marie, sounding hurt, "that we *did* make that arrangement. But there's such a difference between saying it and meaning it! Ahhh . . . I ran immediately back to Carl. I was there the next day. I was sitting on his doorstep waiting for him to come home. And I never told him that I'd been to bed with the other man . . . nothing like that. I told him, only, how much I had missed him; and I asked him to please take me back. He said: 'Yeh, sure, I think we should get married.' And I said, 'Oh, I think we should get married too!'"

Her lighter shot up a jet of flame, and she lit her cigarette, inhaled. "Unfortunately, that's just what we did."

Security

The marriage, in one swoop, was to set all past moral wrongs right. If she'd engaged in premarital sex, and felt that was "bad," she would now be a respectably married woman. Sex was, however—not on moral but on other, less abstract grounds—a perennial problem. For, from the unpleasant beginning of their sexual involvement, she'd found sex with Carl completely distasteful. Marie had never had an orgasm with *him;* she had, though, experienced orgasm in that other, brief love affair with the man she'd met at work. Sex, in that second intimate relationship, had been intensely good and gratifying; but then, the affair had ended with such bruising suddenness. She'd come away feeling she *had* learned her lesson: she'd been slapped hard in two efforts to find a different sort of man . . . a man less like her own father. "I ran back to security," she explained, "which is the only way I can account for what I did. . . . Opted, you know, to have sex on a permanent basis with a guy I wasn't even sexually *attracted* to!"

It was terrible, from the first day onward. The marriage was unworkable, in fact, from the night of the honeymoon itself. And it continued, according to Marie, to wax progressively more bitter and unhappy over the course of the subsequent three years: "We fought like cats and dogs; we fought over everything. Over money, over telephone conversations, friends—you name it, and we managed to fight about it. We would hurl the laundry basket at one another about the question of which one would do the laundry! I couldn't keep the house neat enough; couldn't do anything well enough . . . except, perhaps, cook. He was constantly on my back about everything, *hated* everyone I knew. And slowly, I was becoming friendless . . . because, by the time the fourth year rolled around, he'd started not showing up. We'd make plans to go out with another couple and he just would not show."

Why, did she think, I asked Marie, that Carl had married *her?*

"I believe I was a kind of a status symbol for him," she answered swiftly, as if having already given this matter some thought. "I was better-educated and much brighter than most of the women he knew. I don't think he realized initially how dependent I actually was. I believe, when he understood that fully, that was—for him—when the whole thing started to fizzle."

It sometimes seemed to her, she added, that she had been under a hypnotic spell at the time of her marriage. She had married a man so strangely *like* her father! Not that the resemblance was physical: Carl, whose mother was a German Lutheran, had pale eyes, dark hair, and a fair complexion; he was also somewhat taller than her father. But the two were—and she'd realized this with ever-growing clarity—not only brothers, but twins, beneath the skin. They liked the same things and behaved in a very similar fashion. They had identical requirements when it came to the behavior of wives.

"Both my father and my husband wanted one thing above all from a wife," said Marie. "And that was subservience. Carl's *own* father told me, on more than one occasion, that a woman's sole purpose in life was to keep house for a man and to raise his children. And this was, of course, the role my own mother had been given, too."

Marie was now indisputably involved in a marriage that was a replication—even a caricature—of the marital situation of her parents. Being *in* her mother's position made her understand, she recounted, just how much her mother had been dismissed, put down, ignored as someone who was dumb or ineffectual. "I found myself in the same circumstances in which *she'd* always been: expected to sit at home and wait, with dinner in the oven, for three, four, five hours; it didn't make any difference. You weren't supposed to complain. You weren't even supposed to have an *opinion* of your own! It was only then, when it was happening to *me*, that I *realized*—" She stopped, her eyes beginning to fill with tears.

She'd been depressed, Marie thought, almost from the outset of her life with Carl. But, if their relationship had been difficult initially, it continued, over time, to become ever more disordered, confused, even physically violent. She was becoming what she called "inactively suicidal": she was fantasying, a lot, about dying, but making no real efforts to end her life. "I wanted to do something which I used to call, in my own mind, a 'suicide test'; that is, to go through the motions of killing myself and see if the shock value wouldn't serve to wake Carl up, to alleviate the craziness of the situation. What I didn't want, though," she confessed, "was to really kill myself—not then. But stupid as it sounds, I couldn't think of any other way to break the deadlock. Or, for that matter, to get out of the marriage."

They were moving, now, into their fifth year together. Although continuing to inhabit the same apartment, Marie and Carl were living "parallel but totally unconnected lives." She was continuing, she recounted, to "stash away all the pills I could get—some Valium here, a little Darvon there. And Carl was drinking hard and using amphetamines; he was doing more and more bizarre things, while I—oh, God!—I was falling deeper and deeper into what was, for me, an almost unimaginable depression. I can't *imagine* any physical pain that could truly be worse than the things that were going on in my head at that time! I felt at times . . . I can't put it into words. It was agonizing . . . I didn't have the faintest idea what to *do* with myself. . . ."

She'd been into and out of bad periods (mostly *into*) since the outset of their life together. But *this* depression, paralyzing her in pain and indecision, seemed unremitting, unrelenting, never-ending. It was a part of her, and felt as though it had been, always. She experienced it as stretching far backward into the rememberable past and forward into the imaginable future—a barren eternity of hopelessness. She was in a place, psychically speaking, where she'd never been before, nor known about, in the entire course of her life.

"Not," reiterated Marie, "that there weren't some pretty difficult episodes—depressions—right from the start. There were. I was working, at that time, as a secretary in the department of psychology at Harvard; and I was coming home every night to an empty apartment. Carl had, after just a few months of marriage, started that business of just not coming home after work . . . it was my father all over again. And that very first spring together, as soon as it got warm enough, he began working on a boat that he kept.

"I never saw him at all after that," she continued, her voice low and strained, "and I hadn't—at that time—a car of my own. I'd come home at night, by bus, to those empty rooms; and ugh, how I hated that, coming inside! It was so quiet . . . even the air, when I opened the door it just hit me in the face. The feeling of it was so terrible: it was a feeling of 'You are *alone*.' And I remember, at this time, not really knowing anybody. I didn't make friends very easily. There weren't any young people in the apartments. I came home one night and had the feeling that I didn't even want to *eat*—it was just one more meal by myself. I sat down on the living room rug and started leafing through the newspaper, just turning the pages, and all of a sudden I started crying and crying and crying. Oh, God. Oh, I felt so abandoned, alone, lost, discarded . . . it was just total desolation. And I must have cried so loud and so long that my next-door neighbor, an older widow, could no longer *bear* it. Because there came a knock on my front door. . . ." Marie stopped speaking, swallowed. I waited, saying nothing.

"I opened the door," she resumed after several moments, "and she came in and grabbed me by the hand and said 'I don't know about *you* but I've had enough of this!' And she literally marched me into her apartment, sat me down, and cooked me my supper." Marie sighed. "For a long time, then, she was my only close friend. But she never said a word to me about my husband."

The Idea of Dying

The marriage endured for a full eight years. When she finally did move out, Marie said, it was in the wake of a physical brawl and a marital rape: "Don't tell me there's no such thing as a sexual attack in a marriage, because that's what he did; he raped me!" The note she left sounded (and this was something that she had, afterward, wondered much about) exactly like a suicide note.

It read: I NEVER MEANT TO DO THIS, BUT I JUST CAN'T GO ON ANY LONGER. LOVE, MARIE. "Can you *imagine* that?" she interrupted her narrative to demand, "I actually signed it 'Love'! Carl later on, presented that note in the courtroom when he was disputing the divorce; he was trying to show that I was mentally unbalanced. And in a way," she added ironically, "I think I probably *was*. If anyone had just picked up this note, they'd surely have expected to find me in the bathroom, dead."

Confused and frightened as she was, she believes, now, that "leav-

ing" was in her mind the equivalent of "dying." No one in her family,
until the moment of the rupture itself, had known that anything was
wrong with her marriage. There was no soul that she could count
upon to protect and take responsibility for her: "I didn't know what I
was going to *do* with myself! It hadn't ever occurred to me that there
would come a time when I'd really have to take care of myself. I went
from a sheltered childhood home to a marriage with somebody whose
job was supposed to be to take care *of* me! And my persistent
thought, throughout much that was going on, was: 'How dare he not
take care of me?'" She stopped, reached over to her leather purse, took
out a fresh, unopened pack of cigarettes. She tore open the top of the
package shakily.

"You know, I think now that from about the fifth year we were together, I was probably depressed nonstop. But then we had our *sixth*
anniversary and our *seventh*. We'd been married for seven years; I
was nearing thirty; I was utterly and inconsolably depressed. I prayed
every single night that Carl would drop dead; and then felt guilty as
hell for *having* such thoughts. Every night that he didn't show up—
and he was out all night many times by now—I really hoped he'd been
smashed up on the turnpike somewhere. I really did. But then he'd
come through the door and my stomach would turn. I'd think: 'God-
damn, you made it home alive again!' I hated him so much . . . it just
turned my stomach, having to sleep with him. Having to deal with
him. I detested him and despised myself. At the same time I kept
thinking that there must be something awfully *wrong* with me . . .
because if there wasn't, why didn't my husband ever want to come
home?"

During this entire period of years, the store of hoarded lethal drugs
had grown to overkill, megaton proportions. She had, certainly, no
practical reason for not taking what was coming to seem like the only
possible option—the one way to end this state of confusion and pain.
And one night, after Carl had failed to show up for a dinner they'd
planned in celebration of her twenty-sixth birthday, Marie decided
she'd have to take that option. But, instead of taking an overdose of
drugs, she called up the parish priest of her local church, sobbing and
threatening hysterically to kill herself.

The priest that she contacted that evening was someone she'd never
met; she'd never even heard of him, for she'd not been attending
church. But he heard her out on the telephone, and then insisted that
they get together at once. They spent several hours with one another
that evening. He let her ventilate her feelings; and also suggested,
quietly, that she might contemplate the possibility of a separation.

"This was," admitted Marie, "a step that I couldn't, at that time, even consider."

The idea of dying—and this, as I've seen over and over again, is strangely common among women who are depressed and unhappy in the context of a destructive, unworkable marital relationship—seemed to be, somehow, easier than just *leaving*. Marie had gone back to school, moreover, and felt she *couldn't* leave Carl because she simply wasn't self-supporting. "I didn't think I could go back home," she explained. "I didn't think my mother would have me."

"Why not?" I asked.

"I didn't think she loved me." Her eyes dropped; she stubbed out her cigarette slowly and carefully.

The Deadly Game

If one were to trace out—like a continuing golden thread in a vastly complex pattern—the particular course that Marie's life had taken between her twelfth and twenty-eighth year, why one would discern a circle. In early adolescence the impulses and the movement had been outward. She'd been engrossed by her explorations of the world (and of who she might *be* in that world). She had been making the right moves and doing the right psychological work—in terms of making it away. But beneath this apparently adequate surface adaptation, there had been profoundly regressive and backward surges . . . in terms of unfinished business in the family.

Marie was experiencing, from her mother's side, envy, disapproval, dislike. She believed her mother didn't care for her, because—from the point of view of Daddy's affection—she was clearly the winner. And so she was: in a game where the winner always loses. In the short range she'd been able, of course, to gain ascendancy, to win a large stake of the family power. Her father was indisputably the one who *had* most of it (the power); and *he* was under her spell. But in the long range, the costs were enormous. They included the possibility of any workable relationship with her mother; and also a certain amount of seductive role playing in the interaction with her father.

Even now, at the present time, she had to labor to keep the relationship with her father in its proper perspective. "I realize," she once told me, when we were reaching the end of our interviews, "that my father plays a kind of game with me, and that I play into it. It's always *been* a game that he and I played, but I've become, recently, very conscious of it. Perhaps it has to do with the fact that you and I have been talking, laying these cards all out on the table, so to speak. But he sometimes behaves as if . . . as if he's courting me. I mean the two of us will go out to dinner, and he'll work so hard to be charming and to entertain me—as if he were my *date*, really, and not my father!" She tossed her head, ran a quick hand through her short red-brown hair.

"I'm trying hard *not* to play that particular game with him anymore. I'm realizing that it is deadly . . . as I've begun to believe the whole business of acting coquettish really is." She hesitated. "That's the way I was with most of the men I knew, until about two years ago. And of course, the method works. I'd flirt and I'd get whatever I wanted . . . whether it was from a male friend or from my father. It's just a way I behaved—with people at school, or on the job, whatever. But you know, since Carl and I separated, I've become more self-confident. I've been through a course in assertive training, for one thing—and I've learned that there are *other ways* to deal with men. And I've stopped playing goo-goo pretty much with everyone but my father. I think he's the only one I still continue that 'little cutie pie' sort of a game with . . . ?"

The statement ended, and she looked at me, as if she'd meant it to be a question. I answered: "Maybe you've never gotten over your sense of his power over you. I mean that maybe it's possible to stop playing that game in every other aspect of your life, but the real seduction game is *there*. In terms, that is, of your behavior toward your dad really saying 'I know you have the power, but I know how I can retain my power over *you*.'"

Marie was staring at me. "I hadn't faced this so baldly until just the other day. My mother's going away in a couple of Sundays to a huge Italian feast day; they're holding it in New York. I was the one who had the notion about our going, first of all. She went ahead and got the information, made plans with some friends of her own age, and we'd all planned to go together. But I got busy, and had to back off. And jokingly, she made some offhand remark the other day, saying 'You know I got into this whole scheme in the beginning because you were the one who wanted to go there, and to taste all the different foods, and so forth.' Well, my father perked up at that instantaneously, and he said to her: 'What is this? Where are you going?' When she explained, he seemed happy and said to her, 'Oh, don't worry about a thing.' He turned to me, then, and said: 'The two of *us* will go out to dinner; that'll be much more fun anyway.' I mean, he literally lunged at the chance. And I had to say, 'Well, gee, Dad, I don't know. The reason I backed off was because I had made other plans.' He got *annoyed* at that; he really did."

Back to "Go"

The course of her life had, from puberty onward, resembled a great outward-directed arc. Now, at twenty-eight, the "golden thread" had cycled around to its originating place and enclosed a period of living within its circumference. She was back, once again, where she'd begun; she was working on issues never resolved. Most of these were old concerns, and among the questions of her earliest adolescence. Such as: "Does my father love and value me more than he does my mother?" (How delicious! How dangerous! How unthinkable!) And, even deeper and more fateful, that buried emotional explosive: "Can my mother, then, possibly *not* hate *me?*" If her mother, rightfully outraged, couldn't abide or love her, then was love only to be had in the guise of seductress? Her father had crowed, in his outburst of delight at her return, "How often do you get to raise a daughter twice?"

One certainly had the sense of a cast of characters that, with the un-canniest dexterity, had maneuvered themselves into a former set of po-sitions in order to replay some crucial scene. Marie's surname was, now, different from that of her parents, it's true. But, as if to turn the clock back even more definitively, she was living in her home and at-tending school (a schoolgirl!) once again.

In the remarkable book *Adaptation to Life*, Dr. George E. Vaillant makes a beautiful and beautifully succinct observation. Adolescence is, writes psychiatrist Vaillant, a time of painful self-differentiation, a time when "Family shibboleths are cast aside, and an identity is formed that is the individual's alone. Identity formation in adolescence is fostered by a curious fact of human nature; *as we lose or separate from people that we love, we internalize them.*"

Those powerful and powerfully worshiped idols of our early child-hood become, as we separate from them in the confusion, strain, and tumult of the adolescent period, "inner voices" or "internal instruc-tors" who will (as they speak to us from within) help to guide us into our adulthood.

The infant and child's first caretakers become part of the adolescent and the mature person. Psychologically speaking, we are thus living memorials of those we have loved. But the growing woman who can-not, like Marie, internalize her mother (because the fear of being-like-mother is too overwhelming) or who—because her mother genuinely *dislikes* her—must internalize a critical, disapproving parent, is caught in a human trap. She will be, in the first instance, empty. In the second, she'll have the Enemy (the harsh, unfriendly, hostile voice) coming at her from within. It was this latter set of considerations that led one, indeed, to wonder whether Marie Sirotta's disastrous wrong choices had been predicated by an inner need to get punished for that early adolescent triumph—to make sure she got what she "really deserved" for having been so deep-down rotten . . . for having been the winner.

Certainly, the outward events in her life had faithfully portrayed the picture of her inner distress; her crime and the working-out of the deserved retribution. But that had been in the past, and now she was home. She'd gone back to a certain juncture in her life, where so many bad things seemed to have begun. Now she was busily reworking that relationship with her mother—and, less easily, with her father too. I hoped that Marie would really make it the next time . . . the next time she tried moving out.

CHAPTER FIVE

On Promiscuity and Depression: Sandy

Going Through That Door

Sandy had come into therapy because she was, as she phrased it, "puzzled by my promiscuity"; she was feeling upset and strange about the ways in which she was living her life and yet felt so helpless and powerless when it came to effecting any kind of a change. Her respect for herself had plummeted steadily downward over the course of the past six months; she felt cheap and discardable and could not fathom "why my relationships are so shallow." Her general affect, or emotional tone, was that of a depressed person; she was sad, down, discouraged, and feeling that little in her life gave pleasure or had meaning. But Sandy's was not the kind of overwhelming mood disorder that suggested the use of drugs or medications. The pervasive feelings of shame and self-hatred that she was experiencing seemed so clearly reactive—related to her feelings of loneliness and of loss.

Sandy Geller showed none of the standard biological—the so-called "neurovegetative"—signs and symptoms of a clinical depression. Queried, during that first "intake" interview, about recent changes in her sleeping and eating patterns, as well as her general levels of energy, she reported that there really *hadn't been* any. She wasn't snapping awake in the night, or toward early morning; nor was she suffering from insomnia. Her appetite was all right. It had not, at least so far as she'd noticed, fallen off; it hadn't, alternatively, increased with drastic suddenness. There had been no decline in libido, or levels of sexual interest. "If anything," she had responded to this question with nervousness, "the shoe is on the other foot."

This was, as a matter of fact, the thing she needed to talk to someone about: her sexual life had gotten so mixed up, so crazy, so erratic. She was feeling awfully *rotten* about it.

She'd been involved, over the course of this past year, in a good deal of complicated and yet mostly random activity—sleeping with men she knew casually or well. Men she met at work, or at singles bars, or at social gatherings: at a variety of different places. It was O.K., of course, Sandy hurried to say, for she was divorced, independent, and on her own. It was just that she'd been feeling increasingly weird about it, and unhappy . . . uncomfortable too.

She didn't quite like herself these days. And these feelings: she needed to talk them over with somebody.

Sandy didn't have very far to go, geographically speaking, when she decided to enter treatment. For she was an R.N., working at the Dartmouth-Hitchcock Memorial Hospital in Hanover, New Hampshire (cardiac unit); the Dartmouth-Hitchcock Mental Health Center, which maintains a busy outpatient service, is directly across the street. And yet it had seemed to Sandy, in terms of psychological distance, to be as remote, as distant as an astral star. "I myself had worked on psych-units, and so forth," she said to me much later, "but when it came to actually making that step myself—when *I* had to go through that door—I kept debating, up to the very threshold, about whether or not I wanted to do it. Did I really *need* to see a psychiatrist? I just wasn't sure. But I was feeling troubled enough, and down enough, so that I thought: 'I've got to, at the very least, unburden myself of some of these things. Even if nothing else comes of it, I've got to *talk* about it all to someone!' "

She came in, I remember, in her white uniform; she'd managed to remain relatively fresh-looking and unwilted on what was one of the hottest afternoons in August. Sandy Geller was twenty-five and an attractive—not beautiful—woman. She was tall and slender, occasionally awkward, even gawkily shy in her movements. Her sand-colored and very fine hair was pulled back, that day, in a smooth and cool-looking bun.

I myself was spending several months at the Dartmouth-Hitchcock Mental Health Clinic, engaged in what was becoming a very extended period of research into the subject of women and depression. Having become intrigued by the idea of such a study, Sandy volunteered to be interviewed by me periodically. She was the first of (and certainly representative of) a type of person I was to encounter again and again. That is, the woman who becomes promiscuous in a frantic effort to ward off feelings of isolation, abandonment, and depression.

The Denial of Dependence

Without plunging too far ahead of my narrative, let me say that it's now been two years since the time that Sandy and I began our series of conversations; and we've talked to one another, at intervals, over the course of this entire period. She's twenty-seven years old now. But when she came in, she had just passed the quarter-century mark; she had one child, Julie, who was a year and a half old. Sandy Geller had been divorced for just over a year (a year and two months, to the day) on the hot summer afternoon when she'd finally made her decision and had come in.

Here were some of the ways in which she described her mood and the state of her feelings during that phase of her life: "unhappy"; "self-critical"; "disappointed in things." She believed that much that she'd done, and was doing currently—most especially in terms of her relations with men—was contributing to her leaden and pervasive sense of discouragement, of pessimism, of being a failure. She was questioning her own behavior, unsure about its meaning and purpose, and why she was doing some of the things she was doing. She was, as she put it, "not respectful of the person I perceive myself as having become." And, in terms of psychological pain, it was undoubtedly true that this lack of self-esteem was hurting.

"If my mother *knew* what was going on in my life," reflected Sandy, somewhere in the midst of the first interview that we had, "I think she'd literally turn over in her grave. And my mother," she'd added suddenly, "is not even *dead!*" Realizing at once how very odd that statement sounded, she emitted a short, embarrassed laugh. "I was not brought up like this," she explained swiftly, a flush turning her pale, smooth skin to a raw-looking color. "And what I need to figure out is *why* I'm doing so many of the things that I am doing. All that I do know now—and this is a feeling that's been coming upon me more and more—is that even though it is true in a sense that I'm using these men, I feel as if they're the ones who are using *me*." She was, remarked Sandy, in a voice that had dropped in register and become almost a whisper, feeling "low-down rotten and cheap." She felt like a "thing" that is just being passed from person to person; and is (she punctuated this with a dispirited shrug) "just not worth that much to anyone."

Intellectually speaking, she could eloquently defend her right to her own sexual liberty and freedom. The problem was that this line of reasoning, which she could expound with impeccable logic, seemed to be a position she'd taken at a "thinking" but not a "feeling," emotional level. For deep within her psyche there appeared to be a very different, indeed almost opposite kind of an agenda: another set of needs, quite entirely, which were clamoring more and more loudly for a hearing. And these had to do with desires for such things as security, intimacy; for safe shelter within the harbor of a trusting and gratifying relational bond. These wishes were, however, going unrecognized. Sandy was, at this point in her life, either denying that they existed or managing to keep them at bay, at the periphery of consciousness. Either she considered dependent needs, and the need for love, dangerous or inappropriate—or perhaps, beyond the boundaries of what she might hope for, i.e., of possibility.

But the facts of her existence were these: she was obtaining sex and sensual pleasure. What she wasn't getting was communication between human beings, intimate sharing—whatever items one wants to pull together under the general category of "trust and loving affection." Her relationships with the men she was sleeping with were haphazard, full of lies and petty deceits. They were also freighted with a certain undeniable hostility.

For Sandy both needed men (or "a man") and needed to devalue them. The second need, curiously, proceeded from the first. That is, the wish to devalue the sexual partner seemed to be part and parcel of a desperate attempt to deny any feelings of dependence. "I am trying to understand," said Sandy, during that same first session together, "just why it is that when I begin one affair I have this—this panicky feeling—that I've got to get something *else* going simultaneously! I am not sure myself about why it has to be like this. Why do I have to get into these situations where I'm—you know—conning everybody?" Her expression, as she'd asked this question, had been one of vulnerability, of confusion. But it changed, before I could reply, and she became defiant: "In a way, anyhow, I've got every right to do exactly what *I* want to do! It's my own life, really, and my own body . . . and I'm at a place, now, where I don't owe a damn thing and no special allegiance to anyone. I mean, I do to my child, of course . . . but *not* to any man!"

A few moments afterward, however—as if the air of her anger had seeped out of her body as rapidly as it leaves a balloon—she sagged back against the back of the vinyl-covered blue chair she sat in. "I still do feel it, though," she confessed. "This wrongness, this badness . . . it's as if there is this mean, nattering little voice inside me, telling me that I'm weak and a bitch; that I have no control over myself, or over anything, and that something—some awful, awful punishment—is going to happen. To me, or to Julie . . . I don't know. A punishment that I, for some reason, *deserve*." With these words she turned on me an expression so agonized and devastated that I'd have believed it if Sandy had told me that her "punishment" *had* already happened!

Just Skin Touching Skin

Most psychiatrists are not very comfortable with the word "promiscuous." It is a word that is loaded with moral judgments (negative ones) and special meanings (special to the female sex). It smells of the double standard. For it is true that a male, who may be behaving promiscuously in his sexual life, rarely finds this term being used to describe his behavior. The adverb tends to be used in describing the activities of a *woman*. And a moral verdict is generally implied, i.e., *she* is being *bad*.

Not only is the word promiscuous itself in therapeutic disfavor—and for what are clearly valid reasons—but one isn't likely to find it in the index of any recent psychiatric textbook. There's not much more information to be found on the subject than the definition given in a psychiatric dictionary: "Indiscriminate, casual sexual encounters; high frequency of sexual relationships with a large number of partners," etc., and some scattered papers on promiscuity that can be discovered in the literature. But that's about it. If there *is* such a problem, and if patients such as Sandy Geller become disturbed and perplexed by it, then the modes of dealing with such issues must be idiosyncratic—without a clearly delineated and understood disturbance, treatment must depend on the views and values and the tack taken by the individual therapist.

Of course there is—and most especially in a time of shifting sexual mores—a certain dilemma inherent in any attempt to categorize and "treat" sexuality. For when is an active sex life, with a large number of partners, to be viewed as high spirits, and when is it sexual acting-out? When is a person's sexuality an affirmation of life, and when is it to be seen as self-defeating, masochistic, hurtful of the self (and of others)? These questions are extraordinarily complex ones to try to answer. But some people do, as did Sandy Geller, need to explore them . . . fearing and feeling that they are "wicked" or "sick" (or both).

To the question of "How much sex is too much sex?" there appears to be no sweeping medico-psychological response. The question, nevertheless, continues to be asked. I have noticed, in the course of much interviewing of a large number of women, that there is a not inconsiderable subset of people whose issues revolve around an active, but relationshipless sexual life; they come in, feeling wretched and unvalued, and wondering about whether their behavior is ill, wrong, crazy, etc. Not infrequently, a high degree of sexual wheeling and dealing appears to exist *in tandem with* sectioned-off, contained, but very powerfully depressive feelings. The woman's suddenly increased sexiness seems to be, in this sort of instance, a kind of anti-depressant maneuvering. It can be highly successful; one raises one's level of excitement and therefore one doesn't feel depression. The beneficial effects of such a strategy may be partial; they may be only temporary. But sometimes the enhanced activity and the gamesmanship provide, as it had for Sandy, some psychic balm . . . at least for a while. It helps to stave off (because one is after all so preoccupied and busy) those frightening and perhaps even potentially overwhelming feelings. Feelings of sadness and of anxiety—fears that one will experience oneself as totally abandoned and alone.

Just skin touching skin: it is, in itself, a form of reassurance. Body contact, and being with another human being, may be the real reward for the woman: as mentioned earlier, touching may be more important than is the relief of sexual tension. As psychiatrist Marc Hollender has suggested in another of his intriguing papers on the topic of "the wish to be held and the wish for sex," some women regularly trade off coitus for cuddling, and the feelings of security it gives. "Body contact," writes Dr. Hollender, "commonly provides feelings of being loved, protected and comforted. The need or wish for it is affected by depression, anxiety and anger. . . . For some women such a connection is acceptable; for others it is not. The latter may camouflage their child-like wishes with the veil of 'adult' sexuality. . . ." The craving for closeness to another person's flesh (and for the sense of protection it represents) is sometimes, note Hollender et al., a key determinant of promiscuity.

This may be a part, and even an important part, of the larger picture. It is certainly true that one frequently sees a period of heightened sexual activity at a time of distress and intensified emotional need. What Sandy Geller called her "frantic fucking" phase had not occurred out of the blue, or in any kind of an environmental vacuum. She was a year out of her divorce from Lee. And often it happens in just this way. That is, a person becomes highly promiscuous in the wake of the rupture of a crucial—and crucially important—emotional bond or attachment.

A Short-term High

In the aftermath of a trauma, a deeply wounding emotional loss, there may actually be (if one calculates coldly, in terms of costs and benefits) some short-term adaptive advantages arguing in favor of promiscuous behavior. First of all, there often exists a pressing need to get into other relationships rapidly—no matter how shallow—rather than wait for who knows what length of time, until a serious one can develop. And then, it's a way of reaffirming one's own attractiveness: a vital concern for the woman who, like Sandy Geller, may have just weathered a humiliating and almost intolerable rejection. It's a way, too, of getting oneself held, embraced, cuddled, caressed, and cared for . . . no matter how briefly this interpersonal-tranquillization may last. It is, as psychiatrist Hollender has noted, a pseudo-adult means—at a time of distress, when childish longings are intensified—of having one's "baby needs," one's need to be held, satisfied.

To be promiscuous is, moreover, a way of being *angry* at men. Because in such a situation a woman has made herself available for one thing and one thing only: and that is sexual intercourse. Sex like this, i.e., in the absence of intimacy and tenderness and loving communion, reduces the Other to a human dildo. To thus offer one's body, and at the same time withhold the self, is a wonderful way of expressing a good deal of underlying fury and anger—and it is wonderfully confusing for the other person.

So: the available woman can get hugs, on her own terms, and subtly express hatred . . . on her own terms, too.

What are the *other* potential adaptive "pluses" that might flow from a spate of promiscuous behavior? There is, as I mentioned, that sense of enhanced excitement. And if one thinks of a woman who is (as was Sandy Geller) just on the far side of a breakup that has occurred under insulting and demeaning circumstances, there *is* the problem of damaged self-esteem mixed in with mourning over the love that has been lost and with a sense of having been diminished, hobbled by grief. The situation itself—being rejected—is almost sure to produce very negative feelings about the self. It contains the living elements that can so easily breed and multiply—can spawn serious depression. Becoming promiscuous can keep a person busy, interactive, and it can provide its own kind of a high; as such, it may serve as an excellent short-term antidote.

That sense of aliveness, of making things happen, serves to combat

—admittedly not completely, and not for an extended period of time —those feelings of abandonment, of emptiness, of helplessness, of being half-a-person (i.e., the remaining portion of what was formerly a couple, a unit). One gets oneself into funny, intriguing, and perhaps even dangerous encounters; there are whimsical occurrences and a changing cast of characters; there isn't nothingness . . . the awful sense of annihilation, of not being sure one exists. Sleeping around can, in short, counter those feelings of eventlessness—of one's world having stopped and become eerily still. (And of course one supposes the advantages would include the reaping of some real sexual pleasure.)

Promiscuity, like amphetamines, promotes a short-term high. It surely won't cure feelings of despair, grief, and depression (neither will amphetamines, which tend to bring about a pharmacological and psychological rebound—a low of fatigue, irritability, and increased depressive feeling) but it may keep them at bay, keep them contained for a while. And it's true, when one thinks about it, that behaving promiscuously is a way of externalizing The Danger. By this I mean that when one is running certain *real* risks—for example, that of possibly being caught by someone's wife or by another lover; and/or beaten up by a partner; or perhaps even the risk of contracting venereal disease— they divert the promiscuous person's attention to all of the juggling pins she's got flying in the air. They keep attention away from the juggler herself.

And so, the psychic risk changes from an inner one—that one may be an unattractive, desperate, undesirable, deserted individual—to an outer one, such as the risk of being discovered or harmed. Such a real-world, palpable threat keeps The Danger, The Monster, *on the outside*. But in this sense, promiscuity isn't awfully different from other kinds of risk-taking, fate-challenging, dangerous, and exciting behaviors. It is like accident-proneness or like driving an automobile much, much too fast. A person who does these kinds of things—who lives very hard, gets into many accidents—is frequently viewed as someone attempting to limit, or not experience, very powerful subjective feelings of depression. Many experts see such behaviors as "depressive-equivalents," or "depressive-masks." The Danger is being projected onto the environment and to what may happen in reality. It is, thus, a way of avoiding (not feeling) the painful and potentially overwhelming situation that exists within.

And one more point to be made about promiscuity. When a woman becomes sexually indiscriminate (as Sandy had done) after the breaking of—I should say breakdown of—an important love-bond, her behavior may represent an avoidance of an inevitable time of grief and mourning. It's a way of acting out, of keeping busy, of not taking into oneself the resultant sorrow and the hurt. But the net results of this type of avoidance strategy are, in one particular way, peculiar. Because it is a human truth, as Freud pointed out many years ago, that to become psychologically ready for a new relationship, a bereaved person must first go through the "work" of mourning.

This is true whether the bereavement has resulted from death itself, or from the death of a love-bond. Without taking into oneself the pain and the suffering, and without working through it, there is no emerging on the other side. The person who avoids the process—thereby avoiding the suffering that accompanies it—doesn't become psychologically ready, at liberty for a fresh try, a meaningful new relationship. The promiscuous woman is thus, in some extraordinarily curious way, remaining faithful to the old love-tie, the one that has been severed. Her real emotional connection, her true bond, is with the person whom she hates and has lost.

For Sandy Geller, sex with an ever-changing cast of partners had been—in the months subsequent to her separation from Lee, and the divorce—like the systematic changing of a psychic Band-Aid. Who the man might *be* didn't matter. What mattered, and desperately, was having somebody there. "I had a terror," she later recounted, "of simply being *alone*. And I think the men I went with . . . they knew it. I didn't say it, of course, but this was something I believe they were able to sense. There's no other explanation," she put it ruefully, "for why I went through so *many*." She laughed, but the laugh quickly faded. "I mean, I would meet someone, and I'd date him and be in bed with him—all in no time. But nothing would ever happen, not *ever*, in terms of—you know, a relationship. There was just something about me. Was it my neediness, my dependency? I'm not sure. I scared them away. And if that *didn't* happen and the guy *didn't* take off, I would be the one to get bored or irritated at something about *him*. All of this, mind you, would happen pretty fast."

Every start had had to be, in other words, the beginning of a finish. Sandy herself hadn't been able to comprehend the nature of that desperate searching—why it was that she was running through so many partners so rapidly. She hadn't quite made the mental link between her behavior and the massive impact that her ex-husband's betrayal had actually had upon her. For Lee's ultimate indifference, his lack of concern, had in fact awakened much older, much deeper and profoundly more painful memories and feelings—horrible, untenable feelings of having been unnurtured and uncared for.

These were, in truth, old feelings, ones that had existed throughout Sandy's lifetime. Her marriage to Lee had, supposedly, solved and ended what had been, for her, a lifelong quest. The search for someone to nurture her had seemed, then, to be over. She could rely on her husband to be her Caring Person—to admire, protect, emotionally invest in, and adore her. These are, clearly, the qualities one most expects to find in the doting and loving parent. And it had turned out quite differently. Lee's faithlessness had, when it exploded upon her, touched an inner panic button. It had sent Sandy off, at an enormously intensified velocity, on a renewed search for someone who would cherish her, nourish her, who would *care*.

Very frequently, I've found, it is the lack of such a nurturing person—not only in the individual's present but, more importantly, in her early history—that is the true underlying basis, the underground substructure of what later becomes "promiscuous behavior." This is true not only for women but for men. The Promiscuous Female and the Don Juan are both engaged, in general, in a similar—and similarly desperate—kind of quest. Their search is the search for a Caring Parent. And the search is fueled by great fear and great rage.

Some of that anger may stem from current events; but much has accumulated from the past—from not having been cared for when one did so much *need* care and when one was so helpless and so vulnerable. Which is to say, when one was a child. The inner rage, then, is ultimately expressed by diminishing others: by "using" people for pleasure alone, and thereby transforming them into things, into mere objects. The sexual act is thus made into a biological happening—a source of sensations, of extracting one's needs from another body, of exploitation of another (faceless) creature. But sex is robbed of its most rewarding and human elements, which have to do with loving communication and intimacy and the mutual reinforcement of self-esteem . . . and with the shelter and security of being immersed in an emotional bond.

But a true tie can't, of course, be established. Loving any man means that one can't love *one* man in particular! And indeed, so charged with rage and resentment is this sort of search for love that no real person will actually do. Once the metaphor has been set into motion in the outer world, the perfect knight, the beloved one is the *next* person—the flawless one, still to be met, somewhere around the corner of the future. This is the kind of searching that precludes by its very nature the possibility that one will find.

Repairing the Past

Their marital difficulties, according to Sandy Geller, had begun in earnest when they'd brought the baby back home from the hospital. Before Julie's birth—a year when they'd lived together, and two when they'd been married—she and Lee had maintained a workable, if occasionally tense and difficult, relationship with each other; they'd also maintained a busy and active young couple's life. Lee, a psychologist with a Boston-based firm, was outward-oriented, flirtatious, on the rise, and restless, by nature. Sandy had enjoyed much about their life together; but felt rattled by Lee's "party personality" (his ebullience with other women) and his increasingly different "home personality" (his silence and non-communicativeness) even before their daughter was born.

After Julie's arrival, Lee had become increasingly dismissive, somewhat sarcastic, and even hostile: almost enraged, as Sandy later realized, by the fact that she was no longer concentrating as much of her attention on him. The new mother, rattled by the demands of the infant and by the emotional withdrawal of her husband, became offended on her own part; she began seeing Lee as egocentric, as a "demanding show-off," and she, too, became more and more mistrustful and withdrawn. She'd begun wondering about and doubting this man she was married to: had he even the most minimal capacity, in terms of his basic personality structure, for ever becoming a caring, nurturant, sharing person? She *needed* him to be those things, at this time, for she needed someone to take care of *her*. And it was, she later believed, this kind of problem (that is, issues relating to Who Was Supposed to Take Care of Whom) upon which their marriage eventually crashed, splintered, and foundered.

"I was unsure," Sandy recounted much afterward, "about my own capacities to be a really good mother. It's in that area that I feel that *I* have—what you might call 'a learning problem.' Because my own mother, while she taught me a lot of things, taught them to me negatively. And I've had a struggle, on my own part, to relearn them with my own kid. I want to do the same things, sure, but I want to do them *positively*."

I shook my head, indicating that I didn't understand what she meant. "Well, I suppose," continued Sandy earnestly, "that my mother does love us dearly—she certainly enjoys us more as adults than as children. But she did resent us bitterly. This was something she never made any bones about. We heard it, often, when we were little . . . I don't think any of us has been able to push it away. She told us that she'd *never* wanted children, though she did have four. It was only my *father* that did."

"She told you that?" I asked.

Sandy nodded, then added quickly, as if coming to her mother's defense, "Oh, I'm sure she actually did love us! She put so much time and energy *into* us . . . but . . . I still try to figure it out. My father is a very passive man, very quiet; and he was always unconditional in his love. I mean he'd let you know that he would always love you, no matter what you did! Mom, though; she is just the opposite. She would come down very hard." There was a moment's silence. "My mother's an angry person," she commented then, "very angry and hostile."

"So then," I put in, "when it came to being a mother yourself, you felt you had to improve on, to change what had been your own basic working model? That you had, maybe, not quite gotten the right messages?"

"Oh, there were *lots* of messages!" Her laugh was short, brittle, tense. "That kids were a lot of work, and that they're not worth it. I can't blame my mother entirely, though—she was an only child and had a terrible relationship with her own father . . . at least that's what she says. She resents—not only babies and older kids—she truly resents *men!* She'll say things like, well, 'Men will get you every time.' And: 'They'll take advantage of you; don't take any crap from a man. They have the world by the tail. You just have to stand up and demand what you want. . . .' She's an aggressive—not assertive—lady."

I smiled: "What's that distinction you're making?"

"My mother will fight," explained Sandy, "and she loves a good fight. But the upshot of it is: it just doesn't work. She'll scream and she'll yell, but she won't succeed in making things *happen* differently. She may go on and on, but my father is just a bit hard of hearing. And if he doesn't hear, he doesn't do whatever it is she wants. She will go on with the complaining, in any case—no matter *what* he does. Because it won't be right. It's never right. Oh, my mother! You could never please her!" She threw wide her arms, as if entreating the heavens, and then laughed guiltily.

"And you yourself?" I said. "Were you able to please her?"

Sandy's expression was guarded. "Oh, I tried very *hard* to please her. We were close . . . in some ways . . . and we did share some things. But I was always pretty careful; I wouldn't tell her too much." She hesitated, and I thought for a moment that there would be nothing more that she'd want to say. But then she resumed, her voice tempo slow and thoughtful: "I guess I had my few rebellions, and I think that after I went to nursing school—that was a very significant break. But I realize now, in my own struggle to be a mother to my own child, that she was . . . she was wrong in many things. All those messages, you know, that men are no good and that children are so draining and terrible."

As she said these words, she herself looked very young. It was as if she were play-acting, automatically, her own self as a vulnerable child.

"I can see, though, that my mother's had a great deal of effect on me —as all parents do. I sometimes do catch myself, no matter how hard I may be trying, behaving in ways that are exactly *like* my mother's!" Now her expression was disapproving. "I try to fight that," said Sandy, leaning forward in her chair, looking at me intently. "I try to take from her what she does have—in terms of the things I admire about her—and to be the opposite in the other things. I mean, my mother didn't *like* kids, and never had any fun with them; she resented the whole burden and blamed my father. But look at me: I *did* want Julie! And I'm trying hard, with all that I'm worth, not to resent her and to take really *good* care of her!"

She looked, in that instant, bright and passionate; two spots of color stood on the high planes of her cheeks. But they were gone in a moment, and she sat back again, looking as if her thoughts had taken another sort of turn. They had. "I suppose," she remarked, "that what got Lee so mad was my having a reaction to all this, my trying to go so much the *opposite* way. I was being so gung ho about not rejecting the baby. About being a super-good, super-caring mother."

She became quiet, then, and so did I. I was thinking about how frequently this kind of repairing process gets set into motion in the experience of new motherhood. That is, in the intensified identification with her *own* mother (intense, at this point, because she's now become a mother herself) the new mother sets about making up to the baby for all of the hurts and injustices that she herself has suffered. Because she is identifying with her own mother, as "mother," her baby is identified with herself ("herself-as-baby"). This is, psychologically speaking, a fresh opportunity for making restitution. In the mother's unconscious fantasy, she is redoing her own early history. By being a nurturing, caring mother *to her own child*, she makes right again those things that once were beyond her control and so wrong, so awry.

At some level, the new mother tries to remake her own past, or at least aspects of it, symbolically and magically.

His Most Unforgettable Remark

The reality of their divorce, when it became one, was shocking. Sandra Geller had retained, in the months after the separation, an underground belief that—although she *wanted* the divorce—it would really never happen. Like the death of a person often can be, even though it comes at the end of a long illness, the event itself was surprising; it was a finality for which, at some level, there simply was no complete preparing. The decree was final; it recognized the severance of the unit, of the bond, of what had been a tie in the real world. And she'd felt, in the aftermath, unlike a complete person. She felt like a half, a leftover, from what had once been a full oneness, a functioning organism.

It was at this time, when she had felt so uncertain, so incomplete, so rejectable and discardable, that Lee had made "his most unforgettable remark." Sandy was, by then, long gone from Boston. She had taken the job at Dartmouth-Hitchcock Hospital and had worked out a life in Hanover for herself and for Julie. She was seeing some male friends, and having a sexual life when and where it was possible. There were no strings attached, in terms of future relationships or emotional ties, or love. Sex was a commodity being traded for the relief of loneliness, for transient kinds of companionship.

As for love, it wasn't that Sandy didn't value it; it was just not to be hoped for. "Love," she once said, shortly after coming into therapy, "I couldn't possibly *believe* in it. I couldn't believe that there might be some guy out there"—she gestured with her head toward the window, and the outer world—"who would love me for the rest of his life; no way! . . . Because, for a long time after we separated, I believe I still did love Lee. At least I needed him. And he said something to me, once when we were fighting—this was just at the time we divorced—that I've never forgotten. That I never could forget! He said that he had never, *ever* actually loved me!"

Her face, as she repeated this remark (made more than a year earlier) was aghast. "I said to *him*," she continued, "that that was nothing but bullshit! I said: 'I lived with you for five years, and we had a child and now you can turn around and say that you never *loved* me?' I can't remember what he said to that. But after that conversation, I just felt that, oh, oh, God, there is absolutely nobody. That there never *would* be anyone, no person in this world, who'd love me as much as I could love them! And it seemed so unfair, because all that I'd ever wanted, really, was—was—" She stopped, as if searching in her mind for a word, or embarrassed by the one that was there.

I guessed and asked: "Just—a husband?"

At this Sandy laughed and answered that it wasn't necessarily that, but that it *was* the same kind of thing that you would find in a husband. The tone of her voice was, nevertheless, unsure. "You mean, then," I hazarded, "a commitment?"

She nodded, looked pleased by the introduction of that word. "Yes, just that," she answered. "But I mean—a real one."

Unfinished People

According to Dr. Frederick Burkle, Jr., who became Sandra Geller's therapist, the eruption of that sexual tantrum—happening, as it did, around the breakup of her marriage—followed a not uncommon pattern. Lee Geller, in their last year together, had become involved with several other women. This had been the manifest problem, at the time of the rupture; the latent and more powerful issues had had to do with their inability to meet each other's needs, their mutual frustration, anger, and disappointment. Sandy was, in her promiscuity, living out her fantasied version of what her *husband's* life had been like during their last months together. She was also, by means of the rapid shift of partners, denying any wish or desire for real human relationship, for dependency.

Her behavior was, observed Dr. Burkle, typical of that shown by many people in the months ("even a year or more") after the breaking apart of an important relationship. "The person, when she comes for therapy, has just been having an outburst—one that's been being expressed in terms of her sexuality. And she's been just rolling from man to man, off on an extended toot of a kind. But underneath there's been this nagging, growing question: one that has, finally, to be confronted. And what she'll come in, finally, and ask the psychiatrist, is this: 'What the hell am I *doing?*' . . . because sooner or later she begins experiencing real worry, real fear. . . ." He paused, then plunged off on a further explanation: "She's been running from guy to guy, you see, falling in 'love' every weekend. And everything's piling up, all happening at once, getting confusing. There may be—often are—transient feelings of being on the verge of going crazy, or of wanting to commit suicide, in this kind of situation as well."

Very frequently, noted the physician, one discovers that the relationship that a patient like Sandy Geller has had with her husband has had a recognizable tone . . . a familiar flavor. That is, the relationship (which tends to have been a marriage, and an early one) is characterized by both great hostility and an intense mutual dependency. It's been characterized, also, by a lot of emotional—and perhaps even physical—abuse.

The central problem appears to be that the partners have gotten together at a point in their lives when both are still "unfinished people." Each still has the strongly dependent needs more appropriate to very early youth and to childhood. Neither member of the couple has yet managed to complete (or nearly complete) the developmental tasks of adolescence and of becoming a young adult. Neither has essayed the crucial work of what Jung called "individuation"—which is to say, the work of becoming autonomous; the work of becoming the individual that one wants and *needs* to become.

Both the female and the male parts of the pair are, thus, still dependent and still in need of further parenting. While the partners, in such a case, may have all the outward appearance of mature peers who are getting together to establish a secure base in the world—the kind of adult emotional bond which will provide safe shelter for both— they are in fact "needy babies," and ashamed and angry about being so. Naturally, each person becomes, for the other one, a source of intense frustration and disappointment; both feel that their deepest hopes and expectations have been betrayed.

For the wife cannot be—nor can she become—loving peer, doting mother, and approving father, all rolled up into one perfect caretaking being. Nor will the husband be—or become—adoring lover, cherishing father, and the facilitating, understanding, protective mother that she has, at some unconscious level, bargained for and expected. Each one *cannot* fulfill, for the other, those needs to be parented that are so profoundly unmet. Those intense ("childish") dependency needs become, as a consequence, mixed with intense rage and anger. The Dream of Love, which has been in large part a dream of being fully and completely nurtured, begins to develop rents and holes in its shimmering, gossamer surface—it begins to shred, to disintegrate, to fall to the earth in soiled and disagreeable tatters. And the underlying conflict, there from the beginning, emerges and grows.

Catching Up

An emotional relationship of the type just described—which is to say, one characterized by a mixture of strong dependent and strong hostile feelings—is often one that's been formed when the two partners are rather young, either under or just around the age of twenty. (Sandy had been *just* twenty, and Lee twenty-three, when they'd married.) For this is an age, a point in human life, when one is technically adult, but when certain monumental developmental tasks may not have been completed; in some instances, they haven't even been *undertaken!* I'm referring, of course, to the important psychological tasks of separation —the difficult work of renouncing one's attachment to one's first loves, one's first protectors, one's parents. And also, to the allied task of individuation, or becoming one's own self: that is, a separate (from mother and father) and autonomous being. In the late teens and early twenties, suggested Dr. Burkle, these psychic labors have either not been completely accomplished, or they have not yet solidified, fallen into place. "The consequence for both members of the couple is," he explained, "that they've become locked into the relationship or marriage, at this early, immature level. Both of them have gotten 'stuck,' so to speak, in a kind of developmental arrest."

Generally speaking, in late adolescence and in early adulthood, an individual undergoes an expectable and inevitable amount of personality shift—of growth, of change. This is a transition point in the life cycle; one's priorities, needs, values, will show some natural alteration. This comes about not only due to an altering set of *inner* needs, but simply as a result of accumulating real experiences in the world. In order to become an autonomous, mature individual, one must have a certain amount of experience under one's belt—a few turns at falling flat on one's face, at failing, and realizing that one *can* pick oneself up. A person has, in short, to be put into situations where self-sufficiency is required; situations in which Mom, Dad, or some other rescuing figure cannot be depended upon . . . in which one must depend on *oneself*.

It is only as a result of such experiences, and in the course of standing alone and learning who one is as a separate being, that one becomes an individual, an autonomous "me." But in the late teens and early twenties, a person often hasn't *had* that many experiences. If the young pair—lovers or married couple—become locked into one of those mutually dependent/mutually furious emotional bonds, they won't be at liberty to explore such questions, to become his or her "self," to grow. Often, in fact, the rush into an early decision—in terms of an exclusive attachment—has masked terrible fears about the *loss* of dependent relationships (i.e., leaving home and one's parents), about finding autonomy, about being alone.

The prospect of existing on one's own, and of taking responsibility for that existence, has been just too frightening. And so both individuals have managed, as had Sandy and Lee, to replace a felt neediness vis-à-vis the parents with great dependence and neediness vis-à-vis the spouse. The problem with such solutions is, nevertheless, that there are *still* powerful urges arising from within—urges that impel the developing adult toward individuation, toward becoming a person, "becoming me." One has foreclosed, though, much of one's potential for new experiencing, for discovering the nature of one's self in a variety of situations. In the rush for safety and under the gun of that powerful need—to find someone *to depend upon*—one has renounced opportunities for testing other possibilities (including other emotional relationships) out.

Now usually what will develop, in such early-decision relationships, will be conscious—but unwelcome and guilt-inducing—impulses to try out those Other Voices in those Other Rooms that have been so precipitously foregone. For there is still that underlying need to discover "Who I Am," the "Me That Would Be" in very different sorts of situations, relationships, circumstances. But to do that, to explore in such directions, would involve betrayal of the partner. *He* or *she* becomes, then, the inhibiting force—the person preventing one from growing. The *partner* stands between one's straining personhood and individuation, and the *relationship* itself is perceived as (and may well be) the impassable obstacle blocking psychic growth, change, and development.

If a dependent/hostile relationship of the kind that I've been describing should eventually self-destruct—and in terms of marriages, those entered into below the age of twenty seem to do so more than twice as often as marriages entered into after the age of twenty—then both partners will be forced to confront the crisis of their individual identities. Both the male and the female must face the existential music: must try to answer that terrifying human question, "Who am I, when I am just me, and I am standing all alone?"

For the woman, such an encounter with the Self is often more threatening, more difficult, more truly frightening, then it is for the male. For some females—in fact a not inconsiderable number of females—haven't ever really contemplated the idea of taking care of and being themselves. "When it comes right down to the time of the divorce itself," said psychiatrist Burkle, "most of the women I know—either in treatment, or as colleagues, or as friends—seem to become truly panicked. Because, whether she's now twenty-five, or thirty, or thirty-five, that woman is having to face issues that she may never have had to face squarely before. And what *scares* her is"—he hesitated briefly, then grinned—"well, it's an awareness that she really does, now, have to shit or get off the pot.

"I mean," he continued hurriedly, "that she has to work on *who* she is as an independent person, when there is no one else to fall back on. When there isn't any 'them,' in terms of parents, or any 'him,' in terms of lover or spouse to depend upon. Or for that matter to *blame* . . . for all of those missed and lost opportunities to explore."

The newfound freedom *to be* can be (and often is) experienced as potentially overwhelming. When the decree itself comes through, and the divorce is completed, many women go through a period of heavy drinking or of behaving in a regressive, adolescent manner. "They are scared," remarked Dr. Burkle, "and they're acting lost, like a Man without a Country. . . ." In therapy, the initial needs are for parenting, in terms of advice and some controls. For women like Sandy Geller are, in some sense, going back in their lives to pick up what is unfinished psychological business. It was certainly true, as I realized increasingly (both in the extensive interviews we had alone, and in the occasional three-person sessions that were attended by myself, Sandy, and Dr. Burkle) that her concerns were in reality the concerns of the late adolescent.

That was, of course, the phase of her life that she had been in when she'd become involved, then locked into, that angry/dependent relationship with her husband. But that was a life-bet, a bet for safety, that she had made and she had lost. Now she was alone. She was, as well, back where she'd been *before* Lee: in terms of individuation, she was still eighteen years old, she was behind in the growing-up game. And maybe this was another among the complex motivations for her having gone into such a frighteningly high gear in terms of seeking out new emotional relationships. For among the other things she was doing at that time was simply this: she was catching up.

The Danger

For the physician, pain is an explanatory phenomenon. One can't cure or alleviate suffering without first getting the patient's help in locating just where the hurt is. And for Sandy Geller, as soon became apparent, the pain all radiated from the central problem of intimacy. But to reach it, to get to that precise place, there was much stumbling about in surrounding areas, in a confusing fog, a welter of emotions and feelings.

There was so much anger—angry feelings that she harbored toward her ex-husband—whom she nevertheless, in some deep way, continued to depend upon. No matter how much rage she really felt toward him, it was still Lee who, she believed, would come to her rescue when she needed rescuing—a fantasy-belief which, until she let go of it, would make each failure to do so, on his part, be experienced as a fresh and devastating assault. There was anger, too—much harder to admit and to deal with openly—toward the now almost two-year-old Julie. For it was the baby's arrival, as Sandy surely realized, that had ultimately upset the fragile balance of their marriage.

There were feelings of anger toward herself, as well; times when she felt whipped by that inner voice nattering at her about everything that she had been and now had become. How dirty she felt, then; and how crazy! How much she felt that she had "messed up everything in my life that actually matters"; and how utterly she thought she had failed. Her rage and her fury weren't only, in short, being directed outward to those she blamed and held responsible; much of this untenable and painful feeling was coming *inward*, in the form of self-abuse.

And there was little, in reality, going on in her life to counter her own accusations against herself. There was nothing happening that would aid her in defending against that nattering voice—with its messages to the effect that she was a worthless, valueless, essentially unlovable person. She did have two things: she had excitement, and she had sex. But she was experiencing almost nothing of that sharing of honest feelings, that empathy, which is the scaffolding of real human relationship, and which builds each partner's sense of worthfulness, of individual self-esteem.

It must also be remembered that she had been in that marriage to Lee for half a decade: for five years, one fifth of her entire lifetime. And bad as some aspects of their relationship had been, they'd both remained in it because there *were* some parts of it upon which both had truly depended. When the marriage did end, the very pedestal upon which her sense of self rested had seemed to Sandy to fall away, abruptly, from beneath her. The "self" she'd been for five years, which was pretty much the "self loved by Lee" was gone, as a psychic organizing principle; it was vanished, lost. And the root, the germinal source of human depression *is* Loss.

The impact of that trauma had been widespread, affecting not only Sandy's views of her past but, more to the present point, her thinking about her current life—and a deep-down hopeless, impotent, powerless sense that she had of a possible future. She *was* completely without hope and devoid of trust. Once, for example, during a three-way session (attended by Sandy, her therapist, and me) she described the short life of a friendship that she'd had with one of the young physicians working on her ward.

Her relationship with Bruce, begun several weeks earlier, was a platonic one (a new way for her to be relating to a man). And, a couple of days before the particular conversation from which I'll be quoting, they had gone out on a long hike—climbed a mountain—together.

During that walk, she had found herself *talking*. She had found herself sharing with Bruce certain intimate and very dangerous kinds of thoughts and feelings. She never was quite sure, afterward, how that had happened—what in particular had gotten her started. "We talked a lot about love," she told Burkle and myself, "and I told him how I'd felt about what happened with Lee—about Lee's having said that he hadn't ever cared for me, about his not loving me. And I guess I admitted to Bruce something that I'm surprised that I'd ever come out and say like that . . . I told him that I couldn't believe, deep down, that someone, some man, ever *would*." She laughed, but the laugh sounded wobbly. "I told him things that . . . when you say them to someone of the opposite sex . . . tend to get really heavy. And after that, the next time I saw him, I just had to be real distant, to push him away."

She shook her head, flushed slightly, looked embarrassed. "I started behaving in a way that said, you know, 'I just don't need you anymore.' Feeling rotten about it, too, at the same time. For the past day or two, now, I can't look at Bruce without feeling"—she shrugged—"I don't know—" She stopped, glanced at me, then stared at Dr. Burkle. I didn't know whether she was awaiting chastisement or illumination.

"Without feeling—what?" he prompted.

"I can't quite answer," replied Sandy slowly. "I was going to say . . . guilty. Because I do feel I've been rejecting of Bruce . . . he'd gotten too close to me. I mean that I gave him a piece of Me; something that I don't give to *anybody*. And after that happened it was as if I had to say, 'O.K., that's it; and now, good-bye and forget it.' "

"What piece was that?" pursued Dr. Burkle gently.

Sandy's eyes, fixed upon his face, seemed to have grown larger, widened. "Oh. How I really felt about my emotional wants, and stuff. Which I had never really unloaded, just like that, to anybody."

"Not even to Lee?" The therapist's eyebrows shot up; he sounded surprised.

She hesitated. "I didn't really say—well, I mean that I probably gave it to Lee but it wasn't ever received." There was a silence, and then Sandy turned to me.

"Lee didn't seem to hear it?" I asked.

She nodded: "Yes, it was not favorably taken. His reaction to that kind of effort was very rejecting. And you know, it was hurtful in that I kept trying to reach out and he was just putting down. When that kind of thing keeps happening, you get to the point where you just aren't reaching out anymore. That's pretty much what I did, I suppose: I shut up. I never tried telling anybody, anymore, about the things that I needed. But that had all been way back when, with Lee, you know. I'm feeling now that the way I've behaved with Bruce— after the close, good talk that we had—was just plain irrational. But the way I *talk* to him . . . I can't believe, myself, some of the things that come out of my mouth!" She let out a short giggle, then stopped.

"So what are you doing and saying that's so irrational?" inquired the therapist.

"I've just been being very *sarcastic* to him," responded Sandy abashedly. "Instead of talking to him *humanly*, I'm continually putting him down. Picking on him unmercifully, every chance that I get. And then acting as if we don't really know one another; as if we haven't ever had any friendship or connection at all. I have these cool conversations with him, about the weather, about the patients—about work." She shrugged.

There was another silence, and then Dr. Burkle said, "So, it just got a bit too dangerous, huh?"

To which Sandy replied, her voice dismal, "Yes, it did. And I just shut him off completely. . . ." She folded her arms akimbo, across her chest, as though to protect herself and to say (wordlessly): "I can shut you out too." Then she turned and looked away out the window.

Burkle said, his voice quiet, "So. That's the way it has to be, you being hurt all the time, and you always hurting someone else?" He paused, but not long enough for her to answer. "I have a hunch, Sandy, that you think you'll be *in* this dilemma forever . . . that things are going to be like this, always, for the whole rest of your life."

She wheeled back to face him: "I do," she said passionately, "and it's *pitiful*. But still, it's not going to come as any big shock to me if this *is* the way it is, and if my life *doesn't* change!" No one said anything; but in the succeeding few moments her expression underwent a subtle series of transformational steps, moving from defiance to one of defeat. "You know," she began recounting, with an air of helplessness, "I was at a Parents' Meeting at Julie's daycare center, and we were all being asked to talk about a good thing that had happened that day. And a funny thing, nobody there was able to come up with anything, not a *thing*." She laughed. "I mean, nothing good had happened to a single one of us. It's not me alone; we're *all* depressed!" Sandy seemed mollified momentarily by the thought; diverted and amused. But then, her posture, her voice tone, her expression gloomed over once again. "Even if a good thing does happen the good feelings don't last. At least, that was the way all of us felt." She slouched down a bit farther on the sofa, as if pushed down physically by the thought of all this sadness, of everyone's burdens.

"Depression," observed Burkle, "means not trusting in any of the good things."

If Sandy heard him say this, she gave no reaction, no response, no signal. At last, however, after another soundless interval, she said—in a voice that sounded oddly small and distant, as if coming from far away—that she felt she *had* to resign herself to not-hoping and not-trusting. "Not in any thing; not in any person. Because that way," explained Sandy, "there will be no *disappointment*." She paused, then added wanly: "I've always had an insecurity problem, though. That was a part of my marriage."

It was an extraordinarily astute, self-comprehending statement. She was moving ineluctably closer to a face-to-face view of what was her great and profound fear. This was a fear of a loneliness that wouldn't be endurable: the kind of aloneness that might be experienced by a terrified, immature child. That is, of being isolated, helpless, and abandoned. Her terror of ultimate aloneness was *that* terror—the lost child's terror—which had to do, in the deepest ways, with fears about one's very survival. To be alone is (for the person who has not yet mastered the adult capacities to take care of and to take responsibility for the Self) to confront (without, perhaps, feeling capable of doing so) the possibly crushing forces of the environment, all on one's own. This was part of the reason why Sandy had needed to have someone—anyone—to hold her, caress her, and be *there*.

To have someone there. This had been her strategy, serviceable and even adaptive for a period of time, in terms of fending off grief, panic, sorrow, depression, anger . . . anger at being lost in unfeeling space, at being a person for whom *no one cared*. Her promiscuity had provided her with just plain company: with some needed moments of solace and gratification, and with a subterranean means of expressing those frightened-child aspects of her self that so bubbled with fright and the hostile, revengeful feelings it engendered. Ultimately, however, this particular party would have to be over, and the depression underlying it encountered. For Sandy, there was going to be no way out but to go *through* that depression. And it was here, in the very therapeutic interview I've been describing, that I believe she first made conscious contact with her sense of loss, of deprivation, of mourning, of desperate "unfinishedness." She began the process of experiencing and processing her pain.

A Human Milestone

The capacity to be by oneself, and to tolerate that aloneness well, represent a human milestone, a developmental landmark. When Sandra Geller, R.N., began—after some fourteen months in therapy—to verbalize a need for and an enjoyment of her privacy, it spoke for the fact that she'd attained a new and more secure sense of herself. In the midst of a conversation that we two had around that time, Sandy mentioned that an intern she'd been dating had wanted to spend time with her on the Friday and the Saturday of the previous weekend. "I just didn't feel like it," she reported casually, "because things were so *pressured* on the ward the entire week before. There was a whole lot of stuff piled up at home, too . . . and I wanted to spend some time alone with Julie. I wanted, too," she admitted, "a space of time for myself; I mean, not talking to anyone grownup." It was the first occasion, as I remarked to her then, on which I'd ever heard her speaking so positively about the experience of being alone.

The next time we met was on an afternoon in late December. Sandy took up, at that time, this theme we'd begun discussing: the theme of "being able to be alone." "What's funny now," she reflected, "is how much I *cherish* times that can be put aside all for 'me,' for myself! It's now become a real luxury to me, something that I thoroughly *enjoy!* . . . Which is shocking, when I think about it, because that was the one thing that was so *impossible* for me to handle. That was, among everything else that was so hard and so tough, tougher than any other thing I can think of!" She laughed, then, shook her head in amazement.

It was now just about a year and a half since that sweltering summer afternoon when she'd hesitated before "going through that door" and admitting a need for help (even if that help took no other form but someone to *talk* to!). She looked younger, however, and more relaxed. Her hair, now cut short, capped her head tidily; her forehead was smooth and unfurrowed. "I've become stronger as an individual," Sandy said, rather proudly, that afternoon. "And you know what?" she added, "I'm beginning to *love* me, to love being Sandy Geller!" I nodded, acknowledging that she *did* exude that sense of herself; she smiled.

Sandy had, in the months since she had entered treatment, moved from what had been "simultaneous" to "serial" kinds of sexual relationships with the procession of men she was meeting. At the time of our previous interview, the man of the hour had been that young intern who had wanted to spend the weekend with her—his name was Philip—whom Sandy had described as "tall, handsome, blond and twenty-two." In the beginning, she had been "simply overwhelmed—he *was* so beautiful as a human being, as a male." But when they had talked enough, and been together a certain amount of time, she had realized that the two of them hadn't very much in common. "He was *young*," Sandy commented. "Not that I didn't have a good enough time with him. We'd go out drinking, in bars and stuff; and we would meet his friends and we would all party. I can't say, honestly, that there was ever an occasion when we went somewhere and I didn't have a lot of fun. But when it got right down to going home and going to bed with him—well, Philip was inexperienced. I realized, pretty soon, that there wasn't going to be much in it—nothing in it that I needed. And then, too, the way he was with Julie; well, he didn't know how to relate to a little kid; he didn't know how to handle her. He tried, though, in a way . . . I guess he was better than some of the other men I've dated had been. . . ." Her voice trailed off, and her manner was hesitant, uncertain.

Then she veered away from the topic of her daughter. "I guess what finally happened was that Philip and I went to this big party; that was over the Thanksgiving holiday. And he just dropped me, *left* me there." Sandy frowned, and I asked: "You mean, just this past Thanksgiving?"

"This past Thanksgiving, sure." She smiled, then, added cheerfully: "He went off and danced a lot with a girl who had big boobs, and who was just his age. For about an hour, I felt just *awful;* as if I'd been deserted all over again. But I said to myself, 'Fuck this'; and I went and asked a few of the guys to dance, and it was fine . . . it was great. He quit dancing with her finally and went over to a side wall where a big bar had been set up. And I came up to him and I said: 'Philip, are you aware of the fact that you've been being a perfect bastard this evening?' And he said that no, he wasn't. I explained that he'd simply dumped me, forgotten me for most of the evening. I said that I didn't mind if he danced with her, or with anyone else for that matter, but that it would have been decent for him to just *check* with me, at some point, to find out how I was *doing!*"

She was indignant, not humbled. I remember being surprised, as I listened to her recount that scene, by her air of authority and composure.

"Philip took me home that night," Sandy went on, "and that was pretty much it. I suppose I saw him a few times after that in the elevator and in the halls; I agreed to have lunch with him one day. I told him, then, that he just wasn't what I wanted; I leveled with him, too, about the things that he did that just weren't ever going to be for *me.* I said that I thought we should forget the whole thing—that as far as I was concerned, that was O.K." She smiled again, but added with an almost maternal indulgence: "I chalked the whole thing up to his being twenty-two years old, and single. He just couldn't possibly understand me—no way!"

These were, for her, newly objective sorts of observations. Sandy was now able, in a much more active and instrumental way, to articulate her own needs and to try to go about getting those needs and demands met. She was able to set her own rules and regulations instead of being moved around helplessly by other people—by men—and by their wishes, impulses, and whims. Philip had, for instance, during the time when the pair of them had been dating, complained that her baby was "pesky." "I was on Julie's side," related Sandy. "I didn't feel that I had to try to force her to behave like a china doll just to please *him*. He was, you know," she went on, with a brief nod of her head, "just out for a good time. I think that I was, for a while, trying to make something else—something more—come of the relationship. More than there was or ever possibly *could be* there." However, she concluded offhandedly, what had been different in this particular situation was that "I didn't hang around too long." Sandy had become, clearly, a far more autonomous, far more self-governing individual.

If You Don't Love You Can't Lose

I want to digress, very briefly, and think again about that presenting problem that had first brought Sandy Geller into treatment; I mean, of course, her distress about her promiscuity. I've characterized this sort of behavior as representing a frantic search for a Caring Parent; but other writers have viewed the matter otherwise. In a book called *Sexual Problems: Diagnosis and Treatment in Medical Practice*, the British clinician Stanley Willis suggests that promiscuity may in fact be the mode in which a person *avoids* emotional involvement. For, by means of brief and transient sexual encounters, one reduces the chances of ever feeling emotional grief, pain, rage, or frustration— feelings which may be experienced in close and deep relationships with other human beings. It is, according to Dr. Willis, *unconscious fears relating to the loss of a loved one* that makes the promiscuous person keep his or her psychological distance. That is, If You Don't Love in the First Place, You Cannot Lose.

The notion here is that promiscuity, which might appear to be a way of promoting approach to others, actually maintains an emotional avoidance. Writes Willis: "It is a form of withdrawal by togetherness, rather than the apparently frantic search for love that it appears to be on superficial observation." But it still is, he says, an "illusory facsimile" of what should be a significant and intimate involvement with another person. Any relief brought about by such brief and transitory couplings is, therefore, temporary—such sexual transactions produce more anxiety than they cure, and they "fail to allay the deeper and more central tensions present in the participants. . . ." In a way, the explanation offered by Willis is a variation of the one that I have been proposing. My suggestion has been that promiscuous behavior patterns represent a desperate search for an Ideal Nurturer. What Dr. Willis is saying is that it's a way of maintaining a distance, an emotional barrier; and that it is a solution of sorts for the individual who deeply fears the losses that may attend upon a deep emotional commitment, upon "being in love."

For "being in love" involves, very clearly, more than just sexual desire; and more, too, than the wish to hold onto a partner who is seen as particularly desirable. It involves a component that the psychoanalyst Sandor Rado termed "magical love": which is a vesting of the other person with all of the good attributes of the ideal, caring parent. When one falls in love one unconsciously assigns to the Other the capacity to make *oneself* feel safe and secure. The beloved partner then becomes—in the present—the One who can fulfill what are the leftovers and derivatives of our archaic childhood needs. These have to do with the wish to feel cared for, protected, secure that emotional supplies will be forthcoming. And, as anyone who has been in love knows very well, no one else but one's partner (with whom one shares a deep commitment) will really do. In this the adult lover resembles the eight-month-old baby who loves and recognizes Mother. Other mothers may be able to care for the child quite adequately. But for that infant, who has become emotionally attached to that mother, no other parent will do.

But this is, of course, what human loving and human love-bonds are all about. It follows, of course, that investing a beloved partner with such magical attributes has an element of danger: for that person attains a certain degree of the power that the parent or parents once had. I mean that one becomes profoundly dependent upon the partner —and there is a sense of fear and vulnerability about possibilities of loss and separation. To "be in love" involves, therefore, a not inconsiderable emotional risk. And in Dr. Willis' formulation, the promiscuous person is someone who has either had too painful an experience to chance that risk again, or someone who has been too poorly parented to dare to try trusting and depending on another human individual.

In any case, though, mature love—or "being in love"—does surely involve bringing into an adult relationship some of the childish parts of the self. I mean, a certain degree of faith in the other person's capacity to Take Care, and to Make it All Better . . . an ability to trust, and to depend upon another individual. This kind of loving is, nevertheless, at a certain distance on the dependency-continuum from the kinds of dependence that had been shown by Sandy Geller. In her marriage, she'd been overly clinging, overly needful (as had Lee); afterward, in her promiscuous phase, the angry-and-dependent child parts of herself had been acted out in her counterphobic—"I don't need any *one* man!"—pattern of behavior.

It was this pattern of behavior, or way of being, that appeared to be in a termination process by the time of our conversation that December. For, as became clear in the context of that discussion about herself and Philip, Sandy had begun to recognize her growing and very legitimate desires for a real relationship. She'd begun articulating to herself, as well, the kinds of ingredients that would necessarily go into the establishing of a commitment. Mere sex—or for that matter, mere company obtained by means of sex—would no longer suffice.

The thing that was gone was that frantic quality: that overwhelming sense of needfulness that had seemed to pervade her entire existence. And while it was true that nothing much in the outward circumstances of her life had changed—she was still a divorcée in her mid-twenties, a nurse, who had a young child and who lived alone with that child—*she herself* had actually changed dramatically. She was now someone who could treasure the time she spent by herself, and the time she spent with her baby: she could even speak, as she'd done with such conviction, of loving being Sandy Geller! No longer was it necessary for her to act out a repetition of that desperate drama (of which the unwritten title could have been: I Am Not At All Dependent). Nor was she so fearfully aware of inner lack, of inner emptiness, that she had to hang onto any relationship—to clutch at the crumbs from any emotional table—too long. She could stand alone, as long as was necessary, and until she found someone with whom she could become interdependent—in an emotionally satisfying way.

A Revelation: Or, What Never Happened Between Me and My Mother

When we talked again, which wasn't until the following May, Sandy had already ceased her weekly visits to the Dartmouth-Hitchcock Mental Health Center; she was doing so well on her own. Almost on the heels of our last interview, she told me, a widespread change had begun taking place in her life. A neighbor of Philip's, a divorced man with whom the two of them had occasionally partied, had called Philip and asked if there were now any objections to *his* asking Sandy out. "This fellow, this man—his name's Henry Pace—has got nothing to do with the hospital. He's a local businessman. But he did ask Philip, and Philip said: 'Well sure, it's O.K., I don't care.' And so he called me, and I was flabbergasted. I said: 'What, you want to go out with *me?*'" Sandy's voice was animated, even gay, as she play-acted her surprise and her flattery.

"I did go out with him," she continued, "and it was—it was just fantastic. It *is* fantastic, the way everything has been happening! I mean, I'm not saying that I love him; I *don't*. . . ." She paused, looked at me; I had given a start of surprise at those words. "I have a strange feeling, at times, of being almost *indifferent* to him. . . ." She had hesitated again, but then hurried on as though carried upon a fresh wave of her enthusiasm: "But he is totally dedicated, to Julie and to me; and he's been divorced himself, married and divorced. Henry is just thirty-one . . . and it's all, oh, just gone along like *clockwork!* To the point where, really, I feel as if I'm married to this guy, and have been for years. We are like a *family!* I mean, Henry's not my *boy friend*. I can't say he is my boy friend: I cannot tell people that! I just say, when I'm introducing him to anyone: 'This is *Henry!*'" She drew herself up, looked prideful and proprietary. "I've noticed, too, that there's been all this love for Julie that just comes spilling out recently. It's something that's obvious to other people, I guess, because they've been telling me that I'm much different—much better—with her. And she's calmer too, not so wild, not bouncing off the walls all the time."

Sandy smiled, added, "We both, Henry and I, give her a lot of attention. And I stopped coming to see Dr. Burkle, you know, when it got to the point where Henry had become so involved in my life . . . to the point where I could talk to him, and he would understand. I didn't think, then, there was anything more that Dr. Burkle could do for me."

As she spoke, I was jotting a comment into a notebook. It was a question I wanted to remember to raise later (without interrupting Sandy now). But I looked up, startled, when she remarked suddenly: "I really don't know if Burkle *did* do anything for me!" I glanced at her—a look of question and surprise. "Oh, obviously he did," she said thoughtfully, in the distracted tone of someone who is doing some private thinking aloud. "After eight months or so I'd gotten to the point where I could stand on my own two feet and feel good about doing it. He helped me to become my own person, and to recognize my own feelings for what they were. Maybe the biggest thing was that second one—I haven't been too talented, throughout my life, in admitting to a lot of the feelings I really do have, and then responding to them as if they were—you know, O.K. . . . legitimate." She smiled: "I have always been an 'ought' kind of a person. Paying a lot more attention to the things I 'ought to' rather than the things I really *do* feel!"

"For instance—what sorts of feelings?" I asked her.

"*Anger*," answered Sandy, making a ferocious mock-angry grimace. "Being able to be angry and to even, when it was possible, *tell* the person who was making me feel that way that I *was!* Just to be able to do that, and not always have to deny that that was there, and to hold it all down, all in. I've surprised myself recently, not only in the ways I'm able to get off a lot of bad feelings in jokes and stuff, but by actually spouting off and flying into a rage about something!" A flush of color had appeared on her cheeks: "This is something I've never been able to do before. I'd go home and maybe pound on the walls, or feel lousy, or behave in lousy ways with Julie. But I just had no *way*, ever, of being angry with someone my own age, or older. I'd worked so hard, throughout my childhood, to be pleasing. I was the nearest you can get to being the perfect child! Ah well . . . I tried. . . ."

We began talking, again, about her parents. She felt closer to her father than she did to her mother, admitted Sandy; but she had never been able to "really talk" to either one of them. She was trying hard, now, to understand her mother and just why it was that she couldn't really like her. "I've come to realize something recently," Sandy's words emerged one by one, now, as if being chosen separately and with care, "and that is, that even though I don't *like* my mother, I still do, in my own way, love her. But she's an individual, and I have become one too. The past is over and can't be . . . anything other than what it was. Still, there are times when I *do* want it all to be different! At Christmas time, when Julie and I were with them, I had this urge to blurt out my whole life story, and everything that had happened with Lee and afterward . . . and try to come up with some answers. But I couldn't. The time wasn't right . . . I didn't think it was necessary . . . something." She shrugged.

"One thing did happen during that visit, though," she added suddenly, and with the excitement of someone who's come across something unexpected. "This was an incident when my mother was being incredibly bitchy—which she has a reputation for—and which I've always responded to by either storming off or by slinking away. I mean, that is how it was a lot of the time, between the two of us; pretty uptight, pretty tense. We never got along in any relaxed way; we never were friends. But *this* time what I did was different. I turned around—we were in the kitchen—and I said: 'Mom, I don't know what's bugging you, but we all still love you.' And she started to cry, and I just went over and hugged her, and started crying myself. . . ."

I felt so moved, and such a tightness in my own throat, that I said: "You're practically making *me* cry too."

"It was all like a revelation to me," resumed Sandy, her pale, green-flecked eyes alight. "Somehow there was a breakthrough—and there I was, mothering my mother. It may be something that she hadn't done to me. But what she said, then, was that she didn't mean to be all bitchy and fly off the handle and stuff, but that she was going through menopause. She said that sometimes these awful mean things just came blurting out of her mouth—that she had no control over it." Sandy stopped speaking, turned to look out the window.

I did too. We sat, staring for several seconds at the waving limbs of a young willow tree, executing a wind-inspired dance. "My mother and I didn't do much communicating," she continued then, "and we still don't, to this day. There was always a kind of an impassable barrier between us. I felt her to be a *cold* person, an unsatisfiable person, all during the time I was growing up. I guess I favored my father, always. But I never was able to talk to them, not throughout the entire ordeal of my breakup with Lee, about how I really felt about that whole thing. I just had to carry the load myself, including Julie . . . and there was this awful feeling, you know, that *nobody else is there*." She sighed, murmured: "I think that's how I felt, even before I started all that screwing around. As if I'd been totally deserted; it was just me, myself, all alone . . . and no one really understanding what I was going through. At least, no one *caring*."

Her glance had been fixed upon my face, but fell now to her lap. I saw that she had her hands folded, one over the other, and that she was wringing them slightly. "I have never said to my mother that I love her," reported Sandy, and the communiqué seemed to come out of the blue. "I never *could* get myself to the point where I could do that and not feel—I don't know—insincere. I've almost thought, sometimes, that I'm trying to substitute intimacy with a man for what never happened between me and my mother. I've sometimes had a notion like that was what was going on, in a way, between myself and Lee. I don't know. She and I never just got close, somehow. . . ." The tone in which Sandy made this statement wasn't bitter. It was a voice that recognized that there had been a cause for sorrow. But it was that, a sorrow and sadness. It wasn't a voice of defeat.

Things Like Commitment and Trust

She had stated, and with a seeming sureness and certainty, that she did *not* love Henry, that she felt "almost indifferent" to him. Yet she'd gone on to describe him, in a manner that radiated her own joy and pleasure in the relationship, as a being who was "special" to her, who was *not* just a boy friend, but much more like the husband and the father in her little family! I found that remark about her indifference so peculiar that I came back to it, believing that I must have mis-heard something. "Did you say, earlier, that you don't actually *love* Henry, Sandy?" I asked her, sounding dubious. And she replied without hesitation: "I don't think that I do."

I smiled the kind of smile that one bestows on a naughty but charming child. "I don't get it, because you sound as if you *do* care . . . quite a lot." I cocked my head to one side, looked at her inquiringly. Sandy smiled back; she was, as a matter of fact, beginning to blush. "I'm not sure," she said. "Before I came over here today, to tell the truth, I was trying to figure out what it is I *do* feel toward Henry. We'd been spending our weekends together, you know—from Saturday afternoon to Monday morning—and there were times when this just got to be too much for me. Having another adult around . . . and I told him that. I said to him: 'Look, I just can't handle having you here for forty-eight hours, or whatever. I like my time alone. I need to have some time alone.' And he said: 'Well, O.K., whatever' . . . but lately, it's been the whole weekend again, and I like it. I'm not really objecting to him being there so much of the time now."

"And yet," I asked, "you're not ready to use a word like 'love' for this good thing that has been happening?"

"No." The response was quick and firm. "I don't love him. There are times when I feel grateful to him—the way he's taken over my responsibility with Julie . . . which is something I never asked him to do. But this is something that—well, that's Henry! He just came along, and he did it. And I appreciate him, but I wouldn't say I *love* him, for doing that. . . ." She hesitated, as if deciding about whether or not to continue; but then she did: "There are just things about him . . . I don't know. It's as if we are *both* holding back too much. Because he's been hurt a lot too. It was Henry's wife who left *him*. And he's been through several relationships since that happened . . . all ending in disaster. So we're both pretty hesitant about making any sort of a commitment. He hasn't told me he loves *me*—not to my face, I mean—but once, when we'd gone together to the movies, he wrote on the back of my car, in the snow, 'I love you.'" Sandy giggled: "At the time I thought that was pretty corny! But the two of us . . . it's a pretty mature relationship. I just feel so much older, so much wiser now. I think that explains the feeling I have, of being married to him. It's just settled down, in this way, into a marriage."

A marriage, it seemed, without spoken vows of love and commitment. *These* seemed to be, for both of them, what was ultimately most dangerous. There were parts of herself, Sandy admitted, that she was by no means ready to share. "Since my marriage broke up," she explained, "there hasn't been *any* relationship that I've been in for that long a time. With Henry, it's been only three months now. And maybe in a year—if it went on for that time—I could be ready. I could turn around and say to him: 'Well I feel secure enough, with you, to just be "me," to totally let myself go.'"

I asked her then—if that did happen—what might be the most intimate, the most frightening, the most truly terrible confidence that she could share?

"Hah!" burst out Sandy, taking me aback completely. "I suppose— that I love him!"

I stared. "What would be so terrible about that?" And she responded, with an eruption of anger and of incoherence that such a confession might lead to the loss of her liberty and her freedom—it might lead to marriage.

I was puzzled, for she'd said that she considered her relationship with Henry to have settled already into a marriage. "Suppose, though," I asked, "that a year from now, or four months, or seven months, he were to say to you"—my voice dropped into stentorian, male tones—"Sandra Geller . . ."

"He wouldn't *say* it!" she broke in, pink-faced and schoolgirlish.

"—he were to say 'Sandy, I think I really do care for you; that I love you. How do you feel about me? Seriously, as a commitment?' . . ." I had abandoned the imitation, and I looked into her face directly and asked: "How would you feel? What would your response to that be?"

"I don't know," she responded hastily, "because that's a hypothetical thing." But then she added: "There have been times when he's expressed some emotion to me and I've said, right out, 'But I don't love *you.*' And I've said that, or things like that, on more than one occasion. It's true that I feel comfortable with him; that there have been times when I've thought: 'Henry, it would be awfully easy to turn around and say to you that I love you.' But I never do say it, because the day before I might not have felt that way; and the day after, I might not either. Until I was sure I did feel it *all of the time*, it'd be hard for me to tell anyone that I loved him."

"But do you think that's for real?" I inquired. "Most people, in a relationship, have fluctuations—"

"—To me, in the past, it *has* been," she interrupted. "I think I loved Lee, in the sense of the word I've been using. But maybe"—her expression turned doubtful—"maybe this is a different kind of love. Just the way old people get married, you know, mostly for companionship.

There's a lot of that feeling, of that comfort, which is *nice*, in Henry's and my relationship."

Our session together, which I'd been taping, was concluded. The hour-long spool had wound down to its very end. I pulled the plug from the socket, began wrapping it around my tape recorder. But I had a feeling of unfinished business. "How is it between the two of you sexually?" I asked, while stashing the recorder into my canvas tote.

To which Sandy answered, sounding uneasy: "I don't want to go into all of that now. But we have problems. He's been unable to maintain an erection long enough for me to get any satisfaction out of it. But," she defended Henry at once, "foreplay, and everything else, is just beautiful."

I'd put on my corduroy jacket, and was buttoning it. "He has a very quick ejaculation, then?"

Sandy, who had stood up, sat down again. "Yes, and it's been messing him up something awful. He's said to me that it just never has been like this for him before—and that he can't understand it."

I sat down, too, then, and unbuttoned my jacket again. We stayed there for almost another hour, talking . . . about male potency, and the ways in which it related to such matters as feeling secure, feeling loved, feeling safe, and to things like commitment and trust.

CHAPTER SIX

Body and Mind

A Mood, a Symptom, an Illness

It's time to pause here for the moment and to say what I mean, exactly, when I talk about "depression." For that word can be used by one person who means it in one sense; and heard by another, who hears it in quite another one. The word is a word for all seasons: it's confusing, because depression can be so many different things—a mood; a symptom of an illness; the illness itself. As a clinical syndrome depression is, of course, a psychological and physical disturbance; it has its own very recognizable, clear-cut set of symptoms. But depression can be one of the symptoms of *another* illness: flu, for example, includes among its common assortment of possible symptoms that of "depressive mood." And there are other bodily diseases which list depression among their frequent symptoms: ulcers and rheumatoid arthritic conditions are among them.

States of depression can emerge, moreover, secondary to alcoholism: this is often seen as a chicken-and-egg problem; it's not clear whether a primary depression has brought on the alcoholism or the use of alcohol has brought about depression. For alcohol is essentially a central-nervous-system depressant. (An initial spate of euphoria, one of the immediate effects of the drug, is the delightful effect we're all most familiar with. But this gives way, over an evening's drinking, to the numbing, anaesthetic effects of the liquor; our common alcoholic beverages are quite similar, chemically speaking, to the drug ether. And it may be that the "depression" that heavy drinkers develop has to do with the long-term depressant effects of the use of the substance itself.)

The depression associated with alcoholism might, on the other hand, stem from the obvious fact that alcoholics eventually do *get* into terrible quandaries and difficulties in their working lives and in their personal relationships. They get themselves into life-positions that can only be described as depressing. Who can say, then, by the time that the alcoholism has become established, whether that person's drinking began as a self-treatment of a prior depression, or developed because of the awful situations in which she (or he) eventually found herself? Or whether the depression is a straightforward *consequence* of the abuse of what is after all a powerful chemical substance?

A depressive disturbance can be, then, a primary illness or it can occur as a secondary symptom of some other primary illness. Most frequently, however, we use the word lightly, to designate a passing and ephemeral mood. A person who says: "I feel depressed when my hair gets dirty," or: "I felt so down and depressed after my conversation with Harry" is obviously referring to a temporary state of mind. There's nothing unfamiliar about these evanescent emotional states; we all experience them, and they are part of daily dealing with events (which includes the inevitable frustrating and saddening ones). But these normal, everyday, and passing dysphoric states are quite different from the clinical disorder called "depression." For the latter meaning implies an enduring life mood, a persisting state of emotion, thinking and feeling, which doesn't—somehow—pass and fade away as fresh events occur.

Depression is like the worst of bad moods, doggedly continuing, deepening, failing to end. And it involves a truly staggering array of profound psychological and physical changes. What is most strange though is that this disturbance, which is really widespread among the population—estimates vary upward into the 40-million-persons bracket in this country,* and of course most of those persons tend to be female ones—can and frequently does go unrecognized as the serious affliction that it is. An individual may be experiencing what is subjectively a mood of persisting unhappiness; and yet she may still fail, even in the privacy of her inmost thoughts, to own up to the degree of suffering that's actually being endured. What I've seen, often, is the stout efforts to pooh-pooh the psychological pain in this way. The game seems to be to "not know about it consciously"—at the same time hurting, and hoping, ostrichlike, that if one doesn't look it will all go away.

* A special 1973 report on the depressive disorders, published by the National Institute of Mental Health stated that: "In a national sample of randomly distributed respondents (ages 18–74) 30% were scored as having high distress. . . ." Thirty per cent of the American population is on the order of *sixty-five million people!*

That's rarely, I believe, a successful strategy for dealing with whatever must be dealt with . . . whatever is, to that person, the "matter"
or the content of the depression. But there are such large numbers of
people who go along, just muddling through, while never acknowledging the extent of the hurting that's really going on! A young married woman, Brenda Keyser, springs to my own mind in this particular respect. Brenda, the wife of a junior-level Harvard administrator,
came to talk to me about a thesis she was doing as a part-time
Hampshire College student. She wanted to interview me, actually, for
she was doing a master's thesis on the subject of "successful career
women." I was supposed to be one of those women. She questioned
me at length about the shape of my working and my professional life.

It was an interesting couple of hours. But why did I come to suspect, during the meeting that we had, that this eager and forthright
woman might be fighting against some pretty threatening depressive
feelings? Maybe it was a certain note in the lower ranges of her voice
tone, like the throbbing song that wails in some of the alto notes of
the violin. I can hear that note or sound—whatever it is—very frequently in the voices of women that I interview. Sometimes, from the
voice changes that have occurred from one interview to the next, I
can almost plot the upward or downward turn of a person's mood
state after just a very few words of greeting have been said. But at
any rate, that day, something prompted me to ask Brenda Keyser
whether—having finished asking *me* questions—she would be willing,
herself, to answer some questions for a study on "Women and Depression"?

She seemed taken aback. She said she would think about it and that
evening called to say that she was agreeable. "I don't know how helpful I'll be to you, though," she cautioned. "Because I'm not depressed.
All I am is a bit down, you know, once in a while." And with this advance warning we commenced what became, in fact, one of the
longest among the series of interviews with depressed women that I
actually carried out. Brenda was, as it developed, *not* in therapy of
any kind. She was, however, in the midst of a painful marital crisis and
struggling with issues having to do with a father whom she kept trying (and failing) to please. I hadn't, as I realized by the close of our
first talk, mis-heard the violin's note in the back of this attractive
young woman's voice. For she wasn't merely depressed; she was
actively suicidal, inasmuch as she was making "plans." Brenda Keyser
was saving up: sleeping pills, tranquilizers, any pills that she could get
prescribed to her (by her family doctor) for treatment of her massive
difficulties with anxiety and with disturbed sleep.

But I still do believe that *she* believed herself free of any illness called depression. Despite the fact that she seemed to be living out her days under a dark, threatening, and unrelieved cloud, she considered herself to be simply "just a bit down" every once in a while. Brenda hasn't thought of herself in terms of having a "condition" that might be ameliorated or cured. She was simply so damned miserable that the only way *out* she was considering was that of dying. This seemed to her, in her private and secret imaginings, the only thing that could possibly afford release.

The Biological Symptoms

Depression is a total bodily disorder. It involves virtually every one of the great organ systems within the human frame. The depressed person isn't, for instance, merely feeling sad, hopeless, inferior, powerless, and as if life has lost its meaning; she or he is experiencing a host of *physiological* changes as well. It is important to realize that the recognizable "mental changes"—that deeply lugubrious, too-sorrowing state of feeling—exist in tandem with a profoundly altered kind of *biological* functioning.

Some of the biological accompaniments of depressed states, such as drastic shifts in levels of sexual libido, appetite for food, etc., have been recognized for centuries, at least by physicians. But there are, as recent studies have shown, a wide range of other, subtler, abnormalities. One is the change in the body's salt balance, which shifts during episodes of depression. More salt than is usual is retained within the cells, and more salt often involves more water retention; this may be reflected in feelings of "puffiness." Salt is, moreover, an important ingredient in conducting nerve-impulses; the higher salt concentration brings about an imbalance in the electrical charges within the nervous system.

There are, during episodes of depression, strange alterations in the functioning of the body's endocrine system as well. For example, cortisol, a hormone which ordinarily comes into play in situations of physical stress (such as extreme coldness) or emotional emergency (being insulted, angry, fearful), is produced in abnormally large quantities. Generally, cortisol production will show a diurnal rhythm, peaking in the morning and reaching its low point early in the evening. But in the body of the depressed person, cortisol peaks earlier than usual—around 4 A.M.—and remains elevated throughout the day.

Perhaps it's this increase in cortisol levels, promoting a state of alertness or defensive wariness that explains the widespread sleep disturbances of depressed persons. For sleep disorders of every variety—insomnia, middle-of-the-night awakening, early-morning awakening—are in fact the biological bridesmaids of depression.

Brenda Keyser, though, hadn't made any connection between the state of her feelings, her general unhappiness, and the fact that she'd been plagued for months by a tendency to snap awake at the early-morning hour that Ingmar Bergman has called "the hour of the wolf." She did, it's true, find these sudden awakenings debilitating and scary. It was impossible to get back to sleep. "A lot of times," she told me, toward the close of our first conversation, "when I wake up in the night like that, and I'm feeling kind of shitty about existence and stuff, I don't even know what *hour* it is . . . whether it's still the night, or it's gotten to be morning, or what. Like, last night I woke up and looked at my watch and I thought it was O.K. I read the time as six-thirty, and I was wide awake. I thought, well, all right, I can get up and go to the bathroom and put on some coffee—it's time to be up by now. I went to the john, then, and put on my glasses . . . and I discovered that it was only four-thirty. And I was just—amazed. Because when I'm feeling depressed it's hard—" She broke off, gave me a suspicious look. "I'm not comfortable with that word. What does it mean, 'being depressed'?"

I shook my head, shrugged: "Let's just say 'down' instead."

"Okay, 'down' then," agreed Brenda. "But what I mean is, I guess, that what you said about waking up early is true. When I'm feeling shitty about things in my life, and lethargic, moody, quick to strike out—verbally, I mean—I *do* that. I wake up early. But you know, that's nothing so special to me. I have a part-time job, doing typing, and I was talking with a couple of women there about not being able to sleep. And they both said they do that snapping-awake-at-4 A.M. number too. One of them; she's about twenty-one years old, and she's been married for a couple of years; she said that when she gets up real early like that she simply does her sewing. She can't do that around her husband because *he* thinks she's taking the time away from him. . . ." Brenda's voice ran down, as if she'd lost the point of what she'd started out to say.

"And how about you?" I asked. "Does it bother you a lot when you snap up like that, early in the morning?"

"Sometimes," she answered slowly, "I find it weird. I feel as if I'm—all alone, the only one awake anywhere. I mean I *know* Seth is still in bed, there, and he's sleeping. I'm *not* alone . . . but I feel frightened."

Hyperarousal and Inner Disorder

Sleep disturbances of the sort Brenda described are among the more clear-cut and obvious symptoms of a clinical depression. But there are other, less readily apparent, shifts in the customary pattern of a person's nightly sleep. There is, for example, a total loss of Stage IV (called "delta wave") sleep. Delta wave is the deepest and most restful stage of slumber. There is also a constant movement from one sleep stage to another, instead of the typical orderly progression from one stage to the next. The depressive wakens, moreover, unduly easily, in response to small noises that wouldn't disturb the normal (nondepressed) sleeper.

Other strictly physical concomitants of depressed states include heightened heart and respiration rates. And there is *hyperponesis:* taut, clenched, rigid musculature. Although this high state of tension is invisible to the naked eye, it can easily be picked up on an electromyograph (a device for recording muscle tension). One of the researchers studying muscle tension in depression told me that very frequently a patient who is actually improving on antidepressant medication—but still *feels* miserable and as if nothing can help, ever— will give early-warning signals of improvement on the electromyograph. She or he may be, subjectively speaking, as low in mood as ever; still, those taut facial muscles will have begun to relax.

The entire biological situation seems to be, in brief, one of hyperarousal. And a good deal of the recent research on the physiology of depression does seem to suggest an irritability, a disorganized hyperactivity, of the central nervous system. This is just the opposite, really, of what one would expect. For the depressed person often *appears* so slowed down, so fatigued, so sluggish, that one would suppose that individual's body processes to be turgid, halting, barely cranking along. That is anything but the case.

For within the body, there is that state of abnormal high speed. Studies of the brain waves of depressed people indicate that the nervous circuitry is operating *super-rapidly but unusually inefficiently;* for instance, it takes a depressed person measurably longer to respond to a visual stimulus (such as a flash of light) than it does a normal person. According to psychiatrist Peter Whybrow of Dartmouth Medical School, it's as if "all of the circuits were overloaded somehow. Everything's bouncing back and forth in there."

The processing of perceptions just doesn't proceed in its usual orderly fashion. And there seems to be more random firing within the central nervous system as well. A single nerve cell, responding to a flash of light, can trip off all other kinds of neurons: ones which, ordinarily, would not become involved. This might be, speculated Dr. Whybrow, who is an expert on the biology of depression, the *physical* analogue of that tendency to ruminate, that inability to make decisions, those feelings that one's thought processes are clogged of which so many depressive complain.

Brenda talked of this inner confusion, this difficulty in completing a thought or action sequence, and the problems in concentrating on anything (or even reading) as somewhat like "slogging one's way through a great deal of mental mud." Everything was, she said, during periods when she felt bad, "slowed down, low pace, and very slow, mindwise, too. People will be talking," she explained, "and I'll pick up on something when the conversation's at a particular point. And then what I'll do is say, 'Hey, wait a minute; what's going on?' I'll start talking about something that everyone's already finished with. It's as if my mind's not working; I just can't keep up. . . ." She paused. "It's like that with getting things accomplished, too. Like last week, I took time off from my part-time job in order to finish up work on the thesis I'm doing. And I cleaned up my study; I put things in order, so that I could go in there and could type. But I just couldn't fucking *sit down* at my typewriter! I read my introduction, and my conclusion; I read them both about three or four times. But I couldn't *do* anything. And I feel, now, as if there's a harness on me or something. It's holding me back from doing the things I ought to be *doing*."

She had, she said, been flagellating herself almost all week about not making progress on the paper. "I'd think to myself, 'well if you're not typing, why aren't you looking at the library for this goddamned book by this goddamned turkey?' I had rejected the book entirely, and then, writing my introduction, I'd referred to the person who wrote it. So I thought if I wasn't doing anything else, I should go back to it and figure out whether I wanted to quote that author's argument or not. At that point, though, I get into the indecision bit: 'Yes I want to go to the library; no, I don't.' I don't have a car, and my bike is fucked up at the moment. And I have all this other stuff to do. Like, our apartment's in need of a thorough cleaning. And I *am*, usually, a pretty good housekeeper. So I keep making decisions and then disassembling them. You know. It's this internal kind of jigsaw puzzle that is almost impossible to complete; it never seems to get finalized, to finish itself *off*." She sighed. "The arguments that I have with myself! I could do a million things, work on my annotated bibliography, or on the regular one. I've got the regular bibliography typed; but I have things to add."

The problem was that, although there were many tasks, there seemed to be no particular one on which she could proceed. "I can't resolve on what I should, or should not be doing, or what's wrong with me, and why I'm not doing things right, and what's wrong with my adviser, my husband, and everyone *else* in the world!" She laughed, but the sound was unhappy. "I tell myself it's simple; there's this one thing you want to do—complete this task. And it's all out there, ready for me to do. But I can't seem to move forward, to complete one act. It's like a paralysis. I can't even take one *little* step." She kept trying to tell herself, Brenda added, how good it would feel if it all happened and she completed her paper on "successful women." "But I don't know," she said helplessly, "I've done all the advance preparatory work. But I just can't get moving and *do* it!"

Hunger and Sex

Other bodily changes she'd experienced had to do with her appetite for food, and appetite for sex as well. Both have a tendency to fall drastically during attacks of depression; in Brenda's case, both had shifted upward and were experienced as unusually intense. She was, she remarked, getting "fatter and more frustrated all the time." She felt far more highly charged than was customary and said "My sexuality is nuts, sometimes. A little too much, I feel; and resolving that creates a problem in my relationship with Seth. He just doesn't seem to feel the same kind of drive that I do, anyhow, and so I masturbate a good deal. Once a day or night, something like that. But the truth is, no matter how hungry I may be feeling, unless Seth is up to sex, sex doesn't happen between us. And the way I deal with that, if I make any overtures to him and he just doesn't seem to be interested—or he doesn't say anything to me, or doesn't seem to want that—I just kind of wait until the lights are out, and wait until he's breathing evenly, and then I just masturbate. . . ." She'd been looking away from me, resolutely failing to meet my eye. But now she turned, gave me a grim and defiant look.

"I don't know why it is that when I'm feeling down I should also feel so damned horny. But a week can go by, me feeling that way, and Seth utterly uninvolved. So I end up—well, I'm willing to do it on my own. I don't need him sexually all the time. I used to, but I don't anymore."

An Internal Vulnerability: Everything Changes

In depression, then, everything changes: brain physiology, body physiology, mental processes, one's entire mode of thinking, and of experiencing. There are shifts in sleep patterns, appetite, libido, and an array of less visible physiological changes as well. The entire inward portrait of a mood disorder seems to be that of a widespread perturbation of the system, a loss of biological orderliness, of equilibrium. It is as if whatever forces ought to have counteracted or checked the mood have failed to come into play, and so the feelings of grief and defeat have continued to hold sway, and to intensify.

Everyone, of course, has to cope with failures, frustrations, and losses over a lifetime; some manage to rise above them with only transient pain. But a certain proportion of people can't, or don't. These are the individuals who, as Peter Whybrow observed, seem to have an internal vulnerability—"that is, the biological capacity"—for becoming depressed in the clinical sense.

A Change in the Inner Environment:
Mood, Symptom, Syndrome, and Side Effect

Brenda Keyser's depression seemed, like a desert flower, to have taken root and bloomed in a landscape of desolate relationships. It had everything to do with where she was in her life, and the things that were happening in her world. But a depressive disturbance can come into being by a far more biological route: it can emerge as a result of a change in a person's *internal* environment. When depression is a "symptom" of some other illness—for instance, flu—its origins are obviously more physical than mental. Another way in which the clinical disturbance has been known to emerge is as a side effect of some kind of drug or medication.

I think, in this regard, of a thirty-nine-year-old editor, Lucy Harris. Her very serious depression was brought on by the use of a certain medicine, *reserpine*. This drug, prescribed to her by a prominent and respected Manhattan internist, was given to her in treatment of a high-blood-pressure condition. What her doctor appeared to be unaware of, however, was that reserpine had already acquired something of a bad reputation. The drug, as several medical journals had reported, could tilt some people into severely depressed states. But Mrs. Harris received no warning about this. Her physician never mentioned it; and perhaps, incredible though it seems, he really did not know.

At the time she began taking the medication, Lucy was a senior editor in a large New York publishing firm. In the summer, she and her husband and daughter came to a second home in Hanover, New Hampshire. She'd been drifting, throughout the winter of 1975-76, when she was using reserpine, into a depressed, hostile, somewhat anxious and agitated state. She'd also become sexually frigid. Lucy Harris had never, however, associated the medicine she was taking for her hypertension with the terrible ways she was feeling.

The doctor she'd been consulting was, for his own part, satisfied. For he was treating her high blood pressure; and the reserpine had, in fact, brought it down to a very acceptable level. He either didn't know that the medicine brings about depression in some 15 per cent of the people using it—or he neglected to ask her, specifically, about her mood. During the eleven months that she was using the drug, Lucy's psychological state was in fact deteriorating slowly. By summer she was in a painful depression.

Still, it took her more than a month to come to the Dartmouth-Hitchcock Mental Health Center for outpatient treatment. "I'm arrogant," she told me, later on, at a time when she was already dramatically better. "I suppose I just thought that I was as smart as anyone else going: no one could tell me anything about my problems that I didn't already *know!*" During the full year it had taken her to accept the fact that she did need help, however, she'd gotten embroiled in an unending series of angry interpersonal situations. She was, by then, being eased out of what had seemed to be an impregnable editorial position at the firm where she worked. Her marital circumstances, which she described as "never ideal" had shifted from an inactively troubled to an actively volcanic state. She was also involved in nagging, nattering quarrels with her adolescent stepdaughter.

Lucy, a passionate mountain climber, said that she'd decided in advance of her appearance at the psychiatric unit that summer, that it was "either come here for treatment or throw myself over a cliff: one or the other." And it was in the course of an initial interview with one of the senior therapists, whom she was consulting on a private basis, that a routine question was raised: were there any medications that she was, at present, using in the treatment of any prior physical or psychological difficulties? It was a most standard inquiry. And yet, when she mentioned that she was taking reserpine, Dr. Gary Tucker, a Professor of Psychiatry at Dartmouth Medical School, became alerted immediately. He looked at her: "Did your physician happen to mention," he asked carefully, "that reserpine can occasionally precipitate a depressive disturbance?"

Her doctor hadn't, of course; she didn't know. But a change of her high-blood-pressure medication, prescribed immediately, brought about—over the course of a few brief weeks—an almost Cinderella-like cure. Her mood, her relations with others, her flexibility and ability to cope . . . all underwent an almost magical change.

Once she'd stopped using the drug, the depressive feelings, the hostile and agitated tone of her conversation, and her behavior, had dissipated. So had her disgust with, and rigid aversion to, sex. A darkness that had seemed to envelop her, to create the climate and the conditions under which her life had to be lived, had simply melted away . . . and all she'd done was to quit taking that drug.

The costs, despite this fairy-tale-like lifting of the enchantment, had been enormous. I mean the real-world costs. For, in the year preceding, Lucy Harris had managed to offend and disturb so many authors and publishing colleagues that she'd been eased downward into a less responsible position at her firm. Her general standing in the field of publishing had, as a consequence, fallen. And so, if the inner cloud had broken apart, shredded, pretty much disappeared, she was now under an outer cloud that patently existed. It wasn't at all certain that she could get back to where she'd been *before* the depression had developed.

Her marital relationship, despite the sexual renaissance, was something she'd come to recognize as "probably irretrievable . . . even if I *wanted* to retrieve it. And I'm not sure that I would. . . ." Her dealings with her stepdaughter, whom she did love, were marked by insecurity and tension. Would the three of them, as a threesome, be splitting up? And if they did, who would end up meaning what to whom?

The lifting of Lucy's depression hadn't at all returned her to GO; she wasn't, by any means, in the same life-space she'd occupied *before becoming depressed*. Many aspects of her existence, as if in the wake of a natural disaster, had been disorganized, upended, torn apart . . . to some degree, wrecked beyond repair. And an attack of depression can be, in this respect, compared to other kinds of disaster—to floods, earthquake, typhoon, and so forth . . . in that there's a lot of mopping up and a lot of restoring that has to be done in its wake. In some cases, things never are the same again afterward. The damages can't be made good and all of the losses replaced.

Now in the Lucy Harris instance, most obviously, the depression had been brought about by some subtle shifts in the functioning of her nervous chemistry (triggered by the use of reserpine; this disaster wasn't really, thus, a natural one). It was almost as if the medication had made possible the tripping of some inner biological switch. Lucy had moved, as a result, from what might be called the AC of normal functioning (the circuitry of everyday coping with normal problems; adapting to shifting sets of circumstances, etc.) to a kind of depressive feedback loop of sorts . . . the DC of depressive functioning, which for her involved a sense of physical fatigue, a simmering anger, and feelings of utter helplessness. "The best way that I can describe what it felt like," she once said, "was that it was like being dead. Except that one had to go through the motions of being alive . . . and it was —pain."

Hers was what is called an *iatrogenic illness*—an illness precipitated by medical care. But what it pointed up, and with great precision, was the great difference that could be made by virtue of the fact that her *internal environment* had been altered. It wasn't, obviously, that Mrs. Lucy Harris' bag of life problems and daily difficulties had changed: her ability to cope with them, from a purely biological standpoint, was what had in fact been altered.

And her neurophysiological functioning had been altered in such a way that a depressive disturbance now became "possible." Not everyone who becomes stressed and discouraged by difficulties encountered in their lives becomes, as Brenda Keyser had done, clinically depressed. Some people don't have what Dr. Peter Whybrow has spoken of as a kind of biological permission. That is, they don't have the constitutional makeup that allows for that switchover into the nervous circuitry of depression. The mysterious physiological component that *permits* the development of a mood disorder happens not to be there.

In Lucy Harris' instance, the missing ingredient had been, it seemed, supplied by reserpine.

Susceptibility

Clearly, there are some individuals (and these people might be thought of as being at one end of a spectrum) who are apparently invulnerable to depression. No matter what degrees of pain, unhappiness, loneliness, loss, and sorrow they're called upon to weather, they manage to do it without developing a depressive disturbance. And there are others (who might be thought of as being at the opposite end of that spectrum) who seem to have a very special and salient "biological permission," enabling them to be pitched into extremes of mood state by what appear to be no more than the routine trivia of ordinary existence.

These extremes can be manias (uppers) as well as depressions (downers):

Many clinicians believe, as a matter of fact, that long episodes of euphoria represent what is really a flight from an underlying despair. A patient who comes to my mind in this context is Judith (see "Mood and Medicine"). Judith experienced three extraordinarily frightening attacks of elation. In each instance, just prior to the onset of the "happiness attack," a transitional life event was in the works. On the first occasion, she'd been involved in a move across the country. The second episode had gotten under way in the wake of the death of her grandmother, and just before a trip back to her beloved California. The third mania had begun during a period when she was being seriously considered for academic tenure as a historian of film. (The job opportunity vanished, "largely," she admitted later, "because of my impossible behavior.")

Now every one of these life situations could, to some degree, be considered to be stress-producing. They were all circumstances involving a mild, or more than mild, amount of challenge and coping; some degree of adaptation would necessarily be required. What they were *not*, however, or so it seemed to me, was the stuff of major emotional disturbance.

That is, unless one invokes the notion of that "special biological permission." In Judith's case, nevertheless, these events were all that was necessary in terms of "environmental input" in order to set in motion those mysterious, ill-understood changes in central nervous system functioning that apparently underlie disorders of emotion and of mood. She was simply *more vulnerable* to the stresses and tensions of human living than are those individuals who are elsewhere on our imagined spectrum.

A nice analogy would be with something like vulnerability to flu. Let's take an example in which we imagine that an audience of about a hundred people, attending a meeting or a concert of some sort, are exposed to an active strain of influenza virus. Among those individuals there would be some who would catch the flu and then go on to develop "cases" of varying degrees of seriousness: some would be out of commission for a short, and some for a longer, while. Others, exposed to the same germs, might develop just a minor symptom or two —a mildly sore throat and a case of diarrhea, for instance. But these people wouldn't ever fall victim to anything clearly recognizable as clinical illness or disease.

In other words, some individuals might be slightly affected by the exposure to flu virus, and others might be affected to the point of becoming frankly sick. A much smaller subset among those taken ill could, moreover, not only become infected and catch the influenza but go on to develop pneumonia—and a few might *die* as a result of being in that room with those germs abroad! Still another subgroup of individuals, in the same room with the same influenza virus, might manage to resist not only illness but any symptoms whatsoever. The point, or the analogy I'm making, is the following: in emotional disturbances involving mood—in depression and in mania—losses, setbacks, and miseries; stress, worry, loneliness; concerns, griefs, fears, and disappointments; threats of many kinds and varieties—all are the flu germs or environmental pathogens. An exposure to a taxing or stressful situation, or an experience of loss (perhaps not even a single, discrete event, but something occurring over a period of months or even years) very frequently sets the stage for what are known, in psychiatric terminology, as the *affective disorders*.

The *affects* are another name for the emotions; for feelings. And the affective illnesses are the severe disturbances of mood state. They involve a person's being too happy, or too miserable, to be true. In the case of depression, as in the flu analogy, some individuals, having taken sick, do get sicker and then go on to die. Depression is, in fact, the only psychiatric disorder which involves a high mortality rate. This is because the common symptoms of depressive disorder include suicidal thoughts and feelings.

But the other side of that same coin is that the depressive disturbances actually show an enormously high recovery rate. Estimates have it that for any given attack of depression that a person experiences, there is a 95 per cent chance of recovery. These are, as any rational bettor knows, very palatable odds indeed. The problem is, though, that depressed people are not rational and they're not processing thoughts in their customary fashion. They are on that other, that depressive circuitry. And thus, the 95 per cent chance of complete remission is cited in most textbooks with the *caveat* that a given patient is quite probably going to get better "unless suicide intervenes."

A Matter of Timing

Another important factor that can't be left out here, is the matter of timing. Whether or not one contracts an illness—be it flu, depression, or some other disease—has to do not only with "exposure" but with one's state of functioning at the time that it happens. For no one's biology is static. A person may be completely resistant on one occasion, and then quite vulnerable on a subsequent one. An individual may be resistant, for instance, to emotional disorder in the wake of a severe stress—say, the death of a parent—at one point in life; and yet, at another, respond to the same kind of major event with a serious and prolonged depression. The impact that a particular environmental insult—a loss, an injury, a separation, a trauma of any variety—has upon a particular individual depends not only on the force or degree of the stress (that is, the virulence of the flu germs) but upon that person's own state of being at the time that the stressful life experience is encountered.

Timing is, then, another crucial and delicate involvement. There is always this matter of the interplay of inward and outer events and forces . . . the myriad of necessary ingredients coming together at a particular life juncture. When the combination of outward challenges and interior, biological state "allows" it to happen, the alchemical transformation into the depressive being results.

Across the Life Arc: What Does a Woman Want?

What is most central, what "matters most" to a person, shifts, changes, alters over time. If one conceives of that person's life as a kind of continuous "thread," then depression is a place of snarling, of tangling, of stoppage. An individual becomes, for some reason, incapable of moving onward; she doesn't go into a life mood so much as she becomes possessed *by it*. The depressive state is an entire way of being.

And depression is, when it emerges, a signal of adaptive failure. It communicates a person's real incapacity to manage within the context of some life situation—a breakdown of the normal abilities to carry on with one's everyday functioning. If one thinks of this in terms of a "road of life" metaphor, then it involves pulling over to one side, allowing everyone else to go whizzing by—due, either to failure of the mechanism, problems of the road itself, or difficulties coming from within the driver. This kind of forced halt is, though, something that that biological and psychological and social organism—the depressed human being—is experiencing at *a particular point* or phase of her own very human existence.

For our social and intimate relationships are, as I remarked earlier, not stationary, but are in a process of flux and shift merely by virtue of our movement through time; our movement from one life place to another. Separations and losses are an inevitable aspect of the sequence, but for some people they can't be tolerated, can't be encompassed, can't be endured. In some instances, the loss of a valuable, powerful attachment—an attachment that seems to provide all of the meaning and purpose in a certain person's existence—is equated, by the person who's gotten herself into this vulnerable position, with the end of all meaning and purpose in life.

As psychiatrist Leston Havens has observed in a moving paper on the suicidal patient, there are instances in which there is only *one* individual in a particular human being's world who stands between him (or her) and the desire to die. Writes Dr. Havens, "What if that person is lost, moves away or has a falling out with the patient? The individual . . . will be as much deprived of vital nutrients as if he (she) had stopped eating. . . ." Certain losses, at certain moments of our lives when we feel unready, unprotected, unconfident of our ability to cope with and transcend them, may be experienced as emotional starvation, as annihilation, as death.

Clearly, on this journey through the life cycle—this survey of the key issues and concerns that crop up, to oppress and depress women— we've already encountered some very recognizable themes. They are so familiar, really, that like the Andy Warhol soup can, one comes upon them with a sort of alarmed surprise. Yet by looking carefully at what went wrong at a particular period of a person's life—what appeared to make it so problematical or impossible to traverse or navigate—much can be discerned about the nature of the things that need to be going right (and the kinds of capabilities and capacities that need to be in place) at certain stages and critical phases of every woman's life.

Some of the issues that have been, and will be, discussed are age-related: leaving home and finding new commitments are, by and large, the business of adolescence and young adulthood; the childbearing years and the experience of menopause are biologically defined, and widowhood is generally encountered in the latter adult years. Other issues are the overarching psychological business of a lifetime: the negotiation and renegotiation of problems of separation and independence, and the achievement of inner autonomy.

Freud, during one of his famous lectures, observed rather ironically that one of the unanswerable riddles was the question: "What does a woman want?" His own efforts to formulate a reply had, he confessed, met with but little in terms of demonstrable success. But here, in these accounts or "case histories," what I am trying to do is actually turn the question from a semimocking one to a perfectly serious one—to ask what it is that, when *lacking* in a woman's life, can lead to states of depression? What do women, at the various stages of their lives, require in order to live?

In the Thirties

CHAPTER SEVEN

Turning Thirty: Kath

Out of the White Organdy

Her father had died when she was thirteen. Still, she spoke of him with a present-tense kind of intensity. The very words that Kath Barrie used, in describing her relationship with her father, bore a haunting similarity to the words, ideas, expressions that had been used by Marie Sirotta.

Kath, a twenty-eight-year-old, first-year medical student, said: "I think, truly, that my mother was extremely *jealous* of my father's and my closeness to one another. I'm almost identical to him just in terms of physical appearances—light skin, given to freckling; strawberry-blond hair; the general cast of our features. Everyone's *always* remarked on this very strong resemblance between us! And then, we were always alike in other ways: in, oh, being overly sensitive to rejection or to personal confrontation. Which ties in, I suppose, with an ability to get totally absorbed in whatever work one happens to be doing. This was always a *drive* for my father—to be doing something —he had to, and I am the same way. As for my mother, well"—the muscles under Kath's cheeks and around her chin tightened slightly, like a Jell-O that's just beginning to set—"she is a very intelligent woman, but she's never done a thing about that intelligence—nor has she any desire to do so."

There was a brief silence. We were sitting in my study (a euphemism for office) at the Center for Advanced Study in the Behavioral Sciences, at Stanford, California. Kath Barrie, a student at the Stanford Medical School, had attended a small, informal gathering at which I'd spoken about the book I was writing. The next day she'd telephoned me at the Center, told me that she'd been seriously depressed a year earlier, and volunteered herself as a guinea pig for a series of interviews. I agreed, though I warned her that I had so much material already, that our talks were unlikely to make their way into my book (I was wrong). She was, she said, just on the other side of what had been an overwhelming and frightening experience, and she would be interested in discussing it with me, no matter what I did—or didn't do—with the interviews.

She looked so young. She looked closer to sixteen than she did to age twenty-eight. Her body was slim and boyish; and she wore her long, straight hair pulled back in a smooth ponytail. Her skin was fresh, clear, without makeup; and her manner somewhat reticent, vulnerable, shy.

She looked like a girl whom you might see riding horseback, on a beach, very early in the morning. The general expression on her face, including a slight habitual smile; the distant, if slightly anxious look around the eyes: a loner, at once proud and fearful. She didn't in any case look like someone who'd just emerged from an acute, and at one point suicidally depressive, disturbance. But she had. "I never actually attempted to kill myself," she explained carefully, "but fantasies about doing so began, at one time, to engross my thinking to a pretty frightening degree."

One of the first things she'd needed to tell me about herself had been that her father had died when she was thirteen. I'd responded by asking what disease or illness it was, he had actually died of.

"Heart attack," she replied, then fell silent.

After a few moments, I ventured, "And do you remember . . . how it was? The way it happened?"

"Vividly." She leaned forward slightly, her eyes wide. "I believe now that he had probably had a heart condition for a year or two . . . because I don't think it came as a surprise to him. But he didn't tell anyone. And when he had the first real out-and-out *heart* attack—I was off skiing that weekend, and when I came back, he was in the hospital. That was fine, he was O.K. and he recovered. He was home for six weeks, then had another heart attack. Then," her voice didn't waver, "he died."

Kath had recited this sequence of events in an affectless tone; now she stopped speaking, as though having come to the end of a prepared speech or a statement. She looked at me expectantly, however.

"And then, how did you feel about your mother at that time?" I inquired. She shifted in her seat, and her expression altered subtly, as it had at the last mention of her mother. "Were you angry at her in any way?" I was prompted to ask.

"I would say that when my father died my relationship with my mother began to deteriorate badly. I saw her in the ways that I never had wanted to admit to myself; saw her ways of being. I'd always felt, from her, a whole lot of pressures and restrictions. She saw *me* as someone who had to grow up to be the perfect little lady with the perfect kind of manners. That whole thing—it was a tension between us, before anything at all had happened. But *then*, I mean when my dad died, she didn't ever openly express *grief!* She didn't *hurt!*—I remember that when he had his first heart attack her big concern was that I might not be able to continue in the fancy private school that I was going to at that time! And I . . . that was my last thought on earth, at that point! I was so—so—" She had no word with which to complete the sentence, to describe her own sense of devastation.

"So you felt, then," I suggested, slowly, "that your mother was seeing him more as a meal ticket, as someone to support a style of living, perhaps more than anything else . . . ?"

"Yes, exactly. I don't think," she put in guiltily, "that that was the *only* way my mother saw him. She had difficulty—she always has had difficulty—in expressing her emotions. And that's why we didn't, and still don't, get along that well. But at that time I could only—" again Kath could find no appropriate word; she merely shrugged.

"What I mean is that she was really concerned, most of all, about being able to support our lives together in terms of material things. At least, that was all the feeling that she manifested. I didn't hear anything like: 'Oh, I have lost my husband!' or 'Oh, how I loved that man!' . . . just none of that!" The young woman's voice was bitter. "And yet that was all *I* could feel. That I *missed* him so agonizingly—so agonizingly *much*. I didn't care if we were on poverty row!" She tossed her head haughtily, contemptuously; and yet, the last words had come out as a wail.

I could, in that moment, see the desperate thirteen-year-old reincarnated—siding with her helpless, hopelessly lost dead father and resenting her live, "unfeeling" mother furiously. "Did you think, perhaps, that if *she'd* only been a better wife to him then perhaps your father wouldn't have died?"

Kath jumped slightly, gave me a startled glance. "At the time, I didn't," she answered. "I would tend to say *now* that I—well, I don't blame my father's death on my mother, not by any means. But I do see my father's dying at that point in time because of. . . ." She paused, and the pause lasted until I thought she'd decided not to continue.

She began the sentence anew. "I guess I see him dying because of a host of linking reasons. My father was an inventor and a computer scientist. He had a big reputation and he was, well"—her face had slowly come alight—"he was really a genius. He'd just completed work on a huge project that had to do with the Apollo mission. I didn't understand it; but whatever he'd done was supposed to have been this tremendous success. But you know, there he was, and it was all over. He'd been engrossed in this great gigantic effort, and the whole thing had come to an end. I think"—her voice was moving, now, from enthusiasm to mournfulness—"that *many* people go through complicated emotional responses when they come to the end of something that's been involving them completely."

She hesitated, then added: "He got a little depressed. It was just all over."

I nodded my head in a vague gesture of assent.

"Exactly," said Kath. I wasn't sure what she'd thought I'd communicated. But she continued: "When that intense work thing was over, I could, all of a sudden, begin to see the conflicts that were there between my parents. That *had* been there, I suppose; but which I hadn't recognized or known about before this particular time. My father was getting bored, unhappy with the things he was doing; he wanted to move on. My mother didn't want to leave California, to part with the big house in which the three of us were living. *He*, though, had this pervasive restlessness about him, and my mother—it drove her crazy!" Kath laughed slightly, as if at an amusing, tender memory.

"Restlessness? Of what kind?" I looked at her, shook my head.

"Oh"—she cocked her own head to one side—"he would have been very happy to stay with us for a month, and then go off to work in Germany with his friends who were computer scientists and who had some big new project going *there*. But my mother wouldn't hear of such a thing. So that was an issue. My father, too, spent all of his money on patents—thousands of dollars on patents. My mother thought this was all an outrageous *waste*. So there was a real conflict, for him, between his work interests and his home and family. And I can really see, objectively, how he was just torn between these things. *He*, I think, was the one who made sacrifices. My mother never made any—she got her way."

These last two remarks emerged in such a caustic way that Kath felt she had to explain: "Long before my father's death—though things were very far from having come to a head—my mother and I were at odds with one another. Because she, I think, realized even then that I was heading towards being what she didn't want me to be." What her mother *had* wanted, Kath added quickly, was a daughter who was a perfectly mannerly little doll of a female.

"I was very rebellious; I resisted practically everything she was trying to force upon me. All the limits and restrictions. . . ." She laughed: "I mean I'd been a very good little girl for a number of years; but at that point, around twelve and thirteen, I wanted *out* of the white organdy!"

"And your father . . . before he died . . . was he taking *your* side?"

The smile disappeared, and she looked thoughtful. She seemed to consider her reply with great care, as if she were a witness giving testimony. "My father—I think—at that point—was having a very difficult time. He was trying to be the objective person in this whole little—I don't know what to call it—this *drama*—this tension between my mother and me. Because there was *also*, you see, a great tension between *him* and her! And he certainly didn't take sides openly; in fact, he'd get mad at me on her behalf, quite a bit. Still, I knew. It was clear to me that he saw . . . I mean I really came through with the notion that what he wanted was a normal child, not a female puppet. 'Normal' in the sense that he didn't think it was the end of the world if I broke a rule or got into a little trouble once in a while. But there we go again. *She* wanted a little Miss Vanderbilt, or something—I don't know what it was—it was absolute social perfection!"

Had she ever, later on, felt guilty about there having been so much tension in the family at that particular time? "Did you ever," I asked her slowly, in a tip-toeing, tentative voice, "have guilty thoughts, thoughts that you were, somehow, responsible—because of the quarrels between you and your mother at the time of your father's heart attacks? No?"

She had been shaking her head vigorously, in the negative, long before I got to the end of these questions. "No, I didn't. If anything, as I said, my father's big difficulty was in adapting, after he'd stopped working on that big project. My father was very very much of a genius, really; and it was *painful* for him to have to come back down to earth and to deal with the practical matters of life." Her voice was filled with daughterly pride.

She added, then, wistfully: "He just wanted to run around the world, and to work in all kinds of different places. It was, I think, impossible for him to be married and to do that. . . ." She was staring at something on the wall behind me and I, turning, saw that it was a painting that I'd recently purchased from the artist-wife of one of my Center colleagues. I was about to comment on it when Kath added, almost in a tone of afterthought: "If I blamed my mother for anything, at the time, it was because I saw her as someone very *cold*. I guess I didn't blame myself for my father's death . . . because I felt so close to him."

"You were grieving," I said, and met her eyes, saucer-round and brown.

She nodded, murmured: "Oh . . . oh, *agony*. I was just distraught."

The Best

The Barries had been forced, after the father's death, to make what Kath's mother considered a wrenching move. They had had to sell their sprawling home, perched on a grassy bluff in the Pacific Palisades area of Los Angeles, and move into a tiny, nondescript bungalow. "I see the years after my dad died as an awful, painful time," recounted Kath quietly, her eyes narrowing slightly as though she were squinting at faded pictures from the past. "My mother's overriding concern, her obsession was only this: that I *do* well; that I be the best. But she didn't have to *force* me to do well! I always *had*, because I'd always enjoyed school. There were difficulties about this, between us, even so—endless, unsolvable quarrels. I avoided her as much as I could. I literally spent ages, hours of time, in my room, studying: I was always being the best! I did it," she added lightly, "so that when I got into trouble, she wouldn't be able to get that mad at me. The truth is, though"—there was offended pain in her voice—"I was the model student in my school. At home, you wouldn't ever have known it."

I picked up the word "trouble," raised an eyebrow, asked her about it: "What kinds of trouble did you get into?"

"Oh, well. I didn't start getting into trouble until I was about sixteen or seventeen, when men sort of were coming into the play of things. Before then, I didn't actually know any boys—she'd managed to keep me going in the private girls' school that I'd been attending before my father died. The 'trouble,' though, had to do with things like staying out late on dates, or kissing boys, or whether I'd started to smoke. In the later teens, my relationship with my mother was terrible. She was in her middle fifties, probably going into menopause. She was alone. All the ideals of her life certainly were far from having been realized. . . ." The daughter's voice, nevertheless, was filled with the chill of disapproval.

"What do you think, now, in looking back," I interjected, "that those ideals and goals actually were?"

Kath hesitated, but only momentarily: "To be living in a luxurious home. To have all the amenities of life. She had *none* of that, though, after my father died—she was just out of everything. She wasn't plugged into the kind of social world that she'd expected and that she wanted; not in any way."

"Did she have friends?"

"Yes. Yes, she did. My mother is a very capable woman; but she didn't want to *use* that. She doesn't respect certain kinds of competence—at least, not in a woman. So she has trouble in understanding *me*. I wasn't right, somehow. I didn't dress in the superfeminine way that she wanted me to; I didn't behave or act in the ways that she considers right. The difficulty was in the ways my mother *dealt* with what she didn't approve of or like; she gets very heavy and severe. It would be this incredible *disdain* about my being the person that I was."

The punishments were sullenness, silence, and sarcasm. Her mother would, related Kath, conjure up images of a world that found the adolescent girl immoral and unacceptable—that disapproved of her in every way possible. "At that point, in reality, I'd had absolutely zero sexual interaction with *anyone*. But she was always imagining me as guilty of—God knows what! Every imaginable erotic vice and crime! She'd go on and on at me, saying things like: 'You've no respect for your mother. Look at you!—No decent boy is going to like you the way you are! Just imagine what people must be thinking of you—you are nothing but a disgrace!' . . . and so on, and so on, and so on.

"I'd try to answer," continued Kath, "by saying: 'I think my life is *fine*. I have friends who like me, and their families like me; I'm obviously doing well in school; I feel very *happy* with my life; my life is *fine!*'" She shook her head, from one side to the other, as if to say such protestations had simply never penetrated. "That was what it sounded like," she explained, "the typical beginning of a session. But she'd go on hammering at me about how everyone *scorned* my character and my behavior, and she'd bring in the guilt things like: 'What would your father say?' As if *he* would disapprove if he were alive!"

"Also," Kath went on, "she'd say: 'What would your grandmother think?', although the issues were always something innocuous: for instance, my getting in a half-hour late. Literally! This entire scene would result from nothing more than my having gotten in at midnight, rather than eleven-thirty, from a date!" Her expression was bitter. She unclasped the barrette holding her hair up in its long ponytail, let the hair fall loose around her shoulders and back. Then she combed through the long strands absently, with her long, white fingers. After that, she swept it all back, refastened the round amber comb holder around it. Her long, fine, soft hair remained as she'd arranged it, in place.

I thought, for some reason, of the beautiful ripening young maiden in the fairy story "Snow White." What could explain Kath's mother's rage and her harshness if it hadn't been for her own sense of being displaced? She was the older woman (the "evil queen") experiencing her own sexual power as diminished or gone while her daughter, the lovely innocent, was emerging into her own future—the assumption of her own sexual powers. In *this* version of the tale, the king (whose affections had been torn between them) was dead. Under the influence of her mother's spell, however, Kath remained (as had Snow White) "under glass" and in a seeming sleep until she was, eventually, wakened by the kiss of another. The pity for both women was that Kath's father—her mother's husband—had died at the height of their rivalry. They'd never, therefore, been able to resolve those unspoken, inarticulate, inchoate dilemmas about who was in fact the best, most lovely, most loving female—the fairest, in every sense of the word, of them all. Instead, they'd remained locked in a mutually confrontational, enraged and almost paranoid battle which could only end (so Kath believed) with her getting out of the situation entirely.

A Preliminary Person

When she'd gone off to college, at Berkeley, Kath Barrie felt "preliminary." She was uncertain, at that juncture, not only about who she was but about who she might ever become. "I'd almost bought my mother's stance towards a future life, in spite of everything. You know, you do well, and everybody will see you as a wonderful person —and as soon as possible, you get married. That kind of thing. I'd done my own part, done everything I was supposed to, up to this point, but it became a difficult time for me. I'd thought that just *getting away* from my mother would solve so many of my problems, would make so many things fall into perspective." She smiled, then, but the smile was rueful: "I was wrong, and it was a painful time, really. I was struggling with so much, all at once. Trying to define what I *wanted*. It was also a tricky time, the late nineteen sixties, in terms of social changes and radical movements; there was a lot of upheaval not only within but *around* me." Kath paused.

"Also," she paused again, "I became sexually involved with someone. The first man that I ever went to bed with—" She stopped: "Did you want to ask me something?"

"No. Yes. I mean, go on and talk a little about that."

"Oh." Her voice was offhand, casual, almost bland. "It was nice, in general. I felt good about it, happy. And we spent a lot of time with one another; we spent two years together." Her tone was, nevertheless, affectless and disinterested. "But during that time," she went on, "I think I was getting angry and annoyed, underneath. Because he and his friends—who were *my* friends too!—just weren't going anywhere. They didn't seem to be . . . well, I got the feeling that they weren't attempting to define themselves, or to—look for anything. I, to be honest, didn't know what it was that *I* wanted! But I just had the sense that this . . . this wasn't *it*."

"You had what you called your father's 'restlessness'? That urge to be *doing* something?" I smiled.

"Yes, exactly. That is very much *me*. So I spent a whole lot of time, those first couple of years in college, feeling bored. You'd sit around in the afternoons and nobody would *do* anything. They'd be smoking dope or going out to a party . . . and I'd often write papers for other people, just to alleviate my own boredom. Still, I didn't know what I wanted." Looking for something, anything, in which to immerse herself, Kath had taken up painting. But this, like love and school work, had failed to absorb her energies, to give any meaning to her being.

"I think this was a basic unhappiness," she could reflect, now, some years later, "though I would certainly not have articulated the feeling then." She had looked forward, so, to the escape from her mother; she had believed her own life would become so free, so magical! But it had turned out to be somewhat aimless and empty and drab. Getting away was—a disappointment.

Relationships as Mirrors

When had that first sexual relationship ended?

"It didn't end," recounted Kath wryly, "it simply dissolved." The reasons had to do with her restlessness and the general lack of intellectual stimulation coming to her from her partner. "He didn't have anywhere *near* the amount of direction that I had, so I would smolder with resentment. Instead of seeing him as being"—her tone of voice was equable and tolerant—"someone who was *different* from me. I kept pushing him to be more like me so that we—so that *I*—could be happier! But it wasn't, and couldn't *be*, that way."

She had just passed her twenty-first birthday. She was becoming, admitted Kath, interested in another man. She drew in a deep breath, like a swimmer who's touched one side of the pool after a lap and now must cross back over a very similar stretch of territory. "We decided to move in, and live together openly, this new person and I," she stated, adding: "That was *the end* as far as my mother and I were concerned. I mean to her it all meant: 'Oh my God, she's ruined!'—all that sort of thing. I was being very self-righteous about it all. I was deciding that I wasn't going to be hypocritical." She flushed slightly, seemed embarrassed. "Of course this was all a real stab in the back."

"Or at least," I agreed, with a nod of the head, "a way of telling her off."

Kath nodded: "I know. It was. I don't think I really did want to break relations, in the final sense; but there was a feeling of having to bring everything to a head. I had to make a statement about my being separate; that I was going to do what I wanted; that I was going to pay for the last year of my education. That whole year was so filled with anger and resentment towards her!" Her entire body, as she spoke, seemed charged with angry energy, with excitement. "At the same time," acknowledged Kath, "there was a whole lot of conflict. I felt so guilty, so sorry for her; she was so lonely." The very words she was uttering seemed to be having a deflating effect, for she leaned against the armchair at the end of that sentence, looking drained and soggy. "I kept wondering," she added, her voice dropping, "I kept thinking things like: 'Does it really have to *be* this way? Is it so because she doesn't like me?' All of these thoughts kept rolling around and around in my head."

She stopped speaking. We were, at that point, in the middle of our second interview. I leaned forward, met her eyes frankly, and asked her if she'd like some feedback. Kath said that she would. "Here, then, are a couple of things that I'm hearing," I told her. "You've talked about two long love affairs that you'd been involved in, by the time of your early twenties; and you've said that you even went to *live* with the second person for what was an extended period of time. But you've not once, ever, called him by *name!* Nor have I ever heard the name of the previous lover!" I hesitated, then asked: "Am I hearing correctly? Aren't you talking about your mother more than you are about either of these men?"

She reached back to pull at the back of her hair; she brought the brown-blond sheaf of the ponytail forward and began curling the ends with her fingers abstractedly. "Right," she admitted. She was silent then. "You're right." She was silent again. After a few moments, she commenced, in the slow voice of someone constructing her thoughts as she goes along: "I see both of those men as being somewhat—oh, just sort of instruments—in resolving the difficulties that I had with my mother. I mean, they certainly gave me things that came from their being the people that they were. But for me, I think, *both* those relationships were like mirrors in which I could see all the things that I had to work out. So that I could feel free in actuality—free to be involved with someone—" She stopped, looked at me, asked: "Does this, what I'm saying, make any sense to you?"

I nodded, and she continued.

The two love affairs, which had involved an acting out of her feelings about her mother (in terms of being the sexually "free" woman that her mother had so scornfully predicted) were followed by a phase of life in which Kath began to experience herself as someone different. "All of a sudden, I was turning inward. I stopped blaming my mother for everything and began trying to get a better view of who *I* was; aside you know, from the person who was *her* angry child. I had gotten, somewhere around this time, involved in some group therapy. I did it because I was feeling so oppressed—maybe, in a mildly depressed mood. In that group, I learned a lot of things about myself. That I'm somewhat lazy, and I have a way of putting things off; getting immobilized; and then blaming my mother for my feelings of unhappiness. So I awoke. I learned that if I really wanted to *do* things for myself, I would do them—but I didn't. It was at this point in my life—an incipient point of finding out who I wanted to be, in terms of finding a career—that I realized that I wanted to leave California and to go East. I made that decision; and it was as though, all of a sudden, *I* could take that responsibility. The funny thing was that I experienced this with very little sense of pressure. I knew I would find whatever it was that I was looking for. This just needed growing time.

"You know," she interrupted her own narrative to remark, "there was a real difference—a huge difference—between those 'career' and 'identity' issues that I worked through in that group-therapy experience; and between the massive depression that I went through last year. I just don't know how to phrase it, exactly; I don't know how to put it into words. I guess it was true that during the time when I was worrying about what I would do with myself I did feel, at times, paralyzed. I did feel down, low, and all of that; but that was . . . a general life dilemma. Underneath, somehow, I always knew that it was something I could work out—because the control was in *my* hands. Totally. I mean, ultimately I would go out and do what I needed to do! I would, at some point, realize what it was that I wanted and I'd figure out how to go about working on getting it. . . ." She halted, shook her head; the long ponytail flipped over her shoulder, disappeared behind her neck.

"Surely," said Kath, "there were 'issues' and I did get depressed at times. I'd realize how much I deceived myself about things—how much I didn't know about who I was or what I wanted—how much I let people *tell me* who I was and what I wanted. Still," Kath's voice had risen, so much that I began to feel concern about my noise-conscious office neighbor, "it was nothing—not remotely—like what I went through after the breakup with Philip. That was something that . . . I honestly believed, at times . . . I wasn't going to be able to survive. . . ."

Philip. It was the first man's name she had mentioned. I half smiled, leaned forward, and started to say so. But Kath wasn't in the mood for interruptions: "I really thought I might not get past that, when it all started happening," she continued urgently. "I lived for months in just *pain;* I thought I would never get out of it. And I'd never felt that way, ever—that something was so hopeless and beyond my power. That I was so . . . so unutterably depressed . . . so beyond any chance of redemption. That there was nothing that I, or anyone—including Philip himself, finally—would be able to *do*." A buzzer sounded, suddenly, in my office; we both jumped, looked at each other in amazement.

I explained to her, at once, that this meant that I had a phone call. The Center's system (which is directed toward protecting the resident Fellows) is to have no telephones in the studies, in order to lower the rate of disturbing interruptions. The call could be ignored if I didn't press an answering buzzer . . . which I didn't. But Kath, at that moment, rose and wandered up and down the small room aimlessly, as if to release some energy. She went and stood quietly, then, looking out the large plate-glass window, looking down upon the long row of Fellows' offices halfway down a pachysandra-covered hillside, directly below mine.

Had Kath Barrie, I wondered, never before felt helpless, hopeless, despairing—never felt that her life was totally out of control? What, then, had been her sense of things during the traumatic period surrounding her beloved father's sudden, almost unimaginable death?

Falling in Love

In a small book called *Secrets in the Family,* psychotherapists Lily Pincus and Dr. Christopher Dare have this to say about the transition from late adolescence into early adulthood: "Across the whole area of psychological choice, in life styles, attitudes, preferred role in relationships, leisure activity, political and religious affiliations, and so on, the . . . [burgeoning adult] . . . tries to find a match between his own self and the repertoire available in the real world. The actual range of choice depends on what society makes available to the individual within his background, at that time. But the particular mixture of styles a person finds himself adopting is his attempt to fulfill his needs for personality growth and self-enhancement. A job, a profession, a faith will be chosen partly because it is available; but also because *it fits the person's needs* [my italics]. In later adolescence, as in the remainder of life, relationships are entered into in order to give a sense of completion and fulfillment of the self. . . ." Who one chooses to become is, in short, a curious admixture of what the environment has to offer and what "feels right" or corresponds to one's profoundest inner expectations.

Insofar as the establishing of love-bonds is concerned, no one can quite locate or describe the complex array of conscious and unconscious wishes, of longings, fantasies, and desires that must be activated —must move into place—to produce that inner click, that "knowing," that recognition of the Other Person. What is involved is some deep knowledge of the appropriateness of a particular partner, though it's difficult to articulate just what makes that individual so special, so *right*. One just "knows," often with an overwhelming suddenness and intensity. There is that whole feeling of something within that fits and meshes with something within the Other—falling in love is a finding of the person whom, for some inexplicable reason, one belongs *with*. Few people, if any, can say why, and on what basis, a love choice has been made. The whole process of falling in love defies all objective and rational explanations. This is because the underlying explanations are, by and large, unconscious.

Yet, according to authors Lily Pincus and Christopher Dare, the choices are uncannily accurate. They seem to be made frequently "very quickly, on the basis of relatively little conscious knowledge, and with, as it turns out, great . . . complementarity and fit of personalities." To put the whole thing very simply, the woman who yearns, albeit unconsciously, to know great suffering in a love relationship will be precise and unwavering in her ability to select the man—or procession of men—who will know best about how to be uncaring, and how to inflict cruelty and pain. We all, observe Dr. Pincus and Dare, "have a tendency to get into repetitive patterns of relationships that are motivated by the persistence of wishes in unconscious fantasy form. . . . Sometimes, in marriage, the repetitive aspect of sequences of partnership is remarkably literal, as when a woman whose childhood was damaged by her father's alcoholism finds herself marrying a man who turns out to be an alcoholic,* divorces him and then gets into the same situation once more. . . ." Falling in love involves an intertwining of past and present needs, desires, and fears. The explanations dip into the most primitive parts of a person's past and of her or his deepest being.

Needless to say, these observations extend to nonmarried as well as married partners. They surely are at play in long and intensive relationships, such as the one which flowered between Kath Barrie and her lover and "roommate," Philip.

The Making of Commitments

She went to Boston almost by chance. The decision had been to go East, but she could really have gone anywhere. She had, however, a friend who was living there; and, two years after her graduation, the friend invited her to come for an extended visit. Within weeks, she'd found an interesting job, doing research for a psychologist; and she'd met The Man. "I started seeing Philip very shortly after my arrival," said Kath. "He was, or is, a musician. He was, at that point, very seriously playing classical piano. Like, eight hours a day . . . he was *serious*. I saw that—that in itself—as something terrific. He was very motivated, very self-disciplined; he knew what he wanted. Great. Also, he had the kind of background that I could appreciate. He'd gone to Harvard; he was very intellectual; and yet he was also very sensitive. Very much attuned to women's issues and well, the sorts of problems that we face."

"Such as . . . ?"

She shrugged. "Such as trying to fit ourselves into society . . . he was a very sensitive man."

"How old?"

"My age exactly. Philip was twenty-four, almost twenty-five." A shadow of gloom seemed to come over her; she slumped down in her chair.

"Was he working as a musician or was he studying?" I asked, as much to keep energy in our conversation as for any other reason.

"He was just working part time to support himself. Doing odds and ends; painting, that kind of thing." She shifted in her chair, sat upright, then said with a sudden spurt of vivacity: "The relationship was, in the beginning, extremely passionate. Tremendously *alive*.

* See Chapter Eighteen.

Well, I don't mean it was that way only in the beginning—even to this day there's a great deal of passion that still exists between us. But we are"—she pursed her lips in an unreadable little grimace—"no longer *involved*." It was the first time ever, she added, that she'd truly loved a man; and yet realized that they couldn't get along on a daily basis at all.

"We couldn't live together well, though we *did* live together. Ah, well, you see. . . ." Whatever Kath had started out to say ended in a sigh.

When she spoke again, it was in a tone of exploration, as if she was unsure, each time she began to phrase a thought, where and to what the thought might be going to take her. "I was more mature, in many ways, than Philip was," she said uncertainly. "It was as if I had, in some way, a stronger sense of who I was . . . and this was, I think, threatening to him. So he would push me away and be rejecting. And yet . . . I always understood. I understood this, and didn't drag him into long hassles about it; I was pretty tolerant. I think I'd already learned something about understanding where the other person was: *not* to want him to be just like me and *not* to insist on him being some-one other than he was . . . I'd learned these things. With Philip, though, it was the first time; the first time I ever became that involved. And yet it didn't work out. I *knew*, almost at once, that it wouldn't work—" Her eyes swung to meet mine directly, and she gave me an almost pleading look. "I wonder if all this sounds contradictory? Or if I'm even making any sense?" I was thinking, as she said these last sentences about Kath's efforts to "change" her man. Her mother had done this with her father all the time—and she, as a young girl, had taken note, and disapproved.

She wanted feedback from me. "Let me tell you," I answered, "what I hear you as saying. That you were more deeply in love, and more empathetic, and more giving and willing to understand the 'otherness' of the other person than you ever had been before. That, even so, the relationship failed—as you said you *knew it was going to do*. But tell me," I asked, "what it was that actually caused the whole thing to sour?"

"Oh. I realized that Philip was, in no way, ready for a commitment. And I knew, knew with a certain intensity—even a pressure—that I *did* want that. Not in the sense that I wanted to get married," she amended immediately, "but what I wanted was just more of a feeling of commitment in the tangible, everyday ways. That he would be there for me. That he would give me more than I was getting."

I shook my head: "I'm not sure I understand." Kath gazed at me blankly. "I mean," I explained, "tell me what you're saying in terms of an example."

"It's—hard. Philip is very obdurate, very stubborn. When he gets too close, he gets scared too. And instead of just saying: 'I need to be alone' or 'I need a little space' he withdraws himself emotionally, in a very cold way. I did understand this to a point—but beyond that point, I didn't care whether I understood it or not! I just wanted him to be more receptive to me; and I knew, at the same time, that it wasn't only me: what I wanted of him—he simply couldn't do it. He hadn't enough of himself to *spare*. No matter whom he'd fallen in love with he'd never be able to give . . . at least, not at that particular time of his life. His focus, his energies, were going elsewhere. And I was feeling that, and hurting. I was really wanting that 'more.' . . ."

A smile flitted wanly across her features: "I still haven't," she acknowledged, "given you your example."

We sat quietly for a few minutes. "Oh," she said, then, leaning forward, folding her hands in her lap. "Well, here's a pretty concrete one. This happened after we'd stopped living together, but were still seeing each other fairly frequently. I got flu, and Philip came over—he was going to take care of me, he said. He was wonderful that first day, but on the second, he'd simply had enough. I wanted him to go out and get me some ginger ale; but he'd had it. He simply didn't want to *do* any more! So I ended up having to go out myself, with this temperature, this 104 degree temperature, to get it . . . because he'd had enough. This kind of thing—I couldn't even comprehend it! It drove me crazy. . . ."

Telling that story had stirred other memories. "Even *before* that," she swept on, with scarcely a pause, "when we were living together, social interactions were always very difficult. Philip *demanded*, always, that he be the center of attention; he got impatient when other people began talking about themselves. He couldn't stand it. He was very powerful, too. For one thing, he's six feet six inches, a very big man; so he takes up space, and he took over easily. I always felt *angry* about that. He could be so juvenile, I mean, in the way he had to have everybody's attention. Why couldn't the two of us be together at a party, you know? And just be, well, two of the people in the room?"

"You mean," I asked, "that Philip, somehow, took up all the air?"

"Yes. That's just what he did. So . . . often . . . after we'd gone to see some friends, I'd be *mad*. And he'd be mad about my being mad—he'd see it as an attack on who he was. He thought it was something ridiculous on my part. I mean, who did I think *I* was to constrain and control how *he* should be? He wouldn't let himself get to the point of seeing it . . . that maybe there was something I was trying to say. It was all Hands Off. And Philip, even today, would describe himself as a person who holds himself and those around him quite securely. As someone who opens and closes a door *into* himself, and who controls whether you get in or not. There's no *way* you could just open the door and reach in to him! So there's a closed-off quality about him; only he can open the gate and let you in. And yet," Kath added, with a burst of feeling, "once that way in was open, there was such—such —I had never before experienced a man who was so emotional and so open with his feelings!" She gave a small hitch of the shoulders. "But to *get* that door open. . . ." She nodded her head in the negative, denoting the enormous difficulty of the task. "He controlled the hinge," I suggested.

"Yes." It was not, she added with a hurt look on her face, always worth the struggle to wrench it open: "But in a sense," Kath allowed, "it was always *there*, that way in; and it was always tantalizing."

There were scenes and quarrels after practically every party they went to. "I would say: 'It drives me crazy the way you always have to take over everybody's attention. Why can't the two of us just *be* in the room together? Why do you always have to be the star?' He had a way of detaching . . . he gave me this feeling that it was very threatening to him to just be in a room and say straight out: 'I'm with her.' I felt that; and I wanted him to do that, to acknowledge me. But it was as if he really couldn't make that statement." Kath, remembering, frowned.

"He was always free," I said, but the statement came out as a question.

"He was," she replied. "And it wasn't as if he'd ever flirt with anyone! It was just that he'd ignore me, even though he didn't pursue anyone else. He'd sort of draw attention by proclaiming his presence, but he was always subtly dissociating himself from me. He didn't want me to join any group he was in: not eating dinner; not even in just conversation. If I *did* try to anyhow, I'd find myself disconnected —line cut off, you know—there would be no remarks whatsoever directed at me. So I'd feel shut out, or worse yet, invisible. As if I were someone who wasn't quite *there*." Her voice was angry.

"I'd say to him, afterwards," she continued, "that I couldn't understand why he did this. I'd say: 'Why can't we be in the same place as partners? Because that's what we are, in reality, isn't it?' His response was always that we *were* and we knew it . . . so why did we need to make a big public show?"

The couple's quarrel was a quarrel about the degree of commitment that each was putting into the relationship.

A Matter of Timing

Kath had been, in each of the vignettes that she'd set before me, speaking of her own felt needs for more caring from Philip; more concern on his part, more recognition. He was countering that he *did* have a serious commitment; but the messages being acted out behaviorally were surely confusingly otherwise. For the manner in which he excluded her in those public situations indicated that he did have certain reservations—he either wouldn't, or couldn't present himself as a man who'd made a strong emotional commitment to a special other. At least, not at that moment in time.

Time itself was, as became clear, an issue—in terms of the time of life in which Kath found herself—and Philip found himself—at that phase of their mutual existence. The young partners, troubled and troubling to each other, went to consult a couples therapist. The "timing" issues stood out at once very starkly. "The therapy was helpful," recounted Kath, "in the sense that what these issues were became blatant. Philip was just not ready to make a commitment, not at that point in his life, and I was very ready to make one! My demands weren't, as he'd thought, 'neurotic'! Nor were they all that unreasonable. It certainly wasn't that I was insisting on marriage; I was just ready for, and *wanting*, more of a commitment." She inhaled deeply, let out the breath slowly.

"Certain problems came right into focus, then," she went on. "Philip had, for instance, always said that he had to accomplish 'certain things'—that he had to 'grow up' before he became committed to me. So with the therapist's aid I got him to actually spell out what those things *were* . . . and they were just outrageous. He'd say things like: 'I have to have twenty thousand dollars in the bank,' or 'I have to be successful in what I'm doing, in my musical career.' Things like that. Which made it clear to me that it would take at least another *ten years!*" She was indignant.

"But you realize," I interrupted her, "that what he's saying is: 'I will make a commitment at some point; but I have to prove, first, that I'm a man.'"

"I do realize that," she agreed. "And he said it too, very candidly. He said that he didn't feel he could commit himself to me until he had a sense of security about who he was . . . until he had a sense of his own manhood. He'd say to me, in *tears*, 'I have to do this, I have to grow up.'" Her voice was high with suffering; she stood up again, began pacing up and down the small room.

"What *you* were saying," I remarked, "was: 'I need to be a woman who has a man who loves her and is committed to her.' And what *he* was saying to you was: 'I need to be a *man* before I can make that commitment.'"

She stopped, folded her arms across her chest, stood there staring and yet not quite seeing me: "I know"—she was moved, and her voice cracked in midsentence—"and it was sad . . . very sad. . . . I said to him once that I knew that that was what he needed, to feel like a man. I said: 'But I always *do* see you as a man; I always see beyond the fact that you've got some growing, here and there, to do. What you give me is something so powerful and so wonderful—I could put up with this, if you could learn to accept it.' But *his* answer was: 'I can't.' . . ."

What had been clarified in couples therapy had been the nature of the impasse. It was a deadlock. Philip, wanting her to accept the provisional nature of the commitment that he *could* make, being where he was in his own life. Kath unable to do so, for her own psychological inner clock had been blaring out alarms to the effect that she was overdue, late for something else; that this wasn't the relationship that she needed and wanted. The age of thirty, which she perceived as a kind of watershed, was no longer so far off in the distance.

The upshot had been a decision to part ways—with what Kath called a "loving understanding." It was a decision that was, in one sense, inevitable; and yet, in another, had been almost too excruciating to put into action. "I wanted the split, but God, it was just horrible. The whole thing was *horrible*. Because much as I wanted it, I didn't want to lose him. And we'd cry a lot, and we were angry. I guess I'd thought, when we began therapy, that I did love him and it would all be worked out. But then it became apparent that it *wouldn't*—there was no *way* that Philip was going to get through ten years of future time in a month! So it was very painful. I didn't know what to do. I lived for months in *just pain*. I've never experienced anything like it. I'd never before in my life gotten to such a condition; and I thought I'd never get *out*. There wasn't a day that I didn't cry and feel horrible about it—about the whole thing." She came back to her chair, flung herself down.

"What were you doing, at this time, during the days? Still working?"

Kath shook her head: "No, that research job had ended; and I was only doing a little teaching part time, in a private high school. But I'd already decided to go into medicine and was applying to Penn, Yale, Stanford, and some other places, for the following year. I was taking courses . . . biology, calculus, and so forth."

I smiled: "How were you finding time to cry?"

"Oh, I'd cry anywhere. In the car, driving to school; anywhere. Sometimes even during the lectures . . . I'd just sit there weeping. I was half cockeyed because I was sleeping badly, and I'd stopped eating too. But I still did well in my courses." She grinned wryly. "Not as well as I'd done before, but *quite* well. I was always an exceptionally dedicated student!" We both laughed.

The separation had not been accomplished with a single, cleanly amputating rupture. It had been punctuated by attempts at patching: by doomed efforts at getting together once again. "Philip could think about trying once more as soon as we were apart; but when we did, he simply couldn't handle it. In a way, the hardest thing *I* had to handle was the realization that what I experienced as his coolness or meanness wasn't directed at me personally. He wasn't trying to hurt me, but he couldn't *live* with it. He couldn't be intimate; not on a day-to-day basis, not at that point in his life. I knew he loved me. But he couldn't carry it out, integrate it *into* himself, make it part of who he was." Each try at making it work, however, left Kath feeling more drained and powerless.

She'd been leaning hard on two women friends, and they were becoming alarmed. They'd brought her, almost by bodily force, to the Walk-In Neuropsychiatric Service at Massachusetts General Hospital, one evening at 10 P.M. She'd been weeping, and was making vaguely suicidal statements; they'd been afraid to go home and leave her alone. "This on-again, off-again state of affairs with Philip had been dragging on for months, by then. The people I was talking to were getting really afraid for me"—she smiled suddenly—"and I think I'd also exhausted their patience. At any rate, I got some psychotherapy at that point; and that helped me, gave me strength, to get and to keep the whole thing ended." She sighed, nevertheless.

I was thinking about Philip; Philip the unattainable. The yearned-for person who loved her deeply and truly but who could not—Kath herself had used the phrase—"follow through." I thought, too, about the father who'd been so idolized and beloved and who had died when she was thirteen. He, like Philip, had been serious, devoted to his work . . . somewhat out of reach.

"Kath, I'm going to ask you something that may sound as if it's coming out of left field," I ventured, breaking the silence. "Did you ever make a correlation between the not-ever-quite-havable Philip and your lost father?"

She nodded her head in the affirmative: "I could have told you that even before Philip and I split up. Though not in so many words, perhaps. What I mean is that I both knew it and I didn't know it . . . that somehow, in my relationship with Philip I was working on *that*. I believe I realized this, in some deep way, from the very first minutes onward."

"And now you're in medical school. And the relationship's over. You live in California, and he lives back East. And you're doing well, in general. Do you feel that you have pretty much worked the problem through?"

"I don't know," she responded uncertainly. "I still find myself attracted to this same sort of man. The one who's not quite in reach, the one who's unattainable. Unattainable for some outside reason, or simply unattainable emotionally. I recognize this as a problem, you know. A situation that I'm attracted to or that, for some reason, I find myself in over and over again." She paused: "I am, at this moment, involved with a man who's very giving and loving, but I don't think the problem is worked through . . . because I find it almost impossible to take as much as he's willing to give me. And I know that I am, somewhere deep inside me, on the lookout; still looking for that *other* kind of man. . . ."

It was as though she were, in some profound sense, still courting the suffering love that she'd experienced in that traumatic thirteen-year-old situation where the beloved man, who could not "follow through" suddenly became totally unhavable and unreachable—because he was dead.

Kath was talking, now, about Philip, whom she'd run into at the San Francisco airport a few weeks earlier. He had been short and rude. She'd asked him how things were going; and he'd behaved as though she were prying. He wasn't getting good feedback from the world, insofar as she knew; in terms of making a career, the things he wanted didn't seem to be happening. "We won't ever be friends until it does happen," she said sadly. "We won't, as well as we really know one another, even be able to run into one another in that way and have a normal conversation."

She still found him, obviously, a moving and disturbing person. I asked Kath if she believed he would change, be someone different ten years hence—since she'd suggested that a ten-year developmental gap was the major reason for their separation.

"I don't know, at this point. I'd say perhaps not," she responded. "On the other hand, I know how important the expression of his creativity *is* to him. And if that works out, and he does succeed, he may well be a different person." Her voice was hopeful momentarily, but then she added: "I don't really know," in a tone of doubt. She shrugged.

We were, at that time, reaching the end of our third interview. Kath had spoken fairly extensively about five different men, throughout the course of these talks—including the man who was her lover at this moment—but had referred to only two of them by their names. Kath had mentioned her father's name (Paul) occasionally; and of course, that of Philip.

Orphaned: Or, On Loss in Childhood

I think we can accept as one of the human givens that no one completes the long, complex journey from earliest infancy to young adulthood without having experienced some degree of trauma. Painful experiences and emotional dilemmas appear in the ongoing log of every individual childhood; they are a part of the developmental trip. Individual responses to hurtful events will, clearly, vary widely. The consequences of a traumatic occurrence, in terms of long-term aftereffects, will depend on a host of factors: the suddenness of the happening, the vulnerability of the individual, the quality of the emotional supports that are available . . . to name a few. This is a restatement of a point made earlier, in that "flu" analogy: which is to say that the ultimate impact of a stressful or threatening event will have to do with the interaction between the intensity of the distress itself, and the organism's capacities to cope and general state of health *at that time.*

No matter how benign a particular individual's childhood circumstances may have been, however—and no matter how inherently (constitutionally) psychologically strong she or he may be—there is surely no one who reaches the shores of maturity without having taken on a freightload of unresolved issues. Normally, part of the burst of activity seen in late adolescence and early adulthood is to some degree an acting out of such issues—an attempt to resolve them in the environment and in real life. This endeavor to gain mastery over one's world, and to carry out the emotional repairs that need making, may seem to have nothing to do with the left-behind world of our infancy. Yet many of the decisions taken—to point only to the top of the iceberg, underneath which lies a whole range of ideas, preferences, tastes, views of the self, ambitions, desires, dreams, and so forth—are linked, in the deepest and most intense manner, to the unsolved dilemmas we have brought with us out of childhood.

In the choice of a mate, a profession, a way of living, we may be (all obscured though the knowledge is to ourselves) working on one of these themes: i.e., seeking salve for an unresolved, untreated psychic wound. As Freud noted, in one of his final essays, one of the common ways of dealing with the aftereffects of a painful trauma is to arrange one's life in such a way that one "happens" to get into situations that repeat or re-enact the original event. The individual makes it happen again, in the same way that it *once did happen*, in an effort to gain a sense of control over whatever it was that once left one so injured and conflicted—or perhaps, totally defeated.

By thus staging a revival (or a series of repetitive revivals) of a set of circumstances once perceived as overwhelming and intolerable, one gets to play out—in the world of reality—some sequence of events that reality (real life) once had thrust upon *one's self*. The whole attempt has to do with restaging the too-dangerous-for-bearing scenario and then reassuring one's self that now one cannot be overwhelmed; one is in charge. The problem is, however, that—as in Kath Barrie's instance—the poignantly similar situation may end up in a devastatingly similar loss. The severed relationship with her beloved father, who'd been symbolized in the person of the "creative," "hard-working" (and overidealized) person of Philip, had been severed a second time . . . with the same desperate grief, mourning, and melancholia. It is believed, by many experts, that the loss of a parent in childhood may lead to an increased vulnerability to depression in adult life. Kath had, certainly, responded to the loss of a lover as if to an unquenchable, unresolvable grief.

The similarities between the two men—their high seriousness; their dedication to life tasks that consumed a good deal of their energies—were notable and striking. Both men were so invested in their work that there was, about them, a drawing back, a remoteness, a distance. Both were described as loving her deeply (when she'd secured their attention); but always that bit out of reach. Ultimately, both were unattainable; and both had to depart. Fathers *are*, obviously, unattainable; but Kath's charged relationship with her own father had been terminated with such abruptness—she'd never had an opportunity to achieve the ending on her own terms, and in reality.

An ending for Philip and herself had been, in truth, fore-ordained from the start. "I knew it wouldn't work," she'd told me, at the very outset of our discussion of that love affair. "I knew that right from the beginning." Had this been a part of her unconscious plan? Had this, in itself, been an important part of the psychic package that Kath herself was most interested in purchasing? Philip was, in the thinnest of disguises, such a stand-in for another half-human and half-fantasy hero:

that other person whom she'd loved and felt such a special closeness to; and who'd made that agonizing departure from her life. Philip was to be longed for, yearned for, suffered over—the never-havable, impossible man.

Kath's father had died, as we know, at the very height of that normal thirteen-year-old passionate girlish attraction—her history was special in this very terrible sense.

But a period of pining for the Impossible Man is not very special at all. As child analyst Dr. Albert Solnit of Yale observed to me, in one of our conversations, a phase of yearning for the man-one-can't-have is a frequent feature of late adolescent and early adult feminine development. "Often," Solnit explained, "this romantically idealized person is slightly older—a friend of the family, or an uncle, or a teacher. There is, about him, that somewhat forbidden, cross-generational quality. One feels guilty about fantasizing about this rather inappropriate relative or friend . . . who may be, in point of fact, an age-peer of one's own father."

Such a figure is, suggested Dr. Solnit, merely a slightly camouflaged and somewhat removed representation of the father. "If you were to ask the young woman, though, in what ways that idealized person *differs* from her father, she'd be able to draw a very definite distinction. She'd say: 'What, my *father?* Why, my father's nothing *like* him! My dad looks much older than Joe does, and he's not half as intelligent!' and so forth. Nevertheless, there's a coalescing of the daughter's feelings, a sense of chemistry in this whole crush, that makes for the charged nature of the fantasy and for the sexual excitement."

The archetype of the unconsummated love affair is the daughter's love for the father; and in adolescence, the relationship with that inaccessible and unattainable figure is, with pain and tremendous conflict, usually worked through. The daughter ultimately renounces her male parent and moves to a field that is freed of his presence, and is of her own choice and making.

In Kath's case, however, the slow achievement of this inner independence was interrupted—by the sudden, shocking event that was her father's death. It had happened, that life-changing upheaval, at a time when the three of them (mother, father, child) were experiencing great tensions; when they were all aglow with inner heat and ill-concealed explosive energies. Kath had felt "particularly close" to her father during this period; she'd felt that only she sincerely cared for him (not her mother, who was only interested in material things).

The thirteen-year-old girl was, at that phase, clearly experiencing an upsurge of attraction for her father—as well as guilt, feelings of competition, and the desire to take her envied rival's place. In the midst of this, her father *died!* And it was in the wake of this disastrous loss that the daughter's rage became directed against her non-grieving, "non-caring" mother. (Her mother may have been, in fact, making an effort not to burden her child with her own grief.)

But only *she*, the young girl felt, had really understood and really mourned for her father. (Much later in her life, she was to set herself the task of "understanding Philip.") The catastrophic loss of her father, happening when it *did* happen, thus left the daughter emotionally stranded. She was caught in the middle of a developmental task—a task which is quite complicated even in the absence of a major trauma of this sort—and in the care of a mother who was, herself, feeling disappointed and deprived. Envious, too, perhaps . . . for Kath was at the brink of an adult life in which she would find a sexual partner; someone to love, of her own. Kath had a future.

Her father's death had marked, for both daughter and mother, a definitive rupturing of their own relationship. For the child, it was the loss—not of one—but of both parents. It was the end of her experience of being protected, beloved, nurtured, cared for; she had twisted away, out of her mother's grasp, out of any further need for her. They'd been unable to grieve, to cope, to adapt to a new life together. At thirteen, Kath had taught herself to become sufficient unto herself.

In essence, emotionally speaking, she was orphaned.

Choosing

Did she ever feel, I asked Kath Barrie at the close of our final interview, that if she did commit herself to someone—and that "someone" committed himself to her—that he would then be in danger of dying?

She responded, with a blush: "Oh yes . . . somewhere, deep down . . . there's a deep fear of that."

I looked at her, hesitated, then asked another question: "So in a way your real safety lies in your emotional relationships *not* working out?"

She nodded. "I also think," she replied, "that many women see their careers as . . . oh . . . way to come out and express themselves. I don't. I never have had a doubt that I could do well those ways: I think that for *me* a career is, if anything, a way to avoid how much I need to work on fears about becoming really involved. Terrible feelings that it won't, that it can't *possibly*, ever work out. For me, a career is a way of not facing and confronting those things. As long as I can throw myself into what I'm doing I don't have to *look* at that. . . ."

I stared at her, astonished. "O.K. then," I said, "I'm going to ask you one last question. Suppose I were God and I told you that I would give you a choice of two wishes for what would happen to you in all the years of your future life? Suppose I said to you: 'You can have either rich and flowering success in your career as a physician *or* you can have rich and flowering success in your emotional development?'" I smiled: "Which would you take?"

Kath laughed: "Emotional development."

But she became serious immediately: "I don't mean that only in the sense of developing some wonderful relationship with a man. But what I'm saying is that I think if I were emotionally developed, whether or not I had a career would really not be a big issue for me. I'd be able to accept and know what I was, and wasn't, getting; what I needed to do, and what not. For me, at this point, working is a way of fulfilling a great need in myself. But I see my emotional development, and learning how to love and be loved as a far *harder*, a really much more difficult task than just succeeding at job things *ever* is for me."

In Early Adulthood: The Twenties

Let us draw back from Kath Barrie at this juncture and think of her particular stage of life—the time of the twenties—in ways that are far more general. What, at least in an approximate sense, is this period of life all about? Among other things, it is about the subsiding (in some cases, the aftertremors) of the cataclysms of adolescence.

When, at the close of adolescence, the emotional tumult and confusion of the separation-process has, relatively speaking, begun to clear, the novice adult's personality and character are recognized as altered. It is as though an inner terrain has undergone shift and change—in some instances, complete transformation. Individuation, or the work of becoming the individual that is "me alone" is now under way. There is a feeling, at this phase of living, of a certain existential territory, or boundary of the self, having been (albeit roughly) marked out.

The erstwhile child, if the frightening changes of adolescence have been weathered adequately, has now emerged as a young adult man or woman. And the great change, from dependent youth to mature individual—whether it's occurred with catastrophic, dramatic upheavals or merely with a series of seismic, personality-shifting shudders—has left the person in a somewhat steadier, more integrated state. I don't mean to suggest, for a moment, that the new adult is without dilemmas and difficulties of her or his own. Many deeply felt problems, as well as the inevitable wounds accompanying separation from the care-giving guardians, are encountered and experienced at this time. There is, nonetheless, a certain freeing up of what can best be described as psychic energy or psychological investment—those parts of the self that were absorbed in the powerful relationships with the parents (initially, I mean; and then later involved in the painful process of psychic emancipation *from* them). The ego, the "I" is now transcendent. Young adulthood is the time for making one's way (*my* way) in the outside world.

Gone, by and large, is the adolescent's old, playful, child's sense of limitless possibility. Gone, too, childish beliefs that events are reversible: that if one career or love commitment (made, for eternity, two weeks ago) doesn't seem worth honoring, there will be an endless assortment of possibilities to be explored. Fantasies about potential futures—"If I don't become a musician, I may be a scientist, or marry a rich businessman, or become a ballerina, football player, eminent novelist," etc.—are less believable and satisfying, for they're now subject to the cold blasts of the truths of the actual world. The child's grandiosity and belief in her or his own omnipotence—a belief grounded in an identification with the all-potent-seeming parents—has shrunk to reality's size. Unbounded fantasies about the great prospects that will come into view when one is a "big person" are dissipating or have dissipated. Both the inner world and the outer world seem to have much more definitive and recognizable borders. There is, at this period of living, the dawning realization that one is simply the very human, nonmagical individual that one is (which brings with it those fearful intimations of one's own eventual death).

Events are now hurrying one forward into one's future. It is not only that sense of inner pressure—of an internal biological clock seeming to urge one ahead, to be saying that "It's time now, time to move on" . . . though there *is* this sense. It is the environment itself which seems, as well, to be expectant, to pushing one ahead into a bewildering and yet continually narrowing succession of choices. Will I go on to college; and if I do, what shall I plan to be or do afterward? Will I be accepted? Can I handle the demands? Or should I look for a job immediately? What about money (and remaining dependent on my parents)? After college, will I work immediately, or try to go on for further training? . . . Who pays? . . . And afterward, what then?

Should I be establishing a relationship with a special person? And if I do succeed in doing so, what other things will I be missing? Who am I, deep down, and what is my best way of living and being? Oughtn't I to be utterly and completely free, while young, to explore many different sexual possibilities and partners? Won't this, though, give me feelings of terrible insecurity—that come from no one in particular really *caring?* . . . The questions, and the range of possible answers to them, are endless.

There is, too, a new sense that *wrong* choices carry consequences. For time itself has lost its superabundant, endless quality—it's not got that childhood sense of being something that will go on forever. Time is upon one, and it is time to get moving and to get on with one's tasks. To accomplish and to prove just who one is—not only to the world but to oneself.

This whole testing out of the environment, and testing out of oneself *in* the environment, is obviously a tricky, confusing, and even terrifying process. This is true for both newly adult male and newly adult female; but for the female, faced with changes in the society around her, it's doubly confusing, doubly complicated. For, opinions and views about the person she's expected to be, given that she *is* female, are themselves in a process of flux and change. The confusion within her is mirrored by the vast confusion *without*. And, as she searches her world for appropriate signals, she picks up no orderly broadcasts about reasonable futures that may be part of her considerations. What she picks up are very differing sorts of signals: *some* in direct opposition to each other! a buzzing, raucous blitz of confusion.

The usual early-adult dilemmas about what one may do and who one may be are, for *her*, compounded by those doggedly feminine worries about what is wanted *of her* and what things she can do that will be pleasing to *those she cares about*. She may look around her for the answers; but the answers that come are in a Babel of differing tongues, demands, opinions, points of view. Clear answers about what a woman should be, and the optimal way to live her woman's life, are not beamed to her in the relatively less problematic ways that they are beamed to the young man.

How, really, can a young adult female optimize her chances of happiness? Ought she to marry? And if she does marry, ought she to have children? We are living, at this moment, in the first period of human history in which women have been able to take control of their reproductive potential; and this blessing of science, which has brought new female options and possibilities into being, has also brought a host of new dilemmas along with it. I have, for example, interviewed women whose spouses were strongly insistent on a rational decision *against* having a child. They themselves supported the choice, for a host of sensible reasons, and yet they'd had to be active in suppressing powerful aspects of their female selves. It was, as they acknowledged, a problem that kept getting settled but never *felt* completely settled. For the old childhood fantasies, born out of the relationship with and the identification with one's own mother, spurs the woman on to want to play out the maternal role herself. It seemed to cost a lot, in many cases, to counter these powerful, archaic, primitive, deeply experienced feelings. Some women, having defined themselves as "not maternal" at an earlier point in their lives, were having trouble (usually at the close of the twenties, or in the early thirties) defending those choices to themselves.

Unfinished Business

The years of the twenties are, in essence, a time of self-definition, a time of myriad choosings. The choices that one makes during this period of life can be as mundane as whether or not to wear cosmetics and as life-shaping as whether or not to continue one's studies, pursue a specialized kind of training, set a serious career-goal—or whether to marry. An individual is faced in this decade with an awesome new responsibility; that of taking charge of and caring for the self. The commitments that one makes begin to *feel* increasingly serious.

By this I mean that commitments aren't only more serious in the outer-world sense (i.e., because one will be forced to make good on them). They have a new meaning, internally, too. In one's love relationships and in one's career-objective-setting, the time of the early twenties has involved a delimiting process, a focusing down. There is a sense of playing out some final hands—a new degree of earnestness, of dead seriousness about one's next moves (even if a woman's goal is that of finding her man and marrying him). As Dr. Peter Blos, the great theorist of the adolescent process has observed: "The heir of adolescence is the self."

The task of early adulthood—the twenties—involves, then, figuring out what to do with it!

The latter years of adolescence have, too, meant not only the resolution of some earlier problems but the eruption of some new ones. In truth, as Blos and others have suggested, we never *do* fully resolve the terrible conflicts that are so intrinsic to the separation process. Nor do we, in our heart of hearts, fully succeed in renouncing the deliciously guilty, forbidden attraction to the opposite-sex parent.† The resolution of these core adolescent issues and tasks is, writes Dr. Blos, "at best partial. The part which resisted adolescent resolution becomes the core of a continued effort toward this end; it proceeds within the confines of personal choices such as work, values, loyalties, love." In other words, those concerns, guilts, conflicts, issues, anxieties, which were not worked through and resolved during the adolescent period, are the very issues and concerns that we will (in one disguised form or another) be attempting to master throughout the rest of our lives.

But now, the efforts will be turned outward from the family. We will be working these matters out in the world.

"My Place" in the World

There is of course no cut-and-dried, clearly observable divider between the latter-adolescent and the early-adult life periods. At late adolescence there has been, generally speaking, a honing-down process, an effort directed at formulating what Blos calls "goals definable as life's tasks." Other analysts have referred to this variously. Some have called it the forming of the "vision of one's self in the future."

Dr. Daniel Levinson of Yale, who has been studying personality change during adulthood, has termed this future-life-oriented task-setting as construction of The Dream. The work of early adulthood involves the attempt to implement this vision, with whatever tools of possibility become available in the environment. It is a time of looking for new roles, new relationships, of fashioning a new milieu that *is of one's own choosing*. The ego, beyond the period of greatest pain about the separation from parents, is experienced as stronger; and it becomes absorbed, increasingly, by efforts to make real whatever aspects of the vision may be *made* real. The serious business of creating "my place" in the adult world is now under way.

The newly emerged self of the early twenties can, nevertheless, be compared to a relatively recent geological formation. It is patently there, and has its own contours and outline; it has its dimensions, height, circumference, and breadth. Still, it is subject to underground shudders and tremblings; it is newly formed and not settled; it can still shift in its shape and its structure. It may still experience great af-

† As Erik Erikson notes, in *Identity, Youth and Crisis*, "the 'incestuous' attachment to parent images cannot be considered as necessarily pathogenic. . . . On the contrary, such a choice (i.e., finding a partner who resembles the parent) . . . is part of an ethnic mechanism in that it creates a continuity between the family one grew up in and the family one establishes. It thus perpetuates tradition. . . ."

tershocks. For, whether or not the adolescent transformation has been perceived as a time of earth-shaking alterations, it has—as earthquakes do—involved the release of accumulated strains and pressures at the very core of one's being. It has involved a surging upward of the potent love, guilt, hate, ambivalence that were bound up, contained, in the passionate infantile attachment.

And the psychic separation from our first loves costs us dearly in terms of suffering and of pain. It offers, at the same time, liberation—into new places, new loves, new ways of being of our own. Parting destroys, changes utterly; and, in the same act, makes everything possible. Still, the character formation of the new adult is shaky; or, let us say, provisional.

Early Adulthood, His and Hers

One of the best descriptions of personality change during the young-adult phase is that which has been given by Yale psychologist Daniel Levinson. Unfortunately, the fascinating study carried out by Levinson and his co-workers limited their subjects to males only. Their subjects (who were all between the ages of forty-five and fifty-five) were interviewed intensively, in order to tease out these men's shifting awareness of themselves—and themselves in their worlds—and their inner needs and outer needs—as experienced across the course of time. There has been no such systematic effort to look at what happens to *females* as they pass beyond the teen years, into the twenties, thirties, forties, and beyond. But the Levinson research offers us a standard for useful comparison, in terms of what young men are about during the years of entry into adulthood. The work of this life phase is (for males) fairly straightforward, suggest the researchers.

For the male in his twenties is, generally speaking, engaged in the construction of what Levinson et al. called an "initial life structure." He is busily constructing a home base of his own in the world . . . albeit with a certain withholding of complete self-commitment. At this point, there's a sense that whatever he's building may turn out to be provisional, a "let's wait and see how this actually turns out" kind of feeling. The early-adult period commences with a time of searching, of exploration of the environment, of seeking out of those materials appropriate to the particular man's tasks and his goals. It is a time of scanning the horizon of realizable possibilities—work situations, career options—for paths that will lead him toward the living out of his future-oriented vision, his Dream.

In the course of this searching-out process (which will lead, eventually, to an initial life structure founded upon a small assortment of made commitments), the young adult male will usually find mentors, or one important mentor, along the way. This mentor—that is, an older, experienced, and protective friend who will serve as guide-cum-father figure—will facilitate the younger man's entrance into the serious business of the adult world. The intriguing thing about mentors is that more youthful males find them with such predictable regularity! The younger man will be, then, searching his world for where he can fit in, and for an important "mentoring" patron and friend. He will also be looking around at the women he knows, and, at some level, seeking for The Woman. That special woman who will be his partner and companion in the life-making enterprise in which he's become so engrossed.

This outline, the Levinson outline, is a reasonable account of what happens to most men—and what most men are doing—in the decade between ages twenty and thirty. It has a relative consistency and orderliness. Certainly, individuals will vary in terms of who makes which type of commitment during this period; but this is a pretty good approximate description of the norm. There tends to be a traceable progression from exploration in work and love to commitment in work and love—a style and way of being in the world that contains a movement from A to B to C. That is, in short, coherent.

And what of females during this same life phase? Personality researcher Dr. Wendy Ann Stewart, whose Columbia University thesis was entitled "A Psychosocial Study of the Formation of the Early Adult Life Structure in Women," tried to carry out a Levinson-style study using subjects who were female (Stewart was Levinson's student at the time). The life directions of the women interviewed were, however, a good deal less linear. A woman, during the time of her twenties, seemed to do much more shifting, changing of course, and turning about! In fact, as Dr. Stewart told me, it was difficult even *attempting* to do a systematic study of feminine development during this decade: "Women's lives don't seem to stand still long enough for one to run a good controlled investigation of what may be happening to them psychologically," she acknowledged.

Their lives are far less neat and predictable. "If," observed Stewart, "your subject is in law school and seriously pursuing her studies, there's not any guarantee that she won't decide that the whole competitive, kill-or-be-killed atmosphere is destroying her, changing her as a human being, and as a person, in ways that she finds totally intolerable. The next thing you know she may have moved off in a totally different direction. Or she may have fallen in love and gone somewhere distant with a lover or a new husband—the 'all for love' gamble is something men aren't asked to make, and probably *wouldn't*. Or, she wants a child." Stewart smiled and shrugged: "The point is that she doesn't *have* to achieve out there in the marketplace in the same win-or-lose, do-or-die way that a man does."

Women do have a far wider latitude of possible options (which certainly adds to the confusion about being-for-oneself in contrast to the more traditional female way of being-for-others). What is more, a woman who's committed herself to a particular kind of existence—for example, the marriage and motherhood roles—may not want to go on living in those particular ways. She may, after a time of living out this vision of herself, find that she's moving away from a loving-nurturant-submissive mental set. She still retains the option to return to the world of school or work, just as she had the socially acceptable option of leaving it in the first place. Of course she will, in the meantime, have fallen behind in the career-advancement race—and done so in a way that her male partner, who never did have the same options, clearly *won't* have done. Women have, in other words, more ways of being in the world than do men. As psychologist Stewart noted in her thesis, there was a tendency among women who'd committed themselves to the traditional maternal role early in life (i.e., from age eighteen throughout the early twenties) to want to find their way back to the world and the marketplace sometime in the late twenties or in the early thirties. They were restive by then; and wanted to discover suppressed and only dimly realized parts of the self—to get in touch with other things; with their competitive, assertive, aggressive, "masculine" strivings. But doing so, at this point in their lives, was something they were finding far from easy. The path back into the world of work was blocked, for many reasons; or difficult; or just not readily discoverable.

Most of the women who, on the other hand, had worked on establishing themselves in their careers during their early twenties—and whose career objectives had taken precedence over all *other* goals—began to drift in the opposite direction, toward the close of the twenties and in the early thirties. Noted Stewart, in her doctoral thesis: ". . . even women who attempt to follow a male career development pattern in their twenties feel the need to come to terms with the traditional feminine identity issues of wifehood and motherhood . . . in both a quantitatively and qualitatively different way than is true for men."

The career-oriented women, by the time they'd reached a certain internal turning point around the age of thirty, were suddenly dropping out of the work force: Stewart's "career" subjects were (with one exception) plunging themselves into marriage and motherhood with astonishing and complete absorption. It was as if, she wrote, they were "finally acknowledging that this is what they really wanted to be

doing all along. . . . While they might have been afraid of only succeeding as women rather than as persons as they perceived their
mothers had done, it was probably more terrifying to consider the
possibility of *not* succeeding as women. . . ."

These subjects, although having clearly demonstrated their competence in the adult occupational world, described themselves as "feeling
like children" until they'd become wives and mothers. It was as
though they felt they hadn't yet fulfilled the *real* tasks of mature
womanhood, i.e., marrying and having children of their own.

The Search for a Mentor

One of the most curious findings to emerge from Stewart's research
was that relating to the female's search for a mentor. Apparently,
among women who marry and establish their families during the early
twenties, this friend-parent-guide relationship simply isn't sought out.
While a mentor was of *crucial* significance to the young adult male
setting out to make his way in the world, this figure simply had no
significance for the marriage- and motherhood-oriented woman. It
was *her own mother*, primarily, who functioned as her model of "how
to be" in the adult world.

In terms of this young woman's Dream, or adolescent fantasy of the
future, it had usually been about the happiness of the love relations she
would one day establish. The playing out of this vision, in her early
adult years, thus required no teacher-peer figure. Her behavior could
be something approximate to what her mother's had been (with, of
course, her own improvements added). She perceived herself as the
traditionally supportive, facilitating woman: her investment was in
the *relationships* with her husband and children. Rather than working
out and elaborating a Dream that was her own, she assisted her partner
in *his* elaboration of his own Dream, his destiny; that vision-of-him-
self-in-the-future that he was struggling to make real and true.

Less traditionally oriented young females—i.e., those who were pursuing serious career objectives during the time of the twenties—*did* establish strong relationships with slightly older, more experienced,
mentoring figures. And in this way, noted Wendy Stewart, their behavior throughout this decade of life was indistinguishable from that
of the forward-spurring, ambitious, young adult male. Dedicated career women looked, at this phase of their lives, generally similar to
dedicated career men. But at the close of the twenties, observed Dr.
Stewart, women who "have not married or had children . . . (were
experiencing) . . . an increased sense of urgency to do so." At this

point, practically all of the women in her sample‡ had dropped out of the occupational marketplace; it was as if they'd felt that their biological time, in terms of maternity, was in serious danger of running out.

The women in the Stewart study were all in their thirties at the time of the interviews. They had for the most part, it appeared to me, worked out starkly either-or kinds of solutions. *Either* they had chosen the broad, well-traveled, familiar highway to becoming a mature, adult female, i.e., marriage and motherhood, *or* they had, to quote Stewart, "deviated from the traditional female pattern" by postponing or repudiating these tasks in favor of a sustained and very serious career commitment. No matter which way they'd gone, however, the decade of the thirties had found most of them moving in a completely opposite direction.

Women who'd initially made the traditional moves were now looking for ways of being in the world that were more individualized, more their *own*. That is, they were trying to develop a new Dream, one that didn't just support *his* Dream, his vision of his future; but had more to do with their own "becoming" . . . the development of their own inner selves. This shift in her subjects' priorities was one that, acknowledged Dr. Stewart, she found some difficulty in interpreting. There was a good deal of pain around issues of mistakes having been made and opportunities having been overlooked during the more open-ended time of the twenties. But, wrote the researcher, it wasn't clear whether this turnabout in terms of goals, wishes, desires, preferences, etc., was "indicative of chronic confusion or of a developmental transition." The subjects in the Stewart study who'd sailed directly into marriage and motherhood seemed to be struggling with feelings of: "O.K., this has been accomplished; what's next?" It was as though, in some way, they'd been awakening from the earlier Dream . . . and they were still slightly disoriented and confused.

The women who had careers were, as mentioned earlier, shifting their priorities in the diametrically opposite direction. But they seemed, in general, to be a far more contented lot—almost like young girls exploring the delights of playing house. As Stewart remarks, these subjects, in their descriptions of their husbands, children, lives, homes, neighborhoods, exude an air of relief and discovery, as if saying: "This is it, what I wanted, after all. . . ." They had already demonstrated their competence in the occupational marketplace to their own satisfaction; a few of these women had, in fact, advanced very *far* before making the decision to drop out. (I wondered, on perusing Stewart's thesis, how those subjects would view themselves and their lives if one talked to them ten years hence?)

‡ Eleven women were intensively interviewed in the Stewart research; forty men were in the Levinson sample.

Only *one* of the women who took part in the Stewart study had followed a path analogous to the path taken by men in their twenties. That is, she'd worked on developing a sustained career commitment (a vocational identity) and then—once that task was under way—set about the establishment of intimate bonds, i.e., the tasks of marrying and parenting. For males, the choices relating to working and loving are worked out almost simultaneously but doing both these things in tandem is more problematic and difficult for females. As Stewart observed: "In order to integrate a family and a career, a woman requires a highly supportive interpersonal environment, greater than average personal ambition, the ability to thrive on the complexity and challenge of sequentially ordering two major priorities as becomes necessary without sacrificing either. . . ."

It's a tall order. What appeared to happen, at least to the subjects in her sample, was that the woman—confronted by two major life tasks simultaneously, each of which implied a commitment to certain ways of being—felt compelled to come down on one side or the other. She made a choice. (And by the time of the thirties, she was busily reassessing it.)

The Emergence of Identity

The hallmark of the early-adult epoch of the life cycle is the emergence of identity. It is the coming into being of that sense of self—that which Erik Erikson has described as a *"subjective sense* of an *invigorating sameness* and *continuity."* This new sense of self is there, but it is still shaky. It is rather like the small child's newfound ability to walk upright in the way big humans do, for it is experienced with both victory and huge uncertainty. Practice, and a period of possession, are required before these capacities will feel truly natural; unselfconsciously a part of one's repertoire.

The young adult has "become"; but in a somewhat unclear, unproven, undecided manner. Something yet remains of the child's malleability—and *more* so for young women than for men.

Waiting

This brings me back to the issue, raised earlier (see Chapter Three) of women's strong tendencies to find their sources of self-esteem in the context of intimate relationships. As Wendy Stewart observes, in the concluding section of her valuable thesis, "the Dreams that women form tend to have a strong *relational* component, whereas the Dreams of the men in Levinson's sample were more *individualistic*." If this is the case, in general, then it would follow that the young adult female, on the brink of her adult life, would withhold some aspects of her self and her personality in a "to be completed" state.

For if her Dream must be fulfilled in relation to *him* and *his* Dream then she must await meeting him, and forming an intimate bond with him, before she develops as the person whose ways of being are congruent with those of the beloved partner. If she unites herself (whether in marriage or in a nonlegal but long and important sexual relationship) with a man who is a high school teacher—or lawyer—or electrician—or businessman—or actor, chef, accountant, etc., she will, as a matter of course and of exposure to his occupational community, be influenced to develop those tastes, preferences, ways of existence that make sense in his world (and are supportive of his Dream for the future). Her personality, and very identity, will differentiate and develop in the directions that make most sense in the life structure that her mate is constructing.

The newly matured female, verging on the brink of adulthood and dreaming vaguely bliss-filled dreams of loving union with an as-yet-undiscovered-Other, is thus—and in some profound sense—often waiting to become a fully formed person, to find a way of living and being, *through* that relationship. Perhaps it is this that gives to so many young adult women's lives that zigzagging, haphazard, unpredictable quality. They are remaining pliable.

A sense of very firm ego boundaries, of knowing who one is and what one wants and where one is going, can be a relative disadvantage when it comes right down to the difficult—yet critically important—life business of establishing a love-bond. As psychologists Judith Bardwick and Elizabeth Douvan have written (in an article entitled "Ambivalence: The Socialization of Women") females "use interpersonal success as a route to self-esteem because that is how they have defined their major life task. If they fail to establish a meaningful, rewarding, unambivalent love relationship, they remain cued into the responses of others and suffer from a fragile or vulnerable sense of self."

It is only *after* a woman has achieved security and a sense of worthfulness in her love relations, suggest Bardwick and Douvan, that she is released from her "unendingly anxious" feelings about her personal value. It is only when she's achieved security in an ongoing emotional attachment that she becomes truly internally liberated—able to pursue nontypical, nontraditional, competitive, "masculine" kinds of goals without a great deal of guilt and fear and ambivalence.

And, to turn that same statement around, the unattached female who *does* venture into serious competition with her male peers, often finds herself (or is made to feel as if she is) endangering her eligibility and acceptance as an attractive, feminine person. She must be prepared to accept the consequent flak about her "femininity" . . . which can be horribly wounding. (See Chapter Thirteen and Dr. Terri Funabashi's experience, as an example.)

This dilemma, pointed out explicitly over thirty years ago by sociologist Mirra Komarovsky, is as alive today—and as problematical—as ever. For there are, as Komarovsky shrewdly pointed out, serious contradictions between the two role prescriptions, or modes of being-and-behaving, that her environment demands of the educated, career-oriented woman. One is the role behavior of the feminine "womanly" woman and the other the role behavior of the competitive, assertive go-getter. "The goals set by each role are mutually exclusive and the fundamental personality traits each evokes are at points diametrically opposed," noted Komarovsky. So *much* so that "what are assets for one becomes liabilities of the other, and the full realization of one role threatens defeat in the other."

Young adult females who are, as was that one subject in the Stewart study, trying to develop themselves in *both work and love simultaneously*, are also having to develop two differing kinds of selves simultaneously. In her intimate life, as she relates to her opposite sex partner, this young woman is expected to be someone warm and emotional, nurturant, expressive, noncompetitive, supportive, more compliant, and so forth. (Otherwise, she's "castrating," a "ball-cutter," or, worse yet, "unfeminine.") The built-in conflict, however, and the ambivalent sets of signals with which she must deal, stems from the fact that in her occupational world she'll have to show much more of the typically masculine forms of behavior—self-assertion, competitiveness, control, dominance, a push toward mastery (including mastery over men). The ambitious woman seems to be required, both by inward and outward pressures, to evolve not a single "self" or personality, but two at once!

Little wonder, then, that so many talented women experience a disjointed sense of being tied to two horses about to gallop off in entirely opposite directions! Little wonder, as well, that a goodly number finally choose to disconnect themselves from one or the other of these role options . . . with the idea, feasible or not, that it will be better to return to the career race later on, when other life issues have been settled.

For men, of course, the sexual and occupational role behaviors are far more comfortably synonymous. In both working and loving men are *expected* to be more assertive, aggressive, masterful, and so forth. The shape their lives take, throughout the course of adulthood, reflects this lack of ambivalence; this strain between two very different ways of being. Their psychological development, across time, is more linear, more in the shape of an orderly progression.

It is this progression that Erik Erikson has described in his remarkable *Childhood and Society.* Young human adults, suggests Erikson, move from the crisis that he terms "Identity vs. Role Diffusion"—that is, the finding of one's role in one's society, so that one's society sends back confirming feedback about *who one is*—to the crisis that he terms "Intimacy vs. Isolation." The young adult, writes Erikson, *"emerging from the search for and the insistence on identity* [my italics] is eager and willing to fuse his identity with that of others. He is ready for intimacy, that is, the capacity to commit himself to concrete affiliations and partnerships and to develop the ethical strength to abide by such commitments, even though they may call for significant sacrifices and compromises." Very true—if by "human beings" we mean "men!" Women's life patterns, and the ways in which they go about the business of "becoming," are not by any means so tidy and methodical.

Women's lives, if you look at them over time, rarely follow a straight line from "identity" to "intimacy" and so forth. On the contrary, their unfolding selfhood seems to occur in cycles, or phases, rather than in a movement forward, or in a single direction. If you look at where a woman has been, and what her major goals have been in different ten-year segments of her life, you'll often find sudden discontinuities, surprises—and frequently astonishing ingenuity and invention! There's far more shifting of direction, of moving off in a new way to make up for time lost, and of returning, later in life, to goals and preoccupations that have been abandoned earlier, in a way that might have seemed final then. There is by no means that undeviating male progression from "identity" to "intimacy" to "generativity" (which is "primarily the concern in establishing and guiding the next generation") that Erik Erikson has so tellingly described.

Many of the female subjects in the Stewart study had, for example, taken these developmental tasks of adulthood in a very different sort of order! A goodly subset of these women had worked on issues relating to intimacy in the years of the twenties; and never become concerned about the problems of autonomous identity until much later on! As Drs. Carol Gilligan and Malkah Notman have noted, in an article entitled "Woman's Place in Man's Life-Cycle," Erikson's schema presents *male* psychological development as the norm for psychological development during adulthood. Female psychological development, seen against such a standard, is deviant. For development, in the two sexes, often proceeds in fundamentally differing ways.

"While for men, identity precedes intimacy and generativity in the optimal cycle of human separation and attachment, for women these tasks seem fused," write psychiatrists Gilligan and Notman. "Intimacy precedes or rather goes along with identity, for the feminine self develops as it is known through relationships with others."

Kath Barrie was, as has been seen, very ready to accept an intimate commitment to her lover Philip and to leave those questions—that nagging unfinished business—relating to vocational identity off to one side, until some time later. For Philip, however, this was something absolutely impossible to do. He couldn't permit himself an attachment of this kind, a tie to which he'd committed himself with a great measure of inner finality, before establishing himself in his place in the world—before he'd "become a man." This meant not only finding an occupational role and filling that space in his society; but having his identity *in* that place and role confirmed by the world around him. His adult identity had to go before the making of serious, inwardly binding emotional commitments. First things first; this is the way it had to be.

For Kath, his behavior wasn't entirely comprehensible. For they were a good couple, weren't they? Why couldn't he understand that he was, in her eyes, a man *already?* They were both shouting into the wind; and neither could quite hear the other. For she, in drawing close to the age of thirty, was experiencing inner pressures; the wish for emotional commitment had become transformed into the *need*.

Philip was, however, experiencing the pressure to "become someone"; for him, there was that necessity to do things in their order. He could not say "I am yours" to anyone before saying, to his own satisfaction "I *am*"—and the greater part of this task, was, in fact, still ahead of him. Their dilemma was, as they'd both realized, truly unresolvable.

So they'd parted, with a "loving understanding." But for Kath that parting had pulled away the scab of an older grief, a grief that was of the distant past. She'd grieved then, for almost a full year, not only for the lover that she'd *just* lost; but for the loss experienced much earlier, when she'd been just turning thirteen. In mourning Philip she'd mourned her desperately loved, never relinquished father.

CHAPTER EIGHT

Mood and Medicine: Judith (1)

It's Not Me; It's My Biochemistry

Later, when she was well again, Judith Karlin could point to nothing special in her life, no marvelous happening that might have triggered that bizarre euphoria. The only real "event" she could link it to was a letter she'd received in April, sent to her by a friend living out in California, Frank. Judith had gotten to know Frank the year before: they'd been colleagues, teachers in the drama department at one of the state university campuses. They'd become professional collaborators as well. They were at work on a screenplay, still half finished, but to be completed the following summer. There had never been, as Judith recounted wonderingly, anything remotely romantic about their relationship: "I'd never even found Frank particularly attractive," she shrugged. But now, his letter seemed to her to be invested with intensely personal references, with erotic double meanings, with sentimental innuendos. Judith found herself fantasying about her former colleague: she became, too, preoccupied by the importance, the creative magnitude of the drama they were writing together. Still, she has never believed that it was Frank's letter alone that "caused" her manic attack: "I don't think I'd ever have fastened on him *or* on the manuscript in those ways," she told me, "if I hadn't already been getting crazy at the time his letter arrived."

During late April and throughout May, the screenplay assumed a more and more mystical, an almost religious significance. If Judith found herself unable to sleep, if her thoughts were "continually racing," then the creation of this momentous work was the reason, the justification. But in a way, as she pointed out, when one's mood state is in the process of a remorseless upward spiral such as the one she was experiencing, events in one's life simply *do* feed into it. "Your mind is like a vacuum cleaner," she explained, "and you just suck everything that happens right up into your system."

Her own "manic" system, she continued, in her somewhat breathy voice, had to do, always, with some project that was going to make her extraordinarily famous. "It's a very ambitious thing—like the screenplay. It's going to make me successful, rich; I'm going to win an Academy Award. And I'll be catapulted into another, a kind of a dream life. I'll move into the upper echelons of, oh, worldly and intellectual accomplishment. And not only that, the fantasy—which becomes overpowering—always involves some kind of a crush. Some sort of unattainable man, as Frank really was (being no more interested in *me* than I was in him), who is involved with the big enterprise and who is a friend. I don't know why," she added thoughtfully, "but the person I fasten on has to be a real one; and one with whom I have a professional involvement. But it isn't a person I really am *sleeping* with! . . ." Judith shot me a puzzled look; I merely cocked my head to one side, said nothing, shrugged.

She went on then to explain that the long episode of elation—beginning that April and escalating steadily upward until her trip to California in June—had been experienced as some sort of psychological culmination. "Somehow," she said, her voice throbbing with a natural aliveness and intensity, "becoming manic is like that. It's a coming together of my psyche, my soul, and my life, in a particular work project. It's always involved with writing, but it's *more* than that. More than success, or sex, or love, or self-knowledge alone: it's all of them! The quintessence, although I haven't got words in which to communicate what it feels like, of the quest for understanding of myself."

Slowly, but nevertheless ineluctably, as the weeks of springtime passed, she found herself increasingly alone and isolated. There was no one, not a single friend, who was capable of sharing the tremendously important thing that was happening to her and was "pulling together everything in my life." She could not think about anything other than the cataclysmic significance of the screenplay that she and Frank were preparing. "It was impossible to sleep, eat, to listen to anything that another person was *talking* about! Because what was occurring in my own head had taken on such symbolic significance—and was so mystical, so transcendent, so profoundly religious. . . ." She had no patience with the more prosaic concerns of lesser mortals and became, as she put it, "terrifically irritable." She was losing some measure of meaningful contact with those about her. "One has the sense of being in the midst of this great drama that is going on. And there's a feeling of being inspired, so that one simply cannot be crossed. You can call people jerks whom you couldn't call jerks before. You can say things that *hurt* a lot of your friends, too." Judith paled slightly, and then her skin grew flushed: "That's what I am always sorriest about. That I said damaging things, or did them: did things that made no sense, if I imagine the point of view of those around me. I have had three manic episodes. And in each case, I've spoiled a lot of my relationships."

Judith reached over to a modern, clear-plastic end table and picked up a pack of cigarettes. We were sitting in her Boston apartment, both of us comfortable in slacks and sweaters. It was hard to imagine her as actually embroiled in the situation that she went on to describe.

But clearly, by June, the young film historian—Judith Karlin is in her late twenties, and is quite tall, dark-haired, exotic-looking—was aware that something was a bit wrong with her. "I felt very—precarious; very 'hyper'; very much as though I were on an internal overdrive, going a mile a minute." Boarding the plane for San Francisco, nevertheless, she remembers a feeling that she was "striving hard to avoid facing that knowledge."

The trivial tasks relating to her departure—getting tickets stamped, luggage weighed—had had to be carried out as carefully as a walk on a tightrope. She was tense and hyperexcited, felt she might go out of control. At the same time, every casual conversation—with a clerk, with a waitress—seemed astoundingly insightful, amazing. The world about her was filled with a magical vividness: even the colors of things looked different. "It was like being Dorothy in *The Wizard of Oz*," smiled Judith, lighting her cigarette. "The world, once black and white, had turned to the most vibrant, the most pulsating Technicolor!" She laughed, blew out some smoke, seemed excited by the memory.

She had wafted onto the aircraft on a cloud of fantasies. She and Frank would finish the play this summer, would achieve extraordinary fame, wealth; they would be incredibly happy together. But the mood of joy was peaking; it was fraying at the edges, turning sour. Perhaps it was due to her imminent confrontation with reality (in terms of actually *seeing* Frank) that Judith found herself, during the air journey, feeling more and more disorganized, disoriented; getting downright scared. The stewardess, for instance, seemed to have responded to her quite strangely. "I was sitting by myself, smiling, feeling very happy. And I remember stopping her, as she went down the aisle, and asking the name of the movie. It was something like *Countdown* or *Showdown*; I can't quite remember. But this had, for some unknown reason, great resonance. This was a code word, and it fit right in. I started giggling, you know, as if we were in cahoots of some kind; and I looked at her archly as if to say: 'Right on.' She, of course, found it all strange; she had said the name of the movie, and not anything funny." By the time she reached California, Judith added, she was very likely no longer sane.

When she arrived at the San Francisco airport, Frank was waiting there to greet her. She had called him, before leaving Boston, asking him for this favor: to be there, and to drive her to Santa Cruz, where she'd be staying with their mutual friend, another ex-colleague, Gloria. But on their way out to Gloria's, Frank found himself befuddled by Judith's rapid, incoherent way of speaking. He couldn't follow the sense or meaning of what she was saying: "He later told me that he thought it was just that I talked too fast. Or that he didn't truly remember what I was like. He had not, you know, seen me for a whole year. Or he thought it might be because he himself was stupid, or tired, or it was his fault—the fact that he couldn't follow my meaning. I guess it didn't occur to him, until Gloria took him aside, that there was anything wrong with *me!* I do, though, recall some of our conversation; and I know I was being incoherent. I'd refer to long talks we'd had in my head. And Frank was just very bland and cool; he'd simply nod, keep agreeing. I believe he probably assumed I was referring to something that he'd forgotten—oh, God, it's so embarrassing to think about it!" She jammed her cigarette into a ceramic ashtray, ran a nervous hand through her straight dark hair.

Once they reached Gloria's apartment, however, that shrewd woman—some ten years Judith's senior and twelve years older than Frank—recognized at once that something was terribly wrong. "She told me that I wasn't mentally well, and that I had to call a doctor. But I refused. I felt marvelous: I was an absolutely classic case. And this has been true each time in the three manic episodes I've had now. I've felt marvelous, floating, so beyond any human needs or desire for help! 'Why do I need a psychiatrist?' You know. 'I am writing, and I am wonderful and I am inspired by God—if I am not God myself.'" In the course of the next several days, nevertheless, the sense of confusion and of not being sure what was real and happening outside her head—and what was purely mental, and only happening within—continued to grow.

Before a full week had passed, she was being terrorized by "messages" that were being received over Gloria's very ordinary Sony radio. They were warnings, she recounted now with a recoiling movement of her body that was either a tremor or a shudder, of an impending holocaust. "It all had to do with a huge revolution being touched off, and a war between the leftists and the rightists. And no one else knew about it; God was telling me, in a special language, that only *I* could understand. And everyone I was close to would die, and I would die, and I would not be able to get in touch with my parents. Lord, sheer absolute *fear!*" She shook her head, smiled in self-deprecation. She had believed the bomb was being dropped when they took her to the hospital.

This was the second in a series of three episodes of mood-affecting illness. The first was a small one, a "mini" elation; it had taken place a year earlier. The subsequent one was a severe, life-shattering manic outburst that had ended in a second hospitalization. But all three of these attacks had left devastating consequences, both in Judith's career and in her personal life. "I was transformed, somehow, when I went up and when I went down too, as I did, though not quite as horribly. My perceptions changed; the world around me seemed to have changed; it was like—well, like being possessed. I know, now, that in reality, the *world* was no different and the way I saw things was in my imagining. But oh, the things I did and the things I said! I remember, later on, trying to patch things up and going around saying to people: 'I'm sorry, I'm sorry, I'm sorry. . . .' But in some cases, there is no being sorry enough. And some relationships—well, they will never come right again." She sighed, reached for a glass of Tab that sat close by her. "It's hard to ever get anyone to realize that you've just been responding to the crazy, distorted world that *you've* been living in. . . ."

Judith, now maintained on the drug lithium carbonate, has been attack-free for the past several years (and she is now thirty-four). She wishes, she says, that she had known earlier what she knows now: "Which is that my disturbed moods are *physical* in origin." No amount of psychotherapy has ever, in her opinion, been useful in either preventing or dealing with an attack. Lithium not only controls but prevents episodes. If the "cure" is chemical then, she believes, what is being cured must be along the lines of some biological abnormality. "It really has nothing to do with 'psychological issues' or what's going on in my life at the time that it happens," remarked Judith, and then she added quickly: "It's not *me*, you know; it's my biochemistry."

But this intellectual resolution of the problem—this understanding—is not one that she finds totally comfortable. It lacks what Judith once termed "human sense." "What I have been told—and it's scary to think in that human or psychological way—is that I cannot deal with stress. And I don't like to see myself as someone who can't, for some reason, *deal* with life's ordinary stresses. . . ." She threw her arms wide, as if to say: "What can one do?" Then she shrugged. "The biological explanation, though—that's the end of free will, of a sense that one's in control of one's own life. You hate to think of your soul being captive to your hormones and to the chemicals in your brain!"

Biochemistry and Mood

Is it, in fact, the case that our mood states do correspond to differing biochemical conditions in the brain? Is there such a thing as a physiology of "normal" mood—and a disturbed physiology that underlies abnormal states of mood, such as extended euphorias and extended periods of depression? A personal history such as Judith's argues for the truth of this assumption—and so, of course, does the existence of the many mood-altering drugs now on the market. For if we can (and obviously we *can*) bring about emotional changes by means of medications, then moods must clearly have some physical basis. Otherwise, how could drugs be effective in relieving despair, countering anxiety, and calming mania . . . as they so clearly are?

If the psychoactive drug revolution has made anything clear, it is that changes in the biochemical functioning of the brain are able to bring about mysterious changes in the strictly mental sphere— profound changes in the way a person thinks, feels, perceives her or his world. In Judith's case, lithium carbonate could not only dampen that wild upward mood swing; it could also, it seemed, maintain ongoing control of an inner emotional thermostat. But how, and why, did this happen? What particular brain mechanisms might be involved? The search for answers to questions such as these has in fact absorbed many wise heads in the scientific community. A widespread effort has been under way to discover just what, inside the head, the mood drugs act upon—and just why, precisely, they do work.

A Particular Carburetor Mix

The past ten to fifteen years have actually witnessed an explosion of research into the disorders of emotional state. And an accumulation of scientific evidence now suggests that a particular class of biologically active substances—the *biogenic amines*—may be central to the regulation and maintaining of our moods. These delicate chemical compounds (most important are *norepinephrine* and *serotonin*) are present at certain critical receptor sites in the brain. They are most highly concentrated in neural areas associated with such basic drives as hunger, sex, and thirst. And they seem to be there in a crucial balance, or mix.

That mix might, as one researcher has suggested, be likened to a particular carburetor mix. And what is most decisive for the maintenance of normal mood could well be the balance, the proportions, in which these compounds exist in relation to one another. Too much of one or more of them, active at nerve-cell synapses, may correlate with spiraling mania: too little of one or more of them may create the physical conditions for the experience of acute despair. What the mood-changing drugs might actually be doing, when they bring about what are frequently miraculous results, is reversing an imbalance that has somehow occurred in this complex biochemical system.

The Basic Adaptive Posture

The inner, physiological portrait of a mood disorder is, as described earlier, that of a loss of biological orderliness, of equilibrium. Every organ system in the entire body is affected, including the endocrines, the cerebrovascular system, etc. Sleep patterns; appetite; sexual behavior: all show a marked shift and change. It is as if the organism's homeostatic mechanisms—which normally act to keep the individual in a state of self-regulated balance—have been overwhelmed. But why, when one thinks about it, *do* moods normally run their course and end? Why was it that one acquaintance of mine, having won a National Book Award, was back to his usual state of functioning after a brief, week-long spate of mild euphoria . . . while Judith, subjected to the much milder happy stress of having gotten that letter from Frank, had reacted with a pleasure that had passed to euphoria and finally ended in mania?

During one of our long conversations, I put this question to Dr. Peter Whybrow of Dartmouth Medical School. He raised an eyebrow, shrugged, and said: "The fact that someone's become elated or depressed doesn't *necessarily* mean that an event has 'caused' it; that 'something' has happened. What that elation or depression actually does denote is the absence of some normal self-balancing, homeostatic mechanism. Because one has the impression that whatever counteracting, inhibiting forces there are that ought to be coming into play to end the mood have failed . . . and the mood has continued to grow, unchecked."

That "imbalance," suggested the psychiatrist, probably involves a failure within one or more of the electrochemical mechanisms of the brain's intricate energy system. This renders the system unable to restore its own balance, to return itself to Go, to a central resting mood that is neither too joyous nor inappropriately sad. Long periods of elation, such as Judith had experienced throughout that entire spring; and long moods of depression as well, are deviations from what is the steady state (the mood that is neither way up nor way down) of the organism. And of course it is the steady state that, when one thinks about it, is the basic adaptive posture. In other words, if one is too happy by half, one can't respond to real problems or difficulties in one's life; they are just shut out of consciousness. And, if one is acutely miserable, one is often so without energy and so sure that nothing will make any difference anyhow, that one cannot bring oneself to take care of the ordinary business of Being.

But when a person is in that central mood, she or he is in a position for moving in either direction—for responding realistically and adaptively to the things that are really going on in the environment. Our mood state might, in short, be likened to the ball on the end of a pendulum. When the mood swings out toward the happiness sphere, there's a natural pull, like the force on a pendulum, that brings it back into the central position. Similarly, in states of grief and sorrow, the same thing occurs: a natural thrust, a force, that returns the mood state to a middle range on the emotional spectrum. Obviously, when the ball is in the center, there's maximum adaptive capacity, in terms of being ready to respond—if something good happens, one can move toward the joy direction. If something bad happens, one can move toward the sadness direction. But the further out the mood swings in either direction, the less adaptive is the entire system.

No one has, at the present moment, a biochemical explanation for why moods run their course. According to Whybrow, the reason why they don't normally ascend to enormous heights or fall to great depths—and the reason why they tend to fluctuate within certain well-defined limits—is that the system is a self-regulating one. The underlying regulatory mechanisms have, though, not been teased out. Researchers haven't yet been able to identify what Dr. Whybrow called "the predominant variable, the most potent chemical factor, the King." The current thinking is, he said, that there is no lone chemical substance that correlates with, or underlies states of emotion. "There is, very probably," he observed, "some balance of several brain amines which control the final complexity of behavior."

"*Mood Juices*" *in the Brain?*

Of the known biogenic amines, the ones most studied—and those which appear to be most implicated in mood state—are norepinephrine and serotonin. Norepinephrine is the substance released by nerve cells in the brain when a person takes amphetamines and gets "high." For this compound is somehow related to arousal, alertness, euphoria—and to mania. Serotonin seems, on the other hand, to have something to do with states of drowsiness, with falling asleep (it has been referred to as "sleep juice").

The continual movement of neural impulses into and out of the brain, which goes on as we think, feel, respond, etc., is routinely accompanied by the release of these compounds (which convey information across the gap from one nerve cell to the next). As the "message" is passed along by a neuron, a few drops of the powerful substance are literally squirted out of the root branches of the nerve cell into a synapse . . . which is the tiny gap between two neurons. The biogenic amines are both "manufactured" and stored—in tiny sacs or vesicles—within the nerve cells themselves.

The notion that the biogenic amines might have something to do with states of mood was first seriously entertained in the early 1950s. Doctors had already noticed that the drug reserpine, used in the treatment of high blood pressure, sometimes brought about severe depression as a side effect (as it did, it will be remembered, in the case of editor Lucy Harris). Research on animals revealed that the drug acted to bring about a drop in brain levels of serotonin. Animals being given reserpine excreted unusually large amounts of the chemicals deriving from the metabolic breakdown of serotonin. Also, their brain tissues —examined later—showed a profound diminution in serotonin stores.

This struck some people as a curious finding. Was it possible that depression was caused by reserpine's serotonin-depleting action? It was the first suggestion that the biogenic amines were linked, in some way, to states of mood.

Not long afterward, some new and supportive evidence turned up. A drug being used in the treatment of tuberculosis—iproniazid— seemed to have particularly *euphoriant* side effects. Patients using this drug, for some strange reason, were seen to become joyful, excited, elated. A medical paper, describing this curiosity, even spoke of tubercular individuals "dancing and celebrating in the ward hallways."

(Peter Whybrow told me a tale of a woman he was treating for severe depression, who said that she had experienced real happiness only once in her life—during a religious conversion. After questioning her more closely, he discovered that she'd been in a TB sanitorium at the time and had been being treated with iproniazid. "I couldn't quite bring myself to tell her," he confessed with a wry smile, "that her ecstatic experience might not have come from the Lord but may have been, likely, a biochemical reaction to the medication she was taking.")

Because of its elating side effects, however, iproniazid was soon tried out as an antidepressant. It was found to be fairly effective; but no one knew why . . . until it was shown that iproniazid *blocks* the action of an enzyme that normally breaks down the biogenic amines and renders them biologically inactive. This meant, obviously, higher levels of these chemical compounds would be made available at the synapses.

Subsequent studies of animal brain tissues did, indeed, confirm that those drugs which acted to *increase* supplies of active serotonin and norepinephrine at the receptor sites were the same drugs that brought about a rise in mood state in humans. And drugs that acted to *deplete* reserves of biogenic amines (such as reserpine) in animal brains could bring about depressive states in humans. The "biogenic amine hypothesis," which is to say the suggestion that as biogenic amine levels rose, so did mood, began to look increasingly promising.

But then, the discovery of a completely different type of antidepressants appeared to pull the theoretical rug right out from under it.

·

Up from the Dark Places of the Self

In 1957, the "tricyclic antidepressants" (called "tricyclic" because of their three-ring chemical structure) were discovered by Swiss psychiatrist Ronald Kuhn. The discovery occurred because of a fortunate accident. Kuhn was looking for an antischizophrenic drug; and noticed, while working with one compound, that it appeared to relieve depressive symptoms instead. While the drug did prove useless in the treatment of schizophrenia, its antidepressant action was confirmed in other laboratories. Before long, the large family of drugs now used to combat depression—among them the commonly prescribed Elavil and Tofranil—were being developed.

No one who has seen an individual helped out of a depression by these medications can do anything but marvel; they have been, for many persons, a ladder up from the dark places of the self, from an unrelenting despair. One patient, herself a physician, told me that her own reaction to the drug Elavil, after a period of intense misery, was "that of experiencing a miracle, as if I'd been living in a perpetual fog, a drizzle, or wearing misted-over glasses for a long time, which suddenly had been wiped clean." Everything in her life had, she said, shifted back into focus. It reminded her of her nearsighted son's pleasure when he'd gotten new glasses and could see the world clearly and ride his bike. "Suddenly, things were in place again, and not at all overwhelming. Things became possible . . . above all, I felt *free*."

As far as the biogenic amine hypothesis was concerned, however, these new antidepressant drugs surely did cast doubt on the model. For the tricyclic compounds seemed to have nothing to do with either serotonin or norepinephrine. Yet they were clearly the best and safest medicines available in the relief of depression.

In the early 1960s, the work of Nobel prize winner Julius Axelrod suggested a fascinating explanation for this enigma. Axelrod demonstrated that most of the norepinephrine active at the brain synapses is "recycled"—literally sucked back into the cell and conserved for future use—after the nerve impulse had been relayed. This sucking-back process, called "re-uptake," is the major means by which norepinephrine is "turned off." Many researchers now believe that the way norepinephrine is kept under control is that the nerve ending shoots out a few drops—whatever is needed for transmitting the information —and then pulls the rest right back into the terminal branches of the cell.

Now what the tricyclic antidepressants *do*, as Axelrod showed in a subsequent and most astonishing animal study, is to *prevent* that usual sucking-back process from occurring. In the absence of the customary "re-uptake" action at the nerve cell endings, there was obviously more norepinephrine available and active in the synapses. Once again, then, it had been shown that a drug which relieves depression *also has the effect of increasing brain levels of this important biogenic amine!*

In the wake of Axelrod's major studies of norepinephrine, this compound came to seem to be *the most crucial* to the experiencing of moods. In fact, some scientists were proposing that there could be a simple one-to-one correspondence between "higher spirits" and rising levels of norepinephrine in the brain. This "model of mood" was deeply satisfying, for it was so clean and so simple. Could it *be* so wonderfully simple? Could something so ephemeral, so seemingly unfathomable as human mood states be based upon fluctuations of this mysterious "joy juice"?

The answer, as soon became clear, was No. For it was demonstrated that the tricyclic antidepressants don't block norepinephrine re-uptake alone. They also block the re-uptake of serotonin! It's impossible to say, therefore, whether the relief of depression has to do with the rising levels of one or the other—or with both—of these biogenic amines.

One of the great physician-researchers working in this area, Harvard professor Dr. Seymour Kety, told me that many experts now believe that the critical factor is probably some balance of norepinephrine, serotonin, and perhaps other, lesser-known, biogenic amines—that crucial carburetor mix. If this were so it would help to explain the puzzling effects of the drug lithium. For this medication is not only useful in calming and preventing manias; it also works to counteract the down phases of manic-depressive individuals like Judith Karlin. "But how," I asked Dr. Kety, "can lithium do these two opposite things at the same time?"

It may be, he suggested, that lithium restores levels of serotonin *in relation to* levels of norepinephrine at the synapse. Recent animal studies have shown that lithium does promote synthesis, or manufacture, of serotonin. "Serotonin might not have anything to do with mood states *per se*," he explained, "but might be acting as a modifier, a counterbalance of sorts, keeping those norepinephrine fluctuations within certain bounds at *both* ends of the mood scale." Serotonin might, in short, be the chemical substance that sets a ceiling on "high" moods and a bottom limit on the "lows."

"Suppose," said Kety, by way of example, "you have a person who, for genetic or other reasons, has an inadequate serotonin system. If the serotonin were actually acting as a 'damper' of this kind—at both emotional poles—you can see why such a constitutional deficit might permit a mood to exceed its normal limits. Say, you've got a normal person who's experienced something that has made her very happy; she'd be showing an increased norepinephrine production, but her mood would remain within a certain border, a confine. In the similar kind of situation, excepting that the person has *reduced* serotonin, there would be the same rise in norepinephrine without that serotonin coming into play to block it."

If one visualizes serotonin as having such a "stabilizing" role, then it's easy to see why a mood might go haywire in either the happiness or the misery direction—and why one medication, such as lithium, might be useful in treating both disturbed states.

A Matter of Life and Death:
A Little-known Compound

From the early 1960s onward there has been an enormous research effort directed toward discovering the physical or "bodily" basis of mood. Many investigators have attempted to prove the biogenic amine hypothesis through countless studies of the body fluids of depressed and manic patients. The idea has been, generally, that if mania is associated with too much norepinephrine at the synapses (to take an example) then a patient coming down from wild elation would show steadily decreased amounts of the byproducts of norepinephrine metabolism in her or his urine. This would, of course, reflect dwindling levels of norepinephrine in the brain.

The results of this research have tended, for the most part, to confirm the biogenic amine hypothesis. Still, those results have been attacked on a number of grounds. Most damning of all criticisms was the objection that no one knew, for sure, how much of the norepinephrine metabolites being measured in a person's urine had actually come from her or his *brain!* And if these substances came from elsewhere in the individual's body, what could that have to do with mood?

In the early 1970s, however, two scientific teams, working independently, demonstrated that a little-known compound called MHPG* *does* come largely from the brain. It derives from norepinephrine and has been discovered in both the urine and the cerebrospinal fluid of humans and other species. Some experts, including Harvard Medical School's Dr. Joseph Schildkraut, believe this research is going to have an important clinical payoff.

Schildkraut, a pioneer in the new MHPG work, told me that he thinks biochemical tests that psychiatrists can use routinely are on the threshold of becoming available. Such tests would be invaluable in the diagnosing of depression, because MHPG levels are different in urine samples of patients who are suffering from different *types* of depression.

Psychiatrists have been plagued by the fact that there is no one single illness or disorder that can be called "depression." And two patients, hospitalized with what appear to be identical symptoms and disturbances, might have different underlying disorders that call for different modes of treatment. One person might have depression alone;

* 3-methoxy-4-hydroxyphenylglycol.

the other might have a manic-depressive disorder—but not yet have manifested the "high." Those people will do better, by and large, on differing medication regimes; and yet the doctor can't tell them apart. "A urine test for MHPG can distinguish them," said Dr. Schildkraut. "MHPG values are *lower* in the urine of persons who are depressed but will become manic one day."

Preliminary laboratory studies also suggest that MHPG may prove useful in helping doctors predict how well their patients will respond to the different types of antidepressant medicines now available. Because these drugs are infamously slow to take effect, and can take weeks to do so, the difference in timing can be critical. To play a trial-and-error game with a depressed and potentially suicidal patient is at best an excruciatingly painful process for that person. And at worst it may be a seriously life-threatening situation.

Depression is, as I said earlier, the only psychiatric illness with a significant mortality rate attached to it. But patients almost invariably do recover eventually (the rate of recovery is something like 95 per cent) unless, as the psychiatric textbooks phrase it, "suicide should intervene."

Selecting the right drug at the right time may be, then, literally a matter of life and death.

A Central Theoretical Image

The story I've been telling is by no means a completed—or for that matter, undisputed—one. The biogenic amine "model of mood" has been a matter of controversy almost from the very outset. Some scientists don't buy into the model at all; the evidence arguing *for* it is, they insist, too indirect. For much of that evidence does come from studies of animal brains: and who can say, with certainty, that the drugs that alter moods in humans also act upon norepinephrine and serotonin levels in human brains in exactly the same ways as they do in the brains of animals? To find out directly would involve unthinkable kinds of human research. Scientists would have to conduct brain-tissue analyses in order to ascertain that "mood improvement" did correspond to the rising levels of biogenic amines being made available.

Research of such a sort is obviously out of the question! Also, some experts now believe that the real understanding of human mood disorders is more likely to come from the recent discovery of certain naturally occurring "pain killers" in the brain. These substances (called the enkaphalins and the endorphins) are peptides—they are *not* neurotransmitters. They seem to be internal opiates that the body produces in response to pain. And researchers have now isolated a system of opiate receptors in those brain areas most associated with the experiencing of pain, and with emotional state. So the picture is indeed more complex than earlier investigators had imagined it to be! As one neurochemist put it: "All of a sudden we are seeing a puzzle which had started out to be—well, like when you give a two-year-old a puzzle to solve, and it's only got five or six relatively large wooden pieces. That puzzle, which was our initial set of hypotheses, has fractured in a way; we've now got a puzzle with many more pieces, and it's on the floor, and it's backwards. But it also has got the feel of one that's going to fall into place rather rapidly!"

The biogenic amine hypothesis, now seen as a somewhat simplified picture of the complicated and interactive functioning of the mood juices in the brain, nevertheless remains the central theoretical image in biological psychiatry. Another researcher, commenting upon the conflicting views of the model, said with a summary shrug that it had already survived countless attempts to shoot it down. "And many of those attempts," he added, "were, themselves, discredited before the ink had quite dried on them." It would undoubtedly be foolish, nevertheless, to imagine these powerful neuroregulating compounds as existing in some kind of a biological vacuum—as dominating over, and singlehandedly controlling our moods.

For, while it is clear and evident that there must be some ongoing relationship between these potent brain biochemicals and states of emotion, it must be remembered that the biogenic amines are only one part of what is an extraordinarily intricate physiological energy system—one that is very rapidly changing and extremely sensitive.

They may be an important part—they may be the most important part! They are surely a tantalizing focus of the ongoing research into mood. But one can't focus on the carburetor exclusively and disallow for the significance of other factors necessary to the healthy maintenance of what is obviously a very elaborate, delicate over-all feedback system. More than the biogenic amines alone, it now seems clear, must be involved in keeping the mood motor in equilibrium: we have rich clues, but no completely worked-out solution, to the underlying laws of its functioning.

Wonderfully Female

I've been concentrating here on the ways in which biochemical processes can alter thinking and feeling—how pills and presciptions can change (as Judith Karlin's maintenance on lithium carbonate was doing for her) a person's whole perception of the world and of herself or himself *in* that world. We shouldn't lose sight, however, of the fact that "thinking" alone can alter brain biochemistry: psychological and biological factors constantly interact within our brains to produce the very human experience we call mood.

And it is that reality which, I believe, had somewhat confounded Judith in her attempts to come to a settled understanding of what was happening to her and of the over-all nature of her dilemma. Was she a walking biochemical abnormality? If so, that relieved her of some personal responsibility for many painful things that had happened—but it also seemed so deterministic a view, so reductionistic somehow. If, on the other hand, she tried to assess what had happened in what she called "the human way" so many unsolvable mysteries remained. For, insofar as causes for those manic attacks were concerned, she could come up with—not one set—but a cornucopia of possible interpretations! One had to do with her own mother's physical illnesses between the ages of thirty and thirty-two. "My mother was sick when I was eight years old; and had to be away, for a period of months. She had a really severe back problem and she had to have some serious surgery. And that was—oh, a big separation. It was horrible. I really loved my mother a lot. I think it's horrible when your mother leaves, on principle; but there are mothers and mothers. She and I had really been very close. But what I think about sometimes is that she was thirty when that all started happening; and she had three really bad episodes. And I was thirty when I went crazy—and *I've* been crazy three times."

She shrugged and added that a whole other way of looking at her dilemma was something which she phrased as "women's fear of success." For, on that first occasion of illness—the "mini-elation" she'd experienced just before her move back to the East—she was returning to what was undoubtedly a much better job in Boston. She'd gotten euphoric, the second time, about doing that screenplay with Frank. And the third time the issue had been her upcoming tenure. "Another interpretation I have—also other than chemistry—is that there's a whole self-destructive part of myself that takes over; that when things are going well, I ruin them. The tenure thing in particular. There I was, a triumphant, very productive faculty member, with every chance of being passed through without any problems: then I behaved crazily, and did screw everything up." She hesitated, then observed dryly: "This is where I buy into the whole business of women's underground anxieties about moving ahead in a male world. I mean, that we are programmed to believe that the more we succeed in *that* way, the more we fail . . . as women."

She picked up a cigarette, tapped it on the back of her hand absent-mindedly, but didn't light it. "You mean," I asked, "that the more successful a woman becomes the more she fears being seen as unattractive and ineligible?"

"Yes! Right! And unlovable too." Judith leaned forward, resting her elbows on her corduroy-covered knees. "Unfeeling of her duty and her mission to the species—what she was put into the world to do. To marry and bear children, and to be loved." She sat back, then, leaned over, and picked up a book of matches. "Not to love, mind you, but to *be* loved. That is woman's calling. I always thought that whole bit was something I just wasn't into. I've always been very success-oriented in a male, assertive, instrumental style. Not politics and power struggles in the department; they just don't interest me a lot. But I haven't wanted to hand over my freedom to any man; I've wanted to stay single and in control of my life. Mine has been, and perhaps deep down there's a part of me that believes this is treasonable or punishable—a very *male* definition of success."

She had torn out a match, but then she put both matches and match book down on the table beside her. "Because it does seem that when things are going well I have a strange way of ruining them. I mean, when I come to a place where I'm going to make some tangible achievement, I seem to be—wonderfully female." She broke into a sudden, engaging grin. "At the proper moment I do manage to fuck up."

In the following pages, Judith's story will be continued . . . in the more "human" (as opposed to the biochemical) way.

CHAPTER NINE

Elation and Despair: Judith (2)

The Phantom Passion

The course that Judith's third and most florid manic outburst took
was as typical as the other two attacks had been. Again there was the
at-first-almost-imperceptible, and yet strangely relentless mood of happiness: it was as if something wonderful were going to happen, something almost too wonderful to be humanly true. And in fact, one of
the dreams of her life *might* be about to be realized, for she was in the
process of being considered for academic tenure.

"At first," she said soberly, "I saw this as a tense, awful, horrible ordeal—as achieving tenure *is*, for anyone who has to go through this
experience. But somehow, and I'm not sure when it happened, the anxiety left me and I felt quite happy and optimistic and confident." She
shrugged: "I didn't realize it until later, but I was starting to become
manic."

Judith Karlin, despite her hospitalization for mania the previous
summer—and a shorter, much more easily containable episode of elation which had occurred in the year before *that*—had never yet been
tried on a course of lithium. During her short stay in the sanitorium
out in California, heavy doses of a powerful tranquilizer called
Thorazine had been used to cool the racing motors of her agitation
and excitement. She had gotten well eventually but looked back on
her "tranquilization" with dismay. "In a way, I would rather be crazy.
It's hard to describe just how those things make you feel . . . as if
your mind can't connect, in a way, as if you are a zombie." She
frowned. "I could hardly speak, either; it was as if there were weights
on my throat, holding me down. I felt, all the time I was in the hospi-

tal, as if I were sleep-walking, or the walking dead. Anything," she added wryly, "but a *human*." Still, she'd been able to leave the institution by early August. When she returned to her teaching post in the fall, the whole terrible business was (so she hoped) behind her forever. Her California physicians had suggested that she *not* share the story with friends and acquaintances; it could, realistically speaking, impair her chances of professional advancement. Like Lot's Wife, Judith had been instructed to look steadily to her future—and not to risk what might be destructive glances behind.

She had been being a good patient and following orders. She wasn't attempting to look back at all. But she was, by the time the winter months had given way to the sudden thaws and erratic excursions into spring that characterize mid-March, slipping back into the construction of her "crazy fantasies." Again they involved the production of a "masterpiece." "This time," recounted Judith, "my fantasies were about various political things that were going on in the department too. It all got quite confused, because the man who was supposedly deeply in love with me and the one whom *I* loved so desperately was"—she hesitated, then smiled—"well, he was the chairman of the department. And there was, as before with Frank, absolutely nothing between us. He was friendly; he liked me. I happened to be doing an essay on Sergei Eisenstein's work as a director—and this was something that he, Ralph, had written about himself."

She never did, reiterated Judith, become obsessive about a man with whom she truly *was* sexually involved. "*Never*," she repeated once again; and then added that when she got into these eerily intense fantasy affairs, they were nothing other than "symptoms." She herself had no wish or desire for a consummation in the world of reality: "If anything did really happen," she explained, "I couldn't have my fantasies. What this is, to me," she added, her strong, aquiline-featured face intent, her straight dark hair, usually secured behind one ear, now falling forward over her forehead, "is a retreat from any *actual* occurrence. It's a private, an interior happening . . . a retreat from the exigencies of the outside world and into the world of my fantasy."

Once again there were two long months of good feeling; of a growing sense of joy, anticipation of a glorious future; and of simply being the master of all the things that mattered. She experienced herself as powerful, as centrally important to the scheme of things—as a person in control. "I find it very hard to communicate," she remarked, "the way in which my knowledge of my omnipotency slowly grew and swelled within me. It was just this whole sense, this really manic sense, that something absolutely marvelous is happening to you! And until one goes absolutely off the deep end, it *is* that way: in your inner world you are famous and powerful and you're unquestionably in control of everything! It's rather like the Walter Mitty fantasies; but then, it's more than just being brilliant or beautiful or effective. It is, oh—well, by the time it peaks I am a being with magic powers. I have perceived the secrets of the universe. By then, though, I have become compulsively involved in whatever it is that I'm writing or doing. And in the phantom passion that I believe is becoming stronger and deeper . . . I mean that I'm swimming in fantasies of all kinds. It's difficult to explain, but I am not divorced from the outside world: things on the outside are just feeding into my fantasy world. It's as if I were writing a novel, and it were partly true and partly imagined. . . ."

Her cheeks had grown rosy; her eyes were alight, as she said this. "But I *believe* the part that's imagined! It becomes another act in this great drama that is happening. And it is unimaginably vivid and exciting!"

She was moving, this time by the end of April, from a mood of happiness to one of high irritability. Side by side with that sense of her own importance there was a deep-down knowledge that the balloon might burst any moment; she might be revealed as a being both vulnerable and fragile. "On the one hand I experienced myself as someone inspired. I was a sybil, and I was God, and God was speaking to me and through me. I couldn't be crossed. I could call anyone an idiot or a fool; it was as if all inhibition had disappeared. And oh, Lord, some of the things I did say!" She laughed mirthlessly. "That's what I'll never get over, I suppose. That I said damaging things, and did damaging things, which made no *sense* from the point of view of the people around me!" Some mournful clouds, drifting over her features, now settled upon them as if meaning to stay. "I think part of that irritability of mine came from the fact that I knew, somewhere deep down, that I was going crazy. So that if any opinion were challenged, it became terrifying. Because to me—and I understand that it's a common symptom of mania, this irritability—it was like a statement to the effect that I was crazy. Which was the thing I most expected, and feared, that people would *say!*"

In the early weeks of May she'd taken to rushing into people's offices and making sweeping and outlandish statements with which the hearer was expected to immediately concur. "A few weeks before I really cracked up for the third time," smiled Judith, dissipating the gloom of her expression immediately, "I got very into feminism. I was teaching my first course on women in film; and I saw myself as this great messianic feminist person—" She laughed suddenly: "I was the Amazon of Boston! Well, some of the things I did and said were funny; being manic has its rather funny aspects. But I spoiled a lot of my relationships absolutely irrevocably. . . ." Her voice, and her expression shifted into the "low" registers once again. "And of course, though no one will admit it at all, it had everything to do with what happened about my tenure, and my job."

A Mood of Triumph

At a time when there was every incentive for being cautious and circumspect, Judith Karlin's mood of joy drifted irrevocably upward: her energy, enthusiasm, her insistent "confidence" continued to grow; she was in an amphetaminelike high. She was unable to relax, unable to sleep, unable to let anyone around her even complete a sentence! "The reason was, of course," she recounted, "that I felt that I had all the answers *anyhow*—so how could I permit someone else to finish a sentence? I was just so hyper and so 'up.' And really, there was a whole power thing: I had this feeling that I finally *was* showing everybody! There was simply no doubt in my mind that my tenure was being approved and that they were all working their asses off to give me an offer good enough to convince me to stay! And so I lost my inhibitions and my restraint. For example, one of the middle-aged male professors had been having an affair with a graduate student. She happened to be someone I knew well, a divorcée in her late twenties; and I had felt that he was doing a power trip on her, that he was manipulating her. I mean, he'd done certain things for her which had, in effect, helped to advance her career. But when their affair was over, he'd dumped her not only personally but professionally. *She'd* been, in effect, both unfairly elevated and then treated very shabbily. And my own reaction to all of this had been that she'd let herself be used and discarded; she'd put herself in this passive position vis-à-vis this terribly exploitative man." Judith hesitated. "I wasn't just sympathetic to her plight, you know; I was angry at her too. She'd been playing these manipulative, feminine games; and also, she had been *being* manipulated. I was just working and not playing; which was, I think, better in the end. Anyhow, my mood was one of triumph—of triumphant rage, I suppose! Because I just started ragging that man, and in public. I kept saying: 'How's Nancy? I haven't seen her lately,' and things like that. This person, mind you, had immense weight to swing in the upcoming decision regarding my tenure! And these snide remarks I was constantly making: they were key phrases to everyone present. Oh." Judith shifted in her chair, suddenly, rested her chin in her hand. Looking down at the parquet squares of her living-room floor, she said ruefully: "I was like someone possessed. I was tearing up my whole life. And that's the part that most people don't understand. Unless you are with someone who's knowledgeable about such things, or loves you so much it doesn't matter, I think that such behavior puts an irrevocable blight on your relationship—to *you*, as well as the other person." She looked up, added in a voice full of anguish: "I can't *confront* people who have seen me when I was manic, unless they are people I am so intimate with that they will—you know—take anything."

Certainly, those friends who cared about her had been trying to caution and contain her. A woman colleague, Barbara, had been at a faculty lunch at which some of the male professors had been affectionately teasing Judith. "I was the first feminist in that department, and it was very likely—at that time—that I'd be getting my tenure. And during that lunch they began saying all of these wildly sexist and chauvinist things; they were just joshing around, being playful. One of them, a young professor, was someone who was my age and was a friend. He actually *is* chauvinistic, because he made his wife give up her job to have a baby. But I'm not his wife, and he's a nice man; he's an enemy, but he isn't *my* enemy. At any rate, though, he was saying women should really be subordinate, and things like that—that feminism was all . . . well, I don't remember. Just that 'Oh, you women's libbers' kind of teasing. It was his idea of being funny. But I just got so upset and so angry and so furious at all of them! And Barbara, who didn't even know that I'd ever been manic, but had once had a friend who *had been*, called up that night. She told me that she thought that *I* was different, somehow: 'You know,' she said to me, 'I honestly think you're going into a mania.'"

Judith had responded to Barbara's concern with an angry outburst. "I started yelling," she admitted. "I don't even remember what I said." The suggestion that she ought to consult a therapist was met with an arrogant incredulity. She felt so wonderful, in general; why in the world would she want to go for *help*? She was fine—and not simply fine; she was superb. Her mood was the mood of victory: she was terribly excited about her upcoming tenure appointment, about the writing on Eisenstein's films that she was doing. And above all, she was stirred by the wonderful feelings that come with being in love.

The Glow Wasn't Sickness; It Was Love

"I was never in love, either with Frank or with my departmental chairman, when I was sane," she said, her voice low and uncertain.

"That was a manic thing. I realize that when you're manic you get so elated and supercharged and excited that—well, a woman who was brought up in the way that I was could only attribute that feeling to *one thing*." She smiled: "To being madly in love with someone."

I shook my head, not sure what she meant: Judith stood up suddenly, began pacing around the room. "You are charged with this incredible, unprecedented excitement," she explained. "It's a glow, and the whole world is wonderful. And I was brought up, as so many girls are, to believe that such transfiguration could only come from a man! That's just our sexist upbringing. And so you pour that energy out on whoever happens to be there. Which in this last instance was Ralph, our departmental chairman. I mean, I never said to myself 'I am sick, and something is happening inside me, and *that's* why everything is all aglow.' I certainly didn't think about that. I mean, I'd do so if I ever started going crazy again; at least I *hope* I would! . . . But I never gave a thought to being sick; I was just in love." She stopped her pacing, stared at me, and said: "You'd *have* to be in love to be so excited. But I'd known Ralph for years; I'd been a graduate student in that same department before ever going out to California. And all that time, until I started fixating on him, he was never anything more than a nice person."

Her state of elation, which had been affecting Judith's judgment and understanding, had enabled her to remain impervious to what she now recognizes were advance signals of the impending disaster. So convinced was she, in fact, that she would easily surmount the tenure hurdle, that she purchased an elaborately expensive plum-colored velvet sofa, an antique bookcase, and an oriental rug. Such purchases were, she realized, a bit extravagant, but she would pay for them with her increased earnings; after all, promotion was around the corner! And it would be good to have her place looking just perfect at the time of the celebration party.

Several weeks after these furnishings had been bought, however, her promotion had been passed over and her tenure bid denied. It was clear that she would have to seek a new teaching post elsewhere. And Judith plunged with an almost dizzying rapidity from the exalted heights of her Olympian triumph to the depths of an acute depressive despair.

The Touch of a Malicious Wand

Judith had had three episodes of mania, during one of which she'd become psychotic. (That was of course a year earlier, out in California, when she had received those "messages from God" over the radio.) But this was her first experience of a serious depression. The feminist "Amazon"; the brisk teacher and writer; the energetic scholar; the beloved protégée of the departmental chairmen: all, all had disappeared. She'd been transformed, and totally, as if by the touch of some malicious wand. Her mood, her experience of her life became "black . . . one of blackness, awful hopelessness." She felt as if she had been, in essence, destroyed. Her shell continued to move and to function; but "she"—the real Judith—was dead inside. Or if not dead, worthless. She had nothing to give, and nothing to expect; no, not from anyone. Life was unendurable. She felt totally isolated and alone.

The High and the Low

What Judith Karlin's last and most prolonged attack reflected was the more or less classical outline of a manic-depressive (or "bipolar") mood disorder. She had, for an initial period of three months or so, been feeling too good to be true, too immune to any of the possible difficulties or problems that she ought, rationally, to have been confronting. Now, following upon the rejection of her tenure bid, that too-happy picture had entirely reversed itself; things were too bad to be true. The collapse of her hopes for a rapid and ego-satisfying promotion was being equated with the destruction of her worth and value as a human being. In the wake of what had unquestionably been a defeat and a disappointment, she was calling herself a useless and even "loathsome" individual: she had begun questioning her right —and her willingness—to go on living, as well. In short, the rebuff she had sustained was being magnified beyond all proportion.

The mood of despair was as exaggerated as had been the prolonged experience of happiness that it had supplanted. And in fact, the "high" and the "low," on the surface such strikingly different emotional states, did share one very important feature. They *both* rendered Judith incapable of sustaining realistic contact with her environment. It is this inability to correctly read and assess the signals coming from outside the self that is one of the hallmarks—and dangers—of manic-depressive illness. For our mood states have so much to do with the ways in which we perceive, process, and interpret the information that comes in upon us unceasingly from an ever-changing, ever-challenging, ever-demanding outside world.

The Circular or Cycling Illness

Manic-depressive illness is one of the oldest psychiatric disorders to have been described in the literature of Western civilization. Medical writings, as well as prose and poetry—dating well back into the fourth century B.C.—contain references to individuals who suffer mysterious mood swings, alternating between extreme glee and what the ancients called *melancholia*. One Arateus, a doctor living in the second century B.C., wrote a clinical description of the manic-depressive cycle which remains valid to this day. Such patients, after a prolonged experience of euphoria, were seen to become "sad, dismayed, sleepless. . . . They (are made) thin by their agitation and loss of refreshing sleep. . . . At a more advanced stage, they complain of a thousand futilities and desire death."

So striking in its roller-coasterlike progression of high and low moods is the disorder that in the last century a French psychiatrist, Falret, called it *folie circulaire*—that is, "circular or cycling madness." But the term manic-depressive psychosis was not invented until the early nineteen twenties, when Dr. Emil Kraepelin first used it to delineate a form of mental disturbance most characterized by inappropriate mood; that is, "too joyful" or "too miserable" emotional states.

In Kraepelin's schema, the person who evidenced mania with no sign of depression—as well as the individual who became depressed without any prior phase of elation—was to be classified as manic-depressive. (Actually, mania in the absence of depression is extremely rare; and Judith's first two outbursts, which had not been followed by depressive attacks, had made her an "interesting patient," i.e., a medical oddity. Depression without mania is, on the other hand, as ordinary and common as is the proverbial apple pie.) Kraepelin was, however, making the supposition that even if the depressed person never evidenced any signs of mania, the elated phase had still somehow been there.

More recently, and largely as a result of the development of different types of psychoactive drug treatments, this view has come to seem increasingly questionable. For certain medications, such as the tricyclic antidepressants (Elavil, Tofranil, and the like) may be very helpful in the treatment of "plain" depression. But, compared to lithium, they're relatively ineffective—and may be counterindicated—in the treatment of manic-depressive disorder. If the two patients were really suffering from the same illness, as Kraepelin believed to be the actual underlying situation, then they ought, of course, to be responding to and helped by the same kinds of cure.

Generally speaking, most experts in the field of depression now tend to view manic-depressive disturbance and "plain" depression as fairly separate and distinct disorders. Manic-depressive disturbance is frequently referred to as *bipolar disease*—a mood disorder encompassing both "poles" of emotional state, high and low. And depression in the absence of any symptoms of mania is, in current terminology, *unipolar disease*. The "high-low" sequence is, statistically speaking, a far less frequent occurrence than are periodic episodes of the lows. Within the nation at large, manic-depressive disturbance seems to affect only some 10–15 per cent of the population. But unipolar or plain depression is much more widespread; according to government statistics, it may be affecting up to 30 per cent of the American people. A conservative estimate, given me by Dr. Robert M. A. Hirschfeld, chief of the depression section of the National Institute of Mental Health, comes from that bureau's most recent survey data. The NIMH findings indicate, Hirschfeld told me, that one in every five Americans has at least moderate depressive symptomatology. Such symptoms may include sadness, loss of pleasure in life, indecisiveness, irritability, impaired ability to think and to remember, as well as sleeping problems (early morning awakening is a *signal* of a possible depressive disorder!), appetite changes (loss of interest in food *or* the overeating of the chronically obese), fatigue and loss of drive *or* agitation and hyperactivity. Loss of sexual interest is a common phenomenon—but this drop in libido, which can be accompanied by impotence or frigidity, reflects a broader loss of interest in most things in the world outside the self. The depressed person, like someone with an awful toothache, turns his or her attention inward and has little to give outward; it simply hurts too much.

If we are talking, in any event, about one in every five Americans having at least moderate depressive symptomatology, we are talking about a group of people *on the order of 40 million*. It is, as Hirschfeld acknowledged, a public-health problem of almost staggering proportions. *And two thirds of that group are women.* As noted earlier, *all* surveys of the incidence of plain depression show a routine sex bias, that is, many more depressed women than men!

But this is *not* the case where bipolar depression is concerned. In manic-depressive disorder, which somehow has a more hereditary and biological "feel," nature appears to have provided a certain parity. Here, the sexes are equal: there are roughly similar numbers of manic-depressive women and men.

The Bearer of the Family Dream

Needless to say, there have been numerous efforts to tease out the causes, or triggering factors, that may set off the manic-depressive cycle. One branch of the research has taken the biological high road, viewing the illness as "constitutional" and built into a person's inherent natural makeup somehow. Another branch of the research has taken the "nurture" low road, linking manic depression with particular kinds of rearing practices and certain life experiences. One landmark study of the latter sort, carried out in the mid-nineteen fifties by Mabel Blake Cohen and several co-workers (among whom was Frieda Fromm-Reichmann, the model for the female psychoanalyst in *I Never Promised You a Rose Garden*) was a meticulous study of the family backgrounds of a group of eleven manic-depressive patients.

Dr. Cohen and her colleagues found that their patients had all come from families which had been set off, for one reason or another, from the surrounding milieu or neighborhood. Either the family belonged to a minority group, or had lost money, or an important family member had become mentally ill. Whatever the onus or burden might have been, it was the individual who later became a manic-depressive who had been the one selected to win, or to restore, the family's honor. Often, this child had been chosen for the task because she or he was brighter, more beautiful, more talented, or superior to the other siblings in some other way. "We also found," reported the Cohen researchers, "that the child is usually caught between one parent who is thought of as a failure and blamed for the family's plight (frequently the father) and the other parent who is aggressively striving, largely through the instrumentality of the child, to remedy the situation. . . ."

Is this, then, the particular kind of family and social environment that breeds manic-depressive disease? The findings of the Cohen study, though they continue to intrigue mental health workers, have never been confirmed. Later researches on manic-depressive patients have demonstrated that while many *do* spring from the type of background described by Cohen et al., there are many others who do not. I myself must confess to having been astounded by it, nevertheless. For I'd already been doing extensive interviewing with a sample of women who, like Judith Karlin, experienced "highs" as well as attacks of depression. And the thumbnail family background sketch suggested by the Cohen group seemed to fit what I knew with an accuracy that I found almost eerie.

Judith was, for instance (and I'll cite her history, since she is someone we already know something about) indeed the "golden girl" of
her family. She had had, as a child, the bouncing curls and winsome
charm of a Shirley Temple; she'd also been, as she described herself,
"a bit of a ham" and someone who knew how to maintain herself at
the center of attention. She was not only "brighter, more beautiful,
more talented, or superior" to the other siblings in her family; she had
them beat, hands down. For Judith's brother, three years younger,
had had polio in his infancy, and was slightly crippled; and the youngest child, a sister, was stolid and average—not at all so flamboyantly
superior, so clearly destined for intellectual triumphs later on in her
life.

Judith's father, too, conformed to the familial outline suggested by
the Cohen study: he could have been called "a failure." For, at the
time of her parents' marriage, he had been a promising and already
moderately successful actor—with credits both on the stage and in
films—but his career had, somehow, never consolidated; it had simply
fizzled out. He'd had to go into his family's sweater manufacturing
business, based in Chicago, and he despised what he did (even though
he was an effective executive and had, in fact, made a great deal of
money). To her mother, Judith suspected, the ending of her father's
acting career had been in some sense a betrayal and in every sense a
disappointment. She, the bride of a worldly and glamorous actor,
found herself confined to what she considered the dull, drab milieu
of the business and moneymaking world from which this marriage
had been meant to provide the latchkey, the means of escape. She'd
wed an actor but was married to an ordinary executive. There had
been her mother's recurring back trouble, too, and the sense, for the
precocious and pretty Judith, that things had gone sour in her mother
and father's generation. It was *she* who was the hope of the family, she
who was the family's real investment in the future. And it was she
who—so the unspoken but powerfully present family myth had it—
would someday make all of the things that seemed wrong or disappointing become, at last, magically "right."

I Am What My Dreams Desire Me to Be

For Judith herself, however, such explanations of her present plight
were not in themselves sufficient. "I am not saying," she once told me
dubiously, "that there were not problems in my family. But you
know, my father *could* have been actively destructive and walked out
on the family; he could have done those palpable, terrible things that

happen to a lot of people . . . people who don't go crazy. And again, I know people with difficulties that are severe—objectively severe—and they haven't gone crazy. So it is as simple as that. I mean, the real question is why is it me and not somebody else? I'm not saying that my early life or my current life is totally the *right* life—but what *is* the right life? I believe the answer to why it's *me* is that I have this disease that most people do not have."

Nor did she have great sympathy for the view, common among many psychiatrists, that manic attacks represent a frenzied flight from what is actually an underlying depression. This view is based, to some degree, upon the clinical observation that the joyous person's elated mood is usually accompanied by aggression and growing irritability. (As one therapist remarked to me: "The manic person is feeling good; but it's not a warm glow, nothing that includes other people. It's all focused on the self, and it has to be guarded carefully, protected from intrusions from the outside.") The happy mood has, in other words, an almost desperate quality. And, although the euphoric person's self-references are positive—superpositive, in fact—they appear to be of a very frangible sort. They must be protected, at all costs, from incursions from the real world (hence the tendency to feel threatened, and the irritability). Seen from this standpoint, the manic-depressive individual is someone who, in order to stave off the oncoming depression and all of its attendant negative feelings, has gone to the extreme opposite end of the mood spectrum in order to maintain her or his positive sense of self.

Judith, however, considered this schema to be "absolute bullshit." She didn't believe, she said, that there was any truth in it whatsoever. "It's like saying that being in Heaven is a flight from Hell." Her voice was charged with indignation. "But I have been wildly manic—to a degree that I've never been depressed—and they are, I think, two very *different* places. I mean, you are racing when you are manic; you can do things a depressed person would never be capable of doing! The whole thing about depression is that you can't get out of bed; but when you're manic, you can't get *in* bed; you are totally unable and unwilling to sleep. They are utterly opposite kinds of experiences. You want to collapse and to withdraw when you're depressed. When you're manic, oh!—you just want to be going all the time."

A number of therapists do, nevertheless, view the manic episode as *not only* a denial of an underlying, depressing reality; but as something similar to the acting out of a metaphor, a wished-for dream. The woman who goes on a clothes-buying spree, or redecorates her whole house or becomes sexually promiscuous is really saying to the world: "I am what my dreams desire me to be. In my dreams I am all beautiful, and can wear all the clothes, or decorate the most beautiful house, or absorb all the men in the world. And there are no bounds to my reality—no boundaries to social convention, the limits of my talents and capacities; the size of my pocketbook; the capacity of my vagina; or my body's ability to do without nourishment or sleep." And no doubt this is the reason why the manic person does, for many of us, exert a dramatic and compelling appeal. For we all do have, somewhere deep within us, some part of that same dream; that wish to make our own overly expansive "impossible" fantasies palpable and real.

About Power: Acting Out My Mother's Rebellion

If I were asked to say what Judith Karlin's waking dreams—those three long experiences of elation—had been *about*, and to say so in a word, that word would be *power*. Once, when she'd been describing to me the "differentness" of the ways she thought and behaved when she was manic, I tried to find out whether she'd realized—at the time itself—that she was indeed thinking and behaving differently. "No, no," she replied, almost impatiently. "You think other people are crazy and you are inspired; you know everything; you're God. I mean, it's a whole thing about triumph and domination. And the feeling is: 'I'll finally show them.' It's a little like being drunk; you just lose your inhibitions about what it's possible to do, and what you *can* and *can't* say." We were having lunch together on the day when she made this particular observation. Judith had leaned forward, on the table, her chin in her hands. "The thing is," she continued, "that it happened to me, and I was possessed. It wasn't me; it was the world that had changed, somehow. Because my perceptions of it—the world, I mean —had changed.

"I know," she added, "that in reality the world didn't change; it was only an unending fantasy. But when I think of trying to reproduce for you what it actually felt like—well, I had no sense of it coming from *inside me!* It made perfect sense to me, somehow, the whole crazy new world I was responding to, and seeing, and in touch with. I believed in it; and I was inspired; and it was lovely until the culminating sequence, when I was getting those 'messages,' which were, I now understand, projections of unconscious feelings and psychological whatevers. But, no more than that phone's ringing on the counter over there"—Judith pointed toward the cash register—"did that all feel like it was coming from inside *me*."

For a moment, then, she was silent. The waitress brought us our cheeseburgers. "You know," said Judith casually, her voice tone changed, as if her thoughts had shifted onto a far less emotionally charged topic, "I sometimes think that my manic episodes were like—well, the very obverse of my mother's depressions."

I think I must have looked very startled, when she said that, for Judith's own brown eyes widened in surprise. "You never said," I remarked carefully, "that your mother had been depressed."

She took a bite of her thick sandwich, shrugged. "I don't know that she was—technically. But women *are* more depressed than they are anything else—women are much more depressed, I'd say, than men. And in a way, I was so pushed one way in my life: to be feminine and subordinate and everything . . . to a man. My mother wanted me to achieve, sure she did. But she also wanted me to do this other, this 'girl' kind of thing. So at one level, there was the pressure to behave in a very traditional way; whether or not I wanted to. There was nothing ever said explicitly about that being a lot of shit, and beneath me —or her—or anyone. But I've sometimes felt that I, in my manias, was acting out my mother's rebellion." She took a sip of her coffee, replaced the cup in the saucer with a clatter.

"I might have said that I am manic, instead of depressed, because I am leading a very—not abnormal—maybe 'offbeat' is the word, life for a woman. I mean my *life* is something that I could think is a fantasy!" She picked up the sugar holder, poured a bit into her cup, then stirred it around with her spoon somewhat dreamily. "You can do very funny things when you're manic," she said, "and what I did, especially this last time, was to get terrifically aggressive. And order people about. I was obnoxious, sure; but I was also interesting. I mean, I wasn't just sitting there like a blob . . . and I don't, I never *have* felt trapped. There are a lot of things I could complain about in my life, but feeling trapped is definitely not one of them!"

"What could you complain about," I asked, "if you were complaining?"

"Oh. Not being able to live where I choose to; that is, being dependent on what school finally decides to hire me. Not being able to maintain relationships—because I still don't know where I'll end up being."

I smiled: "Employment problems."

"That's right. It's my whole life. But it's not my *husband's* employment problems . . . that's the only thing that sees me through." Judith was smiling too. "I mean, before I came to meet you today, I was reading a novel about a woman whose husband is an actor. And he's going on tour, and she has to turn down a job. See, this is a situation I wouldn't be *in*. I mean, the only thing that sees me through is that this is *my* employment and *my* choice. And it's not that I've never been terribly lonely—I have been. Every time I move into a strange city, and feel abandoned and miserable, I regret, in a way, not having married. But the minute I get on my feet," she lifted one eyebrow ironically, "I find I quickly *un*-regret it. Really, I would link my becoming manic, rather than depressed, to *that* more than to anything else."

"And if you were a wife—a follower of another person?"

"I think I would be depressed." She laughed: "I would also, I think, be a rather mean bitch. You know," she added, her expression becoming serious, "the fact that I go into uppers, and not into downers—the way most women do—actually relates, I believe, to the fact that I've made a very firm and committed choice not to live in the way that most women *live*. I have my own ambivalences—sure I do. But I don't have the ambivalences of having to follow a husband, to take care of children, and to keep up a home. So I'll tell you what I make of this: it's that most women are told, from their earliest life, that there is only one set of things that will make them happy—a home, children, 'love,' 'fulfillment.' And women then, at some point, get depressed for one of two reasons: either they've gotten these things and they *aren't* happy or they haven't gotten these things so they *can't* be happy! A woman's life is measured in inner states. Whereas for men, the measures tend to be more external—things like 'success' and 'productivity.' "

She lifted her coffee cup, took a sip, put it down again. Her cheeseburger had been barely touched; my own was almost gone. I started nibbling at my pickle and potato chips. "But you know," Judith was continuing, "being 'fulfilled' is a rather static thing. You are," she shrugged, "just so full, and then you can contain no more. You're just standing there, *full* of something!" She grinned, lifted her somewhat discouraged-looking sandwich, took a bite.

"And when you're not being 'fulfilled' or full you are . . . ?" I'd almost been thinking aloud, but the words came out as a question to Judith. She was chewing, but signaled me to wait a moment; then she swallowed. "Obviously, when you're not fulfilled you are empty and frustrated and miserable!" She wiped her lips with a paper napkin, which became smudged with her lipstick. Then she added, with what might have seemed careless irrelevance (but wasn't): "Once, when I was already grown up and an adult, my mother made a remark to me about my father. She said: 'If I once started being angry at him, I would never stop.' To which I responded, I remember, with an inner something like 'Aha!' " She stared at me a moment, her dark eyes bright with intelligence. Then she picked up the soggy cheeseburger, shrugged, took another bite.

The Origins of Depression

Judith was clearly a subscriber to that well-known model or paradigm for how it is that depression originates: the "anger-turned-inward" schema. Many experts do have it that the inflated rates of depression among women are connected with feminine inhibitions about the release of anger. Nice girls don't, as everyone knows, behave aggressively and display their assertive, competitive feelings openly (better yet, as will be seen in Chapter Thirteen, they don't "have" any such tendencies in their general personality makeup at all!). If, nevertheless, a person *is* enraged—and if she is unable to recognize and deal with her own feelings of fury—there is a way of experiencing the emotion without actually threatening her relationship with the one who's enraged her. She can turn her anger *at the other person* around and allow it into consciousness as anger and rage at herself.

Such an individual may be totally, or partially (as was Judith's mother), unaware that she's in a state of simmering fury. In the former instance, she may suppress all awareness of her own hostile feelings because she feels she shouldn't be the sort of person who would *have* such negative, angry thoughts and ideas! In the latter case, she may "know" at some level what she is feeling but consider herself totally helpless when it comes to expressing or communicating the anger that she's experiencing. Her feelings, which can't be released or discharged, are then—like a hand grenade, pin pulled, that the person keeps hanging onto—used destructively against the self. The emotion, transformed, falls down upon the person who's not been capable of releasing it, and in a shower of punishing self-vituperation. The fallout from this sort of self-directed attack is inevitably a drop in self-esteem. And this is, in itself, one of the primary symptoms—the hallmarks—of a depression.

Women actually may, as Judith seemed to assume they do, tend to get depressed more often because they have more trouble with the display of and communication of their anger—and because they frequently try to handle angry feelings in this particular fashion. That is, instead of experiencing and confronting their anger consciously, they turn it around, into weapons destructive of the self. The reason being, of course, that aggression and anger are unfeminine.

Her own mother, she seemed to be saying, had been womanly and depressed. She, Judith, would conduct her own life in a totally different way.

A Model for Mania

No one conveys a more convincing portrait of the utterly happy person than does the individual who is moving into an extended euphoria. I have heard such people discuss their lives and their future prospects in the most wonderful and glowing terms. While it's true that some manic patients may experience a subliminal discomfort, they're possessed by a great exaltation of spirit. The entire mood—the sense that one is "floating on air," "bursting with happiness"—seems the very obverse of depression.

And, in many ways, the two states do seem to be poles apart. For where the euphoric person adores herself, the depressed person detests herself; where the manic individual denies the existence of any realistic difficulties or bars to the realization of her wishes and dreams, the depressed individual exaggerates the size and the scope of the problems that she *does* face; she's overwhelmed. The "high" person is driven and impulsive; she is hyperactive and striving. The "low" person has a sense that she is stuck—paralyzed—and that there is nothing to be done, and that nothing that *could* be done would have any meaning or be of any conceivable use. The elated individual is expansive, friendly, grandiose; her heart is full of high expectations for the future. The depressed person is just the opposite; she believes that nothing good can possibly happen.

And yet, as I mentioned, some of the psychological explanations of mania start with the basic assumption that the mood of joy is essentially a defense—a massive denial of what is in reality an underlying depressive state. Such a "model for mania" has it that the manic person, although *appearing* to be outgoing and friendly, is self-centered, manipulative, actively controlling of others' behavior. Suggests Dr. Lawrence C. Kolb, in a recent textbook (*Modern Clinical Psychiatry*): *These attitudes are based on an emotional need for a dependency relationship.* (My italics.)

Writes Kolb: "The manic would seem to perceive threat and danger in accepting his (her) dependent needs to be cared for by others. To maintain his self-esteem and to defend himself, to maintain his key perception of power and strength, he appears to use those transactions which control others to whom he looks for emotional support. His repertoire of behaviors requires that he must appear extraordinarily independent, needing no one. He thus develops a repertoire of behaviors in which he suggests that he will care for others—his grandiose schemes. He repeatedly attempts to test, manipulate and overcommit others so that he involves others around him to care for him . . . [and thereby] . . . he obtains the needed dependent role while challenging external constraints under the guise of an aggressive pseudo-independence."

The notion here is that the elated person perceives herself or himself as gloriously strong, capable, and competent, *in order not to be aware* of another perception of the self, which may be looming even closer to consciousness. And that is an estimate of one's self as weak, needy, scared, powerless, dependent. The fluctuation between two such radically different appraisals of one's own person may be, as some experts have suggested, a reflection of some vacillation between identification with the submissive maternal figure and with the more powerful father. In other words, the manic-depressive patient, in denying an underlying depressive identification with the mother, acts out an intensely triumphant, strong, victorious, overaggressive role which is in imitation of the paternal figure. It is a way of becoming emancipated from being-like-mother by means of being-like-father; it's also a way of showing the world that one is the person on top.

According to the schema being suggested here, it is the manic-depressive person's failure to attain his or her inflated goal, or dream of glory, that finally forces a renunciation of the identification with the powerful father. The fantasied strength and power vanish with the bursting of the bubble—the fantasied goal that was, in one's imagining, somehow within reach already. And it is in the wake of having to renounce the paternal identification (so goes the reasoning) that the patient becomes so depressed, so utterly helpless.

In a way, this psychological model did match with Judith's situation; and it fit almost as neatly as Cinderella's glass slipper. As she once remarked: "The manic-depressive family pattern is very much tied up with your relationship to your mother and father; this is true. You have all of these ambivalent feelings of love and hate—which are exemplified in those extreme mood swings; in your elation and in your despair. You can't react in any normal way; you are always responding in extremes. And apparently, from what I understand, it also has to do with conflicting expectations."

The Girl Game

Judith *had* had two different sets of expectations that she'd been asked to live up to simultaneously: "I was supposed to be both boy and girl.

I mean that I was expected to be very achieving, like a son, and that part I *did* like. But at the same time I was supposed to be very popular and docile and all of those traditional girl things . . . which was something that I wasn't good at, and that I hated." She hesitated, then said with dubiousness: "I sometimes think of my greatest sin—and maybe even the part of me that is 'crazy'—as being my failure to, you know, be like my mother. She was . . . very beautiful. And she was charming, and into the whole female business of attracting men. I was a disappointment to her; I was offbeat, not very interested in clothes and what she used to call the 'girl game.' The model of the female role that she presented me with—it wasn't for me; I rejected it very early. I knew I wasn't like her, and that I wouldn't make it. I'd just never fit into her categories of 'womanness'; the ways I was weren't her idea of what a woman should be *like*."

She had always, said Judith, felt deeply guilty about not being the person her mother had wanted her to be. Still, she'd had—at the very same time—a certain contempt for this particular feminine vision. She repudiated what she termed the "subordinate, manipulative kind of girl game" and disliked all the pressures about being popular, "developing poise," "having dates," and the other feminine expectations which weighed more and more heavily upon her. "I loved my mother, truly," observed Judith, with the somewhat shamed expression of a misbehaving schoolchild, "but I couldn't, somehow, do those things *right*. At the same time, I knew I had to. Because of course, the idea was that your life *depended*, if you were a woman, on the quality of the man you were good enough to attract!"

Judith sighed. Then she said, with a touch of puzzlement, "Maybe girls aren't growing up with those kinds of assumptions nowadays. But we—oh, we surely did in the 1950s. Nothing was so desperately critical as the 'girl game.' For it was the men who had the power, the real social power. They could give, or withhold from a woman, everything that would matter in her life."

She herself did, she conceded, nevertheless suspect some imponderable link between her mania and her "arrogant" (nonfeminine, nondependent) way and mode of living. Indeed, in speaking of her first hospitalization—the one out in California—Judith had said (not without pride) that when they'd brought her onto the ward, she was "flying." "I was manic, like the *men* there . . . not depressed, you know, like all of the *women*." Maleness was, in her mind, linked with being high, in charge, expansive and active; while femaleness was vulnerability, lowness, dejection, and passivity. To be completely the woman was, in her view, to be completely without power.

A Kind of Biological Command

True understanding of the problem of manic-depressive disorder will ultimately come, I suspect, from the biochemist's laboratory and not from the psychiatrist's office. For, fascinating though it may be to try to fathom the underlying psychology of bipolar illness, one can truly do little other than to produce rather wobbly theoretical constructions. Life events; psychological history; personality structure: all are, one suspects, less significant than are the neurochemical surges and tides which occasionally overwhelm the realities of the vulnerable person's ordinary mental and physical existence. In brief, the feelings of joy or feelings of depression—whether or not they've been triggered by a real happiness, on the one hand, or a sorrow or setback, on the other—cannot be normally handled and worked through by the manic-depressive individual. The feelings, because of some mysterious biochemical disturbance, become self-generating. The mood, whichever it is, doesn't end . . . and, while it's undoubtedly due to some subtle interplay between the person's constitutional predisposition and her or his environment, the major part of the responsibility can almost certainly be attributed to factors that are biological.

In manic-depressive illness, a shift in the functioning of those delicate brain compounds which appear to be necessary for maintenance and regulation of normal moods must be involved. And it is this mysterious inner happening which more than anything else probably sets in motion that marked shift in the manic-depressive person's state of emotional being and of experiencing. Rather than that biological permission to develop a mood disturbance, of which I spoke earlier, the bipolar individual indeed may be subject to a kind of biological command.

The command might be, in fact, a genetic one. There have been, in the recent past, some fascinating investigations into the possibly hereditary nature of manic-depressive disturbance. Before I talk about these carefully controlled laboratory studies, however, I want to mention that it has long been recognized that manic-depressive illness tends to run in certain families and groups. Although it is, as I said earlier, statistically infrequent within the population at large, there are certain peoples among whom it is very common. Jews and Scandinavians, for example, show high incidences of manic-depression; among Jews it is, actually, the most common form of mental illness.

New Genetic Clues

The relatively new genetic evidence has, however, changed what was an intriguing suspicion—that there is some kind of inherited vulnerability which renders some people incapable of adapting to certain types of stress—to a respectable scientific view. The evidence, according to Dr. Gerald Klerman, director of ADAMHA (The Alcohol, Drug Abuse and Mental Health Administration, in Washington, D.C.) comes from three disparate sources. One source is studies of twins; such studies have shown that where one member of a pair develops manic-depressive illness the likelihood that the other twin will do so is extraordinarily high—over 60 per cent. "Also," Dr. Klerman told me, "identical twins have a higher concordance rate than fraternal twins. What that means in nonjargon terms is that if the twins came from the same egg the probability that if one is manic-depressive, the other will be too, jumps even higher."

That, observed Dr. Klerman, is one good genetic clue. Another comes from what are called *pedigree studies*. These are long-range studies of families—running back several generations—of individuals who have been hospitalized with manic-depressive illness. What the pedigree studies have demonstrated is that, in the families of these patients, there are more manic-depressive and depressive relatives than could have been accounted for by chance alone. Furthermore, a large-scale pedigree investigation, carried out in Israel, has implied that the incidence of manic-depressive illness is far higher among the Ashkenazi, or Jews of European origin, than it is among the Sephardic Jews (who are Spanish, Moroccan, more oriental in origin). This study, which was done by a student of Dr. Klerman's, indicated that "almost all of the manic-depressive disorder in Jerusalem seems to be among European families." Added Klerman, with a bemused and intrigued expression, "There seems to be practically none among the North African and Middle Eastern families."

A third type of evidence, also arguing strongly for some inherited predisposing factor in the development of bipolar illness, has come from yet *another* kind of genetic investigation. There are now several studies which have attempted to link the tendency toward manic-depressive disturbance with certain other characteristics—such as color blindness and the Xg blood type—which are known to be passed down from parent to descendants and to be carried on the mother's X chromosome. This research has, in general, supported the notion that the predisposition toward becoming manic-depressive can be correlated with these other genetically transmitted traits.

In other words, one may inherit the vulnerability to manic-depressive disease from one's mother, grandmother, or great-grandmother in much the same way that one might inherit her color blindness or her Xg blood type. And perhaps it is true that among the good fairies surrounding Judith Karlin's cradle—who'd bestowed upon her her superior intelligence; a great creativity; a sense of energy and purpose; an eccentricity, of a sort, that went with her artist's conviction that she was, indeed, someone quite special—there'd been the traditional evil fairy, bestowing the one dark and damning gift, i.e., a tendency to crumble under certain types of stress. She was, if I've not said so, Jewish; and her family was of Ashkenazi, which is to say, European, origin.

Special Biological Permission

This brings us back, once again, to that notion of "special biological permission." Before she'd begun being maintained on the antimanic medication lithium (which has, at this writing, kept her attack-free for a period of some four years), Judith had experienced three upsurges of prolonged mania, and one—relative to the degree of mania—not too severe depression. And what had set these attacks off, in terms of events or environmental input, had been: 1) a move back to the East Coast after a stint of teaching out in California; 2) a letter from Frank, whom she was to see during a summer vacation in California (also, perhaps, the death of an adored grandmother, which had occurred several weeks before Frank's letter actually arrived); and 3) the prospect of receiving academic tenure and promotion.

These were, as I have remarked, all circumstances that would require a certain ability to cope and to adapt—to meet changing situations and the changing demands they involved. They still appear to be, though, far removed from the kinds of massive trauma that would drive a person to madness. Yet "driven crazy" is clearly something that Judith Karlin had been. Something about returning East; and then going back to the West to work on that manuscript; and then about coming up for her tenure, had been sufficient to set into motion those mysterious, ill-understood shifts in central nervous system functioning that appear to underlie disorders of emotion and of mood.

So we return to whatever constitutional factors may underlie that special biological permission. And yet we mustn't, I think, succumb to

a certain temptation to view Judith Karlin in terms, only, of heredi-
tarily transmitted biochemical aberration. It would be easy, foolishly
easy, to begin forgetting her personhood: to see her as essentially a defective molecule, decked out with hair, clothing, parents, friends, a
job, and all of the accouterments of a human personality. But this
would be to ignore the fact that brains—even ones that show the non-
adaptive responses that Judith's did—respond primarily to *psychological and social experience*. And so, while soberly taking into account the obvious relevance of constitutional factors, one mustn't
dismiss the importance of "nurture" and the things that had happened
and were happening in her ordinary, everyday life.

Judith could have had no mind, no "mental life," without the physical functioning of the brain that underlay it. Nor, on the other hand,
could one imagine her having a *brain that functioned in the absence of
a past;* that is, in the absence of psychological learning. The situation
is not an either-or, and one cannot "explain" Judith Karlin's dilemma
solely in terms of neuroregulators and brain biochemistry. As one psychiatrist, Dr. Robert Stoller, has written: ". . . I hope no one seriously
thinks one's past life does not usually influence one's present behavior.
That a medical treatment may quite ignore this past, go directly to the
brain and succeed in changing behavior does not disprove the importance of that past experience in producing the behavior. It may only
indicate the obvious—that the brain is the final common pathway"
through which behavior is going to be expressed.

I am making these points because I do think very seriously that the
notion that hers was a genetically, constitutionally disposed weakness
that rendered her unable to respond adaptively to her environment
might make Judith's problems seem very different from those of
women who are capable of responding in more vital and healthier
ways. And yet the fascinating thing about such abnormal reactions
and about "diseases" in general—and this has been true throughout the
history of medicine—is what they have to tell us about the meaning of
"normality" and of health. Judith's issues, the emotionally laden dilemmas with which she wrestled, were the stuff of her madness: and
yet they were not, by any means, matters remote, alien, or arcane.

She was struggling with a set of difficulties revolving around an uncertainty about which of her beloved-and-resented parents she was
most like. In a sense, certain things that she complained about—having
the expectations of both sexes put upon her—had placed before her
monumental tasks that she had not, somehow, the strength to carry
out. This confusion of sex-appropriate tasks ("Should I marry?"
"Should I have a child?" "Should I try to make it in the world?"
"Should I be passive and receptive, or go-getting and aggressive?") is

a theme that pops up again and again, in the many conversations I've had with depressed, distressed, and also with normally coping women. It is a common problem in a time of changing feminine expectations; and it can only become commoner with the passage of time.

Of course becoming manic is a highly specialized way of responding to stress. For Judith, solving the problem involved becoming all-masculine, and leaving those other dilemmas behind. She'd taken control of her own life, and was relating to power as it exists in a man's world. Once she'd said to me, in a voice throbbing with pride and passion, that she had never been stigmatized for deciding to remain single by women who were jealous of her. "You know," she'd explained with a laugh, "the kind of women who say, 'I too would be teaching, or doing something, if I didn't have the fulfillment of my home and three children.' But really, the fact of being able to be single, and to live alone and have status and dignity; that makes America a great country, and the twentieth century a very lucky time to be living! And that's one thing I'm grateful for—I never thought I'd be allowed to live like this! To live alone, and move about, and do a lot of different things. To read, and to write . . . which is what I want to do more than *anything*. To not see people when I don't care to see them —I mean, women weren't allowed to *do* this, a mere twenty years ago!"

She was engaged, not in the girl game, but in the games of the larger world: in *men's* games, and men's activities. In the political intrigues of the department, which, no matter how disinterested she might have felt, required her to take a position on certain sensitive issues, and to pick and choose her positions correctly. She was, in brief, having to deal with professional decisions, made independently, which would secure her a place in what had been and was still to a large degree, a man's competitive, power-riven universe. Occasionally, the entire power game gave her vertigo. For, whatever obstacles "being female" laid in her path, there were also other issues—issues stemming from what seemed to have been a somewhat faulty problematic identification with her mother and father (and therefore with the male-female aspects of her own inner self). Add to these sorts of difficulty, which are the current and everyday concerns of women searching for ways of being that will "fit" with very disparate sorts of inner needs, that biochemical problem: then you will have a far more accurate understanding of, not only the unusualness, but the very *ordinariness* of the sources of Judith's distress.

For she was trying, as are many women like her, to establish herself in a world predominantly masculine in orientation—a world filled with the kinds of power games that men do, in a variety of ways

(competitive sports being an obvious one) spend much of their childhood time preparing for. Part of *her* childhood had been spent in the
learning of how to be popular, chic, poised, and receptive; little wonder that, when it came to making mistakes, and mishandling some matters, she wasn't always up to managing perfectly, to being tough, and
forthright, and properly aggressive. She was operating now with a set
of underlying rules that she couldn't always completely understand.
For this was not the old, powerless, world of women and the "girl
game." That was the world that had been her mother's and Judith's
uneasy, unfinished task was to find the one that she *could* fit in comfortably—the one that would be her own.

In the Thirties: Loving and Working

Single womanhood, a state that Judith championed with such enthusiasm, has recently become a much more acceptable, and even fashion-
able, style of female living. It is still something that's not that usual in
the early thirties, for many women who've declared against marriage
in their twenties have done a turnabout—as had all of the women in
the sample studied by psychologist Wendy Stewart—by the time their
thirties have rolled around. Most women have married, and many have
one or more children. In terms of numerical figures, it used to be the
case that 95 per cent of the adult population was married by this point
in their lives (that is, nineteen out of every twenty people); now the
figure has fallen to somewhere between 92 and 94 per cent. Rounded
upward, that figure means that some eighteen out of every twenty
people are married by the early years of the thirties: despite the great
lot of talk about the nonexistent future of marriage, getting married is
still something that most people do!

The major issues faced by women who *are* married at this point in
their lives—and who may be mothers of one or more offspring—are,
in many ways, different from the issues and concerns being faced by a
career-oriented woman liked Judith Karlin. The "thirties'-issues" of a
person who is wife and mother, (like Mrs. Laurie Michaelson who'll
be met with in the two succeeding chapters) were much more clearly
and distinctly *female* issues, while for Judith, the concerns weren't
dissimilar from those that *men* face during this self-same period of
their lives.

This phase of a *man's* life has been termed, by adult personality
researcher Daniel Levinson and his Yale colleagues, the "settling
down" period (roughly ages thirty-two to thirty-nine). What is set-

tled is the notion of what one's occupational goals are—the place where one wants to get in the world—what the long-range goals will be. The formation of this inner understanding ushers in a time of focused, ambitious, highly energetic committment to the working out of a Dream, the elaboration of the Quest, the goals one wants to reach —and struggles toward—because it will bring happiness at some point in the future. For the man in his early thirties—and the dedicated career woman in her early thirties—there's a sense of crucial choices having already been made, a career commitment solidified. Now one is scrambling up the ladder, getting there and making it. These are the years of advancement, of discovering the limits to which one can possibly go. The flavor of this life period is the flavor of competition; beating other contenders out, while discovering the far borders of one's own possibilities.

When it comes to this sort of career-building enterprise, it must go without saying, the valued and important qualities would be things like aggressiveness, assertiveness, independence. These traits don't always sit comfortably within a woman's personality—and what's more, women are often criticized for daring to display them (see Chapter Thirteen). Equally important, career-building affects opportunities for daily intimacies. In an instance such as Judith's, clearly, the competition wasn't only with other men but with other women. This would affect the nature of those special friendships that are of such significance in women's lives—those intimate friendships through which women change, develop, and grow.

Female friendships have, in general, a very different quality than do male friendships. Women friends are usually more intimate, in terms of feelings shared; and they're more tolerant and fluid, in the sense of permitting one another to change their minds about an opinion that's been expressed yesterday. (Men can become *indignant* about such easy shifts in views and opinions! They behave, frequently, as though betrayed—as though they'd believed that what she said yesterday had been carved in cement, for all time!) Women's friendships contain more empathy, more mutual nurturing; they allow in certain sorts of shared knowledges and perceptions that would have been filtered out, had one insisted on perfect definition and precision, on statements and opinions made for eternity. And women *need* their friends—and grow through their friends—perhaps using them as nearer images in working out their own individual identities.

Men's friendships are not like that, by and large. Men can, in fact, sustain their friendships at what might be called a buddy level. They *do* things together—work, hike, fish, hunt, climb mountains, bowl, etc.—and share certain experiences. Women *take care* of each other—

and are taken care of—and are willing to switch that caretaking around; to take turns. But this kind of willingness to merge and to trust and to share one's innermost thoughts and feelings can't thrive in a situation of competition. For women who, like Judith Karlin, have placed career commitments foremost, must—as men *must*, in their professional lives—be a good deal more careful. To a certain not inconsiderable degree, Judith had to forego these feminine experiences of self-sharing and loving empathy. She had, perforce, to be prudent; one doesn't expose one's flank to one's competitors. Women's friendships are often subtly (or not so subtly) affected and altered by their assumption of a serious career commitment.

Women become more wary, in this situation, more like men. They tend to keep themselves to themselves to a far greater degree—adaptive behavior, on the career front; but on the other hand, a far lonelier way of being. One is, because one has to be, far more chary of giving away the same degree of "self"; one keeps one's emotional distance. This leaves the woman more isolated, more alone with her own thoughts (which men *are*, more than are most women). Men don't let themselves get involved in the kinds of intimate exchange that would let others into the secrets of their weaknesses—for obvious reasons— and working women, who are moving up a career ladder, must be affected by the same rather practical constraints.

A man, when he shares his intimate thoughts and feelings will usually do it (if he does ever do it) with a woman. A woman, in a relationship with an opposite-sex partner, will often do it with a man. But she'll still tell much about who-she-really-is to her friends, while the man will be much more guarded. Judith Karlin, for reasons stated above, had to show a certain amount of cool appraisal when it came to deciding how much of herself to share with friends who were female. And, when it came to forming a long-term attachment—a commitment to an intimate relationship with a male partner—she was, as she'd made clear, utterly and completely opposed.

Her sexual relationships were "satisfactory" in terms of the life she was trying to live. She had affairs, passing affairs, with men whom she found attractive enough—and whom she liked well enough—and this was really as far as she wanted to go; no further.

Still, I couldn't help but wonder about this when thinking about the specifics of her history. For what, in general, had her manic fantasies actually all been about? It seemed to me that they'd all had a strikingly similar sort of a plot; they were all variations on a particular theme. While Judith herself might disagree with this interpretation, it struck me that each episode had started with a rising euphoria relating to a love affair that was ripening in an almost magical way. There was a mystical, quasi-religious bond growing up between Judith and her fantasy-lover, and it was to culminate in a wonderful production—something that the two of them *created together*.

Now what is it, when one thinks about it, that a man and woman who fall passionately in love with each other and establish a powerful attachment often *do* produce? Judith's metaphor, the waking dream of her mania, sounded to me strangely like the coming together of a couple of lover-partners in order to create a child.

In this, Judith's story is, in fact, not so terribly unusual. It does occur surprisingly frequently that a woman will join her professional creativity with a man, in a business venture; and that together they will work to produce a new being—a product. The relationship between the pair is non-sexual—definitely—but it is charged and energized by that erotic undercurrent. One person is male; the other is female—that's all. In Judith's instance, however, the intellectual engagement seemed to move inexorably from the gratifying to the pathological.

In any case, the "child," in Judith's manic script, had to be an artistic production. Was it, one wondered, because an intellectual creation wouldn't involve a letting go of those competitive, assertive, more masculine parts of the self—of *her*self—which she so valued, because they were seen as the opposite of what is powerless, passive, dependent . . . feminine? Her manias, in some strange way, seemed to me to be almost like disinhibitions of powerful defenses against needs and strange wishes that had been powerfully suppressed, squelched, denied. Only those manic upsurges, rising above the seawalls of her fears and uncertainties, had permitted the inrushing of experiences of loving, and the euphoria that attends it; and the intimate connection that results in that "something new," the pair's mutual creation. It was as though, for the Judith who was in her *right* mind, intimacy was unthinkable; it was terrifying; and to "fall in love" was the equivalent of "to go crazy." Sane, she would stay away from love-bonds entirely; for loving raised the possibility of traumatic separations, such as those terrible experiences when her mother went away to the hospital and she was still a small and dependent child "in love" with her adored caretaker.

In her present life, Judith was protected against any such future shocks; she depended on no one. In the daylight of her daily existence and of her sanity, she was well content to be on her own and without any long-term emotional attachments.

CHAPTER TEN

Postpartum Problems: Laurie (1)

The Ways That Life Really Is

For Laurie Michaelson, the fall into that depressive state was no spectacular or dramatic occurrence. She'd been aware, in the weeks before Christmas of 1975, that her mood state was "slumping," but she had not linked that to anything serious, and certainly not to an illness. What she was going through seemed to be, in essence, something one could hardly put a name to. It was just a dullness, a lack of pleasure, a "dead kind of feeling" that seemed to have invaded every aspect of her life. It was as though the taste of her food and even the colors of the things around her had somehow grown pallid and dim. It was, as she told me later, a feeling that "the whole world had turned to cardboard."

Laurie had heard about something called a postpartum depression—and wondered vaguely if this could relate to what she was presently experiencing. She believed that was something that occurred *just after* the birth of a baby, though—and her daughter Katherine was now over eight months old. Still, the ways she was feeling might well have something to do with the fact that she'd just stopped breast-feeding and could feel her period coming on. There certainly must be massive hormonal changes involved in simply ceasing nursing. And, while she'd had her blue and rotten moods—as does everyone—she had never felt so wretched before. "I just felt my period coming on, and I thought: 'Well, I've got somehow to get through this.' I assumed that what was going on inside my body was connected with what was happening inside my head. Which was basically that I was awfully low, and my spirits were down further than they'd *ever* been. I couldn't understand it, couldn't figure it out—what was making me feel those ways. That my life was meaningless, and I was someone that nobody really needed or cared for. That I was just someone"—she drew in a short, shallow breath, then let it out, saying—"unnecessary." "At another level," she added, "I felt as if I were someone terrible, truly worthless and no good. So these thoughts were just . . . taking over my mind. And I wondered . . . about the hormones." Her voice, trailing off, sounded tremulous and doubtful. She'd had no other explanations to offer herself, for this state that she was in, if not "hormones" and/or "postpartum depression."

Then she recalled that something similar had happened before, when she had stopped breast-feeding Tony, her first child (who was then two and a half). "At that time, too," she recalled, "there had been this funny sort of a feeling. Like, well, that life was awfully *disappointing*. It wasn't what I'd hoped for and expected, perhaps. . . ." She shook her fair head briskly, and met my eyes with her own level hazel ones: "That time," she said, as if in summary, "that mood—the sense of futility and so forth—passed over fairly quickly."

But this time, it didn't. Her menstrual period arrived and left and her mood persisted and deepened. As the Christmas and New Year holidays grew closer, Laurie found herself unhappy to a degree that was becoming truly frightening. There was no rational explanation —at least none that she could fasten upon—which might make comprehensible to her this sense of inner devastation. And yet it went on and grew worse—she had begun accusing herself of every kind of weakness and failing. At the same time, there was a dizzying array of realistic demands to be met. They impinged upon her from every side. She had to perform as mother, as wife, and as an organized working woman (for she taught social work two days a week). And she struggled to keep up with everything being asked of her, to manage well despite the painful mood of sadness and the certainty of her worthlessness and inevitable failure. But she was beginning to worry, with the passing of the days and weeks, not merely about performing adequately in her round of tasks and duties. She was doubting her ability to carry on at all, much longer—to continue this impersonation of an individual who was going about her life, and was functioning.

As far as *doing* anything about the ways she was feeling, Laurie assumed that—being realistic—this was a matter beyond repair. Her feelings had to do with the massive imponderables of human existence, with things that were beyond her own frail understanding. They had to do with dreams not quite coming true; with the hopes that one starts with, and the ways that life really is. If her own lot in life wasn't absolutely perfect, why then, she'd reasoned, what she had to do was to accept what was after all quite an acceptable lot.

There was, nevertheless, that underlying uncertainty about her own capacity to go on; she was in pain, and unsure about her ability to endure. The mood, too, was anything but stationary. It was moving slowly but inexorably downward.

"One night I sat up with my husband, and I cried and cried and cried. I didn't know why: I had Gabe, and we'd had our boy, and then we'd had our girl, and this had been, really, exactly what I'd wanted. But then there was the whole other thing—the set of feelings that seemed to have taken me over, and the kinds of ideas I was having. That I, basically, was a person who—didn't matter. That I was someone who—how can I say it? It sounds so strange—was not really necessary to anyone." She laughed, then, shook her head as if to clear it of the memory of such notions. "It's hard to explain, because I was, I know, a mother of young children. And when are you *ever* more important?" She shook her head again. "So I couldn't fit all of those things into any logical pattern . . . but these were the ways I felt. I mean," she repeated in a low voice, "not very *good*, in general, about myself."

She was quietly shredding a piece of Kleenex that she held in one hand. Laurie Michaelson had told me, at the outset of our first interview, that she was thirty-two years old. But she looked, sitting in the chair next to my desk, like someone's pretty, well-scrubbed, high school sweetheart. "It made no sense," she was saying, again shaking her head, and this time more vigorously. I caught the smell of shampoo.

We were talking in a borrowed office at the Mood Clinic, a treatment facility associated with the University of Pennsylvania. This was where Laurie Michaelson had eventually come for treatment, when the shrinking island of her confidence had left her no further space for living. By then, however, the symptoms of her depression had become unbearable. She felt too stupid, and too inadequate, to go on caring for her children. "I was confused, and afraid I would do something disastrous." She'd also become phobic about going outside, for she was experiencing powerful impulses to end her life—to end this mounting anxiety, panic, and suffering. Laurie had confided, to a horrified friend, that she felt strong urges to just throw herself in front of a subway car, or a bus.

Hormonal Enigmas

I want to stop here, to question the legitimacy of Laurie's assumption —that the "cause" of her severe depression had been hormonal.

As far as the term *postpartum* is concerned, there is a statute of limitations in current medical use . . . and Laurie Michaelson was definitely beyond it. *By definition* the term refers to one of three general time frames: the first ten days after delivery *or* the first three months after giving birth *or* the wider-drawn six-month boundary. Since a full eight months had elapsed since Katherine had been born, Laurie was a couple of months past even the six-month outermost limit. Her depression was not, therefore, postpartum (at least not by definition!). I think it would be useful, nevertheless, to linger on this particular subject for a while. Some things that can be said about it may—even in the set of circumstances we've been discussing—prove to be ultimately clarifying.

One statement that can be made about the postpartum period is that it does involve profound endocrine changes. Although our scientific knowledge of what actually happens during delivery is most incomplete (it's not known, for example, what hormonal factors come into play to trigger the onset of human labor) those studies that *are* available indicate that there are literally massive shifts in hormones and fluid balance occurring in the first ten days postpartum. And these metabolic shifts seem to bring about psychologically vulnerable states—for it is within these ten days that some two thirds of postpartum psychiatric reactions (often depression) emerge.

But an enhanced vulnerability to mental disturbance seems to extend well beyond that small ten-day span. For, as the statistics illustrate with great clarity, new mothers are at a greatly increased risk—some *four or five times* greater—of developing a psychological illness in the first three months after delivery. For the entire first six months after having given birth, moreover, the woman who's engaged in early mothering is far more "at risk" for the development of some psychiatric disorder than are women in general.

Now it may be that it is the fatigue and the stress of the mothering process itself that brings about these inflated rates of mental illness and distress in parturient women. Or it may be that the predominant factors at play have to do with the remarkable amplitude of those hormonal changes. The greater fragility of the new mother could be reflecting an altered physiological state—matters that are primarily internal and biological.

Medical and psychiatric opinions on this subject vary. But the ancient Greek physicians, who certainly recognized postpartum phenomena, considered the new mother's paradoxical reaction (paradoxical in the sense that she became overwhelmed by sadness, grief, even mad delusions of guilt in the wake of what would appear to be a happy event) as an essentially physical occurrence. As long ago as the fourth century B.C., the medical writer Hippocrates was theorizing about the biological basis of this strange sorrow and/or madness that could invade the mind of the new mother. What was occurring, he suggested, was that the bloody vaginal discharge which continues for some four weeks after a woman has given birth (which is called *lochia*, from the Greek *lochias*, or "pertaining to birth") was being suppressed and diverted and transported to the woman's brain. Her emerging distress—which could take the form of confusion, delirium, delusions of guilt, etc.—was linked not only to the drainage failure of the lochia, but to the biological changes presumed to accompany the onset of lactation.

About this latter subject, Hippocrates opined that: "When blood collects at the breasts of a woman, it indicates madness." The modern reader isn't quite sure what was meant by this curious observation! And yet, quaint as it sounds, it does contain a never-discarded notion: that drastic metabolic changes within the new mother's body—connected, somehow, to the recent delivery *and* to the beginning of breast-feeding—create a climate peculiarly ripe for the emergence of depression, madness, despair.

Over the centuries, the notion that the psychological distress that can flare up postpartum is mysteriously linked to the onset of lactation is one that has been strikingly persistent. In the mid-nineteenth century, for instance, "milk fever" was the name given to the mild depressive reactions that frequently follow childbirth, and which had begun to receive medical notice. And the present-day postpartum blues—which everyone's heard something or other about—are often called "third-day" or "fourth-day blues." It's probably more than coincidental that the third or fourth day after delivery is when milk flows into the new mother's breasts.

Both medical observation and ordinary folk wisdom appear to be in agreement on one general finding: the week to ten days after childbirth is a time of high emotionality and unusual fragility for many women. Since some two thirds of postpartum reactions do occur in this time span, this heightened vulnerability *may* be related to the dramatic sequence of internal, biological changes that are—during this period—obviously getting under way.

A Measurable Difference

Now I want to make it clear that I'm not just talking about high emotionality in women who are psychologically unsteady and ill adapted at best; but I'm speaking of a difference, during this time period, in numbers of ordinarily stable and well-functioning people. Research done both in the United States and in Britain has indicated that the postpartum woman is in an emotional state that's unusual *for her;* she's not, so to speak, herself. Her moods tend to swing up and down more easily, and she is uncommonly (for her) prone to crying.

A study of normal women—women who never developed any acute postpartum symptoms of any sort—carried out at Stanford Medical School in the late 1960s, demonstrated that there is indeed a heightened mood lability, and a heightened tendency to tearfulness during this highly sensitized time.

In that particular investigation, the Stanford researchers studied each of the new mothers intensively during three separate ten-day spans in the woman's life. One was a ten-day period late in her pregnancy. One was the ten days just after she'd given birth. The third ten-day span during which she was studied was one occurring eight months after her infant was born.

What emerged from this research was the indisputable and clear-cut finding that in the ten-day period after delivery the woman was *over three times more likely to cry* than she was during the other two ten-day spans during which she'd been studied. And often, the new mother herself was hard put to supply the reasons. Some women reported weeping because they'd read about someone's terrible misfortunes in the newspapers! They seemed extraordinarily prone to identify with others; and unusually empathetic. (Were hormonal shifts of some mysterious kind supporting the emergence of this kind of psychological predisposition? To feel for another is more crucial to the establishment of a good mothering relationship than almost any other quality.)

Others among the new mothers, asked to explain their moodiness, emotiveness, their unusual weepiness, reported fears and worries about their competency to adequately care for their new babies. Others blamed the "emotional" way they were feeling on their husbands', or lovers', behavior. In truth, her mate's behavior—more than any other single factor in her environment—seemed capable of causing the mother's highly unstable mood to plummet. (In another, a British study of postpartum women, one person was quoted as saying that her husband's failure to notify the diaper service had "caused" her desperate depression! In that research, by the way, it was found that 60 per cent of the normal women investigated had experienced transient depression postpartum.) But, to return to the Stanford Medical School study, there was no doubt that the new mother was in a highly susceptible state. When compared to her ordinary self—the person she

was during the other two ten-day segments—she was clearly more
emotionally reactive, and much more easily disturbed by any perceived slight, or hint of rejection.

Any threat that she sensed in her environment could bring forth an
intense and exaggerated response. (This did turn out to be, ultimately,
one of the issues in Laurie's particular case.)

Scientists are very far indeed from a full understanding of the hormonal changes associated with pregnancy, childbirth, and the onset of
lactation. But what is known is that during pregnancy the woman's
brain is being exposed to ever-increasing levels of a number of powerful hormones; and that, following delivery, there is a precipitous decline in levels of different endocrine agents that have been circulating
in her plasma. What this may involve, some researchers have
suggested, is a biologically induced state akin to withdrawal. The new
mother's moodiness and irritability, her tendencies toward depression
and crying, may be similar to the symptoms one sees in a person coming off drugs (barbiturates, for example). In this case, of course, what
would be occurring would be a female-hormone withdrawal. (I might
mention, here, that a good many women experience mild or severe
symptoms, premenstrually—the "premenstrual distress syndrome."
And in the few days before the onset of menstruation, similarly to the
time during and following childbirth, there is an abrupt female reproductive hormone decline.)

In any event, though, it's true that during pregnancy these female
hormones are being churned out in copious quantity. At the onset of
labor, some of the estrogens (estrone and estradiol) are found at levels
some one hundred times higher than they are during the latter (luteal)
phase of the menstrual cycle. Another estrogen, estriol, appears in the
pregnant woman's urine at levels that are about one thousand times
higher than those seen during ordinary menstrual fluctuations! And
the potent hormone progesterone (which means "in support of gestation") is also being produced by the placenta in highly enlarged
quantities. During the last three months of her pregnancy, in fact, the
mother-to-be's progesterone levels have risen some tenfold above
what they are during the luteal phase of her cycle. And they are sixty-
five times higher than when she is in the early, egg-ripening "follicular" phase of the rhythmic menstrual variation—a time of the cycle
when estrogens are higher and progesterone secretion is low.

Female sex hormones are, in short, present in generous and ever-
increasing amounts throughout the course of pregnancy. And so,
curiously enough, are commonly reported feelings of enhanced well-
being. This sense of feeling good is a generality: it is the mirror-

image, though, of the frequently experienced vulnerability and sensitivity that seem to be so general postpartum. In terms of hard facts and statistics, too, there is a *decreased* risk of mental illness among females who are pregnant. In other words, while women are more likely to develop a psychiatric disturbance after the birth of a child, they are *less* likely to do so during pregnancy. To what degree, one wonders, is that shifting risk rate linked to internal, physiological factors—how does it connect to the woman's shifting biology?

Needless to say, many scientists have wondered about the possibly protective effects of certain steroid substances (not only the sex hormones, but thyroid hormone, adrenocortical hormones, etc.) that are found in the gestating woman's blood plasma. For, while women report feelings of well-being, their hormone levels have been showing a gradual and steady increase—and then, with the approach of delivery; during the delivery itself; and in the time just afterward, there is a precipitous decline. Most of these potent compounds have dropped dramatically within the first several days after a woman gives birth. This is, of course, that weepy, emotional time, when symptoms are so much more likely to emerge.

The Hormone Progesterone: A Natural Analgesic

According to Dr. Seymour Levine, of Stanford Medical School—who is one of this nation's leading researchers on endocrines and behavior —the hormone progesterone is one that has been singled out for a good deal of scientific interest. The reason is that this particular hormone appears to have some natural analgesic effects. A vast array of research, carried out on infrahuman mammals (pregnant female rats, for the most part) suggests that progesterone acts as an internally produced sedative. When levels of progesterone are high, in relation to levels of estrogens circulating in the individual's blood plasma, there appears to be some calming influence upon behavior. A pregnant rat, exposed to a noxious stimulus in her environment (such as being moved suddenly from one place to another, or being given a whiff of ether) will respond with less output of stress hormones than will a nonpregnant peer. During pregnancy in humans, progesterone levels are about twice as high as are levels of estrogens. "One might speculate," suggested Levine, "that 'high progesterone' correlates with 'lowered emotional reactivity' not only in pregnant rats but in gestating women."

The Species Is Mammalia

One must be cautious, of course, about extrapolating from the pregnant female rat to the pregnant female human being. (I must say, however, that we do regularly extrapolate in this way when we go about testing drugs!) But as Dr. Levine observed, it would be highly unlikely that progesterone would be having one kind of influence upon female rats and an entirely different effect in the human being. "We are talking about the operation of biological systems, in general," he explained, "which is to say, biological principles that are operative across a range of groups that are all members of a species. That species is *Mammalia;* and it's characterized by this important commonality, i.e., the mother breast-feeds the young. And it would be antibiological thinking to imagine that a mechanism that acts to bring about a particular situation in one species—say, this hormone that has a calming influence on the pregnant female—would serve a completely differing purpose in some other species. If this were so," he added, "we wouldn't be able to talk about 'biological principles.' There would be 'rat principles' and 'dog principles' and 'human principles' . . . which is contrary to all the biological evidence that now exists."

So progesterone brings about a degree of behavioral quietude in rats. The question naturally arises: is there evidence that it does so in humans? And the reply is that there is strong evidence that it does. In one study, carried out at Stanford Medical School, a group of female patients were given progesterone in the midpoint of their menstrual cycle, as treatment for anxiety and depression. They reported increased drowsiness and sleeping—and some mild amelioration of symptoms. Progesterone has also been used as an *anesthetic.* It would be difficult, I suppose, to go beyond that in terms of achieving a state of "behavioral quietude"!

It must be borne in mind, nevertheless, that hormonal actions in human beings are more evanescent, more difficult to discern clearly, than is true in lower mammals. There is, in the infrahuman animal, a much clearer correlation between "hormonal status" and "behavior." For example, if an ovulating female rat who *has mothered in the past* is given some newborns to care for, that female will—within a very short period of time—begin secreting prolactin ("in support of lactation"), which is one of the major hormones associated with nursing. She will begin to lactate, and become capable of breast-feeding the little rat pups. In other words, what is happening in that female rat's environment has a straightforward effect upon the state of her hormones! In humans, the relationship between the female's hormone levels and events in her environment are clearly more indirect and . . . unfathomable. Obviously, a human female, given a newborn *not* her own to care for, will be capable of showing maternally protective and nurturant behavior. But she won't—no matter how much mothering experience she happens to have had—respond physiologically to the mere presence of the infant, and find herself commencing lactation!

We can't say that what is true for the rat is obviously going to be true, with no modification, for the human. But it is very probably the case, says Dr. Levine, that the calmative action of progesterone is present in both female rat and female human. For female humans, like females of the lower animal species, do undergo momentous biological changes that are associated with states of pregnancy and with childbirth, and with lactation. And, while study of these physiological processes in lower mammals can't provide us with *human* answers that are iron-bound in their certainty, this research does provide us with strong and intriguing theoretical possibilities.

The Mother Is *the Environment*

The very suggestion that a hormone related to pregnancy might promote a state of calmness *in the mother* is fascinating. From the point of view of adaption—and of mechanisms that enhance chances of survival—it makes the best of evolutionary sense. For, from the point of view of the growing fetus, the mother herself *is* the environment! It isn't very difficult to see, therefore, why a hormone relating to gestation might be one that acts as a kind of behavioral sedative: keeping the mother relatively quiescent will provide the proper setting in which the embryo can become firmly implanted, and can then grow.

Progesterone is, by the way, the hormone that comes into play during pregnancy to prevent the uterus from undergoing its ordinary, rather violent contractions. Again, this is adaptive: if those uterine muscles were contracting, as they do as a matter of course, expulsion of the fetus would be far more likely to occur. So progesterone does have this clear-cut effect—quieting of the uterine muscles—in rats and in human mothers-to-be. And the possibility is that this potent hormone, impinging upon the brain in ever-enlarging amounts throughout the course of pregnancy, is exercising a mildly tranquilizing effect upon the female's (rat, or human) experiencing and behavior.

A Normal Menstrual Cycle

I want to pause at this point to summarize and then to further elaborate upon some of these various things that I've been saying. Before doing so, however, I think it would be useful to sketch in—for purposes of background and comparison—the rough outline of the hormonal changes that take place within the course of an ordinary monthly cycle. I'll begin with the first day of bleeding, which is the starting point of the cycle, and a time when both estrogens and progesterone are quite low.

This is the beginning of the *follicular*, egg-ripening segment of the menstrual cycle; and in this phase, a group of follicles (ovarian egg containers) are beginning to grow. They are influenced by and responding to a "follicle stimulating hormone," which is being released by the pituitary, or master gland of the brain. As the follicles enter this period of growth and expansion, they secrete and release estrogens in steadily increasing amounts.

During the follicular phase of the cycle, progesterone is present; but the ratio of this hormone to the estrogens is such that the latter are in the ascendant. Estrogens keep rising continuously until the twelfth day, when they peak dramatically. This surge in estrogens is, then, a signal back to the pituitary. A second brain hormone, "luteinizing hormone" is now released. Under the influence of the surge in estrogens, which has brought about a surge in luteinizing hormone, ovulation occurs at midcycle. The egg is extruded from the follicle, and the empty follicle remains. The first half, or *follicular* phase of the cycle is completed.

Once the egg is gone, the empty follicle—the container—which is still being stimulated by luteinizing hormone from the pituitary, changes its structure to become the *corpus luteum* (from the Latin, this means "yellow body"). It is now just that: a little yellow body, not quite the size of the head of a tack. This corpus luteum starts manufacturing and secreting the second ovarian hormone of the cycle —progesterone. This part of the monthly rotation, the second part, is called the *luteal* phase of the cycle.

During this phase, which lasts for fourteen days (if the egg isn't fertilized) the estrogens rise again, this time to a smaller, second peak. But now the estrogens-progesterone ratio has been reversed from that which prevailed in the follicular, egg-ripening part of the cycle: progesterone is now the hormone that dominates and holds sway. This hormone, which in the preovulatory segment of the cycle had been being produced at about the rate of two to three milligrams per day, has shot up tenfold. During the luteal phase, progesterone shows a ten-fold increase, to reach production levels of some twenty to thirty milligrams daily.

But this state of affairs changes suddenly, some four or five days before menstruation. At this point, progesterone levels take a precipitous, abrupt nose dive. Estrogens are, at this same time, also falling rapidly; but they aren't present in the same quantities that were seen earlier, and they don't drop with the same steep sharpness. It is, at any rate, this sudden hormone withdrawal—particularly *progesterone* withdrawal—that some experts believe underlies the mood changes, headaches, tension, anxiety, water retention, irritability, cramping, and so forth, that a large number of women experience premenstrually.

Physicians Frederick T. Melges and David A. Hamburg, in a paper entitled "Psychological Effects of Hormonal Changes in Women," have this to say: "The sedative action of progesterone is important, because it suggests the possibility that the normal rise and fall of progesterone during the menstrual cycle produces a syndrome akin to sedation followed by the withdrawal phenomena associated with sedative drugs."

Some 20 per cent of women seem to experience moderate to severe mood changes or other symptoms during that often rocky four- or five-day time span just before menstruation, when progesterone and estrogens are showing their dramatic decline. Some of the physical symptoms, such as headache, cramping, and edema (bloating) are amenable to treatments of varying kinds; but the best advice, insofar as mood changes are concerned, appears to be instructing the woman to anticipate a time of increased emotional vulnerability premenstrually. Once she recognizes a pattern, she's generally far more able to deal with it. An interesting side note is, by the way, that the edema or bloating of menses—believed to be associated with or even the cause of premenstrual depression, irritability, and anxiety—seems in fact to have nothing to do with mood. For, as recent research has demonstrated, the relief of water retention and bloating has no effect on premenstrual psychological distress. They're unrelated, causally, to one another—both are, however, probably symptoms of that sudden decline in progesterone.

I mentioned, a short while earlier, that the luteal phase of the menstrual cycle lasts fourteen days. This is *always* the case; and it is variations in the earlier, follicle-ripening phase that accounts for the varying lengths of different women's cycles. If, however, the egg happens to be *fertilized* during the process, then obviously the luteal phase of the cycle won't end with the abrupt fall in progesterone, the less abrupt decline in estrogens, and a subsequent menstruation. What will occur instead will be what might be imagined as a continuation of the luteal phase—a steady rise in hormone levels, that goes on and on and on. It is as if a pregnancy is a luteal phase that's stretched out for nine months instead of those fourteen days (with the site of hormone production switching, after some six or eight weeks, to the fetal placenta). For, with the onset of labor—and from its outset to its completion—there is the same dramatic decline in hormone levels that one sees in the few days just before menstruation!

Let me cite just a few of the figures. At labor's onset, two of the estrogens—estrone and the important estradiol—are present (in urine) at levels that are about one hundred times higher than they are in the luteal phase of the menstrual cycle. These estrogens drop dramatically at the time of childbirth and make a slow return to *non-pregnancy levels*—that is, one hundred times lower than they were just before delivery—during the course of the following week.

Another estrogen, estriol, is present, just prior to labor, at urinary levels one thousand times higher than they are during the luteal phase of the cycle. And after delivery, estriol levels don't return to normal for anywhere from two weeks to twenty-one days.

As for the presumably calm-inducing hormone, progesterone, the mother-to-be has been synthesizing it at the rate of about two hundred to three hundred milligrams per day (ten times higher, on a daily basis, than the twenty to thirty milligrams she produces during the luteal—which is the high progesterone—phase of the cycle). After the birth of her child her progesterone levels will be so vastly lowered that they could be termed negligible to the point of nonexistence. And the enhanced risk of mental illness in the postpartum period very probably reflects what is a suddenly and drastically altered internal hormonal status, for these are truly very ample and impressive biochemical changes and shifts.

It may be, I might add, that the sense of relative peace that so many women experience during pregnancy also relates to altering hormone levels—especially increasing levels of the "quieting" hormone, progesterone. We know that the risk of mental illness is *lowered* during the latter months of pregnancy, when the expectant mother's hormones are circulating through the bloodstream at such inflated levels. We know, too, that the postpartum period can be a troubled one for many *normal* women. And for maladapted and neurotic women, the months of pregnancy are frequently a time of feeling surprisingly *good*. As psychoanalyst Therese Benedek has written: "The pregnant woman in her vegetative calmness enjoys her body. Many neurotic women who at other times suffer from anxiety become free from it during pregnancy; others become free from depressions and desperate mood changes. Many women, despite physical discomfort and nausea, feel emotionally stable and have a 'good time. . . .' "

This good time may well be a reflection of the mother-to-be's high progesterone, just as the bad time which so many women do seem to experience during the postpartum period may correlate with the starkly sudden decline in levels of this same hormone—which is believed to be sedating and protective, and to promote an inner state of tranquility.

Was It Hormones?

In order to bring this discussion back to the point of its origin—the possible hormonal origin of Mrs. Laurie Michaelson's depression—we'll now have to take some of the matters we've been considering one or two crucial steps further.

Laurie had, it will be remembered, just stopped breast-feeding her eight-month-old child. She had begun to experience inner sensations, indicating that her first postnursing period was about to arrive, when she felt her mood state commencing its downward slide. The two things clearly had been correlated in her own mind: she'd attributed her depressive mood to mysterious and unfathomable hormonal changes. And she still believed, a couple of years after the fact, that she'd suffered a postpartum depression.

By definition, she actually had not done so. For she was well past the ten days, or three months, or six months postdelivery that could have included her within such a category. But the fact that she *had* just stopped nursing does raise the question of whether endocrine shifts had, indeed, been a contributing factor. Or had quitting breast-feeding and getting depressed merely been coincident in time?

Prolactin and *Progesterone: Natural Analgesics*

Although no one can answer that question with any degree of certainty, some recent research—on lactating rat mothers!—has turned up some rather intriguing evidence. It appears that one of the major hormones associated with nursing, the aforementioned prolactin, has the same analgesic, sedating effects as does the hormone progesterone. That is, both prolactin *and* progesterone seem to provide the mother with some biochemical protection against the experiencing of stress. The lactating female, like the pregnant female, is less emotionally reactive to disturbing events in her environment than is the nonnursing, nonpregnant female (with one important exception! That stressor, or noxious event, will elicit less response from the new mother as long as it has nothing to do with her offspring). What these studies have indicated is, in brief, that both these powerful steroid hormones may be influencing the pregnant or nursing female toward a more quiescent state of being.

That "important exception" is, by the way, extraordinary from an evolutionary point of view. It suggests that hormones associated with nursing are part of an elegant biological system—a system which tunes out irrelevance and tunes the mother into the primary business of successfully raising her offspring. Prolactin and the other hormones that come into play during breast-feeding may, indeed, be acting as an information-filtering mechanism. Studies done in Seymour Levine's laboratory have provided evidence to the effect that lactating mothers (rat mothers) are highly attuned to signals coming from their infants —especially to detect signals suggesting that the offspring needs attention or protection—while being relatively less in touch with and responsive to all of the other things going on in the environment.

If one imagines hormonal effects of this kind upon the pregnant or lactating *human* female, then one can easily picture a situation in which the presence or absence of these biochemical buffering substances might make a person more or less fragile emotionally—more or less vulnerable to outside stress. So I think it worth pointing out that the postpartum "blues" period does occur when progesterone levels are drastically lowered (after delivery); and before the possibly "protective" effects of prolactin (associated with breast-feeding) have yet come into play.

Another arresting fact to be noted is that there is now a well-supported scientific literature demonstrating that the estrogens render the female mammal *more reactive* to stresses and to noxious stimuli in her environment. That is, the estrogens seem to have "arousing," "emotionally activating" effects—but these are, it appears, masked by the dampening influences of progesterone and prolactin, when either of these hormones is in the ascendant.

Again, this research has been carried out on animal subjects—mostly on rat females. But I don't think it inappropriate to suggest the possibility that, in Laurie Michaelson's instance, a buffering process supported by prolactin which had served some protective function—

against the experiencing of emotional stress—was at that point in time actually being withdrawn.

She had just stopped breast-feeding. This meant that not only prolactin and another important hormone associated with nursing (oxytocin) were on a rapid decline. But she was moving, as well, into the "follicular," high-estrogen phase of her returning menstrual cycle. This would be a phase during which the activating estrogens—part of nature's design to promote sexual interest, copulation, fertilization, and eventually a new birth—would be dominant on the physiological scene.

At the same time she was—because she was stopping nursing—moving away from that special state of being which psychoanalyst D. W. Winnicott has termed "primary maternal preoccupation." The connections to her child, both biological (breast-feeding) and psychological, were in the process of loosening. She was tuning in to the environment around her more fully, as both her internal state and her "mental blinkers"—keeping her focused upon her baby—were shifting, and changing. Now she had to experience, as real and as painful, difficulties which had been there all the time, but had existed outside the circle of her attention.

Nothing had, indeed, altered or happened in Laurie's own small environment. Her world was patently unchanged. Her issues and her problems, pushed to one side, were ones that had been there all the while. Now, however, she seemed to be responding to them and experiencing them with a difference—and she was overwhelmed.

As Mind Is to Body, Body Is to Mind

It may sound, from the tone of the above discussion, as if I myself have subscribed to Laurie Michaelson's belief—that it had been a changing endocrine status which had been responsible for the emergence of her very serious depressive episode. But actually, that isn't the case, for I don't believe that her hormones *caused* her to become depressed; at least not on that simple one-to-one basis. There were, in truth, a number of disturbing things that were going on in her life at that particular time: the few paragraphs of our conversation, quoted at the outset of this chapter, are but a small segment of a much longer, and complex set of interviews, to be explored in the pages ahead. Nevertheless, I don't think it irrelevant to ask why it was that she *did* become depressed at this particular juncture—I mean, when she was stopping breast-feeding—and not in the week, two weeks, three weeks, etc., before? For it's quite appropriate to imagine that a shifting hormone status—and most especially, a rapidly declining availability of the hormone prolactin—might have lowered the threshold of her vulnerability.

It would be, I believe, a bit naïve to suppose that shifting reproductive hormones alone could throw a person into a state of profound depression. But I think there must be many instances, Laurie Michaelson's case among them, where hormone changes provide a kind of a push, a biologically induced tilt. In her case, as in that of editor Lucy Harris, whose internal environment had been altered by the use of the antihypertension drug reserpine—as well as in that of Judith Karlin, whose heightened vulnerability was probably a genetically transmitted predisposition—one could easily postulate the existence of some failure occurring at some point in time within the swiftly moving, exquisitely delicate, finely tuned self-regulating systems of the brain. It is so easy, I think, to remember that the mind can affect the body—that worry and stress can produce physical illnesses such as high blood pressure, heart attack, ulcer, asthma, and similarly "psychosomatic" diseases. But the message that emerges from these women's histories is a reminder: the body can affect the mind. Neuro-endocrine events, which are intimately interconnected with the brain's electrical energy system—that is, with neurotransmitter function—can affect a person's thoughts, ideas, feelings, opinions of herself. These internal changes can render a person more emotionally susceptible, less able to deal with matters that she *was* able to deal with otherwise—in a word, less flexible, less able to cope.

There is a particular explanation of what causes depression, which has it that depressive episodes are a response to an insufficiency in the giving-getting or input-outflow balance of a person's life. In other words if one can imagine a human being as a kind of an emotional bank—into which love supplies are being deposited and from which they're being withdrawn in the course of the ordinary commerce of living—then the depressed person is either someone who's suffered a staggering loss in her recent past (bringing about so severe a demand on her emotional assets that she's been emptied out into a state of bankruptcy) or someone who, on a chronic level, finds herself giving out far more than she's getting in. In this schema, it's the lack of enough positive things being taken in—in terms of love, caring, nurturance, support—that brings about the depressive crash.

But what's left *out* of such a model are any notions about the functioning of the "bank's" processes—in this instance, the integrity of the biological organism itself. This is, as mentioned earlier, nothing that is unchanging and static. The same input of good and positive things that had sufficed to keep Laurie Michaelson going when she was nursing Katherine, wasn't adequate at another point in time. When Laurie stopped nursing, her flexibility, her entire ability to cope and to manage had seemed to alter drastically. Her entire mode of perceiving herself—and herself in her world—had changed so utterly that she now considered herself worthless and "unnecessary." The degree and amount of love deposits, coming in to her, weren't different; they just were not, any longer sufficient to keep her in business. She became depressed: unable to take in good things, and fairly disabled when it came to continuing to give them out.

And it happened in the absence of *anything's* having occurred, in terms of provocations in her environment—unless, of course, one wanted to count that article she'd come across in her morning newspaper.

CHAPTER ELEVEN

Great Mother / Bad Wife: Laurie (2)

A Dangerously Inadequate Person

Early in our interviews, Laurie Michaelson told me a story: "By the third week or so after my period had come, I was feeling scared. More than scared—I was desperately *frightened*. To get out of bed in the morning was a task that was almost beyond me. I felt desperate . . . sure that, today, something was going to happen. I wasn't capable of caring for my children." It was at this time, when she was so convinced of her own stupidity and ineptness, that she'd come across that unforgettable newspaper article.

It had been toward the end of December of 1975. The New Year's holiday, with all of its sentimental overtones about the good things to come in the year ahead, was close upon her. At the same time, she was living with a sense that each new day could bring the expected catastrophe. She might—through her sheer clumsiness and inadequacy—do something harmful to her helpless and dependent baby. She felt as if she were moving remorselessly closer to the edge of something—to some unspeakable disaster. In the midst of this, sitting at her kitchen table one morning, she'd read a news item in the paper, about a man and a woman, found dead in their home.

"This was something that I've thought about a great deal, ever since," Laurie said, "for that article was"—her voice was full of tremulousness and hesitancies—"it was very significant to me." She was merely talking about a newspaper story, which she'd read several years earlier. But I understood that she was saying something that she didn't find it easy to say.

"This couple," she went on, "they were parents. And they'd been found just a few days after Christmas. There was a big tree in their house, which was all decorated—and there were gift wrappings, and piles of gifts, and ribbons and so forth, still sitting under it. It seemed to have been, according to the article, a double suicide. And the couple's three children, all very little, had apparently been put to death first." Laurie swallowed. "I can remember reading this, and thinking: 'Yeh, well I can understand it. I can understand how people might want to do something like that! . . . Because I knew very well what it was to be feeling so utterly *low*. Feeling that you just can't go on taking care of your family. That you can't, maybe, even go on with your *life*. When I caught myself thinking those things, though, I recognized that—at any other time—I'd have considered those people crazy! I'd have thought that what they did was absolutely horrible . . . that it made no sense whatsoever."

Laurie's eyes, enlarged in her heart-shaped face, were fixated upon me but not seeing me. What was communicated, as if by the flash of an electric arc, was an instantaneous sense of her remembered panic. But then, as if willfully breaking the current between us, she leaned back against the straight wooden office chair she sat upon. When she resumed speaking, it was with a tone of objectivity and calmness. "That newspaper story was something that, I think, truly frightened me. Because it tuned into a—a whole thing that I was experiencing at that time. An awful sense that I was a useless and worthless person, and not able to care for my children. That I was going to do something terrible—out of my own idiocy. I was going to make a terrible mistake of some kind. I wasn't sure what I would do! But I was just" —she couldn't prevent the sounds of anxiety from creeping back into her voice—"so awfully *afraid*."

I looked at her in puzzlement: "But what, in your fantasies, was the 'terrible mistake' that you thought you were going to make?" For some reason, we both started laughing. Then Laurie shook her head, frowned quizzically: "I don't know. Just fears that I wouldn't watch them closely enough. Or that I wouldn't feed the baby, or wouldn't remember to turn off the stove. It's hard to bring back the whole feeling of that time: the enormous responsibilities . . . the sense of being so thoroughly incapable. I was just, in my own mind, so inadequate. A *dangerously* inadequate person."

She paused, then observed with a good-humored wryness: "In actuality, you know, things went along pretty much as usual. I did the food shopping, and the laundry. I did take care of the children; did continue to function two days a week at my job. . . ."

I raised an eyebrow ironically: "So, during this whole time when you were feeling like such a flop at everything, you were also still teaching a couple of days every week?"

"Yes, I was," she answered seriously. "But when I was in the worst of this—and the depression had become acute—I got to feeling inadequate and inferior *there*, as well."

This had been, Laurie explained, a new development. Earlier, she had been able to leave that mood, that whole sense of impending disaster, behind her. But now the notion that she would not be able to perform capably was following her—a burr that was no longer removable at her front doorstep—out into the world of her job. "When the mood got really low, as low as it ultimately *did* get, I was having those same ideas about my work. That the way I did things was all wrong, you know, and I wasn't doing anything there but taking up space. That my getting my position had been, in the first place, all a matter of bravado and bluster. I felt that I was teaching *badly*—and hadn't the foggiest notion about the things I really ought to be doing. And, oh, that I was a terrible fake, and people were starting to see through my game. Things like that . . . and here, as with that article in the newspaper, was another change that was significant. I mean"—she leaned forward—"when you're at home and feeling a bit rough around the edges, that's one thing . . ." She looked down, momentarily, at a piece of Kleenex that she'd been quietly shredding, as if to examine her handiwork. "But when you get into the work world and you can't pick up and go with it . . . well of course as *you* know, that's different."

She looked up, looked into my face: "And so here it was, this thing, this blight, this depression. It had moved out, and had spread into this whole other area of my life."

On work days, as well as on home days now, she was awakening to an agonizing sense of terror. She would fail today and the results would be irreversible. "I got to the point," recounted Laurie, "where it was something ghastly just to wake up and to get myself out of bed. I mean—" She never said what she meant, but ended the sentence in a self-mocking laugh. She was balling up the Kleenex in one hand; and then, with a sudden movement, she tossed it into a large ashtray on my desk. "That's *my* way of copping out," she observed, her voice droll. "I've always done this a bit, I believe . . . I am *not* insomniac! If there's something I'd rather not think about, I . . . sleep. And that's all I wanted, for a while there; when I opened my eyes in the morning I couldn't face the day ahead. I wanted to sleep . . . to go on sleeping forever." I must have responded to this with a startled expression, for I saw its reflection in Laurie's widened eyes.

"I didn't have any active plans about suicide," she answered my unasked question. "I did, though, sometimes feel afraid about—just going outside." I nodded my head, as she spoke, as if to say that Yes, I could understand that. I was thinking about the fear she'd spoken of earlier, a fear of "going out of control." It seemed linked to apprehensions about poorly contained suicidal impulses—to temptations she'd experienced, such as that wayward desire to hurl herself in front of a bus. "I was trying my best to talk about some of the ways I was feeling," continued Laurie, "and I said things to my close friend Joanna . . . things that I think she found very painful to hear."

"Such as . . . ?" My voice was as quiet as I could make it.

"I told her that I really didn't know why it was that I was going on with my life. I said: 'Boy, it is true, I honestly don't understand why I am living. I *do* see that people around me are going about their business, and they're functioning, and so forth; and they seem to know what it's all about, and what they're doing. But these are the sorts of things I *don't* know! And to me, it doesn't all make sense. I mean I honestly don't know why I, or anyone else, struggles—I don't know what it's all *for!*' And Joanna was—of course—taken aback. She said she didn't know how to answer me. She didn't know what to make of my *saying* such desperate-sounding things!"

Laurie laughed lightly then, and blushed, as if at the memory of a social embarrassment. There was a silence. I heard a telephone ringing, unanswered, in the office next door. "I was crying a lot, around that time," she resumed, "and trying to talk to a couple of other friends, but there was no *way*. They simply weren't feeling the things that I was feeling. And, without feeling as I did, the things that I was saying were simply impossible to understand!"

Her closest confidante, Joanna, had taken the tack of reminding Laurie about all of the positive things in her life. She'd even been brave enough to explore frankly that suicidal comment—to ask Laurie point-blank whether she honestly did plan to throw herself in front of a bus. "She said that if I did want to do a thing like that, it was clear that no one was going to be able to stop me. But she said I should ask myself: 'Is this something you really *do* want to do?' And of course, I didn't. I told her that I knew that none of the things I was talking about made any rational sense whatsoever. I said, too, that I realized I should be grateful for all of the good things that really were there in my life. I said: 'I know I should be happy . . . but I am *not!*'" Laurie's voice, as she repeated this last statement, trembled in a high range. It was that note of indignation, of outrage ("Why *me?*") that is so integral an aspect of grief.

There was another silence. When she spoke again, the sounds that emerged were softer and more burdened. "I was feeling so appallingly miserable, and yet saw no cause for the misery. I'd believed, in the beginning, that it was all just a physical thing: that it'd pass me by if I could just hang in there, and wait it all out. But then, after that first postweaning period had come and gone, I was still feeling the same. No!" She corrected herself hastily, making a quick erasing gesture with one hand. "I wasn't. The fact is that I was feeling steadily worse. There were some three weeks there when I went . . . I think . . . as low as a human being can go."

Her face, as she said this, was a grimace of remembered pain: "One morning, just before going out to work, I told Gabe that I couldn't go on; I couldn't stand it. I was going somewhere, though I didn't yet know *where*. I needed something, some relief, some help, some treatment!"

"*Maybe You Don't Love Me Any Longer*"

Laurie's grimace had shifted (without my having seen the moment of change) into a frown of disapproval. "Gabe said: 'Fine, because I've tried everything I can think of and I'm sure I don't know what to do.'"

I think I must have grinned, for she had inadvertently done a very good imitation of what must have been *his* annoyance. Understanding at once what had caused me to smile, she merely shrugged, sighed, said with fairness: "He was sick of the kinds of things I'd been saying . . . That life was meaningless; that I felt as if I were beginning to crack. I'd go on and on, talking that way, around this time. Initially I'd said: 'Well, it must be this period coming on but I feel as if there's nothing that I'm doing right.' And he would say: 'Well, but you *are*; it's just that you're crying and you're unhappy most of the time.' And another thing he said was: 'Maybe, you know, you aren't happy with me, and maybe you don't love me any longer. But you can't come out with it, and can't admit it—even to yourself. Maybe the real trouble is you not wanting to *be* here. Not with me, and this family, and these children!'" Laurie's cheeks had turned the deep color of brick somewhere between the beginning and the end of the last two sentences.

But she was shaking her head in the negative, as though to say that Gabe's notions had been nothing if not absurd. And she chose that moment—almost as if I'd said something critical to her—to protest that she'd never been one of those nursing mothers who forget their husbands and stay glued to the suckling infant's side.

She and Gabe had managed to get away, just the two of them, for a couple of long weekends (she'd taken a breast pump with her, and expressed the milk, so that it wouldn't dry up). And she had—throughout the eight months when she'd been breast-feeding Katherine—not only been managing the household, but been back at her job from the sixth week postpartum onward. She'd given *nothing* up, she added, almost defiantly.

Then she said: "I wanted to do it all. I wanted to do *everything*, as far as the children were concerned . . . but I also wanted my freedom. So there I was finally, working hard to have it both ways. And I was finding it—oh, it was getting—close to impossible. I was feeling so bad, as if I couldn't bear the sight of another day—another morning. Each time, I thought I wouldn't get through *this* one: that I couldn't make it, couldn't bear it, couldn't go on."

One of Gabe's suggestions, when her mood was approaching its nadir, had been that she go back to work full time. "He said that maybe *this* was what I really wanted. He suggested this, and a number of other possible options. But none of them . . . they didn't seem to have anything to do with it. I didn't want to leave my family. I didn't hate Gabe—I didn't even not love him anymore . . . or at least," her eyelids closed over her eyes in a brief blink, as if to grab a moment of privacy, "I wasn't ready to think that possibility."

Mothering

Very shortly after she'd come to the Mood Clinic for treatment, Laurie Michaelson's mood had swept upward. It was almost perilously swift, occurring within the space of three weeks. It was as if she'd been released by some mysterious underwater grasses, holding her trapped below, and she was now able to surface—out of her depression, into her premorbid emotional state. But, if returning to her normal mood level (i.e., the range of mood shades within which she customarily fluctuated) was accomplished rapidly, it wasn't done without some painful acknowledgments.

For an integral part of "getting better" seemed to involve confronting the ways she felt about her marriage . . . about Gabe. "I found myself, as I was coming out of the worst of it, talking an awful lot about marital problems and the expectations that I had had—about husbands. Not that I," she added quickly, "or anyone else for that matter considered it anything other than that old postpartum syndrome. Most of our friends weren't taking the whole thing that seriously. They all seemed to be thinking things like: 'Poor kid, she's stuck with this baby, and she's needing something.' Still, postpartum or not, I do believe now that there was a part of it that had to do with my relationship with my husband. . . ." She hesitated, shut her eyes for a moment. Then she gave me a thoughtful, assessing look. She decided to continue.

"My feelings during this entire period were—I don't know how to put this—but just general feelings of: 'Gee, I thought life was going to be one way, but here it is, and it's turned out very different.' And . . . to a certain extent . . . I felt trapped. Still I kept trying, in the midst of all that depression, to come back in my mind to just when and why those feelings had started. To figure out, if I could, where it was that they began. . . ." Laurie, as she was speaking, had averted her gaze from mine. She was staring intently at a framed medical diploma that hung on the wall, almost as though she hoped that the answers to her questions might be discovered there, and translated from the Latin.

"I came back, in my thinking, to the time before Gabe and I were married," she continued, in a low voice. "I was in school when we met: then afterward, I held my own job. I was always a pretty independent person, and I managed to hold my own with my husband. Gabe always has the air of being terribly sure of himself; he can be a pretty overwhelming person. But things worked well between us. He was, to be sure, my major absorption, until our first baby—Tony— was born." At these words, almost as if she'd inadvertently committed a *faux pas*, Laurie gave a little leap in her seat.

Expectations

"It wasn't as if I weren't aware that you should still pay lots of attention to your *husband*," she said quickly, as if to forestall a reproach, "and have lots of other things in your life. I did try . . . but the truth was, I really enjoyed being a mother, and having this beautiful baby son. . . ." She seemed increasingly embarrassed. "And I really did get *into* the whole thing. Gabe, I think, had trouble handling that. He felt—as if he'd been, somehow, left out. And he then responded·in ways *I* didn't like; and I responded to the ways *he* was behaving." Her voice had been rising over the course of the last couple of sentences; but when she spoke again, it fell. "He didn't quite meet my expectations," she said dispassionately. It was as if we'd switched to another topic—to slipcovers that didn't fit, perhaps, or the rising costs of energy, or some other manageable, emotionally neutral problem or failure.

"In what way," I asked, in the same neutral, equable tone, "didn't he meet your expectations?"

"I think he felt rejected," she responded, almost appeasingly, as if making excuses on Gabe's behalf. "In the beginning, when we first brought Tony home, I think we were both trying hard to be supportive. But Gabe started staying away a lot . . . more and more, it seemed. Everything was going into the law firm . . . he was always going to take it easier after the next case. But he didn't. He wasn't the father I'd wanted him to be, changing diapers and so forth—taking part. He wasn't an equal participant who was going to share in this whole tremendous experience with me. Not as much as I wanted him to, anyhow." Her glance met mine, of a sudden, and she looked oddly guilty.

"Now if you talked to *him*," she conceded, with a shake of her head, "he'd have his side. He did go to the childbirth classes with me, and he was in the labor room, and did help with the baby . . . at first. He thinks he did his share, but it wasn't quite my expectation—" She stopped, and I looked at her in puzzlement: "Well, which of you is right, do you think?"

"I don't know," she answered enigmatically. "I don't think there's any easy right or wrong, here."

"He did help, though? I mean, did change diapers and—?"

I stopped as she grinned suddenly, showing the trace of a dimple, and shrugged her shoulders lightly: "A little."

"And you breast-fed your first baby, too—and found that was good?"

"Yes, I was really *there*, and found that it was wonderful. But slowly and surely, on Gabe's part, there was . . . withdrawal. It probably didn't reach a peak, though, until our second baby—until Katherine was born. On my own part, throughout this time, what was happening—" She stopped in midsentence as if she'd bumped against a thought that she really didn't want to express. Then she twisted around in her chair, plucked her black leather purse from the side of the chair, where it had been hung by its shoulder strap. She took out a fresh piece of Kleenex. She made no use of it, however; she simply held it in her hand.

"One of the things that I felt obligated to do after our baby was born was to make this man *happy*," Laurie said, hanging the purse back where it had been. "So that he wouldn't leave. After all, we were married and we had this child." Unaccountably, as though she'd run up against the same mental barrier, she stopped speaking again.

For a moment I watched the black purse, gently swinging to a rest. "So what you are saying," I tried to assist her, "is that already, after Tony's birth, you were aware that you had a problem in your marriage?" I waited, then asked: "What was it, that problem? As much as you were able to lay your hands on it at that time—what did you think it was?"

"All right," said Laurie suddenly.

She sounded as if we'd just reached an agreement. I wasn't sure, however, what had transpired. What had happened, as I realized very shortly, was that she'd decided that she would go with me a bit further, go down a particularly guarded and private avenue. She breathed in deeply, like a runner at the starting line, and then she let the breath out. She said: "After the first child, my expectations of Gabe as a father, as a father-dash-parent, as someone who would *share* with me, were really crumbling. I was turned off. I didn't feel that he was participating that much in what was happening—certainly, not as much as I'd have wanted. And he, I think, felt that I was too much into the whole mothering thing—that I wasn't interesting, didn't have other aspects to myself. That I didn't have time enough for *him*. One important difference we had was that he still wanted to go on living as we had before Tony was born. I did try to keep up. But what would happen would be that we'd stay out late at a party, and then on Sunday morning, neither one of us wanted to get out of bed. So I'd get up for two hours and be with the baby, and then he'd get up for two hours . . . this would go on every weekend. The upshot was that we never saw each other, except for a social night out. We were trying to keep up with the kind of life we'd been able to lead before, plus deal with a baby who was up and crying at six."

She hesitated, then added soberly: "That ruined our sex life, for one thing." I understood at once that we'd reached the difficult place about which Laurie had paused before going.

"Well, it didn't ruin our sex life completely," she now amended. "But it put a serious damper on our style. We'd been enjoying ourselves at night, able to sleep late the next day, and to have plenty of time for each other. But there we were, on two-hour shifts the whole weekend long . . . and our sex lives did go down the tubes, a bit. I remember saying—I talked to some friends, and asked what *is* this, after you have a baby? Was it just fatigue, or what was it? I worked out a great theory of my *own*"—she laughed—"and I'm not at all sure that it's wrong! My theory is that when you're breast-feeding you get a lot of cuddling and fondling with the baby . . . and that maybe that nurturing appeases you sexually, and makes you feel somehow . . . not interested. Of course there *is* a whole lot of plain being bone-tired that goes along with this too. But still," her voice sounded quizzical, "the interest in sex seemed so much lessened, on my part.

"I *was* concerned about it," she said immediately, again sounding as if she were hurrying to head off criticism. "I talked to a number of people and the feedback was: 'Oh well, it'll get better' . . . 'You'll get adjusted to having a child' . . . 'Don't worry, it will work itself out.' But that didn't happen. Gabe didn't like it. He criticized, kept on saying: 'Oh, you never have time for me.' He'd complain . . . but I just never really got back up there again, not like before. And you know, it had taken practically no time for me to get pregnant the first time around; but with the second, it took a year and a half, and I still wasn't there! I'm sure," observed Laurie gravely, "that it was the lack of frequency."

Sexual Service

At this point, she continued, when she'd been anxious to begin a new pregnancy, she'd begun taking her temperature so that they could time intercourse to the phase of her highest fertility—and she'd become pregnant within a couple of months. Her interest in sex for the sake of sex had not, however, returned. And Gabe knew it. "My getting the thermometer out was a terrific damper for him," admitted Laurie. He was feeling discardable and said outright that her only interest in him was her interest in having a baby! "It seemed to Gabe that he was just being used. And in a way, he was, I suppose—a little bit—"

I started to laugh: "I'll say!" She laughed too, but only for a moment.

"At the same time," she went on, quickly becoming serious, "he was putting me down a lot, too, and that was a turn-off. I mean the truth of the matter is, we were having a battle."

"And what was his side, do you think, in that battle?"

"His side?" She paused. "Oh, that I wasn't giving him enough attention. That I was ignoring him, not concentrating on him as I'd done before. But you know, I was needing *his* support—and what he wanted from me was *babying*. I found him incredibly egocentric! I felt as if this was another child here, pulling at my skirts, demanding my praise. I was willing and happy to give that out to the babies . . . but instead of helping me with them, he was criticizing. He was angry, because he was so used to being the center of the attention!" She was frowning, breathing little rapid shallow breaths of air, as if she'd indeed set out on a run.

"You felt then," I remarked, so that she could hear my own understanding of what it was she'd been saying, "that Gabe was just another burden, someone else to be nurtured and babied?"

I Wanted Everything

She smiled mockingly. "He wouldn't call it 'babying'; he would call it 'attention.' He wouldn't say to you, either, that he didn't want to take part in the fathering. He'd tell you that he *did*, and that he enjoyed it, and that he was learning how to do it all the time. But just not the way I'd expected him to . . . and it all gets back to expectations. My expectations of him . . . his expectations of *me* . . . I almost feel as if we went from a point in our marriage at which we were each seeing the other as flawless to a point at which we were seeing some more of each other's—reality. After the children came into the picture, though, we both saw the *reverse* side of the first thing. We both saw the absolute worst of one another, and *that* was unreal. Unreal as the other kind of thing had been. . . ." She began tearing a neat little fringe around one side of her Kleenex.

I watched, for quite a while, then asked tentatively: "For you, though, that 'absolute worst' was Gabe's not sharing in the whole parenting thing in the ways that you wanted?" She nodded, seemed so gratified by this summary that I tried another: "And from his point of view, perhaps, *you* were no longer the doting, interested, adoring sexy lady that he'd married? But you were distracted, and in there with the breast-feeding and the babies and the Pablum. . . . And that wasn't what he'd had in mind at all?"

She'd been bobbing her head, in assent, throughout. Her eyes were lowered, however, fixed upon the piece of tissue that she was absent-mindedly fringing. "Our perceptions of each other—" she began, and then halted. "I *did* try," she started afresh. "I did continue to work outside, and I didn't get fat and sloppy and do any of those things you aren't supposed to do. I tried darned hard. In the first months, I tried each of the babies on breast-feeding—and you know, I really enjoyed it. Gabe, when Katherine was still pretty new, arranged to go to Nassau—with some of our friends—for a four-day weekend. I said 'O.K., then, but you're not going without *me*.' So Katherine stayed home with a sitter, and I brought a breast pump along in order to keep my milk supply going. I wasn't going to give up on the nursing, but I wasn't—either—going to miss out on the trip." With a sudden motion, as if rejecting something, she balled up the Kleenex she'd been working on and tossed it into the ashtray. It landed on top of the first one.

We both looked at that overflowing receptacle dubiously. Laurie, without saying a word, picked out both Kleenexes and tossed them into a nearby wastebasket. "I guess that conflict about the trip is part of a conflict that I feel in general," she confessed. "I kind of want to do it all—to do *everything* and not give one part or the other of my life up. I want to be a mother, and to carry on my job: but I still want to be out, you know, being cool, traveling around. I mean, much as I loved caring for the babies"—she blushed slightly—"I didn't want to just talk about diapers!" She laughed suddenly, said in an almost-gay voice: "But the truth was, in a way I *did*—I wanted that too! I liked that part, too. So I tried to do it all and have it all and not to skimp on anything."

She paused, then added mildly: "I certainly did miss the boat, there."

"Which boat?" I asked.

"With Gabe, I think, truly, that a lot of my resentment about not being able to do it all was: 'Why don't you help me? Why don't you *do* more around here? Can't you see that I'm trying so hard to hold it all together, while all that you're doing is *your own job?* You go off to work—you're out for most of the weekday evenings—and when you *are* home, you're not helping! You come in and demand my attention exclusively.' It's: 'Drop everything, concentrate on me now, and have sex!' . . . when you *see* that I'm juggling five different things!" Her face was contorted into a scowl of angry passion. And I, while I was listening to her words, realized that my thoughts were elsewhere. They'd lingered behind, in her narrative, and I was thinking about that Nassau vacation.

Had that invitation been tendered, I wondered, as a kind of a jealous challenge? Had Gabe been saying, simply by making that plan at that time: "Choose between breast-feeding the baby, or going off to the Bahamas, with our friends, for a vacation?" He'd told her that he did plan to go, and that he would—with or without her. "I guess I'm finding it a bit odd," I said aloud, "I mean, the timing of that holiday. It sounds as if you must have been quite involved with the baby, then—as if you were just getting established with the nursing. Is—?"

"Yes," she interrupted eagerly, "but that kind of conflict went on and on. I was trying very hard to please everyone, and eventually, what that led me to . . . I was just out of control. Oversleeping, half crazy, crying all the time," her voice wobbled, now, between anger, complaint, and sadness, "and unable to figure out what, in my life, had become so unbearably wrong."

Parenthood as Crisis

"You know"—she leaned forward suddenly—"when Gabe and I were first dating, he asked me: 'What are your goals in life, Laurie?' And I answered that I didn't know, for sure; they were probably fairly vague. He said: 'Good, because mine are career-oriented and money-oriented.' Maybe it suited him, my own goals being that unclear."

She paused, as if thinking through some issue. I waited, unsure about what she was trying to say. "I suppose, in retrospect," she continued, "my goals, blurry as they were then, had to do with marriage and having children . . . with general happiness. Those are the things that I looked forward to having in my life. But I did go to school, and did enjoy that part too. The *big* priorities were, I suppose, always there in the future—marriage, having children. And Gabe and I were married for several years before having Tony. When we did have him, it was because we'd made the decision.

"So I had my boy," said Laurie softly, "and then later on, I had my girl. It was perfect, just what I'd wanted . . . except that eight months later, I was so down . . . . so unutterably depressed."

I'd had a realization, even as she was speaking these words, of the extent of the crisis that parenthood had actually precipitated. "Do you know," I said, my own voice full of uncertainty, "I have a—a feeling —that the period of your life that began with Tony's birth and ended in the depression after Katherine was weaned, has a quality all its own. It's unlike all the other parts that we've talked about. Is it right, the sense I have—that this phase was somehow different?" I wasn't sure exactly what the thought was that I was struggling so hard to formulate.

But I watched the dawn of the idea suffuse her expression, and she nodded and agreed. I tried to press her further, hoping to understand not only her reply, but my question. "Suppose," I asked, "that segment, or phase of your life were a movie or a play that you were writing? What do you think you'd call it?" She seemed taken aback. "I mean, what would be its title?"

She hesitated so long that I almost offered her the few names that were spinning around in my own head ("Motherhood," "Conflicted Motherhood," etc.). But the answer she gave, when it came, was quite different. She said: "I'd call it 'Great Mother/Bad Wife.'"

Maternalism and Eroticism

"Great Mother/Bad Wife." Laurie's title had, with uncanny deftness, located a certain inherent conflict between two major trends in the feminine personality: the conflict between aspects of the self that are more "motherly" and those parts of the self that are primarily "erotic." I believe that the struggle between these two powerful motivating forces in the feminine self is never so intense as in the crisis of new motherhood. And, as a matter of fact, this underlying truth does seem to be recognized in certain ritualistic practices often seen in primitive societies. Not infrequently, for example, the nursing mother is prohibited—by strong sexual taboos—from intercourse with the father during the early months that are the time of intensest nurturing. In some "uncivilized" societies, as a matter of fact, the lactating woman is literally segregated from her mate until the time of the infant's weaning. Sanctions against her sexuality, thus delivered by the community, do in a sense free the mother from a dilemma. She will naturally expend her loving and libidinous feelings in the establishment of the intense bond with her infant. The conflict between her eroticism and her motherliness is, because the matter is taken entirely out of her hands, mediated and resolved by the prohibition.

And of course, implicit in the widespread establishment of such taboos is the notion that the emergence of "motherliness" can most readily occur when the question of sexuality is, at least temporarily, submerged. The woman is then at liberty to pour the entire vessel of her feeling into the powerful attachment to her infant (the first, most critical love experience of that newborn's life). She will, in this postpartum/nursing period, concentrate her undivided self on the primarily maternal aspects of her being.

A Feminine Existential Crisis

The idea that a woman's sexuality may interfere with her "motherliness" is discussed extensively by Dr. Helene Deutsch in her classic *Psychology of Women*. Psychoanalyst Deutsch writes: "Motherliness may harmonize with the other psychic tendencies or oppose and disturb them, inhibit them, or direct them into false channels. One well known example is its frequent inhibiting influence on eroticism. . . . Conversely, other interests and emotional relations—especially erotic ones—may lead to impoverishment of the motherly feelings. . . ." To be a sexual woman, first and foremost, will affect those trends in the personality that direct one toward being a maternal one. And, while mothering is in the ascendant, eroticism diminishes.

The mothering process is, itself, never so intensive—so insanely preoccupying and demanding—as it is in the weeks and months just following upon the infant's birth. That is why I mentioned that, for the new mother, the conflict between the erotic demands of her mate and the maternal demands being placed upon her by her baby may precipitate a kind of feminine existential crisis. ("Who shall I be for whom, and in what order? And where, in all of this, lie my *own* preferences—where is my 'self'?") Moreover, if I may return momentarily to those sexual taboos that are so widespread in primitive societies, one wonders if they don't embody—in ritual—what is in fact the nursing mother's inner reality. Which is to say, a hormonally based sexually "not-that-interested" trend.

What is clear is that when a woman is lactating (and *not*, therefore, undergoing the cyclic endocrine shifts that are part of the menstrual pattern) her estrogens circulate in her body at levels that are generally lowered. Estrogens are, in the nursing mother, about half as high as are blood levels of prolactin—and estrogens are, it will be recalled, the hormones that support states of heightened reactivity, sensitivity, and excitement. This includes *sexual* reactivity and excitement. But the potent breast-feeding hormone prolactin, "masking" the effects of the estrogen, could well be bringing about an inner situation which promoted a relative diminution of sexual tension (and therefore, sexual interest) in the woman who is nursing.

The breast-feeding mother is, frequently, just plain less arousable. As one obstetrician, Dr. Mavis Gunther, observed in a recent paper: "Many women discover that they are less responsive in intercourse during the early months of lactation. This can reasonably be put down to fear of conception where the risk is run, but this relative frigidity *still happens* [my italics] where contraception is used."

The Nursing Couple

Might it be that the new mother's relatively diminished sexual needs are in fact (as Laurie Michaelson suggested they were) being appeased simply in the process of all that nursing and cuddling? If this were so, then obviously the nursing couple, mother and infant, would be—at least during this early period—a generally satisfied, self-sufficient unit.

In this fashion, the physiologically facilitated inclination of both mother and offspring would show a wonderfully adaptive fit. For a less sexually needy mother would surely be less likely to absent herself from her infant in the pursuit of her erotic gratifications. And the human newborn is, of course, the most dependent newborn in nature. Over the vistas of time that saw the emergence of our species, the general effect of having the caretaking, nurturing, *protecting* mother nearby must have enhanced certain babies' chances of survival. It's far from inappropriate to imagine that certain types of maternal behavior —as well as habitual ways of thinking and feeling—were bred into the human genotype, because experience had proven them useful.

A new mother, relatively able to receive sufficient gratification in the context of the developing relationship with her baby. A young infant, entering life with some crude readiness, some biological preparedness to fall in love with the parent. This is a basic grouping in nature, a biological arrangement that is viable.

The Image of the Madonna

What, then, of the woman's erotic bond to her mate? This would, at least in this early mothering period, naturally shift in its essential quality and its nature. *Her* need for her partner is, at this moment (and no one can say to what degree the hormonal changes she's experiencing are affecting her thinking and behavior) *not* first and foremost a sensual one. What she requires from her partner is that *he* nurture *her* while she struggles to meet the confusing, fatiguing, unceasing demands for caring that are coming to her from the infant. For this segment of time, sexuality and the emphasis upon the erotic aspects of their attachment have moved into the background—for her, at the very least. In this phase, which is the period of her greatest vulnerability, the mother's need is for a supporter, helper, provider, protector.

The image we have of the new mother is not that of a sexual woman. It is the image of the woman-with-her-child, which is that of the Madonna.

The Disappointed Rival

What, then, of the father? He is, most obviously, experiencing nothing in the way of hormonal-biological bodily preparation for this new state of being called parenthood. The changes that he's undergoing are purely psychological—but that isn't to deny the fact that they can be disturbing and difficult. He is, for one thing, experiencing a host of new demands that are being beamed to him from his wife: requests, covert and overt, for extra care, new kinds of assistance, and a degree of parenting of herself.

He is also, very frequently, feeling lonesome and shut out. For there is, as we're all so deeply aware, something so profound and complete and self-contained about the mutually absorbed mother and infant unit. New fathers, especially those who have depended on being the

center of their wives' concerns and attention, may feel intense anger—
may feel that they have been summarily ejected. Although his own
child isn't his sibling in reality, the father may be feeling nothing
other than sibling rivalry!

A husband, watching *his* wife nurse *their* baby, often finds himself
dealing with the reawakening of ancient and painful dilemmas. Many
men do, while watching their wives feed (especially breast-feed) and
care for their own infant, re-experience buried yet smoldering feelings
—powerful jealousies, harking all the way back to early childhood,
that have been stored away in the mental closet where forgotten fantasies and old worries are kept out of sight. They feel within them the
surges of rage they once felt at having to share their own mother's
affections with other members of the family. If the father is (as was
Gabe Michaelson) used to a good deal of loving attention ("babying"), coming to him from his wife, he may respond to his own child
as a quasi-rival.

But this type of reaction is, again, very likely to be occurring out of
reach of his conscious awareness. How could he know about and
admit to such feelings? They have no place in a mature man's thought
and are too ridiculous to be taken seriously in the sober light of adult
reality.

One must add to this scenario, moreover, the mother's postulated
psychophysiological state. She is very probably, as was mentioned
earlier, experiencing a diminished sexual interest during this phase.
She's also absorbed by and preoccupied with her infant. And so the
male partner is, *in actuality*, having to cope with a turning away on
his wife's part. If the present situation happens to coincide with a
painful situation never quite resolved during childhood, then the father's ambivalent and contradictory impulses may make him prey to
feelings of isolation and depression . . . of being out in the emotional
cold.

He may then react—Gabe Michaelson did this—by staying away
from the changed situation as much as possible. As Dr. Therese
Benedek has written (in a paper, "Depression During the Life
Cycle"), the new father's ambivalence to his own child makes him feel
guilty, and the guilt brings about feelings of depression. "Often the
defense against depression is manifest in the father's behavior. Avoidance of the home and even alcoholism may cover up the ambivalence."
So may such things as plain overwork! And there are, as Benedek
notes, numbers of young fathers whose psychosomatic symptoms
(such as ulcers) appear as a reaction to the birth of a child.

The father's *own* need level is, to state the matter simply, unusually heightened during this time. And so, as we see, is the mother's set of needs vis-à-vis him—she needs to do more taking from her mate than she ever will at any other period of life. During this fragile phase, she craves his strong support, nurturance, care.

The Choice

In "ordinary" situations such as this one, misunderstandings may easily begin multiplying. Both partners are extraordinarily unsteady; and when one can't (because he or she is, in fact, so needful) satisfy the other's needs, they imagine they're now seeing the other's true colors. Such considerations make the early-nurturing phase a highly problematical period: the impact of the infant (particularly the first baby) creates a shock wave that reverberates through every level of the couple's relationship.

Basically, the plot line tends to unfold in the following direction: the father of the infant is himself feeling infantile. He withdraws in jealousy and anger, deeply envying the newborn child at his wife's breast. The young mother's dilemma centers around the erotic woman/ maternal woman axis. This is, perhaps, nowhere so clearly symbolized as in the variety of conflicting feelings that lactating women tend to have about their breasts. Many nursing mothers feel peculiar about having their breasts caressed during sexual foreplay—because it feels like a "betrayal" of the baby!

For Laurie Michaelson, developing the maternal side of her self had seemed to necessitate putting her erotic self into a holding pattern. Intent upon the mastering of her mothering role, she'd transformed the wifely role into a rather perfunctory one. She'd spoken of it, in fact, in terms of "oughts" and "should." "I was very aware," she had said, "that one should still pay attention to one's husband, and I really *did* try. But the truth was, I really enjoyed being a mother, and having this baby, and I really did get into it. . . ."

It was almost as though, for this phase of her life at least, a decision had been required. She could be Gabe's romantic partner, or she could be her baby's mother; but somehow, it had proven impossible for her to be both. And Gabe, during the past couple of years, had become as angry, as turned off, as critical of her as any rejected lover might be. Neither of them had been capable of taking the long view, of understanding the pressures of the postpartum period as transient and passing. Instead, they considered it a time when the truth had come out, and they at last perceived the real feelings of each other. So parenthood, having revealed such things, had brought in its train the most intense and painful mutual disappointment.

See-saw

Before she'd gone into therapy, Laurie's conversations with Gabe had had a certain general structure. She would complain about how unhappy she felt; she'd feel guilty about these feelings, and she would weep throughout. Gabe tended, once the conversation had been set into motion, to do most or all of the talking. "It was he," recounted Laurie, "who, when we'd discuss our relationship, would say things like: 'I don't know, but *my* problem is that you never pay attention to me' . . . and things like that. He'd go on and on, telling me about what wasn't working between us, and why it wasn't working, and I would sit there crying, having nothing to say. But then, all of a sudden, as I started getting well—coming *out* of the depression—Gabe began acting like *I* had been acting! All of a sudden it was turned around—*he* was sitting there crying . . . not responding. . . ."

"*He* cried?" I stared at her. It was beginning to sound like one of those marital see-saws. As her mood went up, his had come down. One couldn't help wondering why.

For Laurie, the type of treatment she was receiving (a new mode of treatment of depression, to be discussed in a later chapter) happened to be marvelously effective. It aided her in organizing her thinking—in helping her to put her mental finger upon the real place that was hurting, which is to say the wound of her disappointed expectations. She was depressed, true; but there were reasons.

Her low self-esteem, and the barrage of criticism that she was directing upon herself, didn't stem from sources that were cosmic and phantasmagoric: matters too immense and cloudy to be confronted. She was feeling the ways she felt, as she was to realize rapidly, about "something." And her dilemma wasn't so unresolvably tragic that there was nothing to do but end her existence under a passing bus.

Ambivalence and Anger

Of course some people do have special difficulties in handling their angry feelings toward a person whom they also love and depend upon. Rather than experience their hostility consciously they do a mental sleight-of-hand trick; they redirect their aggressive feelings, and the rage is experienced as rage-against-the-self. Rather than deal with what is perceived as wrongful anger (because "it's bad to feel angry at people you love, and only bad persons would do so"), the feelings are suppressed, ignored, contained. As Dr. Mortimer Ostow writes, in *The Psychology of Depression:* ". . . the depressive process starts at some point in adolescent or adult life as a result of a current challenge. The most common of these depressing challenges is intense ambivalence, that is, irreconcilable hatred and anaclitic (i.e., early infantile) love for the same person. An increase in anger against this ambivalently hated and loved individual often serves to trigger the depressive process in an individual disposed to depression."

Laurie's depressive thought-process had eventuated in furious comments directed at herself. In her anger, she'd called herself a "useless" and "unnecessary" person (in translation, meaning "useless and unnecessary to Gabe"). But the hostility she felt toward *him* was concealed not only from her husband but from herself as well. Laurie's anger bubbled away at a below-conscious-awareness level. The only way in which she became cognizant of the rage she felt was in terms of those vicious attacks on herself. And that her feelings could be described as murderous is evidenced by those strong impulses she felt to throw herself in front of a bus—that is, murder herself.

In psychotherapy, though, the cards of her existence were laid out before her, as tangibly as if they'd been set down before her on a table. In the company of her therapist, she examined those cards; and the most important one, as she quickly realized, was this. Gabe was critical of her, and unhappy with her. He was letting her know this on a daily basis, in a thousand small ways. So was he disillusioned with her, and disappointed by her; *he wasn't pleased to have her for his wife.* He still lived with her, and with the children . . . but in actuality, he wasn't there. The real Gabe, the one who had cared for her, was gone; he was lost . . . and Laurie was horribly disappointed. What was depressing her was not only her realization that there had been a loss, a withdrawal of his affection. It was the *anger* that this deep sense of loss elicited. Laurie hadn't known she'd "felt anger" at Gabe; not at all. But she did feel angry; and the feelings were being deflected inward, against herself.

Within a brief while, as her therapist assisted her in acknowledging and confronting such feelings, Laurie was better and Gabe was the one who'd gone into an odd sort of decline. "At one point," she recounted, "I said to him: 'Gabe, I've been seeing the doctor for five weeks now, and I'm feeling so well. Haven't I been paying *much more* attention to you, just in this recent time?' But he said: 'Yes, just 'cause you've seen this doctor, all of a sudden everything is supposed to be all O.K.! Everything's going to be the way it used to. But you don't like me, and you don't care for me, and I know it.' He always said that *I* was the one who didn't care. But now, everything was all turned around: he was the one who was crying, not talking." It was as if his wife's sudden improvement had sent Gabe into a state of turmoil.

He didn't, he said, trust or quite believe in Laurie's unexpected, rubber-ball-like bounce back into health. He thought the beneficial effects of her treatment would soon peak—she'd fall down, become depressed, begin to ignore him again. "I couldn't understand what was getting him so upset," said Laurie. "Here I was, concentrating on him a lot, giving him lots of attention, and that seemed to be making things worse. He was even *more* unhappy. I asked him what was wrong? I said: 'O.K., it really hasn't been easy between us, these past few years, but what's the problem in the here and the now? What are you feeling at this moment? What do you feel about *me?*' "

She shifted suddenly in her chair, leaned an arm on my desk, and I leaned toward her, as if expecting to hear a confidence. I noticed that the dark pupils of her eyes seemed immense. She said, her voice low: "He cried, then, and said he thought that he didn't love me anymore."

"Oh. Then did—"

Whatever comment I began to make was lost, for Laurie swept on: "I didn't know what to—I asked him if he *knew* he didn't love me, for sure? He said he didn't know, but he just thought it was all over . . . he was sobbing. I asked him if he wanted a divorce or separation: he wanted neither." She said these sentences rapidly, almost like a rote list she wanted to dispose of. But then she added, in a less hurried manner: "He said things to the effect that I'd done a sudden turnaround . . . that I'd been rejecting him and ignoring him, until he'd given up and made up his mind that he could live his life without me. He said: 'All of a sudden you want me again, and you want this marriage to work! And *I'm* supposed to jump right back on the bandwagon!' . . . That," she explained, "was the kind of thing he was saying."

She wondered—who would not have wondered?—if some other person were now involved in this picture. Laurie asked him if he were having an affair. "We talked about his staying away from home so much, seeing clients and so forth. But he insisted that there was nothing like that going on here, and there *was* no such other person. He just wanted time, he told me. He said: 'Let's just wait a little while now. You've had some time to get your act together; now I need time to work on mine! . . .' He wouldn't go with me for treatment, though I wanted him to, so I kept on going myself."

A Telephone Call

Reflecting on that scene much later, and with the benefits conferred by hindsight, Laurie still believes she was faced with an either-or choice: she could believe that Gabe was being honest with her, or believe that he was lying. But what if, in fact, he *was* lying? "What was I going to do? Was I ready to jump out of this marriage?" she demanded. "I thought about it . . . and I wasn't."

And her marriage was improving. In the meanwhile, as part of the treatment, she'd been learning how to concentrate on her own resources, and to take more pleasure from some of the other things in her life. By late in that spring, in fact, she and her therapist had agreed that she was well enough to stop coming in to see him. "My marriage wasn't exactly where I wanted it to be, but I thought we'd resolved some of the major difficulties. If Gabe wasn't the kind of husband I'd expected, and if in fact, he'd been having an affair (which I still suspected), there were still other things in my world. There were friends, and my job, and doing things with the children . . . all pleasurable for me. So he wasn't the only source of enjoyment." She smiled calmly. "The summer was good, with Gabe, and the fall was all right too. Home much more, in the evenings, and so forth." She shifted in her seat: "But then, as the next Christmas came around, he was out an awful lot again. . . ."

"That Christmas would have been," I asked, "the anniversary of your big depression?" She nodded. "As we got closer to the holidays, he was out still more frequently. And more upset, all the time, and crying. We had a scene like that, on New Year's Eve; Gabe sobbing but unable to tell me why. All he could tell me was that he didn't think we were making it—that the right things just weren't happening. That our sex life still wasn't too good: I agreed. I wanted to go, the two of us together, for treatment. 'I don't know what's *wrong* with us,' he kept saying; and I tried to draw him out, make some sense of this . . . but I couldn't get him to talk it through. Not then. Not in the couple of months following. But he seemed upset and suffering a lot of the time. . . ." She stopped speaking, smiled, shrugged. And then said politely, as if offering me my turn: "You know what I'm going to say next."

Slightly taken aback, I answered with the first thought in my head: "Yes, your husband *was* having an affair." She nodded her head dryly. "And how did you learn about that?" I asked.

They had been away together on a brief vacation. The following evening, Gabe had been out—there had been a banquet, a meeting later on with one of the law firm's clients. And very late that night, a telephone call. A woman, refusing to give her name, who simply said: "Do you know that your husband's sleeping around?" Her first impulse, Laurie said, had been to hang up the telephone. She didn't want to hear what this person was going to say. "I wanted to curse and slam down that receiver! But what I did do, in actuality, was ask very quietly: 'Why don't you tell me about it? I really would like to know.'"

What Could I Have Done?

The telephone caller was Gabe's mistress. Here is what happened between them, as reported much later, by Laurie: "The conversation started flowing; and before I knew it, this kinky anonymous phone caller had turned out to be Gabe's girl friend. It was the girl friend who'd *been there this whole past two and a half years!* We spent the whole night talking on the telephone. And I was calm and said: 'Yeh, I really want to know,' and 'What can I do?' She was angry at him, and wanted to take me to some place where he was supposed to be with a girl . . . she thought. She didn't know for sure but thought so! Anyhow, I had a bottle of brandy in the liquor cabinet, and I needed something while I was sitting there. I wanted to be comfortable . . . and I quite honestly wanted the information. I'd asked Gabe, a number of times: 'Are you having an affair? What's going on? Is there some other person?' I *still* feel that I wasn't sticking my head in the sand. When situations came up that sounded fishy, I confronted him. He said No, No, No, down the line. So this happened, and I thought: 'What could I have done?' I could have had a detective; but I couldn't imagine doing that kind of a thing. There was a certain amount of denial on my part—I see that—but I was also dealing with *his* denials. And they were convincing . . . that's what sticks in my throat. How could he tell me these things—'It's you I love; there's no one else'— with such an honest face, when they were *lies?* Why didn't I pick it up? And how could he do it? I don't think *I* could do it! . . . Ah. Well. I still—I have this problem of trust. But anyhow, the girl friend told me the whole story. It had started out as a little sexual fling, and ended up as a love affair. . . ."

"Then how, in terms of timing," I asked, "does that relate to the children?"

"I'd just conceived my second child."

"Oh." I nodded. "I suppose I thought that might be part of the picture." I was thinking about Laurie's having used the thermometer so that they could time intercourse in order to begin her pregnancy.

"That was just after using him for sex service—" said Laurie.

"Yes."

"As *he* perceived it." Her voice was bitter.

"What else did the woman say? That it had become a love affair . . . but now, she thought—?"

"She said—sounding surprised about it—that I sounded like a pretty all-together lady. You know, I was trying to be open and honest, because here it was. I said: 'I've suspected this, but why don't you tell me what's happened, and what is happening now?' And I was sort of ready to go into this big hate thing—the two of us against Gabe. To talk about how awful a guy he was, and so forth. But she, even though she thought he might be cutting out on her, kept defending him! I would say things about him, and she'd object; she said he was a really good person. Here she is, calling his *wife*, and telling on him! And at the same time, she was defending him." Laurie grinned wryly, shook her head: "It was ludicrous. But she cared for him, and she'd believed all along that he was this remarkable guy who was stuck with a depressed wife who was just spoiling everything in his life for him. After we talked, she wasn't so sure. She herself was into a recent divorce; her husband had been running around with her friend."

Again, there was a wry smile, as if to say: "Yes, I know it's all so trite, and yet it *isn't*, when it is happening." Laurie looked down at herself suddenly, as if recalling something she'd neglected to put on that morning: but then, she merely straightened the scarf around her neck.

"At any rate, throughout this whole 'civilized' conversation," she continued, "I was panicking. I thought: 'Oh, yes, here it is, the big thing.' No, I didn't feel panic—not in the sense of 'terror'—I felt numb. And things were going through my head. I thought, what shall I do? Kick the bastard out? Get help? From where? Maybe I'll be sweet and nice, because there are children and financial support involved here. I felt trapped, and kept trying to think through my options. I thought, too, about going around with other men. In a way, I'd always wanted to: I thought, 'O.K., now *I'll* have a good time!'

But in reality, what I did was nothing. I sat there. I sat for a day and a half . . . talked to two of my friends about it."

"And to Gabe?"

To my surprise, she had to think for a moment before replying. Then she said: "I think I waited a day. I told him that I knew the whole story, but wasn't sure about what would now happen with us. I hadn't gotten at all clear about what really had gone on, and what was going on at the moment. I didn't know what my own feelings were. But I *did* say that there was no point in his lying to me anymore. I said: 'The biggest thing that's happened to me is *not* the affair, but all the *lying* you've been doing. You've really hit my Achilles heel with that. I don't know where I'm going to go with *that*.'" She swallowed, looked away.

But then, turning back to me with that bright, composed, cheerleader's smile, she commented: "Where I *did* go was directly back into therapy. And I said: 'Hi, here I am; I'm back again!'" I saw the pucker of that dimple once more. But the light note wouldn't prevail, not this time. Her expression was at once tense and bereft.

"When I came back into treatment, I told my doctor that I needed some help in getting my feelings straight, and wanted someone objective to just hang in there with me. I was hurt, crying a lot; feeling that numbness too. I thought I hadn't ever cared about Gabe; that I hated him; that there was *no way* that we could be reconciled.

"But somehow," she added, with an almost surprised note in her voice, "I wasn't depressed, wasn't hating *myself*, in the ways that I'd done before. I thought that finally—no matter what else happened—all of the cards were face up, on the table. My relationship with my husband was a disaster: but that still didn't have to be equated with *me* being worthless, inadequate, guilty, useless . . . unable to go on with my life. I didn't feel *those* ways . . . the ways I'd felt the other time. I felt unhappy, but not depressed."

She turned a puzzled, wondering look upon me. "Still, even then, I'd think, Oh gee, I wanted a marriage . . . we really *did* like each other a lot. . . . What happened?"

Adultery: A Form of Communication

What, in fact, *had* happened? In order to begin thinking about this, it might be useful to set out a somewhat crude timetable: to take a retrospective glance at what now seemed to have been an inevitable (in some way, even causally linked) succession of phases and events in Laurie Michaelson's life.

To review such a chronological sequence briefly: before having their first child, she and Gabe had been a socially outgoing, rather happy couple, each with a degree of investment in his or her outside career. They had been able, according to Laurie, to find plenty of time for each other; and a mutually gratifying, workable relationship appears to have been established. In short, they worked well as a couple, a pair. And this situation had persisted for the four and a half years they'd lived alone—all the way up until the time of Tony's birth.

For both husband and wife, the transformation of their twosome into a threesome had meant the rupture of the bubble that encased them—the puncturing of their shared fantasy of having found perfect caring in a loving partner. The positive state of affairs, which had lasted so long (". . . we went from a point in our marriage at which we were seeing each other as flawless," Laurie had said) altered suddenly and drastically: it became the very reverse. It was as if, like Dorothy in *The Wizard of Oz*, they were witnessing the curtain of their own illusions falling suddenly away; and what each had then seen in the other was a disappointing and almost shockingly different "true self." Gabe could no longer be the romantic lover, the focus of his wife's adoration, absorption, attention. He viewed her as having become "all mother," as someone who didn't quite care about him and was frigid and rejecting. Laurie thought him narcissistic, too juvenile to assume the role that was realistically his, at this juncture—the role of the participating, involved father. She summed up the nature of their struggle, at one point, in a nutshell: "He wasn't the guy who came home at five o'clock; he was home at seven, with flowers. But I wanted him home at five, and bouncing the kid."

With the arrival of their first child, then, the first salvos in what was to become a state of total warfare—"We were really having a battle," Laurie had commented, when discussing their sexual problems—were sounded. Gabe, within a period of weeks, was telling her about his disillusionment and disappointment, by staying away more and more. He was saying, without words, that he knew she didn't care about him and that he was angry; but his language was the language of behavior—as it was later on, when he ruptured their shared psychological boundary and went outside the marriage to find someone to love who would give *him* her fascinated attention. Gabe's affair was also a message to his wife, for adultery is itself a form of communication.

The Greatest Antiaphrodisiac Ever

Laurie herself was "talking" about her own disappointments and angers: about the failures of her hopes and expectations of Gabe as a father. She was telling Gabe how *she* felt by means of her diminished interest in sexuality. Even when the staggering tasks of early mothering were well mastered and under control, her erotic feelings had, she'd said, "never quite come back." She had been so puzzled by this mystery; but then she'd not been aware of the rage with which she was responding to her husband's withdrawal. There is nothing quite like anger—perhaps the greatest antiaphrodisiac ever—for putting a damper, or extinguisher, on the experiencing of sexual feeling. And what Laurie described to herself as "disappointment in his lack of involvement" was actually fury and outrage at Gabe's creeping disaffection from herself and from Tony.

A good deal was happening in the Michaelson household during this period. But it was all happening beneath their daily life's surface. Nevertheless—and this did strike me as odd—it was against this backdrop of simmering unverbalized resentments that the pair had agreed upon enacting the drama of conceiving, bearing, and caring for still another child. (Had Gabe *really* given his whole consent to this plan, one wondered? And if he had wanted to complete their family with a second baby, why had he become so infuriated about the thermometer, and about having performed that sexual service?) One can only remark, here, that whatever rational arguments one might have made for Laurie's having that child *then*, there was another, nonrational, feeling level at which the idea made no sense. According to outer logic, the timing was good and proper. But the inner logic, the emotional logic, couldn't have been more askew, more wrong.

The act of Katherine's conception must be the next named event in our short chronicle. And, if one thinks of the Michaelsons' relationship as an ever-downhill-flowing stream, then Laurie's getting pregnant was a sudden, steep waterfall. It was a dropping-off place of unmistakable significance. In terms of the couple's relationship, they were now moving—irrevocably so—through another kind of a landscape. They were in a place where they never had been before.

For Laurie had, in Gabe's view, wanted his sperm without wanting *him*. She took from him without caring about him as a person. His sense of outrage, at having been "used" by her, was very shortly afterward being expressed in terms of that affair. (His sperm was, he seems to have decided at that point, the sum total of all that his wife would get.)

Finally, in terms of major happenings, I would leap over the next seventeen months to the time of Laurie's severe depression. Not that I am suggesting that pregnancy and childbirth are insignificant events! But for this pair, this whole phase seems to have been a time of each person's retreating further and further into his or her own corner. If Gabe had turned away completely, and was investing his emotional self elsewhere, then Laurie had been too preoccupied by carrying her baby, and then by nursing, to really register the information. It wasn't until the time of Katherine's weaning that her mother began to know what had been happening around her all along. She wasn't aware of what she knew at a conscious level; the only manifest signs were the symptoms of her depression.

A Baby for a Husband

For as the biological and psychological bond with her infant began to absorb her less totally, the dreadful understanding must have begun to come closer to conscious knowledge. I mean, the understanding that she had somehow traded in having-a-baby for having-a-husband. Had she then, without understanding its source, begun to feel a kind of rage against both baby and husband?

I believe it was feelings such as these, unconscious and totally unacceptable feelings, that were experienced *consciously* as an almost delusory anger at herself. Laurie expressed these feelings only after having transformed them into self-accusatory notions—that she was a worthless person who might lose control, who might crack up, who might (inadvertently) do something that would harm or destroy one of her children. She had been overwhelmed by fears about her own stupidity, confusion, ineptness. She couldn't do anything right. She might not remember to *feed* her still relatively helpless baby! Or she might not watch the baby closely enough. Or she might forget to turn off the stove. So fearful had Laurie become of her own "crazy impulses"—that she had become phobic about just leaving the house, and being out on the street.

She was afraid of bending to one of those winds of strong impulse and simply throwing herself under a bus. This would have been, to be sure, a way of ending the noxious bombardment of inner insult that could hardly be endured much longer! And Laurie *was* enraged to the point of wanting to commit homicide against herself. But, having no rational idea about why she was angry—and what reasons she had for her anger—those powerful feelings of rage, like deflecting arrows, were returning to strike the shooter. They were being experienced as the self-hating and bitter self-castigation of depression.

A Broken Connection

To return to the question we began with: what had happened? Laurie Michaelson, age thirty-two, teacher, mother of two small children, wife of an energetic and successful lawyer, had begun to think of herself as useless and unnecessary in the human world. And in a way, at least in terms of the crucial relationship to Gabe, this was the valid expression of a real and underlying truth. She wasn't necessary; she was superfluous; for he'd abandoned her to her mothering. She had sustained herself throughout the period of carrying and of nursing her baby. But now, returning to resume the erotic connection, she'd discovered that there was nobody there at the other end of the line.

That connection: it had been so bad for so long, so full of static for so long, that until the time of Katherine's weaning, Laurie had not fully taken in—not internalized—the knowledge that it was gone.

But now (and part of the reason may have been that she was no longer being hormonally buffered against the experiencing of stress) she was tuning into the full impact of the message, and hearing all of the signals that she hadn't hitherto been receiving. And the message itself was that there was no one in this wide world who was doing any caring for her.

The message was that she was alone.

The Huge Life Gamble That Is Marriage

I want to digress at this moment from the particulars of the Michaelsons' story and ask a very general question: why do people marry? Why is it that people continue to behave as if true happiness, that forever-after-and-lasting kind of happiness, will be found within the context of this demanding and engulfing commitment? Because, despite dire predictions about the "death of the family," the vast majority of adults do continue to move into marital unions. Most people marry, and most people spend most of their lives (excepting the early adult years) living in families. Not only do most people marry, moreover, but they marry with the hope of being happy. Which might seem to be a rather strange, rather blind kind of behavior, given the evidence of marital misery and marital failures all about them.

Why, given the clear difficulties that can arise, does anyone do it? What is it that is offered to a person that could compensate for the risks involved? I mean, the risks of putting one's sense of worthfulness, of being needed and necessary, esteemed in this world, into the hands of another?

My question contains, I believe, much of its own answer. For what marriage *can* provide, if the risks pay off, is everything mentioned above. The bond provides a mutually shared space in the world, a place of interdependent security. If *my* well-being depends on my partner's existence and well-being, then he is necessary to me; if *his* well-being depends upon my existence and well-being, then I am necessary to him: we are both necessary people. Marriage is, when it operates well, a means with which the couple manages to give each other significance. It provides for the adult what membership in a family once provided for the child: a home ground of the soul, an emotional safe shelter. If it works, it is the best sort of mutual support system, for each partner can bestow upon the other a sense of his or her importance and intrinsic worth. Each one of the pair is, on creation of the marital bond, *part* of a unit—to which the other part is uniquely and wonderfully necessary. (I don't think it coincidental that Laurie Michaelson's despair surfaced in the idea that she was "someone unnecessary." She was mourning, albeit unaware of the source of the misery, over the loss of the sense of being needed and valued by her partner.) In the huge life gamble that is marriage, we put our sense of being "someone significant" into the hands of another—hoping that that person will confirm and validate our worthfulness, even as we do his or hers. The bond thus established creates a clearing in an otherwise frightening and impersonal wilderness. Human love attachments, when they flourish, confer a sense that one's existence *matters*.

The Sources of Self-esteem

But we have all learned a great deal of what we know about loving, long before we reach maturity. As was mentioned earlier, we take in such lessons very early. The love tie that we establish with a peer in adulthood is the same powerful love attachment to the caretakers, now transferred and transformed. The sense of one's worthfulness—of being an all-right person who has value and who matters greatly to another—has come, originally, from the loving relations the child has experienced in the family.

In short, the child's self-esteem derives from having been cared for initially by his or her parents . . . and the parents have an almost limitless power to lower or raise their offspring's self-esteem. To not be loved is, for the young child, much the same as to be no good (which is why the threat of mother's disapproval and withdrawal of affection can be perceived as such a very serious danger). In a way, basic training for marriage occurs very early in life—according to some theorists, it occurs at the mother's breast. According to one family therapist, Dr. H. V. Dicks, it is in the early mothering experience that one learns whether the world is cold, forbidding, and frustrating, or whether others may be trusted to meet one's expectations, gratify one's needs, and to nourish and care. Writes Dicks, in his classic work *Marital Tensions:* "When dependence and receiving, especially, can be lived out in the 'nursing communion,' the first, and perhaps essential step toward a good marriage will have been taken. . . ." Through the parents, adds Dr. Dicks, the child learns how to love as an adult, for the child has "felt adult love on and in himself."

The way it was with the parent is experienced as a kind of inevitability. The way it was with the parent is the model for adult life. It is the pattern beyond all questioning, because—to each particular child— it has a self-evident psychological reality. The way it was tends to become the way it *must be*. Such inner visions, even when one attempts consciously to oppose them, are usually remarkably tenacious. They can, indeed, be acted upon in later life quite literally. In their book *Secrets in the Family*, writers Lily Pincus and Christopher Dare speak of a "woman whose childhood was damaged by her alcoholic father" who marries a man, divorces him when he turns out to be an alcoholic, and then "gets herself into the same situation once more." They quote, too, a case in which a man whose childhood was dominated by his mother's heart disease then married a woman with congenital heart trouble!

Inner Patterns, Inner Truths

These are pathological extremes that I am citing to make a general point. This is that, when one "falls in love," one has already developed an inner pattern. Although, during the painful renunciation of adolescence, we've given up the hopeless fantasy pretense that we'll ever "have" the opposite-sex parent for our own, we're still left with a particular sensitization, a readiness to respond powerfully to an adult *in that parent's likeness.* And many of the powers that the parent once wielded—such as the power to confer a sense of one's value and worthfulness—are then handed into the keeping of the erotic partner. He or she can then regulate, to some degree, the other's self-esteem.

The problem here is that not only do we relove the lost (re- nounced) parent in the loved mate; but there's a great tendency to con- fuse the spouse and the parent. For we each bring with us, from that hazily remembered infantile world, certain unconscious but strong im- ages . . . visions of what The Man or The Woman is really all about. And few adults come to maturity (I don't know of any) without hav- ing been frustrated to some degree, and failed to some degree, by the caretaking parent. So we each carry with us, as adults, inner knowl- edge and persistent notions about the ways in which we have been *and will be* betrayed.

In the early transports of adult loving, moreover, some of life's earliest visions—of being fused and immersed in the being of another, of being perfectly loved, adored, cared for—are reawakened. The partner is idealized as someone flawless, a consummately cherishing, nourishing, caressing figure (the figure of the flawless parent). Now, at last, in the bliss of finding the other—one's own mate—one experi- ences the belief that all that was amiss, or wounding, or saddening, will now come right again. The spouse will replace the imperfect par- ent; and will be an all-understanding, never-frustrating, loving, nurtur- ing care-giver. Love will conquer and love will heal; love itself is probably the wistful expression of our universal desire to experience again the happiness of being a young baby, protected, trusting, and cherished.

And to be caressed, touched upon our naked bodies, to be viewed tenderly by the Other—this is to relive, in other times and places, our most primitive infantile longings. That longing, to be cared for and validated and adored by those loving eyes, is the longing of infancy, now grown up and transformed. The powerful "bucket of love" is now invested in a tender, sexual bond with a partner who is, as the parent never was, available to be one's very own. The difficulty here is, however, that not only have one's most profound hopes of union with the opposite-sex parent been reawakened: so have one's deepest fears about The Man and The Woman. One knows—every adult knows—that he or she may be disappointed and betrayed in the ways that he or she *was* betrayed earlier. And these slumbering perceptions are, like the ecstatic anticipations of perfect love, projected or placed upon the partner. The partner becomes the mirror of one's self, and one can see in him or her the reflection of one's own greatest hopes and most desperate fears. After all, "the only way to be a woman" or "the only way to be a man" has been learned from the child's interactions with the mother and the father. Little wonder that later on, especially in young adulthood when we are so fresh from our families of origin, it's so easy to confuse husband-with-father, and mother-with-wife.

It is so easy, for example, for the young wife whose own father was withdrawn and angry to *perceive* her husband as angry when he's quiet but not particularly angry at all. She may, when the mask of idealization falls from before her, be feeling that she's made a mistake—found herself a man who (as her father was) is full of resentments and is remote. (She may be seeing, underneath that fallen mask, quite another chimera . . . the projection of her own fears and doubts and mistrusts.) Similarly, a young husband whose own mother was cold and rejecting may demand from his wife a degree of attention and maternal caring that becomes increasingly difficult for her to give. And if she shows any flagging in her motherly attentions, he may react with almost paranoid rage and mistrust. The problem is that he's been "expecting" this rejection all along. The Man or The Woman in his own mind is someone who will behave that way. In every marriage, both partners come into the union hoping for happiness ever after—and then proceed to impose images and fantasies of The Woman and The Man of his or her internal world upon the unsuspecting Other. These inner pictures are treated as absolute certainties—and yet they're rarely brought out, verbalized, examined in the open. Both husband and wife assume their certainties are the same—and each takes their own "truth" for granted.

Different Boot Camps

Perhaps one of the greatest difficulties in marriage is that each of us has received our basic training for adult love in differing boot camps —where different rules, regulations, myths, hold their unquestioning and powerful sway. Marriage calls for the merger of two different sets of perceptions and understandings: the working out of a real relationship calls for the dovetailing of two very separate family systems. And each partner has come into the union hoping to make triumphantly real that which earlier had had to be renounced as an impossible dream: that dream of having the beloved Other *all for one's own*. The possibility of being perfectly loved and perfectly cared for, now awakened from wherever in the deep coils of the brain the vision had slumbered, must also, however, raise the possibility of being hurt in the ways that one was *then* hurt. That is why any perceived rejection or betrayal, coming from the part of the spouse (or appearing to) may be seen as something potentially annihilating and devastating. What that can tune into, so easily, is old and primitive kinds of feelings—the emotional wounds and helpless rages of the child. The child, I mean, that once was, in one's own family.

A Man and a Woman

For Laurie and Gabe Michaelson, the first years of marriage had been a time of attending only to the lovable aspects of The Man and The Woman that reigned in their internal worlds. But, if falling in love had enabled them to contact and share and make manifest this beautiful dream, other inner pictures were one day to resurface. These were the inner lessons they knew about being a Mother and Father. At this time, each seemed to have remembered what to fear and distrust and dislike about the other sex. Each had already learned the ways in which The Man or The Woman goes about frustrating and wounding. Those evanescent images of their own parents (especially because Laurie *was*, now, "mother" and Gabe *was*, now, "father") had come to reassert themselves once again and to intrude. The mask of idealization had fallen from each partner's eyes, but underneath it was another illusion.

For Gabe, in the crisis of new parenthood, seemed in some curious way to have seen his wife as Mother, and himself as an ousted sibling. His jealousy and anger, his difficulty in making space in their lives for Tony, cause one to wonder whether he *himself* had felt rejected, in the forgotten world that was his childhood, by his own real mother? Had Laurie's becoming a real mother suddenly activated a long-suppressed trauma—such as intense jealousy and rage once felt about the birth of a younger sibling? Gabe's withdrawal, his staying away more and more often, had been messages about his anger and protest. He seemed, judging by the very force of his response, to have regressed, to be re-experiencing some old and buried, horribly painful feelings, harking back to some overwhelming event, or perhaps some chronically frustrating situation.

Laurie had, in becoming a mother to their child, become for her husband the very bad dream come true. She was, for Gabe, the bad, the disappointing, non-nurturing, frustrating mother. She "gave him" nothing. And she was, on her part, feeling "disappointed" as well. For here was Gabe who, like *her own father*, was withdrawn, smoldering with barely suppressed angers, passive around the household and tending to stay out of his wife's way. It was as if an inner prophecy were being fulfilled, for Laurie's own mother had been "disappointed" too! She, too, had lived with a man who "wasn't there." How subtly do we work to re-create, in the love ties of the present, the old familiar "way it was," the substructure of the past! At any rate, the hopeful visions and images with which each had adorned the other began to fade away like fairies' finery: the Michaelsons now saw the "truth" about the other, which is to say that each saw the ogre-figure that he or she knew from long ago, from ancient history.

Inner Pictures

But the way a woman "really is" and the way a man "really is" were inner pictures that each was projecting onto the other. Gabe had hoped for love, and wanted to trust, but when Laurie turned away to care for the baby, then of course he *knew*. He knew what he'd always known: that "she" didn't care, and that "she" would reject him. And Laurie found herself living with a most familiar figure, the remotely angry father—The Man.

Of course the family of our childhood is, for each of us, the source of the unconscious design. And when we "fall in love," which is to say recognize whom we *can* love, we deeply understand just who it is that can ultimately aid us in bringing our inner blueprints to realization. And these things happen in marriages—for better or for worse.

In the Forties

CHAPTER TWELVE

The Facts of a Life: Diana (1)

Déjà Vu

Turning the bend in the corridor, the one just opposite the nurses' station, I saw Diana seated alone on the small imitation-leather sofa close by the elevators. The light of a winter sun, coming from the windows behind her, spilled over her dark brown hair and gave it a slightly orange tinge. She was waiting for her husband and children, as I knew—the Dahlgrens were coming in this morning for a family meeting. Diana's thoughts, whatever they might have been at this moment, clearly held her preoccupied, engrossed. She, who was usually so hyperaware of others, so elaborately courteous and outgoing—sometimes almost to the point of caricature—didn't seem aware of my presence until I was standing directly in front of her.

For some reason those few instants, the brief span of time during which I walked toward her, have remained fixed in my memory ever since; I've wondered why I should have retained this short reel of experience, this irrelevant happening, so tenaciously. Maybe it had to do with finding Diana so different—so distant, so still. This was not the frantically polite and pleasing person that I knew, but someone unfamiliar, private: to comprehend her required a movement of my own understanding, a shift in my perceptions. And the scene itself—the sunlight, the sofa, the window—seemed to juggle another, older memory as well. I had the slightly eerie sense of having turned the same corner somewhere before, of having come upon this woman sitting alone, enwrapped in her own thoughts.

A couple of days later—without having given much more thought to it—I suddenly realized what it was that the sight of Diana, in that pose and place, had brought to mind. And it wasn't, as I'd thought, a memory from my own past or experience; it was of a scene captured in a Hopper painting—a picture called "Western Motel." It is a view of a woman seated alone on a sofa near a window which looks out on a western American landscape. The painting, which I'd seen on several occasions, had always left me feeling disquieted, uncomfortable.

For one thing, the lone figure in the scene seems to be an overnight guest at a motel; a small suitcase, and a bulging valise, are displayed at one side of the canvas. They appear to be closed and packed: but it isn't clear whether the woman has just arrived or is on the verge of leaving. Is she staying in this blandly furnished but comfortable room by herself—or is there someone here with her? Has that other person, if there is one, stepped out momentarily, perhaps to settle some trivial detail with the clerk at the front desk? Or has "someone" just left, departed irrevocably; is she adrift in this anonymous place with no human anchor?

Impossible to tell what the woman in the painting might be feeling. Her lips curve slightly upward in what might be a smile, but the eyes are bereft, flat, queerly blank. Beyond the large square of the plateglass window are the purple and blue hazily outlined western hills. The quality of the light is ambiguous, though; it could be twilight or dawn. The more one stares at the scene the more the props of what might have been an initial understanding dissipate; the cues become more and more uncertain. Is something momentous—or nothing at all —*happening?* There seems no basis for hypothesizing, for "making up a story" about what might be taking place, about what this person is experiencing. She might be embroiled in the critical event of a lifetime, or no event at all; she could be in the middle of a routine journey, a vacation, or she could be moving from nowhere to nowhere, alone in a human universe, without human attachments. The effect is one of vague fear, even vertigo.

Even the basic identification of "age group" can't readily be made. The woman in the Hopper work might be in her early thirties, in the first bloom of her full mature adulthood. But then she could easily be ten or fifteen years beyond that—in middle or even "older middle age." She could, not impossibly, be someone in her late forties—as was Diana Pharr Dahlgren, at the time of her hospitalization at the Dartmouth-Hitchcock Mental Health Center in Hanover, New Hampshire.

An Infinity of Birthdays

Diana had been forty-eight—or, more precisely, two weeks to the day past her forty-eighth birthday—when she'd entered the hospital; her decision to kill herself had been linked, importantly so, *to* the passage of that birthday. She'd been feeling, for some months before that, unhinged from any meaning, any "real connections," any "sense or purpose in my life's continuation." She'd been depressed, and severely so, but not actively suicidal until the advent of her birthday. Then, the state of misery, which she described as a kind of "boring torture" had intensified. Her mood, which had seemed to have stabilized, albeit at a very low and painful level, had plummeted precipitously. It was beyond enduring. And what frightened her more than anything was the thought of an infinity of future such birthdays, stretching before her.

She had to stop that future. She would, ultimately, be released—through dying. If this happened sooner, it might be better. Better for her, released from this unsharable suffering, and better for everyone else, having to contend with *her* pain. It had seemed, as she later put it, "to be my only sensible option."

Morning Rounds

Patient's Name: *Diana Pharr Dahlgren*. Birth Date: *December 15, 1929*. Marital Status: *Married*. Occupation: *Housewife*. Religion: *Protestant*. Race: *White*. Persons living with patient (Name, age, relationship). . . . The case was being presented routinely at the early-morning (8 A.M.) ward rounds, when the outgoing night staff meets with the incoming shift of nurses and doctors, psychologists, social workers, recreational and occupational therapists, etc., for an exchange of vital information. This meeting is always crowded, and there's often a double tier of chairs around the large oak conference table. Those who arrive after all of *these* seats are gone sit on the floor or stand slouched against the wall. But everyone connected with the ward who can attend, does attend.

There is usually much to be communicated and to be shared during this woefully short space of time. There are, first of all, reports from the night medical staff on what has been happening to the patients—in terms of social interactions (with one another, with nurses and doctors, with visiting family members and friends), in terms of mood and behavior, capacity for sleep or restlessness and wakefulness—as matters have unfolded throughout the long evening hours and across the passage of the night. Then, there are discussions of those patients who are either approaching discharge, or being discharged on this particular day. (Since the Dartmouth-Hitchcock inpatient ward is an "evaluation unit," no patient remains longer than, roughly speaking, a three-month outside limit. And so "being discharged" may involve, in some instances, transfer to a longer-term psychiatric facility. More hopefully, it means the patient's return to home, family, community, the outside world.)

Eight A.M. rounds is the time for the presentation of the new cases, the incoming patients, as well: Diana Pharr Dahlgren was, as it happened, one of four severely depressed women about whom the ward staff were being briefed during one meeting. I was making only desultory notes. *Mrs. Dahlgren's husband, Robert, age fifty, is a chemical engineer, currently teaching at —— * (a small but distinguished college in Massachusetts). *Patient's husband says he knows of no recent losses, and is unable to offer any explanation for his wife's depression. He does speak of Diana's depressive episodes as having increased in frequency—and more recently, in intensity—over the course of the past few years.* This was a first marriage, both for Diana and for Robert Dahlgren. They had been married in 1950, just after Mrs. Dahlgren's twenty-first birthday, and their union, which both described as successful, had remained intact for the intervening twenty-seven years.

The Dahlgrens have four children, three of them still residing in the household. The oldest, a son, Mark, is a graduate of the University of California and is now a doctoral candidate at ——. Mark was, in fact, a graduate student at the University of Washington in Seattle; he was far away, had been told little or nothing about what was happening, and never played any role in the developing family crisis.

Susannah, a senior in high school, is making college applications to schools out in California, too; the Dahlgrens formerly lived in California. Susannah is seventeen, and is nineteenth months older than Wendy, now a junior in high school. The youngest sibling, Frank, is thirteen, and attends ——. Mrs. Dahlgren reported no serious difficulties with any of the children, although she'd mentioned that a school counselor had suggested that Frankie appeared "worried" and that he was having a bit of trouble making friends. *Diana doesn't, herself, perceive this as a critical problem area. She considers her children to be in generally good shape, and speaks quite proudly of them.*

As the case presentation continued, my note-taking became more and more sporadic. I was allowing large chunks, great ice-floes of information to slide past me, unrecorded. For, formidable as had been her attempt to destroy herself—Mrs. Dahlgren had taken an overdose of Elavil, an antidepressant medicine, as well as some aspirin, found in the bathroom cabinet, and she'd been drinking at the time—this was by no means an exotic case history. Diana Dahlgren was still, as far as I was concerned, faceless—and this sounded like the most usual, the most garden-variety type of depressive disturbance. I was already, at this time, closely involved with a number of women on the ward whose circumstances and stories might have been interchangeable with the one now being painstakingly delineated and described.

Diana Pharr Dahlgren, according to the resident in psychiatry who'd handled her admission to the ward, had suffered increasingly depressed episodes during the course of the past few years. *Patient is unable to offer any "reasons," any "cause" for this all-pervasive tone of sadness and dysphoria, which she describes as "feeling as if I'm in mourning for something without having any notion what that something is"* . . . *She says that only recently has this feeling become unmanageable.* I put down my Bic ballpoint on the table next to my notebook, picked up a plastic cupful of lukewarm coffee sitting next to it, took a sip, continued half listening. The doctor presenting the patient was Frederick (Skip) Burkle, Jr., who'd returned to medical school at Dartmouth to do a residency in psychiatry after ten years of practice as a pediatrician in a small, rich Connecticut suburb. ("I felt impelled to come back to school and learn psychiatry," he'd told me once, "because so many of the real problems I was seeing were familial and social—that is, *psychiatric*—problems.") It was Skip Burkle who'd admitted Mrs. Dahlgren, and it was his responsibility to share his information about her, his impressions of her and her circumstances, his initial evaluation of the entire situation with the rest of the assembled staff. He would explain the treatment regime he meant to undertake with her as well.

I looked up and down the long table at the faces of the senior ward psychiatrists, the nurses, the residents in training, the social workers, the two women "alcohol workers"—who dealt with alcoholic patients and their families, and who were, themselves, successful graduates of

Alcoholics Anonymous programs—the activities' therapists, all listening in silence. *Mrs. Dahlgren experienced a severe downward shift in her mood state, which she places as having begun just prior to her forty-eighth birthday, one week ago on December 4. She thinks her state worsened very suddenly in relation to that birthday, and then continued a downhill spiral afterward.* I was jotting along again. I paused, looked up, when Dr. Burkle looked up from his case notes: "Of course this birthday overlaps with the onset of the Christmas holidays, and the beginnings of the school vacations," he said parenthetically. "And Diana felt, she said, unable to cope with all of the things that would need to be done; she felt too spent, too drained, too anergic and miserable to carry out any of the tasks that lay before her."

He began reading from his case notes again: *Patient felt that her state of mind was insidious, was infecting the rest of the family. She decided, apparently, that they would all be better off if she were dead.*

Mrs. Dahlgren had been, during the exploratory "intake" interviews, unable to focus upon or articulate any issues connected to the passage of her birthday—or issues or difficulties of *any* kind that might have been bubbling at the source of (and provided the sudden upsurge of energy for) her impulsive move toward self-murder. There were no overt marital problems, no recent disruptions of important relationships, no special losses, no striking events, nothing that could explain in any way this state, this feeling of inconsolable grief. Nothing of any kind seemed, in short, to have happened. She had simply, on thinking about her future, decided that she hadn't any. *She was alone in the house, and drinking heavily on the night that she made her suicidal attempt. She says that she simply acted on an idea which came into her head at that moment, and that she hadn't been working on any plan or blueprint for killing herself. The family, though, disagrees; they say she'd been making threatening remarks for a period of a few weeks or a month, prior to that particular evening. . . .*

"But where was her husband that evening—the evening when she was drinking alone?" interrupted Dr. Gary Tucker, a senior staff member, his voice at once gentle and riveting. I paused, looked up; there was a rustle of movement throughout the room, a few murmured side remarks. Then everyone stared at Skip Burkle, who blushed slightly under the impact of that attention. Professor Dahlgren was, he explained, active in a wide range of college-administrative, civic, and church affairs. He'd been at a board meeting of his church that evening.

"*Despite* the suicide threats?" asked someone wonderingly.

In the Early Mornings

Predating her suicidal gesture, and for a period of some months, there had been the common psychological and neuro-vegetative symptoms of depression. Mrs. Dahlgren had been feeling de-energized and joyless; she had had crying spells, felt that her existence was pointless and burdensome, that even the very food she ate had lost its taste. She'd been unable to sleep at all unless she'd slithered past the gates of slumber in a state of drunkenness. But, given that liquor *could* put her to sleep, the sleep she obtained was poor and unsatisfying. She erupted into alert, pained wakefulness in the small hours of the morning.

Early morning was the worst time of all. For it was at the outset of a new day (and this is, of course, common among depressed persons) that Diana felt at her most helpless and hopeless; that she felt most inferior and inadequate to the simple demands of a routine day; that she experienced herself as utterly without worth. It was almost as if the worst, the most despicable enemy she could imagine, had crawled inside her head and was directing a stream of hateful comments *about* her from *within* her. The Elavil, an antidepressant drug prescribed to her by her family doctor, had swept her out of the last wave of depression. But it hadn't helped at all in this most recent protracted attack.

A Way of Squeezing Pity

The family is feeling very frightened at the moment. Dr. Burkle looked up, straightened his rimless glasses on the narrow bridge of his nose: "They do report that she'd been talking fairly morbidly, and that she *had* been making threats," he commented, "but none of them had taken the talk that seriously." Because Diana's state of misery had seemed motiveless, unreal, her husband and children had dismissed her talk of killing herself as a ploy, a way of squeezing pity from them, of manipulatively demanding attention. They were tired of focusing on her, frustrated by her unhappiness. They'd simply not been listening—and then she really had tried to kill herself.

After ward rounds were finished, and when the staff members were dispersing, Skip Burkle stopped to talk with me. He mentioned that he had told Diana Dahlgren that I was spending time on this unit, and that I was interested in researching and studying depression among women. "She said she really would like to talk with you," he told me. "She's not just 'willing,' but she actively *wants* to do so." We agreed that I would go ahead and contact Diana Dahlgren, either by phone or by a message at the nurses' station, or by simply knocking at her door; and that then I'd arrange an interview with her sometime within the next few days.

I called. But, by the time I came to see her, she was asymptomatic. There was no longer any depression to discuss. The psychological symptomatology—the crying spells, feelings of self-hatred and disgust, the loss of pleasure, anergia, helplessness, hopelessness—all seemed to have dissipated magically. She was positive and even downright cheerful in her outlook—although she kept hastening to reassure me, almost apologetically, that she "knew she had to get to work on understanding these things, these awful depressions." The organic symptoms had vanished as well. She was sleeping and eating normally; her food "had a taste"; an annoying and perennial constipation was gone.

I had been away from the clinic the day before (a Thursday), and knew nothing of this when I knocked on her partially open door at the time of our Friday-morning appointment. I was greeted by a cordial, composed: "Come in!" She was seated at a Formica desk upon which were stacked several vases, two pretty pots of flowers, a couple of books and an unopened candy box: they were get-well gifts from friends, from neighbors, and she'd ranged them in a row in front of her to inspire her writing of thank-you notes. On a bedside table, and not part of this grouping, stood a lone flower in a green pot—a beautiful and brilliant poinsettia.

Mrs. Dahlgren herself was a pleasantly groomed, ever so slightly plump woman in a black turtleneck jersey and a beige pants suit. She was attractive and trying hard to be helpful and accommodating. But, seated at that Formica desk, chatting so comfortably, she might have been a guest at a Hilton Hotel room somewhere. There was something incongruous about the woman before me and the suicidally depressed patient I'd heard described—who'd been brought to this unit in crisis. It was, somehow, preposterous, Diana Dahlgren's being where she was. And later on in this, our first conversation, she'd voiced exactly this thought: "It's a little hard getting used to this idea, I mean, you know, being a *mental patient*," she'd observed wryly. "There's something about it that's somehow *crazy*." Catching herself on the word "crazy," she laughed, and I did too.

She considered herself, and certainly appeared, completely well.

The Flight into Health

Such astonishing, almost bewildering, spontaneous recoveries are no rarity among newly admitted psychiatric inpatients. This is the so-called "flight into health," often considered to be motivated by an uprush of desperate fear on the patient's part—fear of confrontation with the source, or the severity and depth, of the psychological wound. To become well at once is to avoid getting to the heart of a particular matter, to seal over whatever it is that (as the .person at some level apperceives and "knows") is the hurtful and unknowable psychic truth.

This is the "spontaneous recovery as a means of avoiding the deeper problem" view. But of course becoming hospitalized at once accomplishes a number of things, a major one being that a person is moved from one place (usually, his or her home environment) to another (the hospital). And in many instances, Diana Dahlgren's included, it has seemed to me as if the patient's "presenting symptoms" were like a fantastically staged and elaborate psychological drama, being enacted in the service of procuring aid, help, care. Certainly, if Diana's suicidal move had communicated anything it was that she *would* be helped or she would die. And so the almost absurd speed of her recovery could be seen as related to her having come to the hospital and gotten what she so deeply desired and needed . . . tenderness and attention. Like Anne Munson, she'd been able to take from this institutional setting the nurturance and support that could, apparently, be found nowhere in her "civilian" life.

Emotional Amnesia

In any case, not only those cruelly self-murderous thoughts and ideas were gone. The long, fuguelike depression which had culminated in them had lifted, remitted completely. Diana, within the course of the next several days, did a steady turnabout, becoming positive and then even superpositive about herself, her marriage, her family, her future. The question was, would this new view persist?

It required no cynicism to be highly doubtful. For Diana had done nothing about integrating the sequence of events leading to her hospitalization into her current concept of herself; it was almost as if that other Diana Dahlgren had had no palpable reality, as if those intensely depressive feelings had not only been plowed over, but hadn't quite really existed. It was difficult for the staff—because it was painful for her—to try to get her to return to that time, to focus upon the whole episode. She was splendidly better, and didn't want to follow any line of thinking in a direction that might upset this newfound equilibrium. She basked, for the moment, in the respite of what resembled an emotional amnesia.

Diana Pharr Dahlgren could easily have won, had such a contest been organized, the title of "Happiest Patient on the Ward," hands down. She'd begun to speak of herself as someone who'd been "extremely lucky" and "terribly fortunate" in "having gotten everything I ever really wanted out of life." The question of her discharge would obviously have to be raised momentarily; and yet most of the ward personnel remained dubious, concerned. The acute pain, anxiety, despair she'd felt—like a hole we knew *was down there* in her psychological upholstery—had been so quickly covered over with this bright and distracting coverlet. But how severe was the damage underneath? And how well would she hold together once she returned to her husband, her home, her family?

Diana's "contented" and "gratified" and "satisfied" assessments of her life situation sounded (to say the least) paradoxical. She had, after all, tried to commit the act of murder upon *herself*. Feelings of intense hate and anger—directed against her *self*—had to have been there, had to have energized this act! (Think, after all, about the overwhelming, out-of-control fury most of us would have to be feeling in order to commit homicide. Suicide *is* homicide: the victim is the self.) Do contented and gratified people act upon sudden impulses to end their own existence?

I don't mean to suggest that most people don't, at some point in their lives—some time of crisis, stress, grief, loss—think about wanting to die, or perhaps wanting to kill someone else whom they see as the cause of their pain; suicidal and murderous thoughts are not limited to mental patients. There is, nevertheless, an enormous gulf between the person who merely *has* such thoughts or fantasies, during a period of rage and suffering, and the person who proceeds to *act upon them*. This crucial divide was the one that Diana had crossed; she had *done* a deed, and it seemed imperative that she take responsibility for it—and for all of those thoughts and feelings and ideas that had brought her so close to dying.

But the only explanation she had for having tried to kill herself was the desire to escape—"once and for all"—from those brutal, protracted, torturous depressions. And she was without explanation for *them*. All that she knew was that the first bad attack of desolation and despair had occurred several years earlier. After that, the depressive episodes had kept coming, like waves which rose up on the placid surface of her life, rolled her over and over during a period of intense turmoil, then subsided, dissipated. She was all right, or almost all right, in between: "Just scared about when it might happen again." The last one had been the worst; it had been the longest and most intense; it had become unendurable.

Why Me?

These depressions were, though, nothing that Diana ever "owned," nothing that were "hers" or proceeded from within her. I think that she experienced them as a kind of flu, an attack of disease which came upon her from outside—as if by means of a germ, a virus. The fact that *she* should be getting them sometimes even made her indignant. "I could understand this kind of thing happening to a whole lot of people," she once told me, "who might be, you know, in pretty terrible kinds of circumstances. Without money to feed their families— women who are alone, without husbands to care for them—or people whose kids have gone wild or wrong. But someone like *me* . . . it makes no sense!" She shook her head, looked at me in helpless wonderment: "Why should *I* get into something like that—those awful, unspeakable things, those depressions?"

The Diagnosing of Despair

The meaning of the word *diagnosis*, as explained in the Oxford English Dictionary, is primarily that of "*Determination of the nature of a diseased condition; identification of a disease by careful investigation.*" In making his or her diagnosis of an illness that is *physical*, the modern doctor—like the modern detective—can take advantage of a superb and finely tuned technology. Not only do the patient's medical history, and the physical examination, and the analysis of possible environmental "causes" of the disease yield a useful supply of clues; there is a wide variety of laboratory procedures that can either confirm a diagnosis or point the investigating physician along a different, and perhaps more fruitful trail. Even so, the locating and correct identification of a disease—the first step toward understanding and curing—is still, to some degree, an art form. As one writer, Dr. Leston Havens, has observed: "The tracking down of physical disease has always required the finest sensitivity and intuition, the willingness to follow up what seems hardly present at all, an openness not only to the loud and the obvious but to the obscure and apparently insignificant as well. Medicine is like detective work or safe cracking; it requires fine fingers."

The Treatment of the Soul

If, however, the field of physical medicine requires its modicum of artistry, its sensitive touch, how much more so must the treatment of "mind," of "soul"! For, in the treatment of mental distress, there is no X-ray photography that can lay bare a metastatic growth of anger and despair. No biochemical tests of bodily fluids—of blood, or urine—can explain, or even corroborate the presence of hopelessness, helplessness, feelings of utter worthlessness, the desire to die. The depressive patient can be as mortally ill from "wanting to be dead" as is the cancer patient (and may do his or her dying sooner), but the doctor has little in the way of technological aids or props to support him in his "determination of the nature of the diseased condition. . . ." "It is no wonder," Dr. Havens, a psychiatrist at Harvard, writes, "that we too despair. Confronted by a multitude of obscure human difficulties, with no firm guidelines between the normal and the abnormal or between sickness and sin, we turn back to the challenges of physical diagnosis with relief and confidence. . . ."

How *was* one, in the case of *Diana Pharr Dahlgren; December 15, 1929; Married; Housewife; Protestant; White*, to set about the business of identifying and evaluating her pathology? How could one —except in metaphoric, literary terms—assess the progress of the secret worm in motion within her, the malignant process which had declared its presence in that wild self-attack? What could an "opinion (formally stated) resulting from such investigation" reveal?

How, in short, could she be helped?

Dr. Peter Whybrow, an Englishman in his late thirties, happens to be an expert in the area of the depressive disturbances; he is someone I consulted frequently during research visits to Dartmouth. And once, during one of our many formal (taped) and informal (standing in the hallway) conversations about the nature and meaning of human depression, Whybrow interrupted another sentence he'd started, to say: "Look here, one can sum up practically everything we've been talking about very simply. And that is by mentioning the obvious—which is that much of the business of human living has to do with loving and losing—and that what we call 'depression' has to do with the 'losing' side of that equation."

Of course the loss, as Whybrow added at once, may not involve the loss of another person, an important relationship; the loss could occur at a purely symbolic level. "It might be the loss of a fantasy—about the success that one's talents would bring, or even the fantasy that one would stay young and attractive forever. Or it might be an image of oneself as a supermother, or someone very much in control—whatever it is, you see, that happens to be important for that individual's self-esteem, his or her sense of being a worthy and valued human being." And in the wake of that particular observation, I'd begun wondering, musing, thinking about what loss it was that Diana Dahlgren might have sustained.

Her daily life, as she'd described it, sounded placid and satisfactory, disconsonant with those periodic attacks of self-disparagement and morbid sadness that seemed to come upon her "as if from nowhere." Where, then, was the grief and the loss; what were the seeds of her pain? I was, at that time, poring over the terminology suggested in the *DSM* (i.e., the *Diagnostic and Statistical Manual of Mental Disorders**), that strange little psychiatric guidebook to the various categories of disorders of thought, mood, personality, etc. And I began looking among the various types of the depressive disturbances for the one which most neatly fit the case of Diana Dahlgren.

A Foreigner in New England

There was, among the obvious possibilities, ✕300.4, *Depressive Neurosis*. This is defined in the physicians' manual as being "manifested by an excessive reaction of depression due to an internal conflict or to an identifiable event such as the loss of a love object or cherished possession. . . ." In Diana's instance there seemed no striking event to which she might be reacting, no loss of a loved and needed other person, no

---

* I was using *DSM* II. A new version (*DSM* III) now exists, in draft form.

thing such as a house, job, etc., of which she'd suddenly been deprived. What could she be in this state of mourning *for?*

The first really severe depressive episode, as she recounted, had occurred in the wake of a family relocation. That had been about four years ago, when Robert Dahlgren had changed jobs. Before that he'd taught, for a period of years, at a small, religiously oriented college out in California.

The move from California to New England had not been, according to Diana, any big problem, any trauma: "It's his career, and naturally you go along with it, because it's that that really comes first," she said good-naturedly.

Still, she allowed, she had never felt "the same," never achieved a sense of "really belonging" in the new community. Her emotional roots, better nourished in the church-and-campus life the family had lived out in California, had remained raw and vulnerable. She'd never quite adapted to the patterns of being, never felt taken in to the church that they'd joined and now attended. She was a foreigner in New England, although they'd lived here for the past four years.

Feeling Uprooted

The case could, perhaps, be classified as #307.3, *Adjustment Reaction of Adult Life.* This is described in the *DSM* as: "Resentment with depressive tone associated with an unwanted pregnancy"—in Diana's instance, substitute this example with "unwanted and painful uprooting from a meaningful and supportive environment"—"and manifested by hostile complaints and suicidal gestures." This category of depressive disorder might best capture and explain the nature and quality of Diana's "loss."

An Emptying Family Nest

But then there was also #307.4, *Adjustment Reaction of Late Life.* Chronologically speaking she didn't, of course, qualify. Diana Dahlgren was forty-eight at the time of her hospitalization. But this type of depression is described as: "Feelings of rejection associated with forced retirement and manifested by social withdrawal." And Diana was, at this period of her lifetime, in the process of phasing out of what had been her major "role," the organizing principle of her daily existence: that of center-of-the-family, of mother. She might be mourning the loss of that role and the image of herself as the focal nurturer; she might be suffering from that most mundane of ailments, *empty nest syndrome.* Her adult and near-adult children were in the process of leaving (as Mark, in school in California, had done) and learning-not-to-need-her (as the older girls and even Frankie were doing). She might be feeling unnecessary, abandoned, superfluous, terribly lonely.

The loss of an organizing role can be a monstrous blow to a person's sense of self, of being who he or she *is.* I have seen men, at the time of retirement, literally dying—on psychiatric and on medical wards—over the loneliness and sense of despair attendant upon the loss of the work role. They can't survive the psychological diminishment, the lack of easy entry into, and easy feedback from, the world at large.

For men who become afflicted by *Adjustment Reaction of Late Life* the problem really does arise in late life. But for women, especially those who adopt caring-for-others roles, "retirement" can come some twenty years sooner. And in both sexes it can involve a deadly fall in self-esteem and the pain of loneliness.

The Trauma That Is Loneliness

I want to say a few words, now, about loneliness—though it's truly one of the most difficult of subjects to discuss. The sociologists have a term—*anomie*—which refers to "disconnection from the community-at-large," from the ordinary networks of social living, from interconnection and interaction with others. Anomie means social isolation. Being *lonely*, however, implies not only social but *emotional* isolation. And this painful state, though sung about in many a love song and poem—and explored in some short stories and novels—is largely ignored in most of the psychiatric literature. I have wondered about this strange omission, for "being lonely" is one of the most feared and ultimately horrible mental states.

One of the few attempts to grapple with the problem of loneliness was made by psychiatrist Frieda Fromm-Reichmann. In a little essay called "Loneliness" she remarks upon how hard it is for most people to recall vividly periods of their lives when they *were* very lonely. This is not, suggested the analyst, because the experience isn't striking;

it is because it is almost unbearably so. It presents a threat to a person's integrity, and well-being, the very sense that *one is*. Loneliness is so awful an experience, she noted, that "most people will do practically everything to avoid it." And those who have once suffered from intense loneliness probably develop a degree of amnesia about the experience—and its intensity—because "it is so frightening and uncanny in character that they try to dissociate the memory of what it was like and even the fear of it" from conscious thought, from remembrance. States of loneliness, wrote Fromm-Reichmann, can be so exquisitely painful that even the recollection of them is beyond a person's toleration.

Was plain "loneliness," I wondered, a factor in Diana Dahlgren's recurrent depressions? There was no diagnostic category that leaned on, or even mentioned, so humdrum an explanation. But women do—simply because the structure of their experiences and life-tasks frequently so ordains it—get socially engineered into relatively socially isolated positions. The facts of the matter were these: Diana was alone during the hours when the children were away at school. And she was living at a slight remove from the new community in which she'd found herself: earlier, it had been largely through caretaking of the children, and finding playmates for them, and relating to other parents through school and church activities (again, child-centered) that she'd found her own point-of-entry into the world outside her home.

Now there wasn't quite any shared activity which was meaningful to her, and which brought her into contact with other people. The role of mother, relating to other mothers was sharply attenuated; even the role of wife relating to her husband was woefully diminished, for Robert was increasingly occupied, greatly pressed for time, out of the house during the day and through many evenings—he'd become active on several administrative committees on the campus and was, as he'd always been, highly involved in their church. Diana was a middle-aged woman living in pleasant circumstances in a nice home in a pretty town—and alone a great deal of the time. Alone, and probably lonely.

The Toneless Quality of Loneliness

Had that loneliness become burdensome and then insupportable and finally even terrifying? In his book *Interpersonal Psychiatry*, Dr. Harry Stack Sullivan devoted a few brief passages to the mental distress occasioned by "being lonely." "Loneliness is possibly most distinguished, among the experiences of human beings, by the toneless quality of the things said about it," he commented. It is, nevertheless, a powerful driving force, a state that can be more painful than severe anxiety. "Anyone who has experienced loneliness is glad to discuss some vague abstract of this previous experience of loneliness," observed Dr. Sullivan. "But it is a very difficult therapeutic performance to get anyone to remember clearly how he felt and what he did when he was horribly lonely. In other words, the fact that loneliness will lead to integrations" (the term used by Sullivan to denote "contact" and "satisfying interconnections" with other people) "in the face of severe anxiety automatically means that *loneliness in itself is more terrible than anxiety*."

The italics are mine; Sullivan's point is, though, that even the person who is painfully shy and terribly fearful of being rebuffed or rejected will *try* . . . will make what are costly and gallant efforts to form relationships with other people. In other words, no matter how frightened or anxious or hesitant one may be about making approaches to others, these feelings will often be overridden by that overwhelming need to escape "being lonely." The anxiety which might compel one to avoid others is still *less terrible* than the loneliness one experiences when human contact is diminished . . . or perhaps not there at all.

A Word on the Social Isolation of Women

In my talks with Diana Dahlgren I'd become well aware of her sense of her profound aloneness—an aloneness that she'd been, somehow, helpless to counteract. And I'd begun thinking, as well, how it happens that most (or at least, many) women are thrust, during periods of their lives, into places that are isolated, socially sterile. I remembered a time when, as a gregarious young wife, with a new young baby, in a new apartment, in a strange city, I was adrift for days and weeks, speaking to no one during the daylight hours when my husband was away at work. I seemed to be pushing a baby carriage endlessly across the surface of a remote world. It had no sides, no top, that limbo; there was nothing to enclose, nothing to support, nothing to enfold the mother and new infant. We were communityless, strangers. The day can have a thousand hours during which one learns and relearns the lessons of silence—that self-definition can drip away, erode, and that quiet can become almost too painful for bearing.

But my situation, during this period, wasn't anything particularly atypical. Many women have, or are now, or will in the future adjust to similar kinds of circumstances. I'd simply been boxed, for the nonce, into a socially depriving situation. This can happen very easily and very normally. Indeed, in his moving foreword to a collection of articles entitled: *Loneliness, The Experience of Emotional and Social Isolation,* sociologist David Riesman comments upon the fact that most of the material in this "deeply sad, even tragic volume" is concerned (as it obviously must be) with the social isolation of women.

Loneliness is, of course, not the same thing as depression (depressogenic though it may be). As psychologist Robert S. Weiss, in the lead essay in this book, writes:

> Ordinary loneliness is uniformly distressing. It may be useful to distinguish it from other forms of distress. To begin with, it is different from what is usually described as depression. In loneliness there is a drive to rid oneself of one's distress by integrating a new relationship or regaining a lost one; in depression there is instead a surrender to it. The lonely are driven to find others, and if they find the right others, they change and are no longer lonely. The depressed are often unwilling to impose their unhappiness on others; in any event their feelings cannot be reached by relationships, old or new.

Being lonely is, in Weiss's view, a deficit state, a state of "relational insufficiency." The depressed person, unlike the lonely one, has given up *hope* of finding the satisfying relations desired. But as Weiss, like Fromm-Reichmann and Sullivan, points out, many people cannot *remember* what it was like, feeling lonely. When asked to try, reports the psychologist, they will often say things such as: "Yes, I suppose I was lonely. But I wasn't *myself* then." As Weiss so cleverly remarks, "The self associated with the absence of loneliness is a different one from the self associated with loneliness: it is more engaged by a range of interests, more confident, more secure, more self-satisfied. To someone in this state the earlier lonely self—tense, restless, unable to concentrate, *driven*—must seem an aberration."

Loneliness is a state so threatening to most people, and so difficult to confront within themselves, that they find it difficult to empathize with someone who is currently lonely if they themselves are not. Talk of loneliness is therefore often, notes Weiss, responded to with "absence of understanding and perhaps irritation." He observes:

> Professionals in research and treatment, if they have dealt with their own past experiences of loneliness in this way (i.e., by shutting

them out of consciousness) might also prefer not to disturb their current emotional arrangements. To maintain their current feelings of well-being, they too might be impatient with the problem of loneliness. They might be willing to consider loneliness in an exotic form—the loneliness of the mentally ill or of the Arctic explorer or the alienation of marginal man. But they would be made uncomfortable by the loneliness that is potential in the everyday life of everyone. . . . The frequency and intensity of loneliness are not only underestimated but the lonely themselves tend to be disparaged. It seems easy to blame their loneliness on their frailties and to accept this fault-finding as an explanation. Our image of the lonely often casts them as justifiably rejected: as people who are unattractive, shy, intentionally reclusive, undignified in their complaints, self-absorbed, self-pitying. We may go further and suppose that chronic loneliness must to some extent be chosen.

An Empathic Gulf

The young physicians working on the Dartmouth-Hitchcock inpatient unit were, of course, anything but lonely. They were pressured, harried, overcommitted, *too* busy. Their daily existence stood in a kind of black-and-white contrast to what the emptied, disconnected, solitary life of the superfluous-feeling Diana Dahlgren must have been —before she'd come into the hospital. What an empathic gulf had to be leaped, what an experiential divide crossed, in order for the too-stressed staff to comprehend the lack of stimulation, the barrenness, the "no place to go, nothing to do, no one to be with" loneliness with which Diana had tried (unavailingly) to cope. She'd been alone "a lot"; she'd been out of contact with others. The meeting between oversubscribed and overburdened doctor, on the one hand, and the lonesome, middle-aged patient, on the other, was a meeting between two people for whom the "given conditions," the structure of daily life, was indeed very different. For her psychotherapist to imagine the molasseslike feeling of being stuck in endless time required, I thought, the same leap of understanding that it would take for a superb athlete to "feel what it would be like" to be lame.

But a chronic "deficit state"—loneliness—had played some role, I suspected, in the development of this mysterious affliction, this "motiveless depression." And I entertained a few suspicions too, I'll admit, about whether or not her striking improvement had had to do with simply reducing loneliness! She had, after all, been moved from an environment relatively empty of contact and into one where she was receiving a great deal of nurturance—and just plain simple attention! Her depressions, her suicidal gesture, her becoming a mental patient: these had culminated in her being here, in her getting into relationships.

And now—for the meanwhile—the negative feelings about herself, the pervasive sense of helplessness and hopelessness were gone.

A Personal Rubicon

Strange, this *determination of the nature of a diseased condition*, this diagnosing. Insofar as anything causative was concerned, I'd only come across a couple of possible underlying motives, noxious aspects of Diana Dahlgren's life. And these were trivialities—some loneliness, a move from California to New England. Was this the stuff of depressive illness, of pathological self-recrimination, of neurotic processes that had at last culminated in her desire for death?

That move across the country, when Robert had changed jobs—there was something mysterious about it. It came up unfailingly in every conference that was held with the family. For Diana, it had been a kind of a personal Rubicon; after that upheaval, she'd never again regained her psychological equilibrium. "It wasn't that I'd never felt down, or depressed, or blue in my lifetime *before* then," she'd said in the course of one of these family meetings, "but that was just the same thing as—you know—the way everyone gets down once in a while. It wasn't anything pathological, nothing that was *sick*. . . ." But it was after the move East that she'd embarked on this downward spiral, had drifted from phases of dejection and "feeling blue" to longer, more difficult spells; times of feeling unloved, unworthy, completely useless. She'd become "robotized," had performed her routine tasks like something that's mechanical, dead; she had felt as if she were being watched (or "watching myself") with the cold eye of an enemy.

But it wasn't only Diana who felt that something in the family had gone sour after that move from California. The children all thought so too. They thought that their father had "changed" around that time. Mom had started—obviously—into a decline during this period. But as their oldest daughter, Sue, once remarked thoughtfully (sounding surprised, herself, by the perception): "I think in fact it was you, Dad, who maybe did the changing even before Mom did . . . ?" She'd looked at her father quizzically.

Robert Dahlgren, who usually said little at the family meetings, had appeared startled by the comment. He took his pipe from the side of his mouth and said in his habitually reasonable tone of voice: "Me? I changed? No, I don't think I did. I don't remember doing any particular changing." He looked around at the other members of his family, as if appealing for support.

But they had nodded in assent to Susannah's remark about his "having changed"; they were silent, now. "You got so *busy*, then," persisted Sue. "You know you did."

"But I had to," replied her father. "It was a new *job*."

"You know you changed then, Bob," put in Diana, with a rare aggressive energy. "It wasn't only being busy. You just . . . you weren't the same with us, afterward."

But Professor Dahlgren had continued to look perplexed. "I had no sense of anything like that, nothing at all," he said mildly. "I don't think, I mean I had no feeling of having changed. I really don't believe I *did*."

Alcoholism

I haven't, alas, come to the end of my list of diagnostic possibilities. For the case of Diana Pharr Dahlgren was also a candidate for category ⚕303.2, which is *Alcohol Addiction*. This is suitable for "patients whose alcohol intake is great enough to damage their physical health or their personal or social functioning, or when (sic) it has become a prerequisite for normal functioning. If the alcoholism is due to another disorder, both diagnoses should be made."

For Diana, a *twin diagnosis* would probably be necessary.

She'd been medicating her depression and her anxiety for almost a year preceding the florid events that had culminated in her hospitalization—and she'd been using the only "medicine" that seemed to help matters at all, alcohol.

She'd tried antidepressants, the ones given to her by her family doctor. And these had been helpful, but just up to a point. So had her occasional office visits with this doctor been helpful: he'd permitted, even *helped* her to ventilate her feelings, to openly discuss her distress. But when the aftereffects wore off, she was more alone, more despairing, more "empty" than ever. And the pills he gave her ultimately couldn't do what she needed and wanted to have done. They didn't stop her consciousness, blot out thinking and feeling. . . . She was now a Drinker.

A Family Secret

And here was another vexing aspect of this situation. Although everyone in the Dahlgren household was aware that Diana was on her way to becoming, at the very least, a "problem drinker," no member of the family seemed to have spoken to anyone else about the matter openly! Nor had anyone tried to discuss it with Diana herself, directly. It had been a "family secret," which each person in the household carried alone, on an individual basis. If, during many an afternoon, Mom remained in her bedroom sleeping or crying, that was simply not to be spoken about. It was the way things were. And even Robert Dahlgren, as husband to Diana, as father to the family, seemed disconnected from the problem *as* a problem. It was, curiously, as though Diana's difficulties—her state of despair and her fumbling attempts to deal with and handle that despair—might not be quite "real" if the rest of the family were careful not to give the subject reality by discussing it aloud. It was an odd manner of managing distress—I mean, by denying its very patent and obvious existence. I sometimes thought they'd behaved as if there were a dead body smack in the middle of their living-room floor, and they'd responded by simply walking around it, going on with their daily routines, acting as if it *weren't* there.

Search for Oblivion

But it was. And it was true that her current dependence on alcohol was a complication of formidable magnitude. This was a secondary problem which might become more paramount than the initial one— her depression—itself. For the alcohol abuser is different from other types of substance-abusers. The alcoholic isn't seeking sensation; he or she is seeking oblivion. The alcoholic is looking for a respite—a way out—a means of escaping, even if that "escape" is on a moment-to-moment basis, from a world that's become too difficult, too unmanageable. As Dr. Theodore Nadelson, a Harvard-affiliated psychiatrist, once told me in the course of an interview: "A good metaphor for what can happen when a depressive starts drinking is that of a person dropping a match in a building and starting a small fire. You may, then, address yourself to the problem of putting out the initial fire—say, a depression that's related to a business failure, or to marital unhappiness, or to a sexual problem, etc.—but in the meanwhile the *rest* of the building may have caught fire and *it* may be burning down." The point is that the second symptom—alcoholism—may become an autonomous one, and one that is disconnected from whatever got it going in the first place: "You might cure or at least alleviate the first symptom, the depression," explained Nadelson, "but in the meanwhile the person's become an alcoholic."

One of the pressing questions, at this moment, was whether or not Diana's drinking problem had embarked on an independent career of its own. If her depressions could be halted, even moderated when they occurred, would her dependence on alcohol to take the edge off the pain peel away just as easily? Or had her need already—albeit that heavy drinking had become pronounced just in the past few months—reached the point where it might be "a prerequisite for normal functioning"? Would she, when she went home, have to do a certain amount of drinking just to get through the day?

At this stage of an unfolding story it was impossible to know. A hopeful consideration was, though, that she'd lived forty-eight years of her life already, *without* developing an excessive dependence on alcohol. She might not have totally integrated the need for it into her life style—in Nadelson's terms, "the rest of the building might not have caught fire." But the clinical team working with the Dahlgrens included, from the outset, an A.A. worker, Christine. Christine was, herself, a reformed alcoholic.

Menopausal Depression

I haven't, even yet, exhausted the diagnostic possibilities applicable to Diana Dahlgren's case. Considering the age at which her severe depression erupted, she might have fit into the romantic sounding *Involutional Melancholia*, category ✲296.0. The word involutional means "retrograde" or "regressive"; it refers to processes which are degenerative in nature and have to do with physical aging. In females, there is a special meaning—that of ovarian shutdown and the ending of reproductive life. Involutional Melancholia can, in the case of a forty-eight-year-old woman, therefore be translated as *menopausal depression.*

But this category of mental disorder has recently fallen into psychiatric disfavor. It has been attacked as an anti-feminist label, a medical method for explaining (and then filing away) women in this age group, who are then viewed as unfortunate victims of a deficient plumbing system rather than as persons who may have become depressed about particular factors or problems in their lives.

The whole idea that there is a thing called *menopausal depression—* some kind of a biological time bomb that can explode during those years in a woman's life span when her fertility is in decline or just ending—has, however, been seriously disputed by research dating as far back as the 1920s, and earlier. The ongoing arguments, pro and con, about this entire issue will be discussed extensively in Chapter Fifteen.

Hysterical Personality

Menopausal depression is a large can of worms, and one that I will be examining in great detail. But now, another possible psychiatric classification for Diana awaits us: ⚕301.5, *Hysterical Personality* (*hysteriform personality disorder*). And, considering the very dependent, extremely "feminine" nature of Diana Dahlgren's character structure, she would have been one of the first to receive this particular designation. As the Diagnostic and Statistical Manual describes it: "These behavior patterns are characterized by excitability, emotional instability, over-reacting and self-dramatization. This self-dramatization is always attention-seeking and often seductive, whether or not the patient is aware of its purpose. These personalities are also immature, self-centered, often vain, and usually dependent on others. . . ."

The idea is that such patients depend on others for their emotional supplies; that they take in from others at an excessive clip but are able to give out little; that they are egocentric and overly demanding, preoccupied with the sustenance and satisfaction that they can get from others and empty of their own "inner food." That they lack a sense of that inner self, substance, sustenance that we speak of as *self-esteem.*

Diana Dahlgren might be what the psychoanalyst Sandor Rado called a "love addict," a person whose needs for more love, more succor, more support grow as rapidly as the frustrated people around her try to fill up what is, in effect, a terrible and unsatisfiable inner emptiness.

Accommodating

But I was, like an oculist, trying out these various diagnostic categories as one might go through a series of varying lenses—to see which one, or which combination of them, might best clarify the mystery that was Diana—which one might get her into comprehensible focus. At the same time I was thinking about something that Samuel Butler had said, in *The Way of All Flesh*, which was that all throughout our lives, "every day and every hour we engage in the process of accommodating our changed and unchanged selves to changed and unchanged surroundings; living, in fact, is nothing else than this process of accommodation; when we fail in a little, we are stupid, when we fail flagrantly we are mad."

CHAPTER THIRTEEN

Femininity as Symptom

Made Expressly for Women

It is the last item in my shopping-list of "possible diagnoses" for Diana Pharr Dalhgren which has, clearly, the most judgmental ring. For it raises the suggestion that the fault lay not in Diana's stars nor in the actualities of what might be depressing real-life circumstances; but in an aberrant personality style, a somewhat infantile mode of relating to those around her. While I don't want to argue for or against such a view of Diana Dahlgren, I do want to remark upon the fact that such a judgment is being made, or at least implied—and not necessarily unfairly, because her depressive illness had to be related not only to the stresses and tensions she was meeting with at this particular phase of her life, but to her own individual ways of meeting and dealing with them.

I do want to note, however, that the psychiatric category *Hysterical Personality* might easily be given a tag saying: Made Expressly for Women.

The definition of this mental disorder is anything but subtle in its wording: such patients show "excitability," are "attention-seeking" and "seductive," as well as "immature, self-centered, often vain and usually dependent on others." But of course girls and women are *encouraged*, in every way and throughout their lifetimes, to give special thought to personal grooming, to enhancing physical attractiveness, to being more openly expressive about states of emotion and feeling ("attention-seeking" and "excitability"). Such messages about the "appropriateness" of certain kinds of behavior—coyness and cuteness ("seductiveness") and the display of dependency needs—are bombarded upon all females constantly, upon girl and woman in her family, upon girl and woman in her culture. And so the kinds of personality defects being posited as "hysterical personality disorders"* are ones which strongly resemble characteristics that are commonly considered "normally feminine."

A Bog of Sexual Stereotypes

Trying to talk about or to define what is "normal" is always a treacherous undertaking. One simply *knows* what one means when using the word "normal" or when referring to "normally feminine" behavior. But the fact is that as soon as you try to step forward and say what that *is* you may find the crust of your confidence giving way beneath you, and yourself sinking into a bog of sexual stereotypes. (And as one rather startling set of research results indicated, being "normal" may be something quite different from being "normally feminine.")

Dependency

Take, for example, the normally feminine trait of dependency. Girls and women in our culture are *expected* to show higher dependency needs than do boys and men; this is simply one aspect of the designated sex role about which the infant learns from the moment of birth onward. (I'm not being rhetorical here; psychological experiments have shown that parents hold new babies differently—an infant in a pink blanket, *believed* to be a girl, will be held and cuddled much more.) Thus, as Judith Bardwick noted in her book, the *Psychology of Women*, ". . . the dependency, passivity, tears and affection-seek-

---

* As of 1980, as noted in the last chapter, a new diagnostic system is being adopted. The disorders that I've been discussing are, by and large, contained in the new manual—*DSM* III—but the descriptions of some of them have been altered and revised. Hysterical personality disorder has been rebaptized *Histrionic Personality Disorder;* but the symptom picture is given in ways that don't sound awfully dissimilar. Among other things, the patient is: "Superficially warm and charming, and appealing," "Vain, egocentric, and self-absorbed," "Dependent, helpless, constantly seeking reassurance," and may be given to "Uninhibited displays of sexuality, e.g., Flirtatiousness or coquetry" as well as "Indulgence in frequent flights of romantic fantasy." And—just in case the diagnosing physician has, somehow, missed the point—"In both sexes, behavior that is a caricature of femininity" is given as another indicator for histrionic personality disorder!

ing normal to both sexes are defined as feminine in older children, and girls can remain dependent and infantile longer. . . . This has a very pervasive and significant effect: unless something intervenes, the girl will continue to have throughout womanhood a great need for approval from others. Her behavior will be guided by the fear of rejection or loss of love. An independent sense of self with a resulting sense of self-esteem can only evolve when the individual, alone, sets out to attain goals and, with reasonable frequency, achieves them."

Adds Dr. Bardwick, a psychologist at the University of Michigan: ". . . the American girl rarely achieves an independent sense of self-esteem." But she is speaking, and this must be emphasized, about *normal* femininity. And what Bardwick is suggesting is that the young girl learns to appraise her own worth as a function of the appraisals reflected by others, to value herself insofar as she *is* valued. Being female means never having to be a self-sufficient individual. And girls receive many instructions on this aspect of femininity, throughout the long apprenticeship of childhood.

Now it may well be, theorizes Bardwick, that the greater dependency shown by girls and women is not merely due to the powerful acculturating forces that move them in this direction. There may be inborn biological tendencies that come into play, as well. But in any event, the lack of an *inner* impulsion to break away from the dependent relations of early childhood—and the manifest assumption on everyone's part that she will *not* do so—fosters a situation in which the girl (and later, woman) gives her highest priorities to pleasing others, to being attractive to others, to being cared for and caring for others. "An independent sense of self," observes the psychologist, "can only occur when one has many experiences in which he is responsible while he cannot completely depend upon the original sources of love and support." (I was taken aback by Bardwick's sudden switch to the pronoun "he" in this particular sentence!)

But the over-all point she makes is that women receive ferocious training in the direction *away* from thinking: "What do I want?" We tend to think far more in terms of: "What do *they* want (need) *of me?*"

The Props of Self-esteem

Being successful then translates to being successful in the eyes of others: pleasure has much to do with the act of pleasing. This readily leads to a situation in which good feelings about the self, or self-esteem, become dependent upon the esteem of those around one. Feelings of emotional well-being, a sense of one's worthfulness as a person, are hostage to the moods, the attitudes, the approval of others (or perhaps one critically important Other). One is likable/lovable/significant only to the extent that one is liked, loved, significant to someone else. It follows, therefore, that in a time of interpersonal drought, when sources of emotional supply are not there or are unusually low, the "normally feminine" woman may experience her inner world as emptied of what is good and meaningful to her; the props of her self-esteem may simply collapse. The lack of gratifying input from the environment may, in short—because she has been taught from the cradle onward to depend upon it for her own psychological equilibrium—rapidly eventuate in her becoming far more critical in her assessments of herself, in her feeling worthless, useless, helpless about her particular life circumstances, helpless about her capacity to master or change them. She may become depressed.

This is, I suspect, the point at which "normal feminine dependency" becomes transformed into something which is viewed as pathological, a "symptom." It has to do with some important aspect of that person's life (of which she may or may not be consciously aware) no longer working, no longer giving her the gratification she needs in order to maintain her psychological equilibrium, her own sense of a good and worthwhile inner self.

The Age of Depression

Is it these enhanced dependence needs, which are part of the ordinary feminine sex-role package, that places women more "at risk" for developing one variant or another of the depressive disorders? Women *are*, as I remarked at the outset of this book, more vulnerable to depression than are men—and to an almost staggering degree. I don't mean to suggest that males never suffer from attacks of depression; obviously, that isn't true. But what is true is that for every man diagnosed as suffering from a depressive disturbance, there are generally *two or more women.* (The numbers vary, depending on where the particular study or survey is being done. But there are some studies that indicate that for every male who comes into a particular clinic with a depressive complaint, there are as many as *six* females!) Depression is, as one researcher (female) remarked to me, "predominantly a woman's disease." And it has, in the course of the past couple of decades, reached epidemic proportions. A number of mental health experts have recently suggested, in fact, that the Age of Anxiety of the 1950s has now been succeeded by the Age of Depression.

Most of the sufferers are women: a striking proportion of them are women. This strange disparity between the sexes shows up everywhere, in every clinical situation, in countries throughout the world. More women come to their family doctors with symptoms indicating an overt or disguised depression; more women consult psychotherapists with a primary complaint of depression; more women are hospitalized in psychiatric facilities of all sorts with the severer forms of depression. And, in a study carried out in the late 1960s by the National Institute of Mental Health, it became clear that *70 per cent of the antidepressants being prescribed were being prescribed for women!* (Women were also the major users of the anti-anxiety drugs, such as Librium, Valium, and Miltown.)

The obvious fact that women consume a disproportionate quantity of the antidepressant and anti-anxiety medications has not, as you can imagine, gone unnoticed by the drug companies who are vending these psychic balms. One need only turn to the nearest medical journal to find ad after glossy ad, most of them depicting a pained-looking woman patient, who stares out at the reader-physician imploringly, a pathetic "Please-help-me" expression contorting her features. She is recognizably the typical antidepressant or anti-anxiety drug consumer.

The pharmaceutical companies' adverts are really devilments of ingenuity—for, while they are awful caricatures, they're also real; every physician and psychotherapist *knows* that woman who comes into his or her office with *that* look on her face! I just want to mention, however, that the worst of these drug ads that I've ever personally seen was a Roche Laboratories creation. It was a picture of a woman sitting alone, looking forlorn and miserable, and the text below it went as follows:

M.A. (fine arts) . . . P.T.A. (president-elect) . . . a life currently centered around home and children with too little time to pursue a vocation for which she has spent many years in training. . . . A situation that may bespeak continuous frustration and stress: a perfect framework for her to translate the functional symptoms of psychic tension into major problems. For this kind of patient—with no demonstrable pathology yet repeated complaints—consider the distinctive properties of Valium. . . .

The conflict-ridden feminine role is, here, seen as "pathologically normal": or "normally pathological"—it isn't easy to decide which. At any rate, the intelligent, educated (M.A.) female, functioning in her traditional role (P.T.A. president-elect, mother, wife) is, it is implied, dissatisfied and discontented, anxious and distressed and probably depressed. She needs to be helped, to be drugged.

Masculine/Feminine

Is it possible that those personality traits and characteristics associated with "being feminine" are, in themselves, depressogenic? Isn't it true that the line between "neurotic" dependency and "normally higher" feminine dependency needs is a difficult one to draw? I mentioned earlier that being "normal" and being "normally feminine" might not be quite the same thing. I want to talk now about the witty (if somewhat devastating in their implications) researches carried out by Inge and Donald Broverman and their colleagues. This work was reported upon in the *Journal of Consulting and Clinical Psychology* in 1970.

What the Broverman group did was to devise a deceptively simple list, a brief questionnaire, in which a number of traits considered highly feminine were placed on a scale of 1 to 10 with their "masculine" opposites at the other pole. The Broverman list looked like this:

Very independent _ _ _ _ _ _ _ _ _ _ Not at all independent
1 2 3 4 5 6 7 8 9 10

Not at all easily influenced _ _ _ _ _ _ _ _ _ _ Very easily influenced
1 2 3 4 5 6 7 8 9 10

Not at all aggressive _ _ _ _ _ _ _ _ _ _ Very aggressive
1 2 3 4 5 6 7 8 9 10

Cries very easily _ _ _ _ _ _ _ _ _ _ Never cries
1 2 3 4 5 6 7 8 9 10

Very dominant _ _ _ _ _ _ _ _ _ _ Very submissive
1 2 3 4 5 6 7 8 9 10

Very active _ _ _ _ _ _ _ _ _ _ Very passive
1 2 3 4 5 6 7 8 9 10

Easily expresses tender feelings _ _ _ _ _ _ _ _ _ _ Does not express tender feelings at all
1 2 3 4 5 6 7 8 9 10

Easily able to separate feelings from ideas _ _ _ _ _ _ _ _ _ _ Unable to separate feelings from ideas
1 2 3 4 5 6 7 8 9 10

Very home oriented _ _ _ _ _ _ _ _ _ _ Very worldly
                    1 2 3 4 5 6 7 8 9 10

Never conceited   Very conceited about
about appearance   _ _ _ _ _ _ _ _ _ _ appearance
                    1 2 3 4 5 6 7 8 9 10

Very excitable in   Not at all excitable
a minor crisis   _ _ _ _ _ _ _ _ _ _ in a minor crisis
                    1 2 3 4 5 6 7 8 9 10

Does not hide   Almost always hides
emotions at all   _ _ _ _ _ _ _ _ _ _ emotions
                    1 2 3 4 5 6 7 8 9 10

And so forth. There were 38 such "masculine"–"feminine" personality traits placed in contraposition to one another on the Broverman
questionnaire.

The researchers then sent this sheet around to three different groups
of psychotherapists, with three different sets of instructions. The first
group of clinicians was asked to describe the "mature, healthy, socially
competent woman"—by checking the places, on this scale of normal
personality traits, where *she* would most obviously fall—and the
second group was asked to "think of normal, adult men and then indicate on each item the pole to which a mature, healthy, socially competent man would be closer." The third set of psychotherapist-subjects
was asked, simply, to describe the "healthy, mature, socially competent adult." In this last set of instructions, no sex was specified.

The three groups to which the questionnaire was sent were roughly
similar in composition—they included psychologists, psychiatrists,
psychiatric social workers, of whom slightly less than half were female, slightly more than half, male. When their findings were analyzed, the Broverman workers discovered (to no one's surprise) that
the personality-trait profile of the "healthy adult female" looked very
different from that of the "healthy adult male." On an item, for example, such as "Does not hide emotions at all" on the low-numbered side,
which is opposed to "Almost always hides emotions" on the high side,
"healthy males" were perceived as falling in the 7 or 8 to 10 range,
while "healthy females" were down at the 1 to 4 end of the scale. This
might, of course, be seen as merely a way of rephrasing the obvious:
we all *know* that the feminine sex role leans toward, or one might say
"prescribes," more emotional expressivity. And if adjustment to social
norms is considered to be a part of mental health, the woman who con-
forms to and is at peace with the pressure of these expectations, ought

to be someone "healthier." Her higher level of emotionality is appropriately feminine.

Nevertheless, as Broverman et al. noted, an examination of the overall content of the items, and the ways in which the clinicians responded to them, "conceals a powerful, negative assessment of women." On the face of it, there would seem to be nothing odd about the fact that these psychotherapists expected to see more traits that are stereotypically masculine in the "mentally healthy adult male." Nor is it strange that the "healthy female" was expected to display stereotypically feminine traits. "However," observed the Broverman researchers, in their report, ". . . clinicians are more likely to suggest that healthy women differ from healthy men by being more submissive, less independent, less adventurous, more easily influenced, less aggressive, less competitive, more excitable in minor crises, having their feelings more easily hurt, being more emotional, more conceited about their appearance, less objective, and disliking math and science. This constellation seems a most unusual way of describing any mature, healthy individual."

The difference in the description of the "healthy male" and the "healthy female" wasn't, however, the real kicker in the Broverman study. Their most ludicrous result had to do with that third category —the "healthy, mature, socially competent adult," no sex specified. For this "healthy adult" turned out—when the three groups of answers were compared—to be completely indistinguishable from the "healthy adult male."

Abstract notions about what is "mentally healthy" (as long as sex isn't mentioned) seem to emphasize those "masculine" traits and characteristics that are more prized, more valued in our society. The lesser status, less-valued "feminine" personality traits—less aggression, less dominance, more freedom of emotional expression, more excitability, etc.—were *not* seen as consonant with emotional well-being in the adult individual, sex unspecified.

As far as a general standard of mental health is concerned, the feminine role apparently implies pathology!

An Unfeminine Woman

As the Broverman researchers put it: "For a woman to be healthy, from an adjustment viewpoint, she must adjust to and accept the behavioral norms for her sex, even though these behaviors are considered to be less healthy. . . . (This) places women in the conflictual position of having to decide whether to exhibit those positive characteristics considered desirable for *men and adults*, and thus have their 'femininity' questioned, that is, be deviant in terms of being a woman; or to behave in the prescribed feminine manner, and accept second-class adult status. . . ." The problem is, in brief, that women who display those more masculine, "healthier" personality traits—competitiveness, ambitiousness, adventurousness, who are "not at all interested in own appearance," and who are aggressive and assertive—lay themselves open to the subtle but deeply punishing accusation that they aren't "feminine."

I think, in this respect, of Terri Funabashi, a beautiful second-generation Japanese-American woman who was a second-year resident in psychiatry at a Harvard-connected crisis clinic. Terri volunteered to be interviewed for my "women and depression" study; and I remember being taken aback. She wasn't, by any means, the first female psychotherapist to offer herself as subject, but she did seem so quietly in command of most situations, so self-assured, so composed. "Are you depressed enough to qualify?" I remember asking with a smile, looking at her inquiringly.

"Isn't *everyone?*" she replied lightly.

Later, during the course of our taped conversations, Terri had told me of an incident which, she said, had plunged her into a "raging funk" for most of the fall semester of the previous year. She'd been a new M.D. then, spanking fresh out of medical school, and beginning her psychiatric residency at Harvard. But she wasn't, as she phrased it, "paying too much attention to what I wore, to clothes, to that sort of thing. I mean," she explained, "I was always neat, and whatever I had on was *clean*—but I really wasn't paying a whole lot of *attention*." About six weeks after the term had started, related Terri, she'd been having coffee in the residents' lounge with six or seven of her colleagues (all male) when the discussion of a particular woman patient had arisen.

"This woman had been hospitalized, with a severe depression, on the inpatient unit," Terri told me. "She was a very passive, very dependent person who was in a marriage with a dominant, aggressive, bullying kind of a husband. And part of the problem was, we felt, the fact that she was out of touch with her anger. We all believed she was sitting on some pretty violent rebellious reactions—and turning them in upon herself, because it was too psychologically threatening to experience them in relation to her husband, whom she *needed*." The patient's unacknowledged fury was, everyone agreed, at the core of the depressive reaction. But Terri, her primary therapist, had been (thus far) unable to help her to organize her anger, to make an assertive squeak in her own behalf. "I can't understand it," she'd complained, during this impromptu conference.

To which one of her fellow residents had replied offhandedly: "That's because you yourself are not very feminine."

No one else present, said Terri, had seemed to respond to this statement at all; it was as if her colleague had mentioned the weather, or some other relatively unequivocal matter of fact. The conversation had continued, and she'd managed to maintain her own part in it—inwardly, she'd felt gutted, assaulted, devastated. Even now, over a year later, her eyes widened, started forward in her face with the remembered shock. She leaned backward in her black leather easy chair, as if physically pushed there by the remembered impact of those words.

We talked then, about the thinly disguised hostility, the putting-her-into-her-place impulse that had triggered his cruelly "objective" comment. What, about Terri, had aroused his own anxiety—what had made him want to strike out at her in that way? I asked about whether or not she'd been, at that time, a "free" female, i.e., potentially available as date, as possible lover . . . ? She shook her head "no" at once. She'd been living with someone, a fellow doctor, a man whom she was now engaged to marry. I wondered, aloud, whether the fact that her male colleague seemed to want to devalue and punish her might have had something to do with his feeling some attraction *for* her. I laughed, made some remark about the "sour grapes response." (In her 1932 essay on "The Dread of Woman," Dr. Karen Horney observed that: "According to my experience, the dread of being rejected and derided is a typical ingredient in the analysis of every man, no matter what his mentality or the structure of his neurosis." The need of men, as a group, to disparage women, as a group, is, suggested Horney, based upon "a definite psychic trend . . . a tendency rooted in the man's psychic reactions to certain given biological facts, as might be expected of a mental attitude at once so widespread and so obstinately maintained. The view that women are infantile and emotional creatures, and as such, incapable of responsibility and independence, is the work of the masculine tendency to lower women's self-respect." But what *really* counts here, and what really is at stake, writes the psychoanalyst, is "the ever-precarious self-respect of the 'average man'.")

Terri's fellow doctor had undoubtedly been disturbed by her failure to be womanly in the way that he understood womanliness. She'd failed to conform to the stereotypic blueprint for female behavior insofar as dependence, submissiveness, emotionality, and other traits of the "healthy adult female"—such as low degree of competitiveness, high interest in self-adornment, etc.—were concerned. To be truly feminine, Terri would have had to preoccupy herself more with the kinds of clothing she wore, with making herself more attractive. In the meanwhile (so went her colleague's message) he wouldn't be sexually interested in her even if she had happened to be available—because she was unfeminine. And this put at rest any unspoken, underlying, perhaps never even consciously thought-about issues relating to *who* might be rejecting *whom*. He had retained his own sense of self-esteem and command of the situation . . . if at some cost to Terri.

For what was evident was that now, a full year and more later, the competent young Dr. Terri Funabashi, a second-year resident in psychiatry at the Harvard Medical School, still carried that remark around like a piece of psychological shrapnel that was always capable of acting up. And it did so, every once in a while. It gave her pain, and she did things to avoid that pain—had changed in order to do so. Perfectly capable, at this moment, of understanding what his own needs and motivations might have been, and the essential humor of his entire ploy, Terri nevertheless had—and in the midst of our conversation—done a sudden turnabout.

"Of course," she'd told me, leaning forward and speaking in a voice that picked up speed as she plunged off in a reverse direction, "I did wear my hair differently at that time; I wore it back in a bun. Now," she explained quickly, picking up a glossy black hank as if to underscore what she was saying, "I wear it *loose*. And my shoes," she went on, raising one foot slightly to show me her stylish maroon leather wedgie sandals, "are different too; I used to wear just those Wallabees, you know, whatever was most comfortable and practical."

She was being a good "feminine" girl now. That offhand remark had shot straight to a vulnerable place in her psyche. It had traveled straight to the issue of her sexual identity, the core question of whether or not she was fully and successfully a woman. And she'd shifted, in response to this incident, on at least two of the items on the Broverman questionnaire. She'd moved from the more masculine "Not at all interested in own appearance" and in the direction of the more feminine "Very interested in own appearance."

She'd shifted, too, on a very similar, if more harshly worded item. She'd gone from "Never conceited about appearance" toward "Very conceited about appearance" as well.

Now, a lack of great concern about appearance had been, on the profile of the "healthy, competent adult" one of the earmarks of general psychological well-being. That is, if the sex were unspecified. So Terri was, according to this standard, less "mentally healthy." She was, however, more "feminine" in certain of her attitudes, her behaviors; she was more like the stereotypic view of the "healthy, competent, adult female."

The dilemma was that being a "healthy adult" and a "healthy female adult" were difficult tasks to reconcile. They weren't really the same thing, not at all. And in fact some of the symptoms of *depressed* states—for example, "Cries very easily," "Feelings easily hurt"—were viewed, when they appeared on the Broverman questionnaire, as aspects of normal femininity. So were "Very submissive," "Very passive," "Has difficulty making decisions" considered traits that fell within the "healthy female adult" spectrum. Some of these are, in fact, outright symptoms of depression (for instance, difficulty in making decisions is one) or are a hairsbreadth away from them. (Submissiveness and passivity are not terribly distinct from the psychological symptom of "Feelings of helplessness and powerlessness.")

I'm not, of course, suggesting that the "normally feminine" adult *is* a depressed person. I just want to raise the possibility that the yellow brick road that the "normally feminine adult" follows throughout the course of her life cycle may be bordered by many more depressive gullies and potential "falling-off-places" than is the case for her "healthy, socially competent" male contemporary.

CHAPTER FOURTEEN

Does Anybody Want Diana to Live?
Diana (2)

Disturbed Behavior Is Disturbing Behavior

What could it mean that, in the middle of her life, a woman with no previous psychiatric history, experiencing what were really less than the normally expectable amounts of difficulty with her growing and near-grown children, happily married and "fortunate in having gotten everything that I ever really wanted out of life" had suddenly willed her own execution? It seemed unfathomable, inexplicable, unless in terms of some subtle biological mystery. And the family was, as Dr. Burkle had observed during his initial presentation of the case, "feeling very frightened at this moment." How could they not be? Disturbed behavior as the psychologist Kurt Lewin aptly pointed out, is *behavior that is disturbing to others*. Diana's suicidal move was causing, as it necessarily had to, reverberation upon reverberation deep within the psyche, the being, of every member of her family—and within the family as a whole, a group, a small social system.

There was no fending this off, no defending against its happening. Before the suicide attempt, it's true, Diana's family had managed "not to know," *not* to be disturbed, at any overt level, by her disturbance. A strange ecology of distress seemed, in fact, to have evolved within the Dahlgren household: Diana's misery had been more or less contained by silent though mutual agreement, had been allowed for, "handled" by Robert Dahlgren and by her children. Somehow the rest of the family had been managing to keep her within certain roughly recognized emotional boundaries; they'd avoided the contagion of her wretchedness. But now, the shock of her having tried to poison herself, to die, had upset the morbid equilibrium. *Everyone* had to reorient; they needed help, all of them, in weathering this catastrophe.

A psychiatric hospitalization alone—let alone a suicide attempt!—is usually a profound shock for everyone in the patient's immediate environment. To give them some measure of reassurance, to help them to find their way through a tornado of internal and external turmoil (difficulties that ranged from fear and guilt over her near-death—to social embarrassment over Diana's abortive suicidal try—to anger and rage about who would take over her chores, her housewifely tasks) a series of conferences with all members of the Dahlgren family was arranged.

The family meetings took place, on a weekly basis, throughout the five weeks of Diana's hospital stay. They were attended not only by Diana, and by Bob Dahlgren, and by all of the children (excepting their oldest son Mark who was, it will be recalled, never brought into this crisis at all); there were also Dr. Burkle, Diana's therapist, and the social worker responsible for dealing with "family problems," including financial ones, and assistance in helping them to deal with confusing insurance forms; and there was Christine, too, the "alcohol worker," whose major effort was that of engaging the entire family in the activities of Alcoholics Anonymous. And I was there too, in my role as researcher—and so, occasionally, was a senior staff member, who'd come in as a consultant on the case.

But the sessions weren't held solely for the purpose of helping the family—they were for helping the staff as well, in their own struggle to assess what was happening in the Dahlgren household; the family's strengths and weaknesses; the climate that they, as a self-contained unit, created. It had been, after all, *within* the context of that family setting that Diana had slid into her depression, become at last unable to face the prospect of living. What information could *they* offer about the household as it had been just prior to that florid suicide attempt? How were they, each one of them, responding to what had occurred? And above all, how much help and support were they going to be able to offer Diana when she returned? Answers to such questions would not, of course, be clearly obtainable. But as far as the personnel involved with the Dahlgrens were concerned, why we all would feel grateful for clues.

The Next-to-last Family Meeting

On the morning of our penultimate meeting with the Dahlgrens (the fifth and last session would be devoted to "winding-down" issues) a lazy, thick-flaked snow began falling. As I parked and locked my car in the lot directly across from the Mental Health Center, I heard laughing voices, looked over and saw someone stooping over to make a snowball. A car door, somewhere else on the Dartmouth-Hitchcock lot, slammed shut: a child, excited, asked something about the snow. The mother, murmuring a reply, leaned over, straightened the small boy's snowsuit. There was something festive in the air, even though it was January, even though there'd already *been* plenty of snow. It must have had to do with the large size of the flakes, which were covering the ground rapidly, forming a white rug, a rug that stretched everywhere that one could see. . . . Even inside the hospital one could feel it, that almost childlike sense of anticipation, of wonder at the new snow, padding and muffling the sounds of the outside world. I stamped the snow from my boots.

A Half Hour for Bette Glassman

The Dahlgrens would be coming in at 10 A.M., which left me over half an hour to spend with another patient, Bette Glassman. During this time Bette and I would share, for the most part, the sad bath of her silence—though sometimes she *did* sigh, did offer an occasional comment, which in itself seemed to bubble up from far below the surface, like a communication from a submerged submarine. We had, it's true, exchanged almost two whole paragraphs on the subject of the research I was doing. But that had been over a week ago. The flame of her interest had sputtered rapidly, been doused by a wave of feeling arising from somewhere within; she'd lapsed into her customary apathy, her quiet. Now, the main thing that she managed to communicate to me—and this, unfailingly—was that she expected to see me the following day; and that I must let her know if I wasn't planning to come.

Bette had been on the ward for about two weeks. She'd been brought in, mute, white-faced, withdrawn, by her frantic, almost hys-

terical parents. The daughter of a fairly well-to-do Vermont businessman, the graduate of an Ivy League college, Bette had a good job
as an assistant buyer in the sportswear department of one of the major
Boston women's stores. She was twenty-two years old and her creden-
tials, on paper, were those of an independent, autonomous young
woman. But in some deep and awful sense, she'd never really managed
to leave home.

The story, as the staff had managed to piece it together, was that
Bette, an only child, had been with her parents for a weekend visit
when events had taken the deadly turn that was to end in her hospitalization. It had started, almost ludicrously, as a quarrel about
whether or not she should be permitted to keep—to balance and maintain, that is—her own checking account! Mrs. Glassman had asserted
that Bette, when she wasn't forwarding her statement and checks
home to be balanced, continually overdrew her funds. The daughter
had countered, reasonably enough, that it was her money and her
right to make mistakes with it if she would. Her father had observed,
then, that on the two previous occasions when she'd been permitted to
keep the checking account herself, she *had* overdrawn the account,
and this discussion had escalated into a violent quarrel.

What, I wondered, did Bette's keeping her own checks *mean*—in
fantasy—to each one of them? Was it the end of mutual dependence,
a real separation, the end of everything they had in her childhood—
the end of love, control, or what? The wild words had, in any case,
culminated in a mixture of tears and fury, in Bette's leaping up from
the dining-room table, in her fleeing to her bedroom and slamming her
door so hard that, in her mother's words, "the entire house shook," in
her crying and sobbing and moaning, endlessly, endlessly, refusing to
let them come in. And so most of the night had passed. The next day
the storm was over. Her bedroom door was unlocked, and Bette silent.
So she'd remained, in her bed, curled in a fetal position. The weekend
had slid by but still she'd refused to get up, to go back to work, to
leave. She'd simply remained there, silent and blank-eyed, staring at
the narrow vertical design of her yellow wallpaper. She was uncanny,
frightening, the very parody of the dependent child . . . a fetus.

She had been like that, as much as she could be, during her first
days on the ward. As soon as any possibility for doing so presented itself, Bette had retreated to her room, curled up, dressed or in her
nightgown, lay there under the covers looking, as her father said, "like
a dead baby." To be around her, to sit with her, was to breathe in the
stagnant, hopeless, dead-end quality of her despair. But just recently,
as had been noted with satisfaction at the early-morning ward rounds,

she'd been becoming progressively more communicative. She was, though still relatively silent, growing "more approachable," according to all reports. She was answering questions with a full phrase, or even a sentence, rather than a grudging monosyllable. Either the medication, or her relations with the other patients and with the staff members, were helping. She wasn't better yet; on this everyone agreed. But she was, in some subtle way, improving.

This morning, the morning of the Dahlgren family meeting, I found Bette sitting on the edge of her bed. She was dressed in jeans and a ski sweater; she'd just lit a cigarette, and, blowing out the match, she laid it in a bedtable ashtray. Her legs were idly swinging. When I asked how she was feeling, she shrugged, began—to my surprise—complaining volubly about her parents: "Here I am, a college graduate with a responsible job—a damned hard and *demanding* job—and I'm not even allowed to keep my own *checking account!*" There were two pink spots on her cheeks, signs of life that I'd never seen there previously; she was angry. I told her how much better she looked, and this was true. The change, even from the day before, was Lazarus-like; she seemed returned from the emotional dead.

She had more words at her command today than I'd ever imagined she *would* have. We spent the next half hour in what was, amazingly, a conversation. We talked about the absurdity of the situation, of the money being *her* money, earned by her own labor, and therefore her own to take charge of. Why shouldn't she be able to *make* mistakes with it, to overdraw her account if she were careless—to control what was, after all, her own? And how was it, I was speculating, that a petty conflict such as this one had required resolution on a psychiatric ward?

Bette, secure in my agreement with her view of the situation, was busily erupting in hot gusts of feeling; I was, I think, merely nodding my head, encouraging her to continue. But then, having presented *her* side, *her* arguments, *her* own position about the bank account, she suddenly ran down, ran out of steam, looked at me uncertainly. She looked like a frightened kid. "Of course my mom *is* much better at adding up figures than I am," she admitted. "I mean, I honestly did make the holiest mess of my bank account when I was keeping it." I blinked, stared at her. I wasn't sure whether or not Bette comprehended the leap, the huge emotional turnabout she'd just accomplished.

I was so surprised that I said nothing. I felt, however, the cloud of humid sadness settling over us. The high color had vanished from

Bette's cheeks; she seemed, on the instant, drained of life and energy—the person I'd known her to be, before today. But she answered as if I had, in fact, asked her the questions starting to my own mind: "My parents and I," she said quietly, almost as if she were whispering the information to herself, "are . . . somehow . . . locked in a kind of death embrace. My mother mostly. She needs to control me, and I—for some reason—need to come back to them, to *her*, and be controlled. Sometimes I feel as if I'm being pulled back home almost *physically* . . . as if I'm at the end of a long, invisible string, of a yo-yo."

In the Corridor

That morning I overstayed my time with Bette and was a few minutes late for the ten o'clock session with the Dahlgrens. With luck it wouldn't have started; it was just a few minutes past the hour. As I hurried down the stairway to the first-floor conference room where the family meeting would take place, that phrase of Kurt Lewin's—"Disturbed behavior is disturbing behavior"—popped into my head. The Glassmans, as well we all knew, were preoccupied, absorbed, distracted, terrified by the mute standstill, the end-of-the-line depression to which their daughter had come—on the one hand. On the other, they couldn't seem to play out the reel, to really let go, to let her live independently—to grant her the right to handle her own earnings. And she, on her own side, couldn't make it away, couldn't manage whatever emotional surgery might be necessary for the separation. She'd become "disturbed" instead; that is, seriously depressed. And she was "disturbing," punishing, and frightening her parents by being so. It was, in short, a metaphor of dependence and independence, of conflict over remaining a child or being able (and allowed) to leave, being enacted by both Bette and her parents.

At the turn in the stairwell, I found myself at the heels of two of the staff physicians. Late as I was, it would be bad form to try to push past them. The younger clinician, his voice neutral, was discussing a newly admitted, remarkably beautiful manic-depressive patient, Barbara. "Have you noticed that when Barbara's getting high she runs around the ward without any bra on, and how, when her mood is stabilizing, she puts her brassiere right back on?"

The older psychiatrist turned, acknowledging that I was lagging at their heels and listening: "I want you to notice," he said dryly, "the skilled eye, the *acuity* of the trained practitioner." We all laughed at the joke, but the younger doctor looked mortified.

The Family

When I entered the conference room the Dahlgrens were seated and waiting. I realized with relief that the session hadn't yet gotten under way. My own arrival, creating its brief stir of murmured greetings, was an episode that ended when I took a place on one of the chairs in the circle around a long teak coffee table. The silence, which I'd interrupted, re-formed, rewove after including me. We sat, like attendants at a séance, waiting for the magical happenings to begin.

Who hadn't yet arrived? Glancing around the room half covertly, I checked off staff members—Christine, the alcohol worker, was here, her features set in a cranky expression; she hadn't yet succeeded in getting Diana to attend an A.A. meeting. And Kristi Kistler, the psychiatric social worker was here; she was making use of this few minutes' delay to scribble some notes into a manila-covered folder. The only sound in the room was that of Kristi's pen, moving rapidly across the paper. "I've never noticed, Kristi, that you were left-handed," said Diana, in the strained voice of a hostess breaking the silence.

"Oh . . ." Kristi looked up quickly, smiled: "Yes." There was a long, plate-glass square of a window at one end of the room; beyond it, gusts of snow were skittering and swirling.

It was Skip Burkle, Diana's therapist, who hadn't yet come. Diana herself was seated almost directly opposite me, like a madonna, the visual hub of this scene. Above and in back of her were the window, the kaleidoscopic configurations of moving flakes of snow. Our eyes met briefly, and she smiled at me; she radiated, this morning, a sense of glory, of pride, of real triumph. I was puzzled. What, in this situation, had she found rewarding? Was it that here, in this particular setting, her family was being forced to acknowledge her suffering—and those pained feelings that she'd been unable to stifle, and which now had to be admitted to the world of the real? Or was it simply a case of maternal pride, of having another opportunity to show to the staff what an attractive husband and what attractive children she had?

Bob Dahlgren, Diana's husband, was a tall, lanky man with thinning, slightly curly blond hair, and a perennial half smile hovering at the edge of his lips. It was this smile, perhaps, that gave him a certain air of good-naturedness, of always being in agreement, whether or not he'd assimilated what was being said. He was chewing desultorily, as he often did, on the end of an unlit pipe. Susannah, the oldest of the girls, sat on the chair to his right; next to her was Wendy, a junior in high school, well scrubbed and neat, looking healthy in a 4-H club fashion. And then came Kristi, the social worker, Diana herself, and then Frankie, the youngest member of the family. He seemed on edge and tense; his color was too high, as if it were unbearably hot in the room. I must have been concentrating on him, for he gave me a rueful look, shrugged his thin shoulders. Caught staring, I smiled slightly, moved my gaze back to his mother. Again, I was surprised by her expression, the aura about her—some paradoxical element of victory.

Victim or Victimizer?

Was she, I wondered, the family's victim or its victimizer? Was she martyr or tyrant? Almost as soon as these dichotomies posed themselves in my mind, I realized what a temptation it was to take sides, to settle into one's own views of who was innocent, who was to blame. For, medical though this situation was—and it *was medically dangerous*, for it involved potential death—it was rooted in human needs, thwarted wishes, conflict. And the urge to resolve uncertainty, to make a coherent schema of what one was seeing, to take sides mentally, was almost irresistible. This need, this most human need to make moral or value judgments about the behavior of the family-members, of the patient, etc., crept into these circumstances, inserted itself into one's thoughts and one's statements awfully insidiously. I remember, for instance, one of the senior consultants on the case commenting on Diana's "pathology" about a week after her admission to the ward. "Mrs. Dahlgren has a somewhat hysterical quality," he'd observed, at a mini-meeting of staff members working directly with the family. "She's got a way of seducing you into worrying about her problems, of appealing for help in an extremely manipulative fashion." This was a way of saying, as I later reflected, that the strategies Diana customarily used in her efforts to gain affection were mildly flirtatious, submissive, exaggeratedly feminine ones. She was overly dependent, a drainer of those around her. But these characteristic modes of operation, and the ways in which she tended to relate to others, might not have been at all symptomatic, not at all maladaptive, if they'd only been more *successful*—if they'd procured her the affection and attention that she'd needed!

They *had*, when one thought about it, worked well enough for that long period of her lifetime when she'd been "emotionally healthy." But now, what might otherwise have been seen as her rather typical and commonplace feminine personality traits seemed to have led to an emotional dead end, to blankness, to despair. And, the less functional her behavior had become—in terms of "importing" into her psyche good feelings about herself, a sense of being a valued and needed person—the more submissive, powerless, and ultimately "sick" she had become. Her pathology had to do, in other words, with failing—with an inability to find other, better strategies, an inability to adapt.

A Question of Power

Looking at her this morning, however, perceiving that sense of new-found strength, I speculated about whether or not becoming sick and suicidal hadn't been Diana's ultimate trump card in a desperate game, a contest in which the prize was emotional survival. It was frequently true, as I'd begun to notice with more and more wonder, that depression in women (a disturbance that *she*, on a conscious level, *had* or suffered from) involved deeply buried, subtly disguised, but bitter struggles having to do with powerlessness and with power.

In some cases, a woman's psychological pain, her awful suffering, was all that she actually *possessed* . . . her only means of gaining some measure of control over those about her (and, perhaps, of punishing them for their lack of love, for not caring enough). I'd become impressed, over the course of my interviewing with depressed patients and their families, by the subtle uses to which being sick could, though usually unconsciously, be put. I had, in fact, spoken to a few of the staff members about this. Was this link between a struggle for power, and a person's experience of depression, something that was *real?* Or was I imagining a connection that wasn't actually there?

One psychiatrist, Dr. Gary Tucker, had answered this question with a wide grin and a laugh: "Oh," he'd said, "it's real enough! Much of what you're seeing *is* about power . . . and its allocation within families. And, of course, it's about the *loss* of power."

Diana Dahlgren had, this morning, the palpable proof of her family's, and of the outer world's concern. For here we all were, gathered on her behalf. She—and her problems, her fate—was the significant figure in the discussion to come. It was, I believe, the psychologist Alfred Adler who suggested that the need to attain significance and importance in the environment ("which is," he wrote, "in human terms, always the *social* environment") might be *the* central feature in the development of neurotic illness. What neurotic behavior *is*, in its essence, theorized Adler, is a strategic maneuver, a device that a person has (often unconsciously, and usually because no other way of making it seems available) developed in order to gain power, significance, control, ascendancy *over others*.

Again, one returns to that notion of disturbed behavior being disturbing to others, of psychological hurting being fashioned into the strangest and subtlest kind of weapon ("I will make you suffer by means of my own suffering"). In such a way, powerlessness might be a way of getting power; utter weakness the means of gaining domination. At the very least, becoming ill can be seen as a way of crying for, or passively demanding *attention*. And no one, I think, ought ever to underestimate what a person may do in the service of assuaging this most human of human needs.

Many of the emotional transactions of the Dahlgrens were, it seemed to me, being carried out by means of metaphoric communications. Diana never, for instance, expressed any conscious anger at her husband, blamed no one for her present unhappiness, for the mental pain which she experienced as "being like you imagine physical torture would be. . . ." She seemed to have no particularly aggressive thoughts about anyone in the family. But, if Bob and the children appeared to pass by her, to "walk around her," to avoid her, to pay no attention to her pain; if they failed to listen to her, to care; if they behaved as though she didn't matter, perhaps didn't exist at all . . . well, she had struck back at them. Her attempt to kill herself had been a powerful, if disguised, form of retaliation.

Suicidal acts are *fueled by hate and anger*. (And a suicide which ends in the person's death has been called "the last word in an argument.") Very often, though the deadly blow is being directed at the person's own self, the fury being given expression is meant for *someone else*. Suppressed rage—a rage which the suicidal person may never experience consciously, in his or her own thinking process—is turned back, for some reason (perhaps a belief that it's impossible to be angry at someone you love and need) against the self. This retroflexed anger, this anger-turned-against-oneself is the homicidal fuel that energizes the suicidal act. Suicide has, for this reason, been termed "murder in the 180th degree." Did Diana's sense of ease connect with *this* aspect of the situation, i.e., that she'd survived the suicidal act but had managed to express her angry feelings, to strike out at her family *anyhow?* I saw her reach over to take Frankie's hand, to hold it between hers, to stroke it tenderly. At the same time she glanced across the silent circle at Bob, shrugged briefly, as if to say: "I'm sorry that this happened. I'm sorry that we should all have to *be* here this way." She felt sorry about the depression, about the alcohol problem, about having wanted to die, about having tried to die. She shook her head lightly as if to communicate to him that everything that had happened now seemed incomprehensible, for here she was, in this room, her caring family gathered around her, the snow falling outside on what was a beautiful winter's morning.

The Session

The door opened and Dr. Burkle entered. He apologized for having been delayed, wanted to make up the ten minutes at the close of the hour. Would that be possible for everyone present? We glanced at each other, nodded; then turned toward him expectantly. We were like a little circle of musicians, looking at him in anticipation, waiting for the first note to sound. He took a seat, let the silence reconstitute while we got used to his presence. His first question, directed toward the family at large, was quiet, innocuous: "How have you all been managing this week? How have you been getting along, what with Diana's being here in the hospital?"

The Dahlgrens exchanged glances, unsure of who should be spokesman. The older of the two daughters, Susannah, laughed for no reason, nervously. Then, looking over at her father submissively and slightly flirtatiously, she said: "I don't know. What do *you* think, Dad?"

Bob Dahlgren took his pipe stem away from his lips, rested the empty pipe on his crossed knee. The same pleasant, wry, good-natured smile remained implanted upon his face. He started to speak, deliberately, thoughtfully, trying to fashion as fair an account of what had been happening at home as he possibly could. But one sensed, one experienced, his discomfort; it made me feel, at times, like a violin string, picking up a vibration, humming in unison. It was so hard for him, so palpably antithetical to his nature, these family sessions with their emphasis on "saying it like it is," on open revelation of feeling. He was a private person, a remote person, really. These conferences were for him, I thought, challenges, incursions, advances, attacks upon the hidden citadel of self—that isolated, yet self-contained-seeming place in which he actually did live.

We began in this manner, softly, blandly. Professor Dahlgren related a few isolated family happenings; but there were no special issues, nothing of note that seemed to have occurred during the past week. They had all, in Diana's absence, "been managing as well as could be expected . . . doing pretty well, in fact. . . ." His voice lagged toward the end of this recital, became more hesitant, petered out into silence. We sat, looked at one another. I noticed that Kristi, the social worker, was gazing closely, intently, at sixteen-year-old Wendy, the younger of the two daughters. Wendy, a pretty girl with lightly curling brown ringlets crowning her head in a gentle aureole, was the family placator. She usually tried to soften, defuse, turn off any potentially conflictual discussion. But now she was frowning. "I think, Wendy," prompted Kristi, "that perhaps you don't agree with what your father's been saying—the way he's characterized what it's been like during the course of the week?"

"No, I don't." Wendy spoke with an unaccustomed force and presence; but shot a guilty side glance at Robert. "There've been a *lot* of hassles . . . and a lot of hostility. And what it's been about—"

"Hey, Wen—I don't think that's fair because *you're* the one—" Frankie, half rising from his seat, interrupted his older sister.

"Hold it, Frank," Dr. Burkle put in gently, signaling with a hand motion that he was to sit back. "Relax. And let's hear Wendy out; let's hear what it is she has to say. We'll all get to have our turns."

I was frankly surprised at Wendy's having come forth with an objection to something her father had said, with anything resembling a family issue. She had, throughout the earlier sessions, denied any awareness of problems within the household; denial, of course, was the norm for all of the Dahlgrens. But, when asked directly what *she* thought her mother's motive might have been in making that devastating suicidal try, Wendy had answered with schoolgirlish innocence: "I don't know, I was away at the time. I mean—I was out that evening, at a party with the kids." She'd sounded as if she didn't quite live there, I mean in her home. Wendy, while a good and cooperative child on a surface level, was holding herself aloof from what was happening with an almost desperate intensity.

As well she might, for she was in psychologically perilous circumstances. At a time in her own life when a daughter is working out issues relating to her own sexual identity—and identifying with her mother as a female human being—she was being confronted with two treacherous and scary options. She could *be like* Diana, role-model her own feminineness on her mother's—and be depressed and suicidal. Or she could withdraw and protect herself, forego the customary but complex task of "introjecting" the mother; that is, taking her into one's own self, "being" her, and continuing to grow and develop her own identity. To draw back from this normal and expectable process of identification was to leave a kind of empty place within Wendy's own psyche, her own personality. That place within the self which comes to be, during the process of growth, filled by an internalized image of the mother, was unoccupied. If she couldn't bring her mother *into* herself in this complex but psychologically crucial fashion, a part of her would remain empty, unfilled, desolate.

Wendy's older sister—Susannah—seemed to have elected the second of these two impossible pathways. She would not *be* her mother, wanted to be involved as little as possible, to withhold herself from *their* pain. Toward the end of the last session she'd literally screamed this truth at Diana, crying: "I've got to live my own life, Mom! And not get too deeply entangled in your problems!"

(To which Diana had responded, as if to soot in her eye, with a rapid series of eye blinks.)

"What we've been fighting about," Wendy now resumed doggedly, "has been, mainly, the housework." She paused, looked over at her father again. "It's about the chores." Her voice was taking on a tone of apology. "About who should be doing just *what*."

Robert Dahlgren's fixed, benign expression hadn't been altered by his daughter's unexpected remarks. He had the air of someone watching, rather than taking part in a discussion. He could easily have been at a faculty meeting where no important issues are being taken up; so relaxed was his posture, his appearance. "Well, I guess it is true," he conceded, "that there were a few disagreements about the chores. The girls felt Frankie wasn't keeping up his end, not remembering to make his bed. And we've had a couple of, um, disputes about cooking and groceries. *Who* is supposed to pick up groceries, and that kind of thing. But I'd be inclined—"

"—It's always been unclear, in our house, what you are and aren't supposed to be doing!" cut in Wendy swiftly. I was startled by the frank anger in her voice. She was *here* this morning, psychologically present, rather than a picture of a sweet, scrubbed, conciliatory, well-behaved "good girl." Her skin, usually so clear and shining that it seemed to have been buffed, looked lumpy, as if craters of hidden pus were rising to the surface. She'd have pimples by nightfall, or the next morning. But she was, I knew, confronting something which would have to *be* confronted—now, or at some future time in her life. There wasn't going to be a way, really, around this pain; eventually, she'd have to allow herself to suffer through it. "You know, Mom," she continued, shifting the site of confrontation away from Father to Mother, "that *is* true. You've always given us this sense that we're letting you down, not doing enough, failing you somehow . . . that whatever we're doing isn't really *enough*. I know, for me, if I'd washed the dishes then I'd forgotten to do the sweeping, or not wiped out the fridge. There's never any sense of having finished what I was supposed to finish; that I knew where the job I was doing ended; that I'd done it *right!*"

"You know you do play the martyr, Mom," agreed Frankie, his voice shrill. His small face was looking unhealthily scarlet, and his eyes were wide.

"You hang on a minute, Frankie," said Wendy, for he seemed about to continue. "I was the one who—"

But she couldn't halt his onward sweep: "I mean, like I'd tell you I was going swimming," he went on relentlessly, his voice getting loud, "which is, as you know, a thirty-minute bike ride. And I'd tell you when I'd be home. But the whole summer the same thing kept on happening, where you'd say to me: 'Well, you're kind of late getting back, aren't you?' . . . When you *knew* it was an hour's round trip just on the bike alone, and I wasn't late at all. But the way you said it; it was like I'd done something really wrong." Clearly, Diana had been expressing her dissatisfaction and disappointment in her life in terms of dissatisfaction about chores and lateness. It was, I suspected, *her* way of saying the things she *wasn't* saying otherwise—that her family, by leading their own lives, were letting her down, failing her, abandoning her.

A theme—the chores and people's expectancies—had been stated. Dr. Burkle moved in, now, to organize a discussion about how people could, in the Dahlgren household, get some clearer ideas about what constituted being "bad" and being "good"; how clearer signals could be exchanged about who should be doing which chore, and when. How might responsibilities be more easily and straightforwardly shared? As the talk continued, my eyes slid over to rest upon Robert Dahlgren. His facial expression hadn't changed in the slightest. He'd had no apparent reaction to the children's angry attack upon Diana. Was he, I wondered, somewhat relieved that the conversational ball—initially challenging to him—had veered swiftly off in his wife's direction, that it was she against whom the real play had been made? There would be no way to know. But, even as I toyed with this notion, the action moved down into his court once again.

The talk had turned—and this it always did, as if powered by some subterranean logic, by some subliminally shared family knowledge—to that move from California to the East. After that, things had never been quite the same; an equilibrium then lost hadn't ever been restored. Again Susannah was maintaining that it was Robert who'd done the changing first: "You know you did, Dad; you became so remote then, so unavailable. I just felt," she said sorrowfully, "that I couldn't get your attention anymore."

"We *all* felt that way," nodded Diana.

But once again, Robert seemed puzzled. "I find it hard to believe that I've been withdrawn," he answered uncomfortably. He shrugged lightly; but that wry, good-natured smile still curved the sides of his lips upward. At these words his son quickly sprang to his defense: "Dad spends lots of time with *me*," he asserted boastfully. "We built a snow man. And we play games; he helps me with my homework." There was a pause, into which Frankie added an afterthought: "We have lots of fun with the Frisbee." He drew his skinny shoulders high.

"Ah yes," interrupted Diana, her voice charged with emotion. "And I want to tell *you* something, young man! Which is, Frankie, that I think you make far too many demands on your father's time! The rest of us need to share him too, you know, and there's just so much time to go round. We need to have *ours*, too!" Diana was shaking her finger at Frankie, who'd half jumped from his seat.

He fell back into the chair immediately, though, as if overwhelmed by his mother's verbal assault. "Aren't you really saying, Diana," intervened Kristi smoothly, softly, "that you're really angry at Robert for not spending that time with *you?*"

Diana stopped, turned to stare at the social worker.

"And isn't this anger, which you're directing toward Frankie," continued Kristi, "really meant for *Robert?*"

Diana's eyes remained fixed upon her: "Well . . . yes," she answered Kristi at last. "I think I *am* angry at Robert. I look at them sometimes, out there, throwing that Frisbee on the lawn. And I think: 'Gee, *I'd* like some of that time.'"

At this, Robert took the cold pipe out of the side of his mouth, cradled it in the palm of his hand, shifted position, crossing one knee over the other: "I don't really mind spending time with Frankie," he responded equably.

Dead-end

The flow of conversation ceased. Here was a communicational dead-end. I know that I was confounded: Diana's plea had been, most unambiguously, for more of her husband's time, a larger share of him; he'd answered with an assurance that he didn't resent giving time to *Frankie!*

I looked around the family circle of faces, saw no recognition that anything untoward might have occurred. Only Diana, halted here, staring at her husband, seemed confused. She didn't seem to know what—if anything—had happened. Had she made a request, wrenched out a frank statement of a need? If so, Robert's reply had turned it away so smoothly, had answered to something else, had in fact denied the reality of her demand. I saw Diana's eyelids flutter rapidly, as they did when she was trying to blink something unspeakable out of her thoughts.

My own thought, then, was of something that family therapist Virginia Satir had written, to the effect that "symptoms" and "dysfunctional behaviors" occur when a person is threatened by some event of survival significance, something which says to that individual: "You do not count; you are not lovable; you are nothing." When this occurs, wrote Satir, the person whose self-esteem is already low may attempt to avoid knowing, avoid consciously perceiving this unspeakable threat. If, however, the individual's defenses against an unspeakable possibility "prove unequal to the task of shielding" him or her *from* knowing, "a symptom will take its place. Usually, it is only then that the individual and his community will notice that he is 'ill' and that he will admit a need for help," comments the psychotherapist.

Was the awful knowledge from which Diana was fleeing simply that her marriage wasn't so wonderful after all, and that Bob didn't much *care?* I'd sensed in her a profound need to turn into her marriage, now when the children were going; and she'd once said, with great intensity, that her "worst fear was that of being worthless to her husband as a companion" now that the children were growing up, were separating, were leaving.

A scene flashed into my head: that first staff meeting, the crowded conference room, my somewhat disinterested following of the presentation on Diana Pharr Dahlgren. Dr. Burkle reading from his case notes, stating that the patient had been threatening suicide, and that the rest of the family had gone out for the evening. "*Despite* the suicide threats?" someone had asked. I thought that it was true—a fateful question had to be asked in this as in every instance of attempted suicide. And the question, to be assessed most coldly and objectively, was: *Does anyone want the patient to go on living?*

We remained caught in a growingly oppressive quiet. I experienced a kind of terror. Robert Dahlgren's expression hadn't changed, I noticed, but he kept looking toward the door as if he expected someone —or as if he might jump up and leave. Dr. Burkle's face was impassive; he was allowing this exchange, and the feelings it evoked, to settle into the consciousness of this small congregation. I had to look away from the faces, past Diana, out the window, to watch the flurries of snow whirling and circling. At this moment the psychiatrist, careful around the exposed wound, said softly: "Robert hasn't really answered your question, has he Diana?"

She didn't reply. I stared at the flakes of snow which now seemed to pause in mid-motion, as if waiting for her answer. "No," she said dismally.

"And how does that make you feel?" probed Dr. Burkle, taking it one small painful step further.

"I feel sad," said Diana, her eyes beginning to fill. ". . . sad and hopeless."

Diversionary Tactics

Customarily, after family meetings, there weren't any formal debriefing sessions held by the staff. On this occasion though, after the Dahlgrens had left, everyone lingered. There was a shared need to go over the ground that had been covered, to defuse emotionally, especially after Frankie Dahlgren's eruption. In that instant after Diana's confession of her feelings—that instant when the real source of the hurt seemed to have leaped into view—her son had suddenly begun talking very rapidly, his voice high-pitched and shrill, his face scarlet, his stream of complaints disconnected. He'd become hysterical.

Frankie needed, he insisted loudly, "to discuss my *own* problems." He was having trouble with friends; the other kids didn't like him. He wasn't good at sports. A new kid in the class had appeared to be friendly for a while but then "he must've got the word about me";

he'd dropped Frankie Dahlgren abruptly. The household chores were oppressive; Susannah and Wendy didn't make the rules clear; they weren't any better at this than Mom had been. It was tough coming in from school in the afternoons. "And you, Mom," he added, turning to her accusingly, "when you *are* there, you're always in bed in the afternoon, y'know, crying or sleeping the way you do. . . ." He hurtled on and on, not drawing in any more than the occasional gasp of a necessary breath, not permitting a pause in which anyone could insert a rejoinder, even a calming word. The interview room fairly pulsated with his anxiety. It was as if he'd set off an emotional rocket; we watched in wonder its flare, its explosion, its spread. The discussion of what had passed between Robert and Diana had been precipitously dropped.

Later, at our impromptu conference, Kristi had said: "What's happening is clearly pretty scary for all of the kids. But it's Frankie who still does need his mother the most—and he's the one I'm feeling real concern about."

So was everyone else; there'd been a drivenness, a madly desperate quality to that entire outburst. Had he needed, we wondered, to distract our attention, to shift the action quickly away from that rift between his parents which had shown itself so precipitously? Children in distressed families *will* do this—will behave, quite spontaneously like emotional lightning rods, will try to bring the fire down upon themselves instinctively, fearing that the electrical charge between mother and father may be so powerful as to blow their universe apart. The child's parents are, of course, in large part "the world." And it is, in a way, much safer to take into yourself whatever is bad in the world—to be the disturbed one, the neurotic, the social outcast, the cause of the trouble—than to entertain the possibility that the *world itself* is askew, perhaps going to break apart, perhaps itself sick and uncertain, perhaps totally out of control. Better, in a sense, to take the disturbance inside oneself, to internalize it, to take charge of it. Better to be bad or crazy than to live in a *world* that is. Frankie was, albeit unconsciously, taking steps to preserve his own security, to divert us away from any possible confrontation between Diana and Bob, any possible acknowledgement of pain, misery, disappointment that these two pillars of his universe might be experiencing. Whatever mysteries we might have been nearing, however, he'd acted with swift immediacy, led us off in a different direction and on another chase. The family lid had been kept firmly on, firmly in place. But Frankie was, we feared, on his own way to becoming "a patient."

A complex set of interlocking concerns had to be sorted through—

for complicated decisions had to be made. Diana would be leaving at the end of the following week. Some kind of counseling had to be procured for Frankie; and long, sober thoughts had to be given to the question of *her* survival. For, given the choked state of communications within the Dahlgrens as a group, sending Diana home was a bit like sending a person with vulnerable lungs back to a house next door to a steel mill. She couldn't, on the other hand, become too acclimatized to life as a mental patient; to "help her" in this way would be to do her another sort of disservice.

And yet, and yet . . . once the drama of the situation had subsided, once the family members had slipped back into a customary inattentiveness, what was going to happen to Diana? In the months following an unsuccessful suicide attempt, the risk of successful suicide is awfully, in fact frighteningly, high.

The Quintessential Good Girl

When entrusted with the care of a suicidal person, and attempting to evaluate the risk of *future* attempts, the clinician must carefully assess that person's immediate environment. "The hidden attitude of the relatives will have to be gauged with as much care as those of the patient," psychiatrist Leston Havens has written. "Murderous impulses, especially toward those close to a person, are not easily confessed: the extent of murderousness in the whole human race is not readily acknowledged, despite the facts of widespread war, homicide and suicide. . . . Remarkably active, although unconscious and subtle, efforts may be on foot to rid the world of this person."

These were, insofar as the Dahlgrens were concerned, nightmare thoughts. I happened to be reading Dr. Havens' paper on "recognition of suicidal risks" at the time that I was interviewing Diana: "*Withdrawal* and *silence*," he observed, "are frequently the ways in which 'civilized' people express their rage toward one another."

These comments rolled round and round in my consciousness. And so did the following: ". . . Or there may be only one person in the patient's world who stands between him and the desire to die. What if that person is lost, moves away or has a falling out with the patient? . . ." (Or what, I thought, if none of these overt happenings had occurred, but one simply suspected that the crucially important "other" simply didn't much *care?*)

"I've got no identity in particular," Diana once told me. "I'm not *anybody*, you know, not really a person. I've surrendered that part to Bob."

I wasn't sure what she meant.

She shrugged, sending out a hint of gardenia-scented cologne: "I don't know, exactly. I mean I tried to explain this to Bob—to tell him that now, with the kids about to leave, we're going to have to try to come closer, the two of us. To learn to *be* together in a new kind of way." Her face looked pained momentarily; then she resumed her customary mask of cheerfulness. But the association she'd made, between having "surrendered her identity" to her husband and "needing a new kind of closeness with him" had been unconscious and instantaneous. One had the sense of Diana's inner emptiness, her need of "love nutrients" from Bob in order to merely maintain a sense of self, of being, of personhood.

Diana had always, as she'd only lately begun to realize, achieved the most basic of realizations—i.e., *that she existed*—by means of existing for others. She lived and grew on *their approval*, had been the quintessential "good girl" throughout most of a lifetime. "Before I met Bob, and married him," she said thoughtfully, "it was my mother who did the thinking for me. She was an overwhelming, domineering sort of a person—and she had a lot of illnesses. I think, now, that most of it was hypochondriacal. But I didn't think so, then. And I allowed her (and my grandparents, with whom we lived) to choose my friends, and my clothes, and the places I went and what I liked and what I didn't like." Diana smiled wryly: "I went along with it all. I always was a very, very good little girl."

Diana's parents were divorced; her father, "a pallid, remote kind of person," lived several hundred miles away. He visited only rarely: "Mother and my grandparents, hated those visits." Her mother's illnesses seemed to have begun at the time of her own birth: "I was guilty about them because I knew in some way they were my fault. And I always had to be sure to please her, to make it up to her. And she could really be very warm and giving—but there was a price, and I knew it. She needed *me* to be perfect, because if I was, then people would know that *she* was."

Her mother was, as were her grandparents, sternly religious, fundamentalist Protestants. "I knew I could only do what they—mostly my mother—wanted me to do. If she wanted me to sit still for hours, I would; there was never anything I wanted to do *for myself*. I always took my cues from her, because really, she was in control. And I guess I did do whatever it was she'd decided I should do . . . though how much of it was coming from my grandparents was something I never quite knew. She'd often present a request as something *they* wanted or expected of me, and yet somehow . . . there was a sense . . . I wasn't quite sure."

It was a cloudy, warmish afternoon, the day after that mind-rocking family session with the Dahlgrens, and a week before Diana's scheduled discharge. We were sitting in her room—she on the bed, I on the white chair that belonged to that impersonal Formica desk. From outside the door, which stood open, we could hear the blaring of the TV set in the patients' day room. It often stayed on, playing away into emptiness, with no one at all watching it. "What, exactly," I asked Diana, "were your mother's illnesses about? I mean, what kinds of disease did she say she was suffering *from?*"

She was slow to answer. "I'm not, strangely enough, sure," she said at last. "It all had something vaguely to do with a bad heart. But you see when I grew older and began to study nursing—which I did do for a couple of years before I met Bob—I came to realize that if you *do* have a serious attack, if you *are* close to dying, you go to the hospital and you get treatment and there's really no two ways about it. My mother's 'attacks,' or whatever they were, were nothing like that. She might've had a real condition, brought on by rheumatic fever— which she'd had as a child—but it was just one of those troublesome, minor things. I think, now, that it could have been that she just got a little pain, and got frightened . . . and sometimes so frightened that she was unable to speak. But again, and this was only when I got older, I did begin to realize that the attacks were timed . . . that they often had to do with getting something she wanted, and that often, it was something she wanted from *me.*"

To a child, though, those attacks had been completely terrifying: "Since my father wasn't really part of the picture I was going to lose the only person who was really caring for me, the only one I *had.* And she would say this to me, tell me that I never could manage, never go on without her; and that I didn't know how to do anything for myself."

"Just in case you might've had any idea of trying," I put in sarcastically.

But Diana, absorbed in a memory, didn't quite hear me. "One of the things that I always had to do," she continued, almost dreamily, "was to be especially nice to my teachers, and to the minister of our church, and to the Sunday-school teachers. And an awfully *important* thing, which I'd been taught and told about since way before I could remember, was that I had to be self-sacrificing. Which meant, to me, being prepared in your soul and heart to give up whatever's most needful to you, whatever in the world means the very most *to you*. Once, I remember . . . I must've been around six or seven at the time . . . my mother was having an attack, and she was in pain, and suffering intensely. I knelt at her bedside, praying aloud, and I prayed to God to take her—to carry her to Himself in Heaven so that she wouldn't have to endure this pain anymore. Which was to me, at that time, like saying: 'Oh God, I'm willing to make this ultimate sacrifice.' Because I was also scared about what would happen to me if she did die."

Diana smiled wryly, shrugged. "Kids; you know how kids think! I wanted her not to suffer anymore, and to be with God: to me that *was* the ultimate love, even though I was scared for my own self. But, while I knelt and prayed there, she leaned out of bed and reached over and slapped me across the face. 'How *dare* you pray to God that I should die?' she asked me, and 'What kind of a child are *you* . . . ?'"

At that moment, Diana's phone rang, startling us both. It was the minister of her church, who'd come forward during this crisis, was showing a steady care and concern. While she spoke to him, I stood at the window, looked down. Yesterday's snowfall was looking brownish, starting to melt; much of it was already slush.

"Later on," resumed Diana, after she'd hung up but while I still stood at the window, "I did hear my mother discussing that incident, on more than one occasion."

"Oh? And how did she describe it?" I asked, returning to my chair, sitting down opposite her.

A puzzled expression crossed her face: "She was bragging about it. She'd say, very self-righteously: 'With the last of my strength, I slapped my daughter across the face!' I recall feeling miserably misunderstood . . . and her telling me that if she'd actually died her last act would've been to give me the spanking I deserved!"

"What did that mean?"

She laughed nervously, shook her head: "I don't know. That she'd have physically beaten me, I suppose. I've come to think, in later years, that she really must've hated me. Because she had, herself, had a very restricted life—and she'd never had anything of her own until my father. And it was after *I* was born that she started having all of those illnesses. The illnesses were, I believe, what *she* thought had ruined her marriage."

Diana stopped. We sat in a pool of silence, ruffled only by occasional bursts of cheering from the TV set. It sounded as if it were some sort of game or quiz show program. "When I began to date, which was fairly well along in my teens, she did everything to interfere with those relationships. Most of them never got off the ground, because the person wasn't ever good enough. He wasn't religious, or wasn't in the right profession, or wasn't ambitious, or had the wrong manners, or the wrong background. There was always something that meant that that person absolutely wouldn't *do*." She grinned unexpectedly: "Until I met Robert, of course."

"And *he* passed muster, got the stamp of approval from your mother and grandparents?"

"Oh *no!* Not at *all!*" She leaned forward, her expression alight, her entire body seemingly charged with sudden energy: "My mother detested Robert, absolutely *forbade* the marriage," she declared gaily.

"But why? On what grounds?"

"That's just it; she hadn't any! He was in our own church, and he was religious enough, and he had an education and was ambitious—but she couldn't *stand* him! She opposed us all the way to the altar . . . and afterward, too."

There was another pause, during which I felt her gaiety dissipating, her vigor leaking away almost palpably. "You know, marrying Bob was the only rebellious thing I ever did in my life," she said slowly. "It was the only thing I can remember doing for *me*—ever—I mean, just for myself. But you know, a funny thing, and something I think about now: there never *was* any time at all between living at home with my mother and then going to live with Robert. And I believe it would have been better if there'd been a—space—a time somewhere in between when there wasn't *anyone*, when it was just me alone. Because that same feeling that I'd always had with her, that feeling of not being able to think a thought or make a move that didn't meet with her approval—I think maybe I transferred a lot of that feeling into my relations with Bob."

She spoke in the tones of elegy.

Farewell Scene

On the day of her discharge, the lipstick Diana wore was bright. She appeared happy and alarmed, as tremulous as a bride. The entire family had come in to bring their mother home; it was Frankie who, at his own insistence, carried Diana's suitcase to the elevators. He staggered slightly under the weight, but no one would have dared suggest that he give over this honor to his older sisters or to his father. A small knot of nurses, and of other staff members who'd gotten to know the

Dahlgrens, congregated in front of the elevators briefly; there was an exchange of cheerful farewells. These good-byes weren't final, not by any means, for the family would be returning periodically, for follow-up conferences at the clinic. But the hospital's primary responsibility would end when the Dahlgrens went down, out the front door of the Dartmouth-Hitchcock Mental Health Center, got into their car and drove away. The patient had recovered.

I had a sense of uneasiness, of wanting to cross my fingers behind my back—childishly, for luck. Given Diana's tremendous vulnerabilities, her profound neediness at this juncture of her life, would she make it? Five weeks of being sprinkled with care and attention had surely perked her up; but, when she returned home, would she experience that same withering inner drought? And if she started feeling "like nobody" again, feeling the pain of not-existing-though-she-knew-she-was-alive, would she try to kill herself again? A few weeks in a mental hospital couldn't, I thought anxiously, be much protection against the ingrained and deeply dependent styles of relating which had developed over a lifetime.

Her mood state had become more "iffy" over the weekend, and during the few weekdays prior to her departure. Now, according to the nursing reports, she occasionally seemed a bit "inappropriate"—either too cheerful or too withdrawn and morose. She was clearly worried about what awaited her. The relatively calm passage of the time period spent in the hospital was being succeeded by emotional troughs and swells. But these were only being noted, not considered alarming.

The treatment-recommendations in the case of *Diana Pharr Dahlgren, 48, Married, Housewife; Protestant, White,* were fairly straightforward. She and her husband had been referred for a course of marital therapy—at a community mental health center closer to their home—and Bob had consented to this without hesitation, in his remote, ever-agreeable way. It was also advised that Mrs. Dahlgren, after becoming established in the couples therapy, get some individual counseling for herself—to work on what was seen as her major present complaint, i.e., her overdependence on her husband, and the abrupt plummeting of her own self-esteem when she sensed any drawing back on his part.

She would be continued on the medication regime begun in the hospital—even though, to be sure, no one could be certain what these drugs were doing; she'd gotten dramatically better before they could possibly have taken effect! In some weird fashion her suicide attempt had been, as I've mentioned, the best antidepressant ever. It had been a dramatic expression of the existential horror she'd been experiencing, an abrupt release and outflow of an accumulation of inner poisons. The act had brought the whole thing outside herself, confirmed it as a social reality, let it all hang out in every sense of the word. She'd become a patient. She was all right, even *well*, in this place, at this moment. The medicines she was taking would be monitored—as would her mood state—on a series of follow-up visits, already prearranged.

As for the alcohol problem—well, this too had receded, with astonishing alacrity, as a problem . . . for the duration of her stay on the ward. But here in the hospital, her acute needs for dependency, for relationship, for attention *were* being met; and she had a "role" in life, the role of a patient. She had a place in a social fabric, a place which gave her a purpose (getting well). She was also being given Antabuse, a substance that would produce a severe and unpleasant reaction to the consumption of alcohol.

Once home, however, much of this could change. Once an initial flurry of care and concern on the family's part had subsided, life might well slip back into its familiar grooves. The children would become busy with their own activities, their own movement outward into the world. Bob might well drift into his customary absorption in a range of outside tasks and interests; he might—unless the couples therapy prevented this from happening—eventually become as unavailable as he'd been beforehand. Diana could then ineluctably become bored, lonely, unhappy, "unaccountably depressed," and in time stop taking the Antabuse. She might, eventually, be dutifully complaining about her depressive feelings to a psychotherapist—but still go home, take a drink to ease that pain, those feelings of being superfluous in the world, a "nonentity" and all the anxiety that she felt about it.

This was the danger. And it was Christine, the alcohol worker, who had the last word to say when the Dahlgrens stood in the elevator, the doors about to close in front of them. She'd succeeded, during this past week, in getting Diana to attend an A.A. meeting; now she was reminding her, half cajolingly, half threateningly, that it was vital that she continue to attend. Diana smiled pleasantly. Looking at her standing there, among her family, I understood her pride in them. They *were* attractive. I nodded my head, in an up and down "Yes," as if to tell her so. She waved at everyone nervously. The doors closed, the elevator light turned green, and the Dahlgrens were gone.

I heard a small sigh, turned to Kristi Kistler, the social worker. "Well, what do you think?" I asked.

She shrugged and shook her head. "Do you think she's going to make it?" I persisted.

"I don't know," answered Kristi uncertainly. "It's a big, complicated, scary world out there. And there's so much going *against* her. I'm only hoping, that's what I'm doing. I'm hoping. . . ." I'd actually been asking for some reassurance. But Kristi was, as I realized, looking at me as if she wanted *me* to reassure her! Dr. Burkle, who'd gone to leave a message at the nurses' desk right after the Dahlgrens' departure, now returned along the corridor. He saw us standing there, wordless, looking worried. "What's going on?" he asked.

"It's Diana . . . we were wondering . . . Do you think she's going to be O.K.?"

"It's hard to tell. It depends, so much, on what happens next, on whether the family hangs in there with her." His own voice dropped; his expression was doubtful, concerned, momentarily helpless. He said suddenly, defensively: "It's the same thing in physical medicine, you know. You do what's possible for the patient, but not everyone *does* get better." I realized, then, the depth of his own pessimism, his frustration. There was just so much that a physician could do about Diana Dahlgren's fate. The tubercule of inner anger, loss, sorrow, despair *might* have been arrested. Or it might resume its growth, fester, and flourish anew "out there," in Diana's own world.

The three of us stared at each other, as if caught in a spell. How was it, I've wondered in retrospect, that none of us suspected what the "difference" in her husband had been, since the time of their leaving California? No one did, in fact, correlate Robert Dahlgren's withdrawn quality and his remoteness with the fact that *he himself* was at that time in the throes of a very serious depression. That knowledge would, I've since thought, have affected our speculations about Diana Dahlgren's fate . . . and about her very chances of surviving.

As we stood there, saying nothing, I heard the small "ping" of the elevator bell, looked at the light, and saw that it had turned to a rosy UP glow. "Well," I finally broke the silence, "I'll want to check back with you on the follow-ups, see how Diana's doing. Say, three months from now . . . ?" At this moment, the elevator doors opened; Bette Glassman's parents had arrived.

They asked at once if we happened to know where Dr. Cohen, their daughter's therapist, could be found. "Ask at the nurses' desk," advised Kristi kindly.

Bette's father went over to do so; but Mrs. Glassman pulled me aside. She opened her tan leather purse and took out a sheet of white notepaper. "We've made up a list, and we hope to go over it today, with Dr. Cohen. We've written down all the things that ever happened in Bette's life—everything that might have contributed to her depression." She offered it to me briefly, and I read the top item: Death of her grandfather, when she was four. "She was very close to him," explained Mrs. Glassman anxiously. "They were *so* attached to one another, so loving. It was beautiful; he was my father. And he died very suddenly. Bette kept asking and asking for him; she wanted to know where her Grandpops had *gone* to. . . ."

She glanced past me at that moment, saw her husband signaling in the direction of the opposite corridor. "Oh! Excuse me," she said hastily, putting the list back into her purse and shutting it with a snap. She hurried to catch up with her husband.

In the Fifties

CHAPTER FIFTEEN

The Time of Menopause: Doris (1)

It had rained, that August morning, but the air felt as heavy as if the rain were merely on its way. I went inside the lobby of the Holiday Inn on Whalley Avenue in New Haven; it was a relief to get into its cool, dry, air-conditioned climate. I would be visiting one of the guests there—a Mrs. Doris Nordlund—but I didn't know very much about her. She was a patient at the Yale–New Haven Hospital's Dana Psychiatric Clinic; and was staying at this motel while she went there, three times weekly, for treatment. One of the therapists at the Dana Clinic had told Mrs. Nordlund that I was working on a book on "women and depression." She'd volunteered to be interviewed, and asked the doctor to give me her number. The few facts about her that I brought with me, at the outset, were that she was a woman in her early fifties; that she and her husband owned some kind of citrus farm in Brazil; and that she'd flown to this country, a few weeks earlier, in the wake of an almost lethal suicidal try. But why had she come to New Haven, in particular? I hadn't the faintest idea.

My first impression of Doris Nordlund was of a small-boned, frail, narrow person. I would have called her short.

But later, when she literally had straightened up, I realized that she was a couple of inches taller than my own five feet six. By then, whether because she was under the influence of the antidepressants she was taking, or under the influence of her new surroundings—or both —she'd become infused with a new energy and hope. Or should I say *inflated,* because there was a sense, later, of her personhood having *filled out.* I was to recall, on registering these changes, a remark made to me by Dr. Gary Tucker, Chairman of the Department of Psychiatry at Dartmouth Medical School. "Often, a person who's depressed will look ten years older than her stated age," he'd observed, "while a manic person will look ten years *younger*." Mrs. Nordlund didn't, however, merely begin to look younger over the course of the next several weeks; she began to look like a *different* human being.

I remember, though, being puzzled when she told me, sometime during that initial interview, that she'd been a kind of playgirl during one period of her life, had racketed around the country, had worked as a model. She spoke in a subdued kind of whisper, had a frightened look on her face; and her dark hair hung in limp, bedraggled bangs across her forehead. She had never, she said, in that scared small voice, ever heard of an entity called "clinical depression" before awakening —"indignant at finding myself still alive"—in that hospital in São Paulo, Brazil.

She believed now, as she looked backward in her life with this addition to her understanding, that she'd been ill with this illness for a very long time . . . perhaps as far back in her life as she could remember. And yet she'd not ever doubted, throughout the long agony of these past five years, that hers was a menopausal depression. That is, her depression didn't have to do with *herself* or her own life as she was living it: it had to do with changes, occurring during this epoch of female existence, in an underlying physiological and biological state. Like Judith Karlin, who'd said: "It's not *me*; it's my biochemistry," Doris could say to herself: "It's not *me*; it's my changing female hormones."

In Judith's case, of course, one could readily accept the notion of a "special biological permission," in terms of a genetically transmitted vulnerability to develop a disturbance of mood. And, similarly, in the case of Laurie Michaelson, one could accept the notion of a similar internally based, "postpartum" vulnerability—which had existed for a more delimited period of time, and had been linked to the hormonal changes that accompanied the baby's weaning. Is there, however, a similarly enhanced susceptibility to depression that accompanies the reproductive-hormone shifts of the female menopause?

Doris Nordlund had thought that there was, and that her depressive symptoms were actually symptoms of menopause. But does an entity called "menopausal depression" really exist? Before continuing with Doris' own, extraordinary, history, I'd like to examine the pros and cons of this entire proposition—and to talk, in somewhat general terms, about the concerns of this "middle" period of female life.

In the Climacteric

Doris Nordlund had, at age fifty-two, reached that segment of the life-arc which is called the *climacterium* or *climacteric* (from the Greek word "climacter," which means the round, or top rung, of the ladder). In this instance, of course, the ladder is the ladder of existence itself. The individual, male or female, will now move through a period of life in which the direction is downward, descending. It is, for both sexes, a time of estimating what have been one's profits, and what have been one's losses; a time of looking backward toward what has been and forward toward the shrinking future . . . of estimating what hopes, if any, still may possibly be realized. This is a period of living which, for obvious reasons, can become exquisitely painful. And in the case of the female, it coincides with a biologically timed occurrence.

This is the cessation of menses and the ending of reproductive life: an awesome and final event. It is during this phase of female existence that—so the very widespread folk belief has it—women are unusually prone to develop a depressive disorder, or to become extremely nervous, or even crazily erratic in their behavior. Such menopausal "symptoms" are supposedly correlated with falling rates of production of the important ovarian hormones.

The Depressions of the Menopause

Traditionally, menopausal depression has been viewed as a "special" or "different" type of depressive disorder. The thinking about it has been, by and large, that the decline in levels of certain presumably "protective" female hormones ushers in a period of enhanced psychological instability. "Symptoms," therefore, in a woman of a certain age, can be interpreted as something related to her internal biological condition.

The woman who becomes depressed during the life period when females are most at risk for the menopause (statistically, between the ages of forty-five and fifty-five) is considered, very frequently, to be a distinctive sort of a patient. She wears her malady with a difference. The medical thinking about her has been, moreover, that not only is *she* different but her depression is one that occurs in a distinct and noticeably different kind of a pattern.

The diagnosis *involutional melancholia*—which is the diagnosis that the menopausal woman has tended to receive—is, some experts have claimed, nothing other than a diagnosis of a particular time of life. There is, in fact a growing body of evidence that strongly suggests that a special form of female depression—precipitated by the hormone changes accompanying ovarian-reproductive-system decline—actually doesn't exist at all.

"Involutional Melancholia"

Let me mention, simply in passing, that the tendency to correlate depression and "nervousness" in the female with the dysfunctioning of her generative organs is as old as medical history. It appears, at the outset, in the writings of the ancient Greek physicians. Anxiety states in women were, for example, believed to be caused by the female uterus—which had, supposedly, drifted loose from its moorings and gone wandering through the body until reaching the diaphragm—where it exerted pressure, causing breathlessness and palpitations. (The word "hysteria" actually means "wandering uterus.") I say this, however, merely to note the readiness with which a cause-and-effect association between the distressed female and the status of her reproductive system tends to be made. It seems awfully *easy* to focus blame on this one organ-system within the woman's body!

And in some situations—the postpartum situation is one—a clear link between mental vulnerability and reproductive physiology can be presumed to exist, for a *delimited period of time*.

But in the case of the menopausal woman no such link has been established at all! There is simply no scientific evidence supporting the notion that the hormonal decline of the middle years "causes" the depressions of the female climacteric. Yet the menopausal woman seems to be the most glibly dismissed of mortal beings. The dilemmas of this complex phase of her existence are reduced to a wonderfully simple explanation. Her reproductive organs are losing their function. It is her female biology that is failing her.

It is unfortunate, most sad, of course; but depression is, as Doris Nordlund *was told*, one of the expectable cards that the usual woman in her middle years must look forward to holding in her hand. Her physiology simply ordains a degree of distress and disturbance during the time of the reproductive shutdown. Doris would, so the Brazilian doctors she was consulting kept assuring her, feel better once these highly sensitive and vulnerable years of any woman's life were over. Hers was a melancholy of the menopausal passage.

During this entire phase of her life—I mean the entire time during which she wandered from physician to physician—she was actually still menstruating in what might be called a perimenopausal pattern. That is, her periods were irregular, and she had occasional "flooding" or unusually heavy flow. That was all, aside from her age at the time that she stopped the heavy drinking she'd been doing, and began to "feel" her depression—which was age forty-nine. She was told, nevertheless, that when the full hormonal efflux was over, she would restabilize. Her involutional depression would dissipate, as if by means of magic. But in the meanwhile, aside from hormonal replacement therapy, there was little to do but just wait.

Replacement therapy—an effort to replace her own dwindling supplies of female hormones—was the best that could be offered in terms of treatment. Injections of estrogenic substances would, it was hoped, bring her some degree of relief. Female hormones might help to restore such impalpables as "confidence," "optimism," a sense of self-esteem. Was the underlying rationale a notion that the hormones would restore her to a belief in her own womanly powers?

One doesn't know, for treatment with estrogens partakes of ideas that are, in a way, quasi-magical. If one goes back to the earliest mythologies or if one explores the folklore of primitive cultures, one can see very clearly that females are linked with mystical capacities and mysterious forces by virtue of the fact that they menstruate. Fertility; the ability to create new life: these are awesome powers. There may be an unconscious notion at play in both the doctor who treats his middle-aged patient with estrogens and in the patient herself. The notion being that the loss of the ability to reproduce is a female form of disaster; and that putting in replacement-hormones may stave off fertility's end and the ending of a major phase of the woman's life.

Medically, of course, the rationale for hormonal therapy was that of righting the raging hormonal imbalance which was causing Doris' psychological turmoil. But in any case, the estrogenic medications weren't helping; and her depression was untouched by the treatment.

A Plausible-sounding Fantasy

There is, as I remarked earlier, a school of thought which holds that the entire concept of a biologically based "menopausal depression"—

linked to or caused by falling supplies of the important female hormones—is a totally imaginary construct. According to Yale researcher Myrna Weissman, the tenaciously-held belief in a depressive disorder that women are specially prone to during the climacteric years is a socially shared and plausible-sounding fantasy. But it just isn't true. "It is about as valid, from a scientific viewpoint, as is the notion that witches cause illness and plagues," she observed. "This explanation of the origin of plague and illnesses once seemed self-evident, and not open to question or dispute, as well."

If, for example, being in the menopause rendered a woman far more depression-prone than she would be otherwise, wouldn't it follow that there would be more depression among women in the forty-five-to-fifty-five-year-old age group? The impact of hormonal shifts can certainly be seen in the postpartum situation. Women who have just given birth are at a four- to fivefold greater risk of developing psychiatric symptoms than are women who have not. The idea that hormones play some precipitating role in postpartum depressive illnesses can therefore be entertained with some seriousness. But there *is* no similar surge in rates of depression among women in the menopausal decade. A recent study, carried out by Dr. Weissman, indicates that rates of depression are actually higher among women around the age of thirty! (No "hormonal explanations" are, in the age-thirty cohort, clearly so ready and available!)

Despite the absence of any real proof, however, a certainty that most women's wombs contain a ticking biological time bomb—set to the clock of reproductive functioning and very liable to trip off into depressive illness during the menopause—is taken very much for granted. Menopausal women are, it's believed, susceptible to particularly virulent psychiatric reactions. There is something about the entire belief-model which seems to be inherently satisfying; there's something about it that just feels right; it is as though if it isn't true, it really *ought* to be!

Perhaps the analogy that's being made is from the postpartum and the premenstrual situations. Both do involve an abrupt decline in levels of female hormones circulating in the bloodstream. Both *can*, in some women, bring about a changed inner state which predisposes the person toward an unusual moodiness, irritability, and/or tendency to become depressed. The reasoning is, I suppose, that in the case of menopausal women, a loss of female sex hormones is bringing about a similar loss of coping capacity and flexibility.

But in the first two instances—i.e., the postpartum and premenstrual situations—the hormone changes are steep and sudden. In the few days just prior to menses, estrogens and progesterone levels decline very rapidly. The shift in a woman's hormonal status immediately after she's given birth is, moreover, nothing short of dramatic. But in the naturally occurring menopause, changes in hormone levels have been proceeding apace long before any clear-cut and obvious signs become manifest, in terms of alterations in the woman's bleeding pattern. Long before her periods have become irregular or have ceased, a female's reproductive hormone production has been slowing down, and the cessation of menses is itself no dramatic occurrence, accompanied by clanging cymbals; it's rarely even experienced as an event that can be pinpointed in time. According to Dr. Johanna F. Perlmutter, an obstetrician on the faculty of the Harvard Medical School, the menopause takes place in a nebulous fashion, and happens over a period of anywhere from several months to several years (it can take place over the course of an entire *decade*). "One can only say that the deed has been accomplished," she told me, "when one has gone through an entire year without a period. From a menstrual point of view, once you've been through that year without any bleeding you're considered to have gone through the menopause *a year earlier*. So the statement that a woman's been through her menopause is one that can only be made retrospectively."

The hormonal shifts that occur during the period of reproductive decline are, in a word, so subtle and *gradual*—and they take place over such an extended period of time—that it's difficult to implicate them in the development of menopausal depression. Especially because the existence of "menopausal depression" is, *in itself*, looking very doubtful.

A Special Form of Depression?

In a paper entitled "The Myth of Involutional Melancholia," Professor Myrna Weissman reviewed the evidence for and against a belief in a distinct type of depression to which females became vulnerable during the menopausal years. She went, very wisely, to the medical definition itself, which has it that the patient is someone who had *not* been depressed at an earlier point in her life. The patient is also someone who has become depressed without any apparent or clear-cut reasons. The illness has descended, in short, as a biological bolt-from-the-blue. The underlying explanation being, naturally, that the menopausally depressed woman is suffering from an endocrine derangement.

This argument, which does sound seductively logical, has it that the menopausal female is really suffering from a hormonal deficiency disease. Her psychological symptoms have far less to do with anything that may be going on in her life than they do with the loss of estrogens, progesterone, and other female reproductive hormones. It would seem to be a reasonable enough view of the situation; but Weissman's data speaks strongly for its being a completely erroneous one.

Let me describe the research strategy that was used. Dr. Weissman, who is Director of the Yale Depression Unit, looked over the case histories of 157 depressed female patients who had received outpatient treatment there. She divided the patients who were to be retrospectively studied into three separate age groups. The first were women in their premenopausal years, defined as younger than age forty-five. The second group were those in the menopausal decade, defined as between ages forty-five and fifty-five. The third group of subjects were in the postmenopausal bracket, given as fifty-six and over. After the patients had been separated in this fashion, Weissman studied them carefully, with one paramount question in mind: was the depression of the menopausal woman something special, different, and/or more severe than depressions of the older and the younger women?

First of all, did menopausal women actually show an absence of previous episodes? This is, supposedly, a key clinical feature of involutional melancholia. Weissman found, however, that the women between forty-five and fifty-five were not unusually likely to be suffering their first experience of depression. While 47 per cent of the menopausal women had never been seriously depressed at an earlier point in their lives, 44 per cent of the premenopausal women hadn't either. Nor had 65 per cent of the postmenopausal women. So it would be difficult to say that "hormones" were doing something special in the middle-aged group.

There was, as mentioned earlier, no surge in rates of depression during the menopausal decade either. Nor was there—as the medical definition of "involutional melancholia" claimed—a distinct and clear-cut pattern of symptoms. The depression of the climacteric is, supposedly, "characterized by worry, anxiety, agitation, and severe insomnia. Feelings of guilt and somatic preoccupations are frequently present and may be of delusional proportions. . . ." (A "somatic preoccupation of delusional proportion" would be, for example, that of a woman patient who believed that her reproductive organs were rotting.)

Myrna Weissman compared symptoms shown by patients in the three separate age groups. These symptoms had been carefully tabulated and rated months earlier—just at the outset of each patient's treatment. The researcher, in her retrospective review of the case histories, simply analyzed those ratings. Weissman found *no* different or distinct symptom pattern among the menopausal women.

There was absolutely nothing unique, in terms of anxiety, insomnia, somaticization, or delusions, among women who were in the forty-five-to-fifty-five-year age group. Their symptom patterns simply didn't set them off in any way at all from the women in the older group or in the younger.

Nor was there anything special, in terms of over-all severity of the depression, among women in the menopausal years.

Weissman's conclusion was that there really was no such thing as a "menopausal depression," any more than there was a special "Age-30" or "Age-60" form of depression! It is true, as I said earlier, that the particular diagnosis she was studying (*Diagnosis 296.0, Involutional Melancholia*) is being dropped from the *Diagnostic and Statistical Manual of Mental Disorders* . . . so, in the above discussion, I may seem to have been whipping a dead horse.

But my own suspicion is that, long after this particular definition has disappeared from the psychiatric handbooks, the same powerfully held belief in a change-of-life depression that is "caused" by declining ovarian hormones will continue to persist. It is almost as though there's something deeply satisfying about this entire idea of a menopausal depression, which is more or less expectable, and which is linked to the loss of reproductive capacity.

The Replacing of Hormones

In any event, the prevalent notion that there is a special form of female depression—precipitated by the loss of certain "protective" substances—certainly argues for a preferred form of treatment. That is, replacing those biological substances that are in the process of decline. Estrogen replacement therapy was the major focus of the treatment that was, in fact, given to Doris Nordlund; it hadn't, in her case, proven the slightest bit helpful. But how useful is hormone replacement, in general, when it comes to the treatment of menopausal symptoms?

To attempt to answer that question requires, I think, some definition of what a menopausal symptom actually is—and is not. My reason for saying this is that there are numbers of difficulties and complaints that have been linked to the endocrine changes of female middle life—

everything from depression to hot flushes to dizzy spells, joint pains, swollen ankles, to tingling in the extremities. But only in the relatively recent past has there been any systematic study of the relationship between the types of symptoms that a woman might be experiencing and the realities of her menopausal status. Research on this question has turned up evidence that seems to dovetail most interestingly with the work discussed above. I mean, it supports the position that a special depression of the menopausal years may not truly exist.

For in the mid-1960s, a survey of over six hundred London women was carried out by investigators Sonja McKinlay and Margot Jefferys. In this study, the subjects were divided into three groups: women who'd menstruated within the last three months (premenopausal); women who'd menstruated between three and twelve months earlier (menopausal) and those who'd not menstruated in the past year (postmenopausal). All of the women contacted in the large-scale mailing were between forty-five and fifty-five years of age. They filled out a questionnaire about symptoms they were currently experiencing, and returned it to the investigators.

McKinlay and Jefferys, after analyzing their data, found that the *only* symptoms clearly associated with the onset of a natural menopause were physiological ones—hot flushes, night sweats—and that these occurred in a majority of women. "The other six symptoms specified [on the questionnaire] namely, headaches, dizzy spells, palpitations, sleeplessness, depression and weight increase, showed no direct relationship to the menopause," reported the investigators.

A similar study, which showed similar results, was carried out in Aberdeen, Scotland, by Barbara Thompson, Shirley A. Hart and D. Durno. Again, a postal questionnaire was used; again there was a high rate of response, and the sheet was filled in and returned by 92 per cent of the women who'd received it. Night sweats, it was found, were "markedly associated with the time about and after the menopause." This phenomenon was closely correlated with the hot flushing; it was suggested that the two symptoms might actually be the same thing, but merely happening at a different point in time. *Irrespective of menopausal status*, one third of women complained of depression. All in all, only the vasomotor disorders—flushing and night sweats—were found to be definitely associated with the menopause.

These symptoms are, in fact, related (though no one is quite sure what the nervous mechanisms involved may be) to estrogen loss. With the decline in hormonal secretions, neurovascular control becomes very labile. The blood vessels seem to overrespond to tiny temperature shifts—which may be caused by anger, excitement, being in a crowd, or simply by having one blanket too many. In short, there is a deficiency in the mechanisms regulating heat loss. The red face or bath of sweat that can result from a minor heat change would be more appropriate to a vast temperature change: the woman's body is responding as though she's not just slightly warmer, but as though she's in the midst of the Sahara! Treatment with estrogens is, in fact, effective for women who are greatly disturbed by such symptoms. (The questionnaire studies have indicated, however, that most women are not.)

It may be, though, that such vasomotor instabilities have led to the current notions about the psychological instability of the menopausal woman. If she turns red or perspires, when mildly aroused or excited, she seems somehow more vulnerable, and less under control. In effect, though, her actual psychological responses may be unchanged, while what *is* changed is control of the circulation of blood vessels under her skin.

There is in this particular instance, I believe, a tendency to confound the observable physical symptoms of the menopause with the nonobservable and perhaps nonexistent psychological symptoms. The imprecision and skitterishness of heat-regulatory mechanisms is, objectively speaking, clearly correlated with menopausal status. But there is no real evidence that there is a biologically initiated depressive disorder associated with this phase of female life.

I am not, by any means, suggesting that women can't, and don't, get depressed during the menopausal decade. What I'm suggesting is that the depression a woman may experience during this time has less to do with declining hormones than it has to do with who she is and where she is in her own life. It is, it seems to me, somewhat naïve and simplistic to imagine that the real problems and real difficulties that can emerge during this complex phase of female existence could actually be "cured" by injections of estrogens and other hormones.

When estrogens work, moreover, I believe that they work as a powerful placebo. They treat psychological symptoms, through the mediation of *belief*, rather than anything that's biological or hormonal in origin.

Hormonal Illusions

The medical literature on hormones and hormone replacement is really awfully peculiar. It seems to be filled, from its very commencement, with great claims about the wonderful efficacy of estrogenic treatments—which turn out, in a while, to be claims that are either false or ambiguous. Even before synthetic estrogen was developed in 1930, ovarian substances were being used in the treatment of involutional melancholia, and favorable results were being reported.

Subsequently, when it was found that the substances being used—with "favorable results"—were biologically inert, a number of eyebrows were raised. These medications had had no pharmacological effects whatsoever. They could only have been affecting the menopausal woman's beliefs.

Nevertheless most physicians continued to link the depressive illnesses of the female middle years with the onset of ovarian deficiency. It was expected, therefore, that with the introduction of synthetic estrogens, involutional melancholia would soon become as rare as, say, the tuberculosis of a century earlier. And in 1934, a group of medical researchers reported that estrogenic medications did indeed serve as a superb and specific cure of psychiatric disorders of the menopausal years. Involutional melancholia was in itself, they stated, "only an extreme manifestation of the menopause." It was caused by, and therefore could be cured by, changes in hormonal status.

Other investigators were, however, not coming up with the same grand and glorious results. In that same year, 1934, another group of physicians headed by Pratt and Thomas reported that women receiving estrogens had indeed shown a measure of improvement, but they had gotten better in similar numbers, and at similar rates, as women receiving phenobarbital *and* women receiving out-and-out placebos! If hormones were specific to the treatment of menopausal depressions, why should patients receiving other forms of therapy (including little-pink-pills) be doing just about as well?

Was it possible that there was something about going to the doctor that brought about improvement in a certain number of distressed, menopausal women patients? Some physicians—a very few, because the enthusiasm for estrogen-therapy was mounting, unchecked—began to wonder. In 1951, Dr. John C. Donovan, writing in *The American Journal of Obstetrics and Gynecology*, suggested that the doctor himself was the medicine. It was her ability to confide in and depend upon her physician that actually made the menopausal patient better. Hormone injections did nothing; they were merely a prop in this therapeutic scenario.

Dr. Donovan had, he reported, treated a series of menopausal women with "hormone injections" that were actually salt water. But he had, at the same time, made sure that each patient was given plenty of time and privacy as well, so that she could vent her emotional difficulties. The treatment he offered was, in effect, allowing her the opportunity to talk about the conflicts and problems that she found herself dealing with at this particular phase of her life; and to do so in a dependable and supportive environment.

This physician's findings, which did run counter to the prevailing medical winds, indicated that ovarian hormone decline had relatively little to do with the depressions of the female middle years. These depressions had far more to do with the difficulties being encountered during this complex time of transition. The patient's illness could only, he wrote, "be thoroughly understood in terms of her crucial life experiences, their meanings to her, and her reactions to these experiences. The menopause is one such experience. . . ." If the woman, who'd come in initially for treatment of her "menopausal symptoms," was encouraged to discuss her conflicts and her anxieties for the future, it fulfilled certain dependent needs within her. The doctor-patient relationship provided the setting in which she could work through various troublesome problems: "Clinically, this manifests itself by improvement in symptoms," observed Donovan.

A dependable, trusting relationship with a caring physician was, in short, far more curative than was the treatment of a hypothetical hormonal derangement. A similar opinion was expressed by Dr. Joseph Rogers, of the Tufts University School of Medicine, in a paper published at around the same time. "There is no evidence that the symptoms of anxiety and depression are causally related to estrogen lack," wrote Rogers, "nor is there proof that estrogen administration helps alleviate any symptoms other than the hot flash." But Donovan's and Roger's were not the dominant medical viewpoint. Estrogenic therapies continued to be used; and the problems of mid-life continued to be seen as more biological than they were psychological or social.

Even today, and even in the wake of studies which have linked the possible development of uterine cancer to the use of estrogens, some physicians consider them the treatment of choice for menopausal anxiety and depression. And many women, including many enlightened women, believe that female hormone loss causes psychological disturbances. They *expect* to experience these disturbances during the menopause. It is a myth that, should it ever die, clearly will die a long and painful death.

According to Dr. Edward Sachar, M.D., Chairman of the Department of Psychiatry, College of Physicians and Surgeons of Columbia University, there is a large medical literature on the efficacy of estrogens in the treatment of depression, and "it just doesn't work. Estrogen therapy for those patients simply isn't useful. But the trouble has been," he told me, "that when a depressed woman is in her late forties or early fifties there is often an 'aha' phenomenon. She has entered the menopausal decade and that must be at the root of the problem." Sachar, one of the nation's leading experts on human hormonal function and its relation to human behavior, shrugged at this notion and smiled. "A woman *may* become depressed and she *may* be going through the menopause, concurrently. But the likelihood is that these two occurrences are actually totally irrelevant to one another."

According to Dr. Sachar, those depressions which emerge around the cessation of menses are—like the depressive illnesses that emerge in the twenties, thirties, or sixties—clearly something which occurs in an organism that is biologically vulnerable. But to link that vulnerability to depression to a decline in female sex hormones is, he remarked, a kind of magical thinking. The physician who attempts to treat anxiety and depression with estrogens, added this researcher, ought not to be surprised if these substances prove totally ineffective. "But then"—he sounded almost impatient—"why *should* they be effective? We don't treat the clinical depressions that occur at other times of a woman's life with injections of ovarian substances."

Dr. Sachar's general point was that hormonal decline probably has no relationship whatsoever to the depressions of the female climacteric. How, therefore, could replacement therapy possibly be of help? It is almost as though the physicians who treat the menopausal woman are not treating *her*, but a particular phase of every woman's existence! In many instances, and Doris Nordlund was a prime example, the person's mid-life difficulties are simply defined as "menopausal"—and therefore not requiring further thought or investigation, in terms of preferred treatment. But in Doris' particular situation (which was, as will be seen, a most complex and desperate one) the hormone injections had proven hopelessly ineffective.

"The doctors told me," she later recounted wryly, "that menopause was what the whole thing was all about. They kept saying: 'Here, take a few drops of femininity, and then you can just run along.' And so, of course, that's what I did. But I just kept getting sicker and sicker."

Estrogens and Aging

It may be true that hormones, when they prove useful in the treatment of the menopausal woman's anxiety and depression, are actually "treating" her deep-seated psychological fears about aging, losing her attractiveness, and becoming less womanly, somehow. Symptoms of the menopause in themselves—I mean, bodily symptoms such as hot flushes or sweats—may be, in some cases, terrible reminders of the aging process. The use of the estrogens may, then, enable a woman to believe that she's slowed down the inevitable sequence of events. Estrogens will (she may believe) keep her looking younger and more attractive for a while. They will preserve skin tonus, prevent wrinkling, and retard changes in her physical appearance. They will make those telltale physiological symptoms disappear or diminish. Hormones will (or so many an anxious and depressed female may be assuming) retard the coming of a future in which she will be old. Which means, perhaps, being ugly or unattractive or—most basic fear of all—unwanted.

Has it been demonstrated, however, that female hormones really are effective anti-aging agents? So far as I have been able to discover, there is simply no such proof. The woman who avails herself of hormonal-replacement therapy is medicating the temporary imbalance that may be causing those vasomotor instabilities (flushing, sweats, etc.). She may think that the estrogens are also preserving her femininity and retaining her youthfulness; but she is using potent drugs, drugs which have been linked to the possible development of cancer. And there is an absence of any objective evidence supporting the notion that female sex hormones halt the natural aging process—most especially, changes in appearance—in any clear-cut manner whatsoever.

Why, I wonder, is there such widespread certainty that declining female-hormone levels are responsible for an accelerated rate of deterioration in a woman's physical appearance? Men show as much, or more, facial wrinkling and loss of skin tonus during this same period of *their* lives. This surely isn't due to loss of estrogens, nor is it due to changes in rates of production of the important male sex hormones (which show negligible rates of change over the course of a man's adult lifetime). Why, therefore, should such changes in women be seen as something that has mysteriously resulted from loss of female sex hormones? Isn't wrinkling a part of aging, *in both sexes?*

There is something, it seems to me, rather zany and illogical about this entire, rather widespread conviction that estrogen loss causes physical aging in women. Isn't it possible that women start to look older because they're just *getting* older—in the same way that men do? Why shouldn't aging in women be seen as what it is—aging—and not as a process that is deeply linked to the woman's reproductive status and to her capacity to procreate?

It's an interesting question. But at any rate, hormonal-replacement therapy neither turns back the biological clock nor does it, in all likelihood, do anything about keeping her looking young and "forever female." These synthesized biochemical substances will not keep the wolf of reality—in terms of inner or outward changes—away from any woman's door. According to Harvard gynecologist Dr. Johanna F. Perlmutter, the belief that hormone loss hastens physical aging in females is "total hogwash."

"I can give a woman estrogens from now until doomsday," stated Perlmutter, during one of our conversations, "but she will show skin changes and her breasts will not stand up in the same way as they did at thirteen. Because, in fact, this is part of the aging process. It has nothing to do with loss of estrogens."

A woman's complexion starts looking older, added the physician, well before menopause and well before the decline of the estrogens, in any case.

The menopause is, nevertheless, seen by many or most women as the most shocking of biological markers. And it isn't only because one is bidding adieu to the fertile years of female existence and to that biological capacity that has become a part of self-image itself. It is because of the threat attached to the loss of sexual attractiveness. During one's late forties and the fifties, one's physical appearance is inevitably changing. And the loss of the "self that once was" is, for many a female, the most stunning blow to self-esteem that has been experienced in the course of a lifetime.

A Narcissistic Injury

For some women, the changes in body image that are part and parcel of the aging process are a terrible narcissistic injury. The loss of her youthful looks is, in certain instances, like the loss of an important relationship. The woman is filled with a sense of emptiness and grief, as though abandoned by her beloved. It may be, however, that what she is pining for, during this complex phase of living, is none other than the youthful, sexually appealing person that she used to be. The reaction to such an irretrievable loss may be, as it was for Doris Nordlund, a depressive one. For "attractiveness" had been her most reliable means of obtaining interested attention and the necessary gratifying feedback.

To lose even this potency and this effectiveness would be to lose courage and to lose hope. Doris had, she told me, been profoundly shaken by glancing into a mirror in a small shop in downtown São Paulo, and finding a new reflection there: "It was as if, on that afternoon, I were making the discovery, in a single moment of truth, that I really was no longer seventeen."

She shook her head slowly: "I can't remember now whether I'd even turned forty when that happened. But I was downtown in that store, and I looked into a little round looking-glass. The kind you use for trying earrings on . . . you know? It was aimed upward, in such a way that I saw *this*." She was stroking the bottom of her chin with her forefinger.

"Saw what?" I leaned forward.

"This. Here." She pulled on the skin of her neck, pulled it forward: "This crinkly turkey-crepe under my chin. Hanging so loose that I could have pulled it back, six whole feet I thought." She blushed slightly, shook her head wonderingly: "The last time I'd really looked at that skin it'd been as smooth as a baby's. And here it was suddenly: age."

I paused. Doris Nordlund and I had been talking, on a routine basis, for an extended period of time, by the time this topic came up. We had discussed every personal, emotionally loaded topic imaginable: sex, money, disappointment, failure, depression. But talk about aging seemed to be the most problematic subject that had arisen.

I could see that she felt very constrained. But I asked, hesitantly, what "age"—at the moment she'd made that discovery—had actually meant to her.

Doris' wide eyes grew even wider: "At *that* moment? I was just shocked. I can't be more specific about it. It was as if something had just hit me. My thought was just: 'This is it.' I'd always been an attractive woman—and girl—and suddenly, here it was. The latest news bulletin. It just wasn't true any longer." She laughed, but her expression was somber.

"My feeling was, oh, how could *I* be that thing—that old-looking creature—with all that loose skin hanging down; with that chin?"

She shook her head, then added that she'd begun thinking, almost immediately, about the possibility of having plastic surgery done. "I had the idea that with the proceeds from the very next crop—from our citrus farm out there—I'd have the whole thing sliced off. That was my first idea. But then . . . I began to think about it. And I guess I became more sensible, and started coming to terms with it." She smiled broadly: "I couldn't keep chopping my chin off, after all." She'd laughed.

Then she reached into a waiting pack of cigarettes that were sitting on her lap. Doris took one out, tapped its end briskly, put it between her lipsticked lips: she struck a match, lit the cigarette, blew the flame out. During the time she'd been working on these tasks a change had come over her face again: "It was a special hurt,"—her voice was tight and careful—"because my husband wouldn't give me any of this business . . . I mean, what is it I'm trying to say?"

I shook my head, baffled. "Well, he couldn't comfort," she answered her own question. "He couldn't say things like: 'Oh, it doesn't matter that much; it's not important. Think of the person you are, creatively; think of your brain, your wit, your self.' He had none of *that* to offer. So I had to face the whole thing, the wrinkles and the sagging chin, and—I guess I couldn't manage. I don't think I ever did, not really, until I left him and came back to the United States!" Doris exhaled, coughed slightly on some smoke that had gotten caught in her windpipe.

"You ever did what?" I asked, unsure what she meant.

She swallowed a few sips of coffee, to wash down the blockage. Then she turned those strange blue eyes directly upon me: "Accept age. Accept aging as a process of my own being," she answered quietly.

As a Woman Grows Older

People who respond to the facts of their physical aging with great surges of shock, grief, and fear, may not only be mourning the lost self that "used to be" (so some clinicians have suggested) but be limited in their capacity to relate to others. Was this, in effect, an aspect of Doris Nordlund's fearful reaction? Perhaps so, but if this was her truth, it was only part of her truth. I believe that the mirror reflected back more than an injury to her self-love; it reflected a situation of diminishing options and opportunities that were going to leave her marooned where she was.

That slightly sagging chin was Fate serving notice: she would very likely spend the remaining part of her life in an unsatisfying and ungratifying situation which she was going to be powerless to alter. Doris was, in fact, losing the only power she'd ever perceived herself as ever owning or having—the power that goes along with being an alluring and attractive woman.

Now, her most important ace seemed to have been played (and *when*, exactly, had that happened?). She was getting older—would be *old*—in what was a growingly intolerable relationship with her husband, Eric. Her entire existence was, in itself, organized around that relationship! This was the beginning of the ending segment of her life.

If there remained some underlying fantasies, some hopes of a knight on a white charger who would come to her rescue, these had to be relinquished as too unlikely and too unrealistic. Do knights on white chargers ever *bother* coming after women whose sagging chin folds are showing? The possibility was, she thought, remote.

The hard facts of the matter were that she was stuck. There was no place to go and no place to *be* in the world aside from there, on the farm, in her own position as Eric Nordlund's wife. At the turn of the high forties, recognizing the inroads of physical aging, Doris was probably far less assailed by the decline of hormones than she was by the decline of hope.

Getting Older, Looking Older

"To be a woman is to be an actress," observed Susan Sontag, in an article which appeared in the *Saturday Review* in 1972 (entitled "The Double Standard of Aging"). Being appropriately feminine involves, she suggested, the maintaining of something very like an ongoing theatrical production: attention must be given to such matters as cosmetics, the selection of proper costumes, and to the setting in which one makes one's appearance. Women are trained, from earliest girlhood on, to *care*, in what Sontag terms a "pathologically exaggerated" manner—about the way they look. So severe and so unremitting is the stress placed upon being attractive that most women are, in her view, "profoundly mutilated" by what is a very real and serious societal pressure.

The constant emphasis upon her physical appearance is, in truth, a very hard rap for any woman to beat. One woman I know, a Professor of English at Dartmouth College, told me about a series of lectures that she'd given to a group of returning Dartmouth alumni and their wives. This person's field of expertise is the modern novel; and, in her final presentation, she'd decided to do something risky—concentrate on the works of Thomas Pynchon. Because Pynchon's novels were relatively unfamiliar to that audience, at that time, my friend thought it might be difficult to kindle their appreciation—and she struggled hard and long on that lecture, eager for the material to come fully and vitally alive.

She had, as she later recounted the story, been enthusiastically applauded. "But I'm not sure," she said wryly, "just which aspect of my performance they liked. A number of people in that audience came up, afterwards, and told me that my talk was wonderful. But *many* of the wives complimented me on the suit that I was wearing—asked me if my hair were really naturally curly—wanted to know if I got it cut in Hanover, or elsewhere." She'd laughed: "They were being nice, of course, but the whole thing was ludicrous. *I* was struggling to explain the works of Pynchon, and they seemed more interested in how I looked and what I was *wearing!*" She seemed to feel at once both flattered and annoyed by the recollection of that incident.

It illustrates, however, the ways in which women are urged (even *forced;* see the account of Dr. Terri Funabashi's experience in Chapter Thirteen) to care intensely about their attractiveness and its upkeep. Females are simply *expected,* as Susan Sontag points out, to be narcissistic. It is almost a woman's duty—her feminine obligation—to look at herself in the mirror with great frequency, simply to assure herself that nothing has gone awry, in terms of her act (that is, the attractive presentation of herself to the world around her). And any woman who has watched other women—strangers, friends, acquaintances—deal with her own image in front of a mirror—has certainly observed the seriousness and care with which clothing and cosmetics and hair are checked over. Such behavior is considered routinely feminine: "Indeed, a woman who is not narcissistic is considered unfeminine," notes Sontag, while this sort of devotion to the self reflected in the mirror would be viewed as absurd and ridiculous behavior, in a man.

But then there are, as she points out, very widely differing views about what constitutes "success" for the male and what constitutes "success" for the female—as well as a clear double standard when it comes to the qualities such as effectiveness, independence, autonomy, self-command, competence—traits that might be expected to become more pronounced as a man became older and more experienced in the world. Femininity is, on the other hand, identified more closely with other qualities—warmth, a somewhat charming incompetence, and with more passivity, helplessness, more of an effort to be pleasing to others and to be considered someone "nice." "Age," states Sontag, "does not improve these qualities."

Youthfulness, fragility, and vulnerability are the essence of sexual attractiveness in a female. For most women, aging means "a humiliating process of sexual disqualification." This is the general case, according to Sontag, irrespective of how successful and powerful a woman may become. And in fact it is often the case that a woman who does win power in a competitive profession is seen as intimidating or even castrating: her more "masculine" type of success doesn't enhance her sexual desirability. While in the male's case, getting older tends to operate in his favor—at least, if he "makes it" in the career marketplace.

Many men, remarks Sontag, find that they are much more attractive to women when they are in their forties than they had been earlier in their adult lives. Professional success, increased earnings, and above all, *power* are, she writes, "sexually enhancing." (Certainly, when Henry Kissinger—hotly pursued by so many desirable young females—quipped that "Power is the best aphrodisiac," he was referring to the instance of the nubile woman and the powerful older male. One could not have imagined a similarly plump and fortyish female Secretary of State being chased by a bevy of younger men!) The sexual value of males is set far more by what they have achieved than the way in which they happen to look.

But no matter what she achieves in the world, a woman's sexual value—her desirability—will always be much more bound up with her physical appearance. This is why, says Sontag, throughout adult life so many women experience their aging as a kind of "moveable doom"—an awful threat which always lurks just ahead. Fear of aging is, in her view, the "longest tragedy" of every woman's existence.

It *is* true, most obviously, that in a youth-and-change-oriented society such as our own many *men* are going to be afflicted by fears about aging in the same ways that women are afflicted. But aging, asserts Sontag, is far less disturbing and hurtful for the male, because success, in female terms, is always linked to physical attractiveness. And the woman remains attractive only to the degree that her body and her face are youthful-looking: to the degree that they remain fixed and unchanged.

Indeed her face should be, ideally, "like a mask . . . immutable, unmarked," says Sontag. There is, as she observes, no such thing as an interesting line or a curious scar on a *woman's* (my italics) face— although such testimonies to having been places and had experiences are often seen as attractive, in a man.

The standards of attractiveness that are drawn up for women are, in a word, far, far more stringent: femininity itself is identified with that which is smooth, unwrinkled, and innocently soft—in other words, that which is young and childlike. A billion-dollar cosmetics industry surely testifies to the desperate quality of the female battle against the natural inroads of biological aging! For a much greater part of a

woman's self-esteem—if not to say much of her pleasure in her life—
is threatened, in Sontag's view, merely by the process of her passing
deeper into her adulthood, i.e., getting older. What she calls a "double
standard of aging" ordains that a woman, between thirty-five and fifty,
is becoming sexually obsolete, while a man's sexual power—because
it is tied far more directly to his successes in the world—is frequently
slowing accumulating.

This is why, perhaps, many men seem to be much more fearful of
death, while many women are more fearful about aging. The underlying menace they experience, the real threat, is the loss of that
feminine power *to attract*. This was why, for Doris Nordlund, that
casual glimpse of her sagging chin came as so startling a blow, so
frightened a recognition. It was perceived as an irrevocable statement;
a declaration that her chances for any new relationships in a vague
future that lay ahead were over; and that she'd been left behind. The
loss of her looks, in the particular situation in which she found herself,
seemed to be a verdict.

She'd felt condemned to a terrible loneliness, one that would stretch
on forever. She would remain, until death did them part, on their citrus farm in South America, with her husband Eric.

Menarche and Menopause

Some writers on the psychology of women, Dr. Helene Deutsch
among them, have suggested that an important parallel be drawn between two particularly critical periods of female existence.

The phase of life just around the onset of menses (menarche),
which is of course puberty, may be compared with the phase of ovarian decline (menopause). Both involve a changing biological status,
which ushers in a changing perception of the self, and of the self-in-
the-world. According to Deutsch, "both the pubescent girl and the
climacterical woman clearly display an increase of sexual excitation.
Many aging women who were frigid during the reproductive period
now become sexually sensitive, others become frigid only now, and
often monogamous marriage ceases to gratify their intensified
narcissism." This upsurge of sexual feeling, writes the psychoanalyst
(in *Psychology of Women*) often results in the bizarre, moody, peculiar kinds of behavior that may be seen in young girls around the
time of their puberty.

"In the climacterium, the 'too late' has the same effect as the 'too

early' of puberty," writes Helene Deutsch. Both the pubescent girl
and the menopausal woman are struggling to create a present; but the
former does this with her eye on the future and the latter with her
eye on the past. The woman at mid-life is, in Dr. Deutsch's view,
"under the sign of a narcissistic mortification that is difficult to overcome. In this phase woman loses all she received during puberty. With
the onset of the genital retrogressive processes, the beauty-creating
activity of the inner glandular secretions declines, and the secondary
sex characteristics are affected by the gradual loss of femininity."

Let me say, at once, that I consider these remarks the most arrant
nonsense. Does a woman really lose her femininity, as Deutsch suggests, once she has ended her "service to the species," i.e., her reproductive life? When her inner glandular secretions decline, does she become a dried-out crone within a period of months? Dermatologists
that I have spoken to tell me that there is *no* objective evidence that
estrogens preserve skin tonus or prevent wrinkling. Indeed as one Yale
Professor of Dermatology (Dr. Joseph McGuire, Jr.) remarked: "I
cannot distinguish premenopausal skin from postmenopausal skin in
any way whatsoever. What I can see—in a woman's *or a man's*
skin—is a history of that individual's exposure to the sun!" Deutsch's
characterization of the climacteric woman as someone "peculiar," sexually desperate, grief-stricken over the loss of her fertility and physically deteriorating due to the loss of "the beauty-creating activity" of
the female sex hormones, strikes me as the most sweeping sort of antifeminine bias.

I couldn't agree less with Deutsch's sexually stereotyped view of the
psychology of the female, in the middle of life. But I do agree that the
menarchal girl and the menopausal woman invite comparison. Both are
dealing with major biological discontinuities, which create important
new pressures in the person's life. The capacity to harbor and give
birth to a new human being—and then the loss of that reproductive
ability when it has become an internalized part of who-one-is—involve not only changing physiological processes but a wrenching and
profound psychological reorientation.

Menarche and menopause are times of change and challenge, in the
Eriksonian sense of those words. That is, they are crisis phases which
contain both the potential for gain and growth and for an alternative
defeat and despair. Something new is, at this time, being demanded.
The pubescent girl and the climacteric woman are both facing novel
sets of circumstances which demand new answers to the questions of
"Who am I?" and "Who may I become in the future?"

The great tasks of adolescence are, as we have seen, those of separation and individuation. That is, separating oneself from an old, safe way of living and from the safe base of the family, in order to create a unique self that is "me alone" and a mode of existence that is "mine." In short, the creation of an adult identity. During the pubescent period, the individual is turning away from her family to the larger world. The pain is in renouncing the highly charged emotional relationships of her earliest childhood. The vector is inflexibly outward: into a new environment that is hers alone, and of her own making. The work of this entire life phase is that of becoming a separate, new someone. A someone with a place in the world of her own making (for a woman, this can be accomplished through the making of a career or of a marriage or both).

In middle life, inner and outer pressures are, once again, forcing a woman out of old ways of being and familiar roles—out of whatever zone of comfortable safety, or workable-enough existence she may have created. Shifts and changes in the pattern of her menstrual bleeding itself—which for many years has been not only a reminder of a still-existing reproductive possibility but a comfortable signal that all is well within—creates a feeling of instability, a sense of unease about what might be in the offing. For a woman who has not—as Doris Nordlund had not—ever been able to have a child of her own, a last renunciation must now be made. There has to be a letting go of any last vestiges of unconscious hope, the clinging remnants of any reproductive fantasies.

Separation, for Doris, meant the giving up of any shred of a dream-wish that she would . . . some day . . . give birth. But separation is, as well, a mid-life issue for many women who *have* become mothers. Not only do many individuals have to part with the unspoken underlying notion of having another child one day in the future; they are also in the painful process of separation from their own almost-adult children. "As children move out of the family," Dr. Malkah Notman, a Harvard psychiatrist, has written, "this may revive the memory of earlier separations in the woman's own past and cause difficulty if her own separations are unresolved."

The middle years revive, in other words, the unsolved and unsettled issues of adolescence—which may have lain smoldering for years. This period of her life had brought Doris Nordlund a sense of suddenly awakening, of a rude jolt into confrontation with a painful truth.

She would not ever create another human being; and it was important for her to do *something*—create something of her own—that partook of who she was and her own being. It was as though, looking backward in her life, to where she had been, she'd found that she'd been everywhere and nowhere; she had been drifting. Now there was a sense of shrinking time and diminishing choices. She could, very simply, stay where she was; she could "be" Eric Nordlund's wife. But at that point in her existence "being" Mrs. Nordlund had become a form of "not-being." It had nothing to do with being who she really was, or doing the things she wanted to do. She was, in fact, feeling the pressure to individuate, to become the individual that she needed and wanted to become. But she had, until this point, bobbed along through most of her life without articulating any wants or wishes of her own. These needs, these pressures, were frightening. She'd made no real effort to look the world square in the eye, and to see what would come back to her, in terms of validation. She was fifty-two years old.

And the entire enterprise of changing, of developing oneself, of risking and daring, requires energy, faith, and hope. Doris Nordlund hadn't, for reasons that will be readily apparent, had enough of those things to make it into a truly independent and autonomous young adulthood. When the pressure to change—to change in her sterile marital relationship, and to begin work on becoming the person she needed to be—became manifest, the pressure itself was perceived as something horrible and alien; something totally unmanageable. She'd felt too isolated, too depleted, too unloved and unworthy to strike off in any fresh direction. She simply could not move on her own behalf . . . and she began the relentless slide into what was called a "menopausal depression."

Middlescence

Many women, including women who have spent years of their lives in mothering, face issues similar to those that confronted Doris ("Who am I? And what shall or can I do in the world?") at this particular juncture of their lives. Women, in general, do face the entire problem of creating an identity of their own, far later in life than do most men.

For men, because they simply cannot do what women can do—bring new human life into the world—have to cope, far sooner, with the vitally important concerns and issues involving what they can *do*, what they may *produce;* what they can construct and become. A woman, aware of her inborn gift, her awesome power to give birth to a new being, doesn't truly have to deal (at least not with the same degree of urgency) with the problem of her own creativity.

It is true that research on personality change in the middle years has suggested that, in both males and females, there is a tendency to begin to deal with "cross-sex" issues during the period of the climacterium. That is, for men to start exploring the more subjective, "feeling" side of their personalities and to begin dealing with problems of intimacy and closeness in a manner that is very new to them. A man's attention, during this complex phase of his existence, will often turn from the outer world of deeds, accomplishments, and "making it" to focus upon the inner man, the inner world.

And women will, during this self-same period of living, often be turning their attentions in a diametrically opposite direction—focusing less upon the inner person and looking outward. They will begin dealing, in a far more organized and determined way, with what may have been perceived at an earlier point in time as somewhat more "masculine" preoccupations: with achievement, success in the world, and mastery.

The word *middlescence* seems to me to capture quite well the whole sense of a second upsurge of identity issues—of a second period of existence during which a person feels pushed, by a combination of inner and outer pressures, toward the re-creating of the self, and toward becoming someone tantalizingly and frighteningly new. Painful demands for psychic reorganization are certainly placed upon both female and male, in the middle of their lives.

But the changes required of the woman are, I believe, far more sweeping and more radical. This phase of *her* life contains many more discontinuities, in terms of roles, functions, perceptions-of-self, than does the same phase in the life of the man. (The period of retirement, fifteen to twenty years later, is the male equivalent, in terms of stressful change.) One doesn't, for these reasons, actually need to resort to "hormonal changes" as an explanation for the difficulties and real despair that some women experience during this perplexing state of female existence.

For Doris Nordlund, nevertheless, estrogenic substances of all sorts had been supplied; they were her medicines. It was never suggested to her—not, at least, until she'd nearly died of it—that her disease pertained less to her ovaries and her reproductive system, than it did to her entire life, her entire way of being.

CHAPTER SIXTEEN

Happily Ever After: Doris (2)

It was true, according to Doris Nordlund, that she'd felt much worse over the course of the past few years; it was true, too, that she'd believed, for a long while, that her state of depression would dissipate once the turbulent hormonal changes of the menopause had subsided. But it wasn't until her arrival in New Haven that she realized that waiting for the end of menopause was idiotic: that she'd in fact been walking around with a severe and untreated depressive disorder, for a very long time. It was then, when she'd heard about that illness called "clinical depression," that she'd realized that she'd been rolling in and out of states of despair since as far back as she could recall.

Did she think, I posed her the question, that she'd been depressed when she was a small child? Mrs. Nordlund wasn't sure. She shrugged, observed that whether she'd been out-and-out depressed, or whether she hadn't, she surely had felt *different*. "And to a child, of course, being different is equated with being someone who's not very good," she went on, with a cordial but dispirited kind of politeness. It was early in our first interview, and we were taking stock of each other. She had never been able to sort out what was so wrong with her, she added, but she had always experienced herself as an alien or outcast—someone not really welcome in the human world.

He Made Me Desperate

She sat, her chair facing mine, a puzzled frown upon her scared but exhausted-looking visage. I waited for her to continue. I'd noticed, in other interviews, that a person would often pose a dilemma that seemed to have no apparent explanation—and then offer one, if left to herself, within the next thirty seconds. And Doris Nordlund did so: "My father definitely disliked me," she said, sounding like a radio announcer reporting on a castastrophe. "He felt that way, I now believe, from the day that I was conceived. Maybe because I took away part of my mother's attention, and her love . . . a jealousy thing." But she shook her head, even as she spoke, as though this explanation afforded no satisfaction. "I was the oldest child," she went on doubtfully, "but I've never really been able to understand it. Why he was so *against* me, always! As a small child, I thought about it and thought about it. It made me absolutely desperate."

Mrs. Nordlund was not South American by birth; she was from Michigan, of Scotch-Irish descent. Her husband Eric was an American also—first generation; his parents had come to the United States from Sweden. She was full of apologies, as she gave me these facts; she couldn't be very forthcoming on this occasion, for she was still somewhat depressed. Her medication, she explained, had not yet become fully effective. "I am better, but not well," she said. And it was true that, during the first talk, her depression *was* her personality; the depression was who she was. Later on, as the all-pervasive mood receded, I was to watch Doris Walsh Nordlund's transformation into another and very different person.

We talked a bit, nevertheless, about her mother. Had she too been perceived, I asked, as a completely disapproving figure? The question brought an expression of bitterness, a pursing of lips. "My mother was a rather lazy person, God-rest-her-soul," Doris answered. "She preferred not getting upset about things, and so she found it easier to let a situation such as this one just . . . just coast along. But she *was* aware of it, that I know. Because many years after it had all happened— when my mother was dying, in fact—she admitted to me that she'd known that my father never had liked me. That he'd *detested* me; she used that very word."

"And how did you feel when your mother said that to you?" I responded carefully.

"Relieved!" The word burst forth as swiftly as a bullet: "Because for my own part, it was something I'd always felt was so, and there it *was*. It really was true! It was, and always had been. But, oh, back then, when I was a child, it made me frantic . . . I didn't know what to *do* about it." She swallowed, and I watched her Adam's apple move up and down in her long, narrow throat. "I have no saliva," she remarked suddenly. "My mouth is dry all the time, parched. That's part of the depression."

I nodded my head, as though to say that I knew.

"It isn't from taking the drugs, as it is for some people. I had this *before* I began on the antidepressants; it's from the depression itself." We sat, not speaking, for a brief while. "Your mother," I resumed at last, "when she agreed that your father really did feel that way—did she know the reason?" Doris shrugged, shook her head. A smile, ironic and bitter, came and went: "No, I don't suppose she had any idea, herself."

"And you? What do you think?"

I wasn't sure she'd heard me, for she seemed abstracted, her attention turned away. Her pale complexion had turned even paler; and she seemed to be preoccupied with some inner pain. "I don't know," she said helplessly. Jealousy on his part about the sharing of his wife's attention was the only explanation that Doris had ever been able to come up with. "Also," she added, her voice uncertain, "I resembled him far more than I did my mother. And she was someone whom he absolutely *idolized.*"

I suppose I must have looked startled when she said that, because Doris shot me an amused, almost wiggish smile: "No, no," she shook her finger, as she spoke, like a schoolteacher, "it wasn't your typical miserable marriage that produces the 'disturbed child' . . . they had, basically, a happy relationship. It was just a mistake to have children." She paused momentarily. "In my brother's case, a very clear-cut mistake; because he was a change-of-life baby. He's fifteen years younger than I am. But I, and my sister too, could be classified as mistakes—in the sense that we definitely were not wanted."

"How could you know that that was *really* so?" I shook my head doubtfully. There was a space of silence during which the monotonous hum of the room's air conditioner could be heard. I looked out through the large double window near our two chairs, and examined her "view"—the Holiday Inn's street-level parking lot. There were very few cars sitting out there, in the moist sunshine; and my own was one of them. Several puddles, left by the morning's rain, were sending up steam. "Because of their reactions to us," Doris was saying. "My parents didn't like or want children; but in their generation it was just what was *done.* When you got married, you naturally had children." She shrugged.

"Your mother," I said. "What sort of person was she?"

Mrs. Nordlund seemed taken aback by the question. She asked me how, exactly, I wanted it answered. She frowned slightly, as if I'd posed her a complicated problem. "Oh well," I prompted, "was she, for example, someone you'd describe as outgoing?"

The row of deep furrows that had appeared in her forehead cleared immediately, leaving traces: "Oh—yes. Yes, she was. But in the way of a little girl who hasn't ever grown up; she was happy as long as she had a party or card game to look forward to. Then, she'd be very enthusiastic and bubbly. But when it came to housework, or anything domestic, she wasn't just sulky about it, she was *ill*. With an illness that was nothing but phony . . . and my father just played right along."

"Did you think—do you think now—that she was basically *pleased* with her marriage?"

Doris stared at me, her large, intensely blue eyes very wide. "Yes," she answered guardedly. "I would say that I believe she was." She was toying absently with a silver ornament that hung from a chain around her neck. When she took her hand away I noticed, not without a sense of bafflement, that she was wearing a Jewish Star of David. "Is it your idea, then, that you kids were an interruption in what was otherwise a fairly comfortable relationship? With him playing 'Daddy' and your mother playing 'Baby'?"

She smiled. "Definitely, oh, definitely." She hesitated, then added: "Mother was someone who just wanted to play all the time. And when life proved that you can't play all the time it made her kind of mad. No, not mad: sad. She just sat there and crocheted and waited until the next play time came. But she actually had a *dollhouse*, completely furnished, which my sister and I were never allowed to touch. Dolls, too . . . she had kept it all from her childhood."

I smiled too, asked, "What did your mother look like, physically?"

"Fat." Doris rolled her eyes: "And I loved it when there was a party, because then she'd get very excited and joyous!" The smiling expression vanished as suddenly as if it had been a mirage: "Otherwise, she was ill."

"And how would she spend her time when she was ill?"

"Oh, crocheting. Complaining. She'd do as little housework as she possibly could. And at the dinner table, I'll never forget it, she'd drop her arms on each side of her plate as though she were ready to fall face forward, simply from the exhaustion! And she'd roll her eyes in the back of her head, and take another spoonful of food . . . then drop her arm down to the table with this great display of weariness . . . life was too much."

This was the tenor of life within the household. But outside, in the neighborhood of her childhood and youth, matters had been as bad, or maybe worse.

He Didn't Value Me; He Didn't Care

Doris and I were tape-recording our interviews. We sat, always, in the same chairs, facing each other. In between, on an imitation wood table, we would set my Sony recorder. I checked the spools, every now and then, to make sure that they were still turning—I've always thought, however, that everything that was said in the short conversation reported above was prophetic of all that was to come. What followed, in our hours and hours of discussion, took on all of the qualities of a pattern, a repeating sequence. It had all been said, in those first few moments of winding sound: "My father definitely disliked me." The life that she went on to describe, and all of the experiences that that life contained: everything seemed to be predicated on that initial, dismal statement. Like the declaration of a musical theme, it was to be varied upon and elaborated upon in a variety of differing ways—but never escaped or transcended. "*He* doesn't love or value me," was the relentless refrain. "*He* doesn't care."

The personnel, in terms of who *He* was, surely had changed and shifted over the course of many years of adult living. But at age fifty-two, what she had wanted to die about, was basically that the pattern was so cruelly unchanged. It had always been so—was now—would be forever the same. World without end. She was an unacceptable, worthless, unlovable human female; she was "bad" at the very center of her being.

The Outcast

In the childhood world of the neighborhood, she'd been excluded "as rigidly," said Doris, "as if I'd been a bearer of plague." There'd been a sense, within her, of her own potent badness: a sense of an unforgivable differentness, a differentness that had turned her into an outcast. What, though, had been its origin? A better question might be: what metasignals had she, as a little girl, been giving out?

"I wasn't stupid, I wasn't ugly," the fifty-two-year-old Doris Nord-

lund could relate, in a voice of puzzlement and pain. She still was unsure about what, exactly, had really happened in the childhood environment of grammar school and surrounding streets, so long ago, in
that small town in Michigan. But whatever it was, she'd been consistently set apart. "I looked for reasons, but didn't have them," she said.
"So I suppose I figured that there was something *about* me—that I
must be weird or odd." She shrugged, looked at me questioningly.

I was thinking, as she'd been speaking, about the situation within the
family that she had described. About the father who'd behaved as
though he detested her ("The razor strop was his weapon; that was
used against my bare bottom until I was sixteen," related Doris. "He
was trying to beat something out of me."). About the mother who
didn't defend her child; who liked playing with the dollhouse she'd
had in her *own* childhood and disliked being ruffled or disturbed. Had
these been translated into something that lay outside the home—into
the growing girl's all-pervasive reality?

"There was just something about me that everyone else—all the
other kids—seemed to *know*," she stared at me. "That I was different,
I mean." I was struck by the bald fear in her expression. She stood up,
at that moment and asked me if I wanted a drink of water. When I
said that I didn't, she went and got one for herself, from the bathroom.

Returning to her chair, she adjusted the back of her dark blue Tee
shirt, straightening it over the waist of her paler blue slacks. She sank
back down with a sigh, as though tired by the expedition. "And that
differentness," she resumed, after drinking some water, "I was
punished for it. It was as if—even way back when I was six or seven
years old—there was something about me. Something afraid and confused. I sometimes think that they all recognized this, the other children, and just leaped upon me—in a way that I've seen animals do."

She stopped. Again, I saw fear in those wide eyes. I said that yes,
animals do often go out after the creature who is perceived as being
without any protection. "It sounds, in a way," I added, "as though
you might not. . . ."

"I wasn't! And, you know, a chicken yard is a vicious place. If a
chicken is hurt in the slightest way—if it has just a small bit of blood
on it—the other chicks will attack and keep pecking, pecking, pecking. Often until death, and sometimes even after." Her gaze was still
fixed upon me; and I found the look of fright on her face too intense
to be really bearable. I began to check the spools of my tape recorder.
As I did so, head lowered, I murmured that *she* had, perhaps, been
showing that spot of blood long ago, when she was a small child. "I

might, surely," I heard her agree somberly, "have been attracting everything that was happening."

I straightened up, met her eyes again, found her looking less scared. "I've tried to remember exactly when it was that I discovered I was strange and different." Doris' forehead furrowed again, thoughtfully. "Or was *made* to discover it. But all that really comes to my mind are isolated stories; and they, too, are so difficult to fix in time. Once, though, a boy from the area where I lived was telling someone else that he'd skated with absolutely everyone in the class at the rink that afternoon. And I heard him say—quote—*I even* skated with Doris Walsh—unquote—! As though skating with *me* were—were—"

I shook my head, laughed wryly: "—the last thing that anyone would do! The pits." She laughed her agreement, nodded.

Then she added, speaking slowly: "I have a memory of trying to tell my mother about that incident; and she just brushing it off. I remember trying to ask her: 'What is it all about? And why is it that I'm so different? And why are the other kids reacting to me in this way?' She had no answers; but it *was* true that I'd never been allowed to be like the other children, either. It was as if I always had to be kept under the closest of scrutiny—almost as if I were under guard. The minute the street lights went on in the evening, I had to be inside the house. Everyone was still out there on the street, playing; my parents kept me excluded as much as possible." She shook her head, as if to say she was still helpless to explain what had been going on. But a moment later, she added: "It was as though, somehow, the smallest exposure to any bad influence would corrupt me. As if something—or someone—were out there waiting . . . to bring out my innate wrongness."

She laughed, then, as if to underscore the ridiculousness of the notion; the laugh was without pleasure. Doris turned, took another sip of water. "I suppose," I put it mildly, "that there's really not a living person who hasn't an awful childhood story, like the one about the boy at the ice-rink, that it would be possible to tell. I mean, I think that very few of us manage to grow up without some unforgettable experience of rejection of that sort—isn't that so?" Even as I spoke, though, I was thinking about the uncanny knowingness of young children. They *do* know who among them lacks courage or confidence at a particular period in time . . . and they know how to be very cruel to a disadvantaged comrade, especially if such cruelty has become a local fashion.

Doris didn't answer my question. She merely put the glass of water on the table between us, sighed, nodded vaguely. "I am wondering, about what your major feeling was," I asked, turning the conversation a small notch in a differing direction, "during this time when you were, as you put it, 'discovering your strangeness'? Do you remember . . . ?"

She answered with such suddenness that I jumped slightly: "*Angry!*"

"Angry, angry, *angry*," she repeated. A smile had come to her face, though, as if to soften the harshness of the repetition. "And I recall it all just erupting, all spilling out, every once in a while! A big family Thanksgiving dinner, for instance, when my mother asked me to do something . . . to set the table, I think. I turned to her and I said, just like that: 'Why the hell don't you ever do anything yourself?' And I was appalled just as soon as I'd done it! I'd never even *said* such a word before! She was embarrassed in front of her sisters; and told my aunts that 'Doris really didn't know what she was saying.' I believe I was about ten years old at the time. And *enraged* . . . totally enraged."

"Enraged about what?" Doris shot me a puzzled look. "What was it that you weren't getting?" When she said nothing, I asked: "What did you want, at that time, more than any other thing?"

"Oh," she replied promptly, "*friends*."

She leaned toward me, her blue eyes alive, her voice sounding stronger and less inhibited than it had throughout the rest of the conversation. It was as though she'd been connected up, at that moment, wired in to something . . . those energizing feelings of fury. "Friends," she went on indignantly, "which I wasn't permitted to have." She tossed her head: "Because friends, to my mother and father, were something that would be too dangerous . . . I wasn't ever allowed."

Was she saying, then, that it had been her parents' fault—that it was they who had steered her (or forced her) in the direction of her isolation and differentness? "How *could* your father and mother have stood in the way of your having friends? I'm asking this literally . . . I mean, did they forbid the other kids against coming into your home?"

Even as I asked the questions, she was nodding eagerly: "Yes, and I was not allowed to go to other children's houses," she added, still nodding her head.

"And your younger sister? Was she allowed to have friends?"

Doris paused. "My sister was different," she answered slowly, "more malleable than I was, more easily led, more controllable. She was per-

mitted to have one friend—a girl who lived across the street. It just
happened that way. And also, my mother and father always gave her
more, and trusted her more, than they did me." She hesitated, said:
"They considered her a safer-type person."

I was mystified: "But what *was* it?" I shook my head in puzzlement: "What was this terrible thing that they thought—or you
believed they thought—you were actually going to *do?*" We seemed,
I said, to be skirting some unnamed and inexplicit issue.

She leaned forward, crossed her legs, resting her chin in the hand of
an arm whose elbow was propped on her knee: "I think their main
fear, always, was that 'Doris is a girl, and yet she's strong-willed and
bullheaded . . . liable to do as she likes.'" Doris paused at that moment, and in that space of quiet there was a knock at her hotel room's
door. She stood up at once, murmuring that this must be room service
(she'd ordered coffee for us both). As she was crossing the room,
however, she paused and turned to me: "The thinking was: 'Doris is
going to bring shame upon the entire family. Because she is going to
go out and get herself *pregnant.*'"

I smiled, raised an eyebrow: "You honestly think your parents had
such thoughts when you were five, six, seven years old?" She answered with an affirmative nod: "I'm sure, in a way, it was always
there. The idea that 'Someday we are going to have terrible trouble
with this girl' . . . because I just wasn't the same as my kid sister
Caroline, who was meek and easily led." There was another knock on
the door, and she went to answer it.

I heard her talking to the waiter, who stood in the hall; heard him
make a pleasant joke or remark, heard her answer with a cordial laugh.
Returning with the tray of coffee, Doris Nordlund wore a droll, relatively cheerful expression. "Absolutely all the staff know me by now,"
she explained. "I seem to be the Holiday Inn's only permanent guest."
She had been living in the motel for over three weeks now; and would
be staying for another month, at the very least. "I won't go back to
Brazil," she remarked, "until I'm sure, absolutely sure, that I'm well."
Her hand, as she was speaking, strayed to the Star of David that hung
at her throat. She touched it several times as if it were a magic talis-
man, a charm that would protect her against evil . . . or was it, I wondered, to symbolize her solidarity with whatever had been made
outcast, and whoever had been harmed?

Stirring milk into my coffee, I asked her, at that moment, how she'd
explained the things that were going on to *her own self?* "How, for
instance, did you explain your father's reactions to you—when you

were a small child, I mean? Did it make you feel there must be something very wrong with you? Maybe, perhaps, that you were defective
or wicked, deep down—and that the people around you knew it?"

Doris had been spooning sugar into her own coffee; but she looked
up swiftly: "I had the feeling that I *must* be something terrible because I was so unspeakably unhappy!" Her eyes held that same wide,
round, scared expression: "I *must* be bad!" She repeated. "Otherwise,"
her voice was almost imploring, "why would so many people have disapproved and disliked—even *shunned* me?" She moved her head
slowly from the left to the right, a nod of negation. "I have never, not
even to this day, understood why it happened—why I was so excluded
and so rejected, on all sides. But I was. I mean once, on a rare occasion
when I was walking to school with someone—a neighbor girl—she
suddenly put her books over her face to hide it. She said to me: 'Look
out, don't let Jenny Stavros see me; there she is, and if she sees me
with *you* she won't ever speak to me again!' That literally happened."

"Oh," I said. I put my cup down in the saucer, and it clattered. "By
then," continued Doris, "I was in junior high school, I think."

"But still—no explanation?" I frowned. Doris didn't answer; she
seemed distracted, her thoughts turned elsewhere. And when she
spoke again it was in the voice of someone musing aloud: "I was a talented musician, probably the best oboist that ever went through that
town's school system. I excelled in schoolwork, which certainly
showed up in terms of grades; and I was also a good writer. Or at
least, I could outwrite everyone else who was working on the school
paper. So I wasn't dumb . . . nor was I disfigured, at least not in any
way I knew about. I wasn't too fat, or too thin, or ugly. To this day,
to tell the truth, I've not been able to explain to myself how all of that
got started. Except that it must have occurred when I was a very small
pecked chicken, in that yard full of other chickens. Somehow . . .
they never did let go of me."

Moving, daily, from home to school and from school to home, she
had, said Doris, lugged the burden of her puzzlement: why was she
so unacceptable, so unable to please, so intrinsically *wrong?* She was
doing well at school, in terms of academic successes and musical ones
as well. At home, these reaped no satisfactions whatsoever. "I worked
hard at my school studies, and endlessly at my practicing; but I never
seemed to be doing the right thing, or to be doing it hard enough. I
could *never*," she declared, "ever do enough to reach and to please my
father." She shrugged defeatedly, the resigned gesture of a contestant
who's just dropping out of a race.

"And it was *he*, especially, that you were trying to reach and to please?"

"Of course," she replied, "yes, always. Because he was always the one that *couldn't* be reached; and I wanted, more than any other thing in the world, to do so. At first I wanted him to love me—" She stopped, shrugged again. "Then, years later, I gave up on trying to get him to love me and I tried to settle for his friendship. I wasn't able to get that, either."

She had reached out for her coffee cup; she held it now, near her mouth, and she went on speaking. Her hand was trembling almost imperceptibly; and a few rosy patches of emotion had appeared, here and there on her face. "I was, as I said, a first-rate oboist," she went on, "so good, in fact, that I was offered a musical scholarship—to Michigan State. But my father wouldn't allow me to take it. He wanted me to go to beauticians' school so that I could get right out in the world and earn my own living. He said he just wouldn't support my going to college, and I—well, at that point in my life, I guess I just accepted it, and that was that."

She had put down her coffee cup without having drunk from it. "I gave up on that scholarship without any question; I just folded. To him, you see, everything that I was—my music, my good grades, and so forth—just went for nothing. It was nothing at all to him, ever. It just didn't *matter*." She picked up her spoon, began stirring the coffee around in her cup absentmindedly. Then she dropped the spoon on the side table with a small clatter, looked directly at me. Doris Nordlund's expression was not that of a distressed and depressed fifty-two-year-old woman. She seemed more like a desperate, needful, and frightened small child.

Dutiful Daughtering

The "father problem" that Marie Sirotta had been dealing with (see Chapter Four) had had to do with efforts to free herself from the erotically tinged attention of that parent. It had had to do with renegotiating the relationship in such a way that she would be liberated from his unconsciously seductive ploys and her own excited responses to them—experienced, as she came to realize, with such guilt and such destructive intensity. It had had to do with the rupturing of that electrified connection, or at least the drastic lowering of its kilowattage. For only when she'd resolved that ongoing dilemma about the "unobtainable man" would she be able to renounce the powerful subliminal tie—and attain the inner freedom to love and be loved by a male partner of her own choosing (without the sense of betrayal and guilt which not only colored her choices, but gave her the sense that she ought to be punished). Marie's major difficulty, however—which existed at the time of our intensest interviewing, and for long afterward—was that her father continued, with passion and blindness, to do everything possible to block this effort.

For Doris Walsh Nordlund, the "father problem" had been an almost directly opposite one. For Doris had, from the dawn of memory, been the victim of a paternal boycott. Indeed, the two women's dilemmas, both relating to conflicts around the First-Man-in-One's-Life, represented north and south poles in terms of extremes of psychological danger. For Marie, there had been that acute and vivid attachment, with its lurking, unconscious frights and fears—the impossible incestuous possibility. In Doris' instance, there had been nothing but disinterest and detachment—aside from an occasional episode of violence. For her, the earliest experience of the opposite-sex parent was as a rejection of her person, her existence, and her value and lovability as a feminine being.

Fathers and Daughters

The father is the first stranger to penetrate the biological and psychological unity of the mother and the new infant. As Dr. Tess Forrest has pointed out (in an article called "Paternal Roots of Female Character Development") he is the first representative of the outside world; and he presents the possibility for a secondary, world-expanding relationship, for he is a separate Other. Writes Forrest: "Since paternity, unlike maternity, cannot be established with certainty, it must be built on psychosocial bonds, that is, on faith between mother and father, on the commitment of father and child." The baby, in other words, clearly belongs to the mother: the father must affirm his infant as his own.

Such paternal affirmation is, says Forrest, both giving as an act of will and claiming as an act of love . . . "an avowal of mutual belonging." It is from her father that the girl child needs "confirmation of her desirability as a female and affirmation of her value as a different and separate person. His gentle tenderness communicates to her his pleasure in her femininity. Father, by comparison with mother, has a sharper eye, a firmer grip, a rougher cheek, a deeper voice. He is nonetheless equally tender, loving, warm, and safe, and the infant girl can feel herself lovingly cradled by a man's arms and comforted by a man's voice. . . . Lacking an early contact with her father, the girl is prone to retain toward men the fear of the stranger and the anxiety that characterizes the relations of aliens to each other."

In brief, it is from her father that a female learns to feel basically trustful of the male. Basic trust in her own desirability as a female is acquired, moreover, in these early experiences with The Man. It is of crucial importance, therefore, that the father let his daughter know that she is as he desires her to be—a female, and his own child.

But Doris Nordlund's father had found little that was interesting, and nothing whatsoever that was positive about her. He had, from the time of her first memories, equated her femaleness with her badness; he had never paid attention to her achievements. She grew, but she grew learning that she could not please him. Unsure, rejected, uncertain, how could she develop the hope and confidence that she would be lovable and desirable? She was sly, duplicitous, rebellious, and wanton—in her father's view—and had been so, from time immemorial.

A Desperately Obliging Child

It had always been clear that Doris *would be bad one day*. It was as if, in her father's eyes, this child—his own child—had been singled out to contain and embody all of the wickedness that could ever be found in a woman.

He had predicted over and over what would eventually happen. And she, a dutiful daughter, did emerge as the town's Bad Girl—that is, promiscuous girl—during her adolescence. Doris became, as it had been known that she would become, someone dirty and unacceptable: she moved, in the years of her late teens, from her role as outcast-in-training to full-fledged sexual outcast. And fulfilled, in doing so (as children do) her father's terrible fantasies and imaginings; she made his dreams of her come true.

In return, she got a response—something that good grades and musical achievements had never been able to elicit. She became everything that he had feared (and continually warned her) that she would be. She was all that was disorderly, impulsive, sexual, and outside the moral pale. But of course she would have *had* to act out sexually—

he'd allowed her no other possibility for making a relationship with him . . . or even for capturing his attention.

Father and daughter colluded; and Doris, who considered herself bad and rebellious, was actually nothing other than a most desperately obliging child. She was doing what he wanted and expected her to do.

Madonna/Whore

What, one must wonder (though of course nothing more than speculation is possible) were the myths that were so powerfully operative in Doris Nordlund's father's mind, during that long-ago period of her life? His images of the opposite sex were, one would suspect, rather stark and simplified: a female was either an idolized madonna or a wily, wicked devil. Doris' own mother was the chaste and infantilized baby-wife, adored and worshiped by her husband. In their child, however, resided the baseness and the trickery of the born whore.

Of course that particular dichotomy—Madonna/Whore—is very common in many men's thinking about women. But what seems so peculiar, so inexplicable about the situation that developed in this instance, was that the dichotomy in Doris' father's mind was one which spanned two generations.

The Madonna, Doris' mother, was a dear woman-girl, to be cosseted and indulged. The Whore, his daughter, was everything that was sexually dangerous, forbidden, and bad. (What woman in his own past— what sister, grandmother, aunt—had been the prototype for this misbehaving female? For this hateful yet exciting feminine image?) And her father had struggled manfully to beat the wickedness out of her—with a strap, on her bare bottom.

A Division of Psychological Labor

What shared fantasies and underground myths pervaded and powerfully affected everyone in that family? One can speculate, at this remove, but the answers are lost in time. It is easy to suspect, nevertheless, that whatever badness her father might have experienced within himself or his wife (by "badness" I mean eroticism or sexual impulses) were being projected outward. Whatever was forbidden, sexual, and disturbing was *in their child*. Doris contained and embodied the inadmissible, unacceptable feelings. Or did she? Another view of what was happening might be that her father was displacing his unconscious wishes and impulses onto his child—and then punishing her for having those depraved desires, and for acting upon them.

It is, according to experts who work with adolescents, frequently the case that the teen-ager who "acts out" in one antisocial way or another—i.e., by stealing or becoming promiscuous, etc.—is actually putting into play what are the *parent's* unconscious wishes, fantasies, and deeply forbidden impulses. According to Dr. Adelaide Johnson, who has worked with many such families, the parent is someone who is consciously against—but unconsciously condoning—the child's "unacceptable behavior." For the parent, the offspring's acting out provides a vicarious gratification of his or her own strenuously suppressed and powerfully denied underlying wishes. Those wishes, that badness, those disorderly impulses are completely foreign to the conscious thinking of the parent. The evil is in the child, not in the self. It has to be located, rooted out, attended to, punished.

What is effected is, in a peculiar way, a division of psychological labor. The 100 per cent good and pure parent maintains his view of himself as perfectly moral and clean-minded, while any bad, dark impulses are being acted out by the unfortunate (and dutifully obliging) child. Who is, observes psychiatrist Adelaide Johnson, frequently acting under strong subliminal orders.

The next link in the predictable sequence of events, says Johnson, is that the "bad" behavior itself "serves as a channel for hostile, destructive impulses that the parent feels toward the child." Having unconsciously spurred his offspring into what is perceived as shameful and outrageous conduct, the parent now takes full pleasure in the golden opportunity to come down on the child with a "well-deserved" fury and hatred.

The child, in such a situation, has obviously not been given much in the way of viable options.

Getting Even

"My father," Doris Walsh Nordlund had said in the first few moments of our first interview, "disliked me from the day that I was conceived."

Her use of that word had struck me as odd. It wasn't as though he'd disliked her when she was born and when he first saw her; it was as though he'd hated the very *notion* of her from the instant of her mother's insemination! And she was to choose that particular word, again and again, when attempting to convey to me the nature of the relationship that had always existed between them: "My father made me feel very guilty," she said, almost a year after that initial conversation, "guilty about just being alive. He resented me from the day—from the hour—that I was conceived. Because I took time and affection away from my mother, I suppose." She looked at me questioningly: "That kind of thing's not too rare, is it?"

I shrugged as if to say I wasn't sure, then said: "And you could never win him over, it seems."

"No," she assented, "no, no, I couldn't. But I always, from Day One, felt wicked in some way, as if I were guilty of something. As if my father had his eye on me, all right, and he *knew* I was a rotten, no-good kind of person." She sighed, was silent for a moment, then remarked that she'd always been very conscious of her family, and sensitive about their opinions of her: "No, I don't mean always," she amended at once, "but I do mean well on up into my thirties. Because they were so critical: Puritanism just oozed out of them. And of course," her blue eyes were unblinking, "whenever my father told me about the things I wasn't supposed to do—drink, smoke, have sex—I rushed off to do them immediately, out of some kind of confused desire to fight back. To get even, if you will. But this, too, would turn upon me; and of course guiltiness hit twice as hard. The feelings of being no good, because I *had* smoked and I *had* drunk and I *had* had sex." She smiled ironically: "As quickly as he'd told me about all of these things, and told me I wasn't to do them."

"Do you think," I asked her, "that you were being set up to do that?"

Doris' eyes narrowed thoughtfully. She frowned slightly: "I couldn't answer that," she admitted, after a moment's pause, "because I really haven't ever thought of it that way. I believe that I did a lot of the things that I did because I *knew*, somehow, that man was never going to care for me! I wanted him to care—and oh, God, how I tried! But underneath it all I suppose I realized that anything and everything would be pointless. And I guess I thought finally, well, why not enjoy the game and all the sex and running around, as long as he. . . ." She stopped speaking without finishing the thought.

"And did you enjoy the game?" My voice was quiet, and I met her extraordinary, intensely blue-eyed gaze.

"No," she answered at once, "I didn't."

Neither of us said anything more for a while. I was thinking, even as we sat there, of her having used that word—"conception"—once again in describing the moment of her father's having formed his fatal opinion. The word, each time she used it, was strangely evocative. It brought forth, in my own mind, a visual image of the primal scene. Of her parents actually having intercourse and the seed that was to become Doris Walsh Nordlund being implanted. It was almost as though, in describing the story in this fashion, she were unconsciously catching her father out—in the act of being sexual.

Her conception was, at any rate, living proof of the undeniable fact that he, too, had "done it."

Careening Through the World

The only issues about which daughter and father had ever related were, in a word, those having to do with sexuality and badness. It seemed as though, starving for feedback, the emerging female had opted for that crucial man's hatred rather than settle for indifference. Perhaps it was preferable to be a Wicked Jezebel than not to exist at all! In any case she had been dutiful enough to exemplify all of the sexual immorality that could have existed within himself—but that had to be externalized and thrown off.

Why had he, though, stood over this child's cradle, so long ago, and seen a female who *would one day* become someone wanton and promiscuous and uncontrollable? What disavowed part of himself—or of his own past—could satisfactorily unravel this mystery? The solution of the puzzle is part of the father's story, as is the real truth of Doris' parents' relationship—and it is all lost in the past. But her mother, in her dying, had not supplied any answers. All that she could offer, in that deathbed apology, was confirmation of what Doris had always known to be true; her father had detested her. Before she died, her mother had attempted to excuse herself, saying: "I knew it all the time; but there was nothing, nothing that I could do about it."

Doris Walsh (she was not yet married) was still in her twenties during the period of her mother's dying. But she had been many places and worked at a number of different occupations. Since the time of a violent family scene, which had occurred in her sixteenth year, she had in fact led a fairly disorganized and chaotic existence. The quarrel had been triggered by her parents' finally catching her out; she was involved in her first love affair which had become a sexual relationship. "It wasn't only first love, in my particular instance," said Doris, "but it was my first experience of a real human friendship."

Appropriately enough, her bad behavior had come to light when they'd caught her returning home late one evening *carrying her underpants in her hand*. At sixteen, remember, her father was still spanking her on her bare bottom—the angry provocation, on Doris' part, was not really far from the surface! The escalation of this argument had ultimately involved the boy's entire family; and that first passion had withered in the subsequent poisonous fallout.

When it all broke apart, she felt that something within her—"my last stick of self-respect, perhaps"—had broken too. After that she had gone careening through the world, carried by tides of her own impulses, at best, and by meaningless coincidences otherwise. Thirteen years later, at age twenty-nine, she was still without any special goals or attachments; still unconnected to any person, career, way of life . . . or even to a particular place. At twenty-nine, when she'd come home to help care for her ill and dying mother, she was not someone who'd constructed a home base of her own.

Where had she been in the meanwhile? She had, first of all, acted upon her father's wishes and gone to school to learn to be a hairdresser. She'd worked as a beautician—dutifully—and at that same period of her life, which is to say the late teens, had dutifully become the wildest, most hard-drinking, most scandalously loose young woman in town. She'd moved out of her family's home; but not out of the neighborhood orbit. After all, if they were unaware of the things she was doing, the behavioral communication wouldn't be made. And the behavior itself was meant to carry the message.

Then, acting on someone's offhand suggestion, Doris Walsh left town suddenly, having signed up and joined the WAVES. This was, she believed in retrospect, the wisest thing she could have done at that moment. For life in the WAVES was structured and protected; she made her first friendships with other women, at age twenty, and had some of the successes (and feedback from them) that every person needs in order to build up esteem and respect for the self. For one thing, she'd been among those selected to be trained as an Air Control Tower Operator. The women chosen for this training had to be of exceptionally high intelligence and were, in fact, a Women's Naval Aviation force elite.

For another thing, off duty, she was no one disreputable or unacceptable; she was well liked. As a star of the women's baseball team she became known for the fact that she could "pitch and bat like a man," as she put it. As baseball star Doris earned a pet name, "Danny," because she was as strong a player as any one of the guys. But she was drinking. Off duty, she was using a lot of alcohol—and had been for years.

"The significance of all the drinking I was doing wasn't apparent to me until decades after I'd gotten started," she recounted. "But from the time of my sixteenth year, when my father broke up that silly and wonderful puppy-love-affair, I was drinking *a lot*. For I'd found that I could drink myself right out of reality—reality being, at that time, nothing other than my father." She shook her head: "I didn't want to look at him, I wanted to blot him out."

She'd been drinking a lot when she entered the WAVES; several years later, she was drinking even more. Drinking was part of the folkway on the bases; everyone did it a lot. But she'd begun to chafe, to feel restless. The service was a highly structured sanctuary, and it had been good for her to be in it; but she didn't want to live this life indefinitely. It was fine, and it was fun in many ways; and yet, it lacked meaningful goals. At re-enlistment time, Doris Walsh decided to leave and go back to Michigan—to go to Michigan State, as her father had refused to let her do earlier, and use the GI Bill to pay her tuition and her expenses. She could do so, for she was a Korean War Veteran. And it was time to get to work on what might be some more satisfying, longer-term future.

A Second Try at a Future

As to what that future might consist of, her music was out. She'd not been able to continue practice on her oboe, not during those crazy years as a wild-living beautician and not during the subsequent stint in the service. But she had never lost an interest in writing; and she entered Michigan State as a student of journalism.

She was on her way. Within a few months, too, she'd fallen in love with a fellow student, a senior. (They were actually the same age; but because she'd begun school so much later, he was graduating while she was in her freshman year.) "John was, and I knew it, someone much like my father—cold and demanding," Doris could reflect, many years later. "But I loved him deeply . . . I don't think I have ever loved anyone, not *anyone*, so completely, and so much." They were to marry in August, at the end of the summer after his graduation.

But then, in quick succession, several amazing events occurred.

It began at a party that she and her fiancé attended together. Doris had been disturbed by the attentions that John was lavishing upon a friend she'd introduced him to—a pretty and well-to-do young woman who lived just across the hall. And after that evening, he had indeed stopped calling. When Doris telephoned him, after a week of unexplained silence, he informed her that he and the other girl were, in fact, planning to be married! They had fallen in love, he said, with curtness and with distance.

He was sorry. The wedding would be within the next few weeks.

After that, Doris Walsh stopped attending classes. Always emotionally fragile and vulnerable, she was now frankly depressed. She hid in her room, weeping most of the time, unable to eat or to sleep. There was no point in continuing with her studies, for there was no point in living; and nothing, when one looked it in the eye, really meant anything or mattered. When she was able to leave her room, she left school.

Now, torn loose from any mooring, she'd skidded off on the wind of any notion, mainly recontacting friends she'd made in the WAVES. She would take on temporary jobs of a variety of sorts: a model, in New York; a secretary, out in California. The details of where she lived, the men she slept with, the occupation she had at the moment; these were all of no moment. Nothing was that important, and nothing was that painful anymore. She could have fun and she could laugh. And she was doing a lot of drinking.

It was during this period of her life, the time of the late twenties, that her mother's mortal sickness brought Doris home. There, confronting her as if no intervening time had passed, was the riddle of that deadly relationship with her father. "When she was dying, my father would be calling me continually," she related. "Every time she sank a little he was on the telephone saying: 'You've got to come now, mother's taken a turn for the worse.' And I'd quit whatever I was doing, including a job, and I'd hop on the plane at once—though there was never anything to do when I got there. She was a terminal cancer patient, and she was dying very slowly . . . but whenever my father called, I stopped everything and I came." Doris paused, looked at me questioningly: "I suppose I must have told you, in one of our interviews, that after my mother's death my father sent me a bill?"

I shook my head: "Well he did," she said, "he sent me a bill for all of the items I'd used on those trips back . . . when I was staying in their house."

"A *bill?* For what sort of items?"

She shrugged lightly: "Cigarettes. Shampoo. Deodorant. That sort of thing."

I drew in a jagged breath, almost a whistle of disbelief: "No, you never told me that." I shook my head again, then asked: "What did you do with that bill?"

"Oh," answered Doris, "I kept it for a couple of years . . . then I just threw it away."

The Closest Thing to a Home

Several years after her mother's death, Doris Walsh was working, as a civilian employee, on a naval base in Pensacola, Florida. Her secretarial post wasn't particularly interesting; but in a way, being back on a base was like a return to home. To a *real* home, in terms of a place that felt relatively familiar, affectionate, secure. Her time in the WAVES had been, in effect, the most stable and rewarding period of her entire existence; only on the base had she found a sense of family and community, a sense of any belonging. The life offered plenty of diversions, as always: plenty of alcohol, plenty of parties, plenty of men.

At one party she ran into someone from her home town in Michigan, a Swede named Eric Nordlund. She remembered him somewhat; and he remembered her somewhat; but he was a bit older. He'd graduated from high school even before she'd entered it. He was a Naval Air Technician, had an ex-wife and a child; they lived back there, in that other world that both Doris and Eric knew, in Michigan. It was natural that the two of them would begin to go out together, to drink together, to sleep with one another. Once in a while, the two of them even talked about getting married. There seemed no particular reason, Eric said, that they *shouldn't*.

One day, when they'd both gotten very drunk, they went ahead and did it.

A Bride

It was, perhaps, not the most auspicious of beginnings. The new Mrs. Eric Nordlund was, nevertheless, determined to make it work. This was the start of a new existence: there would be no more of the men, the laughing men, the drunken men, the faceless people who'd been moving in and out of her life. She had had enough of that. There was never to be—ever—any question of her fidelity! She turned her attention to making this partnership operative.

She was a wife.

Perhaps, now, it was possible that she could live the kind of life that many other women lived . . . have her husband and a home, and have their child. Or children. At thirty-one she was still young enough and healthy enough. Doris was told frequently that she was a beautiful woman. She hadn't ever *felt* beautiful. But what did it matter? There was still time to have some of the good, the ordinary things.

Eric, it was true, was often silent and gloomy; this was something that she attributed to his Swedish origins. He did a good deal of drinking. The truth was, he drank through most of every evening. He was often remote, often hard to reach, often controlling and demanding. "His personality did, in fact, invite certain comparisons with that of my father," Doris was to tell me, with a note of discovery and surprise in her voice—as though the idea never had occurred to her before.

Eric also did remind her of John, the fiancé who'd dismissed her so brutally during that brief sojourn at Michigan State. But she had never, curiously enough, seemed to reflect upon the resemblances between these three important men. She'd not discerned any particular shape or pattern to the sequence of her experiences—at least, not until much later.

But, no matter what the problems might be, she was a bride. At last she had found her own place in the scheme of human arrangements— at last. She had someone to depend upon; and someone upon whom *she* could rely for nurturance and protection. And it was over, that other life, that disorganized, formless, promiscuous search for a word of affection, a nod of approval—no matter where it came from! "I don't know whether it was a sudden realization or whether it had come to me gradually, that whole sense that I was losing the only thing I had left to prize. Which was my little bit of pride, my wee bit of self-respect. 'Self-respect'; that had been at a low ebb for years, believe me. And in a way, becoming promiscuous had been a way of saying: 'Yes, Father, I am what you always said I was, and there it is. I am a tramp and I am sleeping around and you can have it all your way: you were right.' But I was terribly afraid all the same."

"Afraid," continued Doris, "of being all alone, and being someone— oh, someone without any value. That fear was with me all the time. It was as though there was a thin skin stretched over it; but underneath, a well of feelings—feeling no-good and afraid."

This part of her life (she'd hoped) was now over. The new one, as Wife, as cherished person, as particularly-chosen-female, was beginning. A commitment had been made. There was someone to whom and with whom she belonged—at last.

As for her family, as for that town in Michigan, they were behind her. She had now quarreled definitively with her father—about the ways he was treating her young brother—and subsequently, there had been no contact. She was in occasional touch with that brother; and with her "well-behaved" younger sister, who had married at seventeen and was divorced now. Caroline's husband had left her, because of her promiscuous behavior; and now she had a lover who was old enough to be her father. In retrospect, one could suspect that all of the children in that family had been somewhat disturbed. But now she, Doris, would make a fresh start, a new beginning. She could, perhaps, create a better, worthier family of her own.

Dutiful Wifing

In a way, by talking about Doris Nordlund's suicide attempt at the very outset, I've already gone far in advance of this particular point in her narrative. And in another way, by having retreated so far back into the story of her pariah childhood and her lethal relationship with her father, I am far behind in terms of explaining and describing what was the nature of the current depressive crisis. There was no other way, however, to make it clear just how much she had riding—in terms of self-image, self-respect, and identity itself—on the success of that marriage.

The central difficulty of her life up to that moment had been simply, the problem of making a viable relationship with a man. And up to now it had been unresolvable. Posed, first of all, in the relationship with her father, the difficult situation had had to be repeated and run through in other contexts, for each run-through was a new attempt at mastery. But men had (or at least the men she chose had) always been dangerous to her. Men had rejected, refused, and abandoned her. They had related to her in one way and one way alone; which is to say, in terms of her sexuality. No man had seemed to take much interest—let alone pride—in her nonsexual achievements.

Her father had, of course, paid no attention to her scholastic or musical successes; his attention had been riveted by her sexual badness, her immorality. Later on, with other men, there had been relatively little in terms of shared concerns, hobbies, intellectual interests—that whole world of relationship that existed beyond physical attraction, and partying and drinking and ending up in bed. She had never taken the opportunity to explore much other than this narrow aspect of her self. Her father simply had not recognized other qualities of her personhood. Doris, traumatized by this initial failure, had begun tentative repair work at Michigan State, in that relationship to her fiancé, John.

But John had of course "invited comparisons" with her father. He, too, had been disapproving and cold; and ultimately a hated betrayer. Only one man among the men she'd known up to the time of her marriage had, Doris Nordlund told me, interested himself in her intelligence, her hopes, her plans, her thoughts. He was older, married, Jewish; she'd known him during those early years when she was still living in her home town, still working as a beautician.

"He—his name was Simon—was a father replacement, I suppose," she said, "but he was a kindly father. He was sensitive, instructive, kind and gentle." He, too, had let her down; she'd become pregnant in the course of their affair and he had insisted on an abortion. She had been devastated by the experience, then became enraged. *No* man, after all, had passed through her life without ending by doing her harm.

Later, she'd come to believe that that abortion had been the only way out. This made it possible to remember this man, who had been unusually understanding and good to her, with much less pain. "Is Simon," I ventured, "the reason for the Star of David that you always wear around your neck?"

"Oh no," she laughed. "I'm what you might call a Scotch-Irish Zionist! I'm dedicated to the preservation of the State of Israel."

I shook my head, as if in puzzlement and she answered the question by saying: "I put this on many years ago when I realized what had happened . . . when I learned about the holocaust. It was just my way of saying that I'm part of it; that I'm responsible simply by virtue of having been alive when such things were going on. I became, long after putting on my Star, close to Simon and also to some of *his* friends. But that wasn't the reason for my wearing it. I had my Star on well before I ever met him."

Even as she spoke, she was touching it—her fingers strayed to it often. I believed that it was, to her, more than a pledge of empathy with others' suffering; it was a charm, protecting her against outward —and inward—evil.

Gypsies

Until the Nordlunds finally had bought land in Brazil—their citrus farm and a small house on the shore of an inland river that Doris called "the river place"—they had spent years in moving from place to place, country to country. "I called us professional gypsies," Doris said somewhat breezily. It was our fifth conversation; she was feeling much better; she added that she had accepted this rootless living for it was the life that her husband's career had decreed. "Eric was—is—a technical adviser, for the Air Force, on a small twin-jet airplane," explained Doris, "but he's a good air-frame man as well."

When I admitted to her that I wasn't sure what that was, she replied: "He knows the *structure* of aircraft as well as being knowledgeable about the running and maintenance of the engine. He's worked on that end of aviation, too." She paused momentarily. "But at any rate," she went on, "this kept us on the move pretty constantly. We'd be three months in one country, a year in another. There was never a *thing*, in terms of working myself up in a job or getting some further schooling, that I could get into."

"I am trying to imagine then," I remarked dubiously, "how you would spend your day?"

"Drinking."

"Drinking?" I raised an eyebrow.

"Well, writing too. Writing letters." She laughed. The depressed, anxious aura that had surrounded her seemed to have dissipated entirely. Was this miracle attributable to her medication? She was being treated biologically with a drug called Parnate, which is chemically similar to those first antidepressants ever discovered—the ones, I mean, which had made tubercular patients experience euphoria (see Chapter Eight). This type of antidepressant is called a "monoamine oxidase inhibitor." Monoamine oxidase is an enzyme that normally breaks down the biogenic amines and renders them biologically inactive. Because the Parnate was inhibiting the action of this enzyme, higher levels of norepinephrine were, theoretically, being made available at the synapses.* She was, she said, feeling clear of mental pain for the first time in many years.

* The monoamine oxidase inhibitors (Parnate, Nardil, etc.) have been re-examined recently. For a while, because of the discovery of the tricyclics, they had fallen into medical limbo and were rarely used.

Or was the miracle—the fact that she was feeling *so much better*—attributable to her having made contact with a caring therapist, and beginning to tackle buried issues that she'd been trying to keep stored away in her psychological closet for far too many years? One couldn't say, for sure. What was clear was simply that, by leaving Brazil and Eric—and their "houseguest," Patricia Halkett—she had removed herself from an unbearable crisis situation.

In His Image

The question of whether antidepressants, therapy, or social change had brought about this vast improvement in her spirits was not, frankly, answerable. It was true that, when events on the farm were moving steadily toward their predictable point of collision, a Brazilian doctor had treated Doris Nordlund with Elavil, one of the tricyclic antidepressants. The depression had proved refractory—but what did that prove? One couldn't conclude, with assurance, that one form of medication was superior to another, for at the point when she was being treated with tricyclic antidepressants she was also facing the probable breakdown of a twenty-one-year-long marriage.

A marriage, moreover, upon which she'd staked almost everything, in terms of sense-of-self; and, in a word, identity. Was there any drug, in the human world, that could have ministered to her plummeting spirits at that moment? She was facing once again the persistent facts of her life: not being valued; not being cared for; being totally abandoned.

Doris had said, during one of our interviews, that when John—the man she'd been engaged to, at Michigan State—had discarded her so abruptly it had been "the worst shock of my entire life." He had, I had answered, behaved in what sounded like an awfully sadistic fashion; his dismissal seemed so cold, cruel, and sudden. "Yes, he was sadistic," she'd agreed thoughtfully. "And I'll have to admit it—my own aim was unerring."

"You mean," I asked, "in finding someone like your disapproving father? To help you recreate the old situation, with everything that was so destructive about it?" She nodded: "It's exactly what I did, found someone in *his* image."

She shook her head as if in disbelief at her own naïveté: "I lined myself up; I was looking for the 'man-who-didn't care,' I now believe! But I didn't realize it until many years later. Until pretty recently, in fact." Doris talked, then, about the cast of uncaring men she'd been involved with; and about the uncanny repetition of this entire sequence of rejection.

Her doom had in fact been, it seemed to me, that of having to assemble the same casts of characters to play in the same central drama in order to rewrite it with a newer, happier ending. With that noncaring man, who'd been given the starring role opposite hers, turning out to be someone who *did* love her and need her. Someone upon whom she could depend.

The drama had, in its most recent incarnation, had a run of over two decades. When this long period of fidelity and commitment to Eric and to their marriage was drawing to a close, Doris was in her early fifties. And realizing, with an exhausted sense of despair and helplessness, that this time, once again, things had not turned out awfully differently.

The story, still to be finished in the living, emerged in the course of our first set of conversations. Everything related to it was then still unresolved; but Doris surely considered herself a married woman—in the sense that she was not entertaining the possibility of never returning to Brazil. But she hadn't yet, it seemed clear, managed to process and understand what had been happening during those last, terrible weeks on the farm, in South America. We came to the telling of the tale itself, I should mention, in a strangely roundabout way.

For Doris was talking about her twenty-one years of marriage and I'd asked her what, during this entire period, her own personal goals had been. "I mean," I explained, "what have you most wanted?"

"Security." She said the word without hesitation.

"Security—defined as what?"

"Oh," she said enigmatically, "yes. Right." I gave her a puzzled look. She responded by saying: "Something very horrible happened to me." She paused, took a deep breath.

"In November of last year," Doris' voice was the voice of someone beginning a long account or narrative, "an English nurse, a woman who we'd met while we were living in Greece, came to visit us at the farm. We'd invited her because I'd been feeling so down; and she and I had become close, and had carried on a long correspondence. Patricia was a sort of a child, a poetic little girl, even though she had been married and divorced. She was still married when we knew her, in Greece. But in any case, she came to see us, and I think I was almost manicky when she first came out! It was such a joy to have a friend, a child-friend; and someone who could speak English, my own *language!*" Doris' eyes were wide: "I think, when she first arrived, I felt as if I were seven feet away from the moon." She looked away, though, and added: "But she fell in love with my husband . . . and that's when I crashed. I realized"—she shrugged—"that her love for him was returned."

"You mean, that they were lovers?"

"No, they weren't." There was no uncertainty in her voice.

"But that he did love her?"

"Yes, he loved her. He told me so over and over again: 'I love the little gal'—that's the way he put it. But I don't think it was physical, then, and I don't think it is now." The woman was, as I learned to my astonishment, still in Brazil and living at the farm. Doris clung, nevertheless, to an unflagging conviction that the two of them loved each other only in a nonphysical sense.

Let me say at once that I did find this belief astonishing. Doris Nordlund was, it appeared, unable to *think* about the situation in any other way. Eric might have a crush on this houseguest-intruder; but a view of him as ultimately loyal and faithful had to be consciously maintained. The thought that he might *not* be would be too unbearable.

The unconscious rage; the unconscious sense of loss; they *were* still being experienced, but as hatred of herself and as loss of self-respect and of self-worth. These feelings are, of course, central to states of depression; and her depression really "knew" about the sense of deprivation and of abandonment from which she was suffering. But she was, as she told me on the muggy August day of our first interview, planning to return to the farm and to Eric.

He had been sending her letters—concerned, reassuring letters, that urged her to return. The Patricia matter was nothing other than a fad, a middle-aged fancy (even though, it was true, that the visitor was *still* in the Nordlund house). Actually, admitted Doris, the thought of having to reconstruct her *own* life, at the age of fifty-two, was an idea completely beyond any bearing.

She was in New Haven for the sole purpose of receiving treatment for her depression. She planned to return home to South America once she was sure she was well.

CHAPTER SEVENTEEN

A Marital Crisis: Doris (3)

The relationship had begun its inexorable process of disintegration, she later realized, at the time when she'd made—and *kept*—a vow to stop the steady drinking she'd been doing since the early days of her marriage. "Living with Eric, especially when I became sober, meant living without conversation," recounted Doris. "With practically no affection, no understanding and no communication about anything more complicated than about how the citrus crops on our farm happened to be coming along. And until five years ago—when I read an article about alcoholism and realized that I *was* one—this was all perfectly O.K. with me."

Compatible Drunks

"Because," she said, "I was a drunk; I saw nothing, felt nothing. Eric is one too, really, to this day. We were plastered when we got married, and we were compatible drunks for many years afterward. Our problems began with my sobering up and beginning to see things more clearly."

One thing that she'd begun seeing before very long was that her husband was lying to her about a variety of trivial matters, and that this was an established habit: "I'd ask him whether he'd had the beef run through the machine twice, at the meat market. Or had he stopped at the post office on the way home? Unimportant, dumb things like that . . . and he'd simply say whatever it was he thought I might want to hear. It just didn't matter what he said, because he assumed I wouldn't remember.

"But you know," she remarked thoughtfully, "when I became a sober, thinking person, Eric's life got really complicated for him. He couldn't say things like: 'My trousers pocket is still torn, and I asked you to sew it up for me last night.' Because I could remember, and I knew he hadn't. I'd say: 'Oh no, you can't do that; I don't blank out anymore, Eric. You said no such thing last night."

I looked at her dubiously: "But why would he want to play such mean little tricks?"

Doris shrugged, shook her head: "Is it spite? I don't know. I don't think Eric really likes women very well; I think he basically hates and fears them. He hated and feared his cold Swede of a mother—and then his first wife ran out on him, betrayed him. There was another man. *Our* relationship was, though, workable enough when we first married. It was probably successful until I stopped drinking. Then he seemed to freeze. . . ." She paused. "You know," she continued after a moment, "I've read a lot of Alcoholics Anonymous material, and mine wouldn't be the first husband to regret his wife's having quit drinking. Because it put more responsibility upon *him*—and Eric isn't exactly fond of that."

He himself continued to drink consistently and heavily. He was convinced, though, that he was *not* an alcoholic, because he never touched any liquor until the end of his day's tasks. He *was* holding down a responsible job—he worked as a technical adviser at a nearby American air base—and he labored on their farm, too, when he came home in the late afternoon. (The major responsibility for the running of the citrus farm was, however, shared by Doris and a hired foreman.) In any event, related his wife, Eric commenced with a generous glass of rum at around four o'clock every afternoon. And from that time onward he continued drinking, without pause or hesitation, until about eight-thirty or nine o'clock . . . after which, he went to bed.

"Sip, sip, sip; I hated it," she grimaced at the remembering. "I didn't know how many ounces were going down. But it bothered me—not because it was alcohol or something that I couldn't have. I didn't want it; but it was taking away from something that I *did* need and *did* want. Everything that went into that sip, sip, sip was taking away the little chance of communication that I had."

Emerging from the haze of alcohol that had blurred and padded her thought process was, she said, like coming up from an anaesthetic. Stopping drinking had been, for her, something similar to Laurie

Michaelson's experience of stopping nursing. Her entire life had begun paining and hurting. "Before that, anything that I didn't like, or anything that made me the slightest bit uncomfortable, sent me straight to the liquor bottle. I'd drink . . . to escape it, not feel it; to forget it or to block it. When I stopped drinking, I lost that protection. Eric and I had been married, by then, for about fourteen years; and for that fourteen years I'd been in one stage of alcoholism or another."

She frowned: "I was drunk on the day we got married, and I'd stayed drunk for all those years. O.K. . . . but then, when I went cold turkey and did succeed in staying off the liquor, the depression started showing. It was obvious that something was awfully wrong; that I wasn't feeling like a human being should feel."

Curiously enough, she and Eric found common ground for agreement when it came to explaining Doris' state. She was in the menopausal years, and obviously, her problem had to do with female hormones. Woman trouble. This must be a menopausal depression. It was true that her monthly cycle hadn't seemed changed in any obvious way: her menstrual bleeding occurred right on schedule, every twenty-six days. The only difference was that the flow tended to be heavier from time to time.

She had stopped drinking and begun experiencing depressive feelings toward the end of her forty-seventh year.

"Please, Can't You Help Me?"

Now she'd begun seeing physicians, seeking relief of her menopausal distress. "I was going, over a period of years, from doctor to doctor. Most of them were obstetricians, oddly enough—or maybe not so oddly—" She stopped, shot me an enigmatic glance. I wasn't sure what she meant to say. Was it that this phase of life, which marked the end point of reproductive possibility (including unconscious wishes and fantasies) would be her last opportunity for communing with those physicians who take care of and nurture the gestating woman? I couldn't be sure, and I simply let the matter drop.

Doris continued: "I went from one to the other to the other. Asking, always, 'Please, can't you help me? I'm afraid all the time.' I was in depression, as I now know: depression as we know it to be. Fear, dread, anxiety. I asked Eric so many times to please just hold me; I felt so afraid and confused."

She shook her head, her blue eyes transformed to blue marbles: "His way was to put his arms around me for a moment, and then, just push me away. The doctors had been telling us that this whole thing was normal; normal functioning. There was nothing to be done about it, because I was in menopause.

"And Eric—" She laughed suddenly. "Before, you know, when I'd asked to be listened to or confided in or simply to have him *talk* to me . . . he'd always said it was 'nerves' and that my period must be coming or it must be going. Menopause, though, was even better, because that *never* quit!" If anything went wrong then, or if she were feeling low, her husband could place the blame upon "menopause." "That made it easy for him to just push me off and walk away from it," her voice was dry, "which was pretty much what he did."

But she had believed it as fully as Eric had—that the underlying explanation of the terrible ways she was feeling were to be found in her female physiology—in her hormones. So, moreover, did the doctors she was consulting; they were giving her female sex-hormone supplements, arcane injections of every conceivable sort. At home, there were drawerfuls of ineffective medications; but neither the hormone shots nor the tranquilizers she was being given seemed to counter her menopausal distress.

Still, the general medical consensus had been that these were the troubled years in any woman's life; and that she would have to struggle, as best she could, through the change. She would feel better when it was over. The fault lay in her altering biology—not in her relationship to Eric nor in their marriage nor in their life together. And her altering biology was something over which no one seemed to have any control.

This was, in general, the situation in the Nordlund household at the time of their friend Patricia Halkett's arrival.

She Was Just Like a Little Child

Doris Nordlund clearly had been in a chronic depression well in advance of her houseguest's visit. Doris had, in fact, pinned a lot of hopes upon Patricia's coming. It was to be a respite, a shelter, a raised dry spot in what seemed like an ongoing stream of pain. The two women had kept up a growingly confidential correspondence; and who knew? Her friend's arrival might even mean her rescue. Doris, on the first night of the visitor's stay, crept out of her bed during the night, wrote in her diary: "Dear Patricia, If you could just come and *live* here! I am so horribly alone."

Later, Doris was to look at that diary entry with amazement: "I wasn't well, admittedly, when she came to us; but I wasn't overwhelmed, either. It was that whole thing that really did it . . . that tipped me under, I mean."

That "whole thing" was, of course, the growing attraction between Patricia and Eric. Doris' first realization that something dangerous was occurring had come about two weeks after what had been a wholeheartedly joyful reunion on all of their sides. It came to her in the form of an announcement from Eric, and it came, she later said, "completely out of the blue." They'd been getting into bed, to go to sleep, when Eric told her that he was going to go in and kiss Patricia good night. " 'You're going to do *what?*' I asked him," recounted Doris. "I was, to be honest, so startled that I didn't know how to react, what to say! He said very calmly that she was lonely, and that he wanted to kiss her good night. So I simply said: 'Well, go, then.' "

Eric left the room and didn't return. "He spent about . . . it seemed like a century . . . but maybe he was in there a half hour with her. Then he came back"—her voice was growing uncertain—"and I think —that's when I started tipping. He said he hadn't done anything; that she was just like a little child. He said he'd only kissed her little breasts. I started going, then, into a deep, deep depression."

She'd stopped speaking. I opened my mouth to make a comment, but at that moment she took up the story: "The next few days, just watching them together, I—well, they'd begun to exclude me from many of the things they were doing. Eric was teaching Patricia to drive so that she'd be able to use the Volkswagen on her own. They'd go down, too, to the little beach by the river, and lie on their towels; her little finger was touching his little finger; and I hadn't been invited."

She drew in, let out a deep breath of air: "When I saw that, those two locked fingers, I felt as if I were dying. I was almost *sick* with fear . . . afraid I was losing my husband. Afraid of him leaving me, not of my leaving him (that was out of the question, at that time). I kept saying to him that I was so scared of losing him: I kept asking him: 'Do you love her?' "

"He'd answer, always, with things like: 'She's already got me. I love the little gal.' But he'd insist that there was nothing physical between them. That it was a sister-brother or parent-child kind of thing."

What her husband had tried to do over and over, was to explain to her that sex really had nothing whatsoever to do with it. Doris had to understand. But she had rapidly passed into a state which was, as she later put it, "beyond trying to understand *anything*. No matter what he'd said, I wouldn't have believed it. Or if I had believed it, it wouldn't have mattered—I was too ill."

Doris Nordlund was now too sick to do much of anything. She was lying in bed most of the time. When she wasn't in the bedroom, she was resting on a hammock on their front porch. "I had no physical energy, almost not enough to move. I couldn't do a thing—couldn't read, couldn't crochet, couldn't write; I could do nothing at all." One afternoon, leafing through an old copy of *Time* magazine, she saw a review of a book written by a man who'd been suicidally depressed and had recovered.

An S.O.S. in a Bottle

She decided to write him a letter. The author's name was "Francis Kirchner" (a pseudonym) and his book was a current best-seller. Doris was, however, so distraught and confused that she misaddressed her letter, mailing it to the New York *Times* rather than to *Time* magazine. This last-ditch effort, this S.O.S. appeal in a bottle tossed out to the world at large, floated around Manhattan for a while; it was finally forwarded to Francis Kirchner, at his home in Connecticut. But during this period of waiting, as her depression deepened, the hope that she would receive a reply from that unknown person diminished. It was the smallest pilot light in an atmosphere of gathering darkness; and it was beginning to sputter and die.

"I would rather," admitted Doris, when talking of her experience of that time, "have all the bones in my body broken, one by one, than to go through *that* again. My nerves were screaming; it was constant, never-ending torture. Every single minute of every hour was torturous: I ate practically nothing; eating was an unspeakable chore. I had to force down every single bite. Couldn't sleep, cried; oh, I wept and I wept! Was I even angry about Eric and Patricia? To be truthful I can't remember. I was so weak, too weak to care; I was just so utterly defeated and down. Down somewhere that—I can't say; I didn't think human beings could feel that bad. I didn't think that you could go down that far—emotionally and psychologically—and still survive. And finally," she added soberly, "I just wanted *out*."

The Afternoon Mail

There was a small unused shack, once built to be a servants' house, off to one part of the property that the Nordlunds called "the river place." In this broken-down structure there was a small bedroom that contained a rickety bed with an old mattress. It was to this shanty that Doris Nordlund went, taking with her a handbag stuffed full of medicines: all of the drugs given to her throughout these past years in treatment of her "menopausal depression." She had brought a pitcher of clear water, as well as this varied collection of medications; and she sat on the edge of the bed, swallowing pill after pill.

Then she lay down, closed her eyes, slept.

There was no note left behind for her husband. "I thought that what had happened would be pretty self-explanatory," she later told me, her voice caustic. But it had been Eric who found her. "He said something much later about the door of the shack having been ajar. He'd noticed it, for some reason; and when I wasn't in the house, he came down there to look for me."

When she awakened, finding herself alive in a hospital in São Paulo, Eric gave her a letter that she'd received in that afternoon's mail. It was a reply to her note to that author—Francis Kirchner. Her own letter had just reached him; and he told her, in tones of urgency, that she could be helped if she would only follow his instructions.

These were: that she buy an airline ticket without delay and leave for the United States *at once!* He himself, Kirchner wrote, had at one time been acutely suicidal. He had been treated, with sophisticated drug therapy, at a place affiliated with Yale Medical School. It was called the Dana Psychiatric Clinic. If she, too, truly needed and wanted help, she must go there without hesitation or backward glances. And she ought to do so (in his opinion) without losing a day, or even an hour, in thinking about it.

Kirchner's statements were made with such strength and conviction that Doris dutifully went ahead and did as she'd been told. Later, she was to realize that—had her letter *not* been forwarded on—she would have returned from the hospital to the same situation on the farm. There would have been Patricia, and Eric, and herself . . . and the vast isolation that surrounded this deadly triangle. Only the strong response from that unknown writer had pried her loose from what would have been, otherwise, an inexorable sequence of events.

The option urged by Kirchner was one that she, in her state of defeat and disorganization, seemed never to have even considered. Instead of dying as a result of the circumstances she'd found herself in, she could do something else: she could simply *leave*.

Other Options

Why, looking back on that day—a day that could easily have closed upon Doris' dying—had she *not* found it possible to consider any of the other alternatives? What, if one strives to look her situation straight in the face, had actually *ordained* that she swallow a cocktail-shakerful of different poisons, and be rushed, half-dead, to the hospital? (Even if her suicide attempt had only been a "cry for help," it was a most dangerous undertaking. Many people who don't really *mean* to die, but who don't understand the potency of the drugs they're taking—or the lethal ways in which different sorts of medications can interact with one another—do end up dead, when they'd only meant to make a loud behavioral statement.) Had this been, in Doris' view, her only means of instilling guilt in—and casting blame upon—her houseguest, Patricia? What about the many *other* options —such as asking Patricia to leave, or leaving herself, or fighting for her rights and having it out with Eric? Doris hadn't, at that point, found it possible to even consider them.

A slogan, running through her mind as she'd stalked down to the shanty by the river, had been: "Peace at any price." "Peace at any price," she'd kept repeating to herself, as she went into the dilapidated shack, the drugs and the water pitcher in her hands. The price she had been willing to pay, had been *ready* to pay, was obviously fantastically high!

But she was angry, tragically unable to be logical; too enraged to think. It is strange, though—and in this she resembled Diana Dahlgren —to realize that she'd never quarreled directly with either her houseguest or her husband! Both Doris Nordlund and Diana Dahlgren were, in effect, too dependent to risk experiencing and communicating their frustration and anger straightforwardly. And in Doris' instance, the ludicrous fact was that her friend Patricia, a nurse by profession, had assumed charge of her care. As Doris sank deeper and deeper into her depressive state, she'd found it less and less feasible to protest any of the things that were in the process of happening; she was too confused, too weak, too powerless. And yet she knew, understood all the while, that this visitor was usurping her house—and Eric—and everything that was *hers*.

Suicide has been called the supreme interpersonal insult that one person (the victim) can deliver to another (the survivor). It is probably true that Doris, when she went down to that old unused river place to find "peace at any price," was really trying to tell her houseguest and her husband off—and in the most striking, dramatic way that was possible. She was, nevertheless, ante-ing up her life itself in order to have her say.

I question whether, in circumstances such as these, it *ever* is worth it. There are a good many ways of expressing one's rage and one's hatred that fall so far short of murder-of-the-self. Doris had, in fact, been carried off to the hospital without having once confronted Patricia directly. But then, the situation of powerlessness itself had had such resonance; it was so *familiar*. It had tuned in so to matters that had been left behind her, yet were still unresolved and unfinished. They harked back to Doris' early life in that small town back in Michigan.

She was now an ailing woman—as her own mother had been. She had striven for Eric's affection and parental support, to elicit the loving care that her father had once upon a time bestowed so tenderly upon her mother. Hadn't her own mother had an indulgent lover-daddy? Eric Nordlund, coldly keeping his emotional distance, was steadfastly refusing of that role. (Doris told me, at one point, that she'd *no longer been able to crochet* when she was in the depths of her depressive illness. That remark evoked an image of her mother—that sickly, fatigued, and complaining woman—who'd spent so many of her own invalided hours doing exactly that!)

It was Patricia's arrival, though, that had ended any lingering fantasy-hopes that Eric might cosset and care for and parent her back to health. Doris was never to be nurtured and protected. Eric was now saying that he "loved the little gal" and it was *Patricia Halkett*, not she, who was being cast in the role of the dearly beloved, indulged, adored, and spoiled little child! This betrayal touched upon the tenderest nerve of that most sensitive emotional tooth; this, this, was unbearable, for the present hurt awakened the hurtful vibrations of the still unexplained, still mysterious, and freshly horrible past.

The impulse to really "do it"—to go ahead and kill herself—was triggered by a small incident, not dissimilar to many of the other small incidents that were occurring around that time. Eric had, that morning, gone out to give Patricia her daily driving lesson; the pair of them weren't back by late in the afternoon. When she'd stormed down to the shack, the medications and water pitcher in hand, a sentence that flashed through Doris' head was: "If this is life, then for God's sake let me out of it!" . . . but the recurring refrain was "peace at any price." And, as she gulped down the pills, swallowing glass after glass of water, her thought was that peace would soon come; the anguish, fear, and panic would soon be over.

She would need no one and no one would be able to harm her. For the first time in a long time she need not dread the future.

Strategies for Dying

I want to remark upon it, because it's such a peculiar finding, that when it comes to devising strategies for dying, men and women do it with a real and systematic sort of difference. The method chosen by Doris Nordlund—self-poisoning—conformed to what is really a female suicidal stereotype. For most women who try to kill themselves, the use of toxic substances is the favored method. They swallow poisonous overdoses of pills or liquid medications; they inhale poisonous gas fumes; sometimes they avail themselves of an ordinary but lethal household fluid. Less frequently, the suicidal woman may cut her wrists. It is very rare, however, that she uses a weapon such as a gun.

Suicidal men favor guns. It is the male's preferred method of dying. The male who wishes to end his own existence turns to the gun as naturally as the female turns to the use of poison. Men will also leap to their death from high places, or hang themselves. These forms of suicide are not that common among women. It is probably true that these deadlier strategies for dying account for the far higher number of "successfully completed" suicides found among males. (Men *die* by suicide more frequently than women. Women make many more attempts that fail.)

Why do women turn to pills and drugs, while men turn to self-hanging, shooting, or jumping off into space? The question is a strange one; and scientists who study suicidal behaviors have not come up with an answer. Some have suggested that the clear-cut sex differences in favored methods may be related to female passivity as contrasted with the male's more activist approaches—even to the problem of ending life. But still, one cannot say for sure that a "typically masculine orientation" or a "typically feminine orientation" is what ordains *his* more energetic and *her* less swift and action-oriented means of committing the deed.

My own suspicion is that the real explanation lies elsewhere. Women, even women who may be seriously intent upon dying, probably have a deep-seated aversion to the idea of mutilating their bodies. Even though one will be dead, and therefore not around to view the ugly scene, most females can't easily tolerate the notion of their own disfigurement. For the mental imagery, the imagined scenario involving being found in that way, is at once both hideous and embarrassing. To a sex so well schooled in the importance of caring for and maintaining one's physical appearance, this is a last gesture of appearing at one's best advantage.

What may be at play, as well, are deep and unspoken fantasies about death as a kind of peaceful and calm "waking-sleep." The notion, that is, that like Snow White, one will someday reawaken, alive and intact . . . and that the problems of the present will, while one has slept, have all vanished magically away.

A Deathly Dance

Here is an explanation of Doris' wild suicidal attempt that would, I think, be considered *fully* explanatory by many or most people: "Mrs. Nordlund, a woman in her early fifties, had tried to kill herself in the context of a growing marital crisis—her husband's attraction to their houseguest and friend, Patricia. Her reasons for wishing to die were that she felt desperately jealous and rejected." But this would be, it seems to me, an oversimplification of a set of deeper, older issues— things that lay buried far below the surface of that particular, very familiar (almost tritely so) sort of marital situation. These issues have to do with profound fears about separateness and aloneness.

In a paper called "Marriage, and the Capacity to be Alone," clinicians Joan Wexler and John Steidl give the following description of the "disturbed couple" who come in for counseling and help during a marital crisis. "When, as couples' therapists," write Wexler and Steidl, "we learn about the spouses' life together before the crisis, we often hear of a life that was dull, dry, without playfulness or imagination. We hear of two gray figures locked in a repetitious, deathly dance. They took measured strides and scrupulous care to avoid recognizing that the relationship had changed and the marriage had become a disappointment. Changes in themselves and the other had to be denied, because change could mean differentness; differentness raises the spectre of separateness and aloneness; and aloneness raises the spectre, for these people, of terrifying, intolerable loneliness. . . ."

This thumbnail description actually suits Doris and Eric Nordlund almost uncannily well. It was the tone and the quality of their marital interaction well in advance of Patricia Halkett's arrival on the scene. When they were sober they had, really, little to say to each other. But for Doris, the prospect of being alone, of *not being* Eric Nordlund's wife, of being on her own, was absolutely terrifying. So terrifying, that somewhere along the line, she'd forsaken her own individual identity.

She'd simply followed her husband through the world, as his appendage; she was, in fact, simply part of *his* identity—she was *his wife* —and without him, she'd be nothing and no one. The underlying fear was, in some substantial part, a fear of ceasing to exist.

On Being Separate Persons

Adults who seek to fuse identities in this manner are, note marital therapists Wexler and Steidl, similar in some important ways to young children who try to cling to their mothers. The toddler, screaming and hanging onto Mother's legs and her skirt, is filled with the most primitive anxiety and fear. The anxiety has to do with the realization of Mother's separateness (which means she can leave) and the fear is that she'll go off and one will be abandoned forever.

The immature, dependent offspring wants desperately to deny their basic differentness as individuals—and so does the immature, dependent adult. The underlying wish, the longing, is to regress to the bliss of infancy, when mother and child were one. Both adult and child, observe the psychotherapists, long to be "engulfed by a caring other." In short, the immature adult—like the young child—can be so terrified by feelings of separateness that she or he rushes to merge her personality into that of another person. Such a problem exists because it has been impossible to accept what every mature person must learn to accept: that we are all, each of us, alone in our own bodies. Each of us must depend, ultimately, on his or her own self.

For some people this basic fact of human existence proves, however, too painful for facing. If one or both partners in a marriage must deny their basic separateness and differentness (a denial of separation which is like the young child's denial that mother is a separate being who can go away) then they may be forced to merge identities—to the diminishment of each person's own individuality. What results from such a fusion is not loving empathy between two separate and adult persons. It is simply a doomed and clumsy effort to regain a state of early "oneness," to regain the lost bliss of infancy, when one was utterly and totally cared for. And it doesn't solve the underlying problem, which is an existential one.

By this I mean that denying one's own identity can't forever delay that final recognition of one's separateness. The knowledge that we are, each of us, alone in our own skins; and that the most intimate relationship with another human being is always, ultimately a finite thing. The denial being made, however, involves not only a denial of one's separateness but of one's eventual death. Because death is, as we all are made to realize during the course of growing and maturing, the final individual experience.

A cosmic, terrible loneliness must accompany so fearsome and profound a realization. Some adults may, therefore, "because they are feeling needy and alone, yearn for and try to recapture with their mates the primitive, continual empathetic exchange of a young preverbal infant with his mother," write co-authors Wexler and Steidl. They may strive to be utterly protected, utterly cared for, in their utterly dependent state—to avoid feelings of separateness and differentness.

This was, I believe, the deeper, truer truth of Doris Nordlund's situation. Clearly, she'd experienced herself as lacking in certain vital things, at the very outset of her marriage. She'd existed, in many ways, at the whim of the other people who'd been passing through her life. She'd had no sense of a good and positive self *within* herself and, indeed, hadn't done much of the adolescent and early-adult work involved in becoming "me, the person that I am." Little wonder that her self-ness, undeveloped as it was, had submerged itself immediately in the requirements and demands of Eric Nordlund's life.

Doris hadn't any demands, nor had she any strong requirements of her own. She could follow her husband anywhere he needed or wanted to go. She could make his wishes her wishes, his tastes and preferences her own. She could be part of who he was, and that was fine; she was fine. But drinking all the while, always drinking.

Old Ghosts

It may be argued that Doris Nordlund, who'd lived alone for such an extended period of her early adult life (in her own apartment, when she'd worked as a beautician; during that stint in the WAVES; later on, at Michigan State, and so forth) had achieved her independence long before her marriage to Eric. But her own experience of herself during that time was far from being one of developing autonomy, a sense of respect for the self, and the confidence that she could sustain herself on her own inner resources. It had been, instead, a kaleidoscope of distractions, of changing relationships, of ungratifying confirmations *from men* about the sort of woman she really was. These relationships were fashioned after that first female-and-male model, her own relationship with her father.

Doris hadn't given a great deal of thought, during those cruising-about, early adult years, to the situation that had existed in her home and the pattern of the things that had happened to her there. But her life *itself* had demonstrated, had indeed predicated itself upon that past. Her way of relating to men knew and was testimony to those old truths of her existence. In any case, during those years of young-adult "independence," she'd been playing out her father's prescription for living. She was the bad girl, *par excellence;* drinking, partying, sleeping around. With her marriage—that jolly, drunken marriage—she'd suddenly tried to turn it all around, to put an end to that style of being entirely. She'd been in flight from being that person, that un-valued person, ever since.

A whole vision of herself as a wife, as a respectable and valued woman, had been what she'd gained as a result of that oddly casual-seeming event. So in a sense, if her marriage now disintegrated, it wasn't only emptiness that she'd have to contend with: it was a void that would be haunted by that old, degraded self-image. If she were no longer the good and faithful wife of Eric Nordlund, who would she or could she be? Once again the bad, evil, alien, disreputable, degraded female of her father's old imprecations and predictions? Her fear wasn't only a fear of being alone; but a fear of being alone and at the mercy of that inner specter.

Finding Emotional Security

Throughout the entire first phase of our interviews—which stretched through August and into the latter weeks of September—Doris Nordlund's primary goal remained that of finding what she termed "emotional security" with her husband, Eric.

"What would emotional security with him actually *be?*" I asked her on one occasion. "Could you describe it? Say what it would be like?"

"Oh, just being able to depend on him," she responded wistfully. "I'm an extraordinarily dependent person, that way. I mean, emotionally . . . I have big requirements."

I smiled: "And what are those requirements?"

"To be held often. To be reassured . . . that I'm of value to him. As a wife, and as a person. And as a friend . . . I'm never, never satisfied about this, I'm never convinced. I have to be told it again and again: that I really am loved and cared for, that I am appreciated. . . ." Her voice trailed off.

I asked after a few moments, whether she thought that her need for reassurances had, perhaps, put unfair demands upon her husband. Doris nodded, murmured that the answers she received never did really satisfy. "That question—'Do you love me?'—It already says you're doubting," she shook her head as if to underscore the wrongness of such an approach. She wagged her finger, too, like a reproving schoolteacher. "And you mustn't doubt. Not after twenty-one years," she added. Then she said: "Eric has his faults, as I have mine; but I know that he's fond of me."

"*Fond* of you?"

She reddened slightly: "I mean there's love between us."

"Oh. When you said 'fond' it sounded like something cooler than love."

"There's love between us," she responded quickly, "and also, he appreciates me as his friend." She would be going back home to their citrus farm in Brazil, a few weeks hence, as Eric had been importuning her to do. The only condition she'd laid down, in advance of her return, was that—chaste though his affections for Patricia might be—Patricia Halkett was to be out of their house.

Officially speaking, i.e., from a medical standpoint, the depressive illness was ended. The patient, Doris Walsh Nordlund, had responded superbly to antidepressant drug therapy combined with some exploration of the psychological dilemmas that had led her to this particular life impasse (and to her suicidal crisis). For the foreseeable future she could remain on maintenance dosages of her medication, Parnate, and she was therefore free to go home.

What, nevertheless, would she be going back to? It was difficult to avoid feeling somewhat pessimistic about what might be awaiting her —and impossible to avoid feeling concerned. For it wasn't only the many questionable aspects of the "best friend and husband" situation

—nor even that Patricia and Eric had been living alone in the same house for the seven weeks that she'd been away—that were the only issues at hand. The gloomy truth was that she and Eric, as a couple, sounded like a sad and pallid pair. Two people, living together locked in a truncated, semi-dead relationship. Their visitor's arrival—like a litmus paper dipped into that invisible yet palpable marital atmosphere —had probably only served to make all that was silently amiss apparent and explicit.

Would maintenance levels of Parnate, despite the real miracles the medication had wrought in New Haven, be equally effective once Mrs. Nordlund had returned to the precipitating, and still stressful circumstances? Doris insisted, at that juncture, that she was perfectly aware of the difficulties she would be facing when she returned to Brazil. She was, nevertheless, feeling more and more positive about her marriage; at least, she was positive about wanting to save it.

Distance, for one thing, and the remission of her depression, for another, were causing her to see a great many matters in a different light. "It is really true," she admitted, during the last interview we had prior to her departure for Brazil, "that Eric isn't intellectually stimulating at all. But I've come to realize that, at age fifty-two, I can't expect to have everything. Am I going to give up everything I *do have* for that English twit? Am I going to give up my farm, for which I've worked and fought, with my own sweat and blood—and my citrus trees, my animals, my parrot, my house . . . all that's mine? Why should I give it all up for *her?*" Her voice was rising, and Doris' blue eyes started forward, seeming to bulge indignantly out of her head.

I shook my own head. But she had, I thought, almost given up *all* of these things very recently. She had come very close to dying. I was remembering, as well, a remark she'd made at some point during our initial conversation. She'd said she knew she ought never to return to Brazil because she might not live if she did so. I asked, now: "What *would* you give all of those things up for—the farm and so forth—do you think?"

She answered, angry and determined, that she wouldn't give them up for anything or for anyone! "No, my husband isn't perfect," she added immediately, "but then, I haven't ever heard of one that is." She'd made her decision.

It was Doris' belief that Eric's love for Patricia had remained nonphysical throughout the entire time of her own absence from the farm. He had assured her of this in his letters repeatedly; and he had kept asking her to return. His affection for their guest was, he'd insisted throughout, a quasi-parental one. He thought of Patricia (in reality only nine years younger than his wife) as just a "little gal," as the child that they'd never been capable of having.

I suppose that Mrs. Nordlund's deep need to believe in this, her husband's, version of events was understandable. But I was astonished to see how much her need to deny what was most probably happening had overwhelmed her ordinary, plain common sense.

In any case, she departed for South America in late September; and by mid-October, she was back.

A New Life

When I saw her again, just after her return to New Haven, I was struck by the difference between *this* Doris Nordlund and the woman I had met initially. She wasn't depressed, when she came back; not even mildly. If I'd been asked to describe her I would have said she was a tallish, attractive, rather competent-seeming woman, who was well able to speak for herself. This, in contrast to the scared, almost shrunken person whose voice volume had rarely risen above the level of a whisper!

The worst had happened. During her brief stay in Brazil she and her husband had parted with finality. They had, she told me, signed a legal and financial separation agreement—the best arrangement that could be effected, she'd added, in a country where divorce laws are nonexistent. "That was the end of it," she remarked wryly, "my twenty-one years of fidelity."

There was about her an almost gay sense of relief; that "glad to be alive" feeling of someone who has just come through a near thing. And she had about her a new kind of energy and purpose as well. Doris Nordlund wanted to talk, that fall afternoon, about the various kinds of next-moves that she was contemplating. But first she wanted to talk about what had happened during that brief two-week sojourn in Brazil.

"I dreaded going back," she confessed now, though Doris had been unwilling to admit to any such feelings in the days just before her departure. "I really didn't want to return to the farm, and to that isolation; but at that time I really couldn't have *seriously* thought of leaving my husband. The idea of it was still deeply inconceivable to me."

I asked her why this was so? "I'm not sure." Her voice was hesitant and full of doubt. "At that time—I guess—I thought I could go back and get busy on a long writing project. And also—take over my tractor again, get back on the farm." She stopped. Her blue eyes had taken on a faraway expression. "The farm, actually, had fallen down in the months I'd been gone." She lifted her shoulders lightly, then met my gaze: "I can't answer your question," she admitted frankly. "It's as though, whenever I started to think about ending my marriage, I wasn't able to continue thinking those thoughts through. It wasn't in my head, really, when I went back. The idea," she explained, "of terminating my marriage."

The choice of that word was so odd that it brought an ironic half smile to my lips: "You were thinking, a bit earlier though, about the possibility of terminating your life . . . ?"

Doris laughed at that notion; and I repeated the question. Why had she been so unable to contemplate the notion of ending her marriage— even *after* acknowledging the fact that, once sober, she had realized that there was nothing there in terms of a real relationship? She was, again, hesitant: "That's a rough one," she said, speaking slowly. "I think . . . well . . . I was sick when I wanted to end my life, and now I was going home well. There was no more of that awful fear I'd been living with; I was free of guilt and anxiety. The feeling was . . . there were some big issues to be worked out at home, clearly, but now *I* was competent. I believed, when I went back, that it would be possible to rebuild our marriage."

She stopped speaking, took a sip of coffee from the mug she held in her hand, then said, "When I got home, I was furious with Eric." Almost like a character actress, asked to step into an old familiar role for a moment, Doris Nordlund took on that *other* personality; she looked tense, tight with unexpressed anger, mildly depressed.

That Old Loneliness

It was I who broke the silence. I asked Doris whether she'd been angry *before* seeing her husband again?

"No," she responded, "not until we'd spent a little time together. I had *reasons* to be angry," she added mysteriously, "but I wasn't. Not until I was actually with him again for a while."

During the long journey home, nevertheless, she'd begun feeling sadder and sadder. To defend herself against bad feelings she had, recounted Doris, made an effort to remember all of the good and supportive—even complimentary—things that her therapist in New Haven, Dr. Julian Lieb, had put into her head. Dr. Lieb had told her that she was actually a strong person, in many ways; he'd told her that she was highly intelligent, unusual and even remarkable. Her effort, on the long flight back to Brazil, was "to concentrate on everything that would make me feel more happy and less sick." (Later, when she'd repeated those compliments to Eric, he'd appeared to be quite puzzled. He'd commented that he couldn't see what that doctor was talking about, for he considered her nothing out of the ordinary!) She was trying to establish in her own mind a good image of herself: "Something that, once back there, I would be able to hold onto. . . ."

"And do you think"—I leaned forward in my chair—"that you could have held onto that image for, say, a year?"

She shook her head at once: "No."

"How long, then, do you think you could have held on—?" Her laughter interrupted me.

"Another three hours, perhaps? *No*," she amended the statement with another burst of laughter, "another hour and a half! . . . *Maybe!*" The mirthful expression disappeared then, and she reminded me quite seriously that she had taken my photograph before her departure. She had also taken a picture of her doctor; and of several new friends that she'd made, in the New Haven area. These photos, scraps of paper were—and she said so quite seriously—what she was depending upon to give her "emotional support" during the difficult readjustment that awaited her in Brazil.

"I arrived with the aircraft at São Paulo," Doris continued, "and Eric swooped down and made a big public display of loving-husband-meeting-wife-after-long-separation. We got into the car, and I felt nothing. Nothing. I was numb. There was simply nothing to say."

As if to underscore those words, she stopped speaking at that moment. She shot me a peculiar, almost unreadable glance; and I realized that she was blushing. Her voice was expressionless and flat, though, when she spoke again. "I'd had a letter from Patricia that arrived—literally—as I was checking out of the Holiday Inn. She berated me for not appreciating my wonderful husband. She also said straight out that she was his mistress."

I jumped slightly, startled; but Doris shrugged. "I wasn't really surprised."

"And Eric?" I asked.

"What?" Her voice was neutral.

"Did he know about your having gotten that letter? Before your arrival, I mean?"

She shook her head. "He claimed he didn't. He claimed he never knew of the existence of such a letter! I'm not sure now that I believe him . . . in my own mind, it's just something I'll probably never know. But in any case, there was a long, fairly silent drive home—a five-hour drive—and then we got up on the hill, heading downward. I could see the farm spread out below, and the house, for the first time. And suddenly that old feeling of loneliness started creeping all over me. It was eerie; I was supposedly cured of my depression. And I thought to myself: 'What's this? I am on this superb antidepressant medicine, so what is this whole gloominess bit? Aren't I better?' "

Revisiting the Battlefield

She knew at that moment that she was going home to an empty house: "It was my first intuition—my first indication—that I wouldn't be able to work things out." She shrugged, sighed.

On the second day, said Doris, she had walked around the place and found it strange. "There was so little there that was of real significance," she related, her voice quizzical, like someone describing a return to a formerly important scene, like a battlefield, and finding the change difficult to comprehend. "It was as if none of this actually had any real meaning for me, after all. There was nothing inside or outside that house that counted; there was nothing there for *me*."

She paused, then corrected herself. "No, that's not completely true. There was a little girl on the farm, Constanza. We'd spent a good deal of time together, and I had been teaching her to read. My little Constanza, as I later realized, was one of the reasons I'd had to come back. She was the child of a couple that worked on the farm, but I'd come to care for her in a motherly way. And there were other creatures on the place—my animals—whom I loved. But on the third day, a kind of an emotional barrier seemed to slam down. I suppose"—her expression was pained—"that was necessary. Otherwise, I wouldn't have been able to do it, to go away and leave them. . . ." Her voice was, again, hazy and uncertain.

But when she resumed the story it was as though a dial adjustment had been made. She spoke more clearly, and with force: "On the fourth or fifth day, I went into the market town nearby. And all of the people I saw there, people I'd known for years, seemed made of plastic. They just weren't real to me, and I knew that I didn't belong there. And I thought: 'My God, this is all killing me, or it will.' Everything was so old, so tired, so closed in. People talking and saying the same things they'd said ten years earlier."

What Doris was describing was a mild experience of what is called "depersonalization." That is, a pervasive feeling of estrangement from a world which seems made of pasteboard: the sense that oneself and one's surroundings are devoid of any true reality. To feel depersonalized is to be in a place without really *being* there (and to feel that the place itself is not there either). In terms of the endangered self, there is safety in nonexistence. If one isn't really there, and if nothing real is happening, then one can obviously suffer no pain. Can pain exist in a vacuum?

I Knew I Could Not Live There

Eric, on that first night of their reunion, was impotent. He told Doris that this had nothing to do with his own sexual powers; the fact was that he just didn't find her attractive. "My therapist had told me," related Doris, her voice even and quiet, "that if ever I *did* decide to leave my husband I would know that I must do so—I would know it with utter and complete clarity. And I did. That's all that my doctor ever said, but when the moment did come, I can tell you that I knew I could not live there."

The statement hung in the air, like the resounding end of a speech. But when these words had died into silence, she took up the theme again: "Nor could I work. I wanted to write, but my energy and creativity had simply drained out of me as if my body were leaking—as if my body were full of holes. I'd look up from my typewriter; and oh, there would be the same scene that I'd looked at so many many times." A desolate expression came and settled upon her features. I could imagine her so easily, sitting at her typewriter in the Brazilian jungle, and straining desperately to write.

"The river, the beautiful river," Doris' voice was musing, "it was like looking at the same lovely painting over and over again, until at last you come to detest it. The scene was a truly beautiful one; but how I loathed it! There was no affection in that place, no joy, no appreciation of the person that I am . . . no warmth, no spirit, no companionship."

She had come to the end of that catalogue of lacks and failures. For some reason I picked up on the last one and asked her: "What would companionship be like?" She shook her head as if to say she didn't comprehend the question, and I said: "How would you describe it?"

The question seemed to be one that she found awkward or difficult to answer: "Oh. Mmm. Discussing things, I suppose." She stopped. "Companions are companions," she went on then, almost impatiently. "They're close; they're sharing. They don't sit off in different corners and say: 'Look, I think it's going to rain tomorrow,' and so that's the end of the conversation, until the next day! Companions *talk* about things," she added wistfully. "Reality things . . . mutual needs . . . wants, desires, dreams, fantasies, gossip." She stopped again. When she resumed speaking, her voice was pensive: "If I could find all of that—and that, to me, would be a big thing to find—" Doris broke off in mid-sentence, shrugged. "But it wasn't there; not in that house; not with Eric. It was a dead world, really. Or if not dead, then stagnant. I knew that, very shortly. I knew that if I stayed there the life would drain out of me. I knew I was going to go under."

Those Great White Spaces

I had first met Doris Nordlund in August; it was October when she returned. The day on which we met again was warm, breezy, and bright; we were in a week of Indian summer. The walls of her not-yet-furnished apartment were painted white, and they reflected the brilliance of the autumn sun. As we talked I would notice her judicious gaze traveling along those empty walls. I thought that, even as she went over what had happened, a part of her mind was preoccupied with thoughts about what would hang where—how she would fill those great white spaces.

Her flat, newly rented, was on the sixth floor of a downtown New Haven apartment house. The sounds of traffic floated up through a partly open sliding glass window. On a nearby dinette table stood an electric portable typewriter; she was at work, Doris said, on the fourth chapter of what was to be a largely autobiographical novel. But writing that book was only one part of her future plans.

She had enough money to live on, at least for the meanwhile; and so she planned to use the next months to do some formal studying of two languages—Portuguese and Spanish—both of them languages in which she had become fluent during her years in Brazil. "I toy, at times, with the idea of teaching . . . ?" The statement ended as a question. But then, everything about her present life was a question. It was all tentative, open-ended, undecided.

It was, she told me, both frightening and refreshing at the same time. She had a lover—a younger man, a fellow student in a writing course she'd taken the previous summer.

Her new love affair was not, she added, going to turn into anything permanent or reliable, but the sex, "after those twenty-one years with Eric," was something renewing and absolutely wonderful. "Now and for some time past, Eric hasn't been potent in the evenings," Doris explained. "It's the alcohol." He'd become accustomed to awakening her when the liquor had run through his system, at about three or four o'clock in the morning. "He'd roll over on top of me, then roll around a little, and that would be that."

She grimaced. "It was pretty awful, even when I was drinking. But much worse when I'd become this cold-sober woman."

She leaned forward, then, with the laugh of a schoolgirl telling a secret: "Poor Eric, though! Imagine trying to make love when the woman's completely clear-eyed and you're fumbling and messing around, half drunk!" She shook her head, hung it as if in penitence for her unwifely sobriety. Then she spoke of her current lover, a part-time playwright and a teacher at a small local college. She had had, she said, more joy in bed during the brief beginning of this affair than she'd had in the past decade, and more, with her husband.

"I am feeling adventurous at the moment," observed Doris, and added that she was also feeling strong enough to explore a world that did, after all, offer possibilities for pleasure and enjoyment. She wanted to *do* things. She wanted to write. "I feel that I can do—and can become—whoever I need and have to be. It's as if I've been blown clear out of a pattern, or way of life, that I'd been struggling to fit myself into for years. And one that, as I've come to realize, always made me desperately uncomfortable."

She rearranged the high collar of her white turtleneck sweater as if the very mention of discomfort had made it feel too tight. "How would you describe it?" I asked her. "That pattern, that uncomfortable way of life . . . ?" I glanced down, at that moment, and noticed that the spools of the tape recorder had stopped turning around and around.

It was the second side of that tape. I was surprised by the realization that we'd been talking for an hour and a half. "Oh," continued Doris, "that of being wife to a man with whom I actually shared no interests —not when we were both sober—and with whom I'd never been able to make a relationship." She stood up then, and strolled casually over to look out of the window.

I pressed the OFF button of the Sony; then I pressed EJECT. The small plastic window flew open, and I took the tape spool out, replaced it in its case. Doris, her back to me, was gazing down at the traffic moving along six stories below. "Light," she murmured, "cars going by. Buildings with *people* in them! Not alligators, lizards, snakes, frogs, toads—*people!*" I walked over, stood beside her, looked down at the scene which so moved her.

Coming of Age

A red Mercedes with an unsightly dent in the rear fender was waiting for the street light to change at a four-way intersection. An old woman, mincing along in what looked like ridiculously high heels was waiting at the same corner, and waiting for the same light to change. "This is, whatever happens, a *living* situation," Doris continued, her voice sounding almost awed. "There's all sorts of life around me, *human* life." A mild breeze, blowing in upon us from that half-open window, moved the brown bangs on her forehead. It exposed a row of furrows in the skin below.

"It's not that I'm not scared when I start thinking about all the uncertainties," confessed Doris, as though responding to a worry alluded to aloud. "I realize that what's ahead of me isn't going to be particularly easy. But being fifty-two isn't, you know, the same thing as being ninety-eight!"

She turned to me, her blue eyes wide and staring: "Before, you see, I was depressed . . . to hope for anything seemed futile. I was incapable of taking any action on my own behalf; even incapable of any clear thought. And I'd *been* like that for so many years!"

Alcoholism, and after that, the surfacing of her depression, had, she said, "delayed my coming of age." She gave her head a brief nod, as if to signify having admitted to and accepted past misfortunes and losses. "I believe, now, that those two long experiences—being a drunk, and then being a depressive—prevented certain things from happening, in terms of my simply growing up. Things that are, strangely enough, just *beginning* to happen! It's hard to explain it: I'm fifty-two years old, and it's crazy, really. But I feel as if I'm experiencing myself as someone very new." She smiled, and I smiled too.

I was getting into my jacket, buttoning the top button. "Who was 'she,' then, the person you left behind? The person who used to be you?" I asked. She stiffened, her expression startled. "Fear," she responded instantly. "Fear was the old self, fear of everything and of nothing. It was my constant companion, with me at all times; but it's just gone now. I don't know why. Drugs? A change of situation?" She shrugged: "All that I know is that I thank God for being here." Her voice was fervent. "Thank God that that nutty letter that I sent out actually was *answered*. Thank God for the fact that I am alive!"

She thought very often—Doris laughed as she said it—about the preposterousness of her having written to that unknown Francis Kirchner on the basis of a review in an issue of *Time* magazine which had actually been a few months old when she'd first seen it! She thought, too, of the outlandishness of Francis Kirchner's tone of command—his telling her where she must go and insisting that she must start out at once. Anything less, anything not quite so demanding, would have been fatal, as she now realized; and she spoke of his letter's arrival with awe, as though she were speaking of a miracle.

It was extraordinary, the fact that that had happened. It was extraordinary that her misaddressed letter to Kirchner had actually been forwarded! It made her feel, she told me, that despite the many hard things that she'd had to deal with in the course of her difficult lifetime, she was an extraordinarily lucky woman.

Saved

Driving home from that interview, I reflected that Doris Nordlund—despite the exotic particularities of her circumstances—was really a very recognizable sort of a person, who'd worked out an easily recognizable pattern of female existence. She was the woman who'd found her place in life, who'd even been "saved" by her marriage. Which is to say that the man she'd found had, like Prince Charming, had a kingdom of his own to offer—a way of life that was his—and it was around this way of being, this world, that they'd worked out a mutual identity. She'd given her life to his life, in every sense of the word. But they hadn't lived happily ever after, for she desperately needed feedback about her value and worth as a human being. And Eric could not or would not give comfort.

Now it is true that depressive disorder is a recurrent illness; and that depressed people can *feel*, to the people around them, like greedy, unsatisfiable babies who can never be comforted, never satiated, never cared for enough. But a most peculiar thing, that I've noticed over and over again in such situations, is that the woman—who *is*, frequently, someone who has been terribly injured early in her lifetime—gravitates toward a certain kind of man. A man who is, as I believe Eric Nordlund probably was, demanding, withdrawn, narcissistic, and ultimately ungiving. Why is it that a person like Doris, who needed *more* support than another woman might have needed had linked herself, and her whole sense of self-esteem, to a man who had far *less* than many other men might have had to give? Does he, on his own part, want his woman weakened and dependent—so that he can control the situation, from a position of strength, and do so by the withdrawal of his affection? And does she cede to him so total and tyrannical a power, which is to say, dominion over her entire sense of worth and value as a human being, *because* of those early wounds? Who can say? Severe depressions such as Doris had suffered surely do emerge in an organism that is *vulnerable* (the biological permission that allows it to happen is there); but they also develop within a certain environment, a particular psychological and social context. In Doris' case, the context had had everything to do with a cold and disapproving man upon whom she nevertheless *depended*. It was to such a context that her very consciousness, her awareness of self, had first wakened. And it was one that she'd been re-creating ever since.

There was always a man who *could* make it all better, and could give her another whole sense of herself, if he *would* . . . but he wouldn't. For the men that she'd loved had, in Doris' words, "invited comparisons with my father." Indeed, that twenty-one years of fidelity to Eric sounded, in many ways, like the first sixteen years of her life, the years of fidelity to her father. In both instances, she'd been in fairly isolated circumstances, and struggling desperately to get some recognition from a man who, on his own part, seemed to have nothing good or positive to give her.

One wondered, in a way, who Eric Nordlund himself would have been, in the absence of Doris. When she'd met him, he was a man who'd detested his mother and had recently divorced his faithless wife; but he always remained, in my own mind, a shadowy figure. Was he depressed himself, and drinking for that reason? It was impossible to know. He was, in a way, a willing actor who'd stepped with sinister readiness into this restaging of Doris' childhood drama. He'd fallen into the male role in the scenario, and stretched her out, almost obligingly, on the rack of her own dismal expectations. As for Doris herself, she'd either found, or subtly fashioned, the man who *would* disapprove of her, fail her, and ultimately reject her entirely.

It was not until this, the sixth decade of living, that Doris had begun to discern the existence of a pattern—and she didn't want to run through it again. She felt, she acknowledged, like someone who's been acting under some form of hypnotic instruction; and who's just beginning to awaken, to look around her in puzzlement, to wonder about the things she's been doing. She'd been able, just recently, to step back and to look at her own life—almost as an interested spectator—and to understand the nature of the relationships that she "happened" to get into, the repeating cycle of the circumstances that had been her early life's conditions. Now that she could *recognize* the system, it would be possible, she hoped, to beat it.

"This is my chance," she told me; on the day that she told me that she and Francis Kirchner had fallen in love. "I know you are going to think it's preposterous," she added at once, with a laugh. I laughed, and agreed that it *was*.

I knew that she and Francis Kirchner had become acquainted after her arrival in the United States—knew that they'd continued seeing one another—knew that Kirchner was single, either separated or divorced. But still, the idea that she and her rescuer had become lovers, and had fallen *in love* with each other! It was preposterous in just about every way that I could think of, and certainly preposterously romantic. It was every disappointed housewife's dream of a saving man, a stranger from far away, who gallops upon the scene to swoop her away from her suffering, who comes in answer to her plea! It was at once ridiculous and quasi-mythical.

But Doris was, in truth, confronting a need to change an entire way of being, a total life structure, everything that had gone before, in fifty-plus years of living. She'd had to walk out of a former existence, and everything it had meant to her—that "twenty-one years of fidelity"—and attempt to replace it with something new. Her circumstances, at the time she'd tried to kill herself, had erupted into what psychiatrist Norman Tabachnick has termed a "creative suicidal crisis"—a powerful wish to die that intervenes between a person's movement away from a life that truly is no longer tenable and a subsequent construction of an entirely new way of being. Doris' depression, and her suicidal effort, had marked the coming to a head of an existential boil.

The old world, the world of the farm in Brazil and the faithful wife of Mr. Eric Nordlund, was no longer only painfully ungratifying; it was lost to her, and would no longer contain her. She couldn't even use the raw materials of what had gone before; she had to make a new life, in a new place, with a personnel that was entirely novel. It was a lot to *do*, at her stage of life, but she thought that now—given much less pain, thanks to Parnate and the insights she'd been gaining into her own behavior—she might be capable of doing things very differently.

Would things, in fact, be different?—or would Francis Kirchner, in the course of time, "show his true colors" and become transformed into that cold, disapproving, and unloving man who'd always been so dreaded, and yet who was, for all that, *the* man—the man of her wishful memories—who was so emotionally familiar? Would this, her most recent love story, turn out to be a *different* kind of story? Or would Francis Kirchner become, because he was scripted to become one, another disappointer and betrayer? The answers to these questions weren't, I realized, to be found in the present. They were ahead on her life's journey, and to be discovered in the future. But one could hope. That was, as Doris told me, one of the main things that was so different about her, at this moment: "Hope," she said, "is something that is possible."

Addendum: Drugs

The antidepressant drug that Doris Nordlund was being maintained on, a drug called Parnate, is actually a tricky and somewhat dangerous medication. Parnate is a compound that is chemically similar to iproniazid—the anti-tuberculosis medication that was discovered to have mood-lifting effects (see Chapter Eight). Iproniazid was the first drug ever found to be useful in the treatment of severe depression; but there were, from the outset, a bag of accompanying difficulties—"side effects" that could range from the problematic to the very serious.

For medications in this group (brand names include Parnate, Nardil, Marplan, Actomol, etc.) interact with chemical substances found in certain common foods, such as sour cream, chocolate, and raisins, in such a way that the person's blood pressure may shoot up suddenly and dangerously. "Side effects" can be anything from severe nausea to dizziness to fainting. The patient using one of these drugs, who eats one among the forbidden foods, may even go into a hypertensive crisis that results in a severe stroke, or in death. That individual must, therefore, be assessed as both very needy and very trustworthy. Taking this kind of medication requires a great deal of self-discipline.

The list of foods that are on the banned list isn't a very long one; but it includes foods that aren't always easy to avoid. Red wine and aged cheeses, such as Stilton and Cheddar, are *absolutely prohibited*. Aged cheeses contain a large amount of a substance called tyramine, which is produced by the fermentation of protein. Tyramine would, in ordinary circumstances, act to raise the body's blood pressure, if it weren't routinely deactivated by the actions of certain enzymes. These enzymes are put out of commission by the antidepressant medication (the drug's mood-lifting effects are theoretically linked to its blocking and inhibiting of the enzyme that breaks down and degrades the important biogenic amines, such as norepinephrine and serotonin). Eating a nice succulent cheese omelet can, therefore, introduce a substance—tyramine—which acts to raise bodily blood pressure without meeting any countervailing internal forces.

The person taking the drugs must be reliable enough to adhere to a fairly punctilious diet. The proscribed foodstuffs are: cheese, wine, beer, pickled herring, sour cream, yoghurt, fava beans or lima beans, chicken livers, canned figs, raisins, chocolate, soy sauce, coffee, licorice, snails, sauerkraut. If this list makes the use of a drug like Parnate sound extremely difficult and somewhat hazardous, then one must balance it against the situation of a Doris Nordlund. Her depression was itself a potentially lethal illness.

She had been depressed enough to desire death, and had come close enough to having her wish come true. She still *did* begin feeling depressed when she tried lowering her medication levels. But she'd been doing well on Parnate, been faithful about the diet; and had been experiencing nothing at all disturbing in the way of side effects. So what was involved was a balancing off of the possible risks that she faced.

The MAO Inhibiting Drugs

Drugs that are similar to Parnate constitute one category of antidepressant drugs: These drugs, as a group, are called the MAO inhibitors. They have, in the recent past, been coming into ever-increasing usage, for they seem to be particularly effective in treating certain *types* of depressive disorders, particularly the "atypical depressions" characterized by great anxiety and phobic kinds of fears. One particular kind of phobia, agoraphobia, which is fear of going outside, can be treated with an MAO inhibitor such as Parnate, with an astonishing and inexplicable success. The drug seems able to calm the panic attacks related to leaving home base—attacks that, according to psychiatrist Dr. Donald Klein, represent a special form of separation anxiety —which would, otherwise, leave the depressed person imprisoned, dependent, terrorized by unnamed fears that kept her rigidly housebound.

The MAO inhibitor medications are also, suggest Dr. Klein and his colleagues at the New York State Psychiatric Institute in New York, the drugs of choice in a particular form of depression to which they have tentatively given the name "hysteroid dysphoria." As its name suggests, this patient is most likely to be a woman. The clinical description has it that she is someone who is exceedingly sensitive to rejection, particularly in a romantic involvement. She is someone who, on losing a lover, is liable to experience a severe depressive crash. At that point, she will go into a leaden paralysis; will be unable to get herself out of bed; and will ruminate endlessly about the lost person. She'll oversleep, and may gorge herself on sweets during this period.

Occasionally, she'll turn to amphetamines and alcohol. What brings her out of the depression, eventually, is either re-establishing the relationship with the same person, or finding someone new. She is someone who can't live if she hasn't got someone else—someone whom she clings to for all he's worth (and often far more).

She overvalues and idealizes that someone. At the same time, she's inordinately demanding of his attention and affection. So demanding, in fact, that she tends to drive the desperately needed someone away—and she tumbles into another depression. Her very vulnerability leads her, then, to repeat the same performance—to grab on to the next "someone" in the same demanding fashion, and holds on to him for dear life. She lurches in this way from one relationship to the next, with a crash to punctuate the end of each of these romantic episodes.

People with this sort of history, and this sort of personality style, seem to do curiously well on the MAO inhibitor drugs, such as Parnate and Nardil. When they stay on the medication, they are protected from the periodic depressive crashing. They become more accessible to therapeutic insight about the self-destructive ways in which they're living, because they are just less driven in their relationships with other people—less clamoring and clinging. That craving for constant attention, affection, and applause appears to diminish; and the person becomes far less of a needy, seductive little baby girl.

This type of patient has been characterized as someone who tends to be narcissistic, vain, and histrionic. "Many of them," Dr. Klein told me, "are actresses, who *have* to have that response from the audience. When they are O.K., they are flamboyant, charming, theatrical, alluring; but when they crash, they're pathetically weak. They feel destroyed."

Needless to say, both the description of the patient and the name of the category of illness itself, sounds like a vulgar sexual stereotype. "Hysteroid dysphoria," from the overeating of sweets to the narcissism and seductiveness, has the ring of a roundup of antifeminine biases! But there does seem to be a group of people who conform to this clinical picture; and drug therapy with an MAO inhibitor *can* produce very marked and striking changes in the whole way in which they go about living their lives! Parnate, Nardil, Marplan, and the like are, for some curious reason, specifically and differentially effective, in treating *this* person, both when she's in a depressive crash and afterward (i.e., when one is working against a recurrence). The peculiarity is that this type of individual doesn't respond, as Doris Nordlund hadn't responded, to the other major type of antidepressant therapy—the tricyclic antidepressants—with any symptom relief whatsoever. But she gets better *and* often stays better, as Doris had, on an MAO inhibitor.

The Tricyclic Antidepressants

The tricyclic antidepressants (the word "tricyclic," by the way, refers to the three-ring chemical structure of these compounds; see Mood and Medicine: Judith [1]) are the drugs that are most commonly prescribed. They are much less tricky, dangerous, and problematic to use; and they are given for the more common kinds of depression, in which the symptoms form a distinct and pretty clear-cut pattern. (See Appendix I.) The symptom picture is characterized, in most instances, by weight loss and sleep difficulty—particularly early-morning awakening. It is this symptom that, according to Dr. Gerald Klerman, Administrator of the Alcohol, Drug Abuse and Mental Health Association, *is the most specific indicator for the use of a tricyclic antidepressant medication.*

There is an unfortunate tendency, Klerman observed, for general physicians to treat sleep disturbances and anxiety in their patients with some form of mild tranquilizer. The doctor, in other words, focuses on one aspect of the problem, but never inquires about feelings of sadness, loss of interest in life, and guilt. The person is, then, given a medication which *won't help*—and *may hurt*—because tranquilizers such as Valium, Librium, and Miltown, are really depressants of the central nervous system. They may make the underlying depressive disorder worse.

A tricyclic antidepressant, such as Elavil (which also has sedative effects) will not only help with the sleep disturbance, but help with the depression as well. And in most cases, Dr. Klerman told me, the person will need antidepressant drug therapy for a delimited period of time.

His own method, he explained, is to build up the dosage until the patient is beginning to feel the improvement: "They say, 'I slept better' or 'I feel less pessimistic' or 'My appetite has improved.' Then I level off the medication for a while; and after the patient reports to me that she or he is back to her normal self, I gradually lower the dosage. People have, by the way, a very good sense of when they're back to normal. They'll say things like: 'I'm halfway there' or 'I'm three-quarters there'; they really do *know*."

The lowering of the dosage level is, he added, rather like a titration experiment in chemistry. It may be that after dropping the dose by 25 milligrams a week the person will say that she didn't sleep well, or became irritable with her children, or that she's lost her zest. "Generally speaking," Klerman said, "I keep lowering the dose, waiting a week or ten days between changes, until reaching the lowest possible levels at which the person can feel like her or his normal self. For the majority of people that will be zero in about three months."

This will mean that both the need for medication—and the depressive attack—are over.

Happiness and Drug Therapy

Shortly after their love affair had begun, when Doris Nordlund and Francis Kirchner were living in a honeymoon of happiness, I asked her how much longer she thought she'd be continuing her use of the antidepressant medications she was using? Doris answered that she and her doctor had tried dropping the dosage of her drugs just recently and that it had been a "real mind-blower . . . a mistake."

"Within a few days," she'd explained, "the fear came back . . . anxiety, dread. It was as though, really, there were just a thin curtain between myself and all of those things. I hadn't realized this; but you know, depressions like mine don't disappear; they don't go away. It's as if it's all still out there, waiting, and the antidepressants keep the symptoms covered all up. When I took away those few milligrams of Parnate, it was just all out there in wait for me. That came," she admitted, "as something of an unwelcome shock."

But *with* the medication, she felt well—more than well; she felt *happy*. And happiness was, she said, something new; something she'd not quite experienced before.

"As you must realize"—she fixed my eyes with her own steady blue-eyed stare—"I haven't been happy, ever, in my lifetime; I just have no happy memories, not even from when I was a little child. I didn't have, really, the faintest idea of what a thing called 'happiness' might *be*. And now I'm living and it *is* difficult to absorb! It's difficult to really believe in, difficult to accept my life now as *real*, a part of reality!" She shook her head swiftly, as if to prove to herself that she was awake. "And Francis"—her face was alight—"he's a great part of it; it's not just *Parnate*. No, oh no. Antidepressants can't warm me, or give me love, or do the kinds of things that Francis does. This compassion; this marvelous, tender, compassionate man, whose very touch is just *compassionate*. You know, my doctor said to me: 'Doris, you've been used all your life, one way or another, by one man or another; and this time it just isn't happening.'" She blushed slightly: "And he's right, it's true. . . ."

As for the drugs, she perceived her own situation in terms of an analogy that Francis Kirchner (whose book on his *own* severe depression had, initially, inspired Doris to write to him) liked to make. The analogy was between the diabetic and the person who is prone to depression: "A diabetic will take insulin for the rest of his life, once the illness develops and is serious. In the same way, I think I'll be on some form of antidepressants for the rest of mine. Because I know, after that little experience of dropping my dosage, that I'll go back into depression if I don't. And that means losing my self—my *real* self, whom I'm just in the process of finding—automatically. Because I *saw* that fear, again," she added, her voice intense, "I *felt* it." She was silent momentarily, then said: "It was right there looking at me."

"Do you believe," I asked her, my voice hesitant as I tried to frame the question that so persistently puzzled me and about which there was such vast and bitter psychiatric disagreement, "that it was *with* you, when you came into the world, this tendency to depression? Or do you believe that it was something that was acquired?"

Doris didn't hesitate before answering, without any rancor in her voice: "It was acquired, I'm sure."

In the Sixties

CHAPTER EIGHTEEN

Alone: Margaret Garvey

Everyone, at least everyone who lives long enough, gets old. Normal people do, and so do neurotics; optimists do, and pessimists do; people who are married, and single people; so do gregarious folk and those who are socially isolated. Each one of us who survives into the decades of the sixties, the seventies, or beyond, becomes—inevitably—an older or elderly person. These statements may seem both trivial and obvious, but in truth, the country of the aged is a land few people think very hard and seriously about before the time of life when they sense that they're *arriving* there. Somehow, throughout much of life, being old seems to be something that happens to other people.

Old age is, in a way, considered alien; and it's true that to reach the years of late maturity is to reach a place where life's conditions are, in many respects, different. This phase of existence will require, as have all important prior life phases, a flexible enough kind of coping and an ability to adapt to new, and often threatening, kinds of demands. But now, great requirements are being placed upon a biological organism that is aging—and is, therefore, less intact and smoothly functioning. An organism that must, moreover, exist in a shrinking social environment—one in which positive emotional feedback will, as a matter of course, be becoming less available.

For it is not unusual for a person to be, at this period of living, dealing with the illness or death of a spouse (an occurrence that's considered to be at the *top* of every list of stressful life events) and with the departures, illnesses, and deaths of other family members, and of close friends. One's children's attentions are diverted elsewhere, into their own families and their own lives: the world seems to have thinned out dramatically. Time itself, once such an abundant commodity, now exists in a limited and ever-diminishing supply.

For each individual, life has been a continuous process, punctuated by periodic normal and abnormal crises. The normal, which is to say normative, crises of maturation in adulthood have had to do with the ability to separate and to individuate; to become the person that one is. This has involved, necessarily, the achievement of an emotional distance from one's family of origin. The family has been converted, during the adolescent and early adult process, from a point at which it occupied an entire inner canvas, or tapestry; it has become one small part of what is a new and emerging design—a design for living that derives, somewhat, from the past; but is still of one's making and really one's own.

Beyond the separation process have come the successive psychological tasks of adult living: the making of commitments to loves that lie outside the family of origin; and then, the maturational task that Erik Erikson has termed "generativity"—the investment in establishing, nurturing, and guiding the upcoming younger generation. Each task, or psychosocial crisis, means the mastery of a new challenge and a new mode of being and relating—or it means maturational failure. The ascending scale of challenges (and possible defeats) is given to us, in the Eriksonian schema, as follows: Identity versus Role Confusion, Intimacy versus Isolation, Generativity versus Stagnation. The final task or set of possibilities that marks the years of late maturity is, as defined by Erikson, Integrity versus Despair.

Integrity is, in his words, "the acceptance of one's one and only life cycle as something that had to be and that, by necessity, permitted of no substitutions: it thus means a new, a different love of one's parents." This sounds somewhat overly schematic and even dogmatic; but what Erikson is positing, I think, is an acceptance of one's origins, and of the life that one has had, including all the mourned and ultimately integrated pain and suffering that one's one and only life cycle may have contained. It means an acceptance of who one is and what one has become.

Integrity refers, I believe, to a kind of emotional closure: one's existence, as one surveys it, seems to have had order and meaning, rather than to have been characterized by haphazardness and waste. There is a sense that one's world has had its measure of value and purpose; that one's life hasn't been, to borrow Macbeth's phrase, "a tale told by an idiot . . . signifying nothing." One doesn't look backward with a sense of existential disgust. The flavor of this period of life is one of discovery: who one was, and what one did are reviewed; this is a phase of final consolidation. One can discern the shape and outline of what has been; and examine the possibilities that remain, in terms of who one still may become. This summing-up process can be an experience that thrums with pleasure and contentment—or it can be a mixed bag—or it can become exquisitely painful. For some people may, having been strapped into the repetitive reconstruction of early childhood dilemmas, now confront the feeling that they've gone nowhere, and done nothing, with their lives. It's been a waste . . . and despair comes.

Despair comes, observes Erikson, when "the one and only life cycle is not accepted as the ultimate of life. Despair expresses the feeling that the time is now short, too short for the attempt to start another life, and to try out alternate roads to integrity." Mrs. Margaret Garvey, who will be met with shortly, *hadn't* had the life that she'd wanted; and now, in the late afternoon of her existence, there had come the realization that she really *would not have* another.

She'd been confronted, in her old age, with what had always been avoided earlier: the task of separating, of acknowledging and integrating her ultimate human aloneness. It was, to her, unbearable; and she was unbearably depressed.

But time was short, and there was no way to do it differently. Something had gone wrong, or been wrong (what was it?) but there was no time, or at least *not enough time*, to solve the problem. And the problem, unresolved, was being experienced with a searing intensity: it was as though, at this point in her life, the psychological bill had come due with a burden of accrued interest; she'd carried it over for too many decades, this bit of unfinished business. She'd avoided facing it by studiously complying with what had been expected of her. She'd certainly been the child her mother expected her to be; she'd repeated carefully, and played out a perfect imitation of the pattern of existence that her mother had led (as Mrs. Garvey's *own* daughter was to commence doing, in *her* time!).

Of course we all do, as Dr. Theodor Lidz observes in his book *The Person*, develop repetitive themes and patterns that color our existence and often determine the ways in which we respond to and try to cope with the tasks of the various phases of our lives: "In the inordinately complex task of seeking to understand an individual," he writes, "we can be guided by finding such repetitive patterns and leitmotifs. . . ." But, adds psychoanalyst Lidz, "sometimes the dominant theme results from an early childhood fixation and reiterates itself, unable to develop and lead onward, remaining in the same groove like the needle on a flawed phonograph record."

A source of despair, in the sixties and seventies, can proceed from a growing realization that one has, in fact, gone round and round in one's life, in repeated attempts to solve a desperately significant riddle —but that the riddle has never become articulated in such a way that one could work on it—could find a stopping-place, a solution. One's life story is approaching its conclusion; and yet, in some deep way, the story hasn't gone forward; the story of one's life feels hardly started. The grief and sense of waste that may be experienced now has to do with never quite having *had* it—the life that was, for want of a better word, authentic, in the sense that it was really one's own. One has to be ready to be finished with having been, when one has never actually succeeded in getting *to be*. Death is approaching and one has, somehow, never gotten *to live*.

As psychotherapists Christopher Dare and Lily Pincus have written (in *Secrets in the Family*): "People who in their childhood have been discouraged from being separate, and thus gaining a separate identity, have difficulties in letting go; they cling. Faced with death they are likely to cling to life, for to die is to accept the last separation, the breaking through the last boundary to the unknown."

For sixty-five-year-old Margaret Garvey, the past had been a sequence of disasters; the present was drab and hopeless; and the idea of the future dismal—but the idea of death, the death that felt nearer at this age, was absolutely *terrorizing*. It was as terrorizing, almost, as being alone: the two states were, in fact, indistinguishable.

A Biological Bolt-from-the-Blue

The diagnosis was a relatively uncomplicated one: unipolar, endogenous depression. The patient, Mrs. Margaret Garvey, was "unipolar" in the sense that her disturbed mood fluctuated in one direction only—downward—but gave no evidence of ever having moved up into the too-happy, ultimately manic emotional pole. She was "endogenous" (the word, as defined in Webster, means, "Produced from within; originating from or due to internal causes") in the sense that there seemed to be nothing happening in her life that could serve to explain so severe a depressive episode. She herself could think of no reasons for these feelings of desolation, awful fear, awful despair. The depression, she said, had descended upon her like a black cloud of devastation, and "it came from out of nowhere." But there was nothing to which she could link it, in terms of a trauma, a grief, a recent loss.

The only actual event in her life—the only thing that had actually *happened* to her—had been a minor foot accident she'd suffered about a year and a half earlier. She had slipped on the ice, Mrs. Garvey told me, and injured her foot and ankle. It had kept her confined to her apartment, and alone most of the time, for almost an entire month.

"I had to have a cast on my leg," her voice was so subdued and flatly affectless that I had continual difficulty in hearing her. "I couldn't get around, and had to spend most of the time in a wheel-chair . . . to do everything by myself." She paused. I moved my chair closer, for it was like trying to listen to a radio on which the volume has been turned too low. "There was no one to care for me, no one at all. My daughter lives in the apartment just above, but she works. She works in an office. She's divorced, and she has to take care of her children. So . . ." She sighed, shrugged; saying any more would be too much of a task. Margaret Garvey shook her head hopelessly.

"I didn't want to be a burden to her, to my daughter, I mean," she offered suddenly, "as my own mother was a burden to me."

Tears welled in her eyes, and I said: "Your mother was a burden to you? In what ways?"

Before her mother's death, two years earlier, explained Mrs. Garvey, she had nursed her through a long and difficult terminal illness. "She wouldn't let me go out; she didn't want me going anywhere. I had to stay by her side always; she didn't want to be left alone. And now, since that thing with my foot, I'm finding myself doing the same thing to *my* daughter. Because she knows that I can't bear it, the being alone, and she deprives herself from going out just for me. I feel depressed about this too. Depressed because I'm doing this *to* her. . . ." The tears, having trembled and shimmered in her eyes momentarily, were now traveling across her cheeks. She wiped them heedlessly away.

We talked for a while about her mother and her mother's death. They had been on good terms when her mother died, except for one thing: "The only thing that I regret was that she didn't want to go to the hospital at the end, and we *had* to send her, because I wasn't capable of caring for her anymore."

"Did you ever think that it might've been getting you down, being kept in the house like that, caring for her and not able to leave her side? I mean that she, a person whom you loved a lot, was also keeping you trapped? Did you ever think about things like that?" My voice was filled with hesitancy, but she shot me a shrewd, almost pleased look.

"Probably," she admitted, seeming engaged by the conversation for the first time. But then she sighed, added, "I don't know . . . it's a question I can't really answer. . . ." The fog had returned.

"Tell me a little more about your mother," I said, feeling odd about asking the question, for Mrs. Garvey herself was in her mid-sixties, a widow and twice a grandmother. But she responded with another show of spirit: "Mother. She was a very *domineering* woman. She was the old school, Irish, and she wanted everything just so and everything right up to par. She babied me a lot . . . and she made me feel like I was nothing, at the same time." Margaret Garvey's tears had dried.

I leaned toward her. "How did she do that, I mean make you feel as if you were nothing?"

She shrugged. "As if no matter what I did for her, I was doing nothing; it was never enough. While in the case of my brother, she was just happy at the sight of him! It was 'My son' this and 'My son' that; and 'Michael this' and 'Michael that.' I knew she must have loved me, but she never showed it in any way."

"But you were the one who took care of her during her final illness," I said, and Mrs. Garvey answered, with asperity, "I was there all the time. My brother would just come to visit, and he went away. But I had to be with her, at every single moment, or else she'd get horribly upset."

Alone

Mrs. Garvey had been widowed for almost a decade. Her husband had died nine years earlier, but she hadn't, she told me, become depressed at that time. "He was an alcoholic," she said, with the slightest trace of a shrug. "We stayed together, but we were not happy." She hadn't suffered a depression, either, in the wake of her mother's death: "I grieved for her," recounted Margaret Garvey, "but I seemed to get over it, in time, pretty well."

Until that injury to her ankle had occurred, some six months later, she thought she'd been managing to get along pretty well. But the long and frightening lonely time that had followed had been an uncannily painful experience: "It was just that—being by yourself all the time—it's something you can't explain. It's as if there's this feeling, and it goes right through you. That you're all alone and the life's gone out of you, and you're just going to *die* . . . or you *have* died and you're not there anymore. There's no life in you, nothing left there at all." Her eyes seemed to bulge and start forward in her face, even as she said those words, and her cheeks were contorted into a grimace. She looked, for the moment, like someone in the intensest physical pain.

Her foot and ankle injuries had, she continued, healed in time, and she'd begun to get around fairly well by the middle of the following month. But the stress of that loneliness seemed to have taxed her far too severely. For her mood and spirits, which had begun to decline during the time of her confinement, hadn't improved once that confinement was over. She'd had to seek treatment, shortly thereafter, of what had now become a frank and full-fledged depression.

And she had, in the eighteen months prior to her hospitalization at Massachusetts General Hospital in Boston, been through one kind of treatment after another. But nothing had helped. By the time she'd entered the hospital she was almost totally immobilized by her depression. Her major presenting complaint had been, in fact, "I can no longer do anything at all."

Psychotherapy, the initial treatment she'd been offered, had been ineffective: Mrs. Garvey seemed almost totally unaware of what that sort of self-scrutinizing process really was all about. "It was just talking," she said. The various forms of antidepressant medications that had been tried had been equally useless. Not only were they useless: she was convinced that they made her feel sicker.

"They gave me a crawly, eerie kind of feeling, those pills," she said, shaking her head as if in refusal, "and three a day just took the life right out of me. I would just lie there like a corpse until they wore off, and then get all confused. I couldn't remember things. Once, when I was taking them, something really drastic happened. It's hard to describe it, but it was just that I didn't know who I was, or where I was—I was just shaking. Then, another thing about those drugs; they made me so dry in the mouth. I couldn't eat—I couldn't swallow, so how could I eat?—and I told my doctor that. He said to take more of the medicine; that it would relieve the depression. But it didn't." Her voice was full of anger and disappointment. "It only made it worse. And finally, I told that doctor that I wouldn't take them anymore. Because I couldn't stand it. I *couldn't.*"

The Dwindles

It was true that in the three months prior to this hospitalization, Margaret Garvey had not been eating. She had actually dropped a full

(and dangerous) thirty pounds of body weight during this brief period. It was, however, much more probable that this weight loss had
been caused by the depression itself rather than by the antidepressants
that she'd been taking. Appetite loss is one of the most common and
pronounced symptoms of the severe, endogenous disturbances that become more frequent in the latter years. In older patients, such as Mrs.
Garvey, this symptom can have a truly dangerous significance.

For the nutritional deficits resulting from a period of self-starvation
—which might be tolerated well enough by a younger person—can be
literally life-threatening in the case of an elderly individual. Malnu-
trition, and the bodily dehydration that results from it can lead to an
irreversible process. If a certain physiological point-of-no-return is
passed, the older person simply loses the ability to absorb and utilize
the life-giving energy that is in our food—and the ability to absorb
that energy doesn't return. The individual may begin eating again; but
the food passes through the body without being taken up and used;
and he or she therefore receives no nourishment. Once this process has
been set into motion, the patient will ultimately die—of what hospital
personnel call "the dwindles."

Mrs. Garvey's depression was life-threatening, in this sense: if it
continued unabated, it might eventuate in just this passive form of suicide.

Her general state of exhaustion was, as well, another complicating
factor. For she was desperately sleep-deprived. Sleep-disturbance is, of
course, a part of the symptom picture, and her sleep was always troubled at best. She tended, as is often the case in these serious, endogenous disorders, to erupt into stunned wakefulness at around 2 or 3
A.M. This was when her depressive mood was at its tortured, snarling
worst: this was the time of her intensest agony. This, too, is "typical." In severe, endogenous depressions, there seems to be a daily variation, with the mood lightening somewhat toward the evening hours
and being at its most excruciating in the small hours of the morning.

Transfixed

All in all, the piercing, intense quality of her depression was something, Margaret Garvey told me, that she felt could not be communicated to other people. "The way I feel is something that you really can't tell to anyone. You can't explain it, because they
themselves—they've never felt that way. So they can't understand

you." She shook her head as if to underscore the futility of trying to translate her feelings into language. "They can't know what it is you're really telling them about." Tears stood in her eyes once again.

She had been an inpatient at the Massachusetts General Hospital for almost three full weeks. During that time, another type of antidepressant drug therapy had been attempted, but the side effects had proven too frightening and disturbing once again. At present, she was unable to eat, unable to sleep, unable to concentrate enough of her attention to enable her to follow the plot of a TV show. "I stay in bed all of the time," she said, "because I haven't the strength to be with the other people. It's as if I can't bother to care about anything. And I'm very edgy all the time, very nervous. Even with my daughter and grandchildren, when they come to visit, I can't—I don't want to get out of bed." She stopped speaking for several moments, wiped tears away from her cheeks with a Kleenex. Mrs. Garvey was, in a word, transfixed.

The following morning she was scheduled to receive the first in a series of what would be anywhere from six to eight electroconvulsive (electroshock) treatments—the number she received would depend on how quickly she responded.

How did she feel about the process on which she would be started? "Very, very nervous," she acknowledged.

"Do you," I asked, "think about not going ahead with it at all?"

Mrs. Garvey shot me an almost frightened look: "Oh no," she breathed, as if she thought I might have gotten some vital matter totally wrong, or might even upset her plans. "I *need* the treatments. I can't go on like this anymore . . . I'm not well."

Electroconvulsive Therapy

Contrary to what is a very widespread popular notion, electroconvulsive or "electric shock" therapy has not become relegated—like dunkings in cold water—to the trunkful of outmoded psychiatric modalities of a less scientifically sophisticated era. ECT is, especially when one considers the unremittingly bad press it has received, still a form of treatment that is in relatively widespread use. Recent estimates made by a Task Force of the American Psychiatric Association (which has made a comprehensive study of the overall efficacy of the therapy) indicates that anywhere from 60,000 to 100,000 persons undergo a course of therapeutic brain stimulation every year.

The reason for this is very simple (although, again, contrary to widespread beliefs). ECT is still one of the most effective treatments available, most especially in the treatment of severe depressions of middle and later life that are accompanied by endogenous or "neurovegetative" symptomatology. By which I mean, the vast appetite, sleep, and energy-level changes that had descended upon a patient like Margaret Garvey—symptoms which, in actuality, had altered every single aspect of her existence.

Typical of these severe, endogenous disturbances of the later years are not only changes in eating, sleeping (especially of the early-morning-awakening variety), etc., but changes in the ability to concentrate, think, make simple decisions, and even to remember—for memory losses can be striking, in depression, and often such losses are mistakenly viewed as senility. The proof that they're *not* due to brain deterioration, during the years of the senium, is there when the depression clears. For very frequently, with remission of the depressive illness, the patient can think and remember once again.

The mood—that awful, weighted, sorrowful mood—is of course a constant factor. So are fatigue, loss of interest, a sense that there's nothing to be done, and nothing that's worth doing. (Mrs. Garvey's major complaint, at the time of her admission to Massachusetts General, said it all in a nutshell: "I can no longer do anything at all.") It is as if the motor of life has just stopped.

The Best Way Out

Feelings of worthlessness pervade, and these can, in some cases, become delusional. A patient may say: "My insides are rotting," or "My brain is rotting," or "I did something to harm my family twenty years ago and I deserve to suffer as I'm now suffering. I deserve to die. . . ." Such delusional self-castigation has at its core, obviously, some profound sense of self-deprecation and self-blame.

Margaret Garvey was of course *not* psychotically depressed; but she did express ideas to the effect that dying might not be the worst that might happen, that it "might be the best way out," all things considered. Still, it was strange to think that a small electrical current, passed through those parts of her brain which are apparently affected by depressive illness—that is, the phylogenetically "older" hypothalamic regions—would in all probability reverse this desperate process. A series of brief electrical stimulations of that brain area which appears to mediate basic biological functions important to survival (such as sleep, appetite, energy levels, sexuality) seems able, in a very high proportion of instances, to restore the severely depressed person's normal functioning—which includes, of course, the living organism's basic wish to survive.

According to Dr. Michel R. Mandel, who is a member of the Task Force that recently reviewed the efficacy of electroconvulsive therapy, and who also directs the Somatic Therapies Consultation Service at Massachusetts General, there is a very widespread—and mistaken—belief that antidepressant drugs can relieve most serious depressions. But this is not, in fact, the case.

"The drugs haven't really produced the universal cures that were initially expected," Mandel told me, during one of our many conversations. (During my Nieman year at Harvard University, I attached myself to the Somatic Therapies Consultation Service and spent several mornings with the group each week as a participant-observer.) "In practice, they prove effective in about 65–70 per cent of the more severe depressive illnesses. But that leaves a large 30 per cent of these patients who are just not having any response. With ECT, as a number of excellent studies have indicated, there's a much higher success rate—on the order of 90–95 per cent. So we're talking about a group of people for whom, as a matter of fact, nothing *but* brain stimulation is really going to be of help."

This may, in effect, be the reason for ECT's survival, as a form of treatment, in a climate of continuing public misunderstanding and downright antipathy.

Antidepressant Side Effects

Another reason for the therapy's continued use, in the face of so much distrust and dislike, has to do with some people's *reactions* to the antidepressant compounds. For these drugs are (make no mistake about it!) powerful ones, and they are not always easy to metabolize. Certain patients, especially older people, find the side effects so overwhelming that the medicines simply can't be tolerated.

In elderly individuals, antidepressants sometimes bring on "toxic deliria," i.e., delirious states. The person feels strangely drunk, confused, unable to remember simple things (such as why she or he has gotten on a bus, and where she was supposed to *go* and so forth); in short, there's a fuzziness in the head, and a frightening sense of being disoriented. "The problem is," said Dr. Mandel, "that you can't get the patient up to a therapeutic dosage before she's gotten panicked by the dizziness, and by the sense that everything around her is spinning." This was the experience described by Mrs. Garvey when she said that the drugs had made her feel "as if I didn't know *who* I was and *where* I was." That had been, for her, an absolutely terrorizing experience.

Additional side effects of antidepressants may come about due to the fact that these drugs are what are called "venous poolers." In other words, they cause the blood to collect and pool in the veins. The upshot is that the blood returning to the heart is restricted, and the heart cannot pump to its full pressure—and so the blood pressure falls. And the patient—particularly an elderly patient—*needs* that pressure kept high enough to keep the brain perfused with blood. If the blood isn't being pumped up in this way, as it should be, the patient faints.

In a word, fainting can be, for some people, a problem associated with the use of the drugs.

So can the problem of cardiac toxicity—heart damage. Among those patients who have a pre-existing heart condition, and then become depressed, the commonly used tricyclic antidepressants (Elavil, Tofranil, etc.) can bring about life-threatening arrhythmias (irregular beating of the heart).

Less potentially lethal, but nevertheless disturbing, are side effects such as the dry mouth of which Margaret Garvey had complained. Another drug-related problem can be difficulties in urinating (a symptom called "urinary retention"). What seems to be involved is a contracting of the sphincter muscles of the bladder. This makes it difficult for the patient to pass water.

And this latter symptom may, in some instances, move from the "minor" to the "major" side-effect category. For it can become terribly uncomfortable: the person experiences pressure but simply can't open the sphincter muscles at all, in order to empty the bladder. This particular side effect, Mandel told me, must then be treated medically; otherwise, serious consequences can result. "If the patient retains fluid chronically, over a period of time, internal pressure in the bladder will affect the ureters, and ultimately the kidneys." (This symptom can be particularly severe in men who have a slight amount of prostate difficulty—which is not at all unusual among older male patients.)

The overall difficulty, when it comes to using antidepressant drugs to treat people who are in their sixties or seventies, is that of getting the person up to a therapeutic dosage level without having devastated her or him with a range of side effects along the way. Because older people are sensitive to drugs in general, the treatment they receive has to be similar, in some important ways, to the treatment of young children. The same rule of thumb, Start Slow and Low, certainly does apply.

But when a person is elderly and depressed, the clearing of the depression is truly a most urgent order of business. For the fact is that untreated depressive illness *has been shown* to correlate with increased probability of death! This higher mortality rate among those suffering from depression is not, as one might imagine, due to suicide, but to a gamut of other, strictly medical causes. As psychiatrists David Avery and George Winokur wrote, in an article published in the *Archives of General Psychiatry*, ". . . a less-known complication (of depressive illness) is non-suicidal death."

Drs. Avery and Winokur are co-authors of one of the more recent of the well-controlled studies of the relationship between "being depressed" and "dying." These two investigators reviewed the case histories of a group of patients whose severe depressions had either *not* been treated somatically, i.e., with antidepressants or ECT, or had been treated inadequately (with dosages of drugs that were so low that they were probably not therapeutically effective); and they compared them with a group of patients who *had* received either adequate drug therapy or a course of electroconvulsive therapy.

They found a mind-boggling differential, in terms of the patient's subsequent health!

The untreated, or inadequately treated depressive's mortality rate—at one year after onset—was 7.3 per cent. The treated depressive's death rate was 1.8. In other words, total mortality, due to suicide *and* medical reasons, was three to four times higher (increased by a 300 to 400 per cent factor) among the individuals whose depressions had remained unresolved!

And three years after the depression's onset, the difference between the two groups persisted. Among the "inadequate treatment" group the death rate was 9.9, while among the "adequate treatment" group, it was 4.0. By now, the gap seemed to have closed somewhat: the "un" or "inadequately" treated patients were only somewhat *more than twice as likely* to be dead! "There is strikingly consistent evidence that patients not receiving somatic therapy have a much higher mortality rate than patients receiving treatment, especially ECT," declared Drs. Avery and Winokur, in summarizing the results of their study.

They could find, interestingly enough, no clear link between depressive illness and the development of cancer. The medical deaths in their sample appeared to be due, for the main part, to cardiovascular illnesses as well as to the nutritional deficits and dehydration that accompany "wasting away."

Data from other studies have, however, suggested an increased incidence of cancer among people who have experienced a recent trauma, life insult, loss, or severe frustration of some sort, and who have responded to it by becoming deeply depressed. These studies were, unlike the Avery and Winokur work, not rigorously controlled: The findings are, therefore, inconclusive. When I asked Dr. Mandel what *his* own view of the matter was, he answered: "My own hunch is that people who are very depressed are more susceptible, somehow, to all types of severe medical illnesses."

It may be that the body's immunological mechanisms are affected and altered by the depressive process, for that process, as was noted earlier (Chapter Six) affects every organ system in the body—salt balance, endocrine function, brain biochemistry, digestion, appetite, sleep, sexual functioning, and so forth. To relieve a depression, and thereby restore the individual's bodily physiology to its normal working operation, might indeed render the person less susceptible to any of the more serious physical diseases. Mandel told me that he himself, in any case, believes that it does.

There are many situations in which ECT is found to be not only the single possible mode of treatment available, but in which it is *literally* a life-saving procedure. When administered, as it presently is, in a drastically modified and modernized fashion, it is among the most side-effect-free and effective forms of antidepressant therapy available. And, according to Michel Mandel, it must be considered when suicidal impulses are liable to overwhelm a distraught and despairing patient. For this treatment brings relief far more rapidly (in days, as compared to weeks) than do the antidepressant drugs.

Therapeutic brain stimulation is actually a good treatment with a terrible reputation. It involves neither massive convulsions—complete with lolling tongue, body bruises, and even fractures—nor breath-stopping electrical shocks—nor memory losses so profound that they transform the reasoning and functioning human being into an amnesic vegetable. Nothing could be further from the truth; but the Back Ward imagery is, as Dr. Mandel once admitted to me, something that he finds embarrassing. "The strange notions that so many people seem to have about the treatment correspond far more to the ECT of thirty or forty years ago. But the ECT of today is so completely different! It's like comparing Kitty Hawk to Apollo 14."

ECT Without Fanfare

Electroconvulsive therapy is administered on the eleventh floor of the sprawling Massachusetts General complex. Baker-11 is actually an ordinary surgical day-care unit—a place in which routine procedures such as minor knee operations, D & Cs, tonsillectomies are carried out. The decision to give the ECT treatment here was, as a matter of fact, made with a certain degree of self-consciousness. It was part of a determined effort, on the part of the Somatic Therapies Consultation Service, to counteract the wild fantasies about the therapy. These exist even in hospitals, even among medical personnel. The underlying rationale was, then, to give the treatments in a very public, mundane, and undramatic setting, so that everyone could see what the procedure was really like, without the mystique and the fanfare.

Every Monday, Wednesday, and Friday morning, at eight o'clock, the patients who are to be treated are wheeled into a line of beds that forms in the corridor, just outside a large, combination operation-and-recovery room. Before the ECT treatments get underway, the "recovery" side of the room is already in a constant flux, alive with movement. Patients, awakening after minor surgical procedures of all kinds, are continually being rolled in—or rolled out—and there are nurses, physicians, orderlies, scurrying busily about.

On the morning that Mrs. Margaret Garvey was to receive her first brain stimulation (a Friday morning) a bright sunlight flooded that long rectangular room. It illuminated the busy scene with such intensity that it made one's very eyeballs ache. She was, as I soon discovered, the second of four ECT patients lined up in a row of rollable cots just outside the door. Before her, and first in the line, was seventy-five-year-old Carl Roehmer, a wan and fragile-looking man.

Mr. Roehmer, like Mrs. Garvey, was suffering from a severe depression; and, like her, he had suffered a recent and very dangerous weight loss. He had a mild heart condition, but there were no real medical counterindications militating against his receiving electroconvulsive therapy. For ECT, contrary to what most people believe, is neither strenuous nor taxing nor heroic. It is a rather benign, routine, surprisingly nondangerous kind of medical procedure.

In terms of deaths associated with the treatment (and mortality is, of course, a reliable guide when it comes to the assessment of danger!) the rate of loss is less than 1 in every 25,000 treatments. This is a very good score when compared to tonsillectomy-related deaths: there, the rate is 1 death for every 10,000 persons undergoing the operation! The low ECT fatality figures are even more surprising when one considers the populations from which each type of patient is drawn. For tonsillectomy patients are usually young and healthy, while ECT patients are—like Mrs. Garvey and Mr. Roehmer—often older and both malnourished and exhausted by lack of sleep.

People like the elderly Mr. Roehmer, with his heart condition, ought (one would suppose) to be swelling those ECT-related mortality statistics. But this is simply not the case; and the reason is that the treatment is just *not* that risky.

On this particular morning, when asked how he was feeling, the patient admitted that he "felt very rocky." Mr. Roehmer seemed eager, almost urgently so, to get on with his treatment; he had, however, not signed a consent form in advance. It was someone's bureaucratic oversight. But it meant that Dr. Mandel had to read a formal statement to him. This was a series of remarks to the effect that, because it had not been possible to treat his depression successfully with drugs, the Somatic Therapies Consultation Service was recommending a course of the new, modified, electrical therapy—"Please," interrupted the old man, with an irritated wave of his hand, "Don't bother with all of that! Just give me the paper, doctor, and let me sign it!"

Dr. Mandel couldn't do that. He explained, sounding apologetic, that the entire statement had to be read. Mr. Roehmer, averting his face and looking annoyed, made it manifestly clear that he definitely would not listen. When the physician stopped reading, the patient took the paper and a pen, and quickly scrawled his signature. Then he lay back against the pillow with a sigh.

"I hope this is going to help," he murmured.

"It will," responded Mandel calmly, affixing an electrode for the electrocardiogram that would monitor heart rate throughout the treatment. "You'll see." The anesthetist, Dr. Bucknam McPeek, was examining the elderly patient's left hand, stroking the top of it as gently as a lover. He was searching for a vein with which to start the intravenous going.

Ten minutes later Mr. Roehmer, already reawakening, had been moved over to Recovery. Mrs. Garvey's bed was being rolled into the treatment area.

"How are you feeling this morning?" Dr. Mandel, speaking gently, leaned over the side of her bed.

She looked pale and frightened: "Nervous," she answered, "terribly nervous." She turned her gaze from his face, then, and stared upward at me.

"You remembered," he asked at once, "that Mrs. Scarf was going to be here this morning?"

"Oh yes." To my surprise, she reached up and took my hand in hers: "I'm glad you're here." She gave me an almost childlike, imploring look: "Promise me you'll stay through the whole thing." Taken aback and moved, I gave her hand a squeeze. I would be there throughout the treatment, I assured her, and would be there when she awoke. The nurse-clinician, Jane Cahill, who works with the Somatic Therapies group, inserted herself between us at that moment. She raised Mrs. Garvey's arm, began wrapping a blood-pressure cuff around it.

"This may feel a bit tight," her voice was cheerfully apologetic, "but I'll be using it to watch your blood pressure, all during the treatment—all right?" She was rapidly inflating the cuff as she spoke. The patient, looking puzzled, merely nodded at the red-cheeked, brisk young woman.

When the cuff was blown up, the nurse scribbled the readings at one end of the pillow slip upon which Mrs. Garvey's head rested. I glanced at the figures, and they seemed high. Jane Cahill, noticing my expression, murmured softly: "That's up, but not abnormally. It just reflects her anxiety about the treatment."

At the head of the table (actually, the rollable bed) Dr. Mandel, working with an associate's assistance, had slipped a rubber strap—it looked like an Indian's headband—around the patient's upper forehead. This strap would hold the recording electrodes firmly in place. The recording electrodes are used for measuring and recording brainwave activity, and they are used to record the rapid electrical firing of the seizure—or a *failure*, if a proper seizure (a grand mal seizure) of both hemispheres of the brain has not been elicited.

I will say more about the seizure itself presently. But the point I want to make first is that these electrodes are used to record and are merely a monitoring device. The *treatment* electrodes, through which the current is actually delivered, would be held in place by Dr. Mandel and Nurse Cahill when the time to give the stimulation had arrived. For the moment, it was the anesthetist, Dr. McPeek, who seemed to be in command of the scene. He was talking to Mrs. Garvey, asking her sociable little questions about which part of Boston she came from; and interspersing this quiet chit-chat with reassurances that she would be unaware of most of the treatment.

"The only thing you'll actually feel"—his words were spoken in a singsong, muted tone of voice—"will be the little pinprick when this needle goes in. I'll try . . . not . . . to hurt you. Good, we got lucky." The I.V. was in place now. "That was the hard part," he said. "Now, all of the medicines we have to use will go right through that needle." In fact, as he spoke, the anesthetist was releasing the first drug into Mrs. Garvey's bloodstream.

It was scopolamine, a drug which acts very rapidly, and which dries up the mouth's secretions. (This would be important, a few moments hence, for reasons which shall be made clear.) The second drug, introduced immediately, was an ultra-short-acting barbiturate called Brevital. "This may sting a bit," said Dr. McPeek, his voice low and hypnotic-sounding, "but it will put you to sleep. And while you sleep we'll do the treatment . . . and when you wake up, it will be over. It will be, for you, like a time sandwich, with nothing at all in between. . . ."

He had not quite finished speaking when Mrs. Garvey, as if on cue, murmured: "I'm feeling sleepy."

She was slipping into unconsciousness. A sense of hurry, in the team around the table, manifested itself immediately. A third and last drug, the muscle relaxant succinylcholine, was released into the patient's bloodstream. Succinylcholine—a drug which is very similar in its action to the better-known curare—essentially disconnects the muscles from their nervous innervations, rendering them completely flaccid. The sense of hurry had to do with the fact that the current would have to be delivered to her brain during the very brief period during which: 1) she was still completely asleep, and 2) her bodily musculature was utterly relaxed so there could be no convulsion.

The succinylcholine would remain effective for a matter of minutes; during this period, the patient's muscles would remain out of communication with her brain. Thus, when the seizure was elicited, the muscle spasms that ordinarily follow a brain seizure—i.e., the convulsion—would be, simply, prevented from ever happening.

The fact that her entire body musculature would be relaxed to the point of total uselessness—paralysis—for a brief period of time was, in fact, the reason for the use of the first drug, scopolomine, which dries the mouth's secretions. For this would prevent Mrs. Garvey from choking on saliva, or from aspirating any fluid into her lungs (which could cause pneumonia). The scopolamine acts, as well, to counter any slowing down of the heart's regular pumping action, which might occur in conjunction with the administration of the powerful muscle relaxant, succinylcholine.

The Brain Stimulation

She was now soundly asleep. The succinylcholine was depolarizing her body's muscles (which are, normally, in a state of oppositional tension). The nurse and the anesthetist, in one well-synchronized movement, had raised the bottom of the cover-sheet, disclosing her lower calves and her legs. The muscles, as the relaxant reached them, were set aquivering. It was a downward-flowing movement, rather like a water current, for the drug follows the pathways of the body's nervous innervations.

"I think we're almost ready now," murmured anesthetist McPeek. He had changed position and now stood at the head of the bed, behind Mrs. Garvey's head. He was holding an oxygen mask over her face, while rhythmically pumping a mixture of air and oxygen into and out of her lungs.

"She's still fasciculating," objected the nurse, pointing to the tiniest ripples of movement that still shivered through the muscles of the calves. "Right, then," agreed McPeek, and there was an extended pause, a momentary cessation of all activity.

I noticed, during that moment, that several of the dials on the front of the square, compact, low-energy console had lit up. This "low-energy apparatus," no bigger than a large-screen television set, has been being pioneered at Massachusetts General and a very few other hospitals in this country. The new machine, which has become available due to recent advances in electronic technology, makes it possible to evoke the necessary brain seizure with what is, comparatively, a mini-current. With this apparatus, a proper therapeutic seizure can be elicited with an electrical stimulus as low as 4 or 5 watts/seconds. This must be contrasted with electrical outputs used in the past: which ranged anywhere from fifty to two hundred or more watts/seconds!

"This new machine," Mandel said, catching my stare at those glowing dials, "has a self-test phase, which tests out the intactness of the circuitry. If it's correct, and everything is O.K. and ready, then that red button lights up—and we push this button here, to treat." The low-energy machine, with its "on-off" designations, looked almost ridiculously simple to operate—rather like a child's toy.

"Are we ready then?" Mandel had turned to the anesthetist. "Good." Now it was he who, with the nurse as *his* partner, executed a smoothly well-rehearsed duet. For as he placed one electrode toward the top of the patient's head, and on the right side (having smoothed as much hair as possible out of the way), Jane Cahill took the other electrode and held it on the right side of the temple, between Mrs. Garvey's eye and her ear.

The Convulsion

The physician pressed the button to deliver the current. Almost instantaneously, the patient's right arm shot up, the fingers clenched in upon themselves in an odd, clawlike fashion. "She's having a full convulsion," said the nurse, who had reached out to hold and to support that rigid arm.

This was, indeed, the convulsion itself and in toto. For the blood-pressure cuff had been inflated to a pressure that was greater than Mrs. Garvey's systemic pressure; and the muscle relaxant had been, for this reason, prevented from getting down into this limb. By permitting the convulsion to occur in this one site in the patient's body, an important piece of information could be obtained. And that was that the stimulation of the *right* side of her brain had spread to the *left* side of her brain, for brain functions "cross over" to the opposite side of the body. The fact that her right arm had convulsed meant that there had been a seizure in the left cerebral hemisphere. And, because the stimulation has been on the right side only, this meant that a total brain seizure had been elicited. A total (grand mal) seizure is necessary, for it is the seizure—involving both brain hemispheres—that makes the patient better.

The *tonic* or rigid phase of the convulsion had endured for the long breath of an instant. It was succeeded by the *clonic* phase, during which the muscles unclenched, in short bursts of movement. Slowly then, and guided gently downward all the meanwhile by the nurse's support, Mrs. Garvey's arm underwent a series of spastic-seeming, fluttery motions. Within a few seconds her arm lay quietly by her side. Both the brain seizure and the "convulsion" were over.

The low-energy ECT console, like a ticker-tape machine, had been sending out a continuous record of brain-wave activity. Dr. Mandel, tearing off the paper, pointed to the seizure-activity and the length of its duration. It had lasted forty seconds, and had required 7 watts/ seconds of electrical energy. This was fairly typical, the physician told me.

"Mrs. Garvey? Mrs. Garvey?" I heard Mandel's associate, Dr.

Charles Welch, calling her back into wakefulness. I turned: her eyelids had opened, and the expression on her face was one of surprise.

"Is it all over?" she asked, in a tone of uncertainty and disbelief. "Am I all right?"

"Yes it is, and you are." Dr. Welch, leaning over, smiled down at her. "How do you feel?" he asked.

"Thirsty," she answered promptly, "awfully thirsty." (No wonder: the drug scopolamine had dried up her saliva; and she was now experiencing that dryness!)

A few minutes afterward, though, she was sitting up in bed and drinking from a white plastic glass, filled with water. "Oh," she said to me, "I've never *been* so thirsty!" I glanced up at the clock on the wall, and saw that it was 8:26. Mrs. Garvey was already awake, alert, and clearly aware of who *I* was.

The ECT administration had begun at 8:15.

Then and Now

Compare this description of an electrical brain stimulation with the following one, written in 1938 by Dr. Ugo Cerletti, an originator of the therapy: "We observed the . . . instantaneous, brief, generalized spasm, and soon after, the onset of the classic epileptic convulsion. We were all breathless during the tonic phase of the attack, and really overwhelmed during the apnea* as we watched the cadaverous cyanosis* of the patient's face; the apnea of the spontaneous epileptic convulsion is always impressive, but at that moment it seemed to all of us painfully endless. Finally, with the first stertorous breathing and the first clonic spasm, the blood flowed better not only in the patient's vessels but also in our own. . . ."

The terrible halt in respiration, as the electrical current is introduced—the spine-arching "tonic" phase of the convulsion and the writhing of the "clonic" muscle spasms—these are the familiar images of what the treatment is like and what ECT is all about. Cerletti was, however, describing "the first electrically produced convulsion in man."[†] In the forty intervening years, the procedure itself has been altered and modified almost beyond recognition. But the terrifying imagery about it has not.

---

* *Apnea,* a temporary stoppage of breathing, brings about *cyanosis,* a bluish coloration of the skin caused by lack of oxygen in the blood.
† To quote Cerletti himself.

The problem has been that the initial success of the treatment—which was, after all, the first *effective* somatic therapy that had become available for the treatment of mental illness, ever—led to its overuse in some quarters; and therefore to its abuse, in some quarters. Ultimately, the abuses of the therapy have become mistaken for the therapy itself!

When, for example, the treatment is abused in Soviet psychiatric institutions, by being administered to political dissenters for nonmedical purposes, many people infer that ECT itself must be an abusive treatment. But this is rather like saying that if heart surgeries, which are bloody, invasive, and very painful, were done on people who didn't require heart surgeries, then all heart surgery procedures ought to be seen as abusive! There is an assumption at work, here, to the effect that electrical brain stimulation is given in a relentlessly malevolent spirit.

What seems to be forgotten by almost everyone is that the treatment really makes a lot of very sick people well, and that it does so very rapidly. And also, that the treatment itself is vastly modernized, vastly changed.

Memories and Thinking

If ECT has changed, been modified, been streamlined, it is due to a much increased understanding of just which aspects of the treatment are therapeutic and which are side effects. It used to be believed, for instance, that memory losses and confusion were what made the patient feel better—that is, the clearing of the depression was related to the blurring of painful recollections. It is now known that this is completely untrue. For a series of elegant researches, carried out by a Scandinavian psychiatrist (Ottoson) in the late 1960s, demonstrated clearly that *it is the series of brief brain seizures, and that alone, which brings about clinical improvement.*

Amnesic problems, like the cardiac symptoms that may accompany the use of tricyclic antidepressants, are unnecessary and unwelcome side effects of the therapy.

Some of the loudest and most vociferous complaints about ECT have had to do, though, with posttreatment side effects relating to loss of memories and/or capacities for retaining newly learned information. Such difficulties are, for the most part, transitory; but some people find them terribly disturbing. (It is true, by the way, that memory loss is another symptom of the depression itself; the depressed person's ability to think and remember is very often badly impaired.) What is now known, however, is that the degree of memory loss experienced does appear to correlate with the amount of electrical energy that has been used in order to evoke the brain seizure. The recent trend, among psychiatrists who are both using and attempting to improve upon the therapy, has been the development of methods for bringing about the grand mal seizure—which means that both brain hemispheres are involved—without the excess of electrical energy that could result in disturbances of memory and of thinking.

A method used by the Mandel group, at Massachusetts General, involves what they consider to be "the most parsimonious use of energy." This is unilateral placement of the stimulating electrodes—in other words, delivering the current to only one side, the *nondominant hemisphere of the brain.* The seizure elicited in that side (usually the right side, as was the case for Mrs. Garvey, for she was right-handed, as are most people) is then permitted to spread, via the corpus callosum, to the dominant hemisphere of the brain.‡

This relatively new "unilateral" technique has, as Dr. Mandel acknowledged, been slow to win acceptance within the psychiatric community. There is some controversy in the literature about whether or not this method is as effective as "bilateral" stimulation—delivering the current to both hemispheres of the brain simultaneously. But there is no dispute at all about the fact that the unilateral method *does* reduce amnesias—both the ability to remember past events and to remember newly learned information—and also posttreatment confusion.

The Somatic Therapies Consultation Service has been using the unilateral technique for the past several years, and they have found it both acceptable and clinically effective. Unilateral electrode placement, in combination with the new low-energy apparatus, has now been used on a series of fifty patients who were admitted to Massachusetts General Hospital and were suffering from depressions that had been resistant to all prior forms of therapy.

According to Dr. Mandel, the results, thus far, have been excellent. "We've not had one patient with a spontaneous memory complaint," he told me. "And complaints of this kind were fairly commonplace before we began using this new 'combination' technique."

‡ Because brain functions "cross over," the left cerebral hemisphere is dominant in right-handed individuals.

How Does It Work?

Why—and how—does this rather puzzling form of treatment actually do its work? Some experts have suggested that brain cells in certain critical areas (the limbic or "old brain" region) may have become sluggish—incapable, for some reason, of producing their proper neurochemical secretions. The electrical stimulation evokes a brain seizure. The seizure, in turn, brings about a sudden outpouring of catecholamines—important biogenic amines (such as norepinephrine) which are, of course, believed to be crucially involved in mood regulation, into the patient's bloodstream. It may be that by inducing a series of seizures in this crucial hypothalamic area of the brain, the cells themselves are being helped to release their neurotransmitter substances more effectively. Who can say?

All that *is* known is that that electrical event, occurring deep within the brain, is related to some neurochemical outflow; and that the biological changes which are then brought about seem to stir most people out of a depression. The result is that the person can eat, sleep, do things, take pleasure in life once again. The best analogy might be to an inert biological pendulum. ECT, like a series of short taps, sets it swinging again; and, after six to eight electrical stimulations, that pendulum of living goes on swinging . . . now by virtue of its own motion and its own force.

What is perfectly plain and beyond any dispute is that electroconvulsive therapy has helped thousands of acutely suffering, debilitated, exhausted, and often suicidally depressed people. One such person, a woman whom I'd interviewed while on a research visit at the University of Pittsburgh's Western Psychiatric Institute and Clinic, told me that she had been desperately ill with depression at two different points in her life—the first time, just after her son went away to college; and the second, shortly after her husband's death.

Nothing *but* ECT had been able to help her, and twice (after other treatments had failed) it had, she said, "restored me to myself."

An Almost Magical Occurrence

There is almost something eerie about seeing a person so seriously depressed as Margaret Garvey had been suddenly brighten and improve.

It is an almost magical occurrence. She, who had literally been dragging herself around for months, and who had described herself as unable to do "anything at all anymore" was steadily reawakening into life. Her transformation, which took place over a period of days, had an inherently dramatic quality. The slower and somehow more comprehensible response to antidepressant drugs doesn't seem so much like wizardry. But the facts were that a small electrical current, delivered to the deep, limbic regions of the brain three times weekly, over a period of two weeks, had rendered Mrs. Garvey able to eat and to sleep, to read and to watch television, and to interact with her daughter, her grandchildren, the medical staff, and the other patients on the ward.

There was something almost irrational about it; but it had happened. "I'm feeling so different now," she told me on the evening of the day of her sixth treatment. "When I came in here, you know, I couldn't talk to anyone—I just didn't have the strength. I wanted to be alone, to lie down in my room all the time. The nurses kept trying to get me to come out . . . and I would." She smiled: "But then, of course, I'd crawl back again as soon as I could."

It was the first real, full smile that I'd seen upon her face, and I said so. She seemed surprised, and told me that it had never dawned upon her that I'd not seen her smiling before! "Those treatments gave me a little push, in some way," she acknowledged. "I shouldn't say a 'little' push; they helped me quite a lot. Now I feel that I want to be with people, and I get into conversations all the time. And I'm kind of *nosy*," she cocked her head to one side, impishly, "kind of inquisitive. I want to find out everything about everyone who's around here!"

She now had much more energy, she reported, and she was gaining weight very nicely: "Before, the food didn't tempt me, I just didn't care. I'd look at it and eat a little bit, but then I just wouldn't have the heart for it. Now I seem to be looking forward to the meals, and I have an appetite." She paused, and added with a child's pridefulness, "I eat almost everything now."

Mrs. Garvey had, she believed, begun coming out of her depression sometime just after the fourth or fifth treatment. The ward staff had, however, noted a subtle "brightening" as early as the third ECT. This happens often with patients on antidepressant medications as well. I mean that the person starts improving, in terms of energy, interest, ability to sleep, etc., before she or he realizes subjectively that the intolerably painful mood is actually beginning to dissipate.

But in any event, six treatments later, the change was apparent to all. The depressive emergency was over. The patient's discharge, and plans for her aftercare, were being arranged.

Departing Time: Margaret Garvey and Anne Munson

Although the therapy had effectively relieved her depressive symptoms—and this was beyond dispute—ECT couldn't, most certainly, be used to treat what were Mrs. Garvey's ordinary human dilemmas. These had to do with the distress and the stress that accompany aging, the thinning out of one's social environment, and the necessary coping with feelings of being superfluous and unneeded. ECT couldn't, in short, treat human loneliness.

And this was something that Margaret Garvey, vastly improved though she might be at the moment, still very much feared. Like Anne Munson, the young patient whom we met in Chapter One, Mrs. Garvey was resisting the thought of leaving the hospital. "The treatments helped me, in my depression, an awful lot," she told me. "But as far as helping me to be on my own, to be alone, I don't know . . . I don't know how it's going to be." A dubious expression crossed her face. There was a sense about her of not wanting to leave the hospital ward ever again. For, as had been true in Anne Munson's case, the hospital was the stand-in for the parenting caretaker.

Mrs. Garvey had, of course, served as caretaker herself for many, many years. Hers had been, in effect, the all-suffering life; the life of service to others (the last of whom had been her dying mother). She didn't want, as she'd stated at the outset of our talks, to become "a burden to my daughter, as my own mother was to me." Yet underneath the powerful wish to care for others resided, one suspected, strong needs and wishes to be cared for herself. Nurturing or *being* nurtured: this was the polarity, the central theme around which so much else in her life seemed to cluster. It was as though life itself—that is, the meaning of life—seemed to hinge on being in that kind of relationship. Either being totally *needed by* or *needing* someone else.

With her own mother's death had come a sense of her own superannuation. She was really no longer necessary to another human being, not in a truly vital way. There was no one deeply dependent upon her; and no one upon whom she had the right to lean heavily. She didn't want to be a burden to her daughter. But she felt so alone in the world. It was fearful, that aloneness: it was the fear, almost, of imminent death.

It was the feeling, she'd said, of either being about to die, or "that you *have* died, and you're not there anymore." Not only had her mother been the last person who'd really depended upon Mrs. Garvey, but she'd actually lived in the same house throughout the patient's entire lifetime. "I'd never left my mother since the day I was born," she said forlornly. "I got married and lived in the same house, in the apartment above hers, until she passed away at the age of eighty-nine." She'd been living downstairs, with her mother, at the time of the old woman's death; and then afterward, she'd lived in the apartment, alone. Her own daughter, and her daughter's children, were now occupying the space upstairs.

Failing to Mourn

Margaret Garvey was, it seemed to me, still struggling with some issues relating to bereavement. She was having difficulty mourning her mother, who'd been both disapproving and loving, such a "burden" in her final days, and yet someone who'd made Mrs. Garvey feel so necessary. In some situations, it seems, to be sad or to grieve is simply too painful. When the loss is, for instance, associated with enormous guilt, the survivor may "not think" about it, in order to avoid the painful and unresolvable feelings that are evoked. When a person dies and one has had both loving and hostile feelings for that person, the whole grief process may be avoided. By *not* experiencing the grief, in both the head and the heart, the individual never gets to work it through; that is, to *have* the experience. Normal mourning is a process, and it has a middle and an end. But failing to mourn often results in that pathology which is called depression.

It is not easy to mourn and to separate from a loved dead person, in any case. But in Mrs. Garvey's instance, there were strong feelings of need, love, anger, and irritation being expressed a full two years after the event. Her mother's passing seemed to have left Margaret Garvey —at age sixty-five—grappling with the same issues that Anne Munson had been grappling with, at the very outset of this book. That is, with the frightening problem of whether or not one contains the inner resources that will make it possible for one to survive on one's own.

The dilemma that both women were dealing with was that of separation. Of separating, acknowledging one's ultimate uniqueness and aloneness, and then going about the business of living on one's own emotional supplies. Mrs. Garvey had collapsed in the face of this human task, which, in the closing years of her life, was perceived as something too terrifying and unbearable. This was why, perhaps, her depression had such a "helpless baby" sort of quality about it. There had been a return to a primitive, regressed, and infantile stand.

There were other analogies as well to be drawn between the young girl and the elderly woman. Not only was there, in both these cases, an ambivalently loving and yet profoundly dissatisfying relationship with the mother (who'd failed to protect the daughter adequately); there was also a sometimes violent, somehow sexually provocative father.

Mrs. Garvey, like Anne, had been threatened, stimulated, frightened by that parent: "My father wasn't an alcoholic, but he went on a binge every once in a while. He'd get drunk and want to throw the furniture out the window. And he wanted to beat us all up. Afterward, he didn't remember it, but he did do those things," she recounted, in an interview that took place as she was in the transition from being desperately ill to being surprisingly well.

She'd hesitated at that point, then smoothed her skirt over her knees absentmindedly. "He—used to put his hands on me, too—especially as I grew older," she announced after a pause. "Even after I was married, too, he always used to come near me and hug me and hold me. He'd put his arms around me . . . touch me . . . in funny ways." She fell silent.

"Did you ever talk to your mom about that?" I asked her slowly.

It was strange, so strange, to be asking this elderly woman about those long-ago secrets. But she'd become extraordinarily absorbed by the conversation: "No"—her cheeks had colored slightly—"I thought about it a lot, but I never told anybody. Not until about a year ago. Then I talked about it with one of the doctors." She hesitated once again, then added quietly: "My father *was* that way. He was very free, very touchy with his hands. He would go near any woman and try to fool around with her, in a joking and kidding way. He'd do that with me, too, long after I was married. He'd say to me, 'Your husband is no good for you' and try to put his hands on me. I'd say 'Pa, what are you doing?' and I'd walk away from him. It always happened when my mother wasn't around. I used to be afraid of being in the same room with him if my mother wasn't there. Even when I was very young. Mine was a threatened childhood, a terrible childhood. I was so fearful, so afraid of what would happen." She had married, while still quite young—in her late teens.

The man she'd married was, like her father, someone who became an alcoholic and who was occasionally violent. Her own daughter (World Without End) had had as traumatic a childhood as Mrs. Garvey's had been. Repetitions of this sort are, at once, always expectable and always mysterious. They have an almost mesmeric quality, as though each generation starts out in the spell of a trance that's been induced by the generation that came before.

And Margaret Garvey's daughter, when her own adult day had come, had repeated the same "mistake." That daughter, now forty-five years old, had a twelve-year-old daughter and a ten-year-old son. It may sound odd to say so, but the most hopeful thing about *her* life was that she'd done something different, she'd gotten divorced! And in fact, at the time of her mother's illness, this middle-aged woman was contemplating the idea of remarrying; her ex-husband had recently died.

Insofar as a new marriage was concerned, Mrs. Garvey's illness had thrown her daughter into a complicated quandary. For she *did* care about her mother deeply, and yet she was, in a way, being almost scripted to give up her life in caring for her parent—which was what her mother had done *for her own mother,* in her own time. Would remarrying mean that she was deserting? Mrs. De Benedetto felt— because her mother's illness had made her so dependent and needful— almost as if working on a future of her own would be a form of abandonment. She'd put off the marriage, during these past months of Mrs. Garvey's depression, because parenting her parent had absorbed most of her available energy and her time.

The electroconvulsive treatments, coming into this complex interpersonal situation as a kind of "override," hadn't really changed anything but the patient's depressive symptoms. The facts and the circumstances of both Mrs. Garvey's and her daughter's and her grandchildren's lives were manifestly unchanged. But the truth was that those facts and those circumstances had been moved around into different positions, almost as if they'd been iron filings, and the ECT a powerful magnet. With the remission of the depression, the facts and the circumstances and indeed the entire picture did look totally different.

At the most basic level, Mrs. Garvey was functioning again. She was able to eat, to sleep, to interact with the people around her. But beyond that, other changes had taken place: one could see it in her newly smiling face, the hair that had been carefully set for her by her daughter; and in the pink cheeks, her energy, her interest in others, and in her readiness to think about her future. That sense of hopelessness was gone. She was beginning, in collaboration with the hospital staff, to plan the shape of the life she would lead when she left.

An entire strategy was being mapped out, in terms of the steps that would be taken. There would be volunteer work in her church, and neighborhood activities designed to meet the needs of the older residents in the area where Mrs. Garvey lived. The goal of these plans was an obvious one—to bring the patient into contact with other people to talk to, people to be "nosy" about, people whose interests she might share. The goal was preventing a fallback into a state of isolation and loneliness. Only in this way could she steer her way through those twin sirens of depression—feelings of aloneness, feelings of being someone superfluous.

Return visits to the hospital were being arranged; and her daughter and her grandchildren were standing by. Friends in the neighborhood were ready to welcome her home: her brother had volunteered to help in any way possible; she really was not alone and abandoned. She could, in fact, face the future with a certain degree of optimism. It would perhaps, be possible to continue with her life, even in the absence of her mother. Separating from her mother—that inner, wrenching psychic separation—had been an almost overwhelming experience. But it looked as though Mrs. Garvey would survive it.

There was, ultimately, an almost dizzying amount of "raw material." After years of work on the topic of women and depression, there were too many interviews in my bulging files for me to hope to quote every one of the patients, therapists, female colleagues, friends, and assorted others whom I'd talked to in the course of the research—or, alas, to deal with all of the issues that had been raised. There were other, rather sensitive problems as well.

I had, in advance of each set of conversations, agreed on a series of ground rules about my ultimate use of the highly charged material that emerged from our discussions. Basically, I was given permission to quote from the talks but asked to change certain basic identifications: names, professions, geographical locations, hair color, etc., things that would proclaim that I was writing about such-and-such an individual and no other person who was very much *like* her. These arrangements had, however, been individually and idiosyncratically made. Midway through my writing, I learned that I would have to have a formal statement from everyone I'd spoken to; and I had therefore to send out a form letter in a large mailing. What it contained was a statement to the effect that the individual signing it knew, at the time of our interviews, that I was engaged in research which would eventuate in my writing a book. The statement was, in short, a legal release. I felt somewhat uncomfortable about having to send it out in that way, but I had to do so, and did.

Most of those forms—all of them, come to think of it—came back accompanied by a personal letter. I'd been out of touch, for almost ten months, with most of the people I'd interviewed (the form letter went out in 1977/78 and I was a Fellow at the Center for Advanced Study in the Behavioral Sciences, across the nation, in Stanford, California). These letters, which were simply spontaneous self-reports, came as a complete surprise to me: for one thing, just about everybody seemed to be doing awfully well! And also to have understood a good deal about *what* had happened to her, and *why*. In a way, my experience was peculiar, for I'd been having a kind of one-way conversation with them, over the past months, communing with them as characters in a book. And now, by means of these letters, they'd asserted their own independence—sprung from my pages to remind me of their own three-dimensional, ongoing, complex, and changing lives.

Anne Munson's letter included a picture. I stared at that photograph for a long while. Her brown-blond hair had some lighter streaks in the front now; and it was cut differently, in an attractive shingle. The harlequin glasses that had almost been her calling-card were gone. She was wearing no glasses at all; I supposed she must have gotten contacts. She looked as if she'd lost some weight since I'd last seen her; and her letter, written on the stationery of the children's portrait studio where she was working as a photographer, confirmed the fact that this was actually the case.

"I'm on a sort of a diet at the moment," she wrote. "I want to weigh 120 lbs. and right now I weigh about 128. It's so hard to lose it, though! My friend's Mom makes granola and I'm so addicted, I gain weight just thinking about it!" She had graduated from high school, and gone back to live in Madison. She wasn't going to college, but was thinking about the possibility of art or photography school: "Just *thinking*," she amended that remark at once, "because I'm really not ready to go back to school yet."

"Let me tell you some of my latest things," her letter continued. "I'm doing TM, and I've moved out of my parent's house. I'm living with the family of a friend—it's a bit out of town, in the country." She was, said Anne, "finally growing independent of my parents. It's a slow slow process, but I can finally understand that our feelings and our ideas are different, and I can feel O.K. about the ways that I feel. I still do feel guilty when I think I'm hurting my Mom, but I'm much more aware of the mind control techniques that she uses on *me*—and I can either point them out to her or ignore them. It's hard making her understand that certain things aren't really her business. Like my relationships. If one thing bothers my Mom it's my *relationships!* I've discovered that she can't stand any of my boyfriends. She doesn't want me to be a sexual woman. I have an off the shoulder dress that's very pretty; and she just hates it. I've finally gotten her to admit why, in an indirect way: she's afraid I'm going to be raped/seduced. But the boy I'm going with is my lover! How do I tell her that I'm actually toying, at the moment, with the idea of *living* with the boy she thinks is going to seduce/rape me?" I myself was taken aback by these remarks. It was as though Anne's mother, who *did* know about the abortion, had taken the view that her daughter had made a "mistake" and it was now plowed over and in the past—as though Anne's virginity had been magically restored, and she had to be protected from the threat of adult sexuality. It was as though, in her mother's eyes, Anne's sexual life had not only ended; it had never been.

On a line of its own, in any event, Anne added: "As if it's all any of her business, anyway!"

She was getting along awfully well, just now, with her father. She could even say that she believed now that he "loves me and respects me. He knows I'm different, older, and he seems to be able to accept that. He even laughed when I told him why Mom doesn't like my dress. I've learned a lot about Mom, because I've been learning a lot about my own self."

She had been watching closely, comparing her ways of doing things with those of her mother: "My Mom is very insecure about putting herself forward and being adventuresome, and she doesn't admit it to herself. She has a funny way of not trying to work out any problems that she has, she sort of walks away and ignores them. What's hard is that she doesn't have any confidence in *me*. I'll have to admit that I can understand her own point of view in a way, but I feel like, well, if I think I can make it, everyone else should too! That's not to say I don't need helping out sometimes, with various things, but I don't have to be totally dependent on any one person. I know I still have a ways to go in overcoming my shyness/insecurity. I know that I'm insecure and it makes me not stick up for myself or my rights. But still I realize that everything takes time. I think I've grown tremendously."

The face that stared up at me out of the photograph did look less uncertain and more composed.

Debra Thierry's note was on the topic of "parents," for the most part, as well. She had, she said, recently discontinued therapy and "on a very happy note." She would not try, she added, to give me the impression that her battles and her conflicts had decreased: quite the opposite, she was involved in much more overt conflict, for "I have become more involved in living."

"My situation with my mother," wrote Debra, "is slowly improving. I think the biggest, most influencing factor as far as that's concerned, has been my realization that I *like* who I am now that I *know* who I am! I can give my parents myself *as* myself. If they don't accept this then I feel let down, sure; but let down, and not crushed. They are getting to know me, and I to know them, and we are finding that, overall, we like each other. . . ."

Sandy Geller was married. She had married Henry Pace, the man

she'd been seeing—and whose potency problems we'd talked about—
at the close of our last interview. She seemed to have no memory of
that discussion, for she wrote: "I can't remember if I was dating
Henry when we last met, I think I was, but in any case I didn't let
him get away; I married him last October. Actually we bought a
house together in July and 'lived in sin' until we were married. Henry
adopted Julie in December, and we celebrated our first Christmas in
our house as a complete family. Life is not without its problems, however. Henry's got a job working nights and I'm working days. Sometimes the separation gets to us and we talk about quitting just so we
can be together. But somehow we manage, and we go on. It has its
benefits, too. I have been able to keep just enough of that independence that was so forcefully thrown at me three years ago. I do
know, though, that when the going is tough Henry is always there.
Julie's behavior change has been remarkable, she's an absolutely
different child. Henry picks her up at daycare every day, and they
spend the afternoon together. For someone who's never played the
role before, Henry is an excellent father. I love them both."

Kath Barrie's interviews had taken place out in California, and so
shortly before the requests were sent around that not enough time had
elapsed for "follow-up" comments. She merely sent greetings, and
mentioned that she'd been in the Stanford area recently and had tried
to telephone; she hadn't found me at home.

Judith Karlin's reply was the last to arrive. She didn't write until
the middle of August. She had been slightly hesitant about doing the
interviews in the first place, and so I thought that her not answering
had been due to a change of mind. But no, she'd been away in Europe
for the summer, and had attended several film festivals. She was, she
wrote, really feeling and doing remarkably well. Because she now had
her academic tenure, and because so much time had now passed, as she
put it, "unclinically," she was feeling much less reticent about many
of the matters that we had discussed. She was willing to "come out of
the closet" about her illness, and let me use the material forthrightly.
"What was, at the time of those manias, an isolating and stigmatizing
experience, is one that I now feel ready to acknowledge and to share
with other people," she said. Since we'd last seen one another she'd
published a book on film criticism; and it had been very well-received
(I had, as a matter of fact, seen a most laudatory review). Things
sounded good.

Laurie Michaelson's interviews, which I knew would definitely be
included, presented me with a problem. I hadn't, in the first draft,
covered her tracks enough: I'd not *changed* her sufficiently. I'd even

mentioned the place where she'd gone for treatment. I worried lest she consider this a threat to her anonymity and privacy, and wrote to ask her how much, in the way of obfuscating changes, she actually wanted? She was, she responded, unconcerned.

"Being associated with the Mood Clinic is definitely O.K." Her handwriting was large, almost like a child's, and she wrote in bright blue ink on a soft blue paper. " 'Laurie Michaelson' has, I suspect, much in common with a number of other women—including blond hair, Philadelphia, the Mood Clinic . . . which is all O.K. by me. . . . 'Laurie' is, you know, in the process of writing her own 'book,' an autobiography. She's somewhere in the middle of the narrative, trying to figure out what is the direction and where her life is really heading. She does, however, have something to say about the Mood Clinic and this whole kind of approach. It was explained to her that she had learned to *think* negatively and could, with work, begin to think more positively. Her negative thinking was based on her own beliefs and attitudes about the world and about her life. Somehow, that took the horror away. This was a teaching-learning situation. I had had successes with that situation before."

She was, added Laurie, rather straightforward with other people about her experience with depression: "Several people, both in my work and in my social life have come to me to ask 'how I got through it.' Twice, just recently, other instructors at the school have come across younger persons who were showing all the signs of depression and I was asked if I'd talk to those students, which I *did* do. . . ."

Doris Nordlund and Francis Kirchner were living together; Doris wrote me a bubbling, almost schoolgirlish letter. Everything, she said, was "solid" between the two of them: "Just recently, my doctor said to me: 'He's becoming quite important to you, Doris.' I exploded. *'Becoming?'* He laughed at me and said, 'Well, I've had trouble believing in you two!' . . . Who hasn't? *We* have trouble believing in us! What we have is so special and profound, and it seems to increase with time. . . ."

But Doris' sense of contentment was belied somewhat by a copy of a letter she'd sent to me. It was a letter to Patricia Halkett, who was still living with Eric, and still at the farm in South America. It had been written, Doris said, "because it came to me that I was doing myself an injustice by carrying around a terrible burden of hatred for her. This letter isn't so much the act of a humanitarian as it is, perhaps, an indication of a giant emotional step forward. My hatred of Eric is also misplaced, for they are both sick themselves. Their conduct towards me two years ago wasn't rational; they behaved like desperately confused people, but the biggest truth is that they served me well. My dignity and ego were battered around fairly badly, yet it took all of that to jolt me out of a stagnant, self-defeating situation. So why hate? My relief is enormous. . . ."

Looking over that odd document, I wasn't so sure. There was something ambiguous about this offer to bury old hatchets; it was, effectively, an original way of bringing those hatchets back *up* into existence! Doris seemed to want to get into correspondence with Patricia and Eric, at this moment—why? Her letter to them was conciliatory; but at the same time, sounded mildly depressed.

I didn't know how to put it together with the more cheerful, even blithe, other note that she'd sent directly to *me*.

There was no response from Diana Dahlgren. I had, unfortunately, left a copybook that contained her address in a stack of materials that were back in my office in Connecticut. I would, I'd decided, contact Diana when I'd returned to the East Coast.

The news of Diana was highly unlikely to be good. Of that I was almost certain. For, on follow-up visits to the Dartmouth-Hitchcock Mental Health Center, I had heard that Mrs. Dahlgren had done badly. After her return home, she'd begun drinking again, and begun making suicidal threats. Early that spring, she had overdosed on aspirin. This time she'd been hospitalized in a psychiatric clinic in Massachusetts. I'd heard no news of her since that time.

I'd had no written statement from my former research assistant, Marie Sirotta, either—but I would see her early in the fall, and therefore hadn't bothered to send her the formal request. We'd been in touch by telephone over the months of my absence, for business reasons; but in late June, she called me, sounding distraught and upset. Marie had been working, during this past year, at Peter Bent Brigham hospital in Boston; but she'd just done something rather awful, and she thought she might even lose her job. "Everything's in a shambles," she said, sounding shaken and even slightly hysterical. The story that emerged piecemeal had to do with a co-worker, an "older woman," a "hostile bitch," someone "perpetually snide and disapproving," with whom Marie had been quarreling. The woman had been baiting her, the other day, and she herself had lost control; she'd actually slapped her! "I'm afraid I'm going to be fired," she told me. She was feeling alternately, "very angry and very depressed."

Marie had not only been in a long-running battle with an "older woman"; she'd been having a love affair with a Catholic clergyman during the many months since I'd last seen her. She didn't feel this was wrong, in the religious sense; she didn't approve of the rules of priestly celibacy and told me that many devout Catholics, like herself and her lover, considered these regulations unfair and outmoded and not worth honoring. But she *did* feel guilty because she simply wasn't that interested in her lover or in lovemaking itself; she was "turned off," tired, unable to work up the enthusiasm for sex. She'd been unable to sleep; and she wasn't eating properly; she felt completely *worn down*. "My mouth feels so dry all the time," she complained.

To which I responded: "You *are* in a depression." She wanted to know if I would be willing to recommend a therapist, someone among the people I'd been interviewing and working with, when I was in the Boston area? I gave her some names.

But when I hung up I continued thinking about it, this love affair with a priest ("Father") and a concurrently erupting quarrel with an older woman, snide and disapproving, a "hostile bitch." There was an imaginative, almost literary quality about this reconstruction of the situation with her parents—and yet Marie had seemed to have such insight, herself, into the game that the three of them had been playing! Here she was, nevertheless, as submerged in the old dilemma as ever. The inner difficulties had not been resolved: if they had been, she wouldn't have started this whole new round, turned it into the reality —the real problems and experiences—going on in her life.

It was so unexpected; she had seemed so perched on the edge of her independence. She had been talking, before I left, about moving out, getting a place of her own, leaving that whole triangulated situation behind her. But she hadn't—obviously. It was as though, intellectually speaking, she could well comprehend the structure of the problem (and what *she* herself should do about it); but emotionally, she was locked into the pattern.

Marie's birthday had just passed; she was now in her thirtieth year.

It was not until many months later that I tried to reach Diana Dahlgren. I apologized for the date on the form, explaining to her that I'd been out in California when I'd sent those statements out, and unable to lay my hands on her address. I wondered if she would mind returning the releases with an accompanying letter about herself? What had been happening to her in this long meanwhile? "You are," I wrote, "the only person about whose subsequent fate I know nothing." (I didn't add that the little that I *did* know had been discouraging and dismal. There was an undeniably high probability that Diana had become institutionalized, on a long-term basis, in the interim . . . or, to look the possible truths in the face, that she had died in the course of a subsequent suicidal effort.)

But the reply that came to me, about a week later, was almost startlingly pleasant and cheerful! "Depression," she wrote, "plays an increasingly small part in my life. I date this from about two years after my hospitalization at Dartmouth, when I finally accepted the fact of my alcoholism at gut level, and set about making Alcoholics Anonymous work for me. It took me a couple of false starts, and it was very difficult for me to come to terms with my alcoholism. But I now have sobriety of almost two and a half years. . . ."

I put down her letter, went to the phone and called her. Mrs. Dahlgren sounded vaguely embarrassed. "I must admit," she told me, "that I remember you only very vaguely. I have only the vaguest memories of so many things that happened to me at Hanover. Someone told me that overdosing on barbiturates is somewhat like electric shock, that you can get an amnesia for the things that were going on during the entire period."

I asked her if she could bring my face to mind, and she couldn't. "Do you remember curly hair, curly dark hair?" She didn't. I laughed. "Then that was me; and you don't remember me, I'd say!"

"It's terrible," admitted Diana, "but you're not the only one—I forgot so much. One of my daughters came home this past summer, and told me 'Mother, do you know it would take you two to three hours to get up, get dressed and eat your breakfast?' And apparently there's something about you that goes, something that's different. I wasn't quite aware of it. But I was living and moving as if I were in a daze." She paused: "I do remember Dr. Burkle ever so slightly . . . but that's about the size of it."

Being slowed down, I told her, could have been a symptom of her depression; it was one of the symptoms.

"Is it? Well, in any case," she answered, "I didn't have any memory, for a long time, and it was miserable." She paused again, then asked politely: "I don't know whether you were aware of it? But at Hanover, they discovered that I have a lithium deficiency. And I've been on lithium ever since I left there. So technically, I'm diagnosed as manic-depressive."

She had never, she added, been manic in the true sense. She was considered to be a manic-depressive depressive—someone who doesn't cycle far upward but who cycles very far down. "It's interesting," remarked Diana, "that I self-medicated with alcohol, which only deepened the depression." She had been killing the pain, in the short run, but using something that would only make things far worse. "I'm no longer at odds with my labels," she added equably. "I don't mind being 'alcoholic'; I don't mind being 'manic-depressive.'"

"But you are *well?*" I asked, as if to hear it from her own lips, once again.

"Oh goodness, yes." She was teaching French part time in a small local elementary school—"eight grades, if you can imagine!" It was fun. She'd become a grandmother in December, when her son Mark's first child was born.

"Basically, things are so much better." Her voice was full of friendliness and of warmth. "I'll tell you, the most profound statement that I can make about myself at this point is—aside from the fact that I am recovered from the depression and that I'm treating my alcoholism in such a way that I don't have to drink any longer—the most important thing I can say about myself is that I finally am beginning to become the person I was meant to be."

"What do you mean by that, Diana?" I asked her.

She hesitated, but just for a moment, then said: "Somewhere along the line I became able to rid myself of my resentments toward my mother. I really just don't feel the same ways about her any longer. I still don't like her very well, but I don't carry that burden all the time. And the very strange thing was that, when I got rid of *that* resentment, so many others left along with it. I have been capable of just going my way and accepting other people, and letting them be themselves—and I am free to be me. I'm no longer forced into comparisons all the time, in an effort to build up my ego."

"What sorts of comparisons?"

"Oh, any sort at all. That's the way my mother raised me. You know: 'My God, did you see her refrigerator, how could anyone *live* like that?' And: 'If I weighed that much I certainly would do something about it!'" She laughed at that moment: "If you recall, *I* weighed quite a little bit when you knew me."

Now it was my turn to hesitate. "You were plump," I conceded.

"Considerably overweight, for me. I had been skinny all my life. I wasn't eating at the time, not at all; it was the booze, I suppose. They tell me some people react that way metabolically, to the alcohol, I mean."

A picture came into my mind at that moment, a remembrance of my first view of Diana Dahlgren, sitting at her desk in her room, writing thank-you notes, dressed in her beige pants suit. "So the extra weight you were packing had nothing to do with anything you were eating, not at all?" I reiterated.

"No, gosh, I wasn't eating. It was simply the booze."

Family counseling, said Mrs. Dahlgren, had been completely unsuccessful. She and her husband had had the notion that the therapist was continually trying to prod them into battle. "We didn't feel like battling. It got worse and worse; and in the end, after another drinking bout, I landed back in the hospital. Bob, of course, didn't understand what it was that was happening to me, and he was doing all the wrong things." She drew in a breath, let it out with a sigh of relief: "He now belongs to Al-anon, an organization that is, you know, for the *spouse* of the one who's doing the drinking, and that makes a big difference." She herself had gone into individual therapy, following her second hospitalization, and had "worked" on some issues of her own during the ensuing year.

"The most tremendous thing that happened to me was being able to deal with my mother," added Diana. "Finally. To be able to rid myself of all *that*."

"So you don't, basically, think that you had anything to renegotiate with your husband?" I asked. "It was mostly memories of your mother—or was it both?"

She thought for a moment. "I don't think there was that much of a problem with Bob. He, naturally, was very upset, disturbed and disgusted with me, during the time that I was drinking. And that showed through. I've always relied on him for approval—in a way that isn't really healthy—because I never had it from anyplace else, I guess. When I was drinking that approval was lacking, because he couldn't, surely, give it. Not under the circumstances. But once I really achieved sobriety, and once *he* began going to Al-anon, the love and the trust that was there between us from the very beginning returned. It came back and it multiplied, really."

"That's just remarkable," I put in, letting myself sound as impressed as I was. "So you really *beat* it."

"I think so." Her voice was quiet and composed. "But of course I make no promises. You can't, if you're an alcoholic. It's just one day at a time. One day at a time, that's the way you take it."

Clearly, there had been more health and strength in the Dahlgren household than anyone could have suspected. They had all, at the time of Diana's hospitalization, been strained out of shape, strained to the point where they'd seemed about to snap apart, to disintegrate, to go flying off into space. But the core had withstood the pressure, and they'd reversed what had looked like an irreversible process. They were a unit, and they'd come back together strongly, once again.

Still, there was some unplumbed mystery here, something about the Dahlgrens as a couple that I couldn't quite understand. I let it go, tried to answer another of the unanswered questions: "Diana, at the time that I saw you, you seemed to be—you were someone who didn't seem to me to have recovered from that move across the country. You struck me, you know, as someone whose roots were raw; you couldn't seem to settle into the new community. Has that happened now? Has that part of your life changed, would you say?"

"No," the reply came with promptness, "and I don't think it ever will. Not for either of us, in the sense of being truly at home. We'll probably be displaced Westerners until retirement, at which point we'll go back. But it doesn't seem to be so abrasive any longer."

There was a silence; I was about to say my thanks and good-byes when Diana Dahlgren embarked on a fresh subject: "Another interesting thing," she observed, "is that when we first came to New England, *Bob* went into a depression; and I think that's when my trouble first began. Because I had always relied on him so *enormously*, and I just didn't recognize what was wrong. I kept trying to pull the whole load without his help, and oh, things just got worse and worse. I went into a terrible depression. I remember those feelings and my thinking of myself as down in a well. A deep, black well, and trying to take two steps up the side, but always sliding back, one step, one step more. I couldn't get *out*. I kept sliding down."

"Did anybody realize, at that time, that Bob was in a depression?"

"No," said Diana, "that never became clear until much later." I thought of her husband's air of withdrawal, during that desperate period when I'd known the Dahlgrens. I thought of Diana's fleeting smile of pleasure and contentment, during that family meeting, and understood well the meaning of her triumph. It was true, she *had* demanded and had gotten what was not being vouchsafed to her in any other form whatsoever—which is to say, Bob Dahlgren's concern and his attention. What had never become apparent was that *he'd* been in need himself. Her husband, it seemed, hadn't known how to recognize what was happening to him, or to ask for her help, so he had broken their connection. This happens. Depressed people have little to give out to others because, during the period of the attack, they are on emotional short rations themselves. He couldn't give out, in his customary way, to Diana. So he'd made some distance between them.

"Was Bob depressed," I asked her, "about moving, or about starting his new job, or what was it?"

"Primarily depressed," she answered, "and he *continues* to suffer from depression about the personality of the chairman of his department. That's about the size of it, right now." She sighed.

"He's just not getting along with the guy?"

"The man's an egomaniac and he makes a lot of unpleasant difficulties. He makes Bob feel, well, unvalued and unrespected. It's just a very difficult situation; and yet the job is, in many ways, one of the best he ever has had. He feels, too, that at this point in his life, it would be hard to find something as good. By and large, he manages pretty well. He does recognize what it is that bothers him. I think he didn't, when he first got here; and it was just as great a shock, coming into these new circumstances, for him as it was for me." She paused, and I thought it was the pause before ending a conversation. But she said: "The man who had been his chairman at home was also his closest and best friend."

"So he expected, I suppose, to get along well with the person? And instead found someone who was going to make him miserable?"

"Yes. So I couldn't go to him for what I was needing."

The conversation halted, momentarily, again. "There's something else," said Diana. "I was *not* meant to be what my mother raised me to be. I was not meant to be fearful and angry and easily hurt—unable to cope with certain kinds of situations. Emotional ones. I do pretty well with practical things, but not with emotional things; that's *not* the way I was meant to be! I think I was meant to be sunny, contented, light at heart and loving toward other people. Not fearful of them, not in competition with them." It was the description of a trans- formation, a pained emergence from the chrysalis of a painful youth. She was in a process of becoming.

As for Margaret Garvey, I hadn't met her until after my return from California, and I'd asked her to sign a formal release at the time of our interviewing. But I checked back with the Somatic Therapies Consultation Service periodically in the weeks and months following her course of ECT and her discharge from Massachussetts General Hospital. Her depressive symptoms, six months after treatment, had not returned. She was doing well, and looking forward to her daugh- ter's forthcoming marriage.

What, in summary, can account for the strangely consistent finding that there is so much more depression among women than there is depression among men? My own view, in the wake of intensive interviewing, in a variety of settings of all sorts, is that it is the female's inherently interpersonal, interdependent, affiliative nature—her affectionateness and orientation toward other people—that underlies her far greater vulnerability. I believe, and much research of the past decade seems to support such a belief, that females are differentially attuned to and interested in the whole matter of relationships and that this greater degree of involvement comes into being very early in life—it begins, pretty much, at birth.

The human infant does, as a number of psychological studies have now demonstrated, come into the world curiously prepackaged to form a powerful love-bond with his or her caretaker. But *female* babies seem to be advance-programmed with a vengeance, for it has been shown that girls are much more reactive and responsive to other human beings than are boys—and this is true as early as at two or three days! Female infants "smile" more (a reflexive or endogenous smile, but the greater number of endearing smiles that newborn girls emit is an arresting observation); and they are more responsive to the cries of other infants in the nursery, and start crying along with another baby more readily than do newborn boys. Girl infants babble more in response to the sight of a human face. At the age of three months, as one fascinating study indicated, female babies will show great interest in and pay a good deal of attention to photographs of human faces. Male babies, at three months of age, couldn't quite discriminate between the photos, and simple line drawings (of both normal and distorted faces); all stimuli seemed equally acceptable to the boys. The girls preferred photos of human faces. These and other research findings seem to suggest an innately stronger "other people" bias in even the littlest female. An innately greater level of inherent

sociability, of attunement to others, of interpersonal sensitivity that
may, in fact, be part of the female's biological heritage—one that
relates to her eventual caretaker role.

However, as psychiatrist Helen Block Lewis observed, after a careful review of the recent "infant research," it "should be emphasized
that a biologically given system is not an automatic unfolding of a
preordained series of events, but one which involves an interaction between genetic factors and life experiences."

Female babies *do*, as Dr. Lewis points out in her book *Psychic War
in Men and Women*, show greater sensitivity to touch, taste, and pain;
and this persists into adulthood. "So a given seems to be at work in
the newborn girl," she writes, "which could permit women to become
more sensitive than men, as befits their bio-cultural role as caretaker-
persons." It is social training, however, that brings the inborn seedlings
of underlying genetic tendencies into the full bloom of female behavior. And women in our society, says Helen Block Lewis, are trained to
devote their lives to others.

"The biological and cultural expectation that they will be mothers
makes it appear natural that they should spend their lives devoted to
others—husbands and children," she points out. "But our society also
scorns people who are not self-sufficient and independent of others.
Women thus learn early that they should be ashamed of the very set
of qualities which are particularly theirs. Ironically, at the same time,
they are constantly threatened by the prospect that if they are not
affectionate enough and as close and loving to others as they ought to
be, they will have failed in their own and others' eyes. They are
ashamed of themselves if they are close to others and guilty and
ashamed of themselves if they are not. . . ."

Who can deny that what she says is true? Women do have to deal
with an unending barrage of contradictory messages and commands,
coming from outside themselves, as well as try to settle conflicting and
often imperious inner wishes, needs, demands. The struggle, for each
woman, is to give shape, pattern, meaningfulness to the existence she is
constructing. To reconcile types of goals which seem to shoot off in
opposite directions; or, if they are irreconcilable, to determine which
of her fantasies, constructed in girlhood, can be carried forth into
adult reality—which dreams fulfilled will, over the course of an entire
lifetime, really bring happiness, really bring satisfaction? The questions she must grapple with have to do with not only Freud's "What
does a woman want?" but with: "What is it that a woman ought *to
be*? What should she *do*?"

Might one imagine, for example, that females who decide to construct a more malelike pattern of living, with a far higher investment in career and work, will be less vulnerable to depression? Perhaps the increasing liberation of women *will*, one day, lead to depressive equality—but the evidence now in hand suggests otherwise. One study, carried out in 1957, and another carried out in 1975, were in agreement: housewives did *not* have more depressive symptoms than did working wives! A very recent investigation, carried out under the auspices of the Yale Depression Unit, compared a matching sample of women who worked and of traditional home-and-family women: *There were, again, no differences in terms of numbers of females afflicted.* (Humorously enough, there was more depression among the husbands of the women who worked!)

The new findings were, however, consistent with previous ones: housewives and working wives were *equally* prone to depression. And both groups of women were *far more* vulnerable than are men. The obvious, and sociological answers to the question: "Why so much more depression among women?" are not all that obvious and clearly correct.

An intellectual road block on this border turns me back in the direction from which I came, and toward what I believe to be the central heart of the issue: the enormous importance and significance of attachment bonds. Women are so very powerfully invested in their affectional relationships—and derive such a sense of self from these vital emotional connections—that their very inner selves become intertwined with other selves, the selves to which they've become so powerfully attached. And then, because those other beings can be lost or devastatingly disappointing, women feel powerless, humiliated, and helpless to correct the situation. It is in woman's willingness to put or ante up so much of her "self" into relationships that she places herself at so much greater risk. For these bonds are so much a part of herself, and are experienced so powerfully, that she often responds to their loss or disruption or disintegration with a full range of depressive symptomatology. Even though, during the course of the life cycle, such losses and disruptions are inevitable—part and parcel, for instance, of such expectable phenomena as growing up, separating, leaving home.

For many women, however, it doesn't *feel* that simple.

I don't mean, for a moment, to be dismissive of the role that might be played by genetics, in terms of transmission of a hereditary tendency to develop a depressive disorder. It is true that in order for a depressive illness to emerge, one would have to have that "biological permission" that I spoke about earlier. Life stress, in terms of losses, crises, negative and threatening and frightening experiences, might, if it were massive enough, be capable of accomplishing the depressive deed alone. There is a point, one would imagine, at which any person would simply be overwhelmed by a set of disasters; and would react with a depression. But generally speaking, when one thinks of the emergence of depressive illness, one thinks in terms of an interaction. The interaction is between stress and the organism's threshold of vulnerability.

It seems clear, given the genetic evidence that has now been gathered and made available, that in particular types of mood illness the role of an internal, biological "predisposing tendency" to develop a mood disorder is really very high. Judith Karlin, for example, was triggered into those wild destructive euphorias so easily, and by such minor life changes and stresses. Most individuals would have coped with those small issues rather efficiently: but they sent Judith's mood state soaring into the skies. If X may stand, then, for "constitutional inborn tendencies" and Y may stand for "stressful life events," it is clear that X had the weightiest and most decisive role in the interaction. Judith's instance was one of a highly fragile and precarious neurophysiology interacting with a set of mildly problematical life circumstances.

It is true, however, that the part played by inborn, inherited, constitutional tendencies of this sort has been well established only in the subtype of depression from which Judith suffered, i.e., manic-depressive disorder. Manic-depressive or "bipolar" (involving both mood poles, euphoria and despair) disease is, as mentioned earlier, the most "biological" of the illnesses of mood. It is a form of depression that affects men and women, moreover, in roughly equal numbers. This is not true of the "unipolar," or "down only" depressions—which afflict women to a far greater degree.

But some experts believe, nevertheless, that unipolar depression—that is to say, a predisposing tendency to develop it—is also transmitted genetically—especially, they argue, in the case of *recurrent* unipolar depressions. The very fact that the episodes recur periodically suggests the existence of an underlying, predisposing (perhaps outright precipitating) biological factor. It is this mysterious, unknown factor—a deficient enzyme, a malfunctioning neuronal receptor—that is "causing" the depressive episodes, and the episodes are unrelated to anything in the person's life. Outbreaks of depression, occurring episodically, point up the existence of a chronic condition—a cerebral chemistry which, so goes this line of reasoning, becomes deranged when the organism is placed upon conditions of stress or threat.

It sounds reasonable, and it could be so. But, despite a good deal of research into the question, the evidence supporting it has not yet been found. There is no solid scientific case that has been made which demonstrates that there is an inherited, predisposing vulnerability in recurring unipolar depressive illnesses. The evidence for a genetic basis for *any form of depression other than manic-depressive disturbance* has, so far, not been definitively established.

If, in the case of repeated depressions, the vulnerability *isn't* demonstrably genetic, where might one suppose that it comes from? No one knows for certain, because it's so remarkably difficult to sort out what might be "inborn" in a particular individual, and what part might be played by that individual's earliest experiences. A case in point is the infant history of someone like Marie Sirotta.

Marie was, it will be remembered, an utterly inconsolable newborn. She was "an impossible baby"; but what, as a matter of fact, really was wrong? Was the initial problem an inborn sensitivity and reactivity on the infant's part, or was it a lack of capacity, on the mother's part, to be nurturant? Marie's mother was, as she later confided to her daughter, then at the low point in terms of her own marriage. The unknown is whether Marie was so naturally overemotional and frustrating a baby that she could not be comforted, or whether her mother, upset and easily frustrated, handled the infant in ways that were impatient and rejecting? What, exactly, *had* happened that had led to so mutually unsatisfying a situation?

The answers to such questions are lost in the mists of time and memory, and also, obviously, matters of personal interpretation. One can only suppose that this squalling daughter, whom she could not seem to care for adequately, made Marie's mother feel inadequate and inferior in her task of mothering. And so the frustration and dissatisfaction must have spiraled.

It is easy to believe that even as a small child Marie experienced periodic bouts of intense dysphoria, of intense despair and uncertainty. For it is in the context of the first affectional bond that, as was noted earlier, the infant first relates to the world; and the mother is, *by the baby*, experienced as the whole world in its entirety. The relationship is, in infancy, engulfing. It is, in its earliest moments, an absorbing duet performed by new mother and newcomer; and it continues, even as others enter the picture, to be the major means by which the developing human being learns about the reliability of the human environment.

For Marie—and for whatever unknown reasons—the lesson was that the world could give no relief or comfort, for she could not be calmed nor helped. Instead of the deeply satisfying duet, the mutually pleasurable and well-fitting set of joyful ballet steps, these partners stumbled over one another; they'd not been able to establish a satisfying, interactive rhythm. It meant anger and frustration on both sides. And Marie hadn't, as a growing child, been in a position to develop that ineffable quality which Erik Erikson called "basic trust" and to which Harry Stack Sullivan had, earlier, given the name of "confidence." What that "confidence" referred to was not a confidence that one would be the winner in every one of life's battles, not at all! Basic trust, or confidence, means an inner assurance that one will know how to go about getting the things that one needs. Ultimately, this is confidence in one's own ability to care for oneself and to survive—on one's own, and independently of one's caretakers. ("Survival" is, in a word, what parents of each generation train their children *for*.)

This basic confidence in the self had not, as we know, developed in the context of the child Marie's ongoing interaction with her mother. It was her father who, as she grew, provided that sense of parental delight and pleasure in his daughter's existence which the mother had been unable to offer. It made up, in some sense, for what the girl experienced as lacking and amiss; but in another sense, it complicated her existence enormously—and was to have abiding effects in her future. For it led her directly into the repetitive situation which was, over and over, Marie's "fate."

There was the triangle, always, and the hostile other woman, and the same seductive, "fatherly" male. The same circumstances, emerging repeatedly; the same concerted efforts, to solve the same old problem. For Marie, the recurring attempts were succeeded by recurring disasters—and recurring attacks of depression. But how could one ever hope to decipher, looking back at her infancy from the vantage point of what had later eventuated in her life, whether Marie had been a vulnerable baby, *at birth*, or whether her depression-proneness had come into being in the context of her earliest experiences in the world? That is, in her relationship to her mother?

The same mystery surrounds the story of Doris Nordlund. Can one suppose "predispositions" to depression, in her terrible story of early blight? (Given the story itself, a "genetic tendency" seems to be a totally unnecessary factor!) Doris' hypocritical, hypochondriacal, and childlike mother had joined forces with her coldly disapproving father; and the pair of them had left their child out in the emotional cold. Why had they behaved so aberrantly? Who can know? What was clear, though, was that Doris—like Marie—had left home without leaving home, and spent many years working on (never working *out*) a particular theme.

Doris Walsh Nordlund had, in truth, spent the major part of her lifetime in reconstructing an elemental situation. She kept "finding herself," time after time, in a state of excessive dependency upon a cold and disapproving man! Isn't it possible that, in both these situations of recurring depression, the recurrence had to do with repeated efforts to solve the same problem—efforts which ended in failure? And that the vulnerability to depression had been established in the context of a malignant early relationship, rather than resulted from a tendency to depressive illness, that was inborn in that individual?

It's just a suggestion. But it makes me think of a slightly different example of early trauma, which was the history of Kath Barrie. Unlike Marie and Doris (who both showed early deficits in social relationships, were isolated, and had little success with peers), Kath was a well-integrated, happy, well-functioning girl until the sudden shattering event, which was her father's death. That loss, occurring when daughter and mother were at the height of their oedipal rivalry, appeared to have triggered a subsequent vulnerability—something that seemed not to have existed before.

For the young girl, still enmeshed in that incestuously toned unconscious love for her beloved and vanished parent, it meant alienation and the hardening of anger at her mother—who, in Kath's eyes, had not loved her man enough to keep him alive. ("*I* would have loved him better had *I* been his wife": such must have been the underlying ideation.) For Kath, the loss of one parent had contained the loss of the other.

At thirteen, then, she'd been emotionally orphaned. And she had remained, ever afterward, in hopeless thrall to the unattainable, unhavable, overidealized, vanishing man. She was alone in the world—in the sense of having no relationship with a trusted, protecting caretaker from her early teens onward—and endlessly pursuing the wonderful male who was just beyond her reach, and not available in terms of an abiding commitment. She suffered recurrent depressions when these relationships reached their inevitable conclusions. Doesn't a story such as hers, and as Doris' and Marie's, make one think far more of a life problem which, like an infectious disease (such as malaria) has been acquired—and which flares up from time to time—than it does of an inherited predisposition to episodes of depression?

Many of the depressed women whom I've interviewed have seemed to be, like Sisyphus, eternally engaged in the reconstruction and re-working of the same dilemma—a problem or task upon which, at some point in her lifetime, the individual has become "stuck" or marooned. Their depressions so often seem to involve the latest collapse of the latest efforts to solve the eternal dilemma (whatever its story line may be).

It is interesting, moreover, to note that *many* people who suffer a single depressive attack, at some point in their lives, never do so again. Fewer than half the people who go through a serious depression will go on to do so again (only about 40 per cent of depressed persons are repeaters). This had led some biologically oriented experts to suggest that the Once Only individuals represent a different strain of the illness, a less "biological" depressive subtype.

If, however, one looked at those Once Only depressions from another point of view one might wonder whether people who suffered a single severe episode—at a particular juncture or stage of living—had in fact been successful in confronting, decoding, and resolving whatever were the central depressive issues? And whether, on the other hand, recurrences involved a failure to locate and to deal with "the problem."

Pernicious childhood experiences cannot, very clearly, serve to explain the far greater numbers of women who suffer depression in adulthood. Men too, it must be presumed, suffer through similarly difficult and pathology-producing early experiences. Neither, as has been seen, can the case be made for a genetic explanation of the higher rates of depression among women. In the most biological of the mood illnesses, i.e., manic-depressive disorder, there is no depressive-disparity. Male and female rates are, roughly speaking, the same. The real explanations lie, in my opinion, in human evolutionary biology. That is, they have to do with—in the most intimate and fundamental way—the entire matter of mammalian attachment bonding.

As Dr. Gerald Klerman observed, in an article written for *Psychology Today*, "Attachment bonds have been useful, even essential, to the survival and development of our species. They are served by a psychobiological apparatus developed through centuries that we have inherited from our mammalian ancestors, particularly the primates. One interesting aspect of the apparatus is that we resist with great biological force any disruption of attachments. We do not give up our bonding without great psychological and physical anguish. . . ." While this is true, obviously, for both sexes, it is even more powerfully true in the case of the female, who is more "people oriented" from the moment of birth; and who tends to value herself and esteem herself in terms of her powerful loving attachments. Women are, I believe, particularly prone to respond depressively to losses, or threatened losses, of love-bonds because they've placed so much more of their own inner substance *in* them.

The female's self, as psychoanalysts Carol Gilligan and Malkah Notman have noted, is more "embedded" in her important relationships. The embeddedness of women, they write, "leads them to appear, when contrasted with men, more contextual in their sense of self, and more responsive to interpersonal cues." According to Drs. Gilligan and Notman: "The evidence of sex differences comes particularly from those studies which tap into women's language and thought, their fantasies and associations, all of which are indicative of certain regularities in women's construction of the relationship between self and other."

The outer membrane of the female's psyche is, somehow, more permeable; it is not distinct and delimited from the psyches with which she is emotionally enmeshed. (Males, in contrast, tend to keep "my own self" and others far more clearly separate; and to have greater conflicts about intimacy, i.e., permitting the other *in*.) But because, in the case of the woman, the context has often been incorporated into the inner being, the loss or threatened loss of a powerful attachment can be experienced as a devastation of the person's own ego, her own self. The loss of that bond *feels like* death itself because the person's entire being has been defined in relation to it. She is then faced with the terrifying question of who she is, and what she is, without it. She is faced with the prospect of living on her own (in terms of giving up dependence on that relationship to tell her who she is and supply her reasons for being). This is, in my view, where the true vulnerability lies: for "aloneness" of this sort is something for which many women are unprepared. *So* unprepared, in fact, that a woman is often readier to experience as guilt, anger, and reproaches directed against the self, what is, in fact, deep dismay and disappointment about a close relationship.

This is, I believe, where so much female depression begins. If one has been disappointed, then the real causes lie in one's own unacceptability, inferiority, unworthiness, unlovability, and guilt (guilt, especially, about underlying anger at the other). Becoming depressed is a way of discharging those awful, negative feelings; and yet leaving the needed emotional bond intact. The depressive stance is a waving of the white flag of powerlessness; and the bottom line, in the depressed female's contract, is that she will not be abandoned. It is a very bad bargain.

It should be recognized, however, that the woman's struggle to be autonomous, to be "me alone" and thoroughly capable of existing on her own, probably flies not only in the face of powerful feminine-behavior shaping—starting in earliest infancy—but of deep-seated biological tendencies as well.

For those modes of perceiving the world and organizing behavior which are more distinctively "female" can't be thought of as having sprung into being in the context of the world we now inhabit. Human culture accounts for only 1 per cent of human evolutionary history. We must think, therefore, in terms of patterns of being and behaving that developed over untold centuries, and which were keyed to survival of the human group in the primitive environment. Such a way of being would have been predicated upon powerful social bonds, "bonds of love," which would serve to keep otherwise more vulnerable individuals in close proximity to protectors. Powerful attachments, in short, between the female and a mate upon whom she depended; and between parents and their offspring; and between the family and the larger social group. This is not the environment of modern life. The very word "dependence" has become something like a dirty word!

For women, the ways in which we now lead and live our lives is, I believe, profoundly antibiological. It is, moreover, nothing that childhood "femininity" training, which encourages affiliativeness, being pleasing to others, being loved, being warm and nurturant, etc., prepares a woman for either. Women, who are both taught to set such an enhanced value upon their emotional bonds and who are *innately ready to learn to do so*, enter the sea of modern adult realities in the leakiest of psychological ships. For, having learned well the important lessons about the vital significance of love-bonds, and the ways in which her humanity and her being are to be defined by them, a woman must then make her way through an ocean of uncertainties in which her attachments may not indeed, help to keep her afloat. Rupture and disintegration are not exceptions; they are cultural norms. To cite just one of the more daunting statistics: for every three marriages entered into, more than one ends in divorce. And the very fact of high geographical mobility, which spells the loss of extended-family ties, friendships, and a lack of stable outside supports must be added to this picture. So must the fact that most women outlive most men by about seven years. So, should a relationship endure throughout a couple's lifetime, the woman—usually a few years younger than the man she's married—will have to look forward to a decade of life alone.

Most women will, at some point in their lives, have to live alone; and most women will have to learn that they can *be*, even in the absence of a strong emotional bond. They are going to have to learn to survive "aloneness" in the same way that men sometimes have to learn they can *be*, even in the wake of a failure. But such learning tasks are, I fear, not going to be easy ones. Depression among women, given the social climate that we inhabit, is not by any means going to disappear, to diminish: it is probably going to afflict women—as the uncertainty of their attachments increases—in greater and greater numbers. We are not about to eradicate depressive illnesses from our midst. The best that can be done is to survive them.

Which involves, in my view, not only getting *out* of an episode of depression but doing so as quickly as possible. This means, in turn, becoming familiar with the common symptoms (which are in fact, fairly glaring and obvious) and, if they're present, thinking about what the underlying issues might be. This *can* involve a process of self-review, or of talking matters over with a trusted friend; and it should involve, surely, going for treatment if treatment does appear to be necessary. But for many people, this latter deed, seems very difficult to accomplish!

How many of the women that I've interviewed have acknowledged that they were depressed for many weeks, months, or even years, and knew it, but said: "I felt that I should be able to get under control and to handle this whole thing by myself." Such bravery is misguided, for —as has been seen in the histories of the women described in these pages—the depressive illnesses can be effectively treated, in a variety of ways. In the histories of Anne and Debra, of Sandy, Marie, and Judith; of Kath, Laurie, Diana, Doris, and Margaret Garvey, a goodly portion of the menu of possible treatments has been explored.

It is true that the natural history of a depressive attack, from beginning to end, is usually somewhere between four and twelve months. Most of these women would, therefore, have gotten well given the passage of enough time. But four to twelve months of misery (possibly longer) for no reason and no purpose whatsoever would represent four to twelve months of needless pain. There are treatments available that can bring relief within a few days or in weeks. Depression is, it's true, a problem that's so widespread that it has been called "the common cold of psychiatric disorders." What must be remembered, in this particular instance, is that this is a cold for which powerful cures now *do* exist!

I have not, I should add, described *all* of the possible treatments of depression that are, at the present time, either in use or now emerging. There are some behaviorally oriented techniques that attempt to guide the depressed person out of her do-nothing apathy and passivity (the "What's the use of bothering?" stance) and into potentially more rewarding forms of activity—which will bring her positive feedback, which will, in turn, give her psychic fuel to continue behaving in a new style. This whole effort is, in a word, directed toward changing the ways a person feels about herself by bringing about change in the things that she ordinarily *does*, on a daily basis.

Another relatively new psychotherapy of depression, developed by Dr. Aaron T. Beck at the University of Pennsylvania's Mood Clinic (which he founded) is called Cognitive Therapy. This mode of treatment is based upon the theoretical premise that the person who becomes depressed is being victimized by her or his own thought-process. The depressive's thoughts or "cognitions" are deeply biased in a negative direction: she or he self-flagellates mercilessly, with a relentless stream of self-denigrating, self-diminishing, self-hating thoughts—thoughts which may not even be completely perceived, but which lie at the margin of consciousness.

It is the bad thoughts, assert Beck and his colleagues, that create the bad (depressed) feelings. Cognitive therapy involves careful analysis of the person's customary *mode of interpreting her world to herself*. The treatment, which involves self-help "homework" exercises, is elegantly designed in such a way as to tinker with the depressive thought-processes. By interrupting the stream of distortedly negative comments being made *to* the self *by* the self, the bad feelings are prevented from happening. This form of psychotherapy has yielded good results* and its effectiveness has been demonstrated in a series of research studies (a rare event in the case of psychotherapy, for the outcome isn't usually rigorously assessed).

Still another new, streamlined, and sophisticated form of treatment has been developed by depression researchers Dr. Gerald Klerman and Dr. Myrna Weissman. This is a brief (twelve to sixteen weeks) therapy, called "Interpersonal Psychotherapy," which is targeted specifically upon the quick relief of depressive symptoms. Here, the therapeutic procedures are based upon the idea that many, or *most*, depressions have to do with something going amiss or awry in a close relationship. There is a loss, or the threat of a loss, of something vi-

---

* Laurie Michaelson, despite the depth and complexity of her difficulties, responded beautifully to this "let's change the way you view your self, your world, and your future to a more positive orientation" type of treatment.

tally meaningful in the depressed person's immediate milieu. And it is this interpersonal loss, or chronic frustration in an important relationship, upon which the therapist's attention becomes focused.

Healing, generally speaking, has to do with dealing intensively and in minutest detail with the difficulties arising in the context of that particular relationship (or, it may be, set of relationships). The interpersonal psychotherapist seeks, at the outset, for a problem in one of the four major areas—possible loci of emotional loss—upon which most of the discussion will be focused. Let me describe these four relational "problem areas" briefly, for they will sound interestingly familiar.

The first is *abnormal grief*, which is to say unresolved issues and angry feelings that have made it impossible for the survivor of a loved person's death to reintegrate her life once again in the wake of the loss of that attachment. (Margaret Garvey was, for an example, someone whose mourning-process had slid into a severe depression.) *Interpersonal disputes*, the second category, refers most frequently to role disputes between marital partners. The disputes have to do with Who wants What from Whom, and Who isn't getting what she or he feels entitled to, and even What is needed for emotional survival. (Diana and Bob Dahlgren and Doris and Eric Nordlund and Laurie and Gabe Michaelson were instances of role clashes of this sort, in which expectations were being disappointed. All had resulted in the woman, who was actually angry and discouraged, becoming sick as a way of handling those feelings. These women were opting to be ill rather than overtly unhappy or disappointed in their marriages—and research evidence indicates that it is in this context, i.e., marital discord, that most female depression emerges.)

Role transition, the third designated "loss" area, has to do with a change in status—for example, going from being a married woman to being a single woman, or from wife to widow—where the central difficulty is in the transition itself, in the reorganizing of the self-concept as one moves from one way of being to another. (Sandy Geller is a cogent example of someone who, in passing from "dependent wife" to "autonomous single woman" passed through a depressed and desperate life interlude.) And the fourth category of possible difficulty, *interpersonal deficits*, covers those instances in which a person, being confronted with a situation in which she or he must count on her own resources, becomes depressed in the face of that unaccomplishable task. This is, most usually, the instance of the young adult who is about to leave home and feels unable to make it. The depression is, in this circumstance, linked to deep feelings that one's resources are not there, in place, and there sufficiently: one can't sustain oneself independently. What this has to do with, really, is a person's sense that she won't know how to go about getting those things that she needs, for her security and for her survival. (This shaky and problematic sense of self was the basic difficulty in the instances of Anne Munson, Debra Thierry, Marie Sirotta.)

The interpersonal psychotherapist, by intensively exploring one of these four major regions of concern, can get rapidly to the core of the depressive pain. The techniques used are, it should be added, the standard tried-and-true techniques of ordinary psychotherapy. They have simply been structured in a most sophisticated way to help the patient confront the source of the hurt in the most rapid and efficient manner. That source is, as the very name of the treatment indicates, assumed to be located in an interpersonal relationship—one which has been lost, or one which is in need of attention, in terms of clarifying issues, or renegotiation of roles and mutual expectations.

The depressive episode itself is seen, in any event, as something that has occurred in a psychosocial and interpersonal setting—and it is the setting itself that is examined very closely. (Drug treatment is, however, sometimes used concurrently, in order to reduce the biological or "vegetative" symptoms of the depression, such as sleep and appetite disorder, loss of libido, fatigue, etc.) It may be true that the person's life context is the major thing that ails her. In this case, that context may need to be altered—or changed radically—in order to cure present symptoms and prevent their recurrence. "Improvement" relates to helping the person to view her situation realistically, and to examine some of the options she may not have been capable of considering.

But in any case curing a depression, or at least curing *a great many depressions*, is viewed by the interpersonal therapist as something deeply involved in curing what is going on in a depressing relational situation. "Curing" may involve a restructuring of that relationship, or the necessity to get out of it completely. This entire approach is, it seems to me, a very promising and practical mode of dealing rapidly and effectively with the emergence of depressive symptoms—and it is, for obvious reasons, one that I think will be very useful in the brief treatment of depressed women.

The great point, however, no matter what type of care one might opt for, is to acquaint oneself with the common, even "classical" symptoms of depression. It is, moreover, to have some working understanding of what the issues might be—and then the range of possibilities, in terms of doing something about it. But never, never to accept depression as a fact of one's life, as something that *is* there and will stay for the predictable while, because it has to do with "the way that life really is." It isn't, or needn't be. But the depressed person can't know that—at least not while she's *in* the depression—because she's suffering from an illness of the body and the spirit.

The central feature of depressive illness is *anhedonia*, the inability to experience pleasure. It is the loss of the capacity to taste one's food, to enjoy one's sexuality, to take an interest in one's ordinarily interesting activities. It is the loss of that capacity, so taken for granted, to wake up refreshed and restored, after a night's normal slumber. To be depressed is to be thoroughly incapable of enjoying one's life. The mood state itself is a filter of experience, allowing nothing cheerful or gratifying to come through.

No one who is in a state of depression can cope very effectively with what may be real-life considerations and pressing adaptive problems. And the person who *is* depressed is in some real way a person who, on being presented with one of life's serious riddles, has thrown up her hands and said: "I don't (or maybe dare not) have the answer!" She has said, behaviorally, that she cannot and will not cope. As long as the mood disturbance remains, she *will* remain in a state of stasis. She is unlikely to gather the energy or spirit to solve or perhaps even to discover what might be the problem.

Diana Dahlgren, for instance, never learned of Bob's own depression until hers had remitted, and she'd been able to stop drinking. All that she did know, at the time that she was slipping into and out of depressions, was that she felt deprived of the nourishment of his care and attention. Sandy Geller, when she was sleeping around compulsively and feeling increasingly bad about it, had not an idea in the world about how she might do it differently—how she could go about establishing a new, lasting, loving connection with a man. In her downcast state, she was moving from one transient relationship to another, finding uncaring men who would then serve to confirm her in her own low ("I'm without value") self-opinion. Doris Nordlund hadn't been able to leave the desolate shell of her marriage—being depressed meant that dying was a more reasonable sort of solution. It was only when she'd become *well again* that each of the women were, in fact, able to find some workable answers to what had seemed to be insoluble, incurable dilemmas.

Each person's answers had, finally, had to do with more than the particulars of her close relationships: getting better meant a capacity to move out of a rigid and uninventive rut, an ability to involve herself in new plans, new options, new jobs in some instances—it meant an energy for life, for the future.

Most of the women that I've talked about in these pages underwent *change* during the time that I knew them. Their stories (or "case histories") were, as has been seen, most various. Some, like those of Doris Nordlund and Debra Thierry, were strange and exotic; and some, like that of Diana, were "ordinary," at least until the onset of the terrible melodrama of a clinical depression. But each person changed: each seemed to see her circumstances and *herself in them* very differently, once the attack of depression had cleared. It was as though, from this bitterest and most piercing of experiences, each woman had managed to snatch a succulent fruit of self-knowledge.

What she learned, moreover, had to do not only with a set of difficulties inherent in a certain phase of the female life cycle, but with a life progression in the direction of autonomy, the capacity to bear one's aloneness and the struggle to be one's own unique self— what Diana Dahlgren had described as the process of "becoming the person that I was meant to be." What she learned had to do with the realization that the self had value, and that that value was something that was contained within.

For some, I suspected, the new self-understanding would fade and become blurry with the passage of time. The painful lessons would have to be learned again—perhaps again and again—over the course of their lifetimes. For others, though, the leap in self-knowledge would be something permanent; it would persist as part of who that woman was, and become part of her way of being. She would, henceforth, be better—in every sense of the word.

Signs That You May Be
Suffering from Depression

A. Are you bothered by feeling sad, depressed, blue, hopeless, down in the dumps? Are you feeling that you just don't care much about things anymore? *And have these feelings persisted for at least two weeks?* Or, on the other hand, have you been having very low, sad days which seem to alternate with days when you feel elated and exuberant?

B. If you would agree that the above description fits you—say, that you're feeling sad, down, and blue, and as though nothing much in life really matters to you—then examine the following list of the common symptoms of depression, and formulate your own individual set of answers:

1. Have your eating habits changed recently?
Although persistent or progressive appetite loss is the more commonly encountered depressive symptom, one sometimes does see the opposite: accelerating food intake, followed by weight gain. This appears to be part of a self-perpetuating obesity-depression cycle: the depressed person stuffs herself, *without* experiencing increased appetite in terms of increased hunger.

2. Have you been having trouble staying asleep; for example, are you snapping awake in the middle of the night, or in the early hours of the morning? Or have you been having trouble *falling* asleep? Are you sleeping unusually much or long?

3. Are you feeling fatigued, tired, run-down, and without your usual energy?
The depressed person's complaints about feeling "exhausted, for no

reason" are frequent, although the reasons for her profound energy loss are not clear. Some of the theoretical explanations of the phenomenon are, in any case, discussed in Chapters Eight and Eighteen.

4. Are you less interested in sex, and do you find sex less pleasurable?

Loss of libido is common in states of depression, as is a diminished capacity for orgasm, in the female (and a diminished ability to maintain an erection, in the male). Some depressed people do, however, seek *more* and more diverse sexual experiences—as did Sandy Geller, whose history is explored in Chapter Five. Indiscriminate sexual encounters, in such instances, seem to feed into the person's overall sense of guilt and worthlessness, and her overall lack of esteem for herself.

5. Are you having trouble thinking, concentrating, or making decisions?

6. Have you been unable to sit still, to the point where it's necessary to be moving about constantly? Or, on the contrary, are you feeling unusually slowed down—as if it's too much trouble to move about and as if there's nothing much worth doing anyhow?

In the first instance, there would be the possibility of an agitated or hyperactive depression, characterized by restlessness, pacing, pressured, repetitive speech. In the second instance, there'd be a question of a retarded, or generally slowed-down depressive state—affecting not only one's abilities to think, talk, and move about, but even one's capacity to recall recent events. A person afflicted by this form of depression will often speak in sentences that are slow and halting; her or his facial expression tends to be flat, fixed, and unchanging.

7. Have you been preoccupied by thoughts of taking your own life —or by wishing that you were dead?

8. Are you more prone to anger, more irritable, more easily annoyed and resentful than is usual for you?

9. Are you feeling extremely discouraged and pessimistic about most things?

10. Are you feeling guilty, worthless, or down on yourself?

11. Have you been brooding about unpleasant things that once happened in the past?

12. Have you been feeling inadequate and self-critical—as though you've recently realized that you're much less attractive or competent than you thought you were?

13. Are you crying more than usual?

14. Have you been feeling needier than at other times? Desperately in need of help or reassurance from somebody?

15. Have you been suffering from physical complaints lately—such as gastrointestinal problems (constipation is a common one) or severe headache or backache—for which no medical explanation or cause can be found?

16. Does your mouth feel dry a good deal of the time, or have you got a persistent bad taste in your mouth?

The reader who has answered the top item, A, in the affirmative, and who can, then, respond to two or more of the subquestions under B in the affirmative, ought to consider the possibility that she is depressed at this time, and that it might be advisable for her to seek some form of assistance, or a consultation, at the very least.

Finding Help

Suppose that, on balance, it seems possible or even probable that you (or perhaps someone you care about) may require antidepressant treatment. How can one know whether drugs or psychotherapy would be preferable in a particular situation? Or, for that matter, whether a combination of *both* forms of treatment would be possible —and whether this type of approach is feasible? And how does one go about finding out? Where does one *start*, when it comes to taking that vital first step?

These are practical and specific questions, which call for practical and specific answers—and they are, for that reason, difficult to talk about in a broad and general sense. Let me attempt, nevertheless, to answer to them with all of the concreteness and specificity that are possible, here.

First of all, as the case histories and situations described in the foregoing pages will surely have made clear, there are different kinds, or subtypes, of depressive disturbances; and these do respond, selectively, to differing types of treatment. Unipolar or "plain," and bipolar (both high and low moods) illnesses are, for instance, both disorders of mood state; but in terms of prognosis, preferred types of treatment, and similarly crucial factors, they are distinct and separate entities.

Within the differing depressive subtypes, moreover, the mania or depression will be experienced at varying degrees of intensity. One person, suffering from a unipolar depression, may feel sad, down, and as if her life is dully painful. Another, also suffering from a unipolar disturbance, may be experiencing it with a needle-sharp intensity. Across the entire depressive spectrum, one can encounter such a dizzying amount of variation—as well as so many masks and forms of disguises—that the disorders of emotional state have been notoriously slippery, and very difficult to categorize. For example, such disparate conditions as hyperactivity in children and senility in older people are viewed, by a not inconsiderable number of experts, as masked depressions that frequently go unrecognized.

Getting the best possible treatment does, however—in depression as in any other form of psychological or biological disturbance—involve targeting, as closely as possible, the particular sort or subtype of illness involved. Has the depression occurred, for instance, in reaction to a recent life stress? Or has it seemed to come out of nowhere? Have there been repeated depressive episodes in a particular person's life that seem to form part of a pattern?

These are things that a competent clinician will need to know. He or she will also need to assess the degree of severity and impairment. Is the depression affecting a particular woman's ability to function in her customary set of roles—in her marriage, family, and in her career, if she works? It is essential to take these considerations into account, for sometimes the depressed woman—like Humpty Dumpty—can't get her life together again, once the attack is over and her normal coping capacities have fully (or almost fully) returned. There are situations in which an effort to delimit the social consequences of the person's depression must be an integral aspect of her treatment.

At the present time, fortunately, a number of very effective psychotherapeutic and biological modes of treating depression are available—and I use the word "fortunately" advisedly, because *none* existed at the beginning of our own century. The problem of finding the right physician, who will then offer the correct form of treatment, is one that still does, nevertheless, remain. Finding a good doctor to treat one's depression is, in a way, something like finding a good clinician to treat *other* kinds of medical problems and conditions. To some degree, it's simply a matter of luck and the breaks; of getting the right referral at precisely the right time. It is still the case, however, that the self-protective health services consumer is someone who informs herself as well and as fully as possible. She doesn't fling her health and well-being and her survival itself into someone else's safekeeping, willy-nilly.

The reader of this book does already, as a matter of fact, know quite a lot. For the case histories that have been discussed will have given her a good understanding of what a depression can *be*, in differing instances, and what kinds of therapy can be used. Knowing what she *does* know, though, and feeling that she herself is in need of attention to a problem, where ought she to think of going?

The best place to begin is with one's family doctor. A thorough medical examination, carried out by a competent internist, is necessary in order to rule out *other* possible causes for your fatigue, disturbed sleep, or other physical or psychological complaints. It may happen that even if you *are* suffering from a depression, it is of a mild-to-moderate and passing kind. Your search for relief may end right here in your general practitioner's office. For many people do experience such transient depressive episodes—often connected to a particular life stress—and the loss of sleep involved is a good part of the problem. A mild sedative or tranquilizer, resulting in a few nights of nourishing sleep, can be all that really is needed. The person's depression subsides.

If, however, the depressive symptoms persist after a period of a few days—*at most*, a week or two—the chances are that, whatever the original and precipitating problem might have been, the depression now has a life of its own.

The primary task, if this is the case—or if your doctor has diagnosed a long-standing depression, on your initial visit—is that of selecting a psychiatrist, either for an expert opinion or for a course of subsequent treatment. If your own family physician has a good understanding of what it means to be depressed, he or she will be very willing to refer you on to someone else—someone skilled and practiced in the treatment of the depressive disorders.

It would be unwise, if you *are* depressed, to drift along with only your general practitioner's care. Or if not unwise, at least not the most prudent thing to do! For most internists have only the most general knowledge of the various types of antidepressant medications; they're neither especially trained nor especially sophisticated when it comes to the use of these drugs.

The commonly prescribed tricyclic antidepressants (such as Elavil and Tofranil), and the somewhat trickier MAO-inhibiting drugs (i.e., Parnate, Nardil, and the like), and lithium carbonate (the form in which lithium is given) are *all* medications which require considerable pharmacological skill and know-how on the part of the prescribing physician. They require more of the clinician's *time*, as well; for dosage levels and possible side effects must be carefully and knowledgeably monitored.

Many general practitioners do, as a matter of fact, view all of the antidepressant drugs as too time-consuming, too troublesome, and too dangerous to monitor. Depressed patients who are also experiencing anxiety—which isn't uncommon—are frequently given a mild tranquilizer, such as Valium. But as Dr. Gerald Klerman has observed (see Addendum, Chapter Seventeen) a drug like Valium will not relieve depression and may, over time, actually *intensify* the problem. Prescriptions for Valium have skyrocketed in number, Dr. Klerman told me; but antidepressants are *under*prescribed, given the prevalence of the depressive disorders.

I'm aware, of course, that family physicians encounter depressed patients—and that they *treat* depressed patients—very frequently. For a particular person, this treatment may turn out to be effective and successful. But I do think it wise to bear in mind that a general practitioner may not offer the correct drug, or may offer too little of the correct drug—and the antidepressants have to reach therapeutic dosage levels before they can possibly provide any relief. It is wise, therefore, to be concerned about who is prescribing your antidepressant medication. A "drug failure" may be due to a lack of knowledge, on the doctor's part, about the most effective use of the varying kinds of antidepressants.

There are problems, as well, with "psychotherapy" offered by an internist or general practitioner. Taking a patient through a course of psychotherapy is something that few G.P.s have had training to do. And the process itself is different from the mere expression of concern and sympathy; tender loving care from a wise and authoritative physician sounds awfully nice, but it won't touch the underlying sore and depressive dilemmas. It would be rare to find an internist with both the requisite skills and the time available to do serious psychotherapy with his depressed patients.

The result of all this may be, unfortunately, an inadequately or nontreated patient. This is why a consultation with a skilled psychiatrist— or with a clinical psychologist or psychiatric social worker, who works in tandem with a psychiatrist who is knowledgeable about the use of these drugs—seems to me to be the most self-protective "ounce of prevention" that is possible, at this particular juncture. A referral to a specialist in the area ought to be as routine as would be a referral to a surgeon, if the question were one of even the most mundane sort of an operation.

Suppose, however, that your own physician is unfriendly to the idea of any outside consultation. It is still your privilege to secure another doctor's input and views, and you may (especially if your discomfort continues or intensifies) want to go ahead and do so, anyhow. In such a situation, the best thing to do would be to call the nearest teaching hospital and request a list of names of psychotherapists and psychiatrists who are well recommended and working in your own particular area. Or, if this option isn't feasible, it might be worth spending a dollar or two on a long-distance telephone call to the nearest university-affiliated psychiatric clinic. Again, one would request a list of names of people practicing in the closest places possible. It sounds haphazard, I know, but it still is better than no care whatsoever.

Mental health care facilities have now, moreover, sprung up throughout the length and breadth of this country; and there will be few readers for whom psychiatric attention will be totally and impossibly out of reach. It is to be hoped and expected, though, that the psychiatry of tomorrow will include the establishment of depression clinics—rather like the clinics for the treatment of diabetes, arthritis, and other commonly occurring disorders that now exist—which would make it much easier for a person to know where to *go* when it became apparent that a problem was emerging. What the clinic approach means for the patient, moreover, is the availability of a *group* of experts—psychiatrists, clinical pharmacologists, psychologists, nurse-practitioners, psychiatric social workers—who, by working together, are pooling their various skills and their knowledge. (A dozen or so such clinics, all associated with leading universities, have been set up within this past decade. A goodly portion of my own research for this book was carried out at one such facility—the Affective Disorders Clinic at the University of Pittsburgh—which has, itself, recently been designated a national research center for the study and treatment of depression.)

And now for a couple of cautionary observations. When it comes to seeking treatment it would be wise, as a general rule of thumb, to try to avoid clinicians who are fully committed to either biological or psychological forms of therapy *exclusively*. Doctor-shopping is, as I well realize, something that is not going to be very easy at this point. But one of the serious difficulties of American psychiatry, at least as it is practiced today, is the therapist's tendency to pledge allegiance to either a psychological *or* a biological approach to the disorders of mood.

It thus happens that one expert prefers using lithium, in every possible situation, while another favors ECT and still another believes that nothing but psychotherapy can ever root out the underlying depressive problems. If you yourself come to one of these psychiatric idealogues for therapy you may find that the treatment you receive has more to do with whose doorbell you've rung than it has to do with anything else! (Including the particular nature of your own problem!)

This is something that every health-care consumer ought to be well aware of. A good rule of thumb would be, in any case, to monitor one's own treatment—and to *not coast along*, for too long a period of time, if the treatment seems to be ineffective. If, after a suitable trial, your symptoms haven't remitted, or if they've worsened, it is time to look further. It is time, at least, to get someone else's expert opinion. There is a range of effective treatments that *is* available; and if one type of therapy doesn't seem to bring results, there are other avenues that ought to be tried. Ask yourself, from time to time, "How am I feeling? Am I getting better?" If not, take responsibility and *be active on your own behalf*.

One final word about that drugs-vs.-psychotherapy controversy. There is no good evidence that supports the notion that antidepressant medications impede progress in psychotherapeutic or "talking" types of treatment. On the contrary, studies carried out by Gerald Klerman and Myrna Weissman indicate that the two types of therapy can be used together, when appropriate, with a very fine degree of effectiveness.

Drug treatments appear to be most useful in ameliorating the *biological* symptoms of depression—such as sleep- and appetite-loss, etc.— while psychotherapy is most helpful in improving the person's social and interpersonal functioning. The two modes of therapy seem to be useful in dealing with different *aspects* of the depression.

Depending on the set of problems and difficulties, a particular person's care and treatment may be weighted more toward psychotherapy and less (or not at all) toward antidepressant drugs. Or, the opposite may be true: the medications may be primary, while psychological treatments play a far less important role. But the two forms of therapy, biological and psychological, are by no means mutually exclusive. And in practice, they are used together very successfully, by many clinicians—and with impressive results.

Do Numbers Lie?

As one might imagine, the consistently sexually lopsided statistics—the undeviating disparity in numbers of females and numbers of males diagnosed as suffering from depression—have presented themselves as a puzzle to experts of every theoretical hue and stripe. And there have been numerous efforts, on the part of psychiatrists, psychologists, epidemiologists (those who study epidemics of illness in the population at large), sociologists, and others, to explain what remains a most peculiar phenomenon. Some among this great group of explainers have taken the position that the phenomenon is, in fact, much *too* peculiar to be true! The statistical findings are erroneous, suggest these writers, because they reflect certain biases in the "counting-up" process. This is the "numbers *do* lie" point of view.

The idea here is that the unequal figures—and the fact that so many more women are in treatment for some form of depression—bears witness only to the eagerness of doctors and psychotherapists to *label* women. The distressed person who happens to be female will get this particular dogtag—DEPRESSION—hung around her neck with undue alacrity. But women are not in actuality, some experts have insisted, one whit more depressed than are their male counterparts.

This is the argument made by Phyllis Chesler in her book *Women and Madness*. Chesler contends that women tend to get diagnosed—i.e., *called*—"depressed" or "disturbed" or "crazy" or "mad" with somewhat sinister readiness. Such psychiatric put-downs are, she maintains, nothing other than a covert societal mechanism—a means for punishing those women who may be deviant in terms of adjusting to and "accepting their femininity" under terms laid down by the male-dominated mental health establishment (which represents the community at large). The woman who fails to accept her female role, along with its attendant inferior social status, isn't "behaving"—and she gets socked with a psychiatric diagnosis. The diagnosis itself is, in Chesler's view, a handy "medical" and scientifically respectable device for keeping women in their place.

What Chesler is suggesting is, in short, that the hefty sex differential in terms of "numbers of persons in treatment for depression" reflects only the ease with which one sex is labeled as being depressed—which in turn reflects social discrimination. It has nothing to do with any objective reality nor with the unbiased truth of the situation.

Could this explain those strange statistics? Might the high rates of depression among women be nothing other than a social phantasmagoria—a "scientific finding" that relates to nothing whatsoever (other, that is, than the biases of psychotherapists and clinicians)? Are females actually no more melancholy, afflicted, anxious, troubled, depressed than are males—but simply seen as being so?

Chesler's views have a certain compelling quality—especially since those depression statistics *are* disturbing, and one would like to explain (since one can't simply wish) them away. But I believe that her argument, as well as the empirical evidence she amasses in support of it, is probably largely false. After four years of studying the problem of women and depression in a wide variety of clinical settings, I myself have not actually encountered anyone whom I suspected to be suffering from a disorder that could be called "psychiatric labeling."

The women that I came to know slightly, or to know well, during this period of time; the women that I talked to at great length, or just a little; the women that I saw just once or talked to over periods of months—they *were* suffering. They were in pain, and in need of help; there just was no question about it. None of them were victims of a "mental health establishment conspiracy" having to do with the blatant and systematic misdiagnosing of women.

One may argue, of course, that the experiences of one investigator—who is, moreover, studying the problem of women and depression in some of this nation's most advanced psychiatric facilities—can't *pretend* to be anything like Chesler's systematic and data-supported overview of the treatment women receive in the entire mental health care system. And I will acknowledge at once that mine is the close-up look, the account of where I've gone and what I've seen; and the kinds of things that happened in the types of places that I happened to go to . . . which is surely open to charges of particularities, quirkinesses, biases.

But so are Ms. Chesler's statistics—or at least her interpretation of them—open to charges of bias. Most epidemiologists consider *Women and Madness* to be a political and polemical book, one that is neither scientific nor objective. The late Dr. Marcia Guttentag, who directed a nationwide study of what many consider to be an "epidemic" of depression among women, made a careful study of the same statistical data that Chesler used. Chesler's figures were found to be based on *absolutes*—that is, on simple head counts of the numbers of women, and numbers of men in county and state psychiatric facilities. Because Chesler found so many more women than men who were age sixty-five and over in these mental institutions, Chesler concluded that anti-feminine bias was rampant among the (mostly male) psychiatric establishment; and that women were being railroaded, via the "diagnosing" track, into geriatric careers as mental patients.

But what she did *not* do was to adjust those figures for age. If there are more women of age sixty-five and over in mental institutions, it is because there are more women of that age in general. *Women live longer.* In fact, given the larger number of women of that age in the over-all population, there were years—the Guttentag study group found—when women were *underrepresented* in psychiatric hospitals. Chesler's claim (that old women are tossed into mental institutions that are actually custodial homes) was simply not found to be substantiated.

Indeed, as one worker on the Guttentag project (which was officially entitled "The Women in Mental Health Project at Harvard") told me, there were years when *men*, in proportion to their numbers in the population, were overrepresented in mental institutions, as a group! Men are, furthermore, far more likely to be committed to institutions against their will. The reason is that male diagnoses very frequently involve problems with *other people*—alcoholism, aggressive acting out of psychological problems, etc.—and they are sent via the courts and brought in by the police.

Women, on the other hand, tend to receive the more "passive" diagnoses. They become depressed, or perhaps schizophrenic—but they don't hurt anyone. For this reason, women are more commonly brought for treatment by their friends or families, and they are committed on a *voluntary* basis.

Each sex does, intriguingly, appear to take the lead in specific types of psychiatric disturbance. Men, as a group, show far higher rates of alcoholism, drug disorder, behavior disorders of childhood and adolescence, etc.—in short, the more action-oriented, disruptive-to-others kinds of difficulty. Where women are concerned, there is one single category in which they hog the diagnostic stage to an almost preposterous degree. And this is, of course, depression.

The peculiarly high rates of depression among women cannot, in all honesty, be explained away in terms of sexist name-calling.

The Guttentag group came away from their own analysis of the mental health statistics with a sense that the finding of *so much more depression among women* was a finding that was discomfiting but real. Not only was there that excess of treated depressions, moreover; there seemed to be vast numbers of women, who were depressed for various reasons—and who had many of the clear-cut symptoms of depression —but who were walking around, not realizing that they "had" anything, and therefore not seeking or receiving treatment.

There could, nevertheless, be a very different sort of a kink in those statistics on women and depression. The fact is that in order to be diagnosed as "suffering from depression," you have to go to a doctor in the first place—and women just plain *do* go to see their doctors more often. Not only do they consult doctors with a demonstrably greater frequency; but they do so about many more minor kinds of problems and of disabilities.

This difference in what researchers call "health-care-seeking-behaviors" springs into being, apparently, sometime just around puberty. Before then, as Dr. Mitchell Balter, a psychologist at the National Institute of Mental Health told me, boys and girls see physicians with roughly the same degree of frequency. The younger males may, in fact, take a slight lead in numbers of visits. But *after* puberty, the picture shifts rapidly. There is a sharp increase on the part of the females, and a decrease on the males' part. And this changed pattern— women seeing their doctors more often—will persist throughout adult life.

Going-to-the-doctor seems to be, in essence, a particularly "feminine" way of coping with stress, and of dealing with a variety of difficulties and problems. Sixty per cent of all patient visits are, in fact, the visits of *female* patients.

If, furthermore, the patient is freely expressive about her sorrows, sadnesses, and life disappointments, and has a few physical symptoms to boot, she may readily be diagnosed as suffering from a depression (by a physician who is well aware that rates of depression are higher in women!). She may be given medications—either tranquilizers or antidepressants—to help her weather her current difficulties. The use of these medically prescribed mood-altering drugs is a very widespread phenomenon—and the majority of those using them (70 per cent!) in toto, are women. A study completed in 1972, according to Dr. Balter, indicated that some 23 per cent of women between the ages of eighteen and twenty-nine (i.e., nearly one fourth the entire age group) had had some psychotropic medication during the course of the preceding year. Among men of the same age, only 6 per cent had done so (and they had used less potent types of medication).

After age thirty, the males' use of mood-changing drugs increased. It doubled to 12 per cent in the years between thirty and forty-four. But among females, there was also a steep rise: from 23 per cent to a hefty 32 per cent. Roughly one third of all the women in this age group (thirty to forty-four) were using prescription drugs to treat their mood. The psychotropic medications were, for the most part, being prescribed by internists and family practitioners (85 per cent of those who said they used mood-altering drugs reported that they had never seen a psychiatrist in their lives). The classic chicken-and-the-egg phenomenon could certainly account for varying rates of male and female patients "in treatment for depression"! For women, if they go to doctors more often, would obviously be being diagnosed and medicated with greater frequency—and therefore joining the roll call when it comes to counting numbers of cases of patients in treatment for depression!

Men, with the same minor symptoms—as well as the same degree of distress and unhappiness—might never go to their doctors at all. And if a man *did* consult his physician with, for example, a digestive complaint, he would be far less inclined to discuss any emotional components of what would be viewed as a physical problem (undoubtedly it is true that the same symptoms, in a male and a female, may be seen as reflecting different underlying problems, by the clinician. Is this antifeminine bias? Or an awareness, on the part of doctors, that women show a much higher rate of depression? Again, the questions and answers here are circular).

In any event, however, the male patient's sex-appropriate behavior will dictate more stoicism, less free expression of sadnesses and weaknesses; and less owning up to physical and mental difficulties. Men are far more reluctant to take on—even on a transitory basis—the "sick role." It is too inconsistent with standard cultural ideals of independence, autonomy, rugged masculinity.

Men and women may, in other words, be *feeling* in much the same dysphoric, unhappy, anxious, depressed ways; but *behaving* very differently. Women may be assuming the culturally "available" sick-and-dependent role, when they are stressed, while men never seek medical attention. The exorbitant numbers of depressed women could be a statistical red herring. Men and women might be equally depressed; but men never counted in as "cases" because they'd never gone in for treatment. It could all be a numerical mirage—a reflection of who is most willing to seek help rather than who actually needs it.

But that just isn't the case. For powerful evidence, coming from so-called "community studies" indicates that women really are more depressed than men—irrespective of who does, or who doesn't go, to the doctor.

What are community studies? Just that: studies of the community at large. What is involved is the selection of a random sample of respondents which is representative of the larger population; and the careful and systematic interviewing of those people in their homes. This bypasses the "going to the doctor" problem. (Because the people being interviewed are, obviously, not being selected on the basis of anything they have or have not done—such as, consulting a physician.)

If the study happens to be an assessment of psychiatric symptoms in the members of the community, then the research interviewer will fill out a long and comprehensive questionnaire that covers many aspects of psychological functioning. For instance, to elicit information about the possible existence of a depressive disorder, initial questions might be: "Did you ever have a period that lasted at least one week when you were bothered by feeling depressed, sad, blue, hopeless, down in the dumps, that you just didn't care anymore, or worried about a lot of things that could happen? What about feeling irritable or easily annoyed?" If the respondent's replies happened to be in the affirmative, then other questions would follow.

These would touch upon sudden changes in appetite, in sleeping patterns, in energy levels, in interest in customary activities, in sexual functioning. And there would be queries about "feeling guilty"; "worthless"; "down on oneself," as well as about problems in concentrating and making decisions—and even, in thinking. There would be questions about thoughts of dying and/or suicide.

Dr. Myrna Weissman, Director of the Yale Depression Unit, has just completed a community study of representative samples of the population, in New Haven, Connecticut. She told me that her survey, like all others that have been done, has uncovered the same phenomenon: an almost frightening amount of depression among women respondents. "Regardless of who is or who isn't going to the doctor—and a number of depressed women that were interviewed were *not* in treatment—women are far more depressed than are men," Weissman said.

Much of the female depression discovered in the community study did, she continued, include milder forms of disturbance. "When you get out in the community, and talk to people in their homes, you draw in the somewhat less severe cases, too. Because you see, for a person to get into psychiatric treatment—he or she has to be in pain and to be really hurting. Getting help takes energy, and it can be expensive; and some feel it's still a bit of a stigma. And so what our nets take in are these people who are doing some suffering; but who aren't in such torment that they can't say, 'Oh well, I can live with it, and besides, what's the use.' They're mildly symptomatic, maybe more transiently symptomatic. But they don't feel bad enough—or maybe don't know enough—to go for help."

In terms of over-all volume—sheer numbers of women who are depressed—Weissman is one among a number of experts who have spoken of what seems to be a steady rise in the course of the past decade. Her own research on suicide attempts among females indicates a similar surge upward; and primarily among younger women. "This has been well documented in several countries over the past ten years," she said. "And while all suicide attempters may not be depressed, I would say that most of them *are*."

As rates of depression among women have increased, the age at which they come to clinics for treatment has been inching downward. Right now, observed Weissman, the typical person who comes to the Yale Depression Unit is a woman, and she is under the age of thirty-five. This age shift downward (in the earlier years of the century, the typical depressed patient was described as someone in the forties, or older) may be due to the fact that women who might have come in later in their lives are now appearing earlier, and with far less serious symptoms. "Or," she added, "it may be due to the fact that help is more available and getting treatment is more acceptable. *Or*"—Weissman smiled, shrugged slightly—"it may be because the treatments—both drug and psychotherapeutic—are themselves so radically improved."

Dr. Weissman, in collaboration with Dr. Gerald Klerman, has written what is considered to be a classic paper on the topic of women and depression. Reviewing all of the possible "explanations" for the strangely sexually tilted statistics, they concluded that the figures represent the real situation, and that the findings are true. Women simply *are* more depressed, in the aggregate, than are men, in the aggregate. Beyond the shadow of a doubt.

The outline below was a very small segment of a long sheet of instructions (called "Directions for Self-Reflection Exercises") which
was handed out in a course on the life cycle, offered at the Harvard
School of Education by Professor Harry Lasker. I was a student of
Dr. Lasker's in the spring of my Nieman Fellowship year at Harvard;
and after that, this small section of that instructions list became the
skeletal understructure of the interviews that I was doing for my
study of depression among women. But because these questions are really supposed to be posed as an exercise in self-scrutiny, my first "subject" was myself. I followed the instructions (my own first life period
was 0-to-3; but some women I've interviewed have started off with an
initial life period that stretched from 0-to-13!). I asked and answered
the questions of myself, speaking them into a tape-recorder. Anyone
who wishes to interview herself or himself in this way will find it an
extraordinary experience. At least it was one—a difficult and fascinating one—for me.

Critical Periods

Break your life into periods starting at as early an age as possible.

1. Group years that seem to go together.
2. Give these years a title.
3. What are the most significant things which occurred during these years?
4. What were the more important episodes you recall in this
   period? What was important about them? What issue or
   theme were you working on?

5. What made that period end?

6. How did you feel during that period?
   —in general?
   —about yourself?
   —about others around you?

7. What did you want most during that period? How much do you feel you achieved of what you wanted?

SELECTED BIBLIOGRAPHY

Akiskal, Hagop S. and McKinney, William T.: Overview of recent research in depression. *Arch. Gen. Psych.* 32:285–301, March 1975.

American Psychiatric Association: Diagnostic and Statistical Manual of Mental Disorders, Second Edition [this is *DSM* II]: Prepared by the Committee on Nomenclature and Statistics, Washington, D.C., 1968.

American Psychiatric Association: Diagnostic and Statistical Manual III *DSM III: Diagnostic Criteria Draft.* Prepared by the Task Force on Nomenclature and Statistics, January 15, 1978.

Ansbacher, Heinz L., and Ansbacher, Rowena R.: *The Individual Psychology of Alfred Adler.* Harper & Row: New York, 1956.

Anthony, E. James: Two contrasting types of adolescent depression and their treatment. *J. American Psychoanalytic Assoc.* 18:841–59, No. 4, October 1970.

Avery, David, and Winokur, George: Mortality in depressed patients treated with electroconvulsive therapy and antidepressants. *Arch. Gen. Psych.* 33:1029–37, September 1976.

Bardwick, Judith M.: *Psychology of Women.* Harper & Row: New York, 1971.

———: *Readings on the Psychology of Women.* Harper & Row: New York, 1972.

———, Douvan, Elizabeth, Horner, Matina S., and Gutmann, David: *Feminine Personality and Conflict.* Brooks/Cole Pub. Co.: California, 1970.

Beach, Frank A.: *Human Sexuality in Four Perspectives.* Johns Hopkins University Press: Baltimore/London, 1976.

Beck, Aaron T.: *Cognitive Therapy and the Emotional Disorders.* International Universities Press, Inc.: New York, 1976.

———: *Depression: Causes and Treatment.* Philadelphia: University of Pennsylvania Press, 1967.

———, and Greenberg, Ruth L.: "Cognitive Therapy with Depressed Women," in *Women in Therapy,* Violet Franks and Vasanti Burtle, Eds. Brunner/Mazel, Inc.: New York, 1974.

Becker, Joseph: *Depression: Theory and Research.* John Wiley & Sons: New York, 1974.

Benedek, Therese and Anthony, James, Eds.: *Depression and Human Existence.* Little, Brown & Co.: Boston, 1975.

Biller, Henry B., and Weiss, Stephan D.: The father-daughter relationship and the personality development of the female. *J. Genetic Psychology* 116:79–93, 1970.

Binder, Jeffrey, and Krohn, Alan: Sexual acting out as an abortive mourning process in female adolescent inpatients. *Psychiatric Quarterly* 48:193–208, 1974.

Blos, Peter: *On Adolescence: A Psychoanalytic Interpretation.* Free Press of Glencoe: New York, 1962.

Bowlby, John: *Attachment and Loss: Vol. I. Attachment.* Hogarth Press: London, 1969.

———: *Attachment and Loss: Vol. II. Separation, Anxiety and Anger.* Basic Books: New York, 1973.

———: The making and breaking of affectional bonds. I. Aetiology and psychopathology in the light of attachment theory. *British J. of Psychiatry* 130:201–10, March 1977.

———: The making and breaking of affectional bonds. II. Some principles of psychotherapy. *British J. of Psychiatry* 130:421–31, May 1977.

Brill, Norman Q., and Liston, Edward H.: Parental loss in adults with emotional disorders. *Arch. Gen. Psych.* 14:307–14, March 1966.

Broverman, Inge K., Broverman, Donald M., Clarkson, Frank E., Rosenkrantz, Paul S., and Vogel, Susan R.: Sex-role stereotypes and clinical judgments of mental health. *J. Consulting and Clin. Psych.* 34:1–7, No. 1, 1970.

Brown, George W., and Harris, Tirril: *Social Origins of Depression: A Study of Psychiatric Disorder in Women.* The Free Press: New York, 1978.

Cath, Stanley H.: Some dynamics of middle and later years. *Smith College Studies in Social Work* Vol. XXXIII, No. 2, 97–125, February 1963.

Chevron, Eve S., Quinlan, Donald M., and Blatt, Sidney J.: Sex roles and gender differences in the experience of depression. *J. Abnormal Psychology* 87:680–83, 1978.

Chodorow, Nancy: "Being and Doing: A cross-cultural examination of the socialization of males and females," in *Women in Sexist Society,* Vivian Gornick and B. K. Moran, Eds., New York, 1971.

Cohen, M. B., Baker, G., Cohen, R. A., Fromm-Reichmann, F., and Weigert, E. V.: An intensive study of twelve cases of manic-depressive psychosis. *Psychiatry* 17:103, May 1954.

Cummings, E. and Henry, W. E.: *Growing Old.* Basic Books: New York, 1961.

Detre, Thomas P., and Jarecki, Henry G.: *Modern Psychiatric Treatment.* Lippincott Press: Philadelphia, 1971.

Dicks, H. V.: *Marital Tensions. Clinical Studies Towards a Psychological Theory of Interaction.* New York: Basic Books, 1967.

Donovan, John C.: The menopausal syndrome: a study of case histories. *Am. J. Obst. and Gynec.* 62:1281–91, December 1951.

Engel, George L.: *Psychological Development in Health and Disease.* W. B. Saunders Co.: Philadelphia/London, 1962.

Erikson, Erik H.: *Childhood and Society,* 2nd Ed. W. W. Norton & Co.: New York, 1963.

———: *Identity Youth and Crisis.* W. W. Norton & Co.: New York, 1968.

Fairbairn, W. Ronald D.: *Psychoanalytic Studies of the Personality*. Routledge & Kegan Paul Ltd.: London/Boston, 1952.

Fieve, Ronald R.: *Depression in the 1970's: Modern Theory and Research*. Excerpta Medica: New York, 1971.

Ford, Caroline S. "Ego-Adaptive Mechanisms of Older Persons," in *Human Life Cycle*, William C. Sze, Ed. Jason Aronson Inc.: New York, 1975.

Forrest, Tess: Paternal roots of female character development. *Contemporary Psychoanalysis* 3:21–38, 1966.

Frankel, Fred H.: Reasoned discourse or a Holy War: Postscript to a report on ECT. *Am. J. Psych.* 132:77–79, January 1975.

Freud, Sigmund: *Mourning and Melancholia*, in the *Psychological Works* of Sigmund Freud, Vol. 4, edited by James Strachey. Hogarth Press: London, 1959.

——: *Sexuality and the Psychology of Love*. Macmillan Publishing Co.: New York, 1963.

——: *Three Contributions to the Theory of Sex*, translated from the German by A. A. Brill. E. P. Dutton & Co.: New York, 1962.

Friedman, Raymond J., and Katz, Martin M., Eds.: *The Psychology of Depression*. John Wiley & Sons: New York, 1974.

Fromm-Reichmann, Frieda: *Principles of Intensive Psychotherapy*. The University of Chicago Press: Chicago, Ill., 1950.

——: *Psychoanalysis and Psychotherapy*. University of Chicago Press: Chicago/London, 1959.

Gilligan, Carol, and Notman, Malkah: *Woman's Place in Man's Life Cycle*. Presented at the Meetings of the Eastern Sociological Association, Philadelphia, March 1978.

Gunther, Mavis. *The New Mother's View of Herself*. Ciba Foundation Symposium 45 (new series), p. 145–57.

Guttentag, Marcia, and Salasin, Susan: *Women, Men and Mental Health*. Presented at the Aspen Conference on Women, August 1–10, 1975.

Hamburg, David A.: "Effects of Progesterone on Behavior," in *Endocrines and the Central Nervous System*. Williams & Wilkins Co.: Baltimore, 1966.

Havens, Leston L.: Recognition of suicidal risks through the psychologic examination. *New England Journal of Medicine* 276:210–15, January 26, 1967.

Havighurst, R. J., Cavan, R., Burgess, E. W., and Goldhamer, H.: *Personal Adjustment in Old Age*. Science Research Associates: Chicago, 1949.

Hollender, M. H.: The wish to be held and the wish to hold in men and women. *Arch. Gen. Psych.* 33:49–51, 1976.

——: Women's wish to be held. Sexual and non-sexual aspects. *Med. Aspects of Human Sexuality* 5:12–26, 1971.

——, Luborsky, L., and Scaramella, T.: Body contact and sexual enticement. *Arch. Gen. Psych.* 20:188–91, 1969.

Horney, Karen: *Feminine Psychology*. Norton Library: New York, 1967.

Johnson, Adelaide M.: "Sanctions for Superego Lacunae of Adolescents," in *Searchlights on Delinquency*. Eissler, K. R., Ed. International Universities Press: New York, 1949.

Josselyn, Irene M.: *The Adolescent and His World*. Family Service Association of America: New York, 1952.

Kernberg, Otto F.: Mature love: Prerequisites and characteristics. *J. Amer. Psychoanalytic Association* 22:743–68, No. 4, 1974.

Kety, Seymour S.: "Biochemistry of the Major Psychoses," in *Comprehensive Textbook of Psychiatry/II. Vol. I.* Eds. Alfred M. Freedman, Harold I. Kaplan and Benjamin J. Sadock, pp. 178–87, Williams & Wilkins Co.: Baltimore, 1975.

Klerman, Gerald L.: *Adaptation, Depression and Life Events*. Paper presented at the Conference "Vulnerable Youth: Hope and Despair," the University of Chicago, Center for Continuing Education, Chicago, Illinois, April 1978.

——: "Drugs, Psychodynamics and Depression," in *Advances in Neuropsychopharmacology*, O. Vinar, Z. Votava, P. B. Bradley, Eds. North Holland Pub. Co.: Amsterdam, 1971.

——: *Psychoneurosis: Integrating Pharmacotherapy and Psychotherapy*. Presented at Symposium on Effective Psychotherapy, Texas Research Institute of Mental Sciences, Houston, Texas, November 19–21, 1975.

——, and Barrett, James E.: "The Affective Disorders: Clinical and Epidemiological Aspects," in *Lithium: Its Role in Psychiatric Research and Treatment*, Samuel Gershon and Baron Shopsin, Eds., Plenum Publishing Corp.: New York, 1973.

——, and Izen, Judith E.: Drug Therapy and Psychotherapy in Psychiatry, in *Perspectives on Medicine Use in Society*, Albert Wertheimer, Ed. Drug Intelligence Publications, 1975.

——: "The Effects of Bereavement and Grief on Physical Health and General Well Being," in *Advances in Psychosomatic Medicine: Epidemiologic Studies in Psychosomatic Medicine*. Franz Reichsman, Ed., Basel, Switzerland: S. Karger, 1975.

Kolb, Lawrence C.: *Modern Clinical Psychiatry*. W. B. Saunders: Philadelphia, 1973.

Leonard, Marjorie R.: Fathers and daughters. *Int. J. Psychoanalysis* 47:325–34, 1966.

Lesse, Stanley, Ed.: *Masked Depression*. Jason Aronson, Inc.: New York, 1974.

Levinson, Daniel J.: *The Seasons of a Man's Life*. Alfred A. Knopf: New York, 1978.

Lewis, Helen Block: *Psychic War in Men and Women*. New York University Press: New York, 1976.

Lidz, Theodore: *The Person: His and Her Development Throughout the Life Cycle*, revised edition. Basic Books, Inc.: New York, 1976.

Lowenthal, Marjorie Fiske, Thurnher, Madja, Chiriboga, David, and associates. *Four Stages of Life*. Jossey-Bass Publishers: San Francisco/Washington/London, 1975.

McKinlay, Sonja M., and Jefferys, Margot: The menopausal syndrome. *Brit. J. Prev. Soc. Med.* 28:108–15, 1974.

Mandel, Michel R.: Electroconvulsive therapy for chronic pain associated with depression. *Am. J. Psych.* 132:632–36, June 1975.

——, Welch, Charles, Mieske, Marlene, and McCormick, Mark: Prediction of response to ECT in tricyclic-intolerant or tricyclic-resistant depressed patients. *McLean Hosp. Journal* 2:203–9, 1977.

Melges, Frederick T.: Managing mood swings in the menstrual cycle. *Medical Aspects of Human Sexuality* April 1975, pp. 81–82.

Mendels, Joseph: Brain biogenic amine depletion and mood. *Arch. Gen. Psych.* 30:447–51, April 1974.

———: *Concepts of Depression.* John Wiley & Sons: New York/London/ Sydney/Toronto, 1970.

———, and Chernik, Doris A.: "Sleep Changes and Affective Illness," in *The Nature and Treatment of Depression.* Frederic Flach and Suzanne C. Draghi, Eds., John Wiley & Sons, Inc.: New York, 1975.

Mostow, E., and Newberry, P.: Work role and depression in women. *Amer. J. Orthopsychiat.* 45:538–48, July 1975.

Nadelson, Carol: "Normal" and "special" aspects of pregnancy. *Obst. and Gynec.* 41:611–20, April 1973.

———, and Notman, Malkah: Conflicts in identity and self-esteem for women. *McLean Hospital Journal* 2:1, 1977.

———: "Emotional Aspects of the Symptoms Functions and Disorders of Women," in *Psychiatric Medicine,* G. Usdin, Ed., Brunner/Mazel: New York, 1978.

National Institute of Mental Health, U. S. Department of Health, Education and Welfare. Special Report 1973, *The Depressive Disorders,* U. S. Government Printing Office, Washington, D.C.

Neugarten, Bernice L.: *Personality in Middle and Later Life.* Atherton Press: New York, 1964.

———, and Kraines, Ruth J.: "Menopausal Symptoms" in women of various ages. *Psychosom. Med.* 27:266–72, 1965.

———, Wood, Vivian, Kraines, Ruth J., and Loomis, Barbara: Women's attitudes toward the menopause. *Vita Humana* 6:140–51, 1963.

Notman, Malkah: Midlife concerns of women: Implications of the menopause. *Amer. J. Psych.* 136:1270–74, No. 10, October 1979.

———, and Nadelson, Carol. Eds. *The Woman Patient: Medical and Psychological Interfaces.* New York: Plenum Press, 1978.

Ostow, Mortimer: *The Psychology of Melancholy.* Harper & Row: New York, 1970.

Parry, Hugh J., et al.: National patterns of psychotherapeutic drug use. *Arch. Gen. Psych.* 28:769–83, June 1973.

Paykel, E. S., Myers, J. K., Lindenthal, J. J., and Tanner, J.: Suicidal feelings in the general population: A prevalence study. *British J. Psychiat.* 124:460–69, May 1974.

Paykel, Eugene, Prusoff, Brigitte, and Myers, Jerome: Suicide attempts and recent life events. *Arch. Gen. Psychiat.* 32:327–33, March 1975.

Perlmutter, Johanna: "A Gynecological Approach to Menopause," in *The Woman Patient: Medical and Psychological Interfaces,* Malkah Notman and Carol Nadelson, Eds. Plenum Press: New York, 1978.

Pincus, Jonathan H., and Tucker, Gary: *Behavioral Neurology.* Oxford University Press: London/Toronto/New York, 1974.

Pincus, Lily, and Dare, Christopher: *Secrets in the Family.* Pantheon Books: New York, 1978.

Poinsard, Paul J.: Psychiatric Problems of Adolescence. *Annals of the New York Academy of Sciences*, Vol. 142, Art. 3, May 10, 1967.

Pratt, J. P., and Thomas, W. L.: The endocrine treatment of menopausal phenomena. *Journal of the American Medical Association* 109:1875–80, December 4, 1937.

Radloff, Lenore: Sex differences in depression: the effects of occupation and marital status. *Sex Roles* 1:249–65, No. 3, 1975.

Robinson, Donald S., et al.: Monoamine metabolism in human brain. *Arch. Gen. Psychiat.* 34:89–92, January 1977.

Rogers, Joseph: The menopause. *New England Journal of Medicine* 254:697–703, April 12, 1956.

Rutter, Michael: *Maternal Deprivation Reassessed.* C. Nicholls & Co. Ltd.: Middlesex, England, 1972.

Sachar, Edward J.: *Hormones, Behavior and Psychopathology.* New York: Raven Press, 1976.

———, Hellman, Leon, Fukushima, David K., and Gallagher, T. F.: Cortisol production in depressive illness. *Arch. Gen. Psychiat.* 23:289–98, October 1970.

Satir, Virginia: *Conjoint Family Therapy.* Science and Behavior Books, Inc.: California, 1967.

Scarf, Maggie: *Body, Mind, Behavior.* New Republic Book Company, Inc.: Washington, D.C., 1976.

Schaffer, Rudolph: *Mothering.* Harvard University Press: Cambridge, Massachusetts, 1977.

Schildkraut, Joseph J., and Kety, Seymour S.: Biogenic amines and emotion. *Science* 156:21–30, April 1967.

———, Keeler, Barbara, Papousek, Mechtild, and Hartmann, Ernest: MHPG excretion in depressive disorders: Relation to clinical subtypes and desynchronized sleep. *Science* 181:762–64, August 24, 1973.

———, Orsulak, Paul J., Gudeman, Jon E., Schatzberg, Alan F., Rohde, William A., La Brie, Richard A., Cahill, Jane F., Cole, Jonathan O., Frazier, Shervert H.: "Norepinephrine Metabolism in Depressive Disorders: Implications for a Biochemical Classification of Depression," in: *Depression: Biology and Treatment,* Shervert H. Frazier, Jonathan O. Cole, and Alan F. Schatzbert, Eds. Plenum Press, New York, in press.

Schneidman, Edwin S., Farberow, Norman L.: *Clues to Suicide.* McGraw-Hill Book Company, Inc.: New York/Toronto/London, 1957.

Schuyler, Dean: *The Depressive Spectrum.* Jason Aronson: New York, 1974.

Selye, Hans: *The Stress of Life.* McGraw-Hill Book Company, Inc.: New York, 1976.

Smith, Stuart L.: "Mood and the Menstrual Cycle," in *Topics in Endocrinology*, Edward Schar, Ed., Grune & Stratton: New York, 1975.

Smotherman, William P., Wiener, Sandra G., Mendoza, Sally P., and Levine, Seymour: *Pituitary-Adrenal Responsiveness of Rat Mothers to*

Noxious Stimuli and Stimuli Produced by Pups. Ciba Foundation Symposium 45 (new series), pp. 5–25.

Solnit, Albert J.: "Depression and Mourning," in *American Handbook of Psychiatry*, 2nd Ed., Silvano Arieti, Ed., Basic Books: New York, 1974.

Sontag, Susan: The double standard of aging. *Saturday Review*, pp. 29–38, September 23, 1972.

Spitz, René A.: The smiling response: a contribution to the ontogenesis of social relations. *Genetic Psychology Monographs* 34:57–125, 1946.

Squires, Larry R., and Chace, Paul M.: Memory functions six to nine months after electroconvulsive therapy. *Arch. Gen. Psychiat.* 32:1557–64, December 1975.

Steele, Carolyn: Obese adolescent girls: some diagnostic and treatment considerations. *Adolescence* 9: No. 33, 81–96, Spring 1974.

Sternberg, David E., and Jarvik, Murray E.: Memory functions in depression. *Arch. Gen. Psychiat.* 33:219–24, February 1976.

Stewart, Wendy Ann: *A Psychosocial Study of the Formation of the Early Adult Life Structure in Women.* Doctoral Dissertation, Columbia University, New York, 1976.

Sugar, Max: Normal adolescent mourning. *Amer. J. Psychotherapy* 22: 258–69, No. 2, April 1968.

——, Ed.: *Female Adolescent Development.* Brunner/Mazel: New York, 1979.

Sullivan, Harry Stack: *The Interpersonal Theory of Psychiatry.* W. W. Norton: New York, 1953.

Sze, William C., Ed.: *Human Life Cycle.* Jason Aronson, Inc.: New York, 1975.

Tabachnick, Norman: Creative suicidal crises. *Arch. Gen. Psychiat.* 29: 258–63, August 1973.

——: Failure and masochism. *Amer. J. Psychotherapy* 18:304–16, 1964.

——: Interpersonal relations in suicidal attempts. *Arch. Gen. Psychiat.* 4:16–21, 1961.

——: Theories of self-destruction. *Amer. J. Psychoanalysis* 32:53–61, 1972.

Task Force on Electroconvulsive Therapy of the American Psychiatric Association: *Electroconvulsive Therapy,* American Psychiatric Association, 1978.

Thompson, Barbara, Hart, Shirley A., and Durno, D.: Menopausal age and symptomatology in a general practice. *J. Biosoc. Sci.* 5:71–82, 1973.

Thompson, Clara: The role of women in this culture. *Psychiatry* 4:1–8, 1941.

Valenstein, Elliot S.: *Brain Control.* John Wiley & Sons, Inc.: New York/London/Sydney/Toronto, 1973.

Valzelli, Luigi: *Psychopharmacology: An Introduction to Experimental and Clinical Principles.* Spectrum Publications, Inc.: New York, 1973.

Weideger, Paula: *Menstruation and Menopause.* Alfred A. Knopf: New York, 1976.

Weiss, Robert, Ed.: *Loneliness: The Experience of Emotional and Social Isolation.* Cambridge: MIT Press, 1973.

Weissman, Myrna: The epidemiology of suicide attempts, 1960 to 1971. *Arch. Gen. Psychiat.* 30:737–46, June 1974.

——: The Myth of Involutional Melancholia. *Journal of the American Medical Association* 242:744, 1979.

——, and Klerman, Gerald L.: Sex differences and the epidemiology of depression. *Arch. Gen. Psychiat.* 34:98–111, January 1977.

——, and Paykel, Eugene S.: *The Depressed Woman: A Study of Social Relationships.* University of Chicago Press: Chicago/London, 1974.

Wexler, Joan, and Steidl, John: Marriage and the capacity to be alone. *Psychiatry* 41:72–80, February 1978.

Whybrow, Peter C., and Mendels, J.: Toward a biology of depression: Some suggestions from neurophysiology. *Amer. J. Psychiat.* 125:45–54, May 1969.

——, and Parlatore, Anselm: Melancholia, a model in madness: A discussion of recent psychobiologic research into depressive illness. *Psychiatry in Medicine* 4:351–78, No. 4, 1973.

Winnicott, D. W.: *The Maturational Processes and the Facilitating Environment.* International Universities Press, Inc.: New York, 1965.

Winokur, George: Depression in the menopause. *Am. J. Psychiat.* 130:92–93, January 1973.

——, and Cadoret, Remi: "The Irrelevance of the Menopause to Depressive Disease," in *Topics in Psychoendocrinology*, Edward Sachar, Ed., Grune & Stratton: New York, 1975.

Wolfenstein, Martha: Loss, Rage and Repetition. *Psychoanalytic Study of the Child.* Vol. XXIV: 432–60, International Universities Press, New York, 1969.

Yalom, Irvin D., Lunde, Donald T., Moos, Rudolph H., and Hamburg, David A.: "Postpartum Blues" syndrome. *Arch. Gen. Psychiat.* 18:16–27, January 1968.

Zilbach, J., Notman, M., Nadelson, C., Miller, J. B.: "Some formulations on aggression in feminine development." Presented at the International Psychoanalytic Congress, New York, August 1979.

Index

INDEX

Abandonment, feelings of, 138

Abnormal grief, 539

Abortion, 12, 13, 15, 22, 24, 26, 516–17

"Accidental" pregnancies, 25

Actomol (drug), 476

Adaptation, failure in, 7

Adaptation to Life (Vaillant), 135

Adjustment Reaction of Adult Life, 342

Adjustment Reaction of Late Life, 342, 343

Adolescence, growth spurt of, 19–20

Adolescent and His World, The (Josselyn), 115, 116

"Adolescent Depression" (Lorand), 42

Adrenocortical hormones, 281

Affective disorders, 184

Affective Disorders Clinic (University of Pittsburgh), 549

Aggression, 20, 87, 255, 261, 270, 271

Aging process, menopausal depression and, 408–16
  decline of hope, 412–13
  estrogens, 408–10
  getting older process, 412–16
  as narcissistic injury, 410–12

Alcohol, Drug Abuse and Mental Health Administration (ADAMHA), 266, 479

Alcohol addiction, 349

Alcoholics Anonymous, 334, 351, 367, 372

Alcoholism, 69, 171, 201, 308, 322, 333, 349–50
  depression associated with, 172

Alienation, 19

Aloneness, 159, 230, 320, 345
  confronting, 33
  See also Loneliness

"Ambivalence: The Socialization of Women" (Bardwick and Douvan), 225–26

American Journal of Obstetrics and Gynecology, The, 406–7

American Psychiatric Association, 493

Anger, 67, 102, 105, 124, 142, 152, 155, 166, 190, 198, 199, 250, 261, 311, 325, 338, 375, 428, 438, 464
  ambivalence and, 310–13
  as an antiaphrodisiac, 318–19

Anhedonia, 541

Anne Munson case, 11–38, 68–69, 70, 510, 516–17, 537, 540
  assessing the danger, 13
  boarding school separation, 18–19
  internalization phenomenon, 26–31
  mother and baby image, 24–26
  mother's helper ambition, 31–32
  notions of the future, 23–24
  pain of separation from parents, 20–22
  parents, 18–22
  patient's knowledge of change, 14–18
  psychiatric consultation, 11–13
  puberty and physical growth, 19–20
  role of being oneself, 20
  sex and nurturance, 32–37
  sexual barter phenomenon, 37–38

Antabuse (drug), 390

Anthony, Dr. E. James, 57, 58, 61

Antidepressant drugs, 238–40, 358, 389–90, 423, 445, 446, 492
  side effects from, 495–98
  See also names of drugs

Anxiety, 13, 33, 44, 83–86, 115, 116–17, 120, 142, 234, 244, 282, 398, 402, 408, 451, 460, 477, 548
  as an early-warning device, 84–85
  as a survival mechanism, 85

Apnea, 505

Arateus, 253

Archives of General Psychiatry (publication), 497–98
Attachment, *see* Human attachment
Attachment and Loss (Bowlby), 79
"Attachment behavior," 75–77
Attachment issues, 87
Attachment-objects, 37
Attractiveness, loss of, 4
Autonomy, 59, 103, 186
Avery, Dr. David, 497–98
Axelrod, Julius, 239

Balter, Dr. Mitchell, 554
Bardwick, Judith, 225–26, 355–56
Barrie, Kath, *see* Kath Barrie case
Beck, Dr. Aaron T., 538
Behavioral tendencies, evolution and, 97–98
Being depressed, experience of, 87
Being oneself, role of, 20
Benedek, Dr. Therese, 286–87, 308
Bette Glassman case, 70–71, 72, 368–71
Biogenic amines, 234–35, 237–38
Bipolar disease, 252, 253–54
Blos, Dr. Peter, 28, 119, 120, 217, 218
Body changes, adolescent growth and, 19–20
"Body Contact and Sexual Enticement" (Hollender), 37, 38
Bouts of panic, 83
Bowlby, Dr. John, 72–74, 75, 77, 79
Brevital (barbiturate), 502
Broverman, Inge and Donald, 359–61, 365
Burkle, Dr. Frederick, Jr., 151, 153, 155, 157, 366, 367, 372, 376, 377, 379, 382, 391
Butler, Samuel, 353

Cahill, Jane, 501, 504
Cardiac toxicity, 496
Case studies, *see* names of cases
Center for Advanced Study in the

Behavioral Sciences, 189–90
Cerletti, Dr. Ugo, 505
Challenges, Eriksonian schema of, 486
Chesler, Phyllis, 551–52, 553
Childhood and Society (Erikson), 227, 228
Child's role, playing (for benefit of parents), 20
Child Study Center (Yale University), 40
Chumship, 118, 119
Climacterium, 397
Clinical depression, 421
Cognitive therapy, 538
Cohen, Mabel Blake, 255
Commitments, making of, 202–5, 271
Confidence, lack of, 46
Corpus luteum, 284
Curare (drug), 502

Dahlgren, Diana, *see* Diana Dahlgren case
Dare, Dr. Christopher, 200–1, 322, 488
Dartmouth-Hitchcock Mental Health Center, 70, 138, 150, 164, 180, 330, 332, 347, 520
Dartmouth Medical School, 235, 396
Debra Thierry case, 39–67, 68–69, 70, 102–3, 517, 537, 540, 542
  "being daughter mother wanted," 64–66
  desire to get away from home, 58–62
  disconnection between facts and realities, 46–50
  early feelings of love, 39–43
  first interview with patient, 44–45
  low self estimate, 43–44
  parental expectations and, 62–64, 67
  self-psychotherapy (care-of-the-inner-self), 56–58
  sham illnesses, 50–54

"Delta wave" sleep, 176
Dependency, 32, 33, 120, 122, 127,
    129, 145, 152, 373
  denial of, 139–41
  feminine trait and, 355–56
Depersonalization experience,
    468–69
Depression, xv–xvi, 3, 13, 171–86
  and body and mind, 171–86
  disparity in numbers (of females
    and males), 537–57
  endocrine system and, 174–75
  in the fifties, 393–481
  finding help for, 545–50
  flu analogy, 183–84
  in the forties, 327–92
  hunger and, 78
  hyperarousal and inner disorders,
    176
  life cycle and, 6–8
  meaning of, 7
  as a mood, symptom, and illness,
    171–73
  mood, symptom, syndrome, and
    side effects, 179–82
  origins of, 261
  sex and, 178
  signs of, 543–45
  in the sixties, 483–542
  surviving, 527–42
  susceptibility to, 182–84
  in the teens, 9–98
  in the thirties, 187–326
  timing factor, 184–85
  in the twenties, 99–186
  vulnerability to, 4, 6, 179
  woman's life and, 185–86
  See also names of case studies
"Depression During the Life Cycle"
    (Benedek), 308
"Depression in Infant Monkeys
    Separated from their Mothers"
    (Kaufman and Rosenblum), 79
Depressive equivalent
    (depressive-masks) behavior,
    144
Depressive neurosis, defined, 341

Depressive theorem, 81–82
Detre, Dr. Thomas, 45, 48, 50
Deutsch, Dr. Helene, 116, 305, 416,
    417
Diagnosis, meaning of, 339–40
Diagnostic and Statistical Manual of
    Mental Disorders (DSM),
    341, 342, 355, 403
Diana Dahlgren case, 69, 329–53,
    354, 366–92, 520, 521–26, 537,
    539, 541, 542
  accommodation process and, 353
  alcohol addiction, 349–50, 351
  communicational dead-end,
    381–82
  déjà vu experience, 329–30
  diagnosis, 339–40
  discharge, 388–92
  disturbed behavior, 366–67, 371,
    375
  diversionary tactics, 382–84
  early morning symptoms, 335
  emotional amnesia, 337–39
  empty nest syndrome, 342–43
  family and, 372–73, 376–80
  "flight into health," 337
  hysterical personality, 352–53
  loneliness, 343–45
  menopausal depression, 351–52
  move from California to New
    England, 341–42, 348–49
  next-to-last family meeting, 368
  pathology, 373–74
  patient and morning rounds,
    331–34
  pity and, 335–36
  question of power, 374–76
  treatment of "mind and soul,"
    340–41
  treatment-recommendations,
    389–90
  "why me" attitude, 339
Dicks, Dr. H. V., 322
Different, feeling, 19
"Directions for Self-Reflection
    Exercises" (Lasker), 558–59

Distance (between oneself and one's family), 18
Distress, 44, 80
Disturbed behavior, notion of, 366–67, 371, 375
Donovan, Dr. John C., 406–7
Doris Nordlund case, 395–481
   519–20, 532–33, 537, 539, 541, 542
   careening through the world, 437–39
   as desperate obliging child, 433–34
   division of psychological labor, 434–35
   dutiful wifing, 443–44
   father image (recreating old situation), 446–48
   "father problem," 431–32
   and "getting even," 435–37
   gypsy living, 445–46
   madonna/whore dichotomy, 434
   marital crisis, 449–81
   marriage, 441–43
   menopause, 395–420
   outcast role, 425–31
   parents and, 421–25, 426
   second try at the future, 439–41
"Double Standard of Aging, The" (Sontag), 413
Douvan, Elizabeth, 225–26
"Dread of Women, The" (Horney), 363
Drugs, 476–81
   basic adaptive posture, 235–36
   biochemical conditions, 234
   biogenic amines, 234–35, 237–38, 242–43
   happiness and, 480–81
   MAO inhibiting, 445, 477–79, 547
   MHPG levels, 241–42
   mood-changing, 234–35
   perception, 243–45
   tricyclic antidepressants, 238–40, 253, 446, 479–80, 496, 547
   See also names of drugs
Durno, D., 404

Dysphoric feelings, 81–82
Early adulthood (the twenties), 214–28
   emergence of identity, 224
   "place" in the world, 219–22
   search for a mentor, 222–24
   searching-out process (male and female), 219–22
   unfinished business, 217–18
   waiting, 224–28
Effectiveness, loss of, 4
Ego immaturity, 21
Elation and despair (Judith Karlin case), 246–73
   love and, 250–51
   "message from God," 251–52
   phantom passion, 246–49
   triumph mood, 249–50
Elavil (tricyclic antidepressant), 238, 239, 253, 335, 446, 479–80, 496, 547
Electroconvulsive therapy (ECT), 493–509, 510, 526, 549
   antidepressant side effects, 495–98
   brain stimulation, 503–4, 505–6
   convulsion, 504–5
   deaths associated with, 499
   effectiveness of, 494
   how it works, 508
   new research and techniques, 506–7
   number of persons receiving, 493
   patient improvement, 508–9
   treatments, 499–502
Emotional amnesia, 337–39
Emptiness, defined, 69
Empty nest syndrome, 344–45
Endocrine derangement, 401–3
Erikson, Erik, 69, 218, 224, 227, 228, 486, 487
Estrogens, aging process and, 408–9
Experience of Emotional and Social Isolation, The (Riesman), 346

Falret, Dr., 253
Feminine existential crisis, 305–6
Femininity, 354–65, 414, 551

cosmetics industry and, 415–16
dependency, 355–56
depression and, 357–59
masculine/feminine questionnaire, 359–61, 365
self-esteem and, 356–57
sexual stereotypes, 355
unfeminine woman, 361–65
"First love" relationships, 68, 71
"Forbidden love," 101–2
Forrest, Dr. Tess, 432
Freud, Sigmund, 103, 145, 186, 211, 528
Fromm-Reichmann, Frieda, 255, 343, 346
Funabashi, Dr. Terri, 226, 362, 363–64, 414

Garvey, Margaret, see Margaret Garvey case
Geller, Sandy, see Sandy Geller case
Generativity, 486
Geographical separation, 30
Gilligan, Dr. Carol, 227, 228, 535
Girard, Helen, see Helen Girard case
Glassman, Bette, see Bette Glassman case
Goals, defined, 218
Goodall, Jane, 79–80
Grand mal seizure, 504, 507
Great mother/bad wife conflict, 292–326
adultery as communication, 316–17
aloneness, 320
ambivalence and anger, 310–13
anger as an antiaphrodisiac, 318–19
existential crisis, 305–6
expectations, 298–301
father's need level, 307–9
having-a-baby for having-a-husband trade, 319–20
husband's love and, 296–97
inadequacy, 292–96

madonna image, 307
marital see-saws, 310
marriage and, 320–26
maternalism and eroticism, 304–5
mothering process, 297–98
nursing and cuddling process, 306–7
parenthood as crisis, 303–4
role choice, 309
sex and, 301
"wanting everything," 301–3
Guilt, 14, 102, 115, 116–17, 118, 120, 132, 402, 436
Gunther, Dr. Mavis, 306
Guttentag, Dr. Marcia, 3, 4, 6, 98, 553–54

Hamburg, Dr. David A., 285
Hart, Mrs. (social worker), 13, 14, 16, 22
Hart, Shirley A., 404
Harvard Project on Women and Mental Health, 3
Havens, Dr. Leston, 186, 340, 384
Helen Girard case, 82–96, 97
anxiety terror, 83–86
embittered relationship with son, 93–96
exasperation feelings, 89–90
Helplessness, feelings of, 26, 33, 46, 85, 87, 365
Heterosexual love object (during adolescence), 39–43
Hippocrates, 278
Hirschfeld, Dr. Robert M. A., 254
Histrionic personality disorder, 355
Hollender, Dr. Marc, 37, 38, 142
Hopelessness, feelings of, 14, 85
Hopper, Edward, 330
Hormonal illusions, 405–8
Hormone replacement, 403–5, 409–10
Horney, Dr. Karen, 363
Human attachment, 70–74, 97, 98, 142, 152, 185–86, 228, 305
"first love," 68, 71
theories of (child's tie to

parents), 71–74
See also Love-bonds
Hunger, depression and, 78
Hyperponesis, 176
Hysteria, 398
Hysterical personality (hysteriform
    personality disorder), 352–53,
    354
Hysteroid dysphoria, 478

Iatrogenic illness, 182
Identity, emergence of, 224
Identity, Youth and Crisis
    (Erikson), 218
Illness pretense, 52
Independence, 18, 25, 35, 59, 87, 138,
    186, 212, 271, 462
    achievement of, 103
Individuation, process of, 152, 153,
    155, 214
*I Never Promised You a Rose
    Garden* (Cohen), 255
Infant, psychological helplessness
    of, 33
Infantile love attachment, 71
Insufficiency, feelings of, 26
Internalization phenomenon, 26–31
Interpersonal deficits, 539–40
Interpersonal disputes, 539
Interpersonal Psychiatry (Sullivan),
    344–45
Involutional melancholia, 351,
    398–99, 402, 403, 406
Iproniazid (drug), 238, 476
Isolation, feelings of, 138, 230,
    345–47

Jefferys, Margot, 404
Jews, 265, 266
Johnson, Dr. Adelaide, 435
Josselyn, Dr. Irene, 115, 116
*Journal of Consulting and Clinical
    Psychology*, 359–61
Judith Karlin case, 229–73, 290, 396,
    530, 537
    elation and despair, 246–73
    maintenance on lithium

carbonate, 233, 234, 243–45, 267
    mood-effecting episodes, 229–34
    "thirties'-issues," 270–73
    See also Manic-depressive cycle;
        Mood and medicine
Jung, Carl Gustave, 152

Kagan, Dr. Jerome, 88
Karlin, Judith, *see* Judith Karlin
    case
Kath Barrie case, 189–223, 518, 533,
    537
    childhood circumstances and
        unresolved issues, 210–13
    choice of emotional development,
        213–14
    falling in love, 200–2
    initial interview, 189–94
    making of commitments, 202–5
    mother relationship (after father's
        death), 194–96
    "preliminary" feeling (college
        years), 196–97
    relationships as mirrors, 197–200
    See also Early adulthood
Kaufman, I. C., 79
Kety, Dr. Seymour, 240
Kissinger, Henry, 415
Kistler, Kristi, 372, 377, 380, 390,
    391
Klein, Dr. Donald, 477–78
Klerman, Dr. Gerald, 266, 479, 480,
    534–35, 538, 548, 550, 557
Kolb, Dr. Lawrence C., 262
Komarovsky, Mirra, 226
Kraepelin, Dr. Emil, 253, 254
Kuhn, Ronald, 238

Lasker, Harry, 558
Laurie Michaelson case, 274–326,
    537
    great mother/bad wife conflict,
        292–326
    postpartum problems, 274–91
Levine, Dr. Seymour, 281, 282
Levinson, Dr. Daniel, 218, 219–20,
    223, 225, 270

Lewin, Kurt, 366, 371
Lewis, Dr. Helen Block, 528
Librium (tranquilizer), 358, 479
Lidz, Dr. Theodor, 487
Lieb, Dr. Julian, 466–67
Lithium, 240, 243–45, 246, 253, 267
Lithium carbonate, 233, 234, 547
Loneliness, 38, 47, 51, 87, 118, 150,
    343–47, 416, 461, 466–68
  social isolation, 345–47
  toneless quality of, 344–45
  trauma of, 343–44
  See also Aloneness
Lorand, Dr. Sandor, 42, 69
Losses, 2–8, 342
  love-bonds and, 68–98
  seriousness of, 4
Lost and abandoned, feeling of, 13
Love
  developmental path leading to,
    118
  early feelings (during
    adolescence), 39–43
  inner patterns and inner truths,
    322–24
Love-bonds, 144, 201, 273, 527
  anxiety, 84–86
  depressive theorem, 81–82
  evolution, 97–98
  forming and mourning of, 68–70
  Helen Girard case, 82–96, 97
  human attachment, 70–74, 97, 98
  losses and, 68–98
  mother-infant pair bond, 77–81
  preprogramming of babies, 72,
    75–77
  process of detaching from, 104–5
  protest, despair, and detachment,
    74–75
  what matters most, 86–87
  See also Human attachment
Luteinizing hormone, 284

McGuire, Dr. Joseph, Jr., 417
McKinlay, Sonja, 404
McPeek, Dr. Bucknam, 500, 501,
  502, 503

Madonna image, 307
Madonna/whore dichotomy, 434
Mandel, Dr. Michel R., 495, 496,
  498, 500, 501, 503, 504, 507
Manic-depressive cycle, 253–70
  genetic studies, 265, 266–67
  girl game, 263–64
  model, 262–63
  notion of "special biological
    permission," 267–70
  power and, 258–60
  triggering factors, 255–56
  See also Judith Karlin case
MAO inhibitor medications, 445,
  447–79, 547
Margaret Garvey case, 104,
  485–514, 526, 537
  alone in widowhood, 490–91
  appetite loss, 491–92
  diagnosis, 488–90
  electronconvulsive therapy,
    493–509, 510
  failure to mourn, 511–14
  intensity of depression, 492–93
Marie Sirotta case, 101–36, 431,
  520–21, 531–32, 537, 540
  attainment of womanhood,
    114–17
  "beating mother out," 117–19
  betrayals, 123–25
  dating and marriage, 126–31
  detaching process (from first
    love-bonds), 104–5
  exploring role, 120
  game playing (winner always
    loses), 133–34
  idea of dying, 131–33
  letting go, 125–26
  love (losing and finding), 119–20
  marital breakup and
    mother/father relationship,
    105–9
  as mother's competitor, 113–14
  "real family" situation, 121–23
  reworking of mother/father
    relationship, 135–36
  spoiled babyhood and early

childhood, 109–13
victorious rival role, 103–4
Marital crisis (Doris Nordlund case), 449–81
"coming of age," 472–73
depersonalization experience, 468–69
doctor-to-doctor seeking relief, 451–52
fear of aloneness, 461–62
finding emotional security, 462–65
friend's arrival and, 452–54
heavy drinking, 449–51, 462
leaving home and husband, 469–70
in new apartment alone, 470–72
new life feeling, 465–66
options, 454–58
separateness, 460–61
suicide and, 458–60
Marital Tensions (Dicks), 322
Marplan (drug), 476
Marriage, 320–26
falling in love, 322–24
merger of perceptions and understandings, 324–25
reason for, 320–21
"Marriage and the Capacity to be Alone" (Wexler and Steidl), 459, 460
Maturity, 32
Melancholia, 253; See also Involutional melancholia
Melges, Dr. Frederick T., 285
Menarche, 20, 416–19
Menopausal depression, 351–52, 395–420
aging process and, 408–16
climacterium, 397
hormones and, 401–8
involutional melancholia, 398–99, 402, 403, 406
menarche and, 416–19
middlescence, 419–20
as plausible-sounding fantasy, 399, 401

as "special" or "different," 397–98
Menstrual cycle, 284–87
follicular, egg-ripening segment of, 284, 289
luteal phase of, 284–85
"Mentoring" patron and friend, 220
Mentor person, search for, 222–24
Michaelson, Mrs. Laurie, 270, 396, 450–51, 518–19, 538, 539
See also Laurie Michaelson case
Middlescence, 419–20
Milk fever, 278
Miller, Dr. Jean Baker, 88
Miltown (tranquilizer), 358, 479
Modern Clincial Psychiatry (Kolb), 262
Mood and medicine, 229–45
drugs and, 234–43
episodes of illness, 229–34
tricyclic antidepressants, 238–40, 446, 479–80, 496, 547
Mood Clinic (University of Pennsylvania), 276, 297, 538
Mother-infant pair bond, 77–81
Mothering (Schaffer), 78
Mother's helper ambition, 31–32
Mourning, 29, 145, 159, 412
Munich, Dr. Richard, 20–21
Murderous impulses, 384
"Myth of Involutional Melancholia, The" (Weissman), 401

Nadelson, Dr. Carol, 11, 13, 14, 15–16, 17, 18, 23, 24, 88
Nadelson, Dr. Theodore, 350–51
Nardil (drug), 445, 476, 478, 547
National Institute of Mental Health (NIMH), 172, 254, 358, 554
"Neurovegetative," signs and symptoms of, 137
Newborn children, mothers in love and, 77–81
New York State Psychiatric Institute, 478
Norepinephrine, 234–35, 237, 238
Notman, Dr. Malkah, 88, 227, 228, 535

Ostow, Dr. Mortimer, 311
Ottoson, Dr., 506

Parents, adolescents and, 18–22
Parnate (drug), 445, 476, 477, 478, 547
"Paternal Roots of Female Character Development" (Forrest), 432
Pedigree studies, 266
Perlmutter, Dr. Johanna F., 410
Person, The (Lidz), 487
Pincus, Lily, 200–1 322, 488
Postpartum phenomena, 274–91
  awareness, 274–76
  endocrine status, 287
  environment and, 283
  hormones and, 287–91
  Mammalia species and, 282–83
  meaning of, 276–78
  menstrual cycle, 284–87
  progesterone levels, 281
  research studies, 278–81
Powerlessness, feelings of, 365
Pratt, Dr., 406
Preprogrammed babies, loving and, 72, 75–77
Primitive infant anxiety, 33
Progesterone, 281, 282, 285, 286, 287–89
Prolactin, 287–89
Promiscuity (Sandy Geller case), 137–70
  aloneness and autonomy milestones, 159–62
  avoiding emotional involvement, 162–64
  catching up process, 152–55
  commitment and trust, 167–70
  decision for treatment, 137–38
  denial of dependence, 139–41
  divorce and trauma, 149–50
  experiencing and processing pain, 155–59
  mother and (what never happened), 164–67
  repairing process (in experience

of new motherhood), 146–49
  short-term high, 143–46
  "unfinished people" partnerships, 151–52
Psychic War in Men and Women (Lewis), 528
"Psychological Effects of Hormonal Changes in Women" (Melges and Hamburg), 285
"Psychological Study of the Formation of the Early Adult Life Structure in Women, A" (Stewart), 220
Psychology of Depression, The (Ostow), 311
Psychology of Women (Bardwick), 355–56
Psychology of Women (Deutsch), 305, 416
Psychology Today (publication), 534–35
Psychosomatic diseases, 290
Puberty, 19
Puppy-love, 27
Pynchon, Thomas, 413

Rado, Dr. Sandor, 163, 352–53
Rage, 33, 261, 375
Relationship, losses of, 65
Reserpine (drug), 179–80, 181, 237, 238
Riesman, David, 346
Robertson, James, 74, 75
Role transition, 539
Rosenblum, L. A., 79

Sachar, Dr. Edward, 407–8
Saline abortion, 12, 26
Salt balance, body's, 174
Sandy Geller case, 137–70, 517–18, 537, 541
  aloneness and autonomy milestones, 159–62
  catching up process, 152–55
  commitment and trust, 167–70
  decision for treatment, 137–38
  denial of dependence, 139–41

divorce and trauma, 149–50
experiencing and processing pain,
    155–59
mother and (what never
    happened), 164–67
promiscuous behavior and, 141–46
repairing process (in experiencing
    of new motherhood), 146–49
"unfinished people" partnerships,
    151–52
Satir, Virginia, 381
Saturday Review, 413
Schaffer, Rudolph, 78
Schildkraut, Dr. Joseph, 241, 242
Schizophrenia, 238
Scopolamine (drug), 505
Secrets in the Family (Pincus and
    Dare), 200–1, 322, 488
Self-destructiveness, 13
Self-esteem, 33, 35, 156, 352, 399,
    416
    intimate relationships and, 224–25
    loss of, 38
    props of, 356–57
    sources of, 321–22
Self-hatred, 83
Self-psychotherapy (or
    taking-care-of-the-inner-self),
    56–58
Separation, 29, 34–35, 45, 63, 69,
    103, 186, 208, 218, 219, 228, 273,
    460
    geographical, 30
    of infant monkeys, 78–80
    mother-infant pair bond, 77–81
    pain of (during adolescence), 21
    from parents, 18–19, 20–22
    playing the child's role and, 18
    protest/despair/detachment,
        74–75, 79
    wishes to return home, 61
    young children from parents,
        74–75
Sephardic Jews, 266
Serotonin, 234–35, 237, 238, 240, 376
Sex and depression, 178
Sex and nurturance, 32–37

Sexual barter phenomenon, 37–38
Sexual interest, loss of, 254
Sexual Problems: Diagnosis and
    Treatment in Medical Practice
    (Willis), 162
Sexual stereotypes, 355
Sirotta, Marie, See Marie Sirotta
    case
Sleep disorders, 175, 176
Social isolation, 345–47
Solnit, Dr. Albert J., 40, 41, 212
Somatic Therapies Consultation
    Service, 495, 500, 501, 507, 526
Sontag, Susan, 413, 414, 415
Spitz, Dr. René, 74
Stanford Medical School, 279–80,
    282
Steidl, John, 459, 460
Stewart, Dr. Wendy Ann, 220–22,
    223, 224, 225, 227, 270
Stoller, Dr. Robert, 268
Stress, 21, 183, 210, 530
Succinylocholine (drug), 502, 503
Sudden impulses, difficulties in
    dealing with, 13
Suicide, xv, xvi, 5, 13, 69, 107, 294,
    338, 367, 374, 375, 458–59
Sullivan, Dr. Harry Stack, 118–19,
    344–45, 346

Thierry, Debra, see Debra Thierry
    case
Thomas, Dr., 406
Thompson, Barbara, 404
Three Essays on the Theory of
    Sexuality (Freud), 103
3-methoxy-4-hydrophenylglycol
    (MHPG), 241–42
Thyroid hormone, 281
Timing considerations, 206–10
Tofranil (drug), 238, 253, 496, 547
Transitional objects, 36–37
Tricyclic antidepressants, 238–40,
    253, 446, 479–80, 496, 547
Tucker, Dr. Gary, 180–81, 374,
    395–96
Tyramine, 476–77

Ugliness, feelings of, 15
"Unfinished people" partnerships,
    151–52
University of Pennsylvania, 276
University of Pittsburgh, 42, 44, 45,
    50
Unwanted baby image (during
    adolescence), 43–44
Urinary retention, 496

Vaillant, Dr. George E., 135
Valium (tranquilizer), 358, 479, 548
"Venous poolers," 496
Victorious rival, role of, 103–4

Walk-in Neuropsychiatric Service
    (Massachusetts General
    Hospital), 208
Way of All Flesh, The (Butler),
    353
Weiss, Robert S., 346
Weissman, Dr. Myrna, 400, 401–3,
    538, 556–57
Welch, Dr. Charles, 504–5
"Western Motel" (Hopper), 330
Western Psychiatric Institute and

Clinic (University of
    Pittsburgh), 42, 44, 45, 50
Wexler, Joan, 459, 460
"What's the point" attitude, 46
Whybrow, Dr. Peter, 176, 179, 235,
    236, 238, 340–41
Willis, Dr. Stanley, 162–63
Winnicott, Dr. Donald W., 36
Winokur, Dr. George, 497–98
"Woman's Place in Man's
    Life-Cycle" (Gilligan and
    Notman), 227, 228
Women and Madness (Chesler),
    551–52, 553
"Women in Mental Health Project,
    The" (Harvard University),
    553–54
Worthlessness, sense of, xv–xvi, 13,
    85, 494

Yale Depression Unit, 402, 529,
    556–57
Yale University, 40, 87

Zilbach, Dr. Joan, 88

8/5